W9-BQT-777

VW Owners Workshop Manual

A K Legg T Eng (CEI), AMIMI

Models covered

All VW Rabbit (inc. Cabriolet convertible), Jetta, Scirocco and
Pick-up 'Mk 1' models with 1.5 liter (88.9 & 89.7 cu in), 1.6 liter
(96.9 cu in), 1.7 liter (104.6 cu in) & 1.8 liter (109 cu in) gasoline
engines, including fuel injection

Does not cover diesel engine or 'Mk 2' models

ISBN 1 85010 098 5

© Haynes Publishing Group 1982, 1984, 1985, 1986

All rights reserved. No part of this book may be reproduced or transmitted in
any form or by any means, electronic or mechanical, including photocopying,
recording or by any information storage or retrieval system, without permission
in writing from the copyright holder.

Printed in England   *(884-12L3)*

ABCDE
FGHIJ
K

THE
BOOK

AUTOMOTIVE
PARTS &
ACCESSORIES
ASSOCIATION MEMBER

Haynes Publishing Group
Sparkford Nr Yeovil
Somerset BA22 7JJ England

Haynes Publications, Inc
861 Lawrence Drive
Newbury Park
California 91320 USA

Library of Congress
85-80230

Acknowledgements

Thanks are due to Volkswagenwerk Aktiengesellschaft for the supply of technical information and certain illustrations. The Champion Sparking Plug Company supplied the illustrations showing the various spark plug conditions. Castrol Limited supplied the lubrication data, and Sykes-Pickavant Ltd provided some of the workshop tools. Special thanks are due to all those people at Sparkford who helped in the production of this manual.

About this manual

Its aim

The aim of this manual is to help you get the best value from your vehicle. It can do so in several ways. It can help you decide what work must be done (even should you choose to get it done by a garage), provide information on routine maintenance and servicing, and give a logical course of action and diagnosis when random faults occur. However, it is hoped that you will use the manual by tackling the work yourself. On simpler jobs it may even be quicker than booking the car into a garage and going there twice, to leave and collect it. Perhaps most important, a lot of money can be saved by avoiding the costs a garage must charge to cover its labour and overheads.

The manual has drawings and descriptions to show the function of the various components so that their layout can be understood. Then the tasks are described and photographed in a step-by-step sequence so that even a novice can do the work.

Its arrangement

The manual is divided into twelve Chapters, each covering a logical sub-division of the vehicle. The Chapters are each divided into Sections, numbered with single figures, eg 5; and the Sections into paragraphs (or sub-sections), with decimal numbers following on from the Section they are in, eg 5.1, 5.2, 5.3 etc.

It is freely illustrated, especially in those parts where there is a detailed sequence of operations to be carried out. There are two forms of illustration: figures and photographs. The figures are numbered in sequence with decimal numbers, according to their position in the Chapter – eg Fig. 6.4 is the fourth drawing/illustration in Chapter 6. Photographs carry the same number (either individually or in related groups) as the Section or sub-section to which they relate.

There is an alphabetical index at the back of the manual as well as a contents list at the front. Each Chapter is also preceded by its own individual contents list.

References to the 'left' or 'right' of the vehicle are in the sense of a person in the driver's seat facing forwards.

Unless otherwise stated, nuts and bolts are removed by turning anti-clockwise, and tightened by turning clockwise.

Vehicle manufacturers continually make changes to specifications and recommendations, and these, when notified, are incorporated into our manuals at the earliest opportunity.

Whilst every care is taken to ensure that the information in this manual is correct, no liability can be accepted by the authors or publishers for loss, damage or injury caused by any errors in, or omissions from, the information given.

Introduction to the
Golf, Rabbit, Jetta and Scirocco

Introduced in 1974 in the UK as a Golf and in 1975 in North America as a Rabbit, the new VW Hatchback soon established itself as a market leader in its class. Together with the mechanically similar Scirocco Sports Coupe, these vehicles set new standards of design integrity which have since been emulated by many of the world's leading motor manufacturers.

Following on the success of the Golf, Rabbit and Scirocco, a more traditional notchback Saloon, the Jetta, was introduced into both territories in 1980 to conform to changing market trends and a demand for a conventionally styled '3-box' saloon in the middle range. To further enhance the appeal of these vehicles a convertible version of the Golf and Rabbit, together with a Pick-up utility vehicle, have also been added to the model line-up.

Such was the demand for these cars in the USA that in 1978 assembly of the Rabbit commenced at Westmoreland Pennsylvania; this plant now being responsible for production of a high percentage of VW vehicles sold in the USA.

Engines fitted to UK models are of 1.4, 1.5, 1.6 and 1.8 litre capacity whereas 1.5, 1.6, 1.7 and 1.8 litre, (89, 97, 105 and 109 cu in) units power vehicles for the North American market.

All models feature a transversely mounted engine/transmission configuration with front-wheel-drive and the now almost universally accepted 'conventional' independent front, semi-independent rear suspension layout. A wide range of trim and equipment options are also available.

Contents

VW Golf Convertible GLi

VW Golf GL (1981 model)

VW Scirocco (UK Storm model)

VW Jetta GLS (UK model)

VW Rabbit L

VW Jetta (US model)

VW Scirocco (US model)

VW Pick-up Truck (US model)

General dimensions, weights and capacities

Dimensions
Overall length
Golf (add 20 mm/0.8 in with headlight washers) .... 3815 mm (150.2 in)
Rabbit Sedan .... 3945 mm (155.3 in)
Rabbit Convertible .... 3923 mm (154.4 in)
Jetta-UK (add 25 mm/1.0 in with headlight washers) .... 4195 mm (165.2 in)
Jetta – North America .... 4325 mm (170.3 in)
Scirocco – UK (add 65 mm/2.5 in with headlight washers) .... 3885 mm (153.0 in)
Scirocco – North America .... 3970 mm (156.3 in)
Pick-up .... 4275 mm (168.3 in)

Overall width
Golf (carburettor engine) .... 1610 mm (63.4 in)
Golf (CIS) .... 1630 mm (64.2 in)
Rabbit Sedan and Convertible .... 1610 mm (63.4 in)
Jetta – UK .... 1630 mm (64.2 in)
Jetta – North America .... 1628 mm (64.1 in)
Scirocco – UK .... 1624 mm (63.9 in)
Scirocco – North America .... 1625 mm (64.0 in)
Pick-up .... 1608 mm (63.3 in)

Overall height
Golf (carburettor engine) .... 1410 mm (55.5 in)
Golf (CIS) .... 1395 mm (54.9 in)
Rabbit Sedan and Convertible .... 1410 mm (55.5 in)
Jetta – UK (with 51 kW engine) .... 1410 mm (55.5 in)
Jetta – UK (with 81 or 82 kW engine) .... 1395 mm (54.9 in)
Jetta – North America .... 1412 mm (55.6 in)
Scirocco – UK .... 1309 mm (51.5 in)
Scirocco – North America .... 1300 mm (51.2 in)
Pick-up .... 1382 mm (54.4 in)

Ground clearance
Golf (carburettor engine) .... 125 mm (4.9 in)
Golf (CIS) .... 117 mm (4.6 in)
Rabbit Sedan .... 122 mm (4.8 in)
Rabbit Convertible .... 142 mm (5.6 in)
Jetta – UK (with 51 kW engine) .... 125 mm (4.9 in)
Jetta – UK (with 81 or 82 kW engine) .... 117 mm (4.6 in)
Jetta – North America .... 117 mm (4.6 in)
Scirocco – UK .... 117 mm (4.6 in)
Scirocco – North America .... 134 mm (5.3 in)
Pick-up (laden) .... 117 mm (4.6 in)

Wheelbase
All models .... 2398 mm (94.4 in)

Turning circle (wall to wall)
All models .... 10.3 m (33.8 ft)

Weights
Kerb weight
Golf 2-door (with 51 kW engine)	800 kg (1763 lb)
Golf 2-door (with 81 or 82 kW engine)	840 kg (1852 lb)
Golf 2-door (with automatic transmission)	830 kg (1830 lb)
Golf 4-door (with 51 kW engine)	825 kg (1819 lb)
Golf 4-door (with automatic transmission)	855 kg (1885 lb)
Golf Convertible	940 kg (2072 lb)
Jetta (UK) 2-door (with 51 kW engine)	825 kg (1819 lb)
Jetta (UK) 2-door (with 81 or 82 kW engine)	865 kg (1907 lb)
Jetta (UK) 2-door (with automatic transmission)	855 kg (1885 lb)
Jetta (UK) 4-door (with 51 kW engine)	850 kg (1874 lb)
Jetta (UK) 4-door (with 81 or 82 kW engine)	890 kg (1962 lb)
Jetta (UK) 4-door (with automatic transmission)	000 kg (1040 lb)
Scirocco (UK) with manual transmission	800 kg (1764 lb)
Scirocco (UK) with automatic transmission	825 kg (1819 lb)
North American models	See sticker on left-hand side door jamb

Trailor load (max)
With brakes (except 81 and 82 kW engine)	1000 kg (2205 lb)
With brakes (81 and 82 kW engine)	1200 kg (2646 lb)
Without brakes	400 kg (882 lb)

Roof rack load (max)
All models	75 kg (165 lb)

Capacities
Engine oil
All except 1715 cc and 1780 cc North American models:
With filter	6.0 Imp pt; 3.6 US qt; 3.4 litres
Without filter	5.25 Imp pt; 3.2 US qt; 3.0 litres

1715 cc and 1780 cc North American models:
With filter	7.9 Imp pt; 4.76 US qt; 4.5 litres
Without filter	7.0 Imp pt; 4.23 US qt; 4.0 litres
Difference between Min and Max on dipstick	1.75 Imp pt; 1.06 US qt; 1.0 litres

Manual gearbox and final drive
4-speed	2.6 Imp pt; 1.6 US qt; 1.5 litres
5-speed	3.5 Imp pt; 2.1 US qt; 2.0 litres

Automatic transmission fluid
Total (from dry)	10.6 Imp pt; 6.3 US qt; 6.0 litres
Service (drain and refill)	5.3 Imp pt; 3.2 US qt; 3.0 litres
Automatic transmission final drive	1.3 Imp pt; 0.8 US qt; 0.75 litre

Cooling system
UK models with expansion tank	1.4 Imp gal; 1.7 US gal; 6.5 litres
UK models without expansion tank	0.99 Imp gal; 1.2 US gal; 4.5 litres
North American models	1.0 Imp gal; 1.2 US gal; 4.6 litres

Fuel tank
Early models	9 Imp gal; 10.8 US gal; 40 litres
Later models (1984 on)	12.1 Imp gal; 14.3 US gal; 55 litres

Use of English

As this book has been written in England, it uses the appropriate English component names, phrases, and spelling. Some of these differ from those used in America. Normally, these cause no difficulty, but to make sure, a glossary is printed below. In ordering spare parts remember the parts list may use some of these words:

English	American	English	American
Accelerator	Gas pedal	Leading shoe (of brake)	Primary shoe
Aerial	Antenna	Locks	Latches
Anti-roll bar	Stabiliser or sway bar	Methylated spirit	Denatured alcohol
Big-end bearing	Rod bearing	Motorway	Freeway, turnpike etc
Bonnet (engine cover)	Hood	Number plate	License plate
Boot (luggage compartment)	Trunk	Paraffin	Kerosene
Bulkhead	Firewall	Petrol	Gasoline (gas)
Bush	Bushing	Petrol tank	Gas tank
Cam follower or tappet	Valve lifter or tappet	'Pinking'	'Pinging'
Carburettor	Carburetor	Prise (force apart)	Pry
Catch	Latch	Propeller shaft	Driveshaft
Choke/venturi	Barrel	Quarterlight	Quarter window
Circlip	Snap-ring	Retread	Recap
Clearance	Lash	Reverse	Back-up
Crownwheel	Ring gear (of differential)	Rocker cover	Valve cover
Damper	Shock absorber, shock	Saloon	Sedan
Disc (brake)	Rotor/disk	Seized	Frozen
Distance piece	Spacer	Sidelight	Parking light
Drop arm	Pitman arm	Silencer	Muffler
Drop head coupe	Convertible	Sill panel (beneath doors)	Rocker panel
Dynamo	Generator (DC)	Small end, little end	Piston pin or wrist pin
Earth (electrical)	Ground	Spanner	Wrench
Engineer's blue	Prussian blue	Split cotter (for valve spring cap)	Lock (for valve spring retainer)
Estate car	Station wagon	Split pin	Cotter pin
Exhaust manifold	Header	Steering arm	Spindle arm
Fault finding/diagnosis	Troubleshooting	Sump	Oil pan
Float chamber	Float bowl	Swarf	Metal chips or debris
Free-play	Lash	Tab washer	Tang or lock
Freewheel	Coast	Tappet	Valve lifter
Gearbox	Transmission	Thrust bearing	Throw-out bearing
Gearchange	Shift	Top gear	High
Grub screw	Setscrew, Allen screw	Trackrod (of steering)	Tie-rod (or connecting rod)
Gudgeon pin	Piston pin or wrist pin	Trailing shoe (of brake)	Secondary shoe
Halfshaft	Axleshaft	Transmission	Whole drive line
Handbrake	Parking brake	Tyre	Tire
Hood	Soft top	Van	Panel wagon/van
Hot spot	Heat riser	Vice	Vise
Indicator	Turn signal	Wheel nut	Lug nut
Interior light	Dome lamp	Windscreen	Windshield
Layshaft (of gearbox)	Countershaft	Wing/mudguard	Fender

Buying spare parts and vehicle identification numbers

Buying spare parts

Spare parts are available from many sources, for example: VW garages, other garages and accessory shops, and motor factors. Our advice regarding spare part sources is as follows:

Officially appointed VW garages – This is the best source of parts which are peculiar to your vehicle and are otherwise not generally available (eg complete cylinder heads, internal gearbox components, badges, interior trim etc). It is also the only place at which you should buy parts if your car is still under warranty – non-VW components may invalidate the warranty. To be sure of obtaining the correct parts it will always be necessary to give the storeman your car's engine and chassis number, and if possible, to take the 'old' part along for positive identification. Remember that many parts are available on a factory exchange scheme – any parts returned should always be clean! It obviously makes good sense to go straight to to the specialists on your car for this type of part for they are best equipped to supply you.

Other garages and accessory shops – These are often very good places to buy materials and components needed for the maintenance of your car (eg oil filters, spark plugs, bulbs, drivebelts, oils and greases, touch-up paint, filler paste etc). They also sell general accessories, usually have convenient opening hours, charge lower prices and can often be found not far from home.

Motor factors – Good factors will stock all of the more important components which wear out relatively quickly (eg clutch components, pistons, valves, exhaust system, brake cylinders/pipes/hoses/seals/shoes and pads etc). Motor factors will often provide new or reconditioned components on a part exchange basis – this can save a considerable amount of money.

Vehicle identification numbers

It is most important to identify the vehicle accurately when ordering spare parts or asking for information. There have been many modifications to this range already.

The vehicle identification plate is on top of the frame by the radiator (photo). On North American models the *Vehicle identification number (VIN)* is on the left-hand side facia or windscreen pillar.

The chassis number is on the top of the right-hand front suspension strut housing, except on 1981 North American models where it is stamped on the bulkhead in the engine compartment.

The engine number is on the cylinder block by the distributor (photo).

The transmission code is stamped on the top of the flange where the transmission joins the engine.

These numbers should be identified and recorded by the owner; they are required when ordering spares, going through the customs, and regrettably, by the police, if the vehicle is stolen.

When ordering spares remember that VW output is such that inevitably spares vary, are duplicated, and are held on a usage basis. If the storeman does not have the correct identification, he cannot produce the correct item. It is a good idea to take the old part if possible to compare it with a new one. The storeman has many customers to satisfy, so be accurate and patient. In some cases, particularly in the brake system, more than one manufacturer supplies an assembly, eg both Teves and Girling supply front calipers. The assemblies may be interchangeable but the integral parts are not. This is only one of the pitfalls in the buying of spares, so be careful to make an ally of the storeman. When fitting accessories it is best to fit VW recommended ones. They are designed specifically for the vehicle.

The vehicle identification plate (UK models)

Engine number location

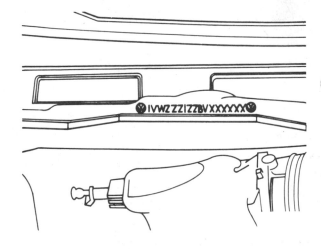

Chassis number location on 1981 on North American models

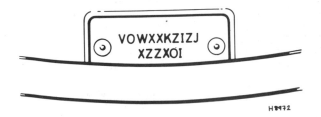

Vehicle identification number (VIN) on North American models viewed through the windscreen

Tools and working facilities

Introduction

A selection of good tools is a fundamental requirement for anyone contemplating the maintenance and repair of a motor vehicle. For the owner who does not possess any, their purchase will prove a considerable expense, offsetting some of the savings made by doing-it-yourself. However, provided that the tools purchased are of good quality, they will last for many years and prove an extremely worthwhile investment.

To help the average owner to decide which tools are needed to carry out the various tasks detailed in this manual, we have compiled three lists of tools under the following headings: *Maintenance and minor repair, Repair and overhaul,* and *Special.* The newcomer to practical mechanics should start off with the *Maintenance and minor repair* tool kit and confine himself to the simpler jobs around the vehicle. Then, as his confidence and experience grow, he can undertake more difficult tasks, buying extra tools as, and when, they are needed. In this way, a *Maintenance and minor repair* tool kit can be built-up into a *Repair and overhaul* tool kit over a considerable period of time without any major cash outlays. The experienced do-it-yourselfer will have a tool kit good enough for most repair and overhaul procedures and will add tools from the *Special* category when he feels the expense is justified by the amount of use to which these tools will be put.

It is obviously not possible to cover the subject of tools fully here. For those who wish to learn more about tools and their use there is a book entitled *How to Choose and Use Car Tools* available from the publishers of this manual.

Maintenance and minor repair tool kit

The tools given in this list should be considered as a minimum requirement if routine maintenance, servicing and minor repair operations are to be undertaken. We recommend the purchase of combination spanners (ring one end, open-ended the other); although more expensive than open-ended ones, they do give the advantages of both types of spanner.

Combination spanners - 10, 11, 12, 13, 14 & 17 mm
Adjustable spanner - 9 inch
Spark plug spanner (with rubber insert)
Spark plug gap adjustment tool
Set of feeler gauges
Brake adjuster spanner (if applicable)
Brake bleed nipple spanner
Screwdriver - 4 in long x $\frac{1}{4}$ in dia (flat blade)
Screwdriver - 4 in long x $\frac{1}{4}$ in dia (cross blade)
Combination pliers - 6 inch
Hacksaw (junior)
Tyre pump
Tyre pressure gauge
Oil can
Fine emery cloth (1 sheet)
Wire brush (small)
Funnel (medium size)

Repair and overhaul tool kit

These tools are virtually essential for anyone undertaking any major repairs to a motor vehicle, and are additional to those given in the *Maintenance and minor repair* list. Included in this list is a comprehensive set of sockets. Although these are expensive they will be found invaluable as they are so versatile - particularly if various drives are included in the set. We recommend the $\frac{1}{2}$ in square-drive type, as this can be used with most proprietary torque wrenches. If you cannot afford a socket set, even bought piecemeal, then inexpensive tubular box spanners are a useful alternative.

The tools in this list will occasionally need to be supplemented by tools from the *Special* list.

Sockets (or box spanners) to cover range in previous list
Splined tools for cylinder head and other special bolts
Reversible ratchet drive (for use with sockets)
Extension piece, 10 inch (for use with sockets)
Universal joint (for use with sockets)
Torque wrench (for use with sockets)
'Mole' wrench - 8 inch
Ball pein hammer
Soft-faced hammer, plastic or rubber
Screwdriver - 6 in long x $\frac{5}{16}$ in dia (flat blade)
Screwdriver - 2 in long x $\frac{5}{16}$ in square (flat blade)
Screwdriver - 1$\frac{1}{2}$ in long x $\frac{1}{4}$ in dia (cross blade)
Screwdriver - 3 in long x $\frac{1}{8}$ in dia (electricians)
Pliers - electricians side cutters
Pliers - needle nosed
Pliers - circlip (internal and external)
Cold chisel - $\frac{1}{2}$ inch
Scriber
Scraper
Centre punch
Pin punch
Hacksaw
Valve grinding tool
Steel rule/straight-edge
Allen keys
Selection of files
Wire brush (large)
Axle-stands
Jack (strong scissor or hydraulic type)

Special tools

The tools in this list are those which are not used regularly, are expensive to buy, or which need to be used in accordance with their manufacturers' instructions. Unless relatively difficult mechanical jobs are undertaken frequently, it will not be economic to buy many of these tools. Where this is the case, you could consider clubbing together with friends (or joining a motorists' club) to make a joint purchase, or borrowing the tools against a deposit from a local garage or tool hire specialist.

The following list contains only those tools and instruments freely available to the public, and not those special tools produced by the vehicle manufacturer specifically for its dealer network. You will find occasional references to these manufacturers' special tools in the text of this manual. Generally, an alternative method of doing the job without the vehicle manufacturers' special tool is given. However, sometimes, there is no alternative to using them. Where this is the case and the relevant tool cannot be bought or borrowed, you will have to entrust the work to a franchised garage.

Valve spring compressor (where applicable)
Piston ring compressor
Balljoint separator
Universal hub/bearing puller
Impact screwdriver
Micrometer and/or vernier gauge
Dial gauge
Stroboscopic timing light
Dwell angle meter/tachometer
Universal electrical multi-meter
Cylinder compression gauge
Lifting tackle
Trolley jack
Light with extension lead

Buying tools

For practically all tools, a tool factor is the best source since he will have a very comprehensive range compared with the average garage or accessory shop. Having said that, accessory shops often offer excellent quality tools at discount prices, so it pays to shop around.

Remember, you don't have to buy the most expensive items on the shelf, but it is always advisable to steer clear of the very cheap tools. There are plenty of good tools around at reasonable prices, so ask the proprietor or manager of the shop for advice before making a purchase.

Care and maintenance of tools

Having purchased a reasonable tool kit, it is necessary to keep the tools in a clean serviceable condition. After use, always wipe off any dirt, grease and metal particles using a clean, dry cloth, before putting the tools away. Never leave them lying around after they have been used. A simple tool rack on the garage or workshop wall, for items such as screwdrivers and pliers is a good idea. Store all normal wrenches and sockets in a metal box. Any measuring instruments, gauges, meters, etc, must be carefully stored where they cannot be damaged or become rusty.

Take a little care when tools are used. Hammer heads inevitably become marked and screwdrivers lose the keen edge on their blades from time to time. A little timely attention with emery cloth or a file will soon restore items like this to a good serviceable finish.

Working facilities

Not to be forgotten when discussing tools, is the workshop itself. If anything more than routine maintenance is to be carried out, some form of suitable working area becomes essential.

It is appreciated that many an owner mechanic is forced by circumstances to remove an engine or similar item, without the benefit of a garage or workshop. Having done this, any repairs should always be done under the cover of a roof.

Wherever possible, any dismantling should be done on a clean, flat workbench or table at a suitable working height.

Any workbench needs a vise: one with a jaw opening of 4 in (100 mm) is suitable for most jobs. As mentioned previously, some clean dry storage space is also required for tools, as well as for lubricants, cleaning fluids, touch-up paints and so on, which become necessary.

Another item which may be required, and which has a much more general usage, is an electric drill with a chuck capacity of at least $\frac{5}{16}$ in (8 mm). This, together with a good range of twist drills, is virtually essential for fitting accessories such as mirrors and reversing lights.

Last, but not least, always keep a supply of old newspapers and clean, lint-free rags available, and try to keep any working area as clean as possible.

Spanner jaw gap comparison table

Jaw gap (in)	Spanner size
0.250	$\frac{1}{4}$ in AF
0.276	7 mm
0.313	$\frac{5}{16}$ in AF
0.315	8 mm
0.344	$\frac{11}{32}$ in AF; $\frac{1}{8}$ in Whitworth
0.354	9 mm
0.375	$\frac{3}{8}$ in AF
0.394	10 mm
0.433	11 mm
0.438	$\frac{7}{16}$ in AF
0.445	$\frac{3}{16}$ in Whitworth; $\frac{1}{4}$ in BSF
0.472	12 mm
0.500	$\frac{1}{2}$ in AF
0.512	13 mm
0.525	$\frac{1}{4}$ in Whitworth; $\frac{5}{16}$ in BSF
0.551	14 mm
0.563	$\frac{9}{16}$ in AF
0.591	15 mm
0.600	$\frac{5}{16}$ in Whitworth; $\frac{3}{8}$ in BSF
0.625	$\frac{5}{8}$ in AF
0.630	16 mm
0.669	17 mm
0.686	$\frac{11}{16}$ in AF
0.709	18 mm
0.710	$\frac{3}{8}$ in Whitworth; $\frac{7}{16}$ in BSF
0.748	19 mm
0.750	$\frac{3}{4}$ in AF
0.813	$\frac{13}{16}$ in AF
0.820	$\frac{7}{16}$ in Whitworth; $\frac{1}{2}$ in BSF
0.866	22 mm
0.875	$\frac{7}{8}$ in AF
0.920	$\frac{1}{2}$ in Whitworth; $\frac{9}{16}$ in BSF
0.938	$\frac{15}{16}$ in AF
0.945	24 mm
1.000	1 in AF
1.010	$\frac{9}{16}$ in Whitworth; $\frac{5}{8}$ in BSF
1.024	26 mm
1.063	$1\frac{1}{16}$ in AF; 27 mm
1.100	$\frac{5}{8}$ in Whitworth; $\frac{11}{16}$ in BSF
1.125	$1\frac{1}{8}$ in AF
1.181	30 mm
1.200	$\frac{11}{16}$ in Whitworth; $\frac{3}{4}$ in BSF
1.250	$1\frac{1}{4}$ in AF
1.260	32 mm
1.300	$\frac{3}{4}$ in Whitworth; $\frac{7}{8}$ in BSF
1.313	$1\frac{5}{16}$ in AF
1.390	$\frac{13}{16}$ in Whitworth; $\frac{15}{16}$ in BSF
1.417	36 mm
1.438	$1\frac{7}{16}$ in AF
1.480	$\frac{7}{8}$ in Whitworth; 1 in BSF
1.500	$1\frac{1}{2}$ in AF
1.575	40 mm; $\frac{15}{16}$ in Whitworth
1.614	41 mm
1.625	$1\frac{5}{8}$ in AF
1.670	1 in Whitworth; $1\frac{1}{8}$ in BSF
1.688	$1\frac{11}{16}$ in AF
1.811	46 mm
1.813	$1\frac{13}{16}$ in AF
1.860	$1\frac{1}{8}$ in Whitworth; $1\frac{1}{4}$ in BSF
1.875	$1\frac{7}{8}$ in AF
1.969	50 mm
2.000	2 in AF
2.050	$1\frac{1}{4}$ in Whitworth; $1\frac{3}{8}$ in BSF
2.165	55 mm
2.362	60 mm

Jacking and Towing

Jacking

The jack supplied with the car is intended only for wheel changing in an emergency. For any other work it should be supplemented by axle stands or blocks. **Do not** venture under the car when it is supported solely by a jack.

To change a roadwheel first remove the spare wheel and tool kit from the well in the rear compartment (photo) on all models except the Pick-up. Apply the handbrake and chock the wheel diagonally opposite the one to be changed. Make sure that the car is positioned on firm level ground. Lever off the bolt caps or hub cover and slightly loosen the wheel bolts with the spanner provided. Raise the jack and locate it under the reinforced area in the sill below the wedge-shaped mark (photo). Raise the jack until the wheel is free of the ground, then unscrew the bolts and withdraw the roadwheel.

Locate the spare wheel on the hub and tighten the bolts lightly. Lower the jack, then finally tighten the wheel bolts and refit the hub cover or bolt caps. Remove the chocks and refit the wheel and tool kit to the rear compartment.

Towing

Towing eyes are provided at the front and rear of the car beneath the bumpers (photos), except on the Pick-up which only has a front towing eye. Providing a fault has not developed in the manual gearbox or final drive, the vehicle may be towed on its four wheels. The same rule applies to models with automatic transmission but the car may only be towed in a forward direction at speeds up to 30 mph for a maximum of 30 miles. If these conditions cannot be met, it is possible to remove both driveshafts, withdraw the CV joints, then refit the CV joints only together with their rubber gaiters to the hubs. Alternatively, tow the vehicle with the front wheels suspended. Towing by suspending the rear of the vehicle is not recommended, and must never be attempted with automatic transmission or Pick-up models.

Spare wheel location on a Jetta

Jacking the car

Front towing eye

Rear towing eye

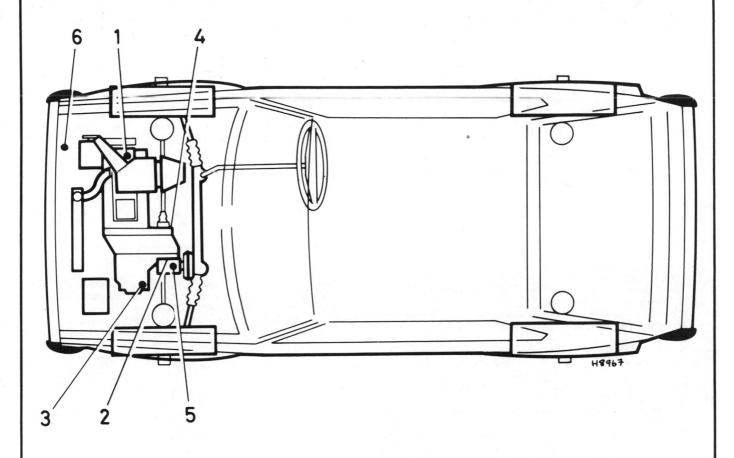

Recommended lubricants and fluids

Component	Lubricant type or specification
1 Engine	Multigrade engine oil SAE 20W/50 or 15W/50
2 Manual gearbox and final drive	SAE 80 or 80W/90
3 Automatic transmission	ATF Dexron
4 Automatic transmission final drive	SAE 90
Steering gear	VW special grease
Rear wheel bearings	Multi-purpose lithium based grease
Hinges, locks and pivots etc	Engine oil
5 Brake fluid	Hydraulic fluid to FMVSS 116 DOT 3 or 4
6 Power steering reservoir	ATF Dexron

Safety first!

Professional motor mechanics are trained in safe working procedures. However enthusiastic you may be about getting on with the job in hand, do take the time to ensure that your safety is not put at risk. A moment's lack of attention can result in an accident, as can failure to observe certain elementary precautions.

There will always be new ways of having accidents, and the following points do not pretend to be a comprehensive list of all dangers; they are intended rather to make you aware of the risks and to encourage a safety-conscious approach to all work you carry out on your vehicle.

Essential DOs and DON'Ts

DON'T rely on a single jack when working underneath the vehicle. Always use reliable additional means of support, such as axle stands, securely placed under a part of the vehicle that you know will not give way.

DON'T attempt to loosen or tighten high-torque nuts (e.g. wheel hub nuts) while the vehicle is on a jack; it may be pulled off.

DON'T start the engine without first ascertaining that the transmission is in neutral (or 'Park' where applicable) and the parking brake applied.

DON'T suddenly remove the filler cap from a hot cooling system – cover it with a cloth and release the pressure gradually first, or you may get scalded by escaping coolant.

DON'T attempt to drain oil until you are sure it has cooled sufficiently to avoid scalding you.

DON'T grasp any part of the engine, exhaust or catalytic converter without first ascertaining that it is sufficiently cool to avoid burning you.

DON'T allow brake fluid or antifreeze to contact vehicle paintwork.

DON'T syphon toxic liquids such as fuel, brake fluid or antifreeze by mouth, or allow them to remain on your skin.

DON'T inhale dust – it may be injurious to health (see *Asbestos* below).

DON'T allow any spilt oil or grease to remain on the floor – wipe it up straight away, before someone slips on it.

DON'T use ill-fitting spanners or other tools which may slip and cause injury.

DON'T attempt to lift a heavy component which may be beyond your capability – get assistance.

DON'T rush to finish a job, or take unverified short cuts.

DON'T allow children or animals in or around an unattended vehicle.

DO wear eye protection when using power tools such as drill, sander, bench grinder etc, and when working under the vehicle.

DO use a barrier cream on your hands prior to undertaking dirty jobs – it will protect your skin from infection as well as making the dirt easier to remove afterwards; but make sure your hands aren't left slippery.

DO keep loose clothing (cuffs, tie etc) and long hair well out of the way of moving mechanical parts.

DO remove rings, wristwatch etc, before working on the vehicle – especially the electrical system.

DO ensure that any lifting tackle used has a safe working load rating adequate for the job.

DO keep your work area tidy – it is only too easy to fall over articles left lying around.

DO get someone to check periodically that all is well, when working alone on the vehicle.

DO carry out work in a logical sequence and check that everything is correctly assembled and tightened afterwards.

DO remember that your vehicle's safety affects that of yourself and others. If in doubt on any point, get specialist advice.

IF, in spite of following these precautions, you are unfortunate enough to injure yourself, seek medical attention as soon as possible.

Asbestos

Certain friction, insulating, sealing, and other products – such as brake linings, brake bands, clutch linings, torque converters, gaskets, etc – contain asbestos. *Extreme care must be taken to avoid inhalation of dust from such products since it is hazardous to health.* If in doubt, assume that they *do* contain asbestos.

Fire

Remember at all times that petrol (gasoline) is highly flammable. Never smoke, or have any kind of naked flame around, when working on the vehicle. But the risk does not end there – a spark caused by an electrical short-circuit, by two metal surfaces contacting each other, by careless use of tools, or even by static electricity built up in your body under certain conditions, can ignite petrol vapour, which in a confined space is highly explosive.

Always disconnect the battery earth (ground) terminal before working on any part of the fuel or electrical system, and never risk spilling fuel on to a hot engine or exhaust.

It is recommended that a fire extinguisher of a type suitable for fuel and electrical fires is kept handy in the garage or workplace at all times. Never try to extinguish a fuel or electrical fire with water.

Fumes

Certain fumes are highly toxic and can quickly cause unconsciousness and even death if inhaled to any extent. Petrol (gasoline) vapour comes into this category, as do the vapours from certain solvents such as trichloroethylene. Any draining or pouring of such volatile fluids should be done in a well ventilated area.

When using cleaning fluids and solvents, read the instructions carefully. Never use materials from unmarked containers – they may give off poisonous vapours.

Never run the engine of a motor vehicle in an enclosed space such as a garage. Exhaust fumes contain carbon monoxide which is extremely poisonous; if you need to run the engine, always do so in the open air or at least have the rear of the vehicle outside the workplace.

If you are fortunate enough to have the use of an inspection pit, never drain or pour petrol, and never run the engine, while the vehicle is standing over it; the fumes, being heavier than air, will concentrate in the pit with possibly lethal results.

The battery

Never cause a spark, or allow a naked light, near the vehicle's battery. It will normally be giving off a certain amount of hydrogen gas, which is highly explosive.

Always disconnect the battery earth (ground) terminal before working on the fuel or electrical systems.

If possible, loosen the filler plugs or cover when charging the battery from an external source. Do not charge at an excessive rate or the battery may burst.

Take care when topping up and when carrying the battery. The acid electrolyte, even when diluted, is very corrosive and should not be allowed to contact the eyes or skin.

If you ever need to prepare electrolyte yourself, always add the acid slowly to the water, and never the other way round. Protect against splashes by wearing rubber gloves and goggles.

When jump starting a car using a booster battery, for negative earth (ground) vehicles, connect the jump leads in the following sequence: First connect one jump lead between the positive (+) terminals of the two batteries. Then connect the other jump lead first to the negative (–) terminal of the booster battery, and then to a good earthing (ground) point on the vehicle to be started, at least 18 in (45 cm) from the battery if possible. Ensure that hands and jump leads are clear of any moving parts, and that the two vehicles do not touch. Disconnect the leads in the reverse order.

Mains electricity

When using an electric power tool, inspection light etc, which works from the mains, always ensure that the appliance is correctly connected to its plug and that, where necessary, it is properly earthed (grounded). Do not use such appliances in damp conditions and, again, beware of creating a spark or applying excessive heat in the vicinity of fuel or fuel vapour.

Ignition HT voltage

A severe electric shock can result from touching certain parts of the ignition system, such as the HT leads, when the engine is running or being cranked, particularly if components are damp or the insulation is defective. Where an electronic ignition system is fitted, the HT voltage is much higher and could prove fatal.

Routine maintenance

Maintenance is essential for ensuring safety and desirable for the purpose of getting the best in terms of performance and economy from your car. Over the years the need for periodic lubrication has been greatly reduced if not totally eliminated. This has unfortunately tended to lead some owners to think that because no such action is required the items either no longer exist, or will last forever. This is certainly not the case; it is essential to carry out regular visual examination as comprehensively as possible in order to spot any possible defects at an early stage before they develop into major expensive repairs.

Every 250 miles (400 km) or weekly – whichever comes first

Engine
Check that the level of the oil and top up if necessary (photos)
Check the coolant level and top up if necessary (photo)

Check the level of electrolyte in the battery and top up if necessary (photo)

Tyres
Check the tyre pressures (photo)
Visually examine the tyres for wear and damage

Lights and wipers
Check that all the lights work
Clean the headlamps
Check the windscreen/tailgate washer fluid levels and top up if necessary (photo)

Brakes
Check the level of fluid in the brake master cylinder reservoir – if topping-up is required, check for leaks (photo)

Removing the engine oil level dipstick (CIS engine shown)

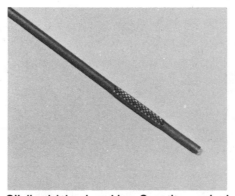

Oil dipstick level marking. Quantity required to raise level from low to high mark is approximately 1 litre (1.8 Imp pints, 1 US quart)

Topping up the engine oil

Topping up the coolant

Topping up the battery electrolyte

Checking the tyre pressure

Checking the windscreen washer fluid level

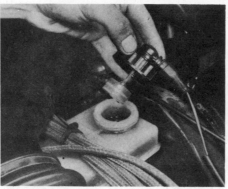

Brake fluid reservoir cap and level switch

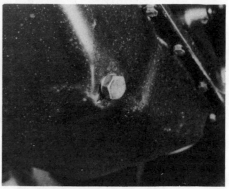

Engine oil drain plug location

UK models: every 10 000 miles (16 000 km) or 12 months – whichever comes first
North American models: every 15 000 miles (24 000 km) or 12 months – whichever comes first

---

This service alternates with the following one at 6 monthly (or the relevant mileage) intervals

Engine

Check clutch play and adjust if necessary
Check antifreeze strength
Check valve clearances and adjust if necessary
Examine all drivebelts for wear, damage and tension
Renew spark plugs
Renew contact breaker points (where applicable)
Check ignition timing
Check idle speed and CO content
Inspect air filter element and renew if necessary
Reset air cleaner intake (where applicable)
Check condition and security of emission control equipment and hoses (where applicable)
Examine engine for oil, water and fuel leaks
Change engine oil
Renew oil filter
Check the power steering fluid and top up to the Full Hot or Full Cold mark on the dipstick (where applicable)
Examine the exhaust system for leaks

Gearbox (manual)

Examine the gearbox and final drive for oil leaks, top up as necessary
Examine the driveshaft CV joint boots for leakage and damage

Automatic transmission

Examine the automatic transmission and final drive for oil leaks. Add automatic transmission fluid and/or gear oil of the specified type, as necessary.

Brakes

Check brake pressure regulator (as applicable)
Examine brake lines and hoses for leaks and damage
Check front and rear brake linings for wear
Adjust rear brakes (as applicable)
Adjust handbrake (as applicable)

Steering

Check tie-rod ends for wear
Check steering balljoints and rubber boots for wear
Check steering gear bellows for damage and leakage

General

Lubricate bonnet lock and door check straps

Examine underbody protection for damage
Check headlights and adjust beam if necessary
Road test car

UK models: first 15 000 miles (24 000 km) or 18 months – whichever comes first, then every 10 000 miles (16 000 km) or 12 months – whichever comes first
North American models: first 22 500 miles (36 000 km) or 18 months – whichever comes first, then every 15 000 miles (24 000 km) or 12 months – whichever comes first

---

This service alternates with the preceding one at 6 monthly (or the relevant mileage) intervals

Engine

Change engine oil

Brakes

Check front brake linings for wear

General

Lubricate bonnet lock and door check straps

UK models: every 20 000 miles (32 000 km) or 2 years – whichever comes first
North American models: every 30 000 miles (48 000 km) or 2 years – whichever comes first

---

Engine

Renew the fuel filter(s)
Renew the air filter element
Adjust the valve clearances
Renew the coolant
Renew the emission control system catalytic converter (where applicable)
Renew the exhaust gas recirculation (EGR) filter
Renew the emission control AIS air filter (where applicable)
Renew the emission control EEC charcoal canister (where applicable)
Renew the emission control OXS oxygen sensor (where applicable)

Automatic transmission

Renew the fluid and clean the oil pan and strainer (where applicable)

Brakes

Renew the brake fluid and check the brakes for operation
Check the brake pressure regulator (if fitted)

Underbonnet view of a Golf GL (air cleaner removed)

1 Vehicle identification plate
2 Alternator
3 Fuel filter
4 Carburettor vacuum reservoir
5 Engine oil filler cap
6 Carburettor
7 Ignition coil
8 Brake fluid reservoir filler cap
9 Windscreen washer reservoir
10 Battery
11 Radiator filler cap
12 Clutch cable adjuster
13 Distributor
14 Fuel purge reservoir
15 Fuel pump

20

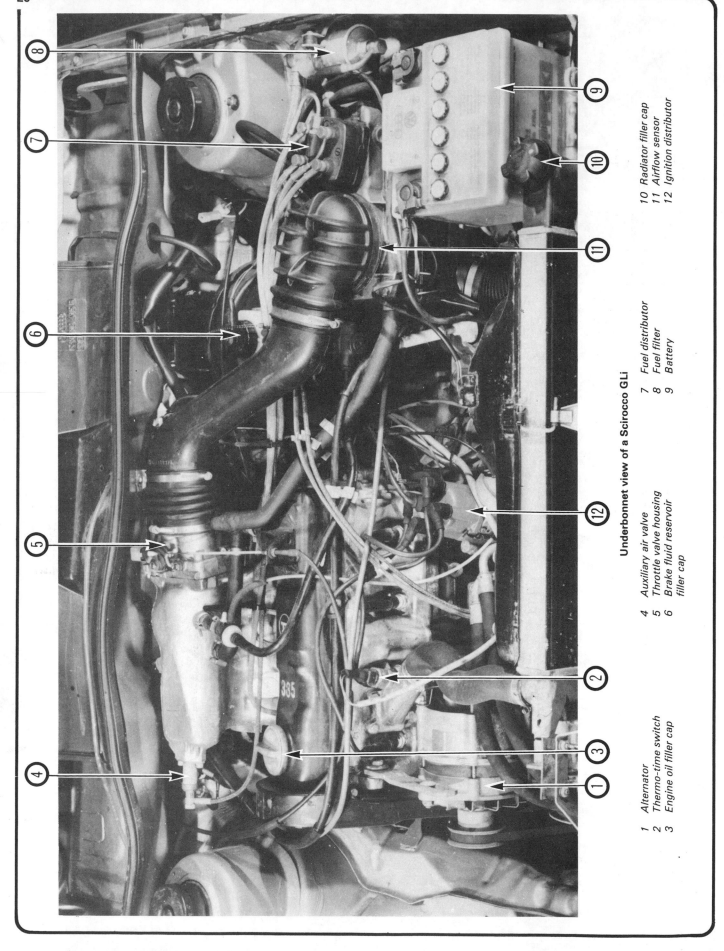

Underbonnet view of a Scirocco GLi

1 Alternator
2 Thermo-time switch
3 Engine oil filler cap

4 Auxiliary air valve
5 Throttle valve housing
6 Brake fluid reservoir
   filler cap

7 Fuel distributor
8 Fuel filter
9 Battery

10 Radiator filler cap
11 Airflow sensor
12 Ignition distributor

Fault diagnosis

Introduction

The car owner who does his or her own maintenance according to the recommended schedules should not have to use this section of the manual very often. Modern component reliability is such that, provided those items subject to wear or deterioration are inspected or renewed at the specified intervals, sudden failure is comparatively rare. Faults do not usually just happen as a result of sudden failure, but develop over a period of time. Major mechanical failures in particular are usually preceded by characteristic symptoms over hundreds or even thousands of miles. Those components which do occasionally fail without warning are often small and easily carried in the car.

With any fault finding, the first step is to decide where to begin investigations. Sometimes this is obvious, but on other occasions a little detective work will be necessary. The owner who makes half a dozen haphazard adjustments or replacements may be successful in curing a fault (or its symptoms), but he will be none the wiser if the fault recurs and he may well have spent more time and money than was necessary. A calm and logical approach will be found to be more satisfactory in the long run. Always take into account any warning signs or abnormalities that may have been noticed in the period preceding the fault – power loss, high or low gauge readings, unusual noises or smells, etc – and remember that failure of components such as fuses or spark plugs may only be pointers to some underlying fault.

The pages which follow here are intended to help in cases of failure to start or breakdown on the road. There is also a Fault Diagnosis Section at the end of each Chapter which should be consulted if the preliminary checks prove unfruitful. Whatever the fault, certain basic principles apply. These are as follows:

Verify the fault. This is simply a matter of being sure that you know what the symptoms are before starting work. This is particularly important if you are investigating a fault for someone else who may not have described it very accurately.

Don't overlook the obvious. For example, if the car won't start, is there petrol in the tank? (Don't take anyone else's word on this particular point, and don't trust the fuel gauge either!) If an electrical fault is indicated, look for loose or broken wires before digging out the test gear.

Cure the disease, not the symptom. Substituting a flat battery with a fully charged one will get you off the hard shoulder, but if the underlying cause is not attended to, the new battery will go the same way. Similarly, changing oil-fouled spark plugs for a new set will get you moving again, but remember that the reason for the fouling (if it wasn't simply an incorrect grade of plug) will have to be established and corrected.

Don't take anything for granted. Particularly, don't forget that a 'new' component may itself be defective (especially if it's been rattling round in the boot for months), and don't leave components out of a fault diagnosis sequence just because they are new or recently fitted. When you do finally diagnose a difficult fault, you'll probably realise that all the evidence was there from the start.

Electrical faults

Electrical faults can be more puzzling than straightforward mechanical failures, but they are no less susceptible to logical analysis if the basic principles of operation are understood. Car electrical wiring exists in extremely unfavourable conditions – heat, vibration and chemical attack – and the first things to look for are loose or corroded connections and broken or chafed wires, especially where the wires

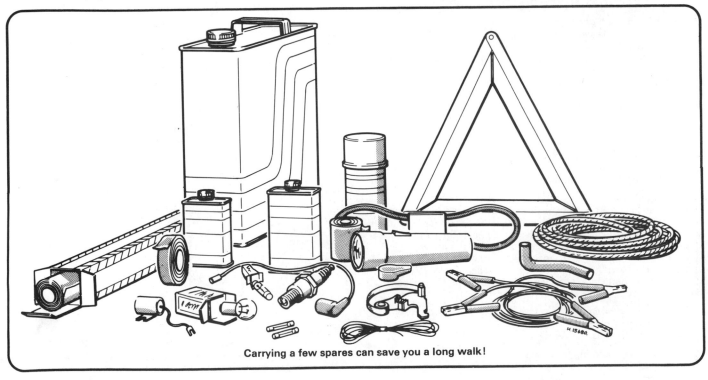

Carrying a few spares can save you a long walk!

pass through holes in the bodywork or are subject to vibration.

All metal-bodied cars in current production have one pole of the battery 'earthed', ie connected to the car bodywork, and in nearly all modern cars it is the negative (–) terminal. The various electrical components – motors, bulb holders etc – are also connected to earth, either by means of a lead or directly by their mountings. Electric current flows through the component and then back to the battery via the car bodywork. If the component mounting is loose or corroded, or if a good path back to the battery is not available, the circuit will be incomplete and malfunction will result. The engine and/or gearbox are also earthed by means of flexible metal straps to the body or subframe; if these straps are loose or missing, starter motor, generator and ignition trouble may result.

Assuming the earth return to be satisfactory, electrical faults will be due either to component malfunction or to defects in the current supply. Individual components are dealt with in Chapter 9. If supply wires are broken or cracked internally this results in an open-circuit, and the easiest way to check for this is to bypass the suspect wire temporarily with a length of wire having a crocodile clip or suitable connector at each end. Alternatively, a 12V test lamp can be used to verify the presence of supply voltage at various points along the wire and the break can thus be isolated.

If a bare portion of a live wire touches the car bodywork or other earthed metal part, the electricity will take the low-resistance path thus formed back to the battery: this is known as a short-circuit. Hopefully a short-circuit will blow a fuse, but otherwise it may cause burning of the insulation (and possibly further short-circuits) or even a fire. This is why it is inadvisable to bypass persistently blowing fuses with silver foil or wire.

Spares and tool kit

Most cars are only supplied with sufficient tools for wheel changing; the *Maintenance and minor repair* tool kit detailed in *Tools and working facilities,* with the addition of a hammer, is probably sufficient for those repairs that most motorists would consider attempting at the roadside. In addition a few items which can be fitted without too much trouble in the event of a breakdown should be carried. Experience and available space will modify the list below, but the following may save having to call on professional assistance:

Spark plugs, clean and correctly gapped
HT lead and plug cap – long enough to reach the plug furthest from the distributor
Distributor rotor, condenser and contact breaker points (where applicable)
Drivebelt – emergency type may suffice
Spare fuses
Set of principal light bulbs
Tin of radiator sealer and hose bandage
Hose clips
Exhaust bandage
Roll of insulating tape
Length of soft iron wire
Length of electrical flex
Torch or inspection lamp (can double as test lamp)
Battery jump leads
Tow-rope
Tyre valve core
Ignition waterproofing aerosol
Litre of engine oil
Sealed can of hydraulic fluid
Emergency windscreen

If spare fuel is carried, a can designed for the purpose should be used to minimise risks of leakage and collision damage. A first aid kit and a warning triangle, whilst not at present compulsory in the UK, are obviously sensible items to carry in addition to the above.

When touring abroad it may be advisable to carry additional spares which, even if you cannot fit them yourself, could save having to wait while parts are obtained. The items below may be worth considering:

Clutch and throttle cables
Cylinder head gasket
Alternator brushes

One of the motoring organisations will be able to advise on availability of fuel etc in foreign countries.

Engine will not start

Engine fails to turn when starter operated
Flat battery (recharge, use jump leads, or push start) (models with catalytic converter must not be push started)
Battery terminals loose or corroded
Battery earth to body defective
Engine earth strap loose or broken
Starter motor (or solenoid) wiring loose or broken
Automatic transmission selector in wrong position, or inhibitor switch faulty (where applicable)
Ignition/starter switch faulty
Major mechanical failure (seizure) or long disuse (piston rings rusted to bores)
Starter or solenoid internal fault (see Chapter 9)

Starter motor turns engine slowly
Partially discharged battery (recharge, use jump leads, or push start) (models with catalytic converter must not be push started)
Battery terminals loose or corroded
Battery earth to body defective
Engine earth strap loose
Starter motor (or solenoid) wiring loose
Starter motor internal fault (see Chapter 9)

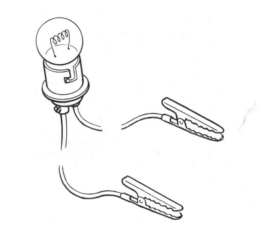

A simple test lamp is useful for tracing electrical faults

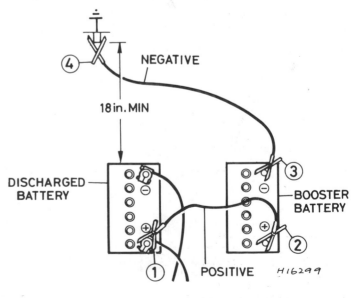

Jump start lead connections for negative earth vehicles – connect leads in order shown

Engine turns normally but fails to start

Damp or dirty HT leads and distributor cap (crank engine and check for spark – photo – but see Chapter 4 for electronic ignition)
Dirty or incorrectly gapped contact breaker points (if applicable)
No fuel in tank (check for delivery at carburettor or fuel distributor) (photos)
Excessive choke (hot engine) or insufficient choke (cold engine) (if applicable)
Fouled or incorrectly gapped spark plugs (remove, clean and regap)
Other ignition system fault (see Chapter 4)
Other fuel system fault (see Chapter 3)
Poor compression (see Chapter 1)
Major mechanical failure (eg camshaft drive)

Engine fires but will not run

Insufficient choke or faulty cold start valve (cold engine)
Air leaks at carburettor or inlet manifold
Fuel starvation (see Chapter 3)
Ballast resistor defective or other ignition fault (see Chapter 4)

Engine cuts out and will not restart

Engine cuts out suddenly – ignition fault

Loose or disconnected LT wires
Wet HT leads or distributor cap (after traversing water splash)
Coil or condensor failure (as applicable)
Other ignition fault (see Chapter 4)

Engine misfires before cutting out – fuel fault

Fuel tank empty
Fuel pump defective or filter blocked (check for delivery)
Fuel tank filler vent blocked (suction will be evident on releasing cap)
Carburettor needle valve sticking (as applicable)
Carburettor jets blocked (fuel contamination) (as applicable)
Other fuel system fault (see Chapter 3)

Engine cuts out – other causes

Serious overheating
Major mechanical failure (eg camshaft drive)

Engine overheats

Ignition (no-charge) warning light illuminated

Slack or broken drivebelt – retension or renew (Chapter 2)

Ignition warning light not illuminated

Coolant loss due to internal or external leakage (see Chapter 2)
Thermostat defective
Low oil level
Brakes binding
Radiator clogged externally or internally
Electric cooling fan not operating correctly
Engine waterways clogged
Ignition timing incorrect or automatic advance malfunctioning
Mixture too weak
Note: *Do not add cold water to an overheated engine or damage may result*

Low engine oil pressure

Warning light illuminated with engine running

Oil level low or incorrect grade
Defective sender unit
Wire to sender unit earthed
Engine overheating
Oil filter clogged or bypass valve defective

Crank engine and check for a spark. Use insulated pliers – dry cloth or a rubber glove will suffice. Do not carry out this check with electronic ignition

Remove fuel pipe from carburettor and check that fuel is being delivered (crank engine on starter)

Slacken fuel distributor (CIS) supply on return unions and check for fuel delivery (ignition switched on)

Oil pressure relief valve defective
Oil pick-up strainer clogged
Oil pump worn or mountings loose
Worn main or big-end bearings
Note: *Low oil pressure in a high-mileage engine at tickover is not necessarily a cause for concern. Sudden pressure loss at speed is far more significant. In any event, check the gauge or warning light sender before condemning the engine.*

Engine noises

Pre-ignition (pinking) on acceleration
Incorrect grade of fuel
Ignition timing incorrect
Distributor faulty or worn
Worn or maladjusted carburettor or CIS
Excessive carbon build-up in engine

Whistling or wheezing noises
Leaking vacuum hose
Leaking carburettor or manifold gasket (as applicable)
Blowing head gasket

Tapping or rattling
Incorrect valve clearances
Worn valve gear
Broken piston ring (ticking noise)

Knocking or thumping
Unintentional mechanical contact (eg fan blades)
Worn fanbelt or other drivebelt
Peripheral component fault (generator, water pump etc)
Worn big-end bearings (regular heavy knocking, perhaps less under load)
Worn main bearings (rumbling and knocking, perhaps worsening under load)
Piston slap (most noticeable when cold)

Chapter 1 Engine

For modifications and information applicable to later models, see Supplement at end of manual

Contents

Specifications

General

Engine type	Four in-line, water cooled, overhead camshaft
Firing order	1 – 3 – 4 – 2
Bore:	
1457 cc	79.5 mm (3.130 in)
1471 cc	76.5 mm (3.012 in)
1588 cc	79.5 mm (3.130 in)
1715 cc	79.5 mm (3.130 in)
Stroke:	
1457 cc	73.4 mm (2.89 in)
1471 cc	80.0 mm (3.15 in)
1588 cc	80.0 mm (3.15 in)
1715 cc	86.4 mm (3.40 in)
Compression ratios:	
1457 cc (except engine code GH)	8.2 to 1
1457 cc (engine code GH)	7.0 to 1
1471 cc (except engine codes FB and FD)	8.2 to 1
1471 cc (engine codes FB and FD)	9.7 to 1
1588 cc (except engine codes EG and FV)	8.2 to 1
1588 cc (engine code EG)	9.5 to 1
1588 cc (engine code FV)	7.0 to 1
1715 cc	8.2 to 1

Crankshaft

Main journal diameter (standard)	54.0 mm (2.126 in)
Main journal undersizes	53.75, 53.50, 53.25 mm (2.116, 2.106, 2.096 in)
Crankpin diameter (standard)	46.00 mm (1.811 in)
Crankpin undersizes	45.75, 45.50, 45.25 mm (1.801, 1.791, 1.781 in)
Main bearing running clearance (maximum)	0.17 mm (0.006 in)
Endfloat (maximum)	0.37 mm (0.015 in)

Connecting rods

Big-end running clearance (maximum)	0.12 mm (0.005 in)
Endfloat (maximum)	0.37 mm (0.015 in)

Pistons

Piston clearance in bore (maximum)	0.07 mm (0.003 in)

Piston diameter (standard) – except 1471 cc:

Honing group A	79.48 mm (3.1291 in)
Honing group B	79.49 mm (3.1295 in)
Honing group C	79.50 mm (3.1299 in)

Piston diameter (standard) – 1471 cc:

Honing group 651	76.48 mm (3.0110 in)
Honing group 652	76.49 mm (3.0114 in)
Honing group 653	76.50 mm (3.0118 in)
Piston oversizes – except 1471 cc	79.73, 79.98, 80.48 mm (3.139, 3.149, 3.169 in)
Piston oversizes – 1471 cc	76.73, 76.98, 77.48 mm (3.021, 3.031, 3.050 in)

Piston rings

Clearance in groove (maximum)	0.15 mm (0.006 in)
End gap – compression rings	0.30 to 0.45 mm (0.012 to 0.018 in)
End gap – oil scraper ring	0.25 to 0.40 mm (0.010 to 0.016 in)

Gudgeon pin

Fit in piston	Push fit at 60°C (140°F)

Intermediate shaft

Endfloat (maximum)	0.25 mm (0.010 in)

Cylinder head

Minimum height	132.55 mm (5.2185 in)

Camshaft

Run-out at centre bearing (maximum)	0.01 mm (0.0004 in)
Endfloat (maximum)	0.15 mm (0.006 in)

Valves

Seat angle	45°
Inlet valve head diameter	34.0 mm (1.339 in)
Exhaust valve head diameter	31.0 mm (1.220 in)
Seat width (maximum)	3.5 mm (0.138 in)
Valve head perimeter width (minimum)	0.5 mm (0.020 in)

Valve guides

Maximum valve rock (valve stem flush with guide):

Inlet valve	1.0 mm (0.040 in)
Exhaust valve	1.3 mm (0.051 in)

Valve timing (nil valve clearance, at 1 mm valve lift)

1457 cc and 1588 cc (except engine code EG from December 1979):

Inlet opens	4° BTDC
Inlet closes	46° ABDC
Exhaust opens	44° BBDC
Exhaust closes	6° ATDC

1471 cc:

Inlet opens	7° BTDC
Inlet closes	43° ABDC
Exhaust opens	47° BBDC
Exhaust closes	3° ATDC

1588 cc (engine code EG from December 1979):

Inlet opens	6° BTDC
Inlet closes	49° ABDC
Exhaust opens	45° BBDC
Exhaust closes	8° ATDC
1715 cc	Information not available at time of writing (see Supplement)

Valve clearances

Cold:

Inlet	0.15 to 0.25 mm (0.006 to 0.010 in)
Exhaust	0.35 to 0.45 mm (0.014 to 0.018 in)

Warm (coolant above 35°C/95°F):

Inlet	0.20 to 0.30 mm (0.008 to 0.012 in)
Exhaust	0.40 to 0.50 mm (0.016 to 0.020 in)

Lubricating system

Oil pump type	Twin gear, driven by intermediate shaft together with distributor
Oil pressure at 2000 rpm, with oil temperature 80°C/176°F	2.0 bar (29 lbf/in²) minimum

Torque wrench settings

	lbf ft	Nm
Valve cover	7	10
Camshaft sprocket	59	80
Timing belt tensioner	33	45
Sump – socket head	5	8
Sump – hexagon head	14	20
Sump drain plug	22	30
Oil pressure switch – tapered thread	8	12
Oil pressure switch – with washer	18	25
Oil filter head	18	25
Sprocket to crankshaft	59	80
Sprocket to intermediate shaft	59	80
Pulley to timing belt sprocket	14	20
Intermediate shaft flange	18	25
Cylinder head bolts:		
10 mm socket head:		
Stage 1	47	65
Stage 2	Tighten further $\frac{1}{4}$ turn	
12 mm socket head:		
Stage 1	29	40
Stage 2	44	60
Stage 3	55	75
Stage 4	Tighten further $\frac{1}{4}$ turn	
Engine front mounting	38	52
Engine side and rear mountings	25	35
Timing belt cover (one-piece)	7	10
Timing belt cover (three-piece):		
Inner	22	30
Outer lower	7	10
Outer upper	14	20
Main bearing caps	47	65
Crankshaft oil seal housing	7	10
Connecting rods big-end nuts (oiled)	33	45
Timing belt tensioner nut	33	45
Timing belt guide	7	10
Camshaft bearing cap	14	20
Oil pressure switch	7	10
Oil pump to block	14	20
Oil pump cover	7	10

1 General description

The engine is of four-cylinder, in-line, overhead camshaft type, mounted transversely at the front of the car. The manual gearbox or automatic transmission is attached to the left-hand side of the engine.

The crankshaft is of five bearing type and the centre bearing shells are flanged to provide a thrust surface to control crankshaft endfloat.

The camshaft is driven by a toothed belt which is tensioned by a tensioner on an eccentric bearing. The valves are operated by bucket type cam followers in direct contact with the camshaft.

An intermediate shaft, which is also driven by the toothed timing belt, drives the distributor and oil pump, and on carburettor engines the fuel pump.

The oil pump is of the twin gear type, driven from the immediate shaft, and it incorporates a pressure relief valve.

The aluminium cylinder head is of conventional design with the inlet and exhaust manifolds mounted on the rear side (as viewed with the engine in the car).

2 Major operations possible with the engine in the car

The following operations can be carried out without having to remove the engine from the car:

(a) Removal and servicing of the cylinder head, camshaft, and timing belt
(b) Renewal of the crankshaft rear oil seal (after removal of the gearbox/transmission, driveplate or clutch as applicable)
(c) Removal of the sump and oil pump
(d) Removal of the piston/connecting rod assemblies (after removal of the cylinder head and sump)
(e) Renewal of the crankshaft front oil seal, intermediate shaft front oil seal, and camshaft front oil seal
(f) Renewal of the engine mountings

3 Major operations only possible after removal of the engine from the car

The following operations can only be carried out after removal of the engine from the car:

(a) Renewal of crankshaft main bearings
(b) Removal and refitting of the crankshaft

4 Method of engine removal

1 The engine together with the gearbox/transmission must be either lifted or lowered from the engine compartment, then the engine separated from the gearbox/transmission on the bench. Two people will be needed for some of the time.
2 A hoist, capacity 3 cwt (150 kg) will be needed and the engine must be lifted or lowered approximately three feet (1 metre). If the hoist is not portable and the engine is lifted, then sufficient room must be left behind the car to push the car back out of the way so that the power unit may be lowered. Blocks will be needed to support the engine after removal.
3 Ideally the car should be over a pit. If this is not possible then the body must be supported on axle stands so that the front wheels may be turned to undo the driveshaft nuts. The left one is accessible from above but the right-hand shaft must be undone from underneath. There are other jobs best done from below. Removal of the shift linkage can only be done from underneath. as can the removal of the exhaust pipe bracket. When all the jobs are done under the car, lower the car back to its wheels unless the unit is being lowered.
4 Draining of oil and coolant is best done away from the working area if possible. This saves the mess made by spilled oil in the place where you must work.

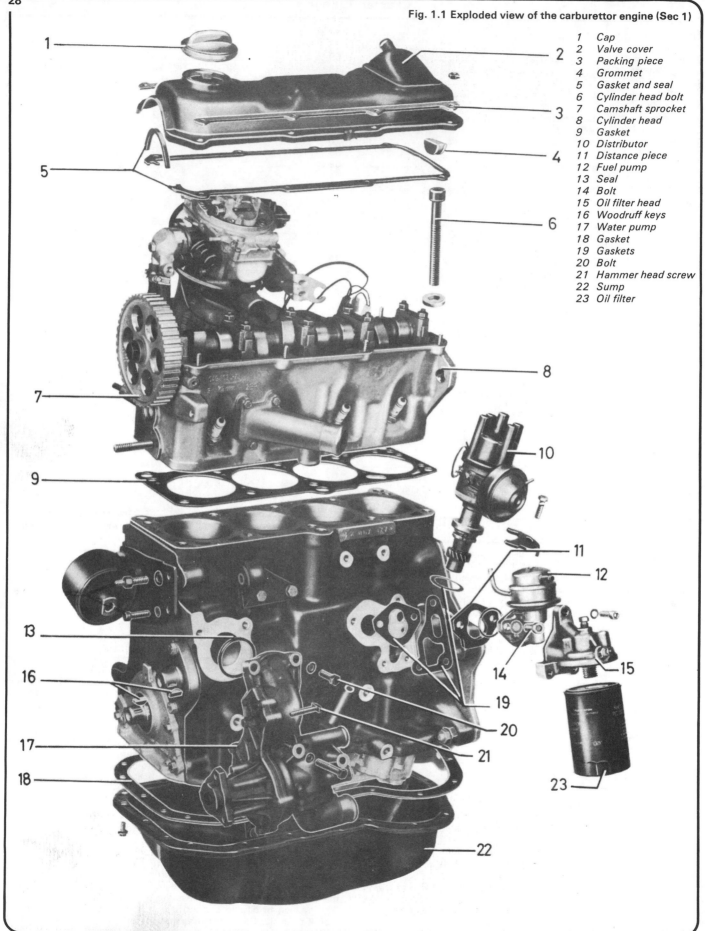

Fig. 1.1 Exploded view of the carburettor engine (Sec 1)

1 Cap
2 Valve cover
3 Packing piece
4 Grommet
5 Gasket and seal
6 Cylinder head bolt
7 Camshaft sprocket
8 Cylinder head
9 Gasket
10 Distributor
11 Distance piece
12 Fuel pump
13 Seal
14 Bolt
15 Oil filter head
16 Woodruff keys
17 Water pump
18 Gasket
19 Gaskets
20 Bolt
21 Hammer head screw
22 Sump
23 Oil filter

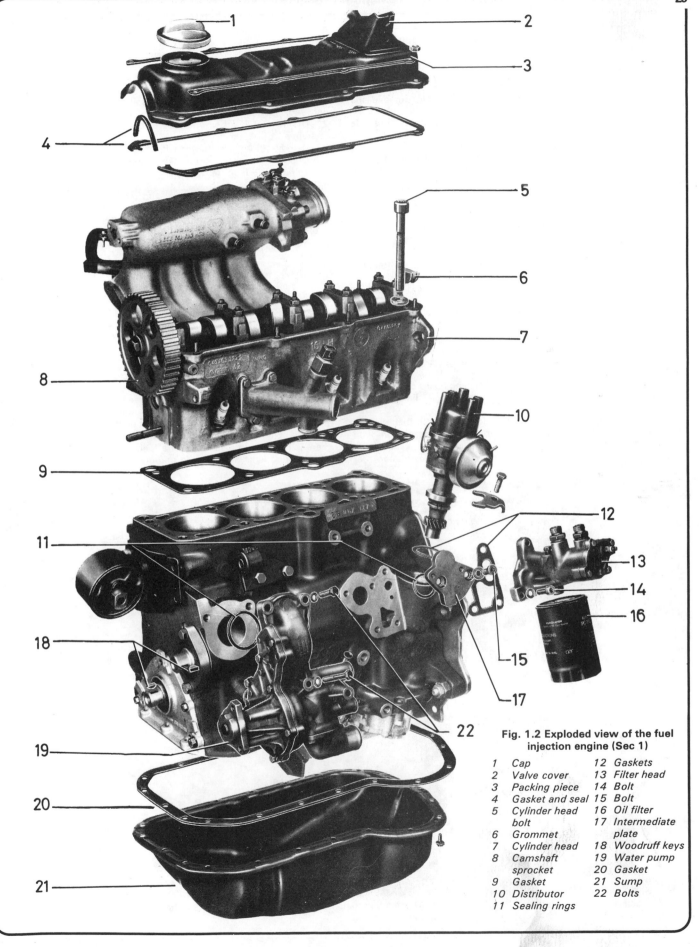

Fig. 1.2 Exploded view of the fuel injection engine (Sec 1)

1	Cap	12	Gaskets
2	Valve cover	13	Filter head
3	Packing piece	14	Bolt
4	Gasket and seal	15	Bolt
5	Cylinder head bolt	16	Oil filter
6	Grommet	17	Intermediate plate
7	Cylinder head	18	Woodruff keys
8	Camshaft sprocket	19	Water pump
9	Gasket	20	Gasket
10	Distributor	21	Sump
11	Sealing rings	22	Bolts

5 Engine and gearbox/transmission assembly – removal and refitting

Note: *Paragraphs 1 to 25 refer to UK carburettor models – refer to paragraphs 26 to 42 for additional information.*

1 Disconnect the battery negative lead. Preferably, remove the battery.

2 Remove the bonnet as described in Chapter 11 and put it in a safe place. Although removal of the bonnet is not essential, it is nevertheless recommended.

3 Where necessary remove the windscreen washer reservoir from the front of the engine compartment.

4 On models with four headlamps, remove the caps and bulbs from the inner headlamps.

5 Remove the air cleaner with reference to Chapter 3.

6 Remove the radiator with reference to Chapter 2.

7 Disconnect and plug the inlet hose from the fuel pump.

8 Disconnect all wiring from the engine, using tape to identify each wire for location (photo).

9 Disconnect the accelerator cable from the carburettor (manual models) and detach the fuel return hose.

10 Remove the vacuum reservoir from the bulkhead and place it on the engine.

11 On automatic transmission models, remove the throttle cable bracket from the carburettor or cylinder head, but do not alter the adjustment.

12 Disconnect the heater hoses and brake servo hose.

13 Remove the speedometer cable from the gearbox/transmission (photo).

14 Disconnect the vacuum hose system, labelling hoses as necessary.

15 Disconnect the manual gearbox gearchange linkage with reference to Chapter 6.

16 On automatic transmission models select 'P' (Park), then disconnect the throttle and selector cables from the transmission with reference to Chapter 6.

17 Unscrew the nuts and withdraw the gearbox/transmission rear mounting, then unbolt the front mounting strut (photos).

18 Disconnect the driveshafts from the gearbox/transmission with reference to Chapter 7, and tie them up out of the way.

19 Unscrew the nuts and withdraw the exhaust system from the manifold. Where necessary detach the brackets from the engine and gearbox/transmission.

20 Attach a suitable hoist to the engine and gearbox/transmission unit and take its weight.

21 On manual gearbox models, disconnect the clutch cable with reference to Chapter 5.

22 Remove the starter motor with reference to Chapter 9.

23 Unscrew the nuts and remove the gearbox/transmission left-hand side mounting, then detach the right-hand side engine mounting (photos).

24 Check that all cables, wiring, and mountings have been disconnected, then lift the unit from the engine compartment, at the same time turning it slightly. Alternatively, lower the unit onto the ground and lift the body over it.

25 Refitting is a reversal of removal, but note the following additional points:

   (a) Attach the mountings loosely at first, then align and centralize the mountings with reference to Chapter 6
   (b) Adjust the throttle cable with reference to Chapter 3 and the clutch cable (manual gearbox) or selector cable (automatic transmission) with reference to Chapter 5 or 6
   (c) Refill the cooling system with reference to Chapter 2
   (d) Refill the engine with oil

UK Jetronic models (additional procedure)

26 During the removal procedure, detach the oil cooler from its location by the radiator – there is no need to disconnect the hoses if the unit is temporarily secured to the engine (photo).

27 Remove the airflow sensor and inlet duct, together with the warm-up valve, cold start valve and injectors as described in Chapter 3 – there is no need to disconnect the fuel lines.

28 Refitting is as described in paragraph 25.

5.8 Disconnecting the wire from the oil pressure switch

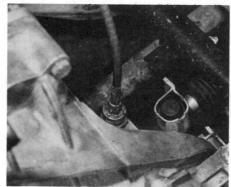

5.13 Disconnecting the speedometer drive cable

5.17a The gearbox/transmission rear mounting

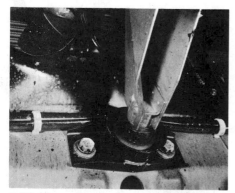

5.17b The gearbox/transmission front mounting and strut

5.23a The gearbox/transmission left-hand side mounting

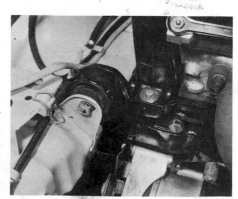

5.23b The engine right-hand side mounting

5.26 Oil cooler location on a Scirocco (UK)

Fig. 1.3 Removal of the compressor (K) and condenser (C) on models with air conditioning (Sec 5)

North American models with CIS (additional procedure)

29 During the removal procedure open the fuel filler cap to disperse any tank pressure.

30 Remove the airflow sensor and inlet duct, together with the warm-up valve, cold start valve and injectors as described in Chapter 3 – there is no need to disconnect the fuel lines.

31 Disconnect the additional vacuum hoses from the distributor advance/retard capsule, EGR temperature valve, vacuum amplifier and vacuum booster (as applicable).

32 Detach the ventilation hose from the valve cover.

33 Disconnect the exhaust system at the front of the flexible pipe instead of at the manifold.

34 Remove the horn from the front body crossmember.

35 Remove the driveshafts completely with reference to Chapter 7, but reconnect the suspension so that the vehicle can be lowered to the ground.

36 Refitting is a reversal of removal, with reference to paragraph 25. Refer to Chapter 7 when refitting the driveshafts. Make sure that the vacuum hoses are correctly routed by referring to the sticker in the engine compartment, or to Chapter 3 of this manual.

North American carburettor models (additional procedure)

37 The additional procedure is as given in paragraphs 29 to 36, with the exception of CIS equipment.

All models with air conditioning (additional procedure)

38 The air conditioning refrigerant circuit **must not** be opened except by a trained refrigeration engineer. However, in order to remove the engine, the compressor and condenser can be removed from the vehicle and placed on a suitable table located by the right-hand side front wing. Access to the condenser is gained after the removal of the radiator.

39 On 1979 North American models, before disconnecting the battery negative lead switch on the ignition and air conditioner, then unscrew the compressor clutch bolt. Using a $\frac{5}{8}$ in x 18 UNF bolt, press the clutch off the compressor shaft, then switch off the ignition and air conditioner and disconnect the compressor clutch wire. To loosen the drivebelt, turn the tensioner until a 10 mm Allen key can be inserted to loosen the bolt.

40 On 1980 on North American models, unscrew the four nuts and dismantle the compressor drivebelt pulley noting the position of the shims. Remove the drivebelt and disconnect the compressor clutch wire.

41 On all North American models, remove the alternator before removing the compressor.

42 Refitting of the compressor and condenser is a reversal of removal, but adjust the drivebelt tension as described in Chapter 11. On 1980 on North American models, the correct tension is achieved by varying the position of the shims (see Fig. 1.5).

Fig. 1.4 Engine right-hand side mounting showing gap (arrowed) which must be uppermost (Sec 5)

Fig. 1.5 Compressor pulley components on 1980 on North American models with air conditioning (Sec 5)

6 Engine and gearbox/transmission – separating and refitting

The procedure is fully described in Chapter 6, Section 2 (manual gearbox) or Section 28 (automatic transmission), however it is only necessary to refer to the paragraphs which have not already been completed by the removal of the engine. The engine must be supported on blocks, or alternatively the gearbox/transmission can be withdrawn with the engine still on the hoist.

7 Engine dismantling – general

1 If possible mount the engine on a stand for the dismantling procedure, but failing this, support it in an upright position with blocks of wood.
2 Cleanliness is most important, and if the engine is dirty, it should be cleaned with paraffin while keeping it in an upright position.
3 Avoid working with the engine directly on a concrete floor, as grit presents a real source of trouble.
4 As parts are removed, clean them in a paraffin bath. However, do not immerse parts with internal oilways in paraffin as it is difficult to remove, usually requiring a high pressure hose. Clean oilways with nylon pipe cleaners.
5 It is advisable to have suitable containers to hold small items according to their use, as this will help when reassembling the engine and also prevent possible losses.
6 Always obtain complete sets of gaskets when the engine is being dismantled, but retain the old gaskets with a view to using them as a pattern to make a replacement if a new one is not available.
7 When possible, refit nuts, bolts and washers in their location after being removed, as this helps to protect the threads and will also be helpful when reassembling the engine.
8 Retain unserviceable components in order to compare them with the new parts supplied.

8 Ancillary components – removal

1 With the engine separated from the gearbox/transmission, the externally mounted ancillary components can now be removed.
2 Unscrew the nuts and withdraw the valve cover, noting where the packing pieces are fitted. Remove the gaskets. On later models it may be necessary to remove the timing belt upper cover first.
3 Unscrew the bolts or nuts as applicable and remove the timing belt cover. As from February 1979 a three-piece fully enclosed cover is fitted, but before this date a one-piece cover is fitted together with a guide located between the crankshaft and intermediate shaft gears.
4 It is now possible to save a lot of trouble when assembling the engine by studying the timing marks. On the intermediate sprocket for the timing belt one tooth has a centre-punch bolt. Turn the engine until this mates with a notch on the V-belt pulley bolted to the crankshaft sprocket (photo). The easier way to turn the engine is to remove the plugs and turn it with a socket spanner on the crankshaft pulley nut.
5 When these marks match, look at the sprocket on the camshaft. One tooth of this has a centre-punch mark. This should be level with the valve cover flange. Having turned the engine until these marks agree now look at the cams for No 1 cylinder, the one nearest the timing belt. They will both be in the 'valve closed' position (photo). Now look through the hole in which the TDC sensor goes where the timing marks show on the periphery of the flywheel and note the reading. Check where the rotor arm points on the distributor, it should point to No 1 plug lead and a mark on the edge of the rim of the base of the distributor (photo). The distributor body is held in position by a bolt and clamp. Using a centre-punch mark the distributor body and the cylinder block in such a way that the marks are adjacent and may be used to set the distributor body at the right position on reassembly of the engine.
6 Remove the clamp, and holding the crankshaft to prevent it turning, lift the distributor body slowly out of the cylinder block. This will cause the distributor shaft to rotate slightly as its skew drive gear moves over the one on the intermediate shaft. Do not allow the distributor body to rotate. Note the amount the shaft has rotated and refit the distributor. The rotor should rotate to the mark on the rim for No 1 cylinder. When you are satisfied that you understand the method of resetting the timing, remove the distributor. If you look down the

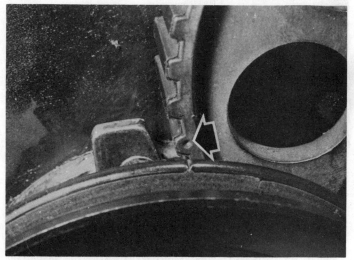

8.4 Intermediate shaft timing mark (arrowed) aligned with the notch in the crankshaft pulley

Fig. 1.6 Camshaft sprocket timing mark (arrowed) with No 1 cylinder at TDC on compression (Sec 8)

8.5a No 1 cylinder cam lobes in valve closed position

8.5b Distributor rotor position with No 1 cylinder at TDC on compression

8.7 Oil cooler hoses on the filter head on a Scirocco (UK)

hole left in the cylinder block you will see the top of the oil pump driveshaft. This has a slot in it. Note the angle of the slot carefully so that it can be set for easy reassembly. It is quite easy to reach and turn with a finger or a screwdriver. It should be parallel to the crankshaft.

7   Remove the oil filter as described in Section 11, then unbolt the filter head from the cylinder block using an Allen key. On models fitted with an oil cooler, unscrew the supply and return hoses from the head and identify them for position (photo). Remove the gasket.

8   Remove the fuel pump as described in Chapter 3, except on fuel injection models.

9   Unscrew the oil pressure switch from the flywheel end of the cylinder head or filter head (as applicable) and remove the washer (if fitted).

10   Remove the alternator as described in Chapter 9, together with the drivebelt.

11   Remove the water pump as described in Chapter 2. Remove all hoses from the engine.

12   Before removing the timing drivebelt check its correct tension. If held between the finger and thumb halfway between the intermediate shaft and the camshaft it should be just possible to twist it through 90°. If it is too slack, adjust it by slackening the bolt holding the eccentric cam on the tensioner wheel. If you are satisfied it can be adjusted to the correct tension remove it and examine it for wear. Now is the time to order a new one if necessary, not when the engine is almost assembled.

13   Remove the crankshaft pulley by taking out the centre bolt and drawing off the two pulleys together. Do not separate them unless

necessary, and if you do, the angular relationship between the pulley keyway and the timing notch on the V-belt pulley must be maintained on reassembly.

14   Where applicable on pre-February 1979 models, unbolt the timing belt guide from the front of the block.

15   Remove the centre bolt from the camshaft driving sprocket and pull it off the camshaft. Do not lose the Woodruff key.

16   On North American models, remove the emission control equipment with reference to Chapter 3.

17   Remove the inlet and exhaust manifolds noting that on carburettor engines there is no need to remove the carburettor from the inlet manifold.

18   Remove the clutch as described in Chapter 5 on manual gearbox models, then unbolt the intermediate plate. On automatic transmission models unbolt the driveplate from the crankshaft, noting the location of the spacer and shim(s).

19   Where fitted remove the power steering pump, as described in Chapter 12.

9   Cylinder head – removal and overhaul

Refer to Section 7, and Section 8 for initial dismantling procedures.

1   Refer to Fig. 1.10. Remove the camshaft bearing caps. These have to go back the same way in the same place. They are numbered (photo), but put a centre-punch on the side nearest the front of the head (where the sprocket was). No 1 is the one with a small oil seal on it.

2   Remove bearing caps 5, 1 and 3 in that order. Now undo the nuts holding 2 and 4 in a diagonal pattern and the camshaft will lift them up as the pressure of the valve springs is exerted. When they are free lift the caps off and the camshaft may be lifted out as well. The oil seal on the front end will come with it.

3   The tappet buckets are now exposed and may be lifted out (photo). Take each one out in turn, prise the little disc out of the bucket by inserting a small screwdriver either side and lift the disc away. On the reverse the disc is engraved with a size (eg 3.75). This is its thickness number. Note the number and then clean the disc and refit it number side down. There are eight of these and they must not be mixed. On assembly they must go back into the bore from which they came. This problem exists also for the valves so a container for each valve assembly and tappet is indicated. Label them 1 to 8, 1 and 2 will be No 1 cylinder exhaust and inlet respectively. No 3 will be No 2 cylinder exhaust and No 4 its inlet valve. No 5 will be the inlet valve for No 3 cylinder and No 6 its exhaust valve. No 7 will be the inlet valve for No 4 cylinder and No 8 its exhaust valve. Note the thickness of all the tappet clearance discs from No 1 valve to No 8 valve for use on reassembly.

4   The next job is to remove the cylinder head bolts. These are hidden away down in the well of the head and to make life easier are socket headed bolts. If you do not have the correct tool (although this is preferable) on early models it may be possible to utilise an Allen key used the wrong way round, that is with the long arm fitted to the bolt. Fit a suitable socket over the short arm and a socket extension bar into the socket (see Fig. 1.11) and proceed to undo the cylinder head bolts in the reverse sequence to that shown in Fig. 1.23. On later models the correct splined tool must be used.

5   When all ten bolts have been removed lift the head from the cylinder block. It may need a little tapping to loosen it but do not try to prise it loose by hammering in wedges. Lift off the gasket and cover the top of the cylinder block with a clean cloth.

6   Take the cylinder head away from the clean area and with a wire brush, blunt screwdriver and steel wool clean off all the carbon from the combustion chambers, valve faces and exhaust ports. When the head is clean and shining wash your hands and take it back to the work area. Remove the spark plugs for cleaning.

7   The valves are not easy to get out unless a suitable valve spring compressor is available. Because the collets and spring caps are set so far down in the head a long claw is necessary on the compressor, and it must be split sufficiently to enable the collets to be removed and inserted. If such a tool is not to hand then find a piece of steel tube about 1 inch (25.4 mm) inside diameter which will fit over the valve stem and press down the spring cover (see Fig. 1.12). The length will depend on the size of the compressor so fit the compressor over the

Fig. 1.7 Timing belt components on pre-February 1979 models (Sec 8)

1	Camshaft sprocket	5 Intermediate shaft	8 Crankshaft sprocket	12 Bolt
2	Bolt	sprocket	9 Nut	13 Drivebelt
3	Tensioner	6 Timing belt guide	10 Pulley	14 Cover
4	Bolt	7 Timing belt	11 Bolt	

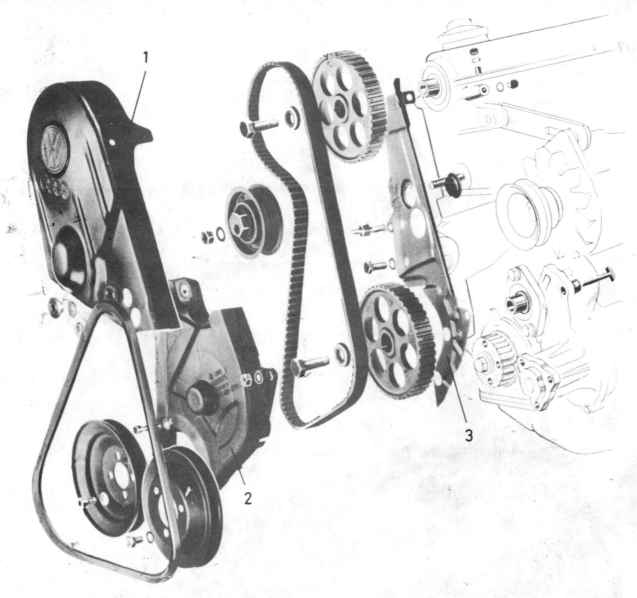

Fig. 1.8 Timing belt components on February 1979 on models. See Fig. 1.7 for identification of common components
(Sec 8)

1 Upper cover   2 Lower cover   3 Rear cover

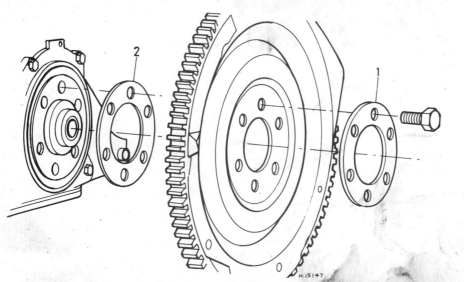

Fig. 1.9 Driveplate components for automatic transmission models
(Sec 8)

1 Spacer
2 Shim

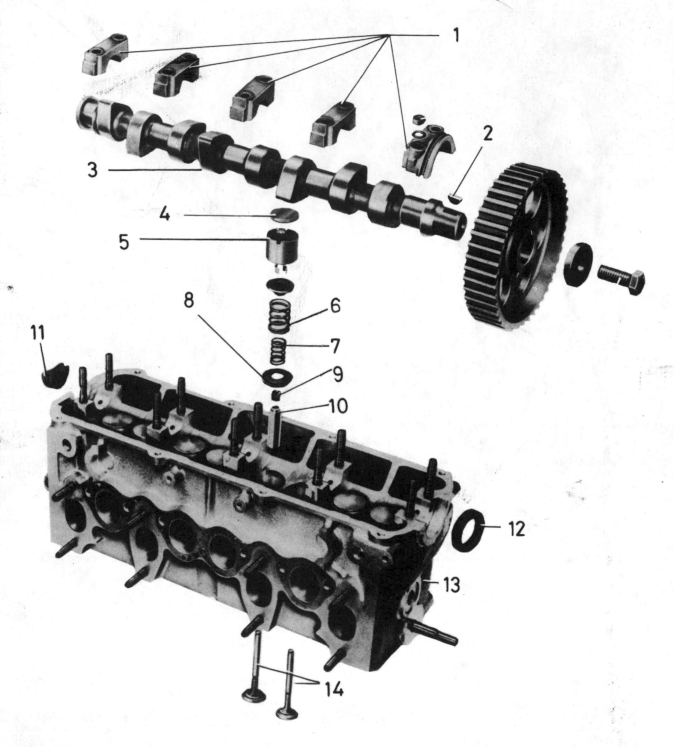

Fig. 1.10 Cylinder head and camshaft components (Sec 9)

1	Bearing caps	5	Bucket tappet	9	Seal	12	Oil seal
2	Woodruff key	6	Outer valve spring	10	Valve guide	13	Cylinder head
3	Camshaft	7	Inner valve spring	11	Grommet	14	Valves
4	Shim	8	Seat				

9.1 Removing a camshaft bearing cap

9.3 Tappet bucket and disc

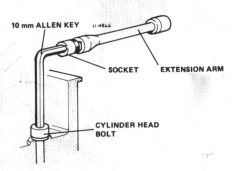

Fig. 1.11 Method of removing cylinder head bolts using an Allen key – early models only (Sec 9)

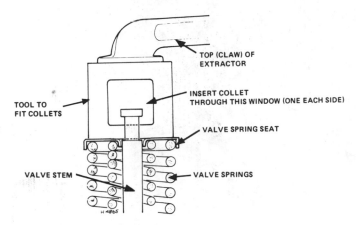

Fig. 1.12 Improvised tool used to remove and refit collets to valve stems (Sec 9)

head fully extended, measure the distance between the claw and the valve spring seat and cut the tube to a suitable length.

8   The next step is to cut two windows of suitable size, say one inch (25.4 mm) long and $\frac{5}{8}$ in (15.9 mm) wide, in opposite sides of the tube. The tube may then be used with the compressor to extract the collets from each valve stem in turn and the valve, springs, collets and seats may join the tappet in the appropriate receptacle, keeping them strictly together for refitting in the same valve guide from which they were taken.

9   The valve springs may easily be checked. It is unlikely that you have a calibrated valve spring compressor, so arrange the spring on the top of a vice with the upper seat in position. Pass a piece of stout wire through the seat and the spring, tie a big knot in the end above the seat so that it will not pull through the hole and hang 100 lb (45.4 kg) on the other end (for the outer spring). The measurement of the length of the spring under this load should be 0.916 in (23.266 mm). If it is less than 0.900 in (22.86 mm) then it needs renewing. Check all the outer springs first and then repeat for the inners (48 lb/21.8 kg and a limit of 0.7 in/17.78 mm). Alternatively, compare the old springs with new ones.

10 The valves should be cleaned and checked for signs of wear or burring. Where this has occurred the inlet valves may be reground on a machine at the agents, but exhaust valves must not be reground in the machine but ground in by hand. Wear in the valve guides may be detected by fitting a new valve in the guide and checking the amount that the rim of the valve will move sideways, when the top of the valve stem is flush with the top of the valve guide. The valve rock limits are given in the Specifications. New valve guides must be fitted and reamed by your VW dealer.

11 Do not labour away too long grinding in the valves. If the valve seat and valve are not satisfactory after fifteen minutes hard work then you will probably do more harm than good by going on. Make sure both surfaces are clean, smear the grinding paste onto the valve evenly and using a suction type cup work the valve with an oscillating motion lifting the valve away from the seat occasionally to stop ridging. Clean the seat and valve frequently and carry on until there is an even band,

grey in colour on both seat and valve then wipe off all the paste.

12 The surface of the head must be checked with a straight-edge and feeler gauge. Place the straight-edge along the centre of the machined face of the head. Make sure there are no ridges at the extreme ends and measure the clearance with feelers between each combustion chamber head. This is the area where the narrowest part of the cylinder head gasket comes – and where the gasket is most likely to fail. If the straight-edge is firmly in place and feelers in excess of 0.004 in (0.1 mm) can be put between the head and the straight-edge then the head should be taken to the agent for servicing or, more probably, a new one.

13 VW recommend that the valve stem oil seals should **always** be renewed to prevent possible high oil consumption. Pulling off the old seal is simple with pliers. With a packet of new oil seals is a small plastic sleeve. This is fitted over the valve stem and lubricated and then the seal should be pushed on over the plastic sleeve until it seats on the guide. This must be done with a special tool (VW 10 204) which fits snugly round the outside of the seal and pushes it on squarely. If the seal is assembled without the plastic sleeve the seal will be damaged and oil consumption will become excessive. If you cannot put them on properly then ask the agent to do it for you.

14 The camshaft should be tested if possible for run-out by mounting it between centres in a lathe and checking the bearing surfaces with a dial gauge. Examine the cam lobes for wear and burrs. Small blemishes may be removed with a fine oil stone, but do not attempt to remove grooves or ridges. If it is necessary to renew the camshaft be careful that you get the right one, there are several kinds which will fit but give entirely the wrong valve timing. Refit the camshaft and its bearings without the valves in the head and check the endplay (see Specifications).

15 When all the parts, head, valves, seats, springs, guides, seals and camshaft have been pronounced satisfactory (photo) then assembly of the head may commence. Insert the valve in the correct guide (photo), fit the inner seat, valve springs and outer seat (photo), assemble the valve spring compressor and possibly the small tube and compress the valve spring until the collets may be assembled to the valve stem (photo). If your fingers are too big, put a blob of grease on the collet and pick it up with a small screwdriver, then insert it into the slot on the valve stem, assemble the second collet and holding them carefully together in place ease off the compressor until the spring seats the collets home. Remove the compressor, put a rag over the valve stem and tap the stem with a hammer. This is to ensure that the collets are seated correctly. If they are they will not come out. Repeat until all eight valves are in position in the cylinder head.

16 Refit the tappets in the bores from which they came (photo) and install the camshaft (photo). Fit a new oil seal at the sprocket end, lubricate the bearings, set the shaft in position, and install bearing caps (photo) Nos 2 and 4, tightening the nuts in a diagonal pattern until the shaft is in place. Now install the other bearing caps, making sure they are the right way round (centre-punch marks towards the drive pulley) and tighten the caps down using a diagonal pattern to the specified torque. Install a new rubber seal at the opposite end to the sprocket.

17 Adjust the valve clearances with reference to Section 23.

18 Loosely fit the valve cover and set the head on one side for assembly to the block in due course. If the engine is not being completely stripped, clean the piston crowns and block face.

19 VW recommend that if the old type (10 mm socket head) cylinder

9.15a Valve, springs, cap and collets

9.15b Installing a valve in the head

9.15c Installing valve springs and cap ...

9.15d ... and valve collets

9.16a Fit the tappet buckets

9.16b Installing the camshaft ...

9.16c ... and bearing caps

head bolts were fitted, they be replaced with the new type (12 mm socket head) bolts.

10 Crankshaft, connecting rods, pistons and intermediate shaft – removal

1 Turn the engine on its side and remove the sump. There may be more oil to run out so be ready to catch it. The oil pump complete with strainer may now be removed after undoing the two bolts. Place it on one side for inspection and overhaul.

2 At the flywheel end remove the six bolts holding the oil seal flange and the gasket to the cylinder block and take off the flange.

3 Remove the intermediate pulley and then undo the two bolts holding the intermediate shaft oil seal flange, after which the intermediate shaft may be drawn out (photos). Remove the O-ring.

4 Undo the five bolts holding the crankshaft oil seal flange to the front of the block and remove the flange and seal.

5 It is important that all the big-end bearing caps are refitted in exactly the way they were fitted before dismantling. This applies also to the shell bearings and pistons. Using a centre-punch mark the connecting rod bearing caps on the edge nearest the front (timing wheel end) using one dot for number 1, two for number 2, and so on.

6 Undo the nuts or bolts from No 1 connecting rod bearing and remove the bearing cap. Whichever are fitted VW recommend that they be renewed on overhaul, so add them to the order list. Gently push the connecting rod and piston out of the block through the top. Do not force it; if there is difficulty then draw the piston back and you will probably find a ridge of carbon at the top of the bore. Remove this with a scraper and if there is a metal ridge reduce this as well, but do not score the bore. The piston and connecting rod will now come out. On the top of the piston there is an arrow which should point towards the front of the engine (photo). Refit the connecting rod bearing cap the right way round and mark the connecting rod and bearing cap with a centre punch so that they may be easily assembled correctly. All this takes time but the effect on assembly more than saves any time spent

Fig. 1.13 Crankshaft and cylinder block components
(Sec 10)

1 Main bearing caps	shells	5 Crankshaft	7 Upper main bearing	9 Intermediate shaft
2 Bolt	4 Centre main bearing	6 Centre main bearing	shell	10 Oil seal
3 Lower main bearing	lower shell	upper shell	8 Oil seal	11 Flange

10.3a Intermediate shaft retaining flange bolts (arrowed)

10.3b Removing the intermediate shaft

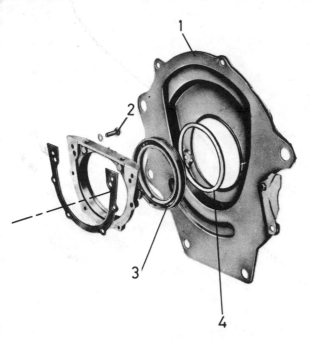

Fig. 1.14 Flywheel end crankshaft oil seal components (Sec 10)

1   Intermediate plate
2   Bolt
3   Oil seal
4   Sealing ring (not fitted to all models)

Fig. 1.15 Main bearing cap number locations (Sec 10)

10.6 The arrow on the piston crown must face the timing belt end of the engine

10.7 Checking the crankshaft endfloat at No 3 main bearing

now on marking parts. Set the connecting rod and piston on one side labelled No 1 and proceed to remove 2, 3 and 4, labelling them likewise.

7   Now examine the main bearing caps. It will be seen that the caps are numbered one to five and that the number is on the side of the engine opposite the oil pump position. Identify these numbers. If they are obscured then mark the caps in the same way as the connecting rod caps. Before removing the caps push the crankshaft to the rear and check the endfloat using a feeler gauge between the thrust washer flanges on No 3 main bearing and the crankshaft web (photo). It must not exceed the specified maximum.

8   Remove the bearing cap retaining bolts, remove the bearing caps and lift out the crankshaft. If the main bearings are not being renewed make sure the shells are identified so that they go back into the same housing the same way.

11 Oil filter – renewal

1   The oil filter is located on the front of the engine beside the alternator (photo).
2   Place a suitable container beneath the filter then, using a strap wrench, unscrew the filter and discard it.
3   Wipe clean the sealing face on the filter head.
4   Smear the sealing rubber on the new filter with engine oil, then fit and tighten the filter by hand only (or as directed on the filter cartridge).

12 Crankcase ventilation system – description

The crankcase ventilation system comprises a hose from the flywheel end of the valve cover to the clean side of the air cleaner.
Periodically the hose should be examined for security and condition. Cleaning will not normally be necessary except when the engine is well worn and sludge has accumulated.

13 Examination and renovation – general

With the engine completely stripped, clean all the components

Fig. 1.16 Cylinder block and piston components (Sec 10)

1	Piston rings	4	Gudgeon pin	7	Big-end bearing shell
2	Piston	5	Connecting rod	8	Big-end bearing cap
3	Circlip	6	Cylinder block	9	Nuts

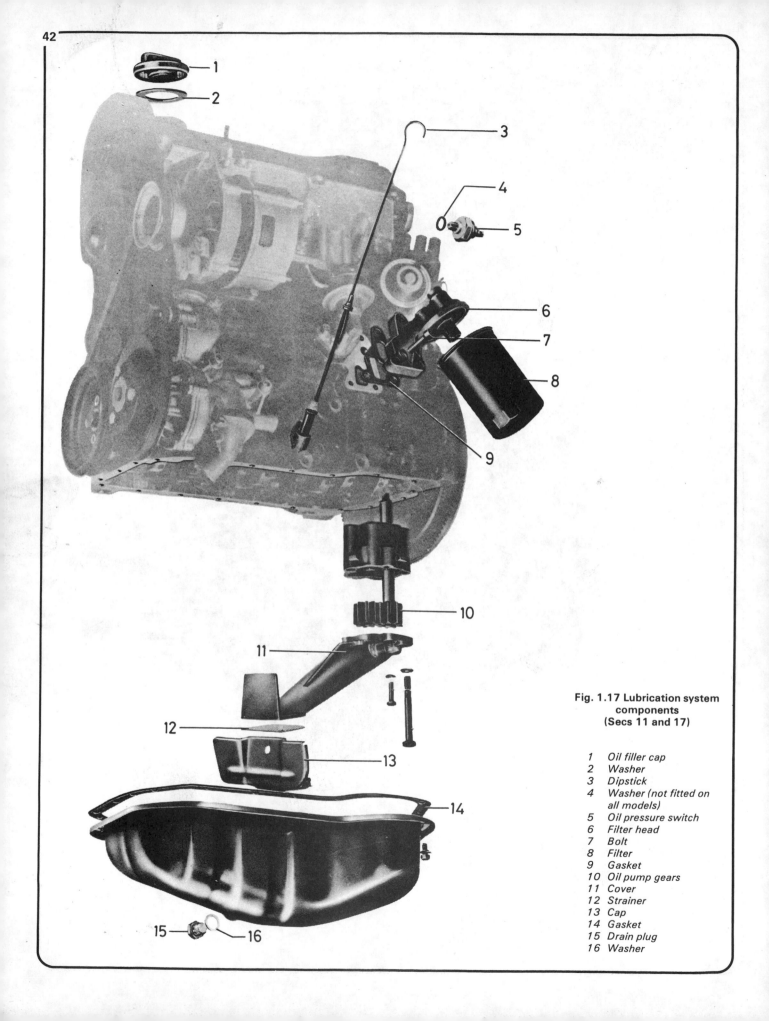

Fig. 1.17 Lubrication system
components
(Secs 11 and 17)

1   Oil filler cap
2   Washer
3   Dipstick
4   Washer (not fitted on
    all models)
5   Oil pressure switch
6   Filter head
7   Bolt
8   Filter
9   Gasket
10 Oil pump gears
11 Cover
12 Strainer
13 Cap
14 Gasket
15 Drain plug
16 Washer

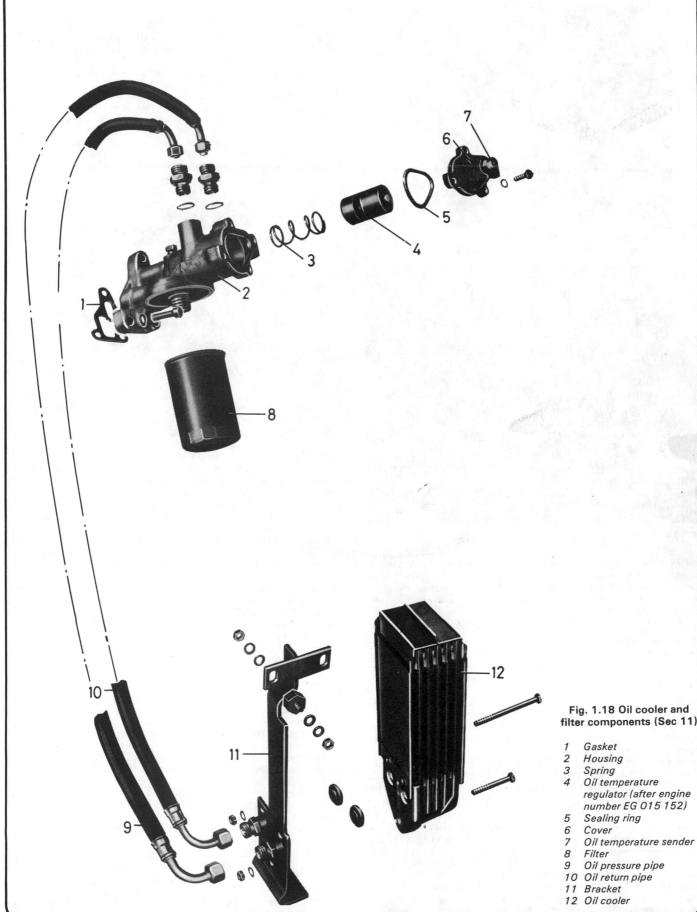

Fig. 1.18 Oil cooler and filter components (Sec 11)

1 Gasket
2 Housing
3 Spring
4 Oil temperature
  regulator (after engine
  number EG 015 152)
5 Sealing ring
6 Cover
7 Oil temperature sender
8 Filter
9 Oil pressure pipe
10 Oil return pipe
11 Bracket
12 Oil cooler

Fig. 1.19 Oil cooler oil temperature regulator location (arrowed) up to engine number EG 015 152 (Sec 11)

11.1 The oil filter

and examine them for wear. Each part should be checked, and where necessary renewed or renovated as described in the following Sections. Renew main and big-end shell bearings as a matter of course, unless you know that they have had little wear and are in perfect condition.

14 Crankshaft and main bearings – examination and renovation

1   Examine the bearing surfaces of the crankshaft for scratches or scoring and, using a micrometer, check each journal and crankpin for ovality. Where this is found to be in excess of 0.025 mm (0.001 in) the crankshaft will have to be reground and undersize bearings fitted.
2   Crankshaft regrinding should be carried out by a suitable engineering works, who will normally supply the matching undersize main and big-end shell bearings.
3   If the crankshaft endfloat is more than the maximum specified amount, new main bearings including the centre flanged ones should be fitted; these are usually supplied together with the big-end bearings on a reground crankshaft.

15 Cylinder block and crankcase – examination and renovation

1   The cylinder bores must be examined for taper, ovality, scoring, and scratches. Start by examining the top of the bores; if these are worn, a slight ridge will be found which marks the top of the piston ring travel. If the wear is excessive, the engine will have had a high oil consumption rate accompanied by blue smoke from the exhaust.

2   If available, use an inside dial gauge to measure the bore diameter just below the ridge and compare it with the diameter at the bottom of the bore, which is not subject to wear. If the difference is more than 0.15 mm (0.006 in), the cylinders will normally require reboring with new oversize pistons fitted.
3   If the degree of cylinder bore wear does not justify reboring, special oil control rings and/or pistons can be fitted to restore compression and stop the engine burning oil.
4   If new pistons or rings are being fitted to old bores, it is essential to roughen the bore walls slightly with fine glasspaper to enable the new piston rings to bed in properly.
5   Thoroughly examine the crankcase and cylinder block for cracks and damage and use a piece of wire to probe all oilways and waterways to ensure they are unobstructed.

16 Pistons and connecting rods – examination and renovation

1   If the engine has covered a high mileage, the pistons must be removed from the connecting rods, the gudgeon pins checked, and the rings renewed.
2   If the piston is worn excessively then remove the gudgeon pin and fit a new piston assembly with new rings as supplied from the VW store.
3   From the outset it must be clear that rings come in sets, if you break one then the minimum purchase is three, so be careful.
4   To remove the gudgeon pin first remove the circlips from each end and then push the pin out. If it is tight, then raise the temperature of the piston to 60°C (140°F) in hot water. Check the play in the connecting rod bush, if the pin seems loose the running clearance limits are 0.011 to 0.025 mm (0.0004 to 0.0009 in) which means if you can rock it at all then either the bush or pin are worn. New bushes can be obtained and pressed into the connecting rod if necessary, but they must then be reamed to size to fit the pin. It is felt that this job should be left to the agent, not because it is difficult, but because it requires an expensive reamer. However, this is rarely necessary.
5   It is almost certain that the rings will require attention. There are three, the top two are compression rings, the lowest one is the oil scraper ring. The compression rings will probably be free in the grooves but the scraper ring may be seized in the groove. This presents a problem, soak the ring in paraffin or some suitable solvent and ease it gently until it will rotate round the piston. This ring must now be removed from the piston. This is done only with care. It can be helpful to use an aid such as a 0.020 in (0.5 mm) feeler gauge. Lift one end of the piston ring to be removed from the groove, and insert the end of the feeler under it. Turn the feeler gauge slowly round the piston and as the ring comes out of its groove apply slight upward pressure so that it rests on the land above. It can then be eased off the piston with the feeler stopping it from slipping into any empty grooves. Note that the compression rings have the word 'TOP' marked on their upper surfaces. Gently remove all carbon from the rings and grooves. Now insert the ring in its groove and roll it round the piston to see that the groove is clear (photo).
6   Clean the cylinder bore and using the piston as a fixture push the ring down the bore until it is 15 mm ($\frac{5}{8}$ in) from the bottom. Now measure the end gap with a feeler gauge. This should be within the specified limits.
7   Refit the rings to the piston spacing the gaps at 120 degree intervals and making sure the top markings are the right way up. With a feeler gauge measure the clearance between the ring and the piston groove (photo). This must not exceed the specified amount.
8   If new rings are to be fitted the gap must be measured in the cylinder and adjusted if necessary with a fine file to the limits shown in the Specifications.
9   If the rings are correct then refit the piston to the connecting rod, making sure the arrow on the piston points to the front, (you marked the bearing cap), refit the circlips and proceed to check the rings on the other three pistons.
10   An expander type oil scraper ring may be fitted; this type is easily recognized by a spiral spring in the ring across the gap. This is where things become difficult. Two types of piston are used in production (Mahle and KS) and there are different diameters for the oil scraper grooves. If you find your vehicle has these rings it would be best to go to the agent, and ask how to refit them according to the latest instructions. The modification is to overcome excessive oil consumption, so if you have this problem and the old pattern rings, a visit to the

16.5 Checking the piston ring and groove for burrs

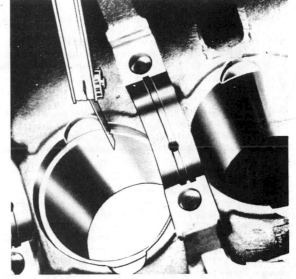

Fig. 1.20 Checking a piston ring gap with a feeler gauge (Sec 16)

17 Oil pump – examination and renovation

1   With the oil pump on the bench, prise off the cap with a screwdriver and clean the strainer gauze in fuel. Refit the gauze and press on the cap.

2   Remove the two small bolts and take the cover away from the body. Examine the face of the cover (photo). As will be seen in the photograph the gears have marked the cover. If the depth of this marking is significant then the face of the cover must be machined flat again.

3   Remove the gears and wash the body and gears in clean paraffin. Dry them and reassemble the gears, lubricating them with clean engine oil. Measure the backlash between the gears with a feeler gauge (photo). This should be 0.05 to 0.20 mm (0.002 to 0.008 in).

4   Now place a straight-edge over the pump body along the line joining the centre of the two gears and measure with a feeler gauge the axial clearance between the gears and the straight-edge (photo). This must not be more than 0.15 mm (0.006 in).

5   If all is well, check that the shaft is not slack in its bearings, and reassemble the pump for fitting to the engine.

6   If there is any doubt about the pump it is recommended strongly that a replacement be obtained. Once wear starts in a pump it progresses rapidly. In view of the damage that may follow a loss of oil pressure, skimping the oil pump repair is a false economy.

16.7 Checking the piston ring-to-groove clearance

18 Intermediate shaft – examination and renovation

1   Check the fit of the intermediate shaft in its bearing. If there is

agent is also required, for this may be the cure for your trouble.

11 Examine the connecting rods for wear and damage. It is most unusual to have to renew a connecting rod but if this has to be done then a complete set of four must be installed.

17.2 Examine the face of the oil pump cover for scoring

17.3 Checking oil pump gear backlash

17.4 Checking oil pump gear endfloat

excessive play the shaft must be compared with a new one. If the shaft is in good order and the bearings in the block are worn this job is beyond your scope, you may even need a new block so seek expert advice.

2   Check the surface of the cam which drives the fuel pump (where applicable). If serious ridging is present a new shaft is indicated.

3   Check the teeth of the distributor drivegear for scuffing or chipping. Check the condition of the timing belt sprocket.

4   It is unlikely that damage to this shaft has happened, but if it has, seek advice from the VW agent.

5   There is an oil seal in the flange for the intermediate shaft. This may need renewal if there are signs of leakage. To do this remove the timing belt sprocket and withdraw the flange from the shaft. The oil seal may now be prised out and a new one pressed in. Always fit a new O-ring on the flange before assembling it to the cylinder block.

19 Flywheel/driveplate – examination and renovation

1   There is not much you can do about the flywheel if it is damaged.

2   Inspect the starter ring teeth. If these are chipped or worn it is possible to renew the starter ring. This means heating the ring until it may be withdrawn from the flywheel, or alternatively splitting it. A new one must then be shrunk on. If you know how to do this and you can get a new ring then the job can be done but it is beyond the capacity of most owners.

3   Serious scoring on the flywheel clutch facing requires a new flywheel. Do not attempt to clean the scoring off with a scraper or emery. The face must be machined.

4   If it is necessary to fit a new flywheel, the ignition timing mark must be made by the owner. The new flywheel has only the TDC mark as an 'O' on the outer face. Where the ignition timing is 0° (TDC), make a notch directly over the 'O' mark using a three-cornered file. If the ignition timing is before top dead centre (BTDC) make a notch 16 mm (0.630 in) to the left of the TDC mark for ignition timing of 7.5° BTDC, or 18.5 mm (0.728 in) to the left of the TDC mark for ignition timing of 9° BTDC. If the ignition timing is after top dead centre (ATDC) make a notch 6 mm (0.236 in) to the right of the TDC mark for ignition timing of 3° ATDC.

5   On automatic transmission models, check the driveplate as described for the flywheel; it will similarly be necessary to mark a new driveplate for ignition timing. If the ignition timing is 9° BTDC, make a notch 21 mm (0.827 in) to the left of the TDC mark.

20 Crankshaft, camshaft and intermediate shaft oil seals – renewal (engine in car)

Crankshaft oil seal (flywheel/driveplate end)

1   On manual gearbox models, remove the clutch and pressure plate as described in Chapter 5. On automatic transmission models, remove the transmission as described in Chapter 6, then unbolt the driveplate from the crankshaft, noting the location of the spacer and shim(s).

2   On all models, carefully prise out the oil seal with a screwdriver or strong wire and wipe clean the recess.

3   Fill the space between the lips of the new seal with multi-purpose grease, then drive it squarely into the housing using a block of wood or suitable metal tubing (photo). If at all possible use VW fitting sleeve No 2003 to avoid damage to the oil seal lip.

4   Refit the driveplate or clutch using a reversal of the removal procedure, with reference to Chapters 5 and 6 as necessary.

Crankshaft oil seal (timing belt end)

5   Remove the alternator as described in Chapter 9, together with the drivebelt.

6   Remove the timing belt cover and timing belt as described in Section 8, making sure that the timing marks are correctly aligned.

7   Unscrew the bolt from the front of the crankshaft, withdraw the pulley and the sprocket and remove the Woodruff key. If the belt is difficult to loosen, have an assistant engage top gear and apply the brakes on manual gearbox models. On automatic transmission models remove the starter motor and restrain the driveplate ring gear with a suitable lever.

8   Prise out the oil seal or extract it with VW tool No 2085, then wipe clean the recess.

9   Fill the space between the lips of the new seal with multi-purpose grease, then drive it squarely into the housing using a block of wood

Fig. 1.21 Flywheel ignition timing marks (Sec 19)

a BTDC   *b* ATDC   O TDC

20.3 Crankshaft rear oil seal

Fig. 1.22 VW Tool 2085 for removing crankshaft oil seal (timing belt end) and camshaft oil seal (Sec 20)

or suitable metal tubing. If available use VW fitting sleeve No 10-203.

10 The remaining refitting procedure is a reversal of removal, but ensure that the timing marks are aligned before refitting the timing belt, and tension it with reference to Section 24.

Camshaft front oil seal

11 Remove the alternator as described in Chapter 9, together with the drivebelt.

12 Remove the timing belt cover and timing belt as described in Section 8, making sure that the timing marks are correctly aligned.

13 Hold the camshaft sprocket stationary with a screwdriver inserted through one of the holes, then unscrew the bolt and remove the washer, sprocket and Woodruff key.

14 Prise out the oil seal or alternatively extract it with VW tool No 2085, then wipe clean the recess.

15 Fill the space between the lips of the new seal with multi-purpose grease, then drive it squarely into the cylinder head using a block of wood or suitable metal tubing. If available use VW fitting sleeve No 10-203.

16 The remaining refitting procedure is a reversal of removal, but ensure that the timing marks are aligned before refitting the timing belt and tension it with reference to Section 24.

Intermediate shaft oil seal

17 Remove the alternator as described in Chapter 9, together with the drivebelt.

18 Remove the timing belt cover and timing belt as described in Section 8, making sure that the timing marks are correctly aligned.

19 Hold the intermediate shaft sprocket stationary with a screwdriver inserted through one of the holes, then unscrew the bolt and remove the washer, sprocket and Woodruff key.

20 Renew the oil seal as described in Section 18.

21 The remaining refitting procedure is a reversal of removal, but ensure that the timing marks are aligned before refitting the timing belt and tighten it with reference to Section 24.

21 Engine reassembly – general

1 To ensure maximum life with minimum trouble from a rebuilt engine, not only must everything be correctly assembled but it must also be spotlessly clean. All oilways must be clear, and locking washers and spring washers must be fitted where indicated. Oil all bearings and other working surfaces thoroughly with engine oil during assembly.

2 Before assembly begins, renew any bolts or studs with damaged threads.

3 Gather together a torque wrench, oil can, clean rag, and a set of engine gaskets and oil seals, together with a new oil filter cartridge.

22 Crankshaft, connecting rods, pistons and intermediate shaft – refitting

1 Place the cylinder block upside down on the bench. Wipe carefully the main journal seatings and fit the main bearing top halves into place. Nos 1, 2, 4 and 5 are plain shells with grooves in them. No 3 has small flanges (photo). If the old bearings are being refitted it is essential that they go back in the same housing the same way round. Lightly oil the shells (photo) and lift in the crankshaft (photo).

2 Fit the lower shells to the bearing caps and install them on the block (photo). These are plain shells. Once again if the old ones are being used they must go back in the same place the same way round. This applies anyway to the bearing caps. They are numbered, one goes next to the timing gears and the numbers on the side opposite to the oil pump.

3 Tighten the bearing cap bolts evenly to the specified torque, and check that the crankshaft rotates smoothly (photo). Some stiffness is normal with new shells, but it must not bind.

4 Lubricate the rear of the crankshaft and using a new gasket install the rear oil seal and flange. Tighten the six bolts to the correct torque.

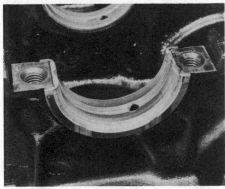

22.1a No 3 main bearing shell in the cylinder block

22.1b Oiling the main bearing shells

22.1c Installing the crankshaft

22.2 Fit the main bearing caps and ...

22.3 ... tighten the bolts

5   Lubricate the front of the crankshaft and fit the front oil seal and flange. Tighten the bolts to the correct torque.

6   Lubricate the intermediate shaft, then install it in the block. Fit the O-ring and flange together with the oil seal, then tighten the bolts. Note that the oil hole must be at the bottom of the flange.

7   The use of a piston ring compressor is strongly recommended. It is cheap enough to buy, but if you cannot get one then make one. A piece of $\frac{1}{16}$ in (1.58 mm) thick sheet metal about 2 in (50.8 mm) wide wrapped round the piston to compress the rings into the grooves is all that is required. It may be held in position with a large hose clip or some similar device. This way the rings go in safely. It is very difficult to coax the rings in one at a time and a broken ring will not only hold up the job for even a week, but a new set of rings must be bought. That will cost more than a ring compressor.

8   Place the block on one side. Fit the ring compressor to No 1 piston and insert the connecting rod (minus bearing cap) and piston into No 1 cylinder (photo). Check that the arrow on the piston points to the front of the block and gradually ease the piston and rings into the block, removing the ring compressor as the rings go into the bore. When all the rings are safely in, pull the big-end bearings to one side of the crankshaft, check that the shell bearing is seated correctly in the connecting rod, lubricate the shell, and fit the connecting rod to the crankshaft journal. Check that the other half of the shell bearing is seated in the bearing cap, lubricate the bearing and fit the cap to the connecting rod (photo). Check that all the markings (made on dismantling) agree and having fitted new bolts or nuts, tighten these to the correct torque. Check that the crankshaft still rotates smoothly, then repeat the process for pistons 2, 3 and 4.

9   Once all the big-end bearings are installed check the axial play (endfloat) of each bearing. Push the connecting rod against the crankshaft web and measure the gap on the other side with a feeler gauge. It should not be more than the specified amount. If it is then consult the agent. Either the bearings are faulty or there has been a possible fault introduced when regrinding the journal. Turn the cylinder block back onto the face to which the cylinder head fits.

10 Wipe clean the mating faces, then install the oil pump and tighten the bolts evenly to the specified torque (photo).

11 Fit a new sump gasket using jointing compound and assemble the sump to the cylinder block (photo).

12 Fit the sprocket to the front of the intermediate shaft and tighten the bolt to the specified torque, holding the sprocket stationary with a screwdriver through one of the holes.

13 Refit the combined V-belt pulley and timing belt sprocket to the crankshaft, together with the Woodruff key, and tighten the bolt to the specified torque. Hold the crankshaft stationary by fitting a lever to two bolts temporarily fitted to the crankshaft rear flange, and use a liquid locking agent on the threads of the pulley retaining bolt.

22.8a A ring compressor fitted to a piston

22.8b Installing a big-end bearing cap

22.10 Installing the oil pump

22.11 Installing the sump

23 Cylinder head – adjustment of valve clearances

1 Valve clearance adjustment is made by fitting discs of varying thickness to the tappet buckets located between the valve stems and camshaft.

2 The 26 different discs progress from 3.00 mm to 4.25 mm in stages of 0.05 mm which seems to indicate that the first thoughts of a sensible man contemplating adjustment of the tappet clearance will be to buy a set of feeler gauges graduated in metric measure. Otherwise, a lot of calculation will be necessary and a set of conversion tables to transpose 0.05 mm steps into thousandths of an inch. However, it is not too difficult referring to the table in paragraph 7, the thinnest disc is 3.0 mm (0.1181 in). The thickness progresses at the rate of 0.05 mm (0.001969 in) and since feeler gauges measure only to the nearest thousandth, 0.001969 in may be taken for practical purposes as 0.002 in. By calculating 25 size increases at this rate the thickest disc 4.25 mm becomes 0.1681 in whereas its true value is 0.1673 and the error over the total range is 0.0008 in which is acceptable.

3 If routine adjustment is to be done with the engine in the car, first remove the valve cover. The procedure is the same except that during an engine overhaul the adjustment disc will already have been removed and cleaned. Further, the size etched on the back of the disc will be known.

4 If the job is done with the engine in the car the discs must be removed and identified if the tolerance is outside the specified limit. The engine will rotate more easily if the plugs are removed. **Do not** rotate the engine by turning the camshaft sprocket, this will stretch the timing belt. Use the alternator drivebelt, or jack up one front wheel and with the engine in gear rotate the roadwheel. Using feeler gauges measure the clearance between the tappet bucket and the cam when the high point of the cam is at the top (photo). **Note:** *Do not turn the engine with any of the discs removed otherwise the camshaft may foul the rim at the top of the bucket.*

5 Repeat this measurement for all the valves in turn and then compare the measurements with the Specifications.

6 Make a table of the actual clearances and then calculate the error from those specified. Suppose on No 1 exhaust valve the measured clearance is 0.15 mm, due say to grinding in a valve. It is 0.3 mm too small so it must be adjusted and a disc 0.3 mm thinner fitted instead of the present disc. As the discs are in steps of 0.05 mm variation the required disc can be selected once the size of the disc at present installed is known. If you have dismantled and reassembled the head then you know the size etched on the back of the disc but if you do not then the disc must be removed to find out. Ideally VW tools 546 and 10.208 (UK) or 4476 (US) should be used but we managed quite well with the tools shown (photo). They were a small electrician's screwdriver and a C-spanner which was just the right size to push the tappet down without pushing the tappet disc (ie pushing the rim down). With the cam turned to give maximum clearance the tappet is pushed down against the valve springs while the tappet disc is levered out and removed by the VW tool or a screwdriver. Be careful, if the spanner slips when the disc is halfway out the disc will fly out sharply (photo).

7 Once all the disc sizes are known a table may be constructed and the sizes of the new discs required may be calculated. Going back to the example, if the present disc is marked 3.60 then one marked 3.30 is required. A table of sizes and part numbers is given below:

Part No	Thickness (mm)	Part No	Thickness (mm)
056 109 555	3.00	056 109 568	3.65
056 109 556	3.05	056 109 569	3.70
056 109 557	3.10	056 109 570	3.75
056 109 558	3.15	056 109 571	3.80
056 109 559	3.20	056 109 572	3.85
056 109 560	3.25	056 109 573	3.90
056 109 561	3.30	056 109 574	3.95
056 109 562	3.35	056 109 575	4.00
056 109 563	3.40	056 109 576	4.05
056 109 564	3.45	056 109 577	4.10
056 109 565	3.50	056 109 578	4.15
056 109 566	3.55	056 109 579	4.20
056 109 567	3.60	056 109 580	4.25

8 As it is unlikely that you will have the spares it will be necessary to wait until they have been obtained before the tappets can be adjusted. If the adjustment was done cold then it must be checked again when the engine is hot, and if the cylinder head has been overhauled it should be checked again, hot, after 500 km (300 miles). The recommended mileage for checking is given in Routine Maintenance.

9 Once the correct clearances have been achieved the cylinder head may be put on one side until required for reassembly. Refit the spark plugs. If the engine is in the car the valve cover should be refitted.

10 One final suggestion. If you have done the job and know the sizes of all the discs this information should be kept in a safe place. It will save a lot of time during the next overhaul.

24 Cylinder head – refitting

1 Turn the engine over and support it on the sump with wooden blocks. Clean the top face of the block. Make a final inspection of the bores and lubricate them. Turn the crankshaft so that the pistons are in the mid cylinder position.

2 If you look at the edge of the block between No 3 and No 4 cylinders on the side above the distributor, the engine number is stamped on an inclined surface. Using this as a datum, install a new cylinder head gasket so that the word 'OBEN' engraved on the gasket is over this datum point and on the top side of the gasket (photo).

3 Lower the head on the block (photo) and refit No 8 and No 10 holding-down bolts. Do not use jointing compound. Check that the gasket is seating correctly and fit the remainder of the holding-down bolts. Now following the sequence in Fig. 1.23 tighten the bolts until the head is firmly held. Using the torque wrench, tighten the bolts in stages to the specified torque following the same sequence.

4 Refit the sprocket to the front of the camshaft, together with the Woodruff key, and tighten the bolt to the specified torque.

5 Turn the camshaft sprocket so that both cams for No 1 cylinder are in the open position and the dot on the camshaft gear tooth is in line with the valve cover.

6 Rotate the crankshaft sprocket and the intermediate shaft sprocket until the dot on the intermediate sprocket and the mark on the V-belt pulley coincide. Install the timing belt tensioner loosely and then the timing belt. Making sure the marks are still in place, put a

23.4 Checking the valve clearance with a feeler blade

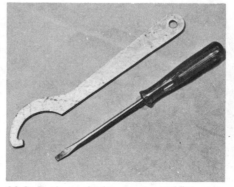

23.6a Tools required to remove and fit tappet bucket discs

23.6b Removing a tappet bucket disc

24.2 Cylinder head gasket on the block

24.3 Lowering the cylinder head onto the block

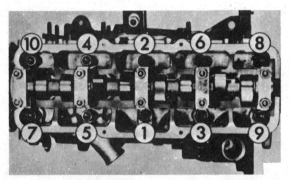
Fig. 1.23 Cylinder head bolt tightening sequence (Sec 24)

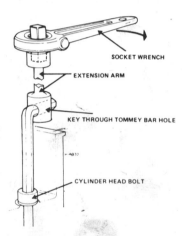

SOCKET WRENCH

EXTENSION ARM

KEY THROUGH TOMMEY BAR HOLE

CYLINDER HEAD BOLT

Fig. 1.24 Method of tightening the cylinder head bolts using an Allen key (Sec 24)

spanner on the adjuster and tighten the belt until it will twist only 90 degrees when held between the finger and thumb halfway between the camshaft and intermediate shaft sprockets. Tighten the eccentric adjuster nut to the specified torque.

7   Refit the distributor as described in Chapter 4.

8   On pre-February 1979 models, refit the timing belt guide to the front of the block, making sure that it is centred between the two sprockets. Tighten the bolts using an Allen key.

25 Ancillary components – refitting

1   On automatic transmission models refit the driveplate together with shim(s) and spacer. Tighten the bolts on the crankshaft to the specified torque. Using vernier calipers, check the distance from the driveplate to the cylinder block as shown in Fig. 1.26. If it is not between 30.5 mm and 32.1 mm (1.20 and 1.26 in) remove the driveplate and fit alternative shims as necessary. Note that the chamfer on the washer must face the driveplate. When the dimension is correct, remove the bolts, coat their threads with liquid locking agent and tighten again to the specified torque.

2   On manual gearbox models refit the clutch as described in Chapter 5, together with the intermediate plate.

3   Refit the inlet and exhaust manifolds (photos). Also on North American models refit the emission control equipment (Chapter 3) and power steering pump (where applicable – Chapter 12).

Fig. 1.25 Checking the timing belt tension (Sec 24)

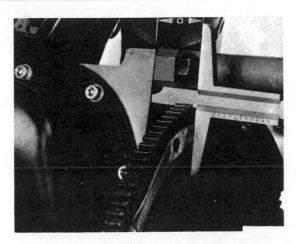

Fig. 1.26 Checking the driveplate-to-cylinder block dimension (a) using vernier calipers (Sec 25)

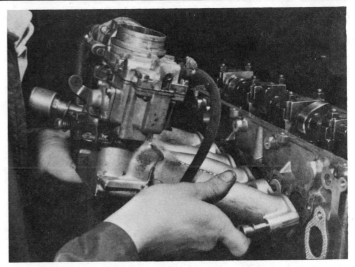

25.3a Installing the inlet manifold

4 Refit the water pump and all hoses to the engine as described in Chapter 2.

5 Refit the alternator and drivebelt as described in Chapter 9.

6 Smear sealing compound on the threads of the oil pressure switch, then screw it into the cylinder head or filter head together with the washer (where fitted). Tighten it to the specified torque.

7 On carburettor models refit the fuel pump as described in Chapter 3.

8 Fit the oil filter head to the cylinder block together with a new gasket and tighten the bolts. On models fitted with an oil cooler, refit the supply and return hoses to their correct unions.

9 Fit the oil filter as described in Section 11.

10 Refit the timing belt cover, and check that it is not touching the timing belt or sprockets.

11 Check that the seal is fitted to No 1 camshaft bearing cap, and that the half round grommet is located at the rear of the cylinder head (photo).

12 Fit the valve cover together with the packing pieces and a new gasket, and tighten the nuts evenly.

13 Refit the spark plugs if not already done and tighten them to the specified torque given in Chapter 4.

14 Refit the gearbox/transmission to the engine with reference to Section 6.

25.3b Installing the exhaust manifold

26 Engine – adjustment after major overhaul

1 With the engine/gearbox refitted to the car, make a final check to ensure that everything has been reconnected and that no rags or tools have been left in the engine compartment.

2 If new pistons or crankshaft bearings have been fitted, turn the slow running screw in about half a turn to compensate for the initial tightness of the new components.

3 Start the engine. This may take a little longer than usual on carburettor engines as the fuel pump and carburettor float chamber may be empty.

4 As soon as the engine starts, let it run at a fast tickover. Check that the oil pressure light goes out.

5 Check the oil filter, fuel hoses, and water hoses for leaks.

6 Run the engine until normal operating temperature is reached, then adjust the slow running as described in Chapter 3.

7 If new pistons or crankshaft bearings have been fitted, the engine must be run-in for the first 500 miles (800 km) as if it were new.

8 There is no need to re-tighten the cylinder head bolts after the first 500 miles (800 km), provided that the new type bolts have been fitted (see Section 9).

9 If new bearings etc have been fitted, it is good practice to change the engine oil and filter after the initial running-in period. This will get rid of the small metallic particles which are produced by new components bedding-in to each other.

25.11 The oil seal (arrowed) on No 1 camshaft bearing cap

27 Fault diagnosis – engine

Symptom	Reason(s)
Engine fails to start	Discharged battery Loose battery connection Loose or broken ignition leads Moisture on spark plugs, distributor cap, or HT leads Incorrect spark plug or contact points gap (where applicable) Cracked distributor cap or rotor Dirt or water in carburettor (if applicable) Empty fuel tank Faulty fuel pump Faulty starter motor Low cylinder compressions Faulty electronic ignition
Engine idles erratically	Inlet manifold air leak Leaking cylinder head gasket Worn camshaft lobes Faulty fuel pump Incorrect valve clearances Mixture adjustment incorrect Uneven cylinder compressions
Engine misfires	Spark plugs or contact points gap incorrect (as applicable) Faulty coil or condenser (as applicable) Dirt or water in carburettor (where applicable) Mixture adjustment incorrect Burnt valve or seating Leaking cylinder head gasket Distributor cap cracked Incorrect valve clearances Uneven cylinder compressions Worn carburettor (where applicable) Faulty electronic ignition
Engine stalls	Mixture adjustment incorrect Inlet manifold air leak Ignition timing incorrect
Excessive oil consumption	Worn pistons and cylinder bores Valve guides and seals worn Oil leak (fuel pump vent hole is common)
Engine backfires	Mixture adjustment incorrect Ignition timing incorrect Incorrect valve clearances Exhaust manifold air leak Sticking or burnt valve

Chapter 2 Cooling system

Contents

Specifications

System type	Thermo-syphon, assisted by belt driven pump, pressurised front mounted radiator, and electric cooling fan

Pressure cap release pressure

UK models with part number suffix A	0.9 to 1.15 bar (13 to 16.7 lbf/in^2)
UK models with part number suffix B and C and all North American models	1.2 to 1.35 bar (17.4 to 19.6 lbf/in^2)

Thermostat

Opening temperature:

UK models up to July 1978	80°C (176°F)
UK models from August 1978	87°C (188°F)
North American models	85°C (185°F)

Fully open temperature:

UK models up to July 1978	94°C (201°F)
UK models from August 1978	102°C (215°F)
North America models	105°C (221°F)
Minimum stroke – all models	7 mm (0.28 in)

Thermoswitch

Switch-on temperature:

UK models up to July 1978	90 to 95°C (194 to 203°F)
UK models from August 1978 and all North American models ...	93 to 98°C (199 to 208°F)

Switch-off temperature:

UK models up to July 1978	85 to 90°C (185 to 194°F)
Uk models from August 1978 and all North American models ...	88 to 93°C (190 to 199°F)

System capacity

UK models with expansion tank	1.4 Imp gal; 6.5 litres; 1.7 US gal
UK models without expansion tank	1.0 Imp gal; 4.6 litres; 1.2 US gal
North American models	1.0 Imp gal; 4.6 litres, 1.2 US gal

Drivebelt tension

Deflection midway between the crankshaft and alternator pulleys	10 to 15 mm (0.4 to 0.6 in)

Torque wrench settings

	lbf ft	Nm
Temperature sender	5	7
Thermostat housing to water pump	7	10
Water pump to block:		
UK models	14	20
North American models	16	22
Water pump cover to body	7	10
Water pump pulley	14	20
Cylinder head outlet elbow (to radiator)	7	10
Cylinder head outlet (to heater)	10	14
Thermoswitch:		
UK models	18	25
North American models	22	30
Radiator mounting:		
UK models	7	10
North American models	4	6
Fan motor mounting:		
UK models	7	10
North American models	6	8

1 General description

The cooling system is of pressurised type and includes a front mounted radiator, belt-driven water pump, and electric cooling fan. The thermostat is located in the water pump, beneath the inlet elbow. The radiator is of aluminium construction.

The system functions as follows. Cold water from the bottom of the radiator circulates through the bottom hose to the water pump, where the pump impeller forces the water around the cylinder block and head passages. After cooling the cylinder bores, combustion surfaces, and valve seats, the water reaches the cylinder head outlet and is returned to the water pump via the bypass hoses when the thermostat is closed. A further cylinder head outlet allows water to circulate through the inlet manifold and heater matrix (with heater control on) and it is then returned to the water pump.

When the coolant reaches the predetermined temperature (see Specifications), the thermostat opens and the water then circulates through the top hose to the top of the radiator. As the water circulates down through the radiator, it is cooled by the inrush of air when the car is in forward motion, supplemented by the action of the electric cooling fan when necessary. Having reached the bottom of the radiator, the water is now cooled and the cycle is repeated.

The electric cooling fan is controlled by a thermoswitch located in the left-hand side of the radiator.

2 Cooling system – draining

1   It is preferable to drain the cooling system when the engine has cooled. If this is not possible, place a cloth over the radiator or expansion tank filler cap and turn it **slowly** in an anti-clockwise direction until the pressure starts to escape.
2   When all the pressure has escaped, remove the filler cap.
3   Set the heater controls to maximum heat, then place a suitable container beneath the water pump.
4   Loosen the clip and ease the bottom hose away from the water pump inlet elbow. Drain the coolant into the container.
5   Remove the thermostat as described in Section 8 and drain the remaining coolant into the container.

3 Cooling system – flushing

1   After some time the radiator and engine waterways may become restricted or even blocked with scale or sediment which would reduce the efficiency of the cooling system. When this occurs, the coolant will appear rusty and dark in colour and the system should then be flushed. In severe cases, reverse flushing may be required, although if a reputable antifreeze/corrosion inhibitor has been in constant use this is unlikely.
2   With the coolant drained, disconnect the top hose from the radiator. Insert a hose and allow the water to circulate through the radiator until it runs clear from the bottom hose.
3   Disconnect the heater hose from the outlet on the left-hand end of the cylinder head, and insert a hose in the heater hose. With the heater controls set at maximum heat, allow water to circulate out through the bottom of the water pump until it runs clear.
4   In severe cases of contamination the system should be reverse flushed. To do this, remove the radiator, invert it, and insert a hose in the outlet. Continue flushing until clear water runs from the inlet.
5   The engine should also be reverse flushed. To do this, disconnect the top hose from the front of the cylinder head and insert a hose. Continue flushing until clear water runs from the water pump.
6   The use of chemical cleaners should only be necessary as a last resort. Regular renewal of the antifreeze/corrosion inhibitor solution should prevent the contamination of the system.

4 Cooling system – filling

1   Refit the thermostat, with reference to Section 8, and reconnect all the hoses. Check that the heater controls are set to maximum heat.
2   Pour coolant into the radiator or expansion tank (as applicable) until it reaches the top of the radiator or the lower mark on the expansion tank.

3   Loosen the top hose clip at the radiator and disconnect the hose temporarily until water emerges, then refit the hose and clip. This is necessary in order to prevent an air-lock forming at the top of the radiator.
4   Top up the radiator or expansion tank and refit the cap.
5   Run the engine at a fast idling speed until the electric cooling fan cuts in.
6   Stop the engine and check the level in the radiator or expansion tank, taking the precaution given in Section 2. Top up as necessary – if an external expansion tank is fitted, top up to the upper maximum level mark. Refit the pressure cap.

5 Antifreeze mixture

1   The manufacturers install G10 antifreeze/corrosion inhibitor mixture in the cooling system when the car is new. At regular intervals (see Routine Maintenance) the strength of the coolant should be checked by a VW garage and if necessary topped up with fresh mixture. It is recommended that the mixture is renewed every two years.
2   Before adding new mixture, check all hose connections for tightness.
3   The proportion of G10 antifreeze and water should be calculated to provide adequate protection against the coldest anticipated temperatures. Refer to the table below, and to the Specifications, to calculate the amount of antifreeze required.

Proportion of antifreeze	Protection down to
40%	−25°C (−13°F)
50%	−35°C (−31°F)
55%	−40°C (−40°F)

4   After filling with new mixture, a label should be attached to the radiator stating the date installed. Any subsequent topping up should be made with the same concentration of mixture.

6 Radiator – removal, inspection, cleaning and refitting

1   Drain the cooling system as described in Section 2.
2   Disconnect the battery negative lead.
3   Pull the rubber cap from the thermoswitch and disconnect the leads. Remove the plug from the fan motor.
4   Disconnect the top hose and expansion tank hose (where applicable) from the radiator.
5   On pre-January 1981 UK models and all North American models, remove the lower mounting nuts and washers, lift the radiator, and slide it from the upper mounting clip (photos).
6   On post-January 1981 UK models, unscrew the top mounting screws and lift the radiator from the lower mountings.
7   Remove the screws or nuts and withdraw the cowling and fan from the radiator.
8   It is not possible to repair this radiator without special equipment, although minor leaks can be sealed by using a proprietary coolant addition.
9   Clean the radiator matrix of flies and small leaves with a soft brush or by hosing, then reverse flush the radiator as described in Section 3. Renew the hoses and clips if they are damaged or deteriorated.
10 Refitting is a reversal of removal. Fill the cooling system as described in Section 4.

7 Fan and thermoswitch – removal, refitting and testing

1   The fan and cowling may be removed from the radiator, or more easily the fan can be removed from the cowling and eased out through the struts. Disconnect the battery earth strap before commencing work, undo the plug connecting the fan to the electric wiring harness (photo), remove the three nuts holding the fan in position and remove motor and assembly together.
2   The fan blades are removed from the motor by undoing the bolt in the centre of the fan hub and levering the plastic blade assembly off the motor shaft.
3   The motor is dismantled by undoing the through-bolts and pulling off the end caps, but there is no point in doing this as spares are not available, the unit is renewed in one piece.

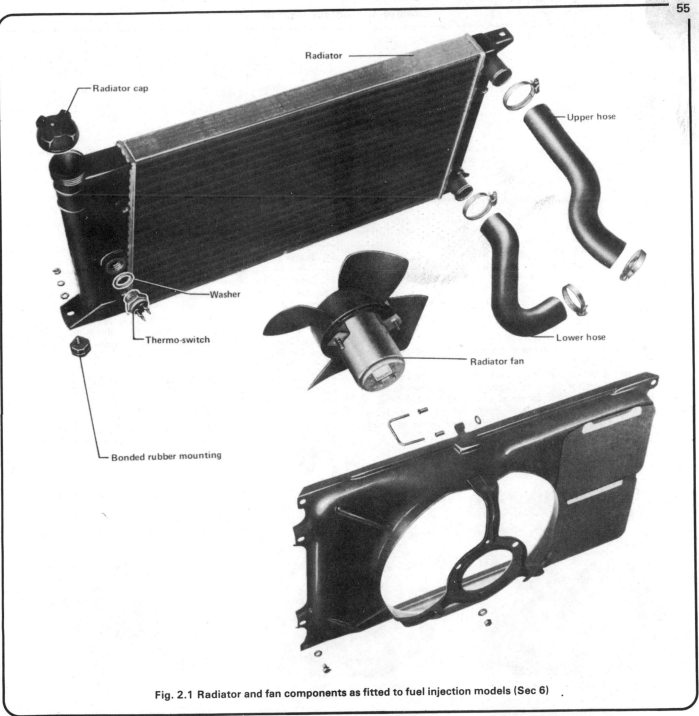

Fig. 2.1 Radiator and fan components as fitted to fuel injection models (Sec 6)

Radiator

Radiator cap

Upper hose

Washer

Thermo-switch

Lower hose

Radiator fan

Bonded rubber mounting

6.5a Radiator lower mounting on pre-January 1981 UK and all North American models

6.5b Radiator upper mounting on pre-January 1981 UK and all North American models

7.1 Disconnecting the electric fan wiring plug

4   To satisfy the curious we removed the through-bolts. Pulling off the end cap was difficult and unfortunately the bearing came off with the shaft (photo). This presented difficulties on reassembly as the cage for the spherical part of the shaft may only be installed when the bearing has been removed from the housing. The shaft and bearing may then be refitted. The commutator and brushgear may be cleaned and then reassembled (photos). Be careful of the two thin washers at the end of the commutator. If one of these is damaged replacements are not available. It is recommended that this unit be renewed if faulty.

5   The fan motor either works or it does not. Supply 12 volts to the plug momentarily. If the motor runs it is satisfactory. Do not allow it to run for more than a few seconds with the fan removed.

6   The thermoswitch is located on the left-hand radiator tank and may be covered with a rubber cap (photo). Remove the cap and disconnect the wires. The switch may be tested by connecting a simple bulb circuit or an ohmmeter across the tags of the switch and observing the point at which the switch closes. The temperature of the coolant in the radiator may then be checked. If the fan does not work after the thermostat has opened and the engine has reached normal running temperature then stop the engine right away. Pull off the leads from the thermoswitch and with a suitable instrument, check whether the switch has closed or not. If it has, then check the fan circuit and do not proceed until this has been sorted out or the engine will overheat. If the switch has not closed, and you are sure the coolant temperature is in excess of the specified amount, then the switch is faulty and must be renewed. To get you home connect the two switch leads together (short out the switch). The fan will then run when the ignition is switched on.

7   Removal of the thermoswitch involves draining the radiator. Once it is empty, using a socket spanner remove the thermo-switch. It may be tested then in a beaker of water in the same way as the thermostat (Section 8,) but using a meter or test lamp to determine the opening point. However, more practically, the switch either works or it does not. If not, fit a new one.

8   Thermostat – removal, testing and refitting

1   The thermostat is located in the bottom of the water pump behind the inlet elbow. To remove it, first drain the cooling system with reference to Section 2.

2   Unbolt the inlet elbow from the water pump and remove the seal and thermostat (photos).

3   Clean the water pump and elbow of any scale or corrosion.

4   To test the thermostat, first measure the dimension 'a' in Fig. 2.2 with it cold. Immerse the thermostat in water and raise the temperature to boiling point. Remove the thermostat from the water and quickly measure the new dimension 'b'. If this is substantially less than the amount shown in Fig. 2.2, the cooling water flow will be restricted and the engine will overheat. If the thermostat is faulty, renew it.

5   Refitting is a reversal of the removal procedure but always fit a new seal, and fill the cooling system as described in Section 4.

9   Water pump – removal and refitting

1   Drain the cooling system as described in Section 2. On models equipped with power steering, remove the drivebelt, as described in Chapter 12.

2   Remove the alternator as described in Chapter 9.

3   Disconnect the three coolant hoses from the pump, then remove the four bolts holding the pump to the cylinder block (photo). The pump will probably be stuck to the block but will come off if tapped gently. Remove the O-ring with the pump.

4   Remove the pulley and then take out the eight bolts which secure the bearing housing and impeller to the water pump housing. The two halves may now be separated (photo) **Do not** drive a wedge in to break the joint. Clean off the old gasket.

5   Remove the thermostat with reference to Section 8.

6   The impeller housing and impeller complete with bearings are serviced as one part, so that if the coolant is leaking through the

7.4a The fan motor housing. The bearing has come out of the cage

7.4b Fan motor brushgear. Be careful of the thin washers

7.4c Fan motor armature. Note the suppressor

7.6 Thermoswitch location in the radiator

8.2a Removing the water pump inlet elbow

8.2b Removing the thermostat

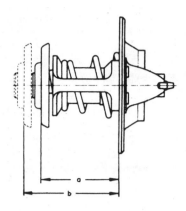

Fig. 2.2 Thermostat dimensions (Sec 8)

a   *Cold dimension – 31 mm (1.22 in)*
b   *Hot fully open dimension – 38 mm (1.5 in)*

bearing or the impeller is damaged the complete assembly must be renewed.

7   Fit a new gasket using jointing compound, then fit the two halves together and tighten the bolts evenly. Fit the thermostat with reference to Section 8. The running procedure is a reversal of the removal procedure, but always fit a new O-ring. Fill the cooling system as described in Section 4 and tension the drivebelt as described in Section 11.

10 Coolant temperature sender unit – removal and refitting

1   The coolant temperature sender unit is screwed into the water outlet to the heater on the left-hand end of the cylinder head (photo). On early UK fuel injection models a switch is fitted instead of the sender unit – the switch incorporates two terminals whereas the sender unit has one terminal.
2   To remove the unit first drain the cooling system as described in Section 2.
3   Disconnect the wire(s), then unscrew and remove the sender unit.
4   On pre-1980 UK carburettor models and all North American models, the sender unit is connected to a temperature gauge on the instrument panel. To test this unit connect it to an ohmmeter and

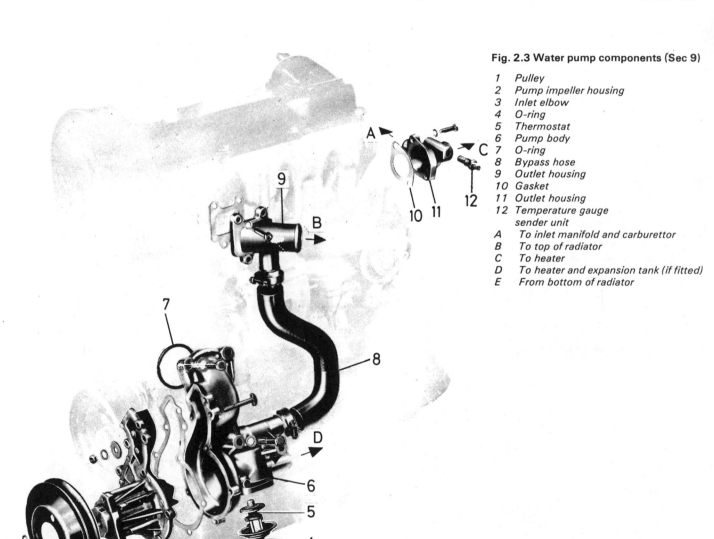

Fig. 2.3 Water pump components (Sec 9)

1   Pulley
2   Pump impeller housing
3   Inlet elbow
4   O-ring
5   Thermostat
6   Pump body
7   O-ring
8   Bypass hose
9   Outlet housing
10   Gasket
11   Outlet housing
12   Temperature gauge
      sender unit
A   To inlet manifold and carburettor
B   To top of radiator
C   To heater
D   To heater and expansion tank (if fitted)
E   From bottom of radiator

9.3 Water pump location (with the engine removed)

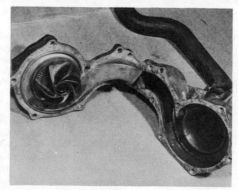

9.4 The two halves of the water pump

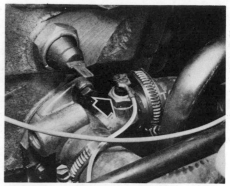

10.1 Temperature sender location (arrowed) on a Golf model

check its resistance when cold and again after being heated in water to the normal engine operating temperature. The cold resistance should be 250 to 300 ohms and approximately half this amount at normal operating temperature. If not, renew the unit.

5   On 1979 and 1980 UK fuel injection models, hot and cold warning lamps are fitted to the instrument panel; 1979 models incorporate bulbs but 1980 models have light emitting diodes (LEDs). A twin terminal switch is fitted and the wires must always be connected as shown in Fig. 2.4. To test the unit, connect an ohmmeter or test lamp and leads to each terminal in turn while heating the switch in water. The cold circuit must be switched on up to a temperature of 60°C (140°F) for the bulbs system or 40°C (104°F) for the LED system. Theoretically the hot circuit can only be tested with the switch installed, as it must be switched on with the coolant temperature above 120°C (248°F).

6   As from 1980 UK carburettor models and 1981 UK fuel injection models, the temperature gauge incorporates an LED which flashes when the coolant temperature is excessive. Testing of the gauge is identical to that for previous models, but testing of the LED involves removal of the instrument panel and connections to the printed circuit board. This work is best entrusted to a qualified automobile electrician.

Fig. 2.4 Coolant temperature switch terminals – fitted to 1979 and 1980 UK fuel injection models (Sec 10)

1   'Hot' control terminal (yellow/red wire)
2   'Cold' control terminal (blue/yellow wire)

---

11   Drivebelt (water pump) – renewal and adjustment

1   The drivebelt should be checked and re-tensioned regularly – see Routine Maintenance.

2   To check the drivebelt, thoroughly examine the inner and outer surfaces for splits, hardening, and deterioration. It will be necessary to

turn the engine in order to check the full length of the drivebelt. On some models the drivebelt cover must be removed.

3   Check the tension by using firm thumb pressure midway between the crankshaft and alternator pulleys. The drivebelt should deflect by

Fig. 2.5 Drivebelt tension checking point. Model without air conditioning shown (Sec 11)

a   Drivebelt deflection

Fig. 2.6 Using a screwdriver to adjust the drivebelt tension – models with air conditioning (Sec 11)

1   Adjusting link

the amount given in the Specifications. If not, adjust the drivebelt as described below.

4   To remove the drivebelt loosen the alternator pivot bolt, using an Allen key where necessary.

5   Loosen the adjustment link bolts and swivel the alternator downwards.

6   Slip the drivebelt from the alternator pulley, water pump pulley, and crankshaft pulley.

7   On models equipped with air conditioning, similarly check the compressor drivebelt tension and if necessary adjust it **before** fitting the water pump/alternator drivebelt. This is particularly necessary where the compressor position must be altered in order to adjust the drivebelt tension since this alters the water pump/alternator drivebelt tension.

8   Fit the new drivebelt over the alternator, water pump, and crankshaft pulleys.

9   Carefully lever the alternator upward until the specified tension is achieved. The alternator must only be levered at the drive end bracket. On models with air conditioning, the drivebelt can be tensioned using a screwdriver as shown in Fig. 2.6.

10 Tighten the adjustment link bolts followed by the pivot bolt, then recheck the tension.

11 On later models with air conditioning, drivebelt tension is adjusted by adding or subtracting shims between the two halves of the compressor pulley. Refer to Chapter 1, Fig. 1.5, for details of this arrangement.

12 Fault diagnosis – cooling system

Symptom	Reason(s)
Overheating	Low coolant level
	Faulty pressure cap
	Thermostat sticking shut
	Open-circuit thermoswitch
	Faulty electric cooling fan
	Clogged radiator matrix
	Retarded ignition timing
Slow warm-up	Thermostat sticking open
	Incorrect thermostat
Coolant loss	Damaged or deteriorated hose
	Leaking water pump or cylinder head outlet joint
	Blown cylinder head gasket
	Leaking radiator

Chapter 3
Fuel, exhaust and emission control systems

For modifications and information applicable to later models, see Supplement at end of manual

Contents

Specifications

General

System type .... Single or twin choke downdraught carburettor, or continuous injection system (CIS); emission control equipment according to model and territory

Air cleaner type .... Renewable paper element, with automatic air temperature control on most models

Fuel equipment
UK models:
    Low compression (8.0 or 8.2 : 1) .... 91 RON minimum (UK 2-star)
    High compression (9.5 or 9.7 : 1) .... 98 RON minimum (UK 4-star)
USA models:
    Without catalytic converter .... 91 RON minimum (regular gasoline)
    With catalytic converter .... Unleaded gasoline

Fuel tank capacity
Golf/Rabbit/Scirocco (early models) .... 10 Imp gal; 12 US gal; 45 litres
Golf/Rabbit/Scirocco (later models) .... 9 Imp gal; 10.8 US gal; 40 litres
Jetta .... 9 Imp gal; 10.8 US gal; 40 litres

Carburettor engines

Fuel pump
Type .... Mechanical, diaphragm, operated by eccentric on intermediate shaft
Operating pressure .... 0.20 to 0.25 bar (2.9 to 3.6 lbf/in²)

Carburettor data – Solex 34 PICT 5
Engine code FH
Carburettor number .... 055 129 015 D or K (manual), 055 129 015 E or L (automatic)
Jets and settings:
    Venturi diameter (mm) 27
    Main jet x135
    Air correction jet with emulsion tube 115z
    Pilot jet .... 52.5 or 60
    Pilot air jet .... 100 or 95
    Auxiliary fuel jet 40
    Auxiliary air jet 140
    Enrichment with/without ball 0.7/without

Accelerator pump delivery .... 1.1 ± 0.15 cc per stroke
Float needle valve 1.5
Cold idling speed .... 2400 ± 50 rpm
Choke valve gap (mm) .... 3.2 ± 0.5
Choke cover mark:
    Suffix D or K 106
    Suffix E or L 130
Idle speed .... 950 ± 50 rpm
CO content at idle .... 1.5 ± 0.5%

Engine code FP

Carburettor number .... 055 129 015 S (manual) or T (automatic)
Jets and settings:
    Venturi diameter (mm) 27
    Main jet x142.5
    Air correction jet with emulsion tube 115z
    Pilot jet 52.5
    Pilot air jet 140
    Auxiliary fuel jet 40
    Auxiliary air jet 160
    Enrichment with/without ball 85/85
    Accelerator pump delivery .... 1.1 ± 0.15 cc per stroke
    Float needle valve 1.5
    Cold idling speed .... 2400 ± 50 rpm
    Choke valve gap (mm):
        Suffix S .... 4.4 ± 0.15
        Suffix T .... 4.0 ± 0.15
    Choke cover mark:
        Suffix S 137
        Suffix T 133
    Idle speed .... 950 ± 50 rpm
    CO content at idle .... 1.0 ± 0.2%

Engine code JB

Carburettor number .... 055 129 022 S or 023 D (manual), 055 129 022 T or 023 J
(automatic)

Jets and settings:	022 S/023 D	022 T/023 J
Venturi diameter (mm)	26	26
Main jet	x135	x132.5
Air correction jet with emulsion tube	100z	100z
Pilot jet	50	50
Pilot air jet	120 (-S), 130 (-D)	135
Auxiliary fuel jet	40	40
Auxiliary air jet	120	120
Enrichment with/without ball	0.9/without	0.9/without (-T) 0.95/without (-J)
Float needle valve	1.5	1.5
Accelerator pump delivery	1.1 ± 0.15 cc per stroke	1.1 ± 0.15 cc per stroke
Cold idling speed	2400 ± 50 rpm	2400 ± 50 rpm
Choke valve gap (mm)	4.8 (-S), 4.6 (-D), ± 0.15	3.8 ± 0.15
Choke cover mark	162	162
Idle speed	950 ± 50 rpm	950 ± 50 rpm
Co content at idle	1.5 ± 0.5	1.5 ± 0.5

Engine code FX (1980 Rabbit, except California)

Carburettor number .... 055 129 024 D
Jets and settings:
    Venturi diameter (mm) 24.5
    Main jet x127.5
    Air correction jet 120z
    Idle fuel jet (size stamped on float chamber) 50.0/52.5/55.0/57.5
    Idle air jet 120
    Auxiliary fuel jet 45
    Auxiliary air jet 155
    Accelerator pump discharge quantity .... 0.8 to 1.2 cc/stroke
    Float needle valve diameter .... 1.5 mm
    Float weight .... 10.5 to 11.5 g
    Cold idle speed .... 2350 to 2450 rpm
    Choke gap .... 3.3 to 3.7 mm
    Idle speed:
        Checking .... 900 ± 50 rpm
        Adjusting (see text) .... 675 ± 75 rpm
    CO content at idle:
        Checking .... 1.0 ± 0.5%
        Adjusting (see text) .... 0.8 ± 0.3%

Carburettor data – Solex 1B3

Engine code JB

Carburettor number	055 129 024 (manual), 055 129 024 A (automatic)
Jets and settings:	
Venturi diameter (mm)	26
Main jet	x122.5 (manual), x120 (automatic)
Air correction jet with emulsion tube	100
Pilot fuel/air jet	50/130
Auxiliary fuel/air jet	37.5/130
Pump injection tube	0.55 mm
Accelerator pump delivery	0.9 ± 0.15 cc per stroke
Needle valve	2.0 mm
Cold idle speed:	
Manual	3900 ± 200 rpm
Automatic	3700 ± 200 rpm
Choke valve gap (mm)	4.3 ± 0.15
Choke cover marking	214 (manual) 213 (automatic)
Idle speed:	
Except Scirocco	950 ± 50 rpm
Scirocco – test value	900 ± 50 rpm
Scirocco – setting value	800 ± 50 rpm
CO content at idle	$1.0 \pm 0.5\%$

Engine code GH

Carburettor number	055 129 024 G (manual), 055 129 024 H (automatic)
Jets and settings as above (engine code JB) except for main jet size:	
Manual	x125
Automatic	x122.5

Carburettor data – Solex/Zenith 2B2 (UK)

Engine code FD

Carburettor number .... 055 129 017 and 017 P (manual), 055 129 017 Q (automatic)

Jets and settings:	017/017 P		017 A/017 Q	
	1st Stage	*2nd Stage*	*1st Stage*	*2nd Stage*
Venturi diameter (mm)	24	27	24	27
Main jet	x115	x125	x117.5	x125
Air correction jet with emulsion tube	140	92.5	140	92.5
Pilot fuel/air jet	52.5/135	70/100	52.5/135	70/100
Auxiliary fuel/air jet:				
017 and 017 A	42.5/130	–	42.5/130	–
017 P and 017 Q	42.5/130	–	52.5/140	–
Needle valve diameter (mm)	2	2	2	2
Float setting (mm)	28 ± 0.5	30 ± 0.5	28 ± 0.5	30 ± 0.5
Marking on choke cover	107		107	
Accelerator pump delivery (slow):				
Cold – cc per stroke	0.9 ± 0.2		1.5 ± 0.2	
Warm – cc per stroke	–		0.9 ± 0.2	
Choke valve gap (mm)	3.5 ± 0.2		3.5 ± 0.2	
Cold idle speed (rpm)	3200 ± 50		3400 ± 50	
Idle speed (rpm)	950 ± 50		950 ± 50	
CO content at idle	1.5 ± 0.5		1.5 ± 0.5	

Engine code FR

Carburettor number .... 055 129 017 T and 023 K (manual), 049 129 015 E (automatic)

Jets and settings:	017 T/015 E to April 78		023 K/015 E from May '78	
	1st Stage	*2nd Stage*	*1st Stage*	*2nd Stage*
Venturi diameter (mm)	24	28	24	28
Main jet	x117.5	x125	x117.5	x125
Air correction jet	135	92.5	135	92.5
Pilot fuel/air jet	52.5/135	40/125	52.5/135	40/125
Auxiliary fuel/air jet	42.5/130	–	42.5/130	–
Progression air jet	–	200	–	180
Progression fuel jet	–	100	–	130 or 100
Needle valve diameter (mm)	2	2	2	2
Pump injection tube	45	–	–	–
Enrichment valve	65	–	65	–
Float setting (mm)	28 ± 0.5	30 ± 0.5	28 ± 1.0	30 ± 1.0
Marking on choke cover	141		141	
Accelerator pump delivery – slow, cold (cc per stroke)	0.9 ± 0.15		1.3 ± 0.2 (-K), 0.9 ± 0.15 (-E)	
Choke valve gap (mm)	4.5 ± 0.15		3.15 (-K), 4.3 (-E), ± 0.15	
Cold idle speed, rpm:				
Manual	3200 ± 50		3200 ± 50	
Automatic	3400 ± 505		3400 ± 50	
Idle speed	950 ± 50		950 ± 50	
CO content at idle	$1.0 \pm 0.2\%$		$1.5 \pm 0.5\%$	

Carburettor data – Solex/Zenith 2B5 (UK)
Engine code FR
Carburettor number .... 055 129 024 C (manual), 049 129 016 F (automatic)

Jets and settings: ....

	024 C		016 F	
	1st Stage	2nd Stage	1st Stage	2nd Stage
Venturi diameter (mm)	24	28	24	28
Main jet	x117.5	x125	x117.5	x125
Air correction jet with emulsion tube	135	92.5	135	92.5
Pilot fuel/air jet	52.5/135	40/125	52.5/135	40/125
Auxiliary fuel/air jet	42.5/130	–	42.5/130	–
Progression air jet	–	180	–	180
Progression fuel jet	–	130	–	100
Needle valve diameter (mm)	2	2	2	2
Pump injection tube	40/37.5	–	40/3.75	–
Enrichment valve	65	–	65	–
Float setting dimension (mm)	28 ± 1.0	30 ± 1.0	28 ± 1.0	30 ± 1.0
Marking on choke cover	218		218	
Accelerator pump delivery, slow cold (cc per stroke)	1.0 ± 0.15		0.9 ± 0.15	
Choke valve gap (mm)	3.9 ± 0.15		3.7 ± 0.15	
Cold idle speed (rpm)	3400 ± 50		3600 ± 50	
Idle speed (rpm):				
Test value	850 to 950		850 to 950	
Setting value	800 ± 50		800 ± 50	
CO content at idle	1.0 ± 0.5%		1.0 ± 0.5%	

Carburettor data – Solex/Zenith 2B2 (North America)
Engine codes FC and FG
Carburettor number .... 055 129 017 B (manual), 055 129 017 C (automatic)

Jets and settings:	1st stage	2nd stage
Venturi diameter (mm)	24	27
Main jet	115	115
Air correction jet	140	92.5
Pilot fuel/air jet	52.5/135	70/100
Auxiliary fuel/air jet	42.5/127.5	–
Enrichment with ball	1.0	–
Accelerator pump delivery (cc per stroke)	0.75 to 1.05	–
Float setting dimension (mm)	28 ± 0.5	30 ± 0.5
Needle valve diameter (mm)	2	2
Choke valve gap (mm)	3.8 to 4.2	
Idle speed (rpm)	850 to 2000 rpm	
CO content at idle	2.0 ± 0.5% (measured in front of catalytic converter)	

Engine code FN
Carburettor number .... 055 129 021, 021 B, 021 D (manual), 055 129 021 A, 021 C, 021 E (automatic)

Jets and settings:	1st stage	2nd stage
Venturi diameter (mm)	24	27
Main jet – except Canada	117.5 (112.5 without converter)	110 (120 without converter)
Main jet – Canada	115	110
Air correction jet – except Canada	130	92.5
Air correction jet – Canada	140	92.5
Pilot fuel/air jet	52.5/135 (140 without converter)	65/140
Auxiliary fuel/air jet	42.5/127.5	–
Enrichment without ball	–	1.1
Accelerator pump delivery (cc per stroke):		
Cold	1.3 to 1.7	–
Warm	0.6 to 0.9	–
Needle valve diameter (mm)	2	2
Float setting dimension (mm)	28 ± 0.5	30 ± 0.5
Choke valve gap (mm)	3.5	5.0
Throttle valve gap (mm)	0.45	–
Idle speed (rpm)	950 ± 50	
CO content at idle (%):		
Manual	1.5 ± 0.7	
Automatic	1.0 ± 0.7	

K-jetronic Continuous Injection System (CIS) engines

Fuel pump
Type .... Electric
Delivery (minimum):
    Electrical connections with screws .... 900 cc/30 seconds
    Push-on electrical connections .... 750 cc/30 seconds

System pressures

	kgf/cm²	lbf/in²
Control pressure, warm, engine oil 50° to 70°C (122° to 158°F)	3.4 to 3.8	49 to 57
System pressure	4.5 to 5.2	65 to 75
Minimum pressure after 10 minutes	1.8	27
Minimum pressure after 20 mins	1.6	23

System adjustments

Idle speed (rpm):
- UK models without electronic ignition .... 900 to 1000
- UK models with electronic ignition .... 750 to 850
- North American models except California .... 850 to 1000
- California models .... 880 to 1000

CO content (volume %):
UK models .... 1 to 2

North American models:

	USA (except California)	California	Canada
Pre-1979	1.0	0.3	1.0
1979 – manual gearbox	1.0 to 1.5	0.5 to 0.9	1.0 to 1.5
1979 – automatic transmission	0.6 to 1.0	0.5 to 0.9	0.6 to 1.0
1980 Pick-up	0.6 to 1.0	0.5 to 0.9	–
1980 (except Pick-up)	0.5 to 0.9	0.4 to 1.2	As 1979
1981 Pick-up	1.0 to 2.0	–	–
1981 (except Pick-up)	0.8 to 1.2	0.8 to 1.2	0.5 to 0.9

All models

Torque wrench settings

	lbf ft	Nm
Fuel pump (mechanical)	14	20
Fuel tank mountings	18	25
Fuel filter check valve (CIS)	14	20
Fuel hose unions (CIS)	18	25
Fuel pump check valve (CIS)	14	20
Cold start valve and hose union (CIS)	7	10
Throttle valve assembly (CIS)	14	20
Thermotime switch (CIS)	22	30
Warm-up regulator (CIS)	14	20
Fuel distributor (CIS)	25	35
Airflow sensor plate (CIS)	2.6	3.5
Exhaust to manifold	33	45
Exhaust manifold to head	18	25
Inlet manifold to head	18	25

1   General description

The fuel system comprises a rear-mounted fuel tank and either a mechanical fuel pump and Solex/Zenith downdraught carburettor, or a continuous injection system (CIS) supplied by an electric fuel pump.

The air cleaner is of automatic air temperature control type on most models, incorporating a disposable paper element.

The exhaust system incorporates a front downpipe and on some models a corrugated extension pipe, an intermediate pipe which incorporates a front silencer on Scirocco models, and a rear pipe and silencer. On certain North American models a catalytic converter is located to the rear of the corrugated front pipe.

2   Air cleaner and element – removal and refitting

1   The air cleaner element should be renewed at the specified intervals, see Routine Maintenance. In dusty conditions, more frequent renewal may be necessary.

Early carburettor models

2   On carburettor engines up to approximately April 1975, the air cleaner is fixed to the right-hand wing inside the engine compartment. To remove the element, unclip the top cover and withdraw the element, then discard it (photo). Clean the interior of the air cleaner with a fuel-moistened cloth, then wipe it dry. At the same time remove the air inlet cap from the carburettor and clean it.

3   Inside the air cleaner body is a spring-loaded temperature control valve (photo). Unclip the body from the wing, then undo the clip holding the crankcase ventilation pipe and pull off this clip. Pull the end of the inlet hose from the exhaust manifold guard and lift the body away from the vehicle. The temperature valve may be quickly checked by pouring hot water over the bulb. The flap will open very quickly, blocking off the warm air inlet and opening the inlet which allows cool air to enter the carburettor.

4   When refitting the body fit the rubber spigots into the wing and settle the case carefully. If the clips seem very stiff stop and resettle the body. It is very easy to split the case. When refitting the air inlet cap to the carburettor make sure that the sealing ring is correctly located in the groove, and lightly smear it with engine oil before pressing it into position.

Later carburettor models

5   On carburettor models from approximately April 1975, the air cleaner is fixed directly to the carburettor and on some models the air intake temperature is automatically controlled in conjunction with engine load. On other models the intake hose is adjustable to draw heated air from over the exhaust manifold or cool air from the front of the car. With the latter type the hose should be directed to the warm air outlet at ambient temperatures below 15°C (59°F) or to the side of the engine compartment at ambient temperatures above 15°C (59°F). To remove the element, unclip and remove the cover and withdraw the element. Note that on some models it is necessary to first loosen the front mounting nut. Clean the interior of the air cleaner with a fuel-moistened cloth, then wipe it dry (photos).

6   Where the temperature control flap is operated by vacuum, check its operation by disconnecting the hose at the element end, then suck and make sure that the flap opens and closes audibly (photo).

2.2 Removing the air cleaner element on an early model

2.3 Air cleaner temperature control valve location

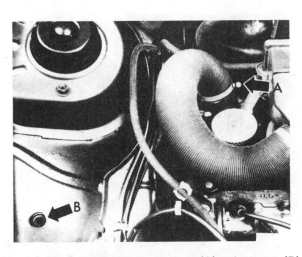

Fig. 3.1 Air cleaner intake hose winter (A) and summer (B) positions – only fitted to some models (Sec 2)

2.5a Unhook the clips ...

2.5b ... remove the air cleaner cover ...

2.5c ... and withdraw the element

2.5d Air cleaner cover mounting

2.6 Air intake temperature control vacuum connection

2.7a On fuel injection models unclip the airflow meter ...

2.7b ... separate the meter from the air cleaner (shown out of car) ...

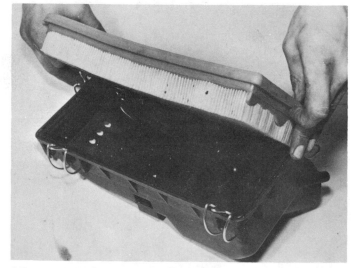

2.7c ... and withdraw the air cleaner element

Fuel injection models

7   On fuel injection models the air cleaner is located beneath the airflow meter on the left-hand side of the engine compartment. To remove the element, unclip the airflow meter and lift it sufficiently to withdraw the element. Clean the interior of the air cleaner with a fuel-moistened cloth, then wipe it dry (photos).

All models

8   Refitting of all types of air cleaner element is a reversal of removal, but where applicable make sure that the vacuum pipes are correctly located.

---

3   Fuel pump (carburettor models) — testing, removal and refitting

1   The fuel pump is located by the distributor on the forward facing side of the engine (photo). To test its operation disconnect the outlet pipe at the T-piece, then disconnect the ignition HT lead from the centre of the distributor cap and (on electronic ignition systems) connect the lead to earth with a suitable connecting wire. Spin the engine on the starter while holding a wad of rag near the fuel pipe. Well-defined spurts of fuel should be ejected from the pipe if the fuel

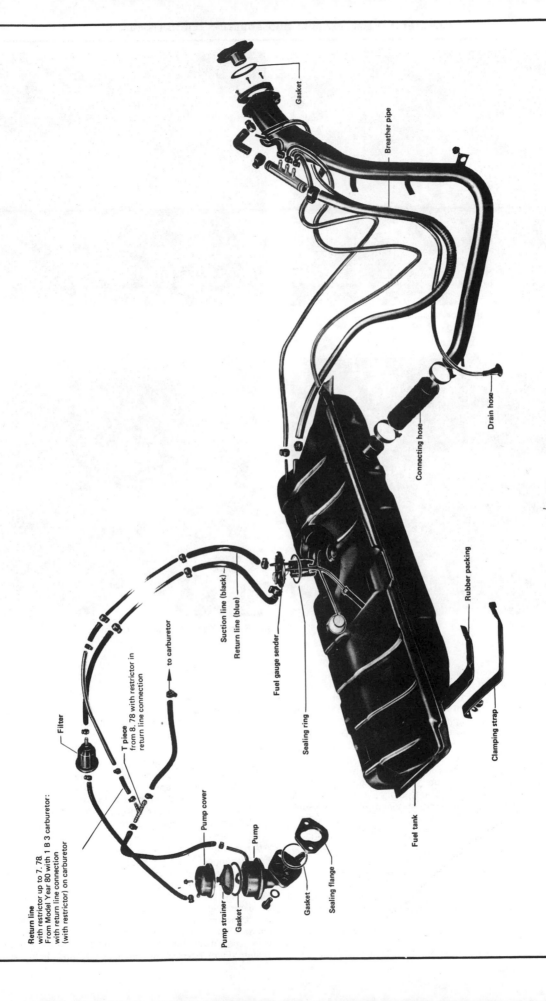

Fig. 3.2 Fuel system components for carburettor engines (Secs 3, 4 and 5)

Return line
with restrictor up to 7. 78
From Model Year 80 with 1 B 3 carburetor:
with return line connection
(with restrictor) on carburetor

Filter

T piece
from 8. 78 with restrictor in
return line connection

to carburetor

Suction line (black)

Return line (blue)

Fuel gauge sender

Sealing ring

Pump cover

Pump

Pump strainer

Gasket

Gasket

Sealing flange

Fuel tank

Gasket

Breather pipe

Connecting hose

Drain hose

Rubber packing

Clamping strap

3.1 Fuel pump location on carburettor models

3.2 Fuel pump cover and internal filter

3.3 Fuel system in-line filter

4.1 Removing the fuel tank filler cap

pump is operating correctly, provided that there is fuel in the fuel tank.

2　If the fuel pump appears to be faulty, first check the internal filter. Unscrew the small screw on the top cover and lift off the cover and filter, inspect the filter and clean it if necessary (photo). Refit the filter and cover using a new sealing ring if necessary.

3　The in-line fuel filter should be renewed regularly — see Routine Maintenance. Make sure that it is fitted the correct way round (photo).

4　To remove the fuel pump disconnect the inlet and outlet hoses, then unscrew the socket-headed bolts and withdraw the fuel pump from the cylinder block together with the sealing flange and gasket. Note that it is possible for an internal seal to fail, causing the engine oil to leak from the vent hole. If this fault is evident, renew the fuel pump.

5　Refitting is a reversal of removal, but clean the mating faces and always renew the gasket.

4　Fuel tank – removal, servicing and refitting

Note: *For safety reasons the fuel tank must always be removed in a well ventilated area, never over a pit.*

1　Disconnect the battery negative lead. Remove the tank filler cap (photo).

2　Jack up the rear of the car and support it on axle stands. Chock the

front wheels.

3　Drain the fuel tank by using a syphon or by disconnecting the bottom filler hose.

4　On fuel injection models only, disconnect the inlet and outlet hoses from the fuel pump, unscrew the mounting nuts, and withdraw the fuel pump from under the vehicle.

All models except Pick-up

5　Disconnect and plug the left and the right-hand side brake hoses, with reference to Chapter 8 if necessary.

6　Unscrew the rear axle mounting nuts on each side, then swing the rear axle down and allow it to hang on the handbrake cable guides.

7　Detach the exhaust system from the mounting rubbers.

All models

8　Disconnect the filler hose and where applicable the return hose from the fuel tank, then unscrew the mounting strap nuts and lower the tank sufficiently to disconnect the breather hoses, fuel hoses, and fuel gauge sender unit wires (photo). Withdraw the fuel tank from under the vehicle.

9　If the tank is contaminated with sediment or water, remove the gauge sender unit as described in Section 5 and swill the tank out with clean fuel. If the tank is damaged or leaks, it should be repaired by specialists, or alternatively renewed. **Do not** under any circumstances

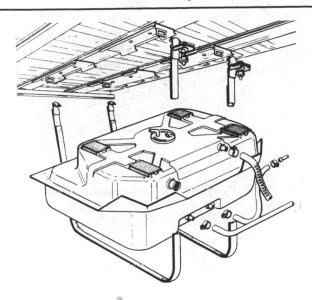

Fig. 3.3 Fuel tank fittings on Pick-up models (Sec 4)

4.8 Fuel tank mounting strap nut

solder or weld a fuel tank.

10 Refitting is a reversal of removal, but always fit the rubber packing strips between the support straps and the fuel tank. Bleed the brakes where necessary with reference to Chapter 8.

11 If a new tank is being fitted to a pre-1980 model it will be necessary to cut the existing breather pipes in order to fit them, and on certain models a new small breather pipe must be obtained.

5 Fuel gauge sender unit – removal and refitting

Note: *For safety reasons the fuel gauge sender unit must always be removed in a well-ventilated area, never over a pit.*

1 Disconnect the battery negative lead.

2 On pre-January 1976 models, drain the fuel tank by using a syphon or by disconnecting the bottom filler hose.

3 On January 1976 on models (except Pick-up), remove the rear seat (see Chapter 11) and remove the sender unit cover (3 screws).

4 On Pick-up models, remove the fuel tank as described in Section 4.

5 On all models disconnect the wiring, and where applicable disconnect the supply and return hoses after noting their position. Also note the position of the wiring for refitting reference (photos).

6 Using two crossed screwdrivers, turn the locking ring to release it from the tank.

7 Withdraw the sender unit and sealing ring.

8 Refitting is a reversal of removal, but always fit a new sealing ring and apply graphite powder to the contact surfaces.

6 Accelerator cable (manual gearbox models) – adjustment

Note: *On automatic transmission models the accelerator cable is connected to the shift control shaft, and the adjustment procedure is fully described in Chapter 6.*

1 Before adjusting the cable check that it is correctly aligned over its full length.

2 Have an assistant fully depress the accelerator pedal. Remove the air cleaner if necessary.

3 Check that the clearance between the throttle lever at the carburettor or throttle valve assembly (as applicable) and the fully open stop is a maximum of 1.0 mm (0.040 in). Note that the throttle lever must not be hard against the fully open stop (ie there must be a small clearance).

4 There are three different cable adjustment arrangements. Where locknuts are provided at the engine end of the outer cable, loosen them, then adjust the cable position and tighten the locknuts. Where a ferrule and circlip are provided, extract the circlip, adjust the cable position then refit the circlip so that it is abutting the ferrule guide. On

5.5a Fuel gauge sender unit on a Scirocco

5.5b Fuel gauge sender unit on a Jetta

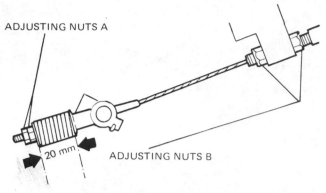

ADJUSTING NUTS A

H 556Z

20 mm

ADJUSTING NUTS B

Fig. 3.4 Accelerator cable adjustment on the PICT carburettor (Sec 6)

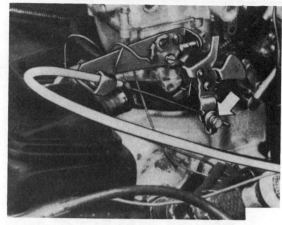

Fig. 3.5 Accelerator cable adjustment on the 2B2 carburettor (Sec 6)

Fig. 3.6 Accelerator cable adjustment on the 2B5 carburettor (Sec 6)

Fig. 3.7 Accelerator cable adjustment on the 4B3 carburettor (Sec 6)

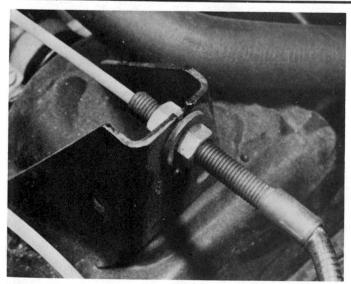

6.4a Accelerator cable adjustment on a Scirocco

6.4b Accelerator cable fixing to throttle valve housing on a Scirocco

some models it is necessary to adjust the inner cable by loosening the clamp screw, repositioning the lever while holding the cable taut, then tightening the screw (photos).

5   After adjustment refit the air cleaner where necessary.

7 Carburettor (Solex 34 PICT 5) – general description

The carburettor is basically a tube through which air is drawn into the engine by the action of the pistons and en route fuel is introduced into the air stream in the tube due to the fact that air pressure is lowered when drawn through the 'tube'.

The main fuel discharge point is situated in the 'tube' – choke is the proper name for the tube to be used from now on – between two flaps, one operated by the accelerator pedal and positioned at the engine end of the choke tube. The other is the strangler, which is operated by an automatic device.

When the engine is warm and running normally the strangler is wide open and the throttle open partially or fully, the amount of fuel/air mixture being controlled according to the required speed.

When cold the strangler is closed, partially or fully, and the suction therefore draws more fuel and less air, ie a richer mixture to aid starting a cold engine.

At idling speeds the throttle flap is shut so that no air and fuel can get to the engine in the regular way. For this there are separate routes leading to small holes in the side of the choke tube, on the engine side of the throttle flap. These 'bleed' the requisite amounts of fuel and air to the engine for slow speeds only.

The fuel is held in a separate chamber alongside the choke tube and its level is governed by a float so that it is not too high or low. If too high, it would pass into the choke tube without suction. If too low, it would only be drawn in at a higher suction than required for proper operation.

The main jet, which is simply an orifice of a particular size through which the fuel passes, is designed to let so much fuel flow at particular conditions of suction (properly called depression) in the choke tube. At idling speed the depression draws fuel from orifices below the throttle which has passed through the main jet and after that a pilot jet to reduce the quantity further. Both main and pilot jets have air bleed jets also which let in air to assist emulsification of the eventual fuel/air mixture.

The strangler flap is controlled by an electrically operated bi-metal strip. This consists of a coiled bi-metal strip connected to the choke flap spindle. When the ignition is switched off the coiled metal strip is cool and the flap is shut. When the ignition is switched on current flows through a heater which causes the strip to uncoil – opening the choke flap after some minutes.

On carburettors from model year 1976 the automatic choke is controlled by engine coolant as well as the electric element. The electric element is controlled by one or two thermo-switches (depending on model) in the coolant circuit, and in this arrangement the electric element is used to open the choke valve during the initial warm-up period, after which the coolant temperature controls the choke valve.

The fuel in the float chamber is regulated at the correct height by a float which operates a needle valve. When the level drops the needle is lowered away from the entry orifice and fuel under pressure from the fuel pump enters. When the level rises the flow is shut off. The pump delivery is always greater than the maximum requirement from the carburettor.

Another device fitted is an electro-magnetic cut-off valve. This is a feature which is designed to positively stop the fuel flow when the engine is stopped. Otherwise the engine tends to run on – even with the ignition switched off – when the engine is hot.

8 Carburettor (Solex 34 PICT 5) – removal, overhaul and refitting

1   The carburettor should not be dismantled without a very good reason. Any alterations of the settings will alter the CO content of the exhaust gas and may contravene the emission control regulations. However, the top may be separated from the body to check the level of fuel in the float chamber and the jets may be cleaned without altering any vital settings.

2   Remove the air cleaner or intake from the top of the carburettor. Clean the carburettor as much as possible externally, remove the nuts from the bolts holding the carburettor to the inlet manifold. Remove the battery earth strap. This will stop any sparks when you remove the wires from the electro-magnetic cut-off valve, the choke and the carburettor earth terminal. The latter is necessary because of the rubber mounting.

3   Disconnect the fuel supply and return hoses as necessary, and where applicable drain the cooling system (Chapter 2) and disconnect the choke hoses.

4   Disconnect the accelerator cable from the throttle lever, then remove the screws and withdraw the bracket from the carburettor. Note that on pre-1980 models the locking tag must be levered from the cable end nut.

5   Disconnect the vacuum pipes and, with all the wires described in paragraph 2 disconnected, withdraw the carburettor from the engine.

6   Where fitted, remove the plastic cover from the automatic choke. Note the relationship of the alignment marks on the automatic choke, then remove the retaining ring (3 screws) or water chamber (1 bolt), and withdraw the heater body and bi-metal spring together with the gasket or cover. Note how the operating lever locates in the spring (photos).

7   Unhook the return spring and remove the five screws holding the top of the carburettor to the body. Lift the top away (photo). Be careful not to damage the gasket. The float may be removed from the float chamber (photo) and checked for leaks. A simple way to do this is to immerse it in warm, not hot, water. Any pin holes will be detected by bubbles as the air inside the float expands. Dry the float thoroughly. It may not be repaired, only replaced by a new one.

8   The needle valve may be unscrewed from the top of the carburettor and checked. Clean out the float chamber, removing any sediment with a soft hair brush.

9   Remove the plug from the outside at the base of the float chamber and then through this hole unscrew the main jet and check that it is clear. Jets **must not** be cleaned with wires or pins. Use compressed air to blow out any obstruction. If wire is pushed in the jet will be enlarged and the delicate balance of fuel mixture upset. If in doubt fit a new jet (see Specifications).

10 On the top rim of the body are two more jets and the air correction

8.6a Automatic choke alignment mark (arrowed)

8.6b Removing the automatic choke cover assembly

8.7a Removing the carburettor cover ...

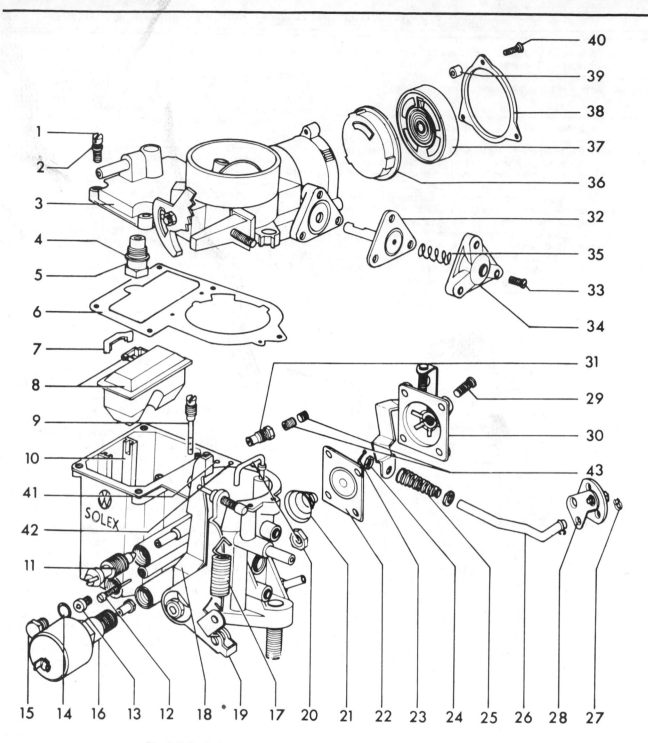

Fig. 3.8 Exploded view of an early Solex 34 PICT 5 carburettor (Sec 7)

1	Cover screw	12	Idle mixture control	22	Accelerator pump	33	Countersunk screw
2	Spring washer		screw		diaphragm	34	Diaphragm cover
3	Top cover	13	Main jet	23	Split pin	35	Spring
4	Needle valve washer	14	Washer	24	Washer	36	Choke cover
5	Needle valve	15	Plug	25	Spring	37	Heater coil and insert
6	Gasket	16	Electromagnetic cut-	26	Connecting link	38	Retaining ring
7	Float pin bracket		off valve	27	Circlip	39	Spacer
8	Float and pin	17	Return spring	28	Bellcrank lever	40	Screw
9	Air correction jet and	18	Fast idle lever		(adjustable)	41	Pilot air jet
	emulsion tube	19	Throttle lever	29	Countersunk screw	42	Auxiliary air jet
10	Carburettor lower	20	Injection pipe from	30	Pump cover	43	Auxiliary fuel jet
	housing		accelerator pump	31	Pilot jet		and plug
11	Bypass air screw	21	Diaphragm spring	32	Vacuum diaphragm		

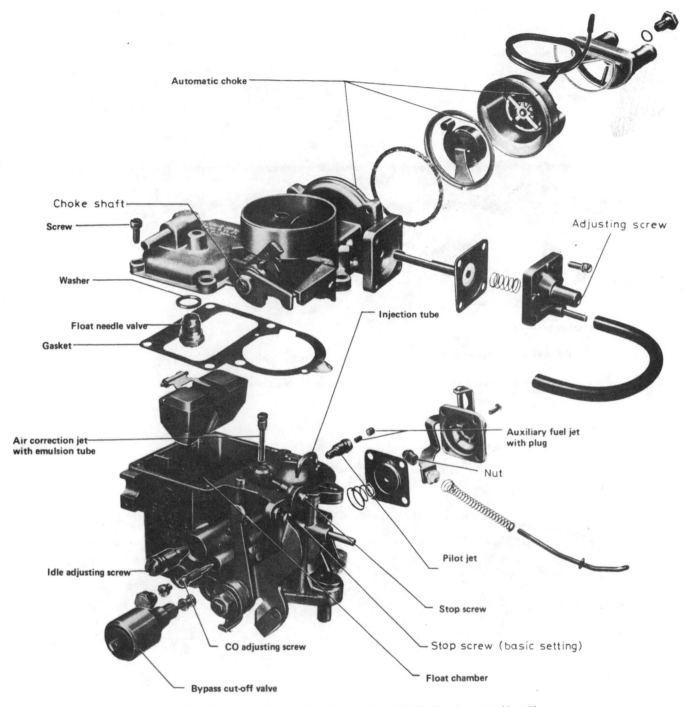

Automatic choke

Choke shaft

Screw

Washer

Float needle valve

Gasket

Air correction jet with emulsion tube

Idle adjusting screw

CO adjusting screw

Bypass cut-off valve

Injection tube

Adjusting screw

Auxiliary fuel jet with plug

Nut

Pilot jet

Stop screw

Stop screw (basic setting)

Float chamber

Fig. 3.9 Exploded view of a later Solex 34 PICT 5 carburettor (Sec 7)

jet with the emulsion tube. Unscrew the air correction jet, take it out and clean the emulsion tube. The jet next to it is the pilot air jet and the one on the outside is the auxiliary air jet. These may be removed and cleaned (photo).

11 There are two more jets to find: the pilot jet and the auxiliary fuel jet. The pilot jet is alongside the accelerator pump cover; the auxiliary fuel jet is approached from the same side as the pilot jet but hides behind a plug, and is not easily accessible.

12 With all the removable jets taken out, blow out all the drillings with compressed air.

13 The electro-magnetic cut-off valve may be removed (photo) and its action tested by supplying 12 volts to the tag terminal and earthing the case. The plunger should first be depressed 3 to 4 mm (0.118 to 0.157 in).

14 The accelerator pump may be dismantled and the diaphragm

inspected for cracks or damage. **Do not** undo the screw on the end of the operating rod or the pump will have to be recalibrated. Take the rod off the lever at the other end. Undo the four screws holding the pump cover and extract the diaphragm. Watch out for the spring and fit it back the correct way. When refitting the cover tighten the screws with the diaphragm centre pushed in. This means holding the operating lever out while the screws are tightened.

15 The choke vacuum diaphragm may be inspected in a similar way. **Do not** alter the setting of the centre screw or the choke opening will need to be reset.

16 There is one other check to made. If the bushes of the throttle butterfly flap are worn and the spindle is loose in its bearings then air may leak past and affect the air/fuel ratio. The remedy is, unfortunately, a replacement carburettor.

17 Assemble all the parts methodically. Put a little jointing compound

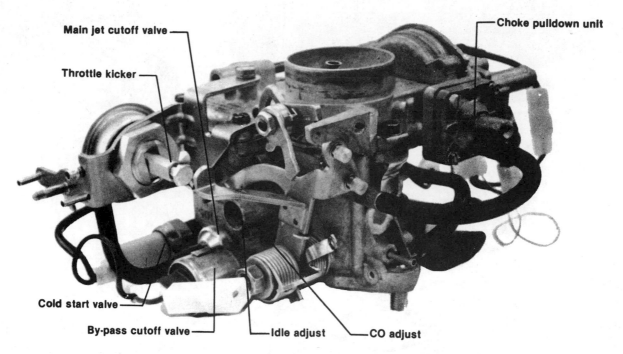

Main jet cutoff valve

Throttle kicker

Choke pulldown unit

Cold start valve

By-pass cutoff valve

Idle adjust

CO adjust

Fig. 3.10 Front view of 34 PICT 5 carburettor fitted to North American models (Sec 7)

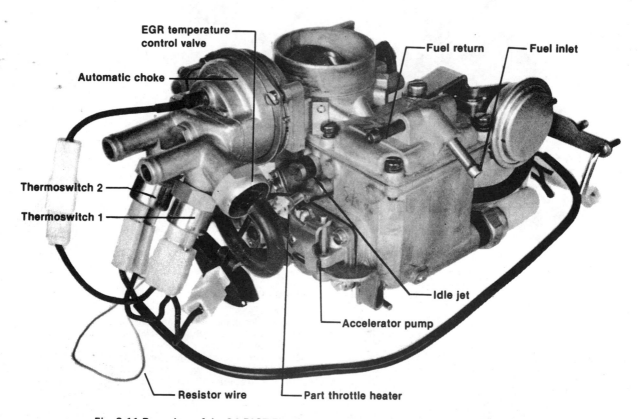

EGR temperature control valve

Automatic choke

Fuel return

Fuel inlet

Thermoswitch 2

Thermoswitch 1

Idle jet

Accelerator pump

Resistor wire

Part throttle heater

Fig. 3.11 Rear view of the 34 PICT 5 carburettor fitted to North American models (Sec 7)

8.7b ... and float (Solex 34 PICT 5)

8.10 The Solex 34 PICT 5 carburettor main body. 'A' main jet plug, 'B' main jet, 'C' air jet and emulsion tube, 'D' pilot air jet, 'E' auxiliary air jet, 'G' main fuel/air delivery tube, 'F' injection pipe from accelerator pump

8.13 Removing the electro-magnetic cut-off valve

Fig. 3.12 Adjusting the choke valve gap (Sec 9)

on the main jet plug. If the gasket is broken fit a new one, do not try to stick the old one in place. The carburettor should not need recalibration as you have not moved any of the adjusting screws.
18 Refitting is a reversal of removal, but always fit a new gasket. All of the adjustments described in Section 9 can be completed with the carburettor in position on the engine.

9 Carburettor (Solex 34 PICT 5) – adjustments and tests

Choke valve gap
1   Remove the air cleaner or intake. Remove the automatic choke cover with reference to Section 8.
2   Close the choke valve and at the same time where applicable position the cold idle speed adjusting screw in the upper notch.
3   Push the choke pull-off rod fully toward the diaphragm, then check that the distance between the choke valve and the carburettor wall is as given in the Specifications. If not, turn the diaphragm adjusting screw as necessary (photo).
4   Refit the cover and air cleaner or intake.

Throttle valve stop screw
5   This screw determines the basic throttle valve opening – on some models the screw is non-adjustable.
6   With the engine idling at normal operating temperature, remove the vacuum advance pipe and connect a vacuum gauge to the outlet on the carburettor.
7   Turn the stop screw clockwise until the gauge registers a vacuum, then unscrew it slowly until the gauge returns to zero. From this point unscrew the screw a further quarter of a turn.
8   Refit the vacuum advance pipe and adjust the idle speed and CO content if necessary.

Accelerator pump discharge
9   The accelerator pump may be adjusted to give the correct quantity of fuel per stroke by turning the nut on the end of the connecting rod (photo). A piece of rubber or plastic tube must be clipped over the

9.3 Solex 34 PICT 5 carburettor adjustments – choke valve gap adjusting screw (A), throttle valve stop screw (B), fast idle screw (C)

9.9 Accelerator pump discharge adjustment (arrowed) on the Solex 34 PICT 5 carburettor injection pipe in the carburettor bore and led out to a measuring cylinder. With the tube in position, operate the throttle until fuel comes out of the tube into the glass. Empty the glass and then operate the throttle five times catching the fuel in the measuring glass. Divide the amount in the glass by five and compare the result with the amount given in the Specifications. To adjust the stroke alter the setting of the nut and repeat the test. Lengthen the rod (ie screw out the nut) to decrease the amount injected. On some early models a different arrangement may be met. This is shown in Fig. 3.13. Screw the screw out to increase the amount injected.

Vacuum valve (float chamber)

10 1.5 litre automatic transmission models fitted with carburettor number 055 129 015 L have an electrically-controlled vacuum valve which channels manifold depression to the float chamber in order to improve move-off performance up to 1800 rpm.

11 To test the system connect a test lamp into the vacuum valve circuit, then start the engine and allow it to idle – the test lamp should light up. Now increase the engine speed to between 1700 and 1900 rpm – the test lamp should go out.

12 The same carburettor also incorporates an automatic cold idle valve which effectively varies the opening of the cold idle valve according to the coolant temperature. The valve is operated by manifold vacuum.

Idle speed and CO content

13 Connect a tachometer and exhaust gas analyser to the engine in accordance with the manufacturer's instructions.

14 Disconnect the crankcase ventilation hose from the air cleaner or intake and seal the exposed hole (ie not the hose) with masking tape.

15 On 1980 North American models, similarly disconnect the charcoal filter hose at the intake and seal the intake hole. Also disconnect the hoses from the air injection valves and plug the valves.

16 On all models run the engine at a fast idling speed until it reaches its normal operating temperature. Switch off all electrical components and only make an adjustment when the radiator fan is stopped.

17 On models equipped with electronic ignition, briefly accelerate the engine in order to operate the idle stabilizer.

All except North American models with electronic ignition

18 Make sure that the choke valve is fully open, then allow the engine to idle and if necessary adjust the idle speed screw until the engine runs at the specified speed (photo).

19 Check the CO content on the analyser and if necessary adjust the mixture to achieve the specified result. Note that on some models a tamperproof plug seals the mixture screw, and its removal may violate current legislation.

North American models with electronic ignition

20 If adjustment of the idle speed or CO content is necessary on North American models equipped with electronic ignition, the procedure is different. First disconnect the plugs from the idle stabilizer and connect them together, then disconnect and plug the vacuum advance and retard hoses. Adjust the idle speed to the specified adjusting value, then reconnect the vacuum advance and retard hoses and adjust the CO content. Now readjust the idle speed if necessary to regain the specified value. Reconnect the idle stabilizer plugs, accelerate the engine briefly, then check that the idle speed and CO content are within the specified checking values.

Fig. 3.14 Testing the vacuum valve system (Sec 9)

Fig. 3.13 Early type accelerator pump discharge adjustment (Sec 9)

Fig. 3.15 Cold idle valve (1) and thermo-pneumatic valve (2) (Sec 9)

9.18 Solex 34 PICT 5 carburettor fast idle cam (A), idle speed screw (B) and mixture screw (C)

All models
21 Finally check the idling speed and make any small adjustment as necessary. Stop the engine, remove the instruments, and reconnect all the hoses as necessary. If the vehicle has been used under frequent stop/start conditions, the CO content may rise after reconnecting the crankcase breather hose, however this is due to the presence of fuel in the engine oil. A long fast drive or an oil change will solve the problem.

Fast idle (cold idling) speed
22 Adjust the idle speed and CO content as described in paragraphs 13 to 21.
23 Set the fast idle stop screw on the third step as shown in Fig. 3.16.
24 Hold the choke valve fully open, then run the engine and check that the fast idle speed is as given in the Specifications. If not, adjust the screw as necessary.

Part throttle heater (North American models)
25 1980 North American models are equipped with a heating element for part throttle channel heating up to 75°C (167°F).
26 To test the heater, connect a test lamp into the supply wire direct from the battery positive terminal — the lamp should light up if the heater is operating correctly.

Main jet shut-off valve (North American models)
27 This valve is controlled by an electro-pneumatic relay in the vacuum control unit, and it cuts off fuel flow through the main jet when the relay voltage is less than 5 volts or when the ignition is switched off.
28 To test the valve, run the engine at idling speed, then disconnect the wiring plug from the vacuum control unit. If the engine does not stall, either the valve or the vacuum system is faulty.

Cold start valve (North American models)
29 This valve supplies extra fuel for up to 2 minutes for starting at temperatures below 16°C (60°F).
30 To test the valve, disconnect the supply wire and connect a test lamp and battery to the terminal. At temperatures below 16°C (60°F) the test lamp should light up.

Throttle kicker (North American models)
31 The throttle kicker increases the idling speed when the air conditioner is operating, in order to prevent the engine stalling.
32 Before testing the kicker the ignition timing, idle speed and CO content must first be checked and adjusted if necessary. An ignition timing lamp (strobe) will be required.
33 Briefly accelerate the engine, then switch on the air conditioner to the coldest temperature and highest blower speed. The ignition timing should not alter — if it does, loosen the locknut on the throttle kicker and turn the adjusting screw as necessary. Tighten the locknut, using a liquid locking agent, when adjustment is correct.

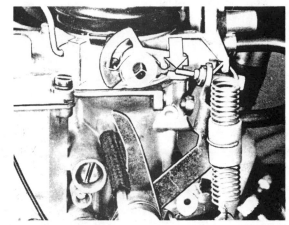

Fig. 3.16 Fast idle stop screw position (arrowed) when adjusting the fast idle speed (Sec 9)

Fig. 3.17 North American carburettor part throttle heating element (A) and supply wire (B) (Sec 9)

10 Carburettor (Solex/Zenith 2B2 and 2B5) – general description

The carburettor has two venturi tubes, two float chambers and two throttle valves. However, it is not, as would seem, two separate carburettors. The throttle valve of stage 2 remains firmly shut until released by the movement to full throttle of the butterfly valve of stage 1. Once the system of locking levers releases stage 2 throttle, it is then controlled by a vacuum capsule and opens according to the depression in the venturis of both stages.

At idling speed most of the fuel is supplied by stage 1. The fuel flows through the main jet to the idling fuel jet and mixes with the idle air supply to form the idle mixture. It is then delivered via drillings in the carburettor body into the choke tube just below the throttle valve. The composition of this mixture is governed by the mixture regulating screw, which governs the CO value.

During the idling period, stage 2 also supplies fuel to its own venturi via a similar system of drilling and jets.

Further supply of fuel during the idle period is provided through the auxiliary fuel jet and auxiliary jet of stage 1. These intermingle in the emulsion tube and enter the inlet via the same passage below the throttle flap of stage 1. The flow of this fuel is controlled by the bypass air control screw. The entire supply can be shut off by the magnetic cut-off valve which operates when the ignition is switched off.

Stage 2 does not have an auxiliary supply system, bypass control screw, mixture regulating screw or cut-off valve. All idle adjustments and mixture control adjustments are done on stage 1.

As the throttle valve is opened the accelerator pump comes into action, delivering fuel to the air stream, and the bypass of stage 1 is further activated. Then the main jet system comes into action and delivers fuel to the atomiser in the venturi. The butterfly valve of stage 2 is still closed, and the only contribution from stage 2 is via the basic idle system.

As full load conditions are approached, the supply of fuel from stage 1 increases through the main jet system and the interlock mechanism of the throttle valve of stage 2 is released, allowing the butterfly valve to open and fuel is supplied via the main jet of stage 2 to the atomiser in stage 2 venturi. The enrichment tube of stage 2 also supplies fuel to the stage 2 venturi.

The position of the butterfly valve of stage 2 is governed by a vacuum capsule which is operated by the increasing depression in the venturi of both stages 1 and 2.

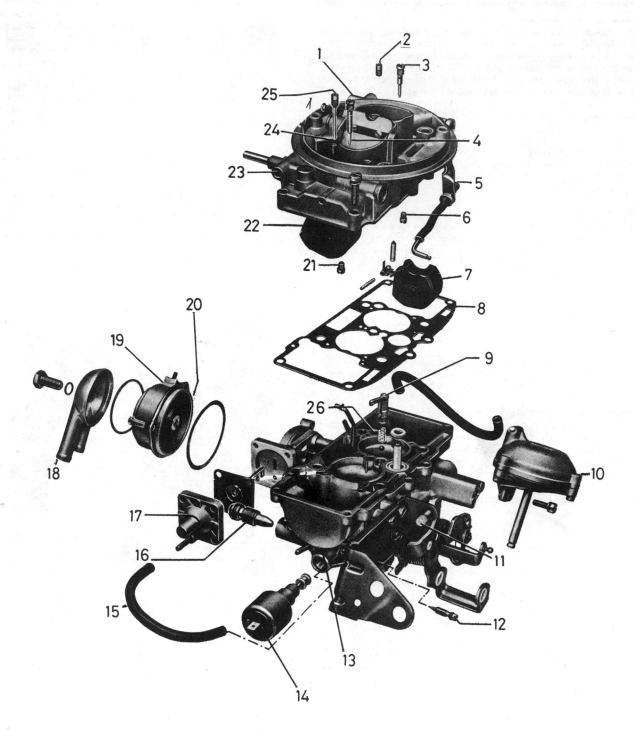

Fig. 3.18 Exploded view of an early Solex 2B2 carburettor (Sec 10)

1 Pilot fuel and air jet (1st stage)	10 Vacuum capsule for control (2nd stage)	19 Choke valve control body
2 Progression air jet	11 Basic throttle setting adjustment screw	20 Choke valve electric element
3 Pilot fuel and air jet (2nd stage)	12 CO content adjustment screw	21 Main jet (1st stage)
4 Choke valve flap	13 Carburettor body	22 Float (1st stage)
5 Injection quantity control screw	14 Magnetic cut-off valve	23 Upper part of carburettor body
6 Main jet (2nd stage)	15 Hose	24 Bypass air fuel jet
7 Float (2nd stage)	16 Idle adjustment screw	25 Bypass air jet
8 Gasket	17 Choke valve cover and adjustment screw	26 Progression fuel jet
9 Injection tube	18 Choke valve cover coolant supply cover	

11 Carburettor (Solex/Zenith 2B2 and 2B5) – removal, overhaul and refitting

1   Apart from cleaning the jets, setting the choke and throttle flaps and checking the accelerator pump injection capacity, the only other repair possible is the adjustment of the float level. These tests are included in this Section because they must be done with the carburettor away from the car. Running tests are described in Section 12.

2   To remove the carburettor, first take off the air cleaner. Disconnect the accelerator cable and the fuel hose. Remove the battery earth strap and then disconnect the wiring from the magnetic cut-off valve, the automatic choke and the microswitch (if fitted) on the accelerator linkage. Tag these wires for easy refitting. Label the vacuum hoses and remove them. Undo the bolts holding the carburettor to the manifold and take the carburettor away.

3   Refitting is the reverse of removal. Be careful when refitting the accelerator cable to secure the outer cable in the clamp on the carburettor so that there is no stress on the butterfly valve of stage 1 when the accelerator is fully depressed. If the pedal is not fully depressed when the valve is exactly at full throttle position of the valve you will be pushing the pedal down and straining the throttle linkage of the carburettor.

4   Refer to Fig. 3.20. The various jets, except the air correction jets and emulsion tubes, may be located, removed and blown out with compressed air. **Do not** clean them with wire or a pin. If they are so blocked that the compressed air will not remove the obstruction then fit a new jet.

5   Remove the screws holding the carburettor top to the carburettor body and turn the head upside down. The main jets are now accessible and may be serviced.

6   The automatic choke is identical with that of the PICT 34 carburettor (see Section 8) except that the heater resistance element has a different value. The method of setting the choke valve gap is identical to that described in Section 9; however, make sure that the

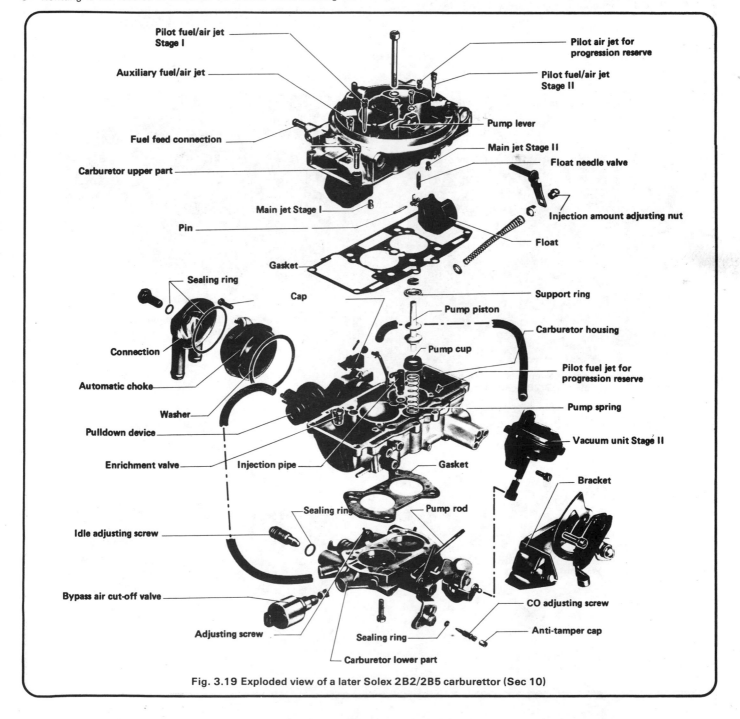

Fig. 3.19 Exploded view of a later Solex 2B2/2B5 carburettor (Sec 10)

Fig. 3.20 Jet locations in top of carburettor Solex 2B2/2B5 (Sec 11)

Fig. 3.21 Location of main jets stage 1 (8) and 2 (9) on Solex 2B2/2B5 carburettor (Sec 11)

1/2 Auxiliary fuel/air jet
3 Air correction jet with emulsion tube, stage 1 (cannot be screwed out)
4 Pilot fuel/air jet, stage 1
5 Pilot fuel/air jet, stage 2
6 Air correction jet with emulsion tube, stage 2 (cannot be screwed out)
7 Progression air jet

Fig. 3.22 Location of progression fuel jet (10) and enrichment valve (11) on Solex 2B2/2B5 carburettor (Sec 11)

Fig. 3.23 Accelerator pump discharge adjustment nut (a) on Solex 2B2/2B5 carburettor (Sec 11)

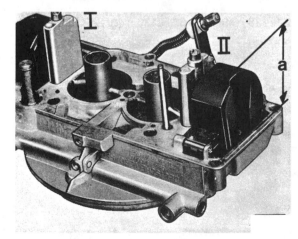

Fig. 3.24 Float level adjustment dimension (a) on Solex 2B2/2B5 carburettor (Sec 11)

Fig. 3.25 Stage 2 throttle valve basic setting adjusting screw (arrowed) on Solex 2B2/2B5 carburettor (Sec 11)

gap is measured against the carburettor outer wall.

7   The stage 1 throttle valve basic setting is made at the factory; however, if it is found necessary to adjust it, proceed as follows.

8   Remove the tamperproof cap and turn out the screw until there is a gap between it and the stop.

9   Open and close the throttle valve quickly, then turn in the screw until it just touches the stop. From this point turn it in a further quarter of a turn.

10 The measurement and adjustment of the accelerator pump output must be done with the carburettor assembled but not bolted to the manifold. Make sure the float chambers are full and that a supply of fuel to the carburettor is available. A piece of hose and a funnel connected to the carburettor inlet will do. Hold the carburettor over a large funnel and operate the throttle lever until fuel begins to run from the carburettor into the funnel. Hold the choke valve in its fully open position. Now hold a measuring glass under the funnel and operate the throttle fully ten times. Allow the fuel to run into the glass and divide the quantity by ten. The correct amount is given in the Specifications. If necessary adjust the nut as shown in Fig. 3.23. Note that on some carburettors (see Specifications) a vacuum valve controlled by a thermo-pneumatic valve in the coolant provides two different accelerator pump injection quantities. At coolant temperatures below 20°C (68°F) vacuum is supplied to the vacuum valve, and above 25°C (77°F) the valve is closed.

11 While the top is separated from the carburettor body the float position may be checked. Refer to Fig. 3.24 and measure the distance shown. If these are not correct (see Specifications) the only adjustment is by bending the bracket.

12 The stage 2 throttle valve basic setting is made at the factory; however, if it is found necessary to adjust it, proceed as follows.

13 With the stage 1 throttle valve in the idling position and the automatic choke fast idle cam set to its hot position, turn the adjusting screw (Fig. 3.25) to give a gap between the screw and the stop.

14 Disconnect the vacuum unit pullrod, and lightly press the throttle valve lever to the closed position to eliminate any play.

15 Turn in the adjusting screw until it just contacts the stop, then on the 2B2 carburettor turn it a further half turn, or on the 2B5 carburettor turn it a further quarter turn. Lock the screw with sealing paint and reconnect the vacuum unit pullrod.

16 Refitting is a reversal of removal, but always fit a new gasket.

12 Carburettor (Solex/Zenith 2B2 and 2B5) – running adjustments

Idle speed and CO content
Models with conventional ignition
1   Connect a tachometer and exhaust gas analyser to the engine in accordance with the manufacturer's instructions.

2   Disconnect the crankcase ventilation hose from the air cleaner or intake (photo) and seal the exposed hole (ie not the hose) with masking tape.

3   Run the engine at a fast idling speed until it reaches its normal operating temperature. Switch off all electrical components and only make an adjustment when the radiator fan is stopped.

4   Check that the fast idle screw is not touching the cam, then allow the engine to idle and if necessary adjust the idle speed screw until the engine runs at the specified speed.

5   Check the CO content on the analyser and if necessary adjust the mixture screw to achieve the specified result. Note that on some models a tamperproof plug seals the mixture screw, and its removal may violate current legislation.

6   Stop the engine, remove the instruments, and reconnect the crankcase ventilation hose.

Models with electronic ignition
7   Carry out the procedure described in paragraphs 1 and 2.

8   To **check** the idling speed, run the engine at a fast idling speed until it reaches its normal operating temperature. Switch off all electrical components and only make the check when the radiator fan is stopped.

9   Check that the fast idle screw is not touching the cam, then allow the engine to idle and check that the idle speed is as given in the Specifications.

10 To **adjust** the idle speed, stop the engine, then disconnect the plugs from the idle stabilizer and connect them together. Adjust the idle speed to 750 to 850 rpm. Stop the engine and reconnect the idle

12.2 Crankcase ventilation hose to valve cover connection

stabilizer plugs, then start the engine again and accelerate the engine briefly. The idling speed should now be as given in the Specifications.

11 To check and adjust the CO content, first disconnect the plugs from the idle stabilizer and connect them together. Start the engine and check that the CO content is as given in the Specifications. If not, turn the mixture screw as necessary.

12 Stop the engine, remove the instruments, and reconnect the crankcase ventilation hose.

Fast idle (cold idling) speed
13 Run the engine until it reaches normal operating temperature. Connect a tachometer to the engine.

14 Set the fast idle adjusting screw on the highest step of the fast idle cam, then without touching the throttle, start the engine and check that the fast idle speed is as given in the Specifications. If not, turn the adjusting screw as necessary – due to its location, access to the screw is difficult and therefore it is necessary to operate the throttle to release the screw from the cam. The screw must be set up again as previously described in order to check the adjustment.

Vacuum pullrod
15 Disconnect the pullrod, loosen the locknut, and adjust the rod so that the dimension shown in Fig. 3.26 is 1 to 2 mm (0.04 to 0.08 in).

Fig. 3.26 Vacuum pullrod adjustment dimension (a) on Solex 2B2/2B5 carburettor (Sec 12)

13 Carburettor (Solex 1B3) – general description

The carburettor components are shown in Fig. 3.27. The general description is similar to that given in Section 7 for the 34 PICT 5 carburettor. However, the accelerator pump is of the piston type, and a part throttle enrichment valve is fitted to improve move-off performance (photos).

As from May 1980 a fuel reservoir is fitted to the front of the engine to purge vapour bubbles from the system (1.5 litre only).

14 Carburettor (Solex 1B3) – removal and refitting

Follow the procedure given in Section 8 for the 34 PICT 5 carburettor (photo).

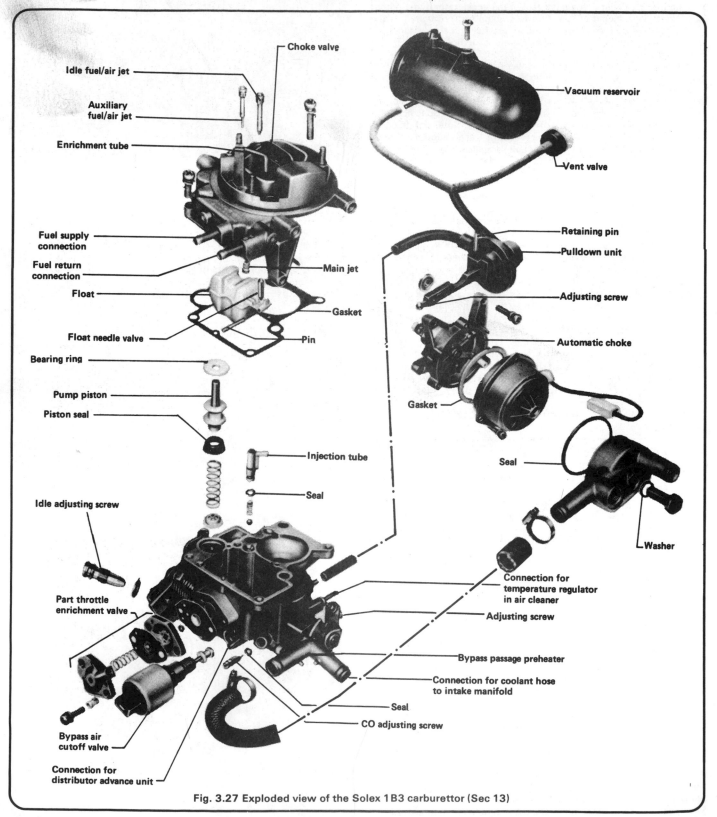

Fig. 3.27 Exploded view of the Solex 1B3 carburettor (Sec 13)

13.0a Side view of the Solex 1B3 carburettor

13.0b Front view of the Solex 1B3 carburettor

13.0c Fuel purge reservoir location (May 1980 on, 1.5 litre engines)

14.0 Solex 1B3 carburettor accelerator cable fixing

15 Carburettor (Solex 1B3) – adjustments

Enrichment tube
1   The bottom end of the enrichment tube must be level with the upper surface of the choke valve when closed. Carefully bend the tube if adjustment is necessary.

Accelerator pump discharge
2   Hold the carburettor over a funnel leading into a calibrated measuring glass.
3   Turn the fast idle cam so that the adjusting screw is not touching it, then fully open the throttle slowly ten times. Divide the amount discharged by ten and compare it with the amount given in the Specifications.
4   If adjustment is necessary loosen the cam plate screw (Fig. 3.28), reposition the cam plate and tighten the screw. Recheck the adjustment.

Choke valve gap
5   Open the throttle valve and set the fast idle adjusting screw on the highest step on the fast idle cam.
6   Using a screwdriver press the choke operating rod towards the pull-down unit, then check that the choke valve to carburettor wall gap

Fig. 3.28 Accelerator pump discharge adjustment on Solex 1B3 carburettor (Sec 15)

a   Adjustment screw   b   Cam plate

Fig. 3.29 Checking the choke valve gap on the Solex 1B3 carburettor with a drill (2) (Sec 15)

Fig. 3.30 Throttle valve basic setting screw (c) on Solex 1B3 carburettor (Sec 15)

is as given in the Specifications, using a drill to measure the gap.
7   If necessary turn the adjusting screw as required.

Idle speed and CO content

8   The procedure is identical to that given in Section 12; however, on this carburettor the choke valve is not directly connected to the fast ideal cam since the former is operated by vacuum. When checking that the fast idle adjusting screw is not touching the cam, it may be necessary to turn the cam.

Throttle valve basic setting

9   The adjustment is made at the factory; however, if it is found necessary to adjust it, proceed as follows.
10 Remove the tamperproof cap, then connect a vacuum gauge in the vacuum hose between the distributor and the carburettor.
11 Start the engine and allow it to idle. Set the fast idle cam so that the adjusting screw is not touching it.
12 Screw in the throttle valve stop screw to give the maximum reading on the vacuum gauge, then unscrew it to give the lowest reading.
13 Unscrew the screw a further quarter of a turn.
14 Disconnect the vacuum gauge and refit the hose.

Fast idle (cold idling) speed

15 The procedure is as given in Section 12, but the adjusting screw is more accessible.

16 Continuous injection system (CIS) – general description

Although the system is sometimes known as the K-jectronic system it does not depend upon electronics, but on the passage of air through a cone and the position of a sensor plate in that air stream. The only electrical components are bi-metallic heaters and solenoids. The fuel pump is also driven by an electric motor but there are no mini-computers or other electronic devices as in the previous Bosch systems fitted to VW/Audi vehicles (photos).

Refer to Fig. 3.31 which shows a diagrammatic layout of the system. Air passes through the air cleaner into the airflow meter and from there via two throttle butterfly valves into the inlet manifold. The engine inlet and exhaust valve arrangements are identical with the carburettor engine.

As the air passes through the airflow meter, the sensor plate is lifted from the rest position. The angle at which it becomes stable depends upon the speed of the airflow, which is of course governed by the engine speed. There is a law of hydraulics and pneumatics which states that a body free to move in a vertical conical air passage will move according to a straight line graph, assuming a stable position governed by the air-flow volume. This simple law is used so that the up-and-down movement of the sensor plate may be used to measure the correct volume of fuel required by the engine.

The sensor plate is mounted on a lever, hinged at the end. In the centre of this lever a rod, bearing on the lever, operates a plunger in the fuel metering unit. This plunger has grooves machined in it which open and close ports in the wall of the plunger bore of the metering unit. These ports connect the input side of the metering unit which receives fuel from the tank via the pump, accumulator and filter, to the output side of the metering unit which has the four injector lines connected to it. As the sensor plate lifts in the inlet air stream, the plunger lifts and fuel is supplied to the injectors in a volume directly proportional to the airflow, which in theory gives perfect combustion. Unfortunately, the engine requires a different air/fuel ratio for differing conditions, and the required ratio is not a straight line graph. The actual requirement is a wave form about this line. A slightly rich mixture at idle, a lean mixture at cruising speed and a rich mixture for acceleration and full load. This is obtained by altering the shape of the cone bore slightly so that it is slightly 'egg cup' in shape. The irregularities in the bore are not defects but the results of very careful calculation and patient experiment.

When the ignition is switched on the pump operates and quickly raises the system pressure to approximately 3.5 kgf/cm^2 (50 lbf/in^2). The pump runs at an almost constant velocity supplying 1.5 litres/minute (2.6 Imp pints/minute). The amount of fuel required is dependent on the opening of the meter valve, so provision is made at the side of the metering unit, for a spring loaded valve which opens at approximately 4.9 kgf/cm^2 (70 lbf/in^2) allowing the fuel to return to the tank via a return pipe.

As the engine is turned by the starter the airflow lifts the sensor arm, opens the fuel ports to the injector lines, and fuel pressure builds up in the injector lines. The injectors are spring-loaded and open between 2.4 and 3.5 kgf/cm^2 (35 and 50 lbf/in^2). Once open they stay open, squirting fuel into the inlet manifold continuously in the vicinity of the inlet valve ports. The volume of fuel supplied per second is governed by the volume of airflow at that time so the combustion is almost complete if the system is tuned correctly.

Obviously there are starting problems for an engine tuned to run efficiently at a high temperature. There are various minor problems too, which are dealt with in the text.

There must be some way of keeping the fuel meter plunger in contact with the sensor arm. This is done by introducing hydraulic pressure to the top of the plunger from the control pressure valve.

Surges and pressure variations are dealt with by an accumulator in the pipe line between the pump and the fuel meter unit. This device also maintains residual pressure in the system for a short time to assist hot starting. Under each of the injector outlets from the fuel meter is a small pressure regulating valve to keep the pressure difference on both sides of the port constant and maintain a smooth continuous supply of fuel to the injectors.

The supply of air to the inlet manifold when the engine is cold at idle speeds, when the throttles are closed, is insufficient. This is overcome by a simple gate valve connected between the air cleaner and the manifold. The gate is closed by a bi-metallic strip heater as the engine warms up. The operation of this valve and its testing are described in the text.

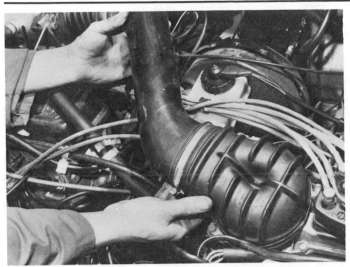

16.0a Air inlet tube (CIS)

16.0b Throttle valve housing (CIS)

16.0c Fuel pump location (CIS)

16.0d Fuel accumulator location (CIS)

16.0e Breather valve on a Scirocco (CIS)

A rich mixture for starting from cold is supplied by a fifth injector in the inlet manifold operating at full pressure for a very short period, varying from 3 to 10 seconds according to the temperature of the coolant. This period is regulated by a thermo time switch. The operation is described later in the text.

The tests and adjustments require the use of meters, measuring glasses, a thermometer, a voltmeter or ohmmeter, a tachometer, pressure gauge with adaptors and an exhaust gas analyser. Given the correct meters the tests are simple and adjustments easily within the grasp of the owner driver. Without the gauges the job cannot be done, so how much you can do yourself depends on the availability of equipment. We have described the method of testing the components in the following Sections.

17 CIS – general dismantling

1   If the engine is to be dismantled, or removed from the chassis, then obviously the fuel system must be dismantled. It is easy to pull off the leads and hoses but quite another thing to put them all back, so, before starting, get a notebook and pencil, plus some labels and tape. Using your own code, label each wire or pipe as it is taken off. Remember that not only has the CIS to go back correctly but the ignition, cooling system, indicator lights, starter and alternator leads,

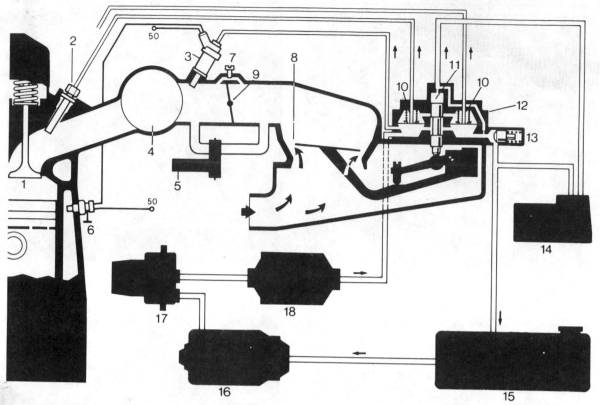

Fig. 3.31 Diagrammatic layout of CIS (Sec 16)

1 Inlet valve
2 Injector
3 Cold start valve
4 Air intake distributor
5 Auxiliary air regulator
6 Thermotime switch

7 Idle speed adjusting
  screw
8 Air sensor plate
9 Throttles (2)
10 Pressure regulating
  valves (1 per injector)

11 Control plunger
12 Fuel distributor body
13 System pressure
  regulating valve
14 Control pressure
  regulator

15 Fuel tank
16 Fuel pump
17 Fuel accumulator
18 Fuel filter

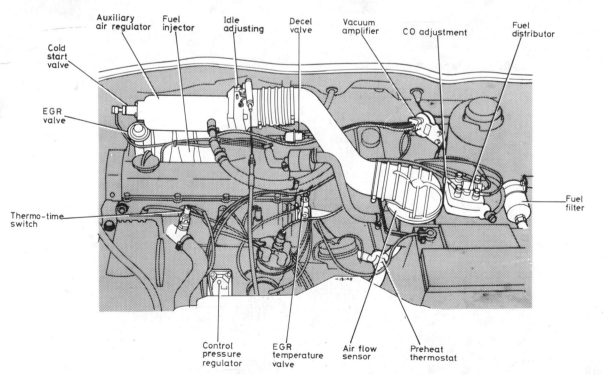

Fig. 3.32 CIS components on later North American models (Sec 16)

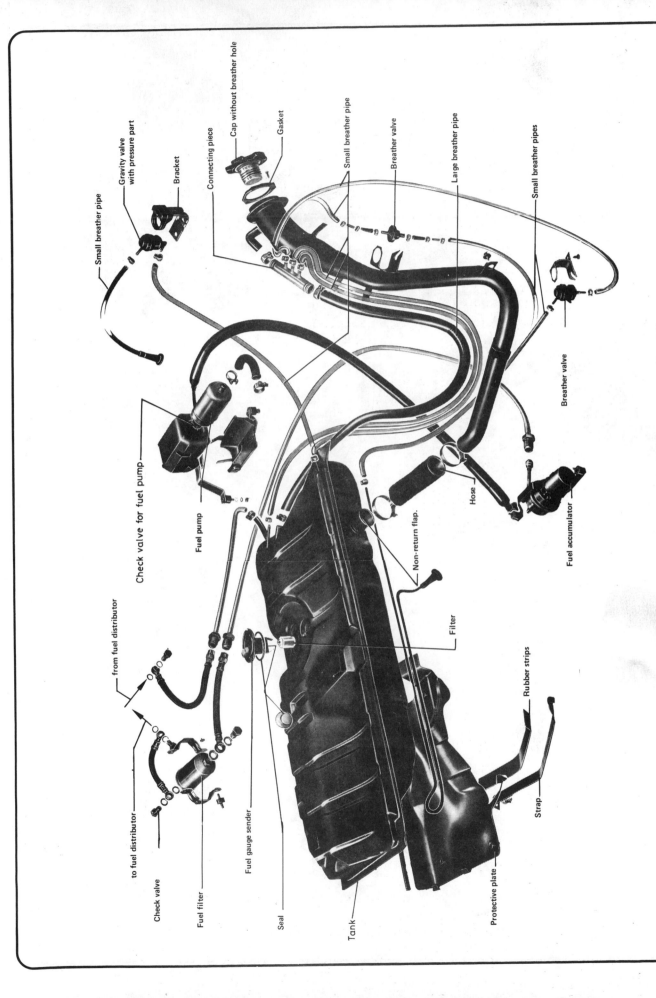

Small breather pipe

Gravity valve with pressure part

Bracket

Connecting piece

Cap without breather hole

Gasket

Small breather pipe

Breather valve

Large breather pipe

Small breather pipes

Check valve for fuel pump

Fuel pump

Breather valve

from fuel distributor

Hose

Fuel accumulator

to fuel distributor

Non-return flap.

Check valve

Filter

Fuel filter

Rubber strips

Seal

Fuel gauge sender

Tank

Protective plate

Strap

Fig. 3.33 Fuel supply components on UK models with CIS (Sec 16)

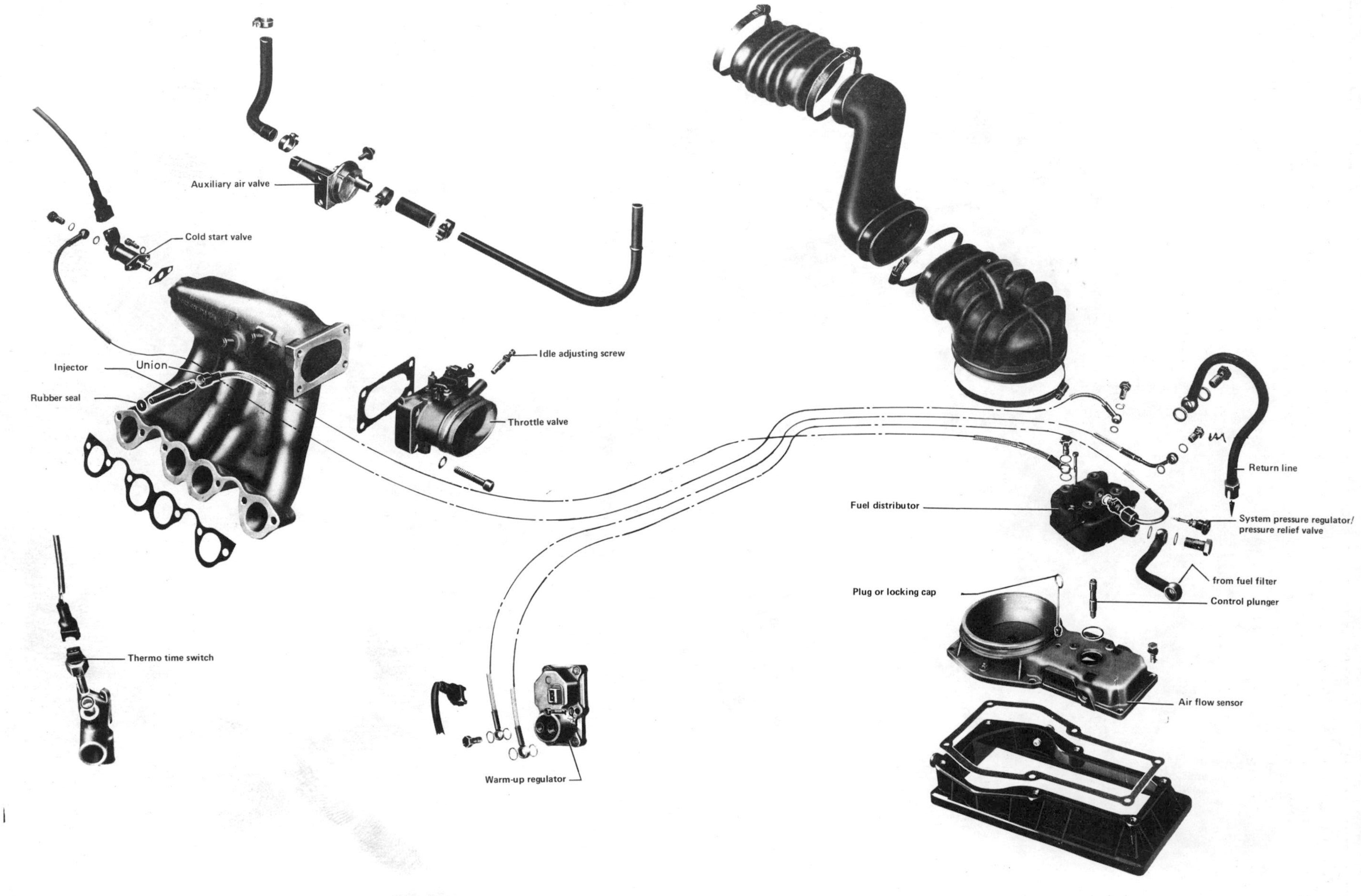

Fig. 3.34 Fuel control components for the CIS system (Sec 16)

Return line

System pressure regulator/ pressure relief valve

from fuel filter

Control plunger

Air flow sensor

Fuel distributor

Plug or locking cap

Idle adjusting screw

Throttle valve

Warm-up regulator

Auxiliary air valve

Cold start valve

Union

Injector

Rubber seal

Thermo time switch

radiator fan and thermal switch and possibly headlamp leads have to also. So, label everything and you will be able to smile when assembly starts again. If you do not you will find a surprising number of ways of making connections incorrectly, some of them possibly expensive.

2 The first lead to disconnect, and the last one to reconnect, is the battery earth strap.

3 VW have a very firm ruling about plastic hoses. If they are removed from the connectors then new ones must be fitted. The old ones must *NOT* be used. It will probably be necessary to heat the plastic hose over the connector in order to pull it off. Do *NOT* cut it off or you may damage the metal connector and a new hose will leak. Heat the plastic with a soldering iron, not a naked flame, until it is sufficiently soft to manipulate and then pull the hose away.

4 It is now necessary to fit a new hose. This must be done without warming the hose. The hose should be gripped in a suitable circular clamp with the amount of hose required to cover the metal of the joint protruding. Push the hose on cold and then remove the clamp and leave the joint alone. VW have a special clamp tool VW P 385 if you are lucky enough to have access to one. If you are not and cannot make up a tool yourself, we suggest you take the old hose complete with connectors to the agent and ask for a new hose to be fitted to the old connections.

5 It is best to fit new washers and gaskets when renewing joints, and to torque tighten connections correctly where a limit is given. Gaskets and joint washers can be damaged by overtightening and leak just as those not tightened enough.

6 Always renew frayed or worn electric wiring. Do *NOT* use insulation tape except as an emergency repair, and fit the correct terminal tags. If you do not have the tools or ability to do this then go to someone who has and get the job done properly.

18 CIS airflow sensor – adjustment

1 To check the position of the sensor plate it is necessary to remove the air intake casing, but before doing this run the engine for a few minutes to build up pressure in the fuel lines.

2 Undo the clip and take off the air intake casing. The sensor plate may now be seen. Check the position of the plate relative to the bore. There must be a gap of 0.10 mm (0.004 in) all round, between it and the bore. The plate surface must also be even with the bottom of the air cone when the fuel line residual pressure is removed.

3 If the level is not correct then the plate should be lifted using a magnet or with pliers but be careful not to scratch the bore. The clip underneath may be bent to adjust the level, using small pliers (photo). Pull the plate up as far as it will come and the job can be done without dismantling anything else. The tolerance is 0.5 mm (0.019 in) but it isn't possible to measure it accurately, so judge the level as best you can by eye.

4 Centering the plate can be easy or difficult. Try the easy way first. Undo the centre bolt, it is fairly stiff as it is held by thread locking compound. Take the bolt out and clean the threads. Now try to centre the plate with the bolt loosely in position. If this can be done then remove the bolt, put a drop of thread locking compound on the threads and refit it holding the plate central. Tighten the bolt to the specified torque.

5 If the plate will not centre then the sensor unit must be removed from the vehicle. It is probably easier to remove the mixture control unit from the sensor unit than to undo all the pipes, but if you do be careful that the plunger does not drop out when you separate the units. Disconnect the sensor unit from the top of the air cleaner. Take the sensor unit out and turn it upside down. Now check that the sensor beam is central in its bearings. If it is not, slacken the clamp bolt on the counterweight and it may be possible to centre the beam in its bearings and at the same time the sensor plate in the cone. If this is possible, remove the bolt, clean the threads, put a drop of thread locking compound on them and refit the bolt with the beam and plate in the correct positions. Failing this a new sensor unit must be purchased for if the plate is not central you will have really major problems (photos).

6 Once the plate is central and level, the unit reassembled, the mixture control unit refitted, and the system recharged with residual pressure by turning the ignition on for a few seconds, it is possible to check the action of the airflow sensor. Turn the ignition off and, using a small magnet, lift the plate to the top of its movement. There must be a slight, but even, resistance, but no hard spots. Now depress the

18.3 Airflow sensor plate adjusting clip (arrowed) (CIS)

18.5a Mixture control unit fuel hose connections (CIS)

18.5b Note the arrow on the fuel inlet (CIS)

18.5c Disconnecting the air inlet hose from the air cleaner (CIS)

18.5d Crankcase ventilation hose location on the air cleaner (CIS)

18.5e Removing the airflow sensor unit (CIS)

18.5f Top view of the airflow sensor unit (CIS)

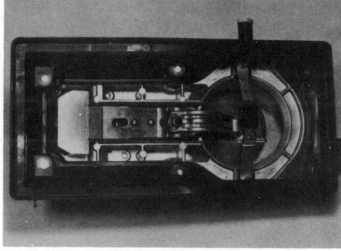

18.5g Bottom view of the airflow sensor unit (CIS)

plate quickly. This time there should be no resistance to movement.

7   If there is resistance to movement, or hard spots in both directions then probably the plate is not correctly central, so check again. If the resistance or hard spot happens only when lifting the plate then the problem is with the plunger of the fuel mixture unit. Remove the mixture unit from the sensor casing and carefully remove the plunger. Wash it well in clean fuel to remove any residue, refit it and try again. If this does not cure the problem then it is probable that a new mixture control unit is needed. *DO NOT* try to remove the hard spot with abrasives; this will only make matters worse. A visit to the VW agent is indicated. He may be able to cure the problem but be prepared to purchase a new mixture control unit.

19 CIS mixture control unit – checking

1   The pressure regulating valve for the system pressure is included in the mixture control unit. Refer to Fig. 3.36, A hexagonal plug on the corner of the fuel distributor casing may be screwed out and inside will be found a copper ring, shims for adjusting the pressure on the spring, the spring, a piston and a rubber ring. Be careful not to scratch the bore or the piston since these are mated on assembly and a new piston means a new distributor body. If the piston is stuck either blow it out with compressed air or work it out using a piece of soft wood. Do not attempt to adjust the system pressure by altering the shims. Always use new seals when refitting the plug.

2   From the tests on the air sensor plate movement the operation of

the plunger will have been checked. If it is suspect then the fuel distributor body must be disconnected from the airflow sensor plate and lifted clear. Be careful that the plunger does not fall out and get damaged. Carefully extract the plunger and wash it in clean fuel. When refitting it the small shoulder goes in first. Do not attempt to cure any hard spots by rubbing with abrasive. If washing in clean fuel does not cure the problem then a new assembly is required.

3   There are three pressure tests and one quantitive test in order to check the operation of the fuel distributor. For these a special pressure gauge is required and a batch of four 100 cc measuring glasses. Before these tests are carried out the pump delivery must be checked and the filter examined.

4   The pressure gauge should be capable of reading pressures from 0 to 7 kgf/cm^2 (0 to 100 lbf/in^2). It must be fitted between the fuel distributor body and the control pressure regulator. Take the pipe off the control pressure regulator and connect it to the input side of the gauge. A further pipe is required to connect the gauge to the control pressure regulator and there must be a tap on the regulator side of the gauge. In effect the original line is connected to one side of a T-piece with the tap and extension pipe on the other side and the gauge on the stem of the T-piece. The official VW tool number is 1318.

5   To check the system pressure close the tap by the gauge, run the engine at idle speed and read the gauge. If the pressure is not between 4.5 to 5.2 kgf/cm^2 (65 to 75 lbf/in^2) then it must be adjusted. VW state that the fuel distributor body should be changed.

6   The control pressure may be checked 'hot' or 'cold'. To check it cold means the engine should not have been run for several hours.

7   For a cold check connect the gauge as in paragraph 4 but open the tap. Remove the electric leads from the control pressure regulator, and auxiliary air valve. Check that the air temperature around the engine is approximately 20°C (68°F). Now start the engine, run it at idling

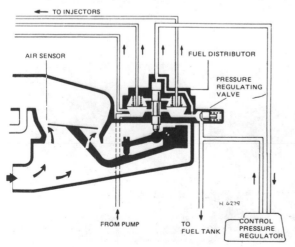

Fig. 3.35 Diagrammatic cross-section of the CIS mixture control unit (Sec 19)

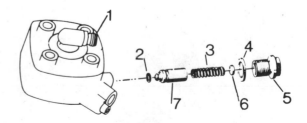

Fig. 3.36 Exploded view of the pressure regulating valve on the CIS (Sec 19)

1	*Fuel distributor body*	*5 Plug*
2	*Rubber ring*	*6 Shims for pressure*
3	*Spring*	*adjustment*
4	*Copper ring*	*7 Valve piston*

Fig. 3.37 Pressure gauge installation when checking the CIS
(Sec 19)

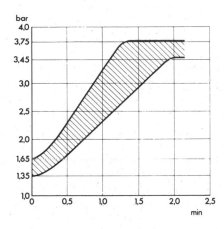

Fig. 3.38 CIS cold control pressure graph for UK models (Sec 19)

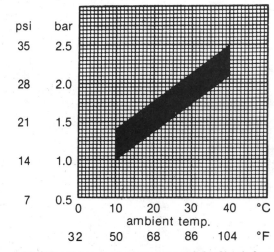

Fig. 3.39 CIS cold control pressure graph for North American
models except California (Sec 19)

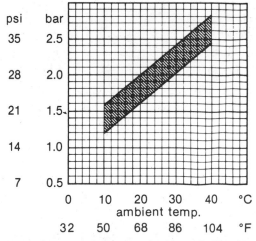

Fig. 3.40 CIS cold control pressure graph for Californian models
(Sec 19)

speed for a few moments and check the pressure. Figs. 3.38 to 3.40 give graphs within which the pressure should lie according to the air temperature. If the pressure is outside these limits VW recommend that the control pressure regulator be renewed, but we recommend that you check the system pressure and the fuel return line for blockage if the 'cold' regulator pressure is high before doing anything drastic. If the pressure cannot be cured this way then a new control pressure regulator is necessary as it cannot be repaired, because too high a control pressure at cold start will prevent the plunger moving up to give that extra rich mixture. Conversely too low a pressure will give too rich a mixture.

8   The 'hot' check means that the engine oil is between 50° and 70°C (122° and 158°F). The gauge connections are as for the 'cold' check but this time leave the electric wires on the control pressure regulator and auxiliary air valve. Start the engine and run it at idling speed for a few minutes. The control pressure should build up to 3.4 to 3.8 kgf/cm² (49 to 57 lbf/in²). If the pressure is outside this limit then the control pressure regulator must be renewed.

9   If all is well on the two previous tests, check the whole system for pressure leaks. With the gauge as for the 'hot' control pressure regulator test, run the engine until the gauge reads between 3.4 and 3.8 kgf/cm² (49 to 57 lbf/in²). Switch off the engine and leave the gauge connected for ten minutes. It should now read not less than 1.8 kgf/cm² (27 lbf/in²). If the pressure is between 1.8 and 2.0 kgf/cm² (27 and 29 lbf/in²), wait a further ten minutes. It should not have fallen below 1.6 kgf/cm² (23 lbf/in²). If the system fails these tests then there is a leak somewhere and trouble with starting will be experienced when the engine is warm as the residual pressure will be lost and the system may even get a vapour lock. The obvious action is to check all the hoses and joints first. Then check the pump to see that the check valve is working correctly and also the accumulator. There is one other unit that is suspect. If the pressure drops with the tap in the gauge line open, but does not drop if you close the tap after running the gauge up to between 3.4 and 3.8 kgf/cm² (49 and 57 lbf/in²) and then waiting ten minutes, the control pressure valve is at fault and must be renewed.

10   The last test on the fuel distributor unit is a quantitive test which will also check the injectors. Pull the injectors out of the inlet manifold and place each one in a 100 cc measuring glass. On the relay/fuse board connect contacts L13 and L14 by means of a lead made up of 1.5 mm² wire and incorporating an 8 amp fuse. See Section 21 for full details. Run the pump and lift the sensor plate slightly, you will have to remove the air duct from the top to do this, so that fuel begins to

emerge from the injectors. Run the pump until one glass contains 100 cc and switch off. The other three glasses should have more than 85 cc in them. If one or more have less than this change the injector of the low one with the injector which gave 100 cc and repeat the test. If the same fuel line shows a low level again, then the fuel distributor is defective, if the same injector shows low again then the injector is at fault. If the fuel distributor is at fault then probably one of the pressure control valves is not working properly. Clean the external

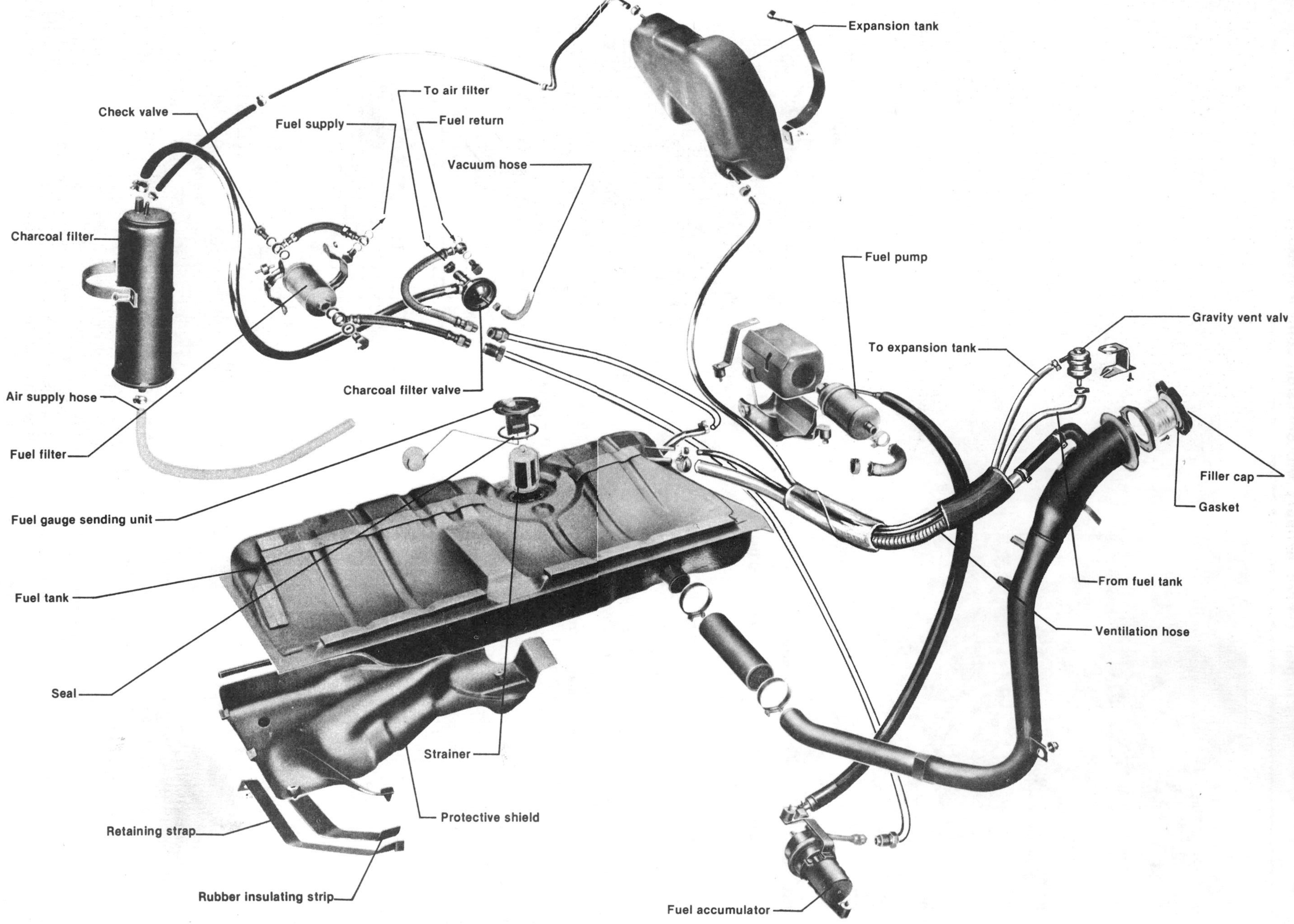

Fig. 3.41 Typical fuel supply components on late North American models with CIS (Sec 21)

parts of the system and take the defective fuel line off the distributor. There may be a fault in the line or the banjo joint, or dirt in the control valve pipe, but failing this a new assembly is required. Before buying one it would be worth having the system checked by an expert.

20 CIS control pressure regulator – checking

1 Disconnect the wiring from the control pressure (warm-up) regulator and auxiliary air valve (photo).
2 Connect a voltmeter across the supply wire terminals and operate the starter briefly – there should be a minimum of 11.5 volts.
3 Connect an ohmmeter across the regulator heater element terminals – the resistance should be between 16 and 22 ohms.
4 Renew the regulator if necessary and reconnect the wiring.

21 CIS fuel supply – checking

1 If the engine is not getting enough fuel, or none at all, then a logical routine should be followed. The tests described below are not exhaustive, but should suffice the owner and enable him to locate and cure the trouble.
2 Undo the fuel return line from the fuel distributor and put it in a jug which will hold a quart, or a 1000 cc measuring glass.
3 Locate the fuse relay box under the dash and find the fuel pump relay. It is second from the right, part no 321 906 059 and has a 16 amp fuse on the top of it. Pull it out and locate the terminals L13 and L14 on the board.
4 Make up a jumper lead of two pieces of 1.5 mm² cross-section wire and an 8 amp fuse. Get someone to hold the measuring glass and the return pipe. Switch on the ignition and using the jumper lead connect L13 and L14 for exactly 30 seconds. Disconnect and see how much fuel has arrived in the measure. The amount must be at least the minimum quantity given in the Specifications. If it is not then you have problems; either with the pump or a faulty filter/accumulator.
5 Refit the relay. Remove the HT lead from the coil and tie it safely out of the way (or earthed on electronic ignition). This time repeat the test operating the starter, with the ignition switched on. Check the amount delivered. It must be at least the specified minimum. If you had this amount the first time but not the second then the relay is at fault. If you did not obtain the specified quantity either time, then the relay is probably all right but the fault is elsewhere.
6 The official way now is to start renewing things but a little thought may save a lot of expense. The official fuse is 16 amps. The fuse in the jumper lead was 8 amps. The maximum current requirement of the pump should be 8.5 amps, and normal consumption 6.5 amps. If the fuse has not blown then it may be that there is no voltage at all at the pump, or that there is an intermittent fault. If the 8 amp fuse has blown then the motor is working too hard or has an electrical fault.
7 It is best to have two people for the electrical tests. Remove the plug from the fuel pump and connect a voltmeter across the plug terminals. Switch the ignition on and read the voltmeter. There should be the full battery volts at these terminals. If the voltage is less, then the problem is in the switch, the relay or the wiring.
8 If the voltage supply is correct, then rig up jumper leads from the plug to the motor with an ammeter in one of them. Switch on and check the current consumption. A high consumption (6.5 amps plus) could mean a number of faults. Perform the following checks:

(a) *Switch off, undo the inlet hose to the fuel filter and hold it in a container. Switch on again and check the current. If fuel is flowing rapidly and the current consumption has dropped then renew the filter*
(b) *If test (a) gives no joy, this time repeat the test but disconnect the hose from the pump to the accumulator at the accumulator. If the fuel flows now with a reasonable current consumption then the accumulator is suspect*
(c) *If tests (a) and (b) give no cure, then either the pump or something between it and the tank is at fault*

22 CIS fuel filter – servicing

1 The fuel filter is attached to the side of the engine compartment by a clip (photo). It will be seen that there is an arrow on the casing. This

20.1 Control pressure regulator location (CIS)

Fig. 3.42 CIS fuel pump relay (Sec 21)

22.1 Fuel filter location (CIS)

must always point in the direction of the fuel flow.

2   The filter should be replaced with a new one at regular intervals –
see Routine Maintenance. No other servicing is necessary, or possible.
Fit new washers on the joints when renewing the filter. Clean the
exterior carefully before removing the pipes and use proper fitting
spanners, not adjustable wrenches, to turn the nuts.

23 CIS fuel injectors – description and checking

1   There is one injector fitted per cylinder. These are pushed into
bushes in the inlet manifold. At first sight this seems odd, but these
injectors spray onto the back of the inlet valve ports so they are
working in a lower pressure than atmospheric pressure and the
tendency is for them to be pulled in rather than blown out at high
speeds. They are pulled out quite easily. Inspect the rubber seal in the
intake manifold. If it is perished or cracked remove it and fit a new one.
Moisten the new seal with fuel before installing it and likewise moisten
the injector before fitting it into the seal.

2   The injector may give trouble for one of four reasons. The spray
may be irregular in shape; the nozzle may not close when the engine
is shut down, causing flooding when restarting; the nozzle filter may be
choked giving less than the required ration of fuel, or the seal may be
damaged allowing an air leak.

3   If the engine is running roughly and missing on one cylinder, allow
it to idle and pull each plug lead off and refit it one cylinder at a time
(not on electronic ignition models). If that cylinder is working properly
this will have an even more adverse effect on the idling speed, when
the lead is pulled off, which will promptly improve once the lead is
refitted. If there is little difference when the lead is removed then that
is the cylinder giving trouble. Stop the engine and check and service
the spark plug. Now have a look at the injector. Pull it out of the seal
and hold it in a 100 cc measuring glass. Plug up the injector hole and
start the engine. Let it tick over on three cylinders and look at the
shape of the spray. It should be of a symmetrical cone shape. If it is not
the injector must be changed because the vibrator pin is damaged or
the spring is broken. Shut off the engine and wait for 15 seconds.
There must be no leak or dribble from the nozzle (photo). If there is the
injector must be renewed as dribble will cause flooding and difficult
starting. If the spray is cone shaped and no dribble occurs then the
output should be checked. Turn back to Section 19; this will tell you
how to do a comparative test.

4   The injector cannot be dismantled for cleaning. If an injector is
removed from the line the new one should be fitted and the union
tightened to the specified torque.

5   The operating pressure is between 2.1 and 3.1 kgf/cm² (38 and 45
lbf/in²). It is not possible to check this without special equipment. If
this is available the opening pressure of the four injectors should not

vary more than 0.6 kgf/cm² (8.5 lbf/in²).

24 CIS inlet manifold – removal and refitting

1   This casing conveys the mixture from the throttle housing to the
inlet ports.

2   Before commencing work on its removal, take off the battery earth
lead (ground strap).

3   Remove the throttle valve housing.

4   Depending upon the operating market there will be different hoses
and leads so remove all electric leads and hoses, labelling them as you
do.

5   For USA vehicles so equipped, remove the EGR vacuum hose and
pipe and then undo the holding bolts and remove the EGR valve.

6   Pull out the injectors and tie them out of the way. Label them 1 to
4. At the end of the casting is the cold start valve. This should have
been disconnected, but take it out and store it safely.

7   For USA vehicles, remove the decel valve.

8   From above remove the two outer holding bolts. From under the
vehicle remove the four lower bolts. A good socket spanner with a
universal joint drive will help a lot when removing and refitting. Always
clean off all old gasket material and use new gaskets when refitting the
casting to the cylinder block. Tighten the bolts to the specified torque.

9   Reassembly is the reverse of removal. Reconnect the earth lead
last.

25 CIS cold start valve – checking

1   Remove the plug from the cold start valve and wrap it in insulation
tape to prevent any sparks (photo) – there will be fuel vapour present.
Take the two screws holding the valve to the inlet out and take the
valve out of the distributor casing. The valve must be left connected to
the fuel supply. Wipe the nozzle of the valve. Pull the HT lead out of
the centre of the distributor and tie it out of the way (earth it on
electronic ignition models). Switch on the ignition and operate the fuel
pump for one minute. There must be no fuel dripping from the nozzle.
If there is, the valve is faulty and must be renewed. Switch off the
ignition.

2   Now put the stem of the valve in a glass jar. Reconnect the plug
to the valve. Take the plug off the thermotime switch and put a jump
lead over the plug terminals. Switch on the ignition and have an
assistant operate the starter. The valve should squirt a conical shaped
spray into the jar. If the spray is correct the valve is working properly.
If the spray pattern is irregular the valve is damaged and should be
renewed. If the valve is working properly refit it in the air intake
distributor and proceed to test the thermotime switch as described in
the following Section.

23.3 Checking a fuel injector (CIS)

25.1 Disconnecting the cold start valve wiring plug

26 CIS thermotime switch – checking

1 To test the switch remove the plug from the cold start valve and bridge the contacts with a test lamp or a voltmeter. The test must be done with a cold (coolant below 35°C) (95°F) engine.
2 Remove the HT lead from the centre of the distributor and earth it with a suitable lead. Have an assistant operate the starter for ten seconds. Depending on the coolant temperature the bulb should light, or the voltmeter register, for a period of between 3 and 10 seconds, and then cease to register. If the circuit is not broken in ten seconds the switch must be renewed (photo). If the bulb does not light at all, and you are sure the engine is cold, then check that there is voltage supplied to the switch. If there is no voltage then the fuel pump relay must be checked.

27 CIS auxiliary air regulator – description and checking

1 The auxiliary air regulator allows air to pass while the engine is cold. When the ignition is switched on the heater resistance causes the bi-metallic strip to deform, turning the rotating valve until the air passage is closed. It remains in this position during normal operation.
2 To check the operation remove it from the engine, disconnect the hoses and look through the inlet pipe. If the unit is cold there must be a clear passage. Connect it to a 12V supply for five minutes and watch the operation through the inlet. At the end of the five minutes the valve should be closed. If it does not operate correctly check the resistance of the heater unit. This should be 30 ohms.

28 CIS – running adjustments

UK models with conventional ignition

1 Connect a tachometer and exhaust gas analyser to the engine in accordance with the manufacturer's instructions.
2 Disconnect the crankcase ventilation hose from the air intake and seal the exposed hole (ie not the hose) with masking tape.
3 Do not connect a pressure gauge to the fuel system during the adjustment.
4 Run the engine at a fast idling speed until it reaches its normal operating temperature. Switch off all electrical components and only make an adjustment when the radiator fan is stopped. Switch the headlamps on main beam.
5 Allow the engine to idle for at least two minutes then check that the idling speed and CO content are as given in the Specifications.
6 If the idling speed requires adjustment, turn the screw on the throttle valve housing as necessary (photo).
7 If the CO content requires adjustment, pull out the plug from the airflow sensor and use the special VW tool P377 to alter the setting.

Take care not to lift or press down on the adjusting screw when turning it, and do not accelerate the engine with the tool in position. Refit the plug when completed and remove the instruments.

UK models with electronic ignition

8 Carry out the procedure described in paragraphs 1 to 4.
9 To **check** the idling speed, allow the engine to idle for at least two minutes, then check that the idling speed is as given in the Specifications.
10 To **adjust** the idling speed, stop the engine, then disconnect the plugs from the idle stabilizer and connect them together. Adjust the idle speed to 750 to 850 rpm. Stop the engine and reconnect the idle stabilizer plugs, then start the engine again and accelerate the engine briefly. The idling speed should now be as given in the Specifications.
11 To check and adjust the CO content first disconnect the plugs from the idle stabilizer and connect them together. Start the engine and check that the CO content is as given in the Specifications. If not, refer to paragraph 7.

Pre-1979 North American models

12 The procedure is as described in paragraphs 1 to 11, but (where fitted) disconnect the purge hose between the air cleaner and the activated charcoal container at the air cleaner end. If there is a decal the permissible CO content will be shown on it.

1979 North American models

13 The procedure is as described in paragraphs 1 to 11, but on Canadian models do not switch the headlamps on main beam.

1980/81 North American models without oxygen sensor

14 Note that tamperproof plugs are fitted to the idling speed and CO content adjustment screws, and that their removal by unauthorised persons normally violates Federal Environmental Protection Agency leglislation.
15 The procedure is as described in paragraph 13.

1980/81 North American models with oxygen sensor

16 Refer to paragraph 14. Run the engine to normal operating temperature and make sure that the radiator fan has operated at least once. The adjustment must be made only when the radiator fan is stopped.
17 Switch off all electrical components.
18 Switch off the engine and connect a tachometer.
19 Connect a duty cycle meter or dwell meter to the oxygen sensor test connection (Fig. 3.43) – the blue wire with the white tracer.
20 Disconnect the plugs from the idle stabilizer and connect them together.
21 Start the engine and accelerate the engine briefly. Allow the engine to idle – the frequency valve must make a buzzing sound and

26.2 Thermotime switch location (CIS)

28.6 Location of CIS idle speed adjuster (arrowed)

Fig. 3.43 Oxygen sensor test connection (arrowed) on 1980 on
North American models (Sec 28)

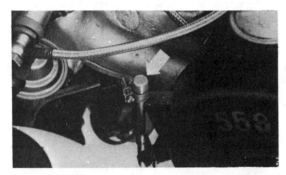

Fig. 3.44 CO tester probe receptacle on 1980 on
North American models (Sec 28)

the duty cycle meter must fluctuate.

22 Check that the idling speed is as given in the Specifications. If necessary adjust the idle speed screw, then switch off the engine and reconnect the idle stabilizer plugs.

23 To check the CO content, first disconnect the crankcase ventilation hose(s) from the valve cover and seal the exposed hole(s) with masking tape. Do not plug the hose(s).

24 Remove the charcoal canister hose from the front valance and point it away from the car.

25 Disconnect the oxygen sensor and make sure that the exposed terminal does not touch the body.

26 Remove the cap from the probe receptacle and fit the CO tester.

27 Start the engine and check that the idle speed is as given in the Specifications. The duty cycle meter reading should be 45° ± 2° (50% + 2%) and the HC reading under 300 parts per million.

28 Check that the CO content is within the specified limits and adjust the screw if necessary.

29 Check and readjust the idle speed if necessary.

30 Stop the engine and disconnect all the instruments, then reconnect the crankcase ventilation hose(s).

29 Emission control – general

1 Some or all of the following systems are fitted to North American models in order to reduce the emission of harmful gases into the atmosphere.

Catalytic converter

2 This item is situated in the exhaust pipe system at the front. A light on the dashboard is fitted to remind the driver that the converter must be changed.

3 It helps to reduce the amount of hydrocarbons (HC) and CO by converting them into water (H_2O) and CO_2

4 To renew the converter, raise the vehicle on a hoist, remove the shield, unbolt the flanges on each end of the converter and install a new one using new gaskets.

Exhaust gas recirculation (EGR)

5 The principle of the system is to extract a portion of the hot burnt gas from the exhaust manifold and to inject it into the inlet manifold where it mixes with the fuel and air and enters the cylinders again. The result is to lower the flame peaks during combustion and so to lower the production of the oxides of nitrogen which are a small but important part of pollution. The exhaust gas passes through a filter which removes any carbon particles and then through a valve which is operated by the depression in the choke of the carburettor.

6 A very basic layout of the early system is shown at Fig. 3.45. To this have now been added several more refinements including a temperature valve and a micro-switch on the accelerator linkage. We do not recommend that the owner tries to adjust this system, however there are a few jobs which can be done. The filter, which is fixed to the exhaust manifold, may be changed. This should be done at the intervals given in Routine Maintenance. Other than this check that all the hoses and wires are intact and then leave well alone.

Air injection system (AIS)

7 This system is fitted in addition to EGR. Its purpose is to provide extra air so that hydrocarbons and CO still in the emission stream may burn in the exhaust system. A basic layout is shown in Fig. 3.46.

8 An air pump belt-driven by the engine, sucks air through a filter and delivers it to the cylinder head by means of a pipe manifold so that air is injected just behind the exhaust valve port into each cylinder. Inserted between the pump and the manifold is a non-return valve called the anti-backfire valve which prevents the gases blowing back into the pump, if a backfire occurs in the exhaust system.

9 When the driver lifts his foot from the accelerator suddenly the throttle closes and the mixture becomes over-rich. This can cause back firing in the exhaust. To prevent this a branch pipe from the air filter supplies air via a control valve to the manifold. The valve is vacuum operated by a line from the inlet manifold.

10 The filter should be renewed at the specified intervals, the belt tension should be checked and adjusted if necessary and the hoses examined for leaks and chafing.

11 If backfiring does occur in the exhaust system it must be cured right away as otherwise damage to the silencers will occur. Backfiring of this sort is usually caused by a defective air control valve, or a leak in the hose system, but it may be an engine defect. We suggest the car should be taken to the dealer right away and checked.

12 The anti-backfire valve is screwed to the air injection manifold. To remove it the manifold must be removed from the cylinder head. It is just below the spark plugs.

13 The filter and the control valve are on the right-hand side of the engine compartment. If the wing nut on the bottom of the filter housing is removed the cover and the filter may be removed.

Evaporative emission control (EEC)

14 The fuel tank is connected to an expansion tank located under the right-hand rear bumper. Be careful when reconnecting the tank to refit the hoses back where they came from.

15 The expansion tank is connected to an activated charcoal filter bolted to the side of the engine compartment. Unless this is damaged it will not require renewing except at the specified intervals. To renew it remove the hoses, undo the screw in the mounting bracket and lift the canister away. When fitting a new one make sure the hoses are correctly arranged.

16 The reason for such a long service life is as follows. When the vehicle is stationary (most of its life) the petrol fumes are ducted to the charcoal filter and stay in the filter. When the engine starts, fresh air is drawn into the filter and then via the connecting hose to the air cleaner. The clean air carries the fuel in the filter into the air cleaner, thereby cleaning the filter for another spell of duty. The fuel is drawn into the engine and burnt.

Deceleration valve

17 This valve is regulated by inlet manifold vacuum, and its purpose

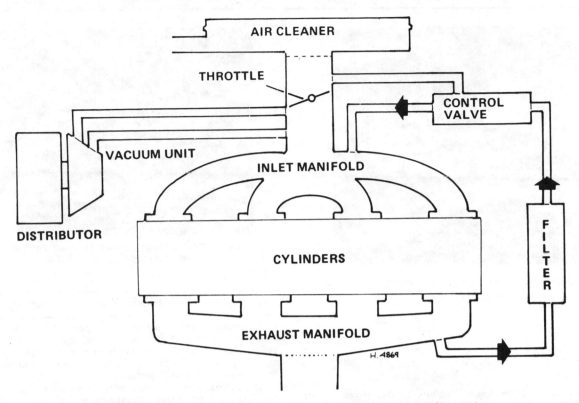

Fig. 3.45 EGR system components on North American models (Sec 29)

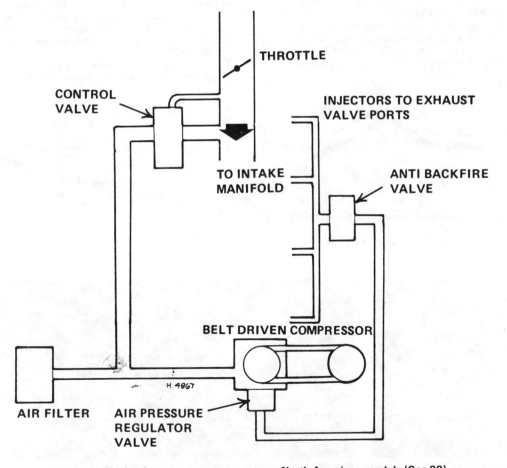

Fig. 3.46 Air injection system components on North American models (Sec 29)

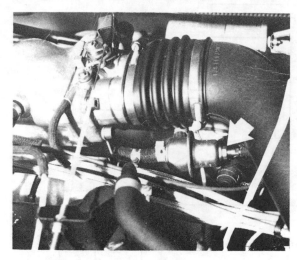

Fig. 3.47 Deceleration valve (arrowed) on North American models with CIS (Sec 29)

Fig. 3.48 Oxygen sensor (arrowed) and supply wire on North American models with CIS (Sec 29)

is to provide a combustible fuel/air mixture to the engine during deceleration. Without it the mixture would be lean, with the resultant emission of hydrocarbons.

Oxygen sensor system (OXS)

18 This system measures the oxygen content in the exhaust gases and regulates the fuel/air mixture by means of a control unit.

19 The oxygen sensor is located in the exhaust manifold and should be renewed at the specified intervals, at which times a warning light appears on the instrument panel.

30 Exhaust system – checking, removal and refitting

1 The exhaust system should be examined for leaks, damage, and security at regular intervals. If a small leak is evident, use a proprietary repair kit to seal it – if the leak is excessive or damage is evident, renew the section. Check the rubber mountings for deterioration and renew them if necessary (photo).

2 The exhaust system components are shown in Figs. 3.49 to 3.52. To renew a section of the exhaust system, jack up the front or rear of the car as necessary and support it on axle stands. Disconnect the mountings and separate the joints. Where the joints are flanged, unscrew the bolts and remove the gasket. Where the joints are clamped, remove the clamp then use a hammer to tap around the joint to free any rust. If necessary, carefully heat the joint with a blowlamp to assist removal, but shield the fuel tank, fuel lines, and underbody adequately from heat (photos).

3 When refitting the clamped type system, position the components on the mountings before tightening the inter-section clamps.

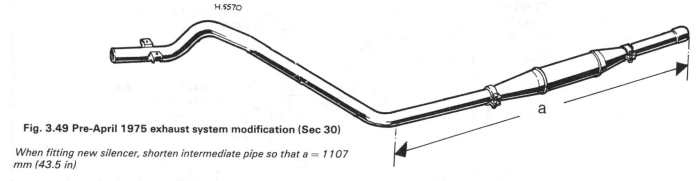

H.5570

Fig. 3.49 Pre-April 1975 exhaust system modification (Sec 30)

When fitting new silencer, shorten intermediate pipe so that a = 1107 mm (43.5 in)

30.1 An exhaust system rubber mounting

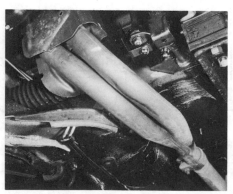

30.2a Front section of exhaust system on a Golf

30.2b Clamp type exhaust system joint

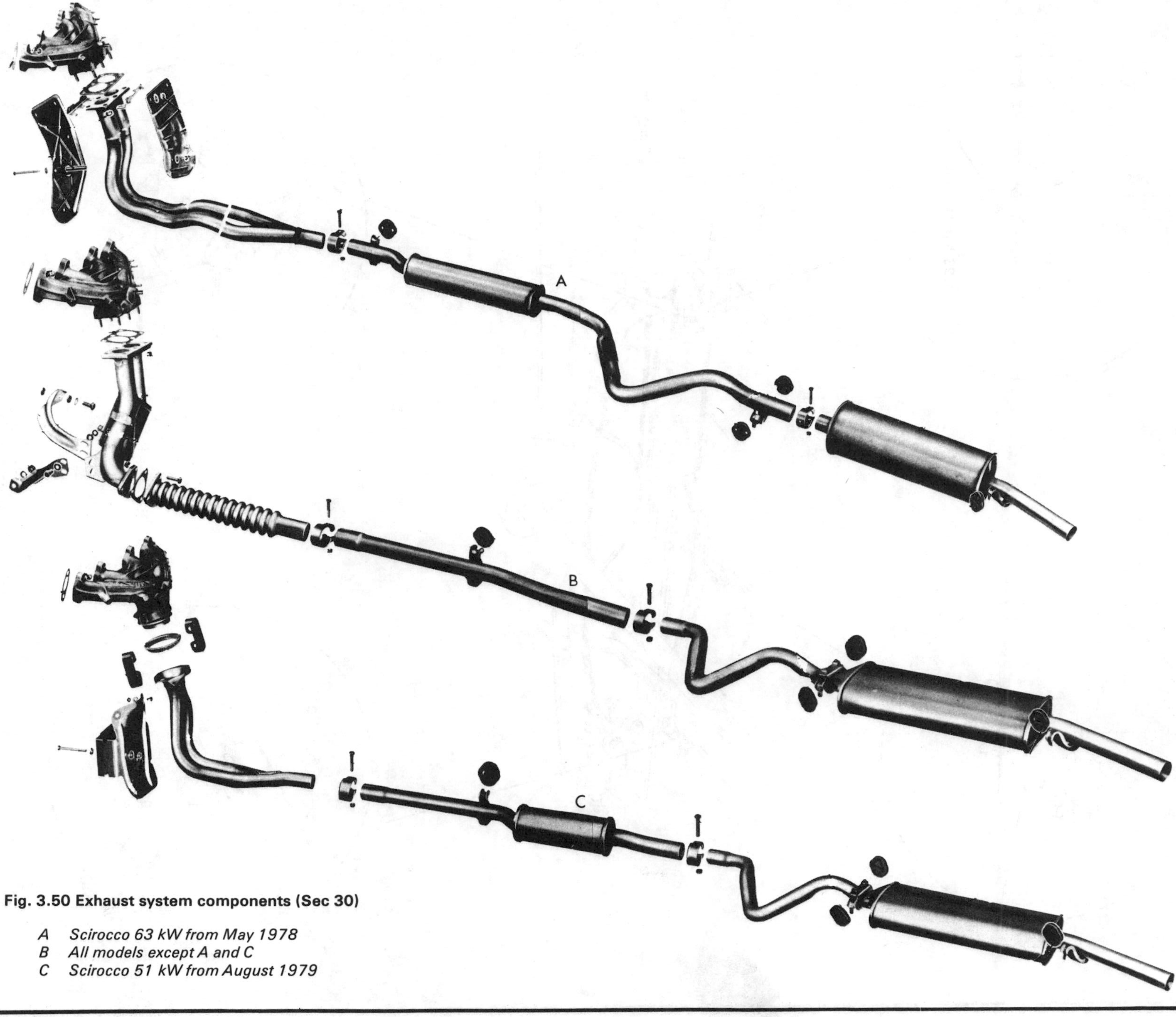

Fig. 3.50 Exhaust system components (Sec 30)

A   Scirocco 63 kW from May 1978
B   All models except A and C
C   Scirocco 51 kW from August 1979

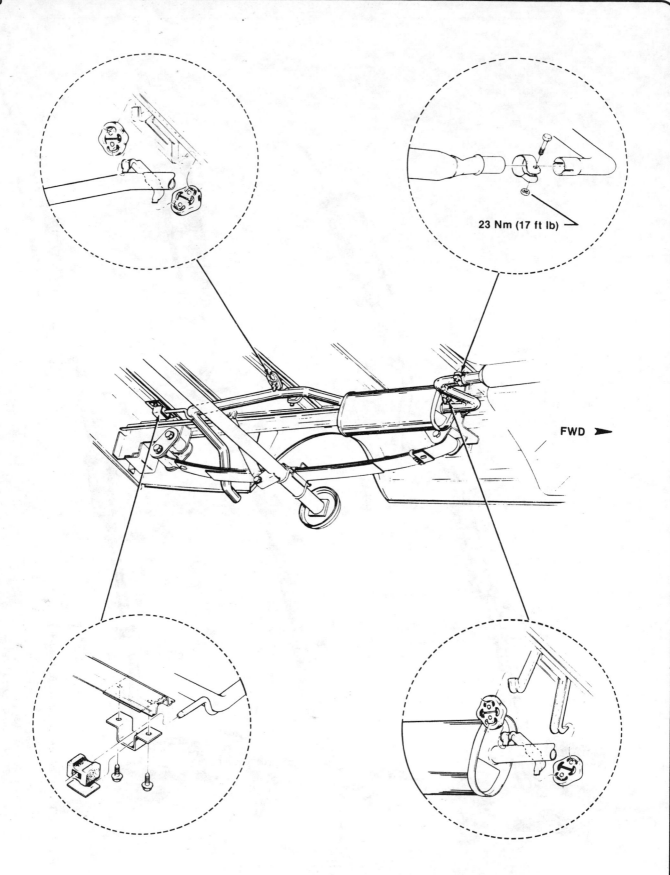

23 Nm (17 ft lb)

FWD ➤

Fig. 3.51 Exhaust system components on North American Pick-up models (Sec 30)

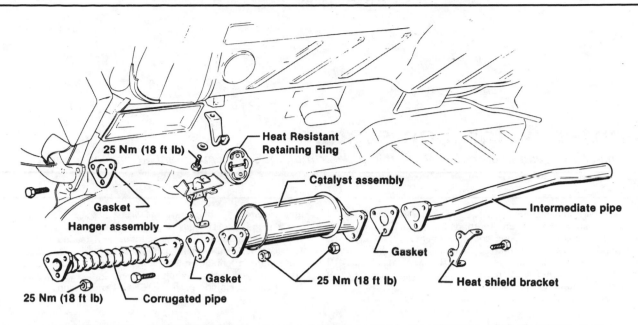

Fig. 3.52 Exhaust system components on North American models with a catalytic converter (Sec 30)

31 Fault diagnosis – fuel, exhaust and emission control systems

Unsatisfactory engine performance and excessive fuel consumption are not necessarily the fault of the fuel system or carburettor. In fact they more commonly occur as a result of ignition and timing faults. Before acting on the following it is necessary to check the ignition system first. Even though a fault may lie in the fuel system it will be difficult to trace unless the ignition is correct. The faults below, therefore, assume that this has been attended to first (where appropriate).

Symptom	Reasons
Excessive fuel consumption	Air cleaner element choked
	Leaks from fuel tank, fuel pump, fuel lines, carburettor or CIS equipment
	Float level incorrect (carburettor engines)
	Mixture adjustment incorrect
	Valve clearances incorrect
	Brakes binding
	Tyres under-inflated
	Catalytic converter blocked (where applicable)
Insufficient fuel supply or weak mixture	Faulty fuel pump
	Inlet manifold gasket leaking
	Mixture adjustment incorrect
	Clogged fuel line filter
	Sticking needle valve (carburettor engines)
	Faulty airflow sensor (CIS)
Stalling at idling speed at ambient temperatures below 15°C (59°F)	Carburettor icing due to high air humidity – use VW petrol additive part number AOS 150 000 03

Chapter 4 Ignition system

For modifications and information applicable to later models, see Supplement at end of manual

Contents

Specifications

General

System type	12 volt battery and coil, either contact breaker points or transistorized system
Distributor rotor rotation	Clockwise
Firing order	1-3-4-2
Location of No 1 cylinder	Camshaft sprocket end

Coil

Primary resistance:	
Contact breaker system	1.7 to 2.1 ohms
Transistorized system, UK models	0.55 to 0.75 ohms
Transistorized system, North American models	0.52 to 0.76 ohms
Secondary resistance:	
Contact breaker system	7000 to 12000 ohms
Transistorized system, UK models	2500 to 3500 ohms
Transistorized system, North American models	2400 to 3500 ohms

Contact breaker points

Dwell angle	44° to 50° (50 to 56%)
Equivalent gap (approx)	0.016 in (0.4 mm)

Ignition timing (static or idle)

Carburettor engines:	
Engine codes, FB, FD, FH, FK and FX	7.5° BTDC
Engine codes FP, FT, FR, FV, GH (with DIS) and JB (distributor suffix M or P)	0° (TDC)
Engine codes GH (without DIS) and JB (distributor suffix K)	9° BTDC
Engine code FN (North America)	3° ATDC
Fuel injection engines:	
UK models	0° (TDC)
North American models	3° ATDC

Spark plug types

UK 1.5 litre models:	
Engine codes JB and GH	Bosch W8D
	Beru 14-8D
	Champion N10Y
Engine codes FH and FK	Bosch W7D, W7DC
	Beru 14-7D, 14-7DU
	Champion N8Y
Engine code FB	Bosch W6D, W6DC
	Beru 14-6D, RS-37
	Champion N8Y
Engine code FD	Bosch W5D, W5DC
	Beru 14-5D, 14-5DU
	Champion N7Y

UK 1.6 litre models:
  Engine codes FP and FR .... Bosch W7D, W7DC
                                                                                              Beru 14-7D, RS-35
                                                                                              Champion N8Y
  Engine codes FN, EM, FV and FT .... Bosch W7D, W7DC
                                                                                              Beru 14-7D, 14-7DU, RS-35
                                                                                              Champion N8Y
  Engine code EG .... Bosch W5D, W5DG
                                                                                              Beru 14-5D, 14-5DU, RS-39
                                                                                              Champion N6Y

North American 1.5 litre models:
  Engine codes FC and FG .... Bosch W175T30
                                                                                              Beru 175/14/3A
                                                                                              Champion N7Y
  Engine codes EH and FX .... Bosch W175T30, W7D
                                                                                              Beru 175/14/3A, 14-7D
                                                                                              Champion N8Y

North American 1.6 litre models:
  Engine code FN (with catalytic converter) .... Bosch W200T30
                                                                                              Beru 200/14/3A1
                                                                                              Champion N8Y
  Engine code FN (without catalytic converter) .... Bosch W175T30
                                                                                              Beru 175/14/3A
                                                                                              Champion N9Y
  Engine codes EE and EF .... Bosch W215T30
                                                                                              Beru D125/14/3A, 215/14/3A, 215/14/3A1
                                                                                              Champion N7Y
  Engine code EJ (except California) .... Bosch W175T30, W7D
                                                                                              Beru 175/14/3A, 14-7D
                                                                                              Champion N8Y
  Engine code EJ (California) .... Bosch WR7DS
                                                                                              Beru RS-35
                                                                                              Champion N8GY

North American 1.7 litre models:
  Engine code EN (USA except California) .... Bosch WR7DS
                                                                                              Beru RS 35
                                                                                              Champion N8GY
  Engine code EN (California) .... Bosch WR7DS
                                                                                              Beru RS-35
                                                                                              Champion N8GY
  Engine code EN (Canada) .... Bosch W8D
                                                                                              Beru 14-8D
                                                                                              Champion N10Y

Spark plug electrode gap
UK models .... 0.6 to 0.7 mm (0.024 to 0.028 in)
North American models .... 0.6 to 0.8 mm (0.024 to 0.032 in)

Torque wrench settings

	lbf ft	Nm
Spark plugs	22	30
Distributor clamp bolt	11	15
Coil clamp screw	6	8

1 General description

The ignition system may be of the conventional contact breaker type, or the electronic transistorized type. Both types of system comprise a battery, coil, distributor and spark plugs; the distributor is driven by a skew gear in mesh with the intermediate shaft of the engine.

To enable the engine to run correctly, it is necessary for an electrical spark to ignite the fuel/air mixture in the combustion chamber at exactly the right moment in relation to engine speed and load. The ignition system is based on feeding low tension voltage from the battery to the coil, where it is converted to high tension voltage. The high tension voltage is powerful enough to jump the spark plug gap in the cylinders many times a second under high compression, providing that the system is in good condition.

With the contact breaker type, the ignition system is divided into two circuits, the low tension circuit and the high tension circuit. The low tension (sometimes known as the primary) circuit consists of the battery, lead to the ignition switch, lead from the ignition switch to the low tension or primary coil windings (terminal +) and the lead from the low tension coil windings (coil terminal –) to the contact breaker points and condenser in the distributor. The high tension circuit consists of the high tension or secondary coil windings, the heavy ignition lead from the coil to the distributor cap, the rotor arm and the spark plug leads and spark plugs.

The system functions in the following manner. Low tension voltage is changed in the coil into high tension voltage by the opening and closing of the contact breaker points in the low tension circuit. High tension voltage is then fed via the carbon brush in the centre of the distributor cap to the rotor arm of the distributor, and each time it comes in line with one of the four metal segments in the cap, which are connected to the spark plug leads, the opening and closing of the contact breaker points causes the high tension voltage to build up, jump the gap from the rotor arm to the appropriate metal segment, and so via the spark plug lead to the spark plug, where it finally jumps the spark plug gap before going to earth.

The transistorized ignition system functions in a similar manner but an electronic sender unit replaces the contact points and condenser in the distributor, and a remotely mounted electronic switch unit controls the coil primary circuit. On some models the system incorporates a digital idle stabilizer (DIS) which automatically advances the ignition timing during idling when the engine experiences additional loads, for example when switching on certain electrical components.

The ignition timing is advanced and retarded automatically, to

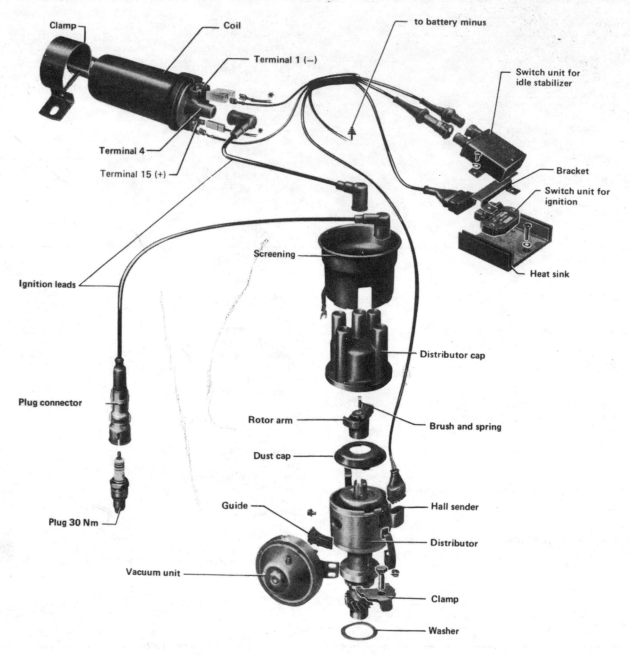

Fig. 4.1 Transistorized ignition components (Sec 1)

ensure that the spark occurs at just the right instant for the particular load at the prevailing engine speed.

The ignition advance is controlled both mechanically and by a vacuum-operated system. The mechanical governor mechanism comprises two weights which move out from the distributor shaft as the engine speed rises due to centrifugal force. As they move outwards they rotate the cam relative to the distributor shaft, and so advance the spark. The weights are held in position by two light springs and it is the tension of the springs which is largely responsible for correct spark advancement.

The vacuum control consists of a diaphragm, one side of which is connected via a small bore tube to the carburettor, and the other side to the contact breaker plate. Depression in the inlet manifold and carburettor, which varies with engine speed and throttle opening, causes the diaphragm to move, so moving the contact breaker plate, and advancing or retarding the spark. A fine degree of control is achieved by a spring in the vacuum assembly.

The contact breaker circuit on some models incorporates a ballast resistor or resistive wire which is in circuit all the time that the engine

is running. When the starter motor is operated, the resistance is bypassed to provide increased voltage at the spark plugs.

On fuel injection models, the distributor rotor arm incorporates a centrifugal cut-out which effectively governs the engine to a maximum speed of approximately 7000 rpm (photo).

2   Contact breaker points – checking and adjustment

1   The manufacturers do not specify a service interval for checking the contact breaker points, however the following information is given for use in the event of breakdown, starting difficulties or power loss.

2   Prise the two clips from the distributor cap (photo). Where an interference screen is fitted, disconnect the earth cable and low tension leads. Remove the cap from the distributor.

3   Pull off the rotor arm and remove the dust cover (photo).

4   Prise open the contact points and examine the condition of their faces. If they are blackened or pitted, remove them as described in Section 3 and dress them using emery tape or a grindstone. If they are

1.0 Distributor rotor arm incorporating a centrifugal cut-out

2.2 Distributor cap location (Scirocco model)

2.3 Distributor rotor arm and dust cover

2.5a Checking the contact breaker points gap with a feeler gauge

2.5b Loosening the contact breaker point retaining screw

3.4 The contact breaker points showing the low tension lead

Fig. 4.2 Adjusting the contact breaker points gap (Sec 2)

worn excessively, renew them.

5   To adjust the contact points accurately a dwell meter will be required, however for an initial setting first turn the engine until the heel of the moving contact is on the high point of the one of the cam lobes. Using a feeler blade, check that the gap between the two points is as given in the Specifications (photo). If not, loosen the fixed contact retaining screw and use a screwdriver in the notch provided to reposition the contact (photo). Check the gap again after tightening the screw.

6   Smear a little multi-purpose grease on the cam and apply a small amount of grease to the moving contact pivot. Apply one or two drops of engine oil to the felt in the cam recess.

7   Connect a dwell meter to the ignition circuit and if possible check the dwell angle while spinning the engine on the starter (refer to the meter maker's instructions). If it is not within the specified limits

decrease the points gap to increase the dwell angle, or increase the points gap to decrease the dwell angle.

8   Refit the dust cover, rotor arm, distributor cap and interference screen if fitted together with the low tension leads, then check the dwell angle with the engine running (if possible).

9   Check and if necessary adjust the ignition timing as described in Section 11.

3   Contact breaker points – renewal

1   The contact breaker points should be renewed at the specified intervals (see Routine Maintenance).

2   Prise the two clips from the distributor cap. Where an interference screen is fitted, disconnect the earth cable and low tension leads. Remove the cap from the distributor.

3   Pull off the rotor arm and remove the dust cover.

4   Disconnect the low tension lead from the connector block (photo).

5   Unscrew the retaining screws and lift the complete contact breaker set from the distributor. Take care not to drop the screw.

6   Wipe clean the contact breaker baseplate, then fit the new contact points using a reversal of the removal procedure; adjust and lubricate the points as described in Section 2 and adjust the ignition timing as described in Section 11.

4   Condenser – testing, removal and refitting

1   The condenser is fitted in parallel with the contact points. Its purpose is to reduce arcing between the points and also to accelerate the collapse of the coil low tension magnetic field. A faulty (short-circuited) condenser can cause the complete failure of the ignition system, as the points will be prevented from interrupting the low tension circuit. An open-circuited condenser will cause misfiring or starting difficulties, and rapid burning of the points.

2   To test the condenser, remove the distributor cap and rotate the engine until the contact points are closed. Switch on the ignition and

separate the points with a screwdriver. If this is accomplished by a strong blue flash, the condenser is faulty (a weak spark is normal).

3 A further test can be made for short-circuiting by removing the condenser and using a test lamp, battery and leads connected to the condenser supply terminal and body. If the test lamp lights, the condenser is faulty.

4 The simplest test is to substitute a new unit and check whether the fault persists.

5 To remove the condenser, remove the distributor as described in Section 9 and clamp it lightly in a vice.

6 Remove the cap, interference screen (if fitted), rotor arm and dust cover.

7 Disconnect the low tension lead from the connector block.

8 Remove the retaining screw and withdraw the condenser and connector block from the distributor.

9 Refitting is a reversal of removal.

Fig. 4.3 Joining the connectors (arrowed) from the digital idle stabilizer (Sec 6)

---

5 Transistorized ignition system (TCI-h) – precautions

1 On models equipped with transistorized ignition, certain precautions must be observed in order to prevent damage to the semiconductor components and in order to prevent personal injury.

2 Before disconnecting wires from the system make sure that the ignition is switched off.

3 When turning the engine at starter speed without starting, the HT lead must be pulled from the centre of the distributor cap and kept earthed to a suitable part of the engine or bodywork.

4 Disconnect both battery leads before carrying out electric welding on any part of the car.

5 If the system develops a fault and it is necessary to tow the car with the ignition key switched on, the wiring must be disconnected from the TCI-h switch unit.

6 Do not under any circumstances connect a condenser to the coil terminals.

7 Take care to avoid receiving electric shocks from the HT system.

Fig. 4.4 Voltmeter connection when testing the transistorized ignition switch unit (Sec 6)

---

6 Transistorized ignition switch unit – testing

1 With the ignition switched off, pull the connectors from the digital idle stabilizer (DIS) unit and join the two connectors together.

2 Disconnect the multi-plug from the switch unit and connect a voltmeter between terminals 4 and 2 as shown in Fig. 4.4.

3 Switch on the ignition and check that battery voltage, or slightly less, is available. If not, there is an open-circuit in the supply wires.

4 Switch off the ignition and reconnect the multi-plug to the switch unit.

5 Pull the multi-plug from the Hall sender on the side of the distributor, then connect a voltmeter across the low tension terminals on the coil.

6 Switch on the ignition and check that there is initially 2 volts, dropping to zero after 1 to 2 seconds. If this is not the case, renew the switch unit and coil.

7 Using a length of wire, earth the centre terminal of the distributor multi-plug briefly; the voltage should rise to between 5 and 6 volts. If not, there is an open-circuit or the switch unit is faulty.

8 Switch off the ignition and connect the voltmeter across the outer terminals of the distributor multi-plug.

9 Switch on the ignition and check that 5 volts is registered on the voltmeter.

10 If a fault still exists renew the switch unit.

11 Switch off the ignition, remove the voltmeter, and reconnect the distributor multi-plug and DIS connectors.

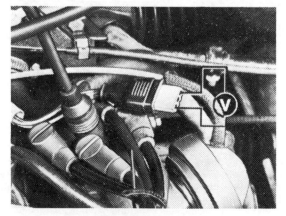

Fig. 4.5 Voltmeter connection when testing at the transistorized ignition distributor multi-plug (Sec 6)

---

7 Transistorized ignition Hall sender – testing

1 Check that the ignition system wiring and plugs are fitted correctly.

2 With the ignition switched off, pull the connectors from the digital idle stabilizer (DIS) unit and join the two connectors together.

3 Pull the HT lead from the centre of the distributor cap and earth the lead to a suitable part of the engine or bodywork.

Measuring plug gap. A feeler gauge of the correct size (see ignition system specifications) should have a slight 'drag' when slid between the electrodes. Adjust gap if necessary

Adjusting plug gap. The plug gap is adjusted by bending the earth electrode inwards, or outwards, as necessary until the correct clearance is obtained. Note the use of the correct tool

Normal. Grey-brown deposits, lightly coated core nose. Gap increasing by around 0.001 in (0.025 mm) per 1000 miles (1600 km). Plugs ideally suited to engine, and engine in good condition

Carbon fouling. Dry, black, sooty deposits. Will cause weak spark and eventually misfire. Fault: over-rich fuel mixture. Check: carburettor mixture settings, float level and jet sizes; choke operation and cleanliness of air filter. Plugs can be re-used after cleaning

Oil fouling. Wet, oily deposits. Will cause weak spark and eventually misfire. Fault: worn bores/piston rings or valve guides; sometimes occurs (temporarily) during running-in period. Plugs can be re-used after thorough cleaning

Overheating. Electrodes have glazed appearance, core nose very white – few deposits. Fault: plug overheating. Check: plug value, ignition timing, fuel octane rating (too low) and fuel mixture (too weak). Discard plugs and cure fault immediately

Electrode damage. Electrodes burned away; core nose has burned, glazed appearance. Fault: pre-ignition. Check: as for 'Overheating' but may be more severe. Discard plugs and remedy fault before piston or valve damage occurs

Split core nose (may appear initially as a crack). Damage is self-evident, but cracks will only show after cleaning. Fault: pre-ignition or wrong gap-setting technique. Check: ignition timing, cooling system, fuel octane rating (too low) and fuel mixture (too weak). Discard plugs, rectify fault immediately

Test lamp method

4   Connect a test lamp and leads across the low tension terminals on the coil.

5   Spin the engine on the starter for 5 seconds and check that the test lamp flickers on and off. If not, the Hall sender is faulty and the distributor should be renewed.

Voltmeter method

6   Pull back the rubber boot from the switch unit and connect a voltmeter between terminals 6 and 3 as shown in Fig. 4.6.

7   Switch on the ignition and turn the engine by hand in its normal direction of rotation. The voltage should alternate from between 0 and 0.7 volts to between 1.8 and battery voltage. If not, the Hall sender is faulty and the distributor should be renewed.

All methods

8   Reconnect the DIS connectors.

8   Transistorized ignition DIS unit – testing

1   Check that the connectors and wiring are fitted correctly to the digital idle stabilizer (DIS) unit.

2   Connect a stroboscopic timing light and tachometer to the engine in accordance with the manufacturer's instructions.

3   Start the engine and run it to normal operating temperature.

4   Accelerate the engine briefly, then allow it to idle and note the ignition timing (refer to Section 11 if necessary).

5   Switch on all the electrical components and lights.

6   Check that when the engine speed drops below 940 rpm, the ignition timing advances; if not, renew the DIS unit. If the engine speed does not drop with the additional electric load, have an assistant engage top gear and very slowly engage the clutch (make sure that the handbrake is firmly applied and the wheels chocked).

9   Distributor – removal and refitting

1   Disconnect the battery negative terminal.

2   Unclip and remove the distributor cap, noting where No 1 spark plug lead enters the cap in relation to the distributor body.

3   Turn the engine with a spanner on the crankshaft pulley bolt until the rotor arm points to the No 1 spark plug lead position.

4   Unscrew and remove the TDC sensor or blanking plug from the top of the gearbox or automatic transmission.

5   Turn the engine until the TDC 'O' mark is aligned with the timing pointer.

6   Mark the distributor body in line with the tip of the rotor arm, and also mark the distributor body and cylinder block in relation to each other.

7   Disconnect the low tension lead or multi-plug (as applicable) from the distributor. Pull the vacuum hose(s) from the capsule.

8   Unscrew the clamp bolt and withdraw the clamp followed by the distributor from the cylinder block. Note by how much the rotor turns clockwise. Remove the distributor body sealing washer and fit a new one on refitting.

9   To refit the distributor first check that the oil pump lug (visible through the distributor aperture) is set parallel to the crankshaft (Fig. 4.7). Check that the TDC 'O' mark is still aligned.

19   Set the rotor arm to the position noted in paragraph 8, align the distributor body and cylinder block marks and insert the distributor. As the gears mesh, the rotor will turn anti-clockwise and point to the previously made mark.

11   Refit the clamp and tighten the bolt. Reconnect the vacuum hose(s), and low tension lead or multi-plug (as applicable).

12   Refit the TDC sensor or blanking plug, and the distributor cap, then reconnect the battery negative terminal.

13   Check and if necessary adjust the ignition timing as described in Section 11.

10   Distributor – overhaul

1   Remove the distributor as described in Section 9.

2   On the conventional ignition system remove the contact breaker

Fig. 4.6 Voltmeter connection when testing the transistorized ignition Hall sender (Sec 7)

Fig. 4.7 Oil pump lug position prior to fitting distributor (Sec 9)

points as described in Section 3, and the condenser as described in Section 4.

3   To remove the vacuum capsule unscrew the retaining screws, and remove the connector block if retained by one of the screws.

4   Extract the spring clip and detach the operating arm from inside the distributor body. Withdraw the capsule and the guide, where fitted.

5   It is not possible to dismantle the distributor further, although it is possible to examine the centrifugal mechanism by prising the blanking plate from the body side.

6   Checking the contact breaker points and condenser is described in Sections 2 and 4. To check the vacuum unit, suck on the outlet tube(s) and make sure that the operating arm moves. Check the distributor driveshaft for lateral movement – if excessive the body assembly must be renewed. Wipe clean the distributor cap and make sure that the carbon brush moves freely against the tension of the spring. Clean the metal segments in the cap but do not scrape away any metal otherwise, the HT spark at the spark plugs will be reduced. Renew all components as necessary.

7   Reassemble the distributor using a reversal of the dismantling procedure; on the conventional system adjust the contact breaker points as described in Section 2.

11   Ignition timing – adjustment

Note: *Accurate ignition timing is only possible using a stroboscopic timing light, although on some models a TDC sender unit is located on the top of the gearbox casing and may be used with a special VW tester to give an instant read-out. However, this tester will not normally be available to the home mechanic. For initial setting-up*

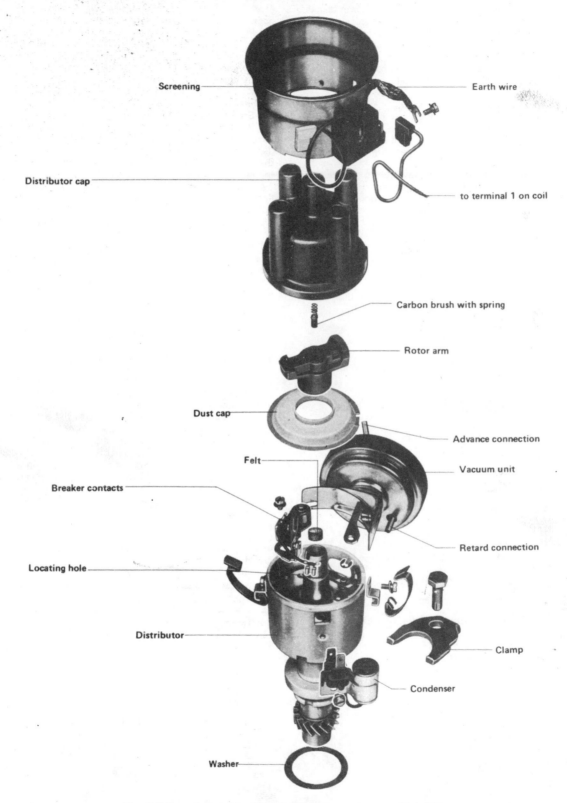

Screening

Distributor cap

Earth wire

to terminal 1 on coil

Carbon brush with spring

Rotor arm

Dust cap

Advance connection

Felt

Vacuum unit

Breaker contacts

Retard connection

Locating hole

Distributor

Clamp

Condenser

Washer

Fig. 4.8 Conventional ignition distributor components (Sec 10)

purposes of the conventional ignition system, the test bulb method can be used, but this must always be followed by the stroboscopic timing light method.

Test bulb method (conventional ignition system only)

1   Remove the No 1 spark plug (crankshaft pulley end) and place the thumb over the aperture.

2   Turn the engine in the normal running direction (clockwise viewed from the crankshaft pulley end) until pressure is felt in No 1 cylinder, indicating that the piston is commencing its compression stroke. Use a spanner on the crankshaft pulley bolt, or engage top gear and pull the car forwards.

3   Continue turning the engine until the line on the crankshaft pulley is aligned with the pointer on the timing cover. If there are no marks

on the timing cover, unscrew and remove the TDC sensor or blanking plug from the top of the gearbox or automatic transmission and align the timing mark (see Specifications) with the timing pointer (see Fig. 4.9) (photo).

4   Remove the distributor cap and check that the rotor arm is pointing toward the No 1 HT lead location in the cap.

5   Connect a 12 volt test bulb between the coil LT negative terminal and a suitable earthing point on the engine.

6   Loosen the distributor clamp retaining bolt.

7   Switch on the ignition. If the bulb is already lit, turn the distributor body slightly clockwise until the bulb goes out.

8   Turn the distributor body anti-clockwise until the bulb just lights up, indicating that the points have just opened. Tighten the clamp retaining bolt.

9   Switch off the ignition and remove the test bulb.

10   Refit the distributor cap and No 1 spark plug and HT lead. Once the engine has been started, check the timing stroboscopically as follows and adjust as necessary.

Stroboscopic timing light method

11   On engines with a distributor incorporating a single vacuum

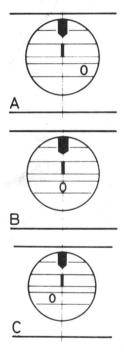

Fig. 4.9 Ignition timing marks (Sec 11)

A   7.5° or 9° BTDC
B   0° (ie TDC)
C   3° ATDC

capsule (ie vacuum advance only), disconnect and plug the vacuum hose. On all other engines do not disconnect the vacuum hoses.

12   If there are no timing marks on the timing cover and crankshaft pulley, unscrew and remove the TDC sensor or blanking plug from the top of the gearbox or automatic transmission.

13   Connect the timing light to the engine in accordance with the manufacturer's instructions.

14   Connect a tachometer to the engine in accordance with the manufacturer's instructions.

15   Start the engine and run it at idling speed.

16   Point the timing light at the timing mark and pointer; they should appear to be stationary and aligned (photo). If adjustment is necessary (ie the marks are not aligned), loosen the clamp retaining bolt and turn the distributor body anti-clockwise to advance and clockwise to retard the ignition timing.

17   Gradually increase the engine speed while still pointing the timing light at the timing marks. The mark on the flywheel (or driveplate) or pulley should appear to move opposite to the direction of rotation, proving that the centrifugal weights are operating correctly. If not, the centrifugal mechanism is faulty and the distributor should be renewed.

18   Accurate checking of the vacuum advance (and retard where fitted) requires the use of a vacuum pump and gauge. However, providing that the diaphragm unit is serviceable, the vacuum hose(s) firmly fitted, and the internal mechanism not seized, the system should work correctly.

19   Switch off the engine, remove the timing light and tachometer, and refit the vacuum hose (where applicable).

12 Coil – description and testing

1   The coil is located on the bulkhead in the engine compartment, and it should be periodically wiped clean to prevent high tension voltage loss through possible arcing (photo).

2   To ensure the correct HT polarity at the spark plugs, the coil LT leads must always be connected correctly. On the conventional ignition system the LT lead from the distributor should be connected to the negative (–) terminal on the coil. Incorrect connections can cause bad starting, misfiring, and short spark plug life.

3   Complete testing of the coil requires special equipment, however if an ohmmeter is available, the primary and secondary winding resistances can be checked and compared with those given in the Specifications. During testing the LT and HT wires must be disconnected from the coil. To test the primary winding, connect the ohmmeter between the two LT terminals – to test the secondary winding connect the ohmmeter between the negative (–) LT terminal and the HT terminal.

13 Spark plugs and HT leads – general

1   The correct functioning of the spark plugs is vital for the correct running and efficiency of the engine. The spark plugs should be renewed regularly (see Routine Maintenance). However, if misfiring or bad starting is experienced before renewal is due, they must be removed, cleaned, and regapped.

11.3 Removing the timing blanking plug from the top of the gearbox

11.16 The timing marks (arrowed) on the crankshaft pulley and timing cover (Scirocco model)

12.1 Coil location on a Golf model

2   The condition of the spark plugs will also tell much about the overall condition of the engine.

3   If the insulator nose of the spark plug is clean and white, with no deposits, this is indicative of a weak mixture, or too hot a plug. (A hot plug transfers heat away from the electrode slowly — a cold plug transfers it away quickly).

4   If the tip and insulator nose are covered with hard black-looking deposits, then this is indicative that the mixture is too rich. Should the plug be black and oily, then it is likely that the engine is fairly worn, as well as the mixture being too rich.

5   If the insulator nose is covered with light tan to greyish brown deposits, then the mixture is correct and it is likely that the engine is in good condition.

6   If there are any traces of long brown tapering stains on the outside of the white portion of the plug, then the plug will have to be renewed, as this shows that there is a faulty joint between the plug body and the insulator, and compression is being lost.

7   Plugs should be cleaned by a sand blasting machine, which will free them from carbon more thoroughly than cleaning by hand.

8   The spark plug gap is of considerable importance, as, if it is too large or too small, the size of the spark and its efficiency will be seriously impaired. The spark plug gap should be set to the figure given in the Specifications at the beginning of this Chapter.

9   To set it, measure the gap with a feeler gauge, and then bend open, or close, the *outer* plug electrode until the correct gap is achieved. The centre electrode should *never* be bent as this may crack the insulation and cause plug failure, if nothing worse.

10   Always tighten the spark plugs to the specified torque.

11   Periodically the spark plug leads should be wiped clean and checked for security.

14   Thermo-pneumatic valve – description and testing

1   Some carburettor engine models are equipped with a thermo-pneumatic valve which regulates the ignition vacuum advance during the warm-up period in order to improve cold driving performance.

2   On early 1.6 litre engines with automatic transmission the hoses are routed as shown in Figs. 4.10 and 4.11. With the engine cold, there is no vacuum advance on the 55 kW engine, and vacuum advance only above approximately 2000 rpm on the 63 kW engine. Full vacuum advance is available when the valve opens, ie at normal operating temperature.

3   On early 1.6 litre engines with manual gearbox and later 1.5 litre engines with automatic transmission, the system incorporates a check valve. During the warm-up period the check valve maintains vacuum advance even after the throttle has been fully opened. With the valve open, the check valve is bypassed and ignition advance is normal.

4   To test the valve, remove it and immerse it in water being heated. Attach hoses to the inlet and outlet parts, then attempt to blow through the valve and check it against the following table:

Engine type	Valve closed below	Valve open above
1.6 litre, 55 kW, automatic	45°C (113°F)	61°C (141°F)
1.6 litre, 63 kW, manual or automatic	52°C (125°F)	68°C (154°F)
1.5 litre, 51 kW, automatic	30°C (86°F)	46°C (114°F)

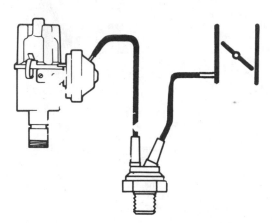

Fig. 4.10 Thermo-pneumatic valve and hoses on early 1.6 litre 55 kW engines with automatic transmission (Sec 14)

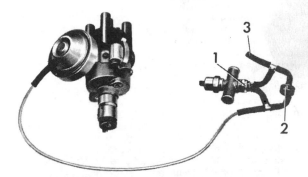

Fig. 4.12 Thermo-pneumatic valve (1), check valve (2), and hoses (3) on early 1.6 litre 63 kW engines with manual gearbox (Sec 14)

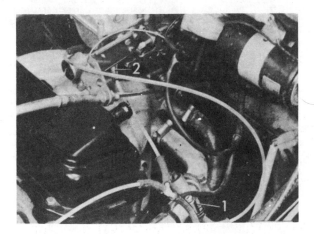

Fig. 4.11 Thermo-pneumatic valve (1) and hose (2) on early 1.6 litre 63 kW engines with automatic transmission (Sec 14)

Fig. 4.13 Thermo-pneumatic valve (1) and check valve (2) on 1.5 litre engines with automatic transmission (Sec 14)

5   To test the check valve (where fitted), remove it and blow through it; the valve must be open when blowing through the white port and closed when blowing through the black port. Always fit the check valve with the white connection toward the vacuum capsule.

15 Fault diagnosis – ignition system

By far the majority of breakdown and running troubles are caused by faults in the ignition system, either in the low tension or high tension circuit. There are two main symptoms indicating ignition fault. Either the engine will not start or fire or the engine is difficult to start and misfires. If it is a regular misfire, ie the engine is only running on two or three cylinders, the fault is almost sure to be in the secondary, or high tension circuit. If the misfiring is intermittent, the fault could be in either the high or low tension circuits. If the car stops suddenly or will not start at all it is likely that the fault is in the low tension circuit. Loss of power and overheating, apart from faulty carburation settings, are normally due to faults in the distributor or incorrect ignition timing.

Engine fails to start (conventional and transistorized systems)

1   If the engine fails to start and the car was running normally when it was last used, first check there is fuel in the petrol tank. If the engine turns over normally on the starter motor and the battery is evidently well charged, then the fault may be in either the high or low tension circuits. First check the HT circuit. If the battery is known to be fully charged, the ignition light comes on, and the starter motor fails to turn the engine, check the tightness of the leads on the battery terminals and the security of the earth lead to its connection to the body. It is quite common for the leads to have worked loose, even if they look and feel secure. If one of the battery terminal posts gets very hot when trying to work the starter motor, this is a sure indication of a faulty connection to that terminal.

2   One of the most common reasons for bad starting is wet or damp spark plug leads and distributor. Remove the distributor cap. If condensation is visible internally dry the cap with a rag and wipe over the leads. Refit the cap.

3   If the engine on models fitted with conventional ignition still fails to start, check that current is reaching the plugs by disconnecting each plug lead in turn at the spark plug end. Hold the end of the cable with an insulated tool about $\frac{3}{16}$ in (5 mm) away from the cylinder block, then spin the engine on the starter motor.

4   On engines with transistorized ignition remove each plug in turn and earth it to a suitable part of the engine with the HT cable connected. Spin the engine on the starter motor.

5   Sparking at the cables or plugs should be fairly strong, with a regular blue spark. If necessary remove the plugs for cleaning and regapping. The engine should now start.

Engine fails to start (conventional system only) – continuation

6   If there is no spark at the plug leads, take off the HT lead from the centre of the distributor cap and hold it to the block as before. Spin the engine on the starter once more. A rapid succession of blue sparks between the end of the lead and the block indicates that the coil is in order and that the distributor cap is cracked, the rotor arm faulty or the carbon brush in the top of the distributor cap is not making good contact with the rotor arm.

7   If there are no sparks from the end of the lead from the coil, check the connections at the coil end of the lead. If this is in order start checking the low tension circuit. Commence by cleaning and gapping the points (Section 2).

8   Use a 12 volt voltmeter, or a 12 volt bulb and two lengths of wire.

With the ignition switch on and the points open test between the low tension wire to the coil (it is marked –) and earth. No reading indicates a break in the supply from the ignition switch. Check the connections at the switch to see if any are loose. Refit them and the engine should run. A reading shows a faulty coil or condenser or broken lead between the coil and the distributor.

9   Remove the condenser from the distributor body but leave the wiring connected. With the points open, test between the moving point and earth. If there now is a reading then the fault is in the condenser. Fit a new one and the fault is cleared.

10   With no reading from the moving point to earth, take a reading between earth and the negative (–) terminal of the coil. A reading here indicates a broken wire which must be renewed between the coil and distributor. No reading confirms that the coil has failed and must be renewed. For these tests it is sufficient to separate the contact breaker points with a piece of paper.

11   If the engine starts when the starter motor is operated, but stops as soon as the ignition key is returned to the normal running position the ballast resistor may have an open-circuit. Connect a temporary lead between the coil positive (+) terminal and the battery positive (+) terminal. If the engine now runs correctly, renew the resistor. Note that the ballast resistor or resistive wire must not be permanently bypassed otherwise the coil will overheat and be damaged.

Engine misfires (conventional system only)

12   If the engine misfires regularly, run it at a fast idling speed. Pull off each of the plug caps in turn and listen to the note of the engine. Hold the plug cap in a dry cloth or with a rubber glove as additional protection against a shock from the HT supply.

13   No difference in engine running will be noticed when the lead from the defective circuit is removed. Removing the lead from one of the good cylinders will accentuate the misfire.

14   Remove the plug lead from the end of the defective plug and hold it about $\frac{3}{16}$ in (5 mm) away from the block. Restart the engine. If the sparking is fairly strong and regular, the fault must lie in the spark plug.

Engine misfires (conventional and transistorized systems)

15   The plug may be loose, the insulation may be cracked, or the points may have burnt away, giving too wide a gap for the spark to jump. Worse still, one of the points may have broken off. Either renew the plug, or clean it, reset the gap, and then test it.

16   Check the HT lead from the distributor to the plug. If the insulation is cracked or perished, renew the lead. Check the connections at the distributor cap.

17   Examine the distributor cap carefully for tracking. This can be recognised by a very thin black line running between two or more electrodes, or between an electrode and some other part of the distributor. These lines are paths which now conduct electricity across the cap, thus letting it run to earth. The only answer in this case is a new distributor cap.

18   Apart from the ignition timing being incorrect, other causes of misfiring have already been dealt with under the paragraphs dealing with the failure of the engine to start. To recap, these are that:

(a)   The coil may be faulty giving an intermittent misfire
(b)   There may be a damaged wire or loose connection in the low tension circuit
(c)   The condenser may be short-circuiting (where applicable)
(d)   There may be a mechanical fault in the distributor (broken driving spindle or contact breaker spring where applicable)

19   If the ignition timing is too far retarded it should be noted that the engine will tend to overheat, and there will be a quite noticeable drop in power. If the engine is overheating and the power is down, and the ignition timing is correct, then the carburettor should be checked as it is likely that this is where the fault lies.

Chapter 5 Clutch

Contents

Specifications

Clutch type .... Single dry plate, non-fulcrum diaphragm spring pressure plate, cable actuation

Free play at clutch pedal .... 15 to 25 mm (0.6 to 1.0 in)

Overhaul data
Clutch disc run-out (maximum) .... 0.3 mm (0.012 in) measured 2.5 mm (0.10 in) from outer edge
Pressure plate inward taper (maximum) .... 0.2 mm (0.008 in)

Torque wrench settings

	lbf ft	Nm
Pressure plate to crankshaft	55	75
Flywheel to pressure plate	14	20
Gearbox end cover plate (4-speed gearbox)	11	15

---

1 General description

Unlike the clutch on most engines, the clutch pressure plate is bolted to the crankshaft flange and the flywheel, which is dish shaped, is bolted to the pressure plate with the friction disc being held between them. This is in effect the reverse of the more conventional arrangement where the flywheel is bolted to the crankshaft flange and the clutch pressure plate bolted to the flywheel.

The release mechanism consists of a metal disc, called the release plate, which is clamped in the centre of the pressure plate by a retaining ring. In the centre of the release plate is a boss into which the clutch pushrod is fitted. The pushrod passes through the centre of the gearbox input shaft and is actuated by a release bearing located in the gearbox end housing. A single finger lever presses on this bearing when the shaft to which it is splined is turned by operation of the cable from the clutch pedal. In effect the clutch lever pushes the clutch pushrod, which in turn pushes the centre of the release plate inwards towards the crankshaft. The outer edge of the release plate presses on the pressure plate fingers forcing them back towards the engine and removing the pressure plate friction face from the friction disc, thus disconnecting the drive. When the clutch pedal is released the pressure plate reasserts itself, clamping the friction disc firmly against the flywheel and restoring the drive.

As the friction linings on the disc wear, the pressure plate will gradually move closer to the flywheel and the cable free play will decrease. Periodic adjustment must therefore be carried out as described in Section 2.

---

2 Clutch – adjustment

1 The clutch adjustment should be checked at the intervals given in Routine Maintenance. To do this, check the free play at the clutch pedal by measuring the distance it has to be moved in order to take up the slack in the cable. If the distance is not as given in the Specifications, adjust as follows.
2 Loosen the outer cable locknut at the gearbox bracket, then turn the serrated disc while holding the outer cable stationary until the pedal free play is correct (photos).
3 Fully depress the pedal several times and recheck the adjustment, then tighten the locknut. Lubricate the exposed part of the inner cable with a little multi-purpose grease.

---

3 Clutch cable – renewal

1 Working in the engine compartment loosen the outer cable locknut at the gearbox bracket, then back off the serrated disc until the inner cable can be released from the operating lever. To do this pull the clips from the lever and withdraw them from the inner cable (photos).
2 Withdraw the inner and outer cable from the gearbox bracket.
3 Working beneath the facia unhook the cable from the clutch pedal, then withdraw it through the grommet in the bulkhead. Note the sealing O-ring on the outer cable ferrule.
4 If necessary prise the guide sleeve from the rubber washer on the gearbox bracket, then remove the washer.
5 Check that the cable locating grommet and washer are secure in the bulkhead.
6 Fit the new cable using a reversal of the removal procedure. Check that the sealing ring is correctly located on the bulkhead end of the outer cable, and lightly lubricate the exposed parts of the inner cable with multi-purpose grease. Make sure that the inner sealing lip of the rubber washer on the gearbox bracket is parallel to the end cap, otherwise the gearbox breather may become blocked with foreign matter. Finally adjust the cable as described in Section 2.

---

4 Clutch pedal – removal and refitting

1 Loosen the outer cable locknut at the gearbox bracket, then turn the serrated disc and locknut anti-clockwise until the inner cable is slack.
2 Working beneath the facia, unhook the cable from the clutch pedal.
3 Prise the clip from the end of the pedal shaft.

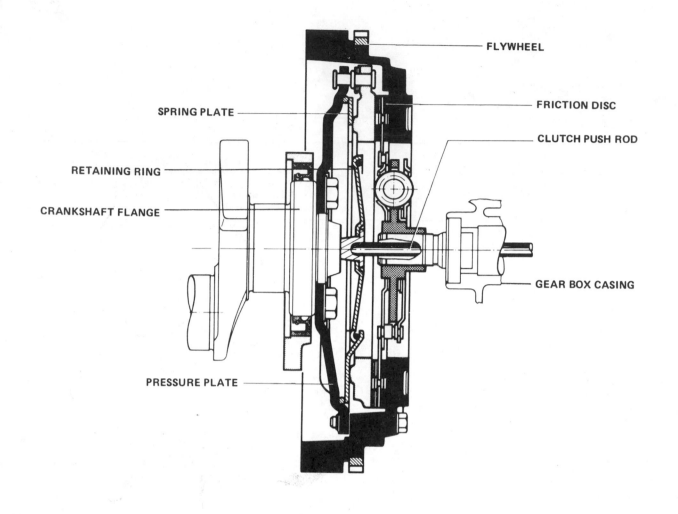

FLYWHEEL

FRICTION DISC

SPRING PLATE

CLUTCH PUSH ROD

RETAINING RING

CRANKSHAFT FLANGE

GEAR BOX CASING

PRESSURE PLATE

Fig. 5.1 Cross-section of the clutch (Sec 1)

2.2a Clutch cable adjuster location on a Scirocco (airflow sensor removed)

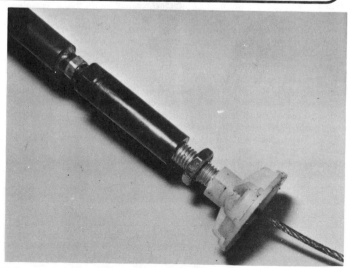

2.2b Clutch cable adjuster and locknut

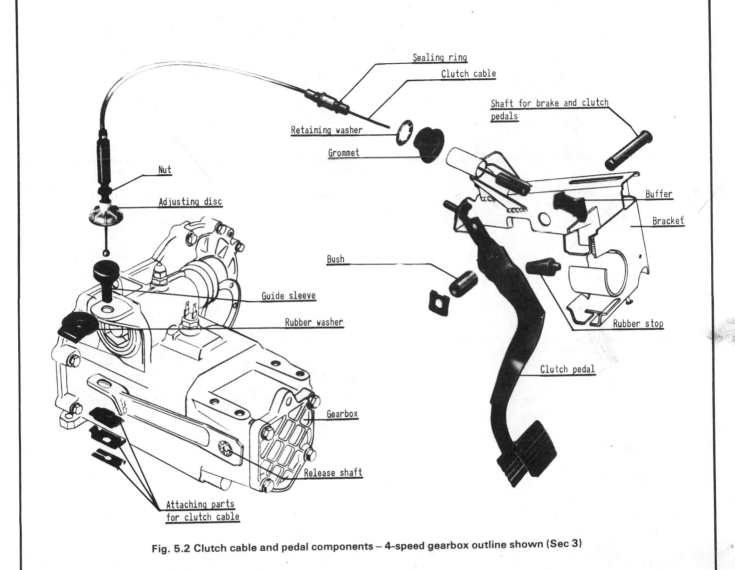

Fig. 5.2 Clutch cable and pedal components – 4-speed gearbox outline shown (Sec 3)

3.1a Clutch operating lever and cable

3.1b View of clutch operating lever and cable connection from below

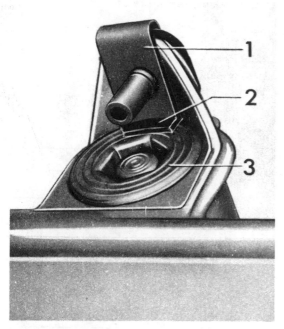

Fig. 5.3 Clutch cable guide rubber washer (1), sealing lip (2), and selector shaft end cap (3) (Sec 3)

4   Slide the pedal from the shaft.
5   Examine the shaft and pedal bush for wear and renew them if necessary. The bush is an interference fit in the pedal and can be removed or installed using a soft metal drift – make sure that the ends of the bush are flush with the ends of the pedal tube.
6   Refitting is a reversal of removal, but lubricate the shaft with a little multi-purpose grease and adjust the cable as described in Section 2.

5   Clutch – removal and refitting

1   Remove the gearbox as described in Chapter 6. Clamp the flywheel to prevent it turning and remove the bolts holding the flywheel to the pressure plate in a diagonal fashion. Release each one half a turn at a time until they are all slack and then take them out. The flywheel and the friction disc may now be removed, but note which way round the disc is fitted and also mark the flywheel and pressure plate in relation to each other. On later models, centering pins are provided to ensure that the TDC mark on the flywheel is positioned correctly (photo).
2   Examine the pressure plate surface. If it is clean and free from scoring there is no reason to remove it unless the friction disc shows signs of oil contamination.
3   If the plate surface is defective then it must be removed. Note exactly where the ends of the retaining ring are located (the ring must be refitted this way later), and prise the ring out with a screwdriver. The release plate may now be removed (photo). The pressure plate is held to the crankshaft flange by six bolts fitted using a thread locking compound. These will be difficult to remove as they were tightened to a high torque before the locking fluid set, so the plate must be held with a clamp similar to that shown in Fig. 5.5 (photo).
4   Refitting is a reversal of removal; use thread locking compound on the bolts securing the plate to the crankshaft flange if they have been removed, and tighten them to the specified torque (photo). Make sure

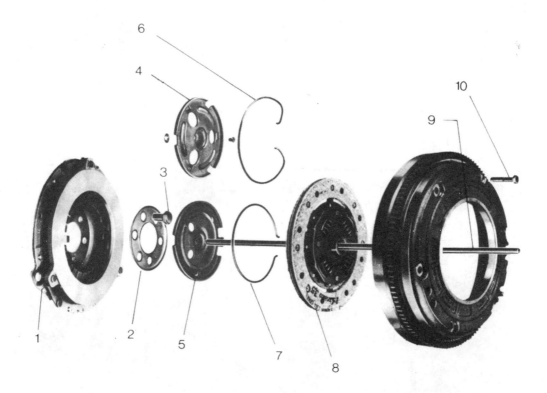

Fig. 5.4 Exploded view of the clutch components (Sec 5)

1   Pressure plate assembly
2   Packing plate
3   Bolt
4   Release plate (200 mm/8 in diameter clutch)

5   Release plate (190 mm/7.48 in diameter clutch)
6   Retaining ring (200 mm/8 in diameter clutch)
7   Retaining ring (190 mm/7.48 in diameter clutch)

8   Friction disc
9   Pushrod
10 Bolt

5.1 Flywheel expanding peg location for centering pressure plate

5.3a Removing the clutch release plate

Fig. 5.5 Special VW tool for holding the pressure plate stationary while unscrewing or tightening the retaining bolts (Sec 5)

5.3b Removing the clutch pressure plate

5.4 Tightening the clutch pressure plate retaining bolts

that the retaining ring is correctly seated (Figs. 5.6 and 5.7). Take care that no oil or grease is allowed to get onto the pressure plate or friction surfaces.

5   When refitting the clutch disc make sure the greater projecting boss which incorporates the torsion springs is furthest from the engine, then fit the flywheel over the pressure plate. Fit the securing bolts and tighten them finger tight only.

6   The next operation is to centre the clutch disc. If this is not done accurately the gearbox mainshaft will not be able to locate in the splines of the clutch disc hub, and it will be impossible to fit the gearbox. The best centralising tool is VW 547 which fits in the flywheel and has a spigot which fits exactly in the centre of the clutch disc hub (Fig. 5.8). If you cannot borrow or hire tool VW 547 then we suggest you make up a tool as shown in Fig. 5.9. Alternatively centre the disc using vernier calipers (photo). Once the clutch disc is centred correctly, tighten the securing bolts in a diagonal sequence to the specified torque and check the centralisation again.

7   When refitting the transmission, put a smear of lithium-based grease on the end of the clutch pushrod at the release plate end.

6   Clutch assembly – inspection

1   The most probable part of the clutch to require attention is the

Fig. 5.6 Correct location of release plate retaining ring ends (arrowed) on the 190 mm diameter clutch (Sec 5)

Fig. 5.7 Correct location of release plate retaining ring ends (arrowed) on the 200 mm diameter clutch (Sec 5)

Fig. 5.8 Using VW tool 547 to centre the clutch friction disc (Sec 5)

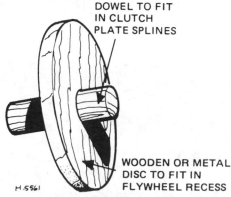

Fig. 5.9 Home-made tool for centralising the clutch friction disc (Sec 5)

DOWEL TO FIT IN CLUTCH PLATE SPLINES

WOODEN OR METAL DISC TO FIT IN FLYWHEEL RECESS

5.6 Using vernier calipers to check the clutch disc centralisation

friction disc. Normal wear will eventually reduce its thickness. The lining must stand proud of the rivets by not less than 0.6 mm (0.025 in). At this measurement the lining is at the end of its life and a new friction plate is needed.

2   The friction disc should be checked for run-out if possible. Mount the disc between the centres of a lathe and measure the run-out at the specified dimension from the outer edge, then compare the result with the Specifications. However, this requires a dial gauge and a mandrel. If the clutch has not shown signs of dragging then this test may be passed over, but if it has we suggest that expert help be sought to test the run-out (Fig. 5.10).

3   Examine the pressure plate. There are three important things to check. Put a straight-edge across the friction surface and measure any bow or taper with feeler gauges.

4   The rivets which hold the spring fingers in position must be tight. If any of them are loose the pressure plate must be scrapped. Finally, the condition of the friction surface. Ridges or scoring indicate undue wear and unless they can be removed by light application of emery paper it would be better to renew the plate.

5   The flywheel friction surface must be similarly checked.

6   So far the inspection has been for normal wear. Two other types of damage may be encountered. The first is overheating due to clutch slip. In extreme cases the pressure plate and flywheel may have radial cracks. Such faults mean that they require renewal. The second problem is contamination by oil or grease. This will cause clutch slip but probably without the cracks. There will be shiny black patches on the friction disc which will have a glazed surface. There is no cure for this, a new friction disc is required. In addition it is **imperative** that the source of contamination be located and rectified. It will be either the crankshaft oil seal or the gearbox input shaft oil seal (or both!). Examine them and renew them as necessary – the procedures are given in Chapters 1 and 6.

7   Whilst the gearbox is removed, it is as well to check the release bearing for satisfactory condition – see Section 7.

Fig. 5.10 Checking the friction disc for run-out (Sec 6)

Fig. 5.11 Checking the taper of the pressure plate friction surface (Sec 6)

7.2 Removing the gearbox end cover (4-speed models)

7.4 Extracting the clutch release lever location circlips (4-speed models)

7.5 Removing the clutch release arm and shaft (4-speed models)

7 Clutch release mechanism – removal and refitting

1   The clutch release mechanism is located in the gearbox end housing and is accessible after the removal of the end cover or plate (as applicable).

2   On 4-speed gearbox models, unbolt the end cover from the gearbox and remove the gasket (photo).

3   On 5-speed gearbox models, first support the engine/gearbox unit with a trolley jack, then remove the torque strut and rear gearbox mounting and lower the jack a few inches. Using a sharp instrument, pierce the endplate and lever it out from the gearbox. A new plate must be obtained.

4   On both 4 and 5-speed gearboxes the release lever is located on the shaft by one circlip (early models) or two circlips (later models). Extract the circlip(s) (photo).

5   With the clutch cable disconnected (see Section 3) withdraw the release arm and shaft from the gearbox and remove the lever and spring (photo).

6   Remove the release bearing (photo) and on 4-speed models only,

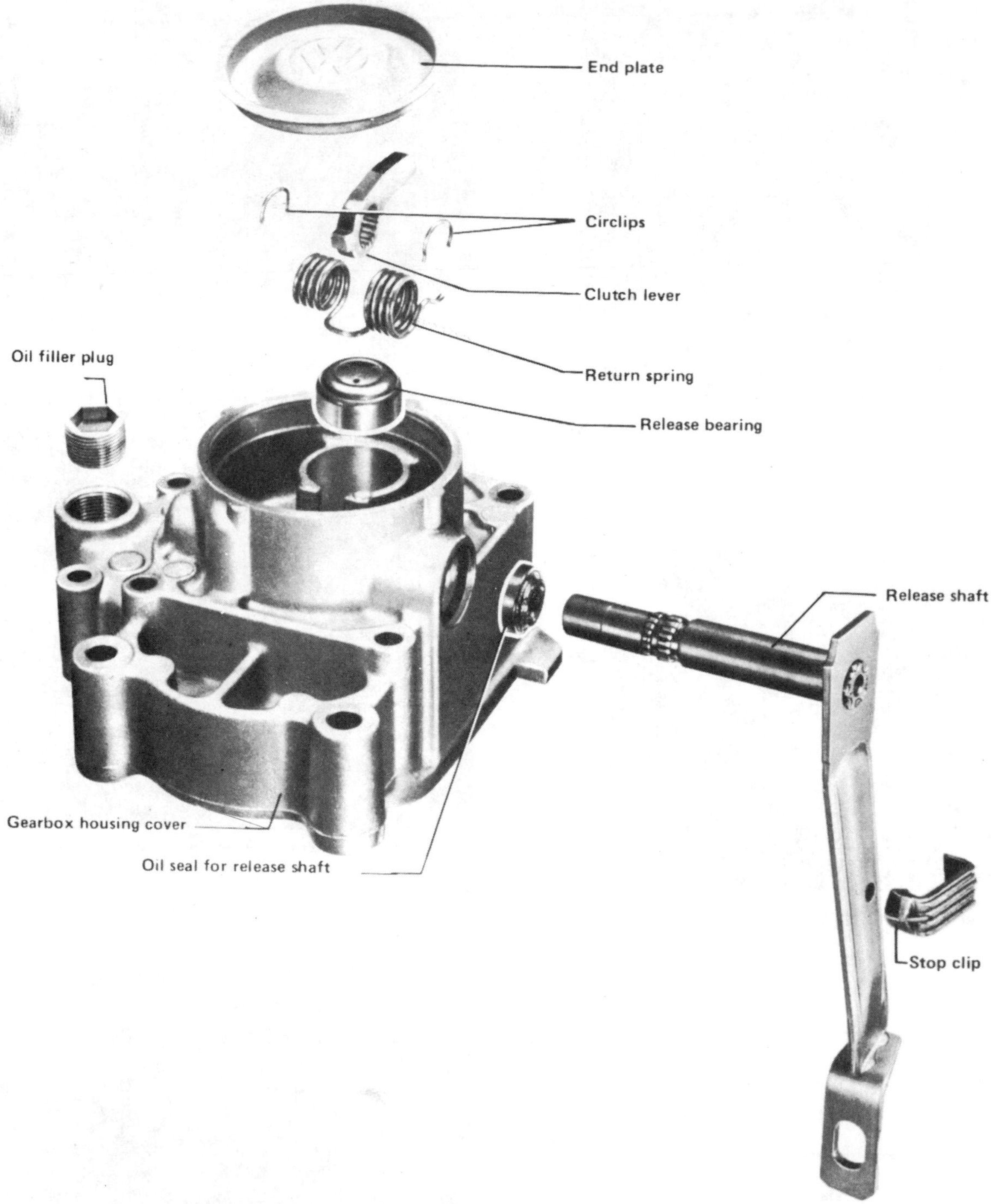

End plate

Circlips

Clutch lever

Return spring

Oil filler plug

Release bearing

Release shaft

Gearbox housing cover

Oil seal for release shaft

Stop clip

Fig. 5.12 Exploded view of the clutch release mechanism on the 5-speed gearbox (Sec 7)

7.6 Removing the clutch release bearing (4-speed models)

extract the guide sleeve. Removal of the pushrod on the 4-speed gearbox is not possible unless the unit is lowered.

7   Rotate the release bearing and check it for wear and roughness; renew it if necessary. Check the shaft oil seal for wear or deterioration, and if necessary prise it out and drive in a new seal squarely using a suitable length of metal tubing. Fill the space between the seal lips with multi-purpose grease.

8   Refitting is a reversal of removal. Note that the release lever and shaft have a master spline, and when fitting the return spring ensure that the bent ends bear against the casing with the centre part hooked over the release lever. Always fit a new gasket to the end cover on 4-speed models, and use a suitable length of metal tubing to drive the new endplate into the housing on 5-speed models.

8 Fault diagnosis – clutch

Symptom	Reason(s)
Judder when taking up drive	Loose engine/gearbox mountings Friction linings worn or contaminated with oil Worn splines on gearbox input shaft or driven plate
Clutch fails to disengage	Incorrect cable adjustment Driven plate sticking on input shaft splines (may be due to rust if car off road for long period) Faulty pressure plate assembly
Clutch slips	Incorrect cable adjustment Friction linings worn or contaminated with oil Faulty pressure plate assembly
Noise when depressing clutch pedal	Worn release bearing Worn splines on gearbox input shaft or driven plate
Noise when releasing clutch pedal	Distorted driven plate Broken or weak driven plate cushion springs

Chapter 6
Manual gearbox and automatic transmission

For modifications and information applicable to later models, see Supplement at end of manual

Contents

Specifications

Manual gearbox

Type .... Four or five forward speeds (all synchromesh) and reverse. Final drive integral with main gearbox

Ratios

4-speed version

1st .... 3.45 : 1 (11/38)

2nd:
    All models up to September 1974 .... 1.95 : 1 (19/37)
    All models from October 1974 (except 1981 Rabbit) .... 1.94 : 1 (18/35)
    1981 Rabbit .... 1.75 : 1 (20/35)

3rd:
    All models up to July 1976 .... 1.37 : 1 (27/37)
    All models from August 1976 (except 1981 Rabbit) .... 1.29 : 1 (28/36)
    1981 Rabbit .... 1.06 : 1 (31/33)

4th:
    All models up to July 1980 .... 0.97 : 1 (32/31)
    All models from August 1980 (except 1981 Rabbit) .... 0.91 : 1 (33/30)
    1981 Rabbit .... 0.70 : 1 (37/26)

Reverse .... 3.17 : 1 (12/38)

Final drive:
    All models except UK Golf/Scirocco manufactured between
    August 1976 and July 1979 .... 3.89 : 1 (19/74)
    UK Golf/Scirocco models manufactured between August 1976
    and July 1979 .... 3.70 : 1 (20/74)

5-speed version

1st .... 3.45 : 1 (11/38)

2nd:
    All models except gearbox codes FM, FD and FK .... 1.94 : 1 (18/35)
    Gearbox codes FM, FD, and FK .... 2.12 : 1 (17/36)

3rd:
    All models except gearbox codes FM, FD
    and FK .... 1.29 : 1 (28/36)
    Gearbox codes FM, FD, and FK .... 1.44 : 1 (27/39)

4th:
All models up to July 1980 except gearbox code FM	0.97 : 1 (32/31)
All models from August 1980 except gearbox codes FM, FD, and FK	0.91 : 1 (33/30)
Gearbox codes FM, FD, and FK	1.13 : 1 (31/35)

5th:
All models up to July 1980 except gearbox code FM	0.76 : 1 (58/44)
All models from August 1980 except gearbox codes FM, FD, and FK	0.71 : 1 (38/27)
Gearbox codes FM, FD, and FK	0.91 : 1 (34/31)
Reverse	3.17 : 1 (12/38)
Final drive	3.89 : 1 (19/74)

Oil capacities
4-speed gearbox	1.5 litres; 1.6 US quarts; 2.6 Imp pints
5-speed gearbox	2.0 litres; 2.1 US quarts; 3.5 Imp pints

Automatic transmission
Type	3-speed epicyclic gear train type incorporating multi-plate clutches and brake, and one brake band. Drive transmitted from engine by torque converter

Ratios
1st	2.55 : 1
2nd	1.45 : 1
3rd	1.00 : 1
Reverse:	
Up to 17th August 1975	2.42 : 1
From 18th August 1975	2.46 : 1
Final drive:	
All 1.5 and 1.6 litre engines, and USA 1.7 litre pick-up	3.76 : 1 (21/79)
1.7 litre models, except USA pick-up	3.57 : 1 (23/82)

Fluid capacity
Total (from dry)	6.0 litres; 6.3 US quarts; 10.6 Imp pints
Service (drain and refill)	3.0 litres, 3.2 US quarts; 5.3 Imp pints
Final drive oil capacity	0.75 litre; 0.8 US quart; 1.3 Imp pints

Torque converter stall speed
Models up to September 1975	1950 to 2250 rpm
Models from September 1975:	
1.5 litre	2250 to 2500 rpm
1.6 litre	2100 to 2350 rpm
1.7 litre	2200 to 2500 rpm

Note: *Deduct 125 rpm per 3200 ft altitude*

Torque wrench settings

	lbf ft	Nm
Manual gearbox – 4-speed		
Selector rod adjustment	11	15
Gearbox to engine:		
M12 bolts	55	75
M10 bolts	33	45
End cover bolts	11	15
Casing bolts	18	25
Selector shaft locking screw	14	20
Reverse shaft screw	14	20
Reversing light switch	22	30
Oil filler plug (without magnet)	18	25
Drain plug (with magnet)	18	25
Oil filler plug (from 1974)	14	20
Manual gearbox – 5-speed		
End cover bolts	18	25
5th gear retaining nut	108	150
Mainshaft bearing retainer	11	15
Reverse shaft	22	30
Casing bolts	18	25
Pinion bearing retainer	29	40
Drain plug	18	25
Oil filler plug	18	25
Gearbox to engine:		
M12 bolts	55	75
M10 bolts	33	45

Automatic transmission	lbf ft	Nm
Oil pan	14	20
Oil strainer cover	2	3
Transmission to engine	40	55
Torque converter to driveplate	22	30
Selector cable to lever	5	8

1 Manual gearbox – general description

The manual gearbox is of the VW type number 020. It incorporates four or five forward speeds and one reverse speed, with synchromesh engagement on all forward gears. The clutch withdrawal mechanism comprises a release arm and lever located at the outer end of the gearbox and a pushrod located in the input shaft.

Gearshift is by means of a floor-mounted lever connected by a remote control housing and shift rod to the gearbox selector shaft and relay lever.

The final drive (differential) unit is integral with the main gearbox and is located between the main casing and the bearing housing.

Drain and filler/level plugs are screwed into the main gearbox casing.

When overhauling the gearbox, due consideration should be given to the costs involved, since it is often more economical to obtain a service exchange or good secondhand gearbox rather than fit new parts to the existing gearbox.

2 Manual gearbox – removal and refitting

1   The gearbox is removed downwards so the vehicle must be raised from the ground sufficiently to withdraw the box from underneath. The ideal is to work over a pit but axle stands or similar support under the body can be arranged. However, note that you must be able to turn the wheels to disconnect the driveshafts. Do not raise it too much or you will be unable to get at the box through the opening in the engine compartment. About 24 in (60 cm) clearance is required.

2   Since the engine will be left unsupported at the rear it is necessary to make provision to take the weight of it. If you have a block and tackle or a garage crane this will be simple, but if not it is possible to make a simple support similar to that used in the VW agency. Fig. 6.1 shows a simple beam which is supported on either side of the vehicle in the channels which house the bonnet sides on the top of the wings. Alternatively the engine can be supported from underneath with blocks placed under the sump, but this method means that the car cannot be moved while the transmission is out of the car.

3   Remove the bonnet as described in Chapter 11 and place it safely out of the way.

4   Having supported the engine, disconnect the battery negative lead.

5   For the purposes of this Section the front is the engine end of the gearbox, left and right are as if you are standing at the side of the car behind the gearbox looking towards the engine.

6   Remove the left gearbox mounting complete and take it away. Drain the gearbox oil (photo).

7   On pre-November 1978 4-speed models, it is necessary to align a cut-out in the flywheel with the right-hand side driveshaft flange to provide sufficient clearance to remove the gearbox. If the gearbox has a bolt as shown in Fig. 6.3 instead of a stud and nut, it is not necessary to align the flywheel. On some 81 kW engines the right-hand side driveshaft flange has a flat on it which must be facing the flywheel in order to remove the gearbox. To align the flywheel, first remove the TDC sender unit using a spark plug box spanner. Turn the crankshaft by pulling on the drivebelt until the lug (or depression) on the flywheel appears in the TDC sender hole; the lug is at 33° BTDC and the depression at 76° BTDC.

8   Disconnect the wiring from the reversing light switch or consumption indicator switch (photo).

9   Remove the speedometer cable and plug the hole to stop the oil running out when the box is removed (photos). Undo the upper engine/gearbox bolts and remove them. Disconnect the clutch cable and tie it out of the way.

10 Remove the starter motor as described in Chapter 9.

11 Remove the earth strap (where fitted) from the gearbox.

12 Disconnect the gearchange linkage from the gearbox and completely remove the selector rod on the gearbox.

13 Remove the torque strut from the body and the engine.

14 Remove the mounting which goes from the gearbox to the main body of the car. It is on the right-hand side of the gearbox but for some reason is called the rear mounting by VW, presumably when referring to the engine and gearbox as an entity. It is best to take it right away from the rubber mounting on the gearbox.

15 Unbolt and remove the exhaust pipe bracket (where fitted).

16 Undo the socket bolts holding the left driveshaft to the gearbox flange with an Allen key and remove the CV joint from the flange. Cover the CV joint with a plastic bag and tie the shaft out of the way. Turn the roadwheels to get at each bolt in sequence, do not try to work on bolts behind the CV joint.

17 Repeat for the right-hand driveshaft. Just below this driveshaft

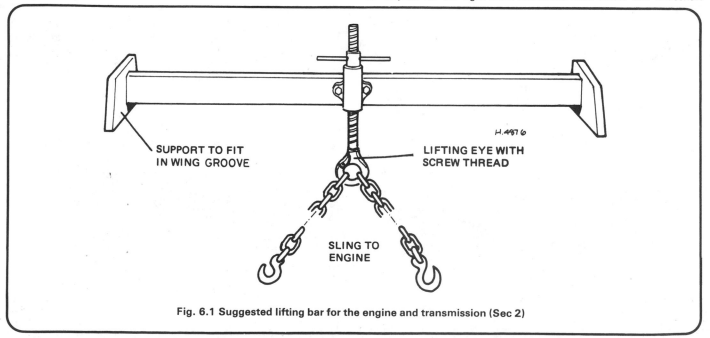

H.4876

SUPPORT TO FIT IN WING GROOVE

LIFTING EYE WITH SCREW THREAD

SLING TO ENGINE

Fig. 6.1 Suggested lifting bar for the engine and transmission (Sec 2)

2.6 Manual gearbox drain plug location

Fig. 6.4 Flywheel alignment mark for removing the gearbox (Sec 2)

Fig. 6.2 Flywheel cut-out (arrowed) on pre-November 1978 4-speed models (Sec 2)

Fig. 6.5 Reversing light switch location on models manufactured between August 1975 and April 1976 (Sec 2)

1   Bracket   2   Selector shaft lever

Fig. 6.3 Bolt location (arrowed) on models without a flywheel cut-out (Sec 2)

Fig. 6.6 Location of the consumption indicator switch (A) and selector shaft peg bolt (B) on Scirocco models from January 1981 (Sec 2)

2.8 Reversing light switch location

2.9a Removing the speedometer drive cable

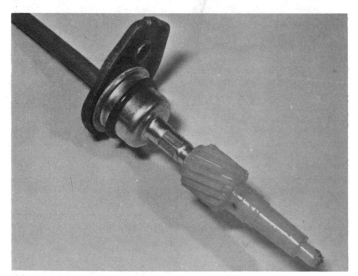

2.9b Speedometer drive cable and driven gear

2.19 Removing the gearbox from the engine, showing the cut-out in the flywheel (arrowed)

flange is a nut or bolt – remove this and then the bolts for the flywheel cover plate and the smaller cover plate on the sump.

18 Now is the time to stop and think. Check round that nothing else holds the box and assess just how it is to be lowered. Apart from the dowels the gearbox driveshaft splines are engaged in the friction disc of the clutch and the box must be pulled back to withdraw the shaft from the boss of the disc. This must be done carefully or there will be damage to the friction disc. In fact, if the box is not kept level the shaft will jam in the splines.

19 **Do not** try to separate the box from the engine by driving a wedge between the flanges, this will damage the castings. This box can be pulled backwards easily enough if it is kept level (photo). The dowels are a tight fit and when they come out of the dowel holes the weight of the box will be felt suddenly. **Do not** let the box drop at all or you will damage the gear driveshaft splines but move it away from the engine until you can see the shaft clear and then lower the box to the ground and remove it from under the car.

20 Finally the question of weight. The box can be lifted and carried by one man but easing it off the dowels and lowering it is too much for even the strongest man. To start with, his arms are not long enough. Nor will a man underneath be able to hold it up. The job requires two men. It is as well to rehearse the way to do the job. It is probably best to do it in two stages: wriggle it clear of the engine and rest it on a support or sling, get a fresh purchase and then lower it. However remember that once it is clear of the dowels it will go down of its own

accord and if allowed to fall will probably need a new gearbox case.

21 Lifting the box back into position after overhaul is much easier as you know the weight problem and can raise the box a little at a time. Make sure the joint surfaces are clean, put a little graphite or molybdenum powder (not grease) on the splines and line the box up so that the gearbox driveshaft will enter the clutch friction disc. Slide the box gently forward over the dowels, install the bolts and tighten them to the specified torque.

22 Refit the remaining items in the reverse order to removal and centralize the mountings as shown in Figs. 6.7, 6.8 and 6.9.

23 Adjust the clutch with reference to Chapter 5, and check that the gearshift mechanism operates correctly. Refill the gearbox with oil.

3 Manual gearbox overhaul – general

The overhaul of the gearbox requires a number of special tools, and adjustments are critical if the job is to be done successfully. For this reason we do not recommend that the home mechanic should attempt a complete overhaul. However, the gearbox can be dismantled and the following Sections describe the dismantling and overhaul procedures.

Overhaul of the differential unit is not considered to be within the scope of the home mechanic, since special jigs and fixtures are required for this work.

Fig. 6.7 Centralized position of the gearbox rear mounting (Sec 2)

Fig. 6.8 Centralized position of the gearbox side mounting (Sec 2)

X = X

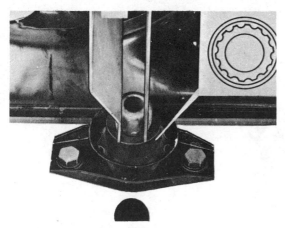

Fig. 6.9 Centralized position of the gearbox front mounting (Sec 2)

4   Manual gearbox (4-speed) – separating the housings

1   Remove the clutch pushrod. Undo the four bolts securing the gearbox end cover plate and remove the cover plate. This will give access to the clutch release mechanism. Lift out the clutch release bearing and sleeve.

2   There are two circlips one on each side of the clutch release lever (Fig. 6.10). Later models may only have one circlip. Remove these and slide the operating shaft out of the main casing, collecting the return spring and release lever as the shaft is withdrawn. Note that there is a master spline on the shaft and that the release lever will fit on the shaft in one way only.

3   Prise out the plastic cap from the centre of the left-hand side drive flange and remove the circlip and spring washer. Withdraw the flange using a suitable puller. Fig. 6.11 shows VW tool 391 being used to pull off the flange (photos). There is no need to remove the opposite driveshaft flange.

4   Remove the selector shaft detent plunger or peg bolt and the lockbolt for the reverse gear shaft (photos). Remove the reversing light switch (photo), or fuel consumption indicator switch.

5   On the side of the main casing below the clutch withdrawal shaft is the cover for the selector shaft. Using a plug spanner, remove this cover and lift off the spring seat, then remove the two detent springs. Later transmissions have only one spring (photo).

6   Withdraw the selector shaft from the main casing (photos).

7   On the end of the main casing (where the clutch withdrawal mechanism is located) are two plastic caps. Prise these out and undo the nuts underneath them. There is a third nut inside the casing from which the clutch withdrawal mechanism was removed, this must also be removed (photos). If these nuts are not removed, the mainshaft bearing cannot be pulled out of the casing and the casing will fracture if pressure is applied to draw it off.

8   Undo and remove the 14 bolts securing the two casings together. Twelve of these bolts are M8 x 50 and two are M8 x 36, note where the shorter bolts are fitted.

9   The casings are now ready for separation. Fig. 6.13 shows VW tool 391 being used. Secure the tool in the holes for the cover plate with two 7 mm bolts and then screw the centre screw down on the top of the mainshaft until it just touches. Fasten a bar or piece of angle across the bellhousing in such a manner as to support the end of the mainshaft and then continue to screw in the centre screw of the tool until the casing is pulled away, leaving the mainshaft bearing complete on the mainshaft. Lift away the main casing (photo). On top of the bearing there may be one or more shims, collect them and label them to ensure that they can be identified at reassembly. The needle bearing for the pinion shaft will remain in the main casing: it can be removed, if necessary, using a suitable extractor.

10 Recover the three clamping screws which retain the mainshaft bearing – they will drop into the gearbox as the casing is being removed. Remove the magnet from the gear carrier housing.

5   Manual gearbox (4-speed) mainshaft, pinion shaft, and differential – removal

1   Refer to Fig. 6.14. The mainshaft assembly can be removed quite easily, but the pinion shaft assembly must be partially dismantled before the pinion shaft and the differential unit can be removed.

2   Remove the two shift fork shaft circlips and withdraw the shaft from the gear carrier housing, then lift away the the shift fork set (photos).

3   Remove the circlip retaining the 4th speed gear on the pinion shaft, then lift the mainshaft out of its bearing in the gear carrier housing and at the same time remove the 4th speed gear from the pinion shaft (photo). The mainshaft needle bearing and oil seal will remain in the gear carrier housing.

4   Remove the circlip retaining the 3rd speed gear on the pinion shaft. This circlip is used to adjust the axial play of the 3rd speed gear and must be refitted in the same position, so label it for identification at reassembly. Remove the 3rd speed gear (photos).

5   Remove the 2nd speed gear and then the needle bearing from over its inner sleeve (photos).

6   To remove the rest of the gears a long hooked puller will be required. Fig. 6.16 shows VW tool 447h being used with a suitable puller (A). Before pulling off the synchro hub/sleeve and 1st speed gear remove the reverse gear by tapping the reverse gear shaft out of its seating, then lift the shaft and gear away.

7   Remove the plastic stop button from the end of the pinion shaft and fit the puller under the 1st speed gear. Note that the pinion shaft bearing retainer has two notches to accommodate the puller legs. Pull the gear and synchro hub off the shaft. Tape the synchro unit together to prevent it coming apart.

8   Remove the needle bearing and thrust washer. Note that the flat side of the washer is towards the 1st speed gear (photos).

9   Remove the four nuts or bolts securing the pinion bearing retainer and lift off the retainer. Note that the retainer incorporates the reverse gear stop on models manufactured from June 1975 – previous to this the reverse gear shaft incorporated a stop bush. The pinion shaft is

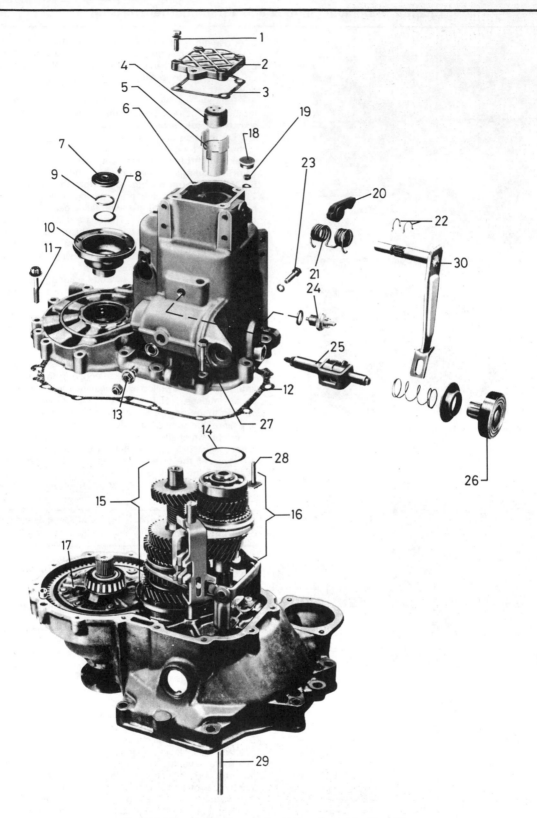

Fig. 6.10 Exploded view of the 4-speed gearbox (Sec 4)

1	Bolt	9	Circlip
2	Cover	10	Drive flange
3	Gasket	11	Bolt
4	Clutch release bearing	12	Gasket
5	Guide sleeve	13	Detent plunger
6	Main casing	14	Shim
7	Cap	15	Pinion shaft
8	Spring washer	16	Mainshaft

17	Differential		switch
18	Cap	25	Selector shaft
19	Nut	26	Selector shaft cover
20	Clutch lever	27	Transmission bolts
21	Return spring	28	Clamping screw
22	Circlips	29	Clutch pushrod
23	Bolt	30	Clutch release
24	Reversing light		shaft

Fig. 6.11 Tool for removing the drive flanges (Sec 4)

4.3a Removing a drive flange plastic cap

4.3b Drive flange showing circlip and spring washer

4.3c Using a puller to remove a drive flange

4.4a Selector shaft detent plunger location

4.4b Removing the selector shaft detent plunger

4.4c Removing the reverse gear shaft lockbolt

4.4d Removing the reversing light switch

Fig. 6.12 Using a spark plug box spanner (A) to remove the selector shaft cover (Sec 4)

4.5 Removing the selector shaft cover and spring

4.6a Removing the selector shaft

4.6b The gear selector shaft (early type)

4.7a Removing the plastic caps to expose the mainshaft bearing clamp retaining nuts

4.7b The three mainshaft bearing clamp retaining nut locations

4.9 Removing the main casing from the gear carrier housing having released the bearing with a puller

Fig. 6.13 Removing the main casing with tool VW 391 (Sec 4)

5.2a Removing a shift fork shaft circlip (arrowed)

5.2b Removing the shift fork set

Fig. 6.14 Gear carrier housing and gears on later models (Sec 5)

1 Stop
2 Circlip
3 4th gear
4 Circlip
5 3rd gear
6 Needle bearing and 2nd gear inner race
7 2nd gear
8 Bolt
9 Mainshaft
10 Shift fork set
11 Bearing plate
12 Pinion shaft
13 Differential
14 Circlips
15 Reverse selector assembly
16 Reverse gear and shaft
17 Gear carrier housing

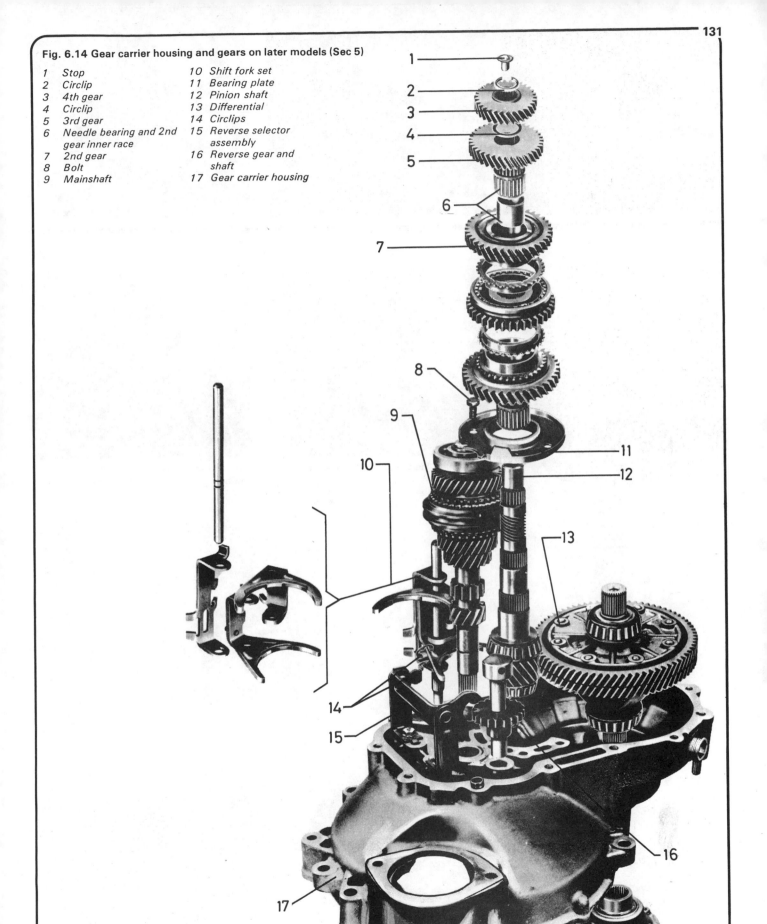

5.3 Removing the 4th speed gear retaining circlip (pinion shaft)

5.4a Removing the 3rd speed gear retaining circlip (pinion shaft)

5.4b Removing the 3rd speed gear from the pinion shaft

5.5a Removing the 2nd speed gear from the pinion shaft

5.5b 2nd speed gear needle roller bearing location

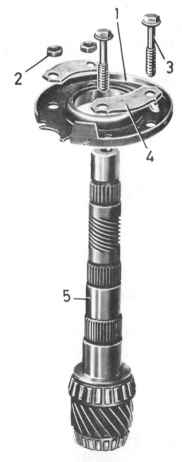

Fig. 6.15 Pinion shaft bearing plate on pre-March 1977 models (Sec 5)

1   Bearing plate
2   Nuts (fitted up to September 9th 1976)
3   Bolts (fitted from September 10th 1976)
4   Reinforcement plate
5   Pinion shaft

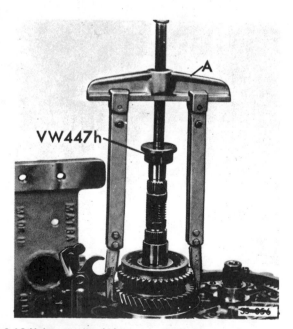

Fig. 6.16 Using a puller (A) to remove the 1st gear from the pinion shaft (Sec 5)

5.8a 1st speed gear needle roller bearing location

5.8b Removing the 1st speed gear thrust washer

5.9a Removing the pinion bearing retainer bolts

5.9b Removing the pinion bearing retainer

5.9c The pinion or output shaft

5.10 The differential unit in the gear carrier housing

6.1 Mainshaft oil seal in the gear carrier housing

6.2 Mainshaft needle bearing in the gear carrier housing

seated in a taper roller bearing, and can now be removed from the gear carrier housing (photos).

10 Remove the second drive flange as described in Section 4 paragraph 3, and then lift the differential unit out of the gear carrier housing (photo). We do not recommend trying to overhaul the differential unit, if it is in any way suspect seek advice from your VW agent.

a suitable extractor. Do not remove the bearing unless it is defective as it is likely to be damaged during removal (photo).

3   If the outer races of the differential bearings are defective then it will be necessary for the casings and the differential unit to be taken to the VW agent for servicing.

4   The starter motor shaft should be tried in the starter bush. If undue wear is apparent, remove the bush with a puller and fit a new one.

6   Manual gearbox (4-speed) – gear carrier housing – overhaul

1   Clean the housing using a grease solvent, remove all oil and sludge. Renew both the oil seals (photo). Fill the space between the lips of the seals with multi-purpose grease before fitting. The drive flange oil seal must be driven as far as it will go. The special VW tool 194 can be used, but a piece of suitable diameter steel tubing can also be used.

2   The mainshaft needle bearing may be removed, if necessary, with

7   Manual gearbox (4-speed) main casing – overhaul

1   There are three oil seals to renew: one for the clutch operating lever, one for the selector shaft, and a large one for the drive flange. In each case prise out the old seal, noting which way round it is fitted. Fill the seal lips with multi-purpose grease and drive the seals squarely into the housing using a suitable mandrel or piece of tubing (photos).

2   On early models the needle bearing for the pinion shaft is difficult to extract unless the correct extractor is available (see Fig. 6.19).

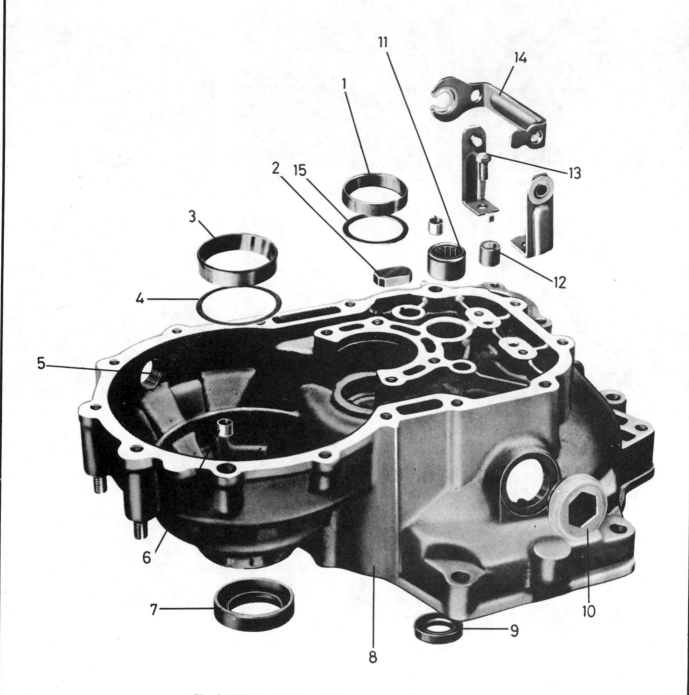

Fig. 6.17 Exploded view of the gear carrier housing (Sec 6)

1	Pinion bearing outer race	4	Shim
2	Magnet	5	Drain plug location
3	Differential bearing outer race	6	Dowel sleeve
		7	Drive flange oil seal
		8	Bearing housing

1 Pinion bearing outer
   race
2 Magnet
3 Differential bearing
   outer race

4 Shim
5 Drain plug location
6 Dowel sleeve
7 Drive flange oil seal
8 Bearing housing

9   Mainshaft oil seal
10 TDC sender unit (early
    models)
11 Mainshaft needle
    bearing

12 Starter bush
13 Bolt
14 Reverse shift fork
15 Shim

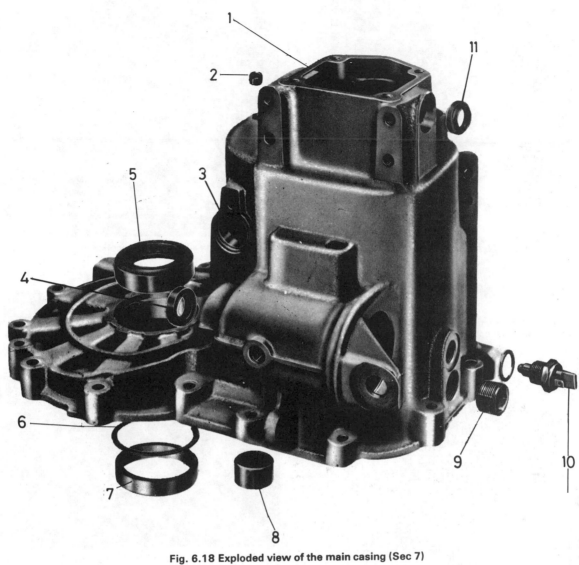

Fig. 6.18 Exploded view of the main casing (Sec 7)

1 Gear carrier housing
2 Oil level plug
3 Speedometer drive aperture
4 Selector shaft oil seal
5 Drive flange oil seal
6 Shim
7 Differential bearing outer race
8 Pinion shaft needle bearing
9 Oil filler plug
10 Reversing light switch
11 Clutch operating lever oil seal

7.1a Clutch operating lever oil seal

7.1b Selector shaft oil seal

7.1c Drive flange oil seal location in the main casing

Fig. 6.19 Using an extractor (A) to remove the pinion shaft needle bearing from the main casing on early models (Sec 7)

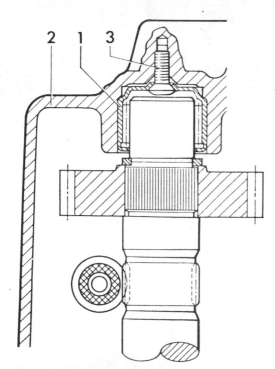

Fig. 6.20 Cross-section of the pinion shaft needle bearing on later models (Sec 7)

1 Needle bearing	*3 Self-tapping screw*
2 Main casing	

However the shaft may be tried in the bearing without having to remove the bearing (photo). On later models the bearing is retained with a self-tapping screw.
3   If the outer race of the final drive bearing is renewed, the complete unit must be taken to the VW agent for setting up with the correct shims (photo).

7.2 Pinion shaft needle bearing location in the main casing

7.3 Differential bearing outer race location in the main casing

8   Manual gearbox (4-speed) pinion shaft bearings – renewal

1   The large and small bearings accurately locate the pinion shaft gear with the crownwheel of the differential. If either bearing is defective then both must be renewed. In the removal process the bearings are destroyed. New ones have to be shrunk on and the shim under the smaller bearing changed for one of the correct size.
2   This operation is quite complicated and requires special equipment for preloading of the shaft and measurement of the torque required to rotate the new bearings. In addition the shim at the top of the mainshaft and the axial play at the circlip of the 3rd speed gear on the pinion shaft will be affected. This will mean selection of a new shim and circlip. There are six different thicknesses of circlip. Therefore it is recommended that if these bearings require renewal, the work should be left to your VW agent.

9   Manual gearbox (4-speed) mainshaft – dismantling and reassembly

1   Refer to Fig. 6.21. Remove the ball-bearing retaining circlip and then, supporting the bearing under the inner race, press the shaft out of the inner race. VW tool 402 can be used to remove the bearing but

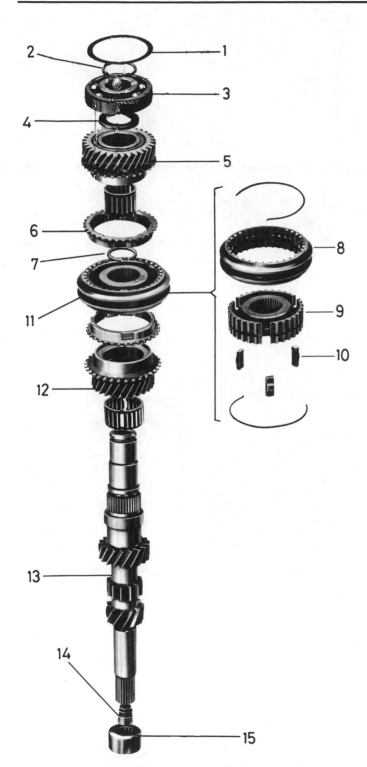

9.2a Removing 4th speed gear from the mainshaft

9.2b Removing 4th speed gear needle roller bearing

a suitable tool can be made from a piece of steel. At assembly the bearing is pressed into the gear carrier housing and the shaft pressed into the race.

2   Remove the 4th speed gear and the needle bearing together with the synchro ring (photos). On early models a thrust washer is also fitted, and the 4th speed gear and washer must be pressed off the shaft.

3   Remove the circlip, then support the 3rd speed gear and press the mainshaft through the 3rd/4th synchro hub. Tape the synchro unit together to prevent it coming apart.

4   Remove the needle bearing to complete the dismantling of the shaft (photos).

5   Should the clutch pushrod be loose in the mainshaft, the bush may be driven out of the end of the shaft and a new bush and oil seal fitted. Note that a modified seal and bush was fitted as from October 1977 (see Fig. 6.22); the original bush and seal must be installed flush but the modified seal must be inserted 0.8 to 1.3 mm (0.031 to 0.051 in) from the end of the shaft. If the shaft is to be renewed then the tolerances will be affected and this means going back to the agent with his special tools and gauges. The problem is the play between the 2nd speed gear on the pinion shaft and 3rd speed gear on the mainshaft when both shafts are fitted. This must be 1.0 mm (0.040 in). Adjusting this also requires a new shim on the top of the ball-bearing between the bearing and the gear carrier housing.

6   If gears on either shaft are to be renewed then the mating gear on

Fig. 6.21 The mainshaft components (Sec 9)

1	Shim	9	Hub
2	Circlip	10	Sliding key
3	Ball-bearing	11	3rd/4th synchronizer
4	Thrust washer (only up to June 1975)	12	3rd speed gear
5	4th speed gear	13	Mainshaft
6	4th gear baulk ring	14	Clutch pushrod bush and seal
7	Circlip	15	Needle bearing
8	Sleeve		

9.4a 3rd speed gear needle roller bearing location on the mainshaft

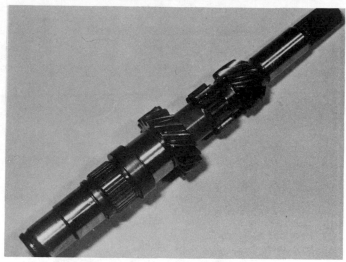

9.4b The mainshaft completely dismantled

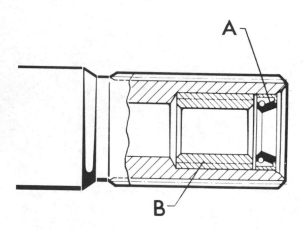

Fig. 6.22 Modified clutch pushrod seal (A) and bush (B) (Sec 9)

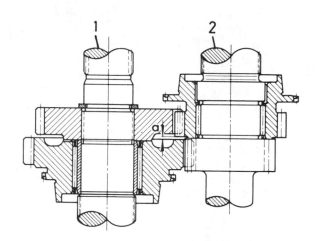

Fig. 6.23 Clearance between 2nd and 3rd speed gears (Sec 9)

| 1 | Pinion shaft | a = 1.0 mm (0.040 in) |
| 2 | Mainshaft | |

the other shaft must be renewed as well. They are supplied in pairs only.

7   The inspection of the synchro units is dealt with in Section 10.

8   When reassembling the mainshaft, lightly oil all the parts.

9   Fit the 3rd speed gear needle bearing and the 3rd speed gear. Press on the 3rd/4th gear synchro hub and fit the retaining circlip. When pressing on the synchro hub and sleeve, turn the rings so that the keys and grooves line up. The chamfer on the inner splines of the hub must face 3rd gear (photos).

10 On early transmissions fit the thrust washer and 4th speed gear. Later transmissions have a ball-bearing with a wider inner race and the thrust washer is not fitted. If the old type bearing is being replaced with a new type, the 4th gear thrust washer must be left out.

11 The mainshaft ball-bearing should now be pressed into the main casing. Ensure that the same shim(s) removed at dismantling are refitted between the bearing and the casing. The bearing is fitted with the closed side of the ball-bearing cage towards the 4th speed gear. Insert the clamping screws and tighten the clamping screw nuts to the specified torque (photos).

Note: *The endplay will have to be adjusted if either of the bearings, the thrust washer or mainshaft have been renewed, so the help of a VW agent with the necessary special tools and gauges will be required.*

---

10 Manual gearbox (4-speed) synchroniser units – inspection

1   The synchroniser unit hubs and sleeves are supplied as a matched set and must not be interchanged. Before dismantling the units, mark the sleeve and hub in relation to each other.

2   When renewing the synchro baulk rings it is advisable to fit new sliding keys and retaining springs.

3   When examining the units for wear, there are two important features to check:

(a) *The fit of the splines. With the keys removed, the hub and sleeve should slide easily with minimum backlash or axial rock. The degree of permissible wear is difficult to specify, no movement at all is exceptional, yet excessive movement will affect operation and result in jumping out of gear. If in doubt consult your VW agent*

(b) *Selector fork grooves and selector forks should not exceed the maximum permissible clearance of 0.012 in (0.3 mm). The wear can be either on the fork or in the groove, so try a new fork in the existing sleeve groove first to see if the clearance is reduced considerably. If not then a new synchro assembly is needed.*

4   The fit of the synchro ring on the gear is also important. Press the ring onto the gear and check the gap with feeler gauges. Refer to Fig. 6.25, the dimension (a) must not be less than 0.5 mm (0.020 in).

5   When installing the springs they must be curved in opposite directions and inserted in different sliding keys.

9.9a Fitting 3rd speed gear to the mainshaft

9.9b 3rd speed gear baulk ring located on the gear

9.9c Fitting the 3rd/4th synchro assembly to the mainshaft

9.9d 3rd/4th synchro hub retaining circlip fitted on the mainshaft

9.11a Fitting the mainshaft ball-bearing into the main casing

9.11b Mainshaft ball-bearing outer race clamp locations

Fig. 6.24 Synchro hub and sleeve alignment mark (arrowed) (Sec 10)

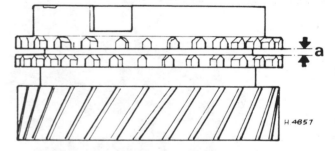

Fig. 6.25 Checking synchro baulk rings (Sec 10)

'a' must not be less than 0.5 mm (0.020 in)

if only the crownwheel is damaged. It is worth asking, but most likely you will need a replacement differential.

11 Manual gearbox (4-speed) differential unit – inspection

1   A faulty differential will cause a lot of noise while the car is in motion. However, it may go a long way making a noise without getting any worse. If you decide it needs renewing then renew it as a unit.
2   There are several problems. If a new differential is fitted then a new crownwheel to an old shaft is inviting noise. It may be possible for the agent to build the old differential if only the taper bearings are at fault, and he may be able to fit a new crownwheel to your differential

12 Manual gearbox (4-speed) differential, pinion shaft and mainshaft – reassembly

1   Refit the differential unit in the gear carrier housing. Using tool VW 391, fit the drive flange to the gear carrier housing and fit the spring washer, retaining circlip and cap.
2   Check that the mainshaft ball-bearing is correctly fitted in the main casing, plastic cage towards the casing, and that the bearing clamp bolt nuts are tight.
3   Fit the pinion shaft complete with its taper bearings into the gear carrier housing, so that the pinion gear meshes with the crownwheel (photo).
4   Fit the bearing retaining plate and the four securing bolts (photo). Fit the 1st speed gear thrust washer with its flat side up (towards the 1st gear). Fit the needle roller cage.
5   Slide the 1st speed gear over the needle bearing. Warm the

12.3 Fitting the pinion shaft into the gear carrier housing

12.4 Tightening the pinion shaft bearing retaining plate bolts

12.5a Fitting 1st speed gear to the pinion shaft

12.5b 1st speed gear baulk ring located on the gear

12.5c Aligning the baulk ring slots with the sliding keys in the 1st/2nd synchro assembly

12.5d Fitting the 1st/2nd synchro assembly to the pinion shaft

12.5e Using a metal tube to drive the 1st/2nd synchro assembly onto the pinion shaft

synchro hub a little and press it into position. The hub will slide on if heated to 120°C (250°F) and it can then be tapped into position. Make sure that the cut-outs are in line with the shift keys in the 1st/2nd synchro to avoid damage to the baulk ring on reassembly. The shift fork groove in the operating sleeve should be nearer 2nd gear and the groove on the hub nearer 1st gear (photos). Fit the 2nd gear synchro baulk ring.

6   The inner race for the 2nd speed gear needle bearing must be fitted next and pressed down as far as it will go.

7   Fit the reverse idler gear and shaft with the shaft aligned as shown in Fig. 6.26. Use a plastic hammer to drive the shaft into the casing. Check that the stop bush is positioned as shown in Fig. 6.27 on early models.

8   Fit the 2nd speed gear needle bearing on the pinion shaft and the 2nd gear with the shoulder downwards.

9   Warm the 3rd speed gear and press it down over the splines with the collar thrust face towards the 2nd gear.

10   Fit the 3rd gear retaining circlip and using feeler gauges measure

the play between the gear and the circlip. It must be less than 0.008 in (0.20 mm). If it is more, a thicker circlip must be fitted. The following table gives the sizes available:

Part no	Thickness (mm)	Thickness (in)	Colour
020 311 381	2.5	0.098	brown
020 311 381 A	2.6	0.102	black
020 311 381 B	2.7	0.106	bright
020 311 381 C	2.8	0.110	copper
020 311 381 D	2.9	0.114	brass
020 311 381 E	3.0	0.118	blue

11   At this stage the mainshaft must be fitted in position on the gear carrier housing. Slide it into the needle bearing in the casing and fit the shift forks in the operating sleeves. Insert the retaining circlips. Fit the reverse gear shift fork (photos).

12   Fit the 4th speed gear and its retaining circlip on the pinion shaft. Finally inspect the stop button (where fitted) for the pinion shaft

Fig. 6.26 Reverse idler gear shaft alignment (Sec 12)

X = X

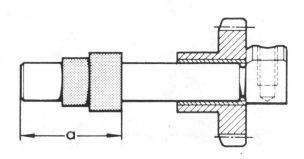

Fig. 6.27 Reverse idler gear stop bush position (Sec 12)

a = 41 mm (1.61 in)

needle bearing in the end of the pinion shaft.

13 The gear carrier housing and shafts are now ready for the assembly of the main casing (photo).

13 Manual gearbox (4-speed) – reassembling the housings

1   Check that the reverse gear shaft is in the correct position (see Fig. 6.26) and set the geartrain in neutral. Fit a new gasket on the gear carrier housing flange.

2   Lower the main casing over the gears, checking that the pinion shaft is aligned with the pinion shaft needle bearing in the casing. Drive the mainshaft into its bearing, using a suitable mandrel on the inner race. A piece of suitable diameter steel tube can be used. Ensure that the mainshaft is supported on a block of wood when driving the mainshaft into the bearing.

3   Insert the 14 bolts which secure the two housings together and tighten them to the specified torque.

12.11a Fitting the mainshaft assembly to the gear carrier housing

12.11b Fitting the shift forks ...

12.11c ... and shift fork shaft

12.11d Fitting the reverse shift fork pivot posts

12.11e Reverse shift fork assembly

12.11f Reverse shift fork location on reverse idler gear

12.13 Gear carrier housing assembly ready for fitting of the main casing

13.4a Fitting the bearing retaining circlips to the mainshaft

13.4b Inserting the clutch pushrod into the mainshaft

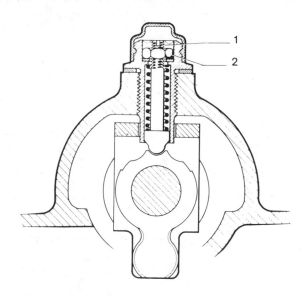

Fig. 6.28 Selector shaft detent plunger for models up to December 1974 (Sec 13)

1   Slotted screw   2   Nut

4   Fit the circlip over the end of the mainshaft, working through the release bearing hole. Insert the clutch pushrod into the mainshaft. Ensure that the circlip is properly seated, then fit the clutch release bearing and sleeve assembly (photos).
5   Fit the clutch release shaft and lever. Ensure that the spring is hooked over the lever in the centre and that the angled ends rest against the casing. The shaft can be inserted in the lever in one position only. Fit the two circlips, one each side of the lever.
6   Fit the clutch release sleeve and bearing.
7   Position a new gasket on the end of the casing and fit the end cover plate and four securing screws. Tighten the screws to the specified torque.
8   Lubricate the selector shaft and insert it into the casing. When it is in position, fit the spring(s) and screw in the shaft cover with a plug box spanner, tightening it to the specified torque.
9   Fit the selector shaft detent plunger (or peg bolt). This has a plastic cap. Only if the housing, selector shaft or plunger are faulty and new ones are required should the plunger need adjusting. If necessary, adjust as follows with neutral engaged:

Models up to December 1974 (side pressure system)
(a)   *Refer to Fig. 6.28. Turn the slotted screw until it contacts the plunger, at which point the nut will commence to move out*
(b)   *Unscrew the slotted screw $\frac{1}{4}$ of a turn, then refit the plastic cap*

Models from January to August 1975 (side pressure system)
(a)   *Refer to Fig. 6.29. Loosen the locknut and screw in the retaining screw*

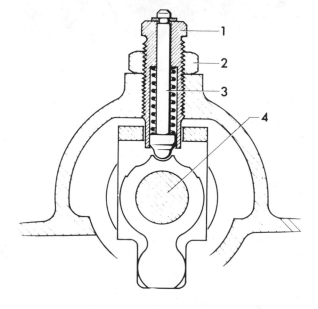

Fig. 6.29 Selector shaft detent plunger for models from January to August 1975 (Sec 13)

1   Retaining screw   3   Plunger
2   Locknut   4   Selector shaft

(b)   *Push in the selector shaft until it contacts the reverse gear catch, then turn out the screw slowly until the selector shaft springs out*
(c)   *Turn out the screw a further $\frac{1}{4}$ of a turn and tighten the locknut*

Models from September 1975 (except Scirocco models from January 1981, which have no adjustment)
(a)   *Refer to Fig. 6.30. Slacken the locknut and screw in the adjusting sleeve until the lockring lifts off the adjusting sleeve*
(b)   *Screw the adjusting sleeve out until the lockring just contacts the sleeve*
(c)   *Check that the lockring lifts as soon as the shaft is turned. Tighten the locknut and fit the plastic cap*

10   Fit the reverse gear shaft lockbolt and the reversing light switch, or fuel consumption indicator switch.

---

14   Manual gearbox (4-speed) gearshift linkage – adjustment

Side pressure system (up to November 1974)
1   Engage neutral and check that the lower part of the gearstick is vertical. If not, loosen the gearstick upper plate bolts and reposition the plate until the gearstick is positioned correctly.
2   Refer to Fig. 6.32 and 6.31 and adjust the selector rod and

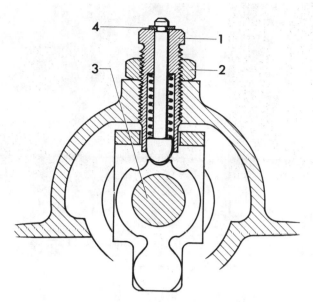

Fig. 6.30 Selector shaft detent plunger for models from September 1975 (except Scirocco from January 1981) (Sec 13)

1 Retaining screw 3 Selector shaft
2 Locknut   4 Lockring

bearing rod to the dimensions given.

3   If the gearshift function is still incorrect, adjust the selector shaft as described in Section 13.

4   Engage 1st gear and check that the gearstick is vertical when viewed from behind. If not, loosen the nuts securing the bearing plate

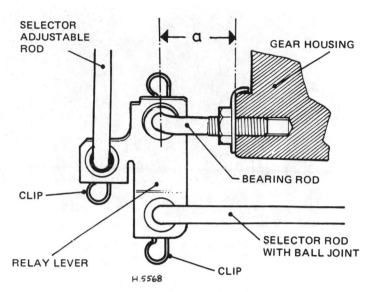

Fig. 6.31 Bearing rod adjustment dimension (Sec 14)

a = 30 to 32 mm (1.18 to 1.26 in)

(see Fig. 6.36) and move the plate within the elongated holes as necessary.

Side pressure system (from December 1974 to August 1975)

5   Carry out the adjustments described in paragraphs 1, 3 and 4. The selector rod and bearing rod are not adjustable.

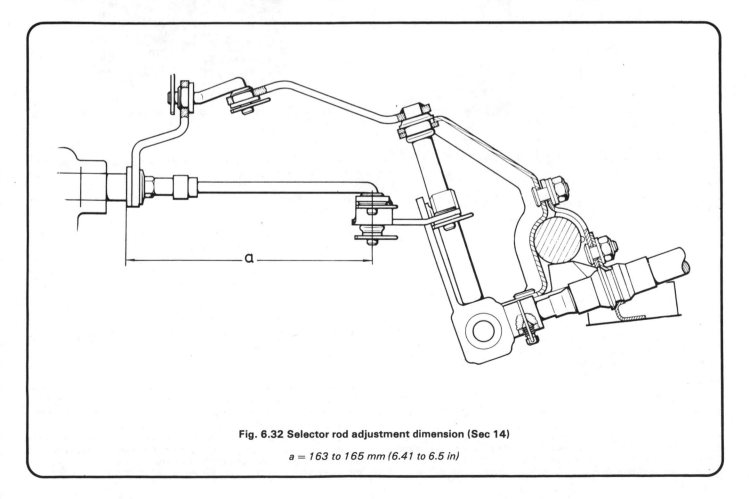

Fig. 6.32 Selector rod adjustment dimension (Sec 14)

a = 163 to 165 mm (6.41 to 6.5 in)

Fig. 6.33 Gear lever housing cover. Arrows show alignment holes
– for A and B see text (Sec 14)

14.7 Gearchange shift rod clamp bolt location (arrowed)

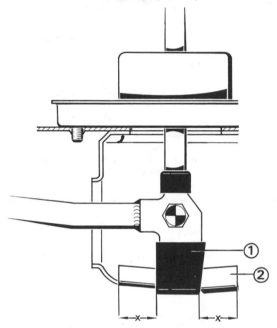

Fig. 6.34 Gearshift finger (1) and stop plate (2) (Sec 14)

$X = X$

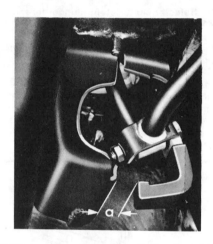

Fig. 6.35 Gearshift rod adjusting dimension (a) (Sec 14)

Downward pressure system (from September 1975)

6   With the gearstick in neutral, align the holes in the lever housing cover plate with the holes in the bearing plate, A in Fig. 6.33, and check that the threaded holes B are in the middle of the slots. If they are not, turn the bearing plate through 180°. Tighten the lever bearing.
7   Slacken the shift rod clamp bolt (photo) to permit the selector lever to move on the shift rod. Pull the boot off the lever housing and push it back out of the way.
8   Refer to Fig. 6.34. Ensure that the shift finger is in the centre of the stop plate and that dimension X is the same on both sides.
9   Now adjust the shift rod so that dimension A in Fig. 6.35 is 0.75 in (20 mm), then tighten the clamp bolt.
10 Check the operation of the gearshift linkage by selecting each gear in turn. If the linkage is spongy or binding check the adjustment of the selector shaft detent plunger; refer to Section 13.

15 Manual gearbox (4-speed) gearchange lever and linkage – removal and refitting

1   Unscrew the gearchange lever knob. Release the rubber gaiter from the gear lever housing and pull it off the lever.
2   Release the boot from under the lever housing, slide it forward on the shift rod and remove the pivot bolt securing the shift rod to the gearchange lever (photo).
3   On the side pressure system, unbolt and remove the gear lever upper plate. Note that the front bolt hole is shaped to point forward. The gear lever can now be removed upward.
4   On the downward pressure system, unbolt and remove the lever bearing bolts, then remove the gear lever and bearing followed by the spacer. If necessary the bearing components can be removed from the lever bearing plate.
5   To remove the linkage refer to Figs. 6.36, 6.37 or 6.38. Note that the 90° end of the upper link locates in the relay shaft. When disconnecting the front and rear selector rods on the downward pressure system, prise back the ends of the plastic clips before pulling the rods off the selector and relay levers (photos).
6   Refitting is a reversal of removal, but lubricate all friction surfaces with molybdenum disulphide grease.
7   Adjust the linkage as described in Section 14.
8   On the side pressure system secure the selector lever square-headed bolt with locking fluid, and make sure that the gear lever upper bearing shell locates correctly in the lower shell.
9   If jumping out of third or fourth gear is experienced on the downward pressure system, fit a relay lever with a cut-out as shown in Fig. 6.38.
10 To assemble the gear lever bearing on the downward pressure system, locate the shells in the rubber guide, press the lower bearing half into the shells followed by the spring and upper bearing half, then push the rubber guide into the lever plate.

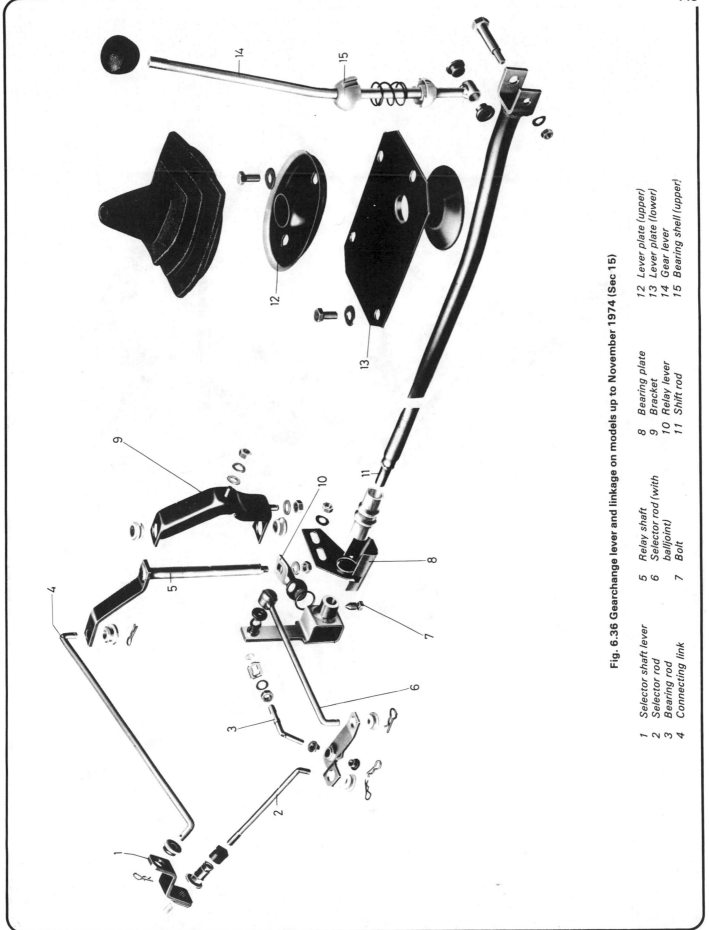

Fig. 6.36 Gearchange lever and linkage on models up to November 1974 (Sec 15)

1 Selector shaft lever
2 Selector rod
3 Bearing rod
4 Connecting link

5 Relay shaft
6 Selector rod (with balljoint)
7 Bolt

8 Bearing plate
9 Bracket
10 Relay lever
11 Shift rod

12 Lever plate (upper)
13 Lever plate (lower)
14 Gear lever
15 Bearing shell (upper)

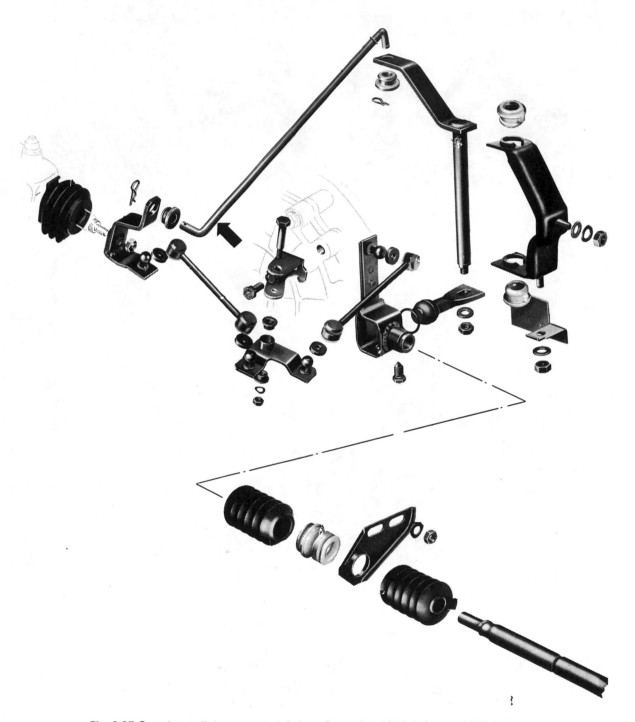

Fig. 6.37 Gearchange linkage on models from December 1974 to August 1975 (Sec 15)

Arrow indicates 95° end of link – other end is 90°

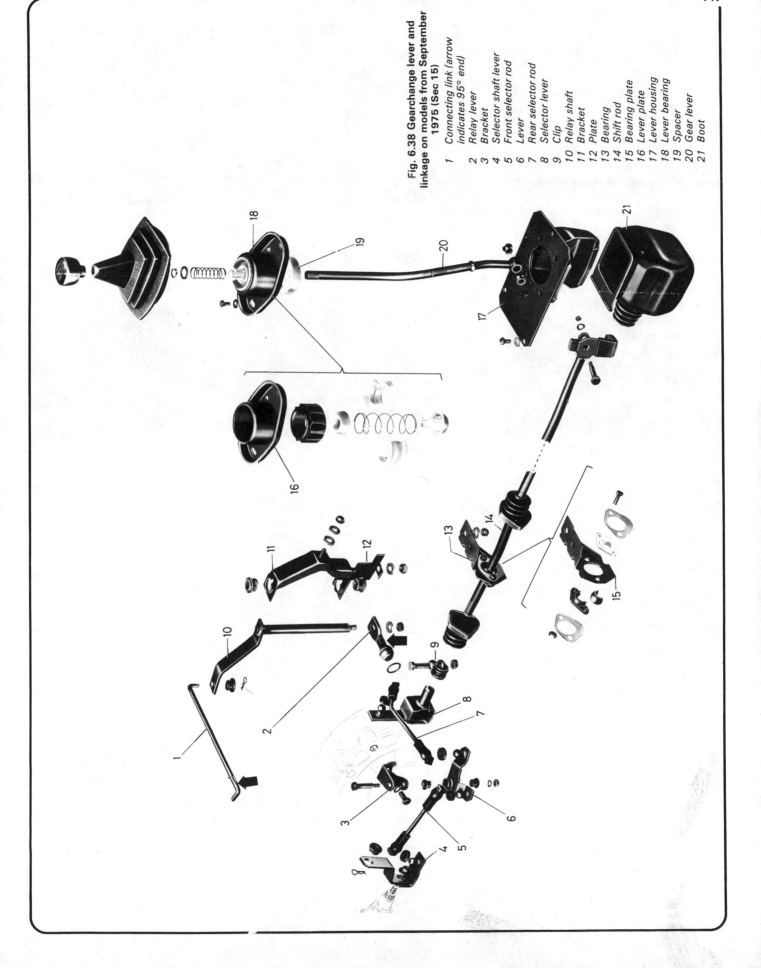

Fig. 6.38 Gearchange lever and linkage on models from September 1975 (Sec 15)

1 Connecting link (arrow indicates 95° end)
2 Relay lever
3 Bracket
4 Selector shaft lever
5 Front selector rod
6 Lever
7 Rear selector rod
8 Selector lever
9 Clip
10 Relay shaft
11 Bracket
12 Plate
13 Bearing
14 Shift rod
15 Bearing plate
16 Lever plate
17 Lever housing
18 Lever bearing
19 Spacer
20 Gear lever
21 Boot

15.2 Gear lever boot location

15.5a Removing the gearchange linkage crank pivot bolt

15.5b Removing the gearchange linkage crank and bushes

15.5c Removing the gearchange linkage crank bracket

15.5d The gearchange relay shaft location

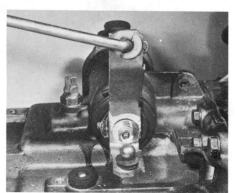

15.5e Selector shaft lever location

16 Manual gearbox (5-speed) – separating the housings

1   Remove the clutch pushrod from the mainshaft.
2   Unbolt and remove the end cover from the main casing. Remove the gasket.
3   Remove the selector shaft detent plunger or peg bolt, the 5th gear retaining screw, and the reversing light switch or fuel consumption indicator switch.
4   Using a spark plug spanner, unscrew the selector shaft and cap and remove the spring.
5   Engage neutral and withdraw the selector shaft. If difficulty is experienced, extract the circlip and drive out the shaft. However, this may cause damage to the shaft components.
6   Unscrew the reverse gear shaft lockbolt.
7   Prise the plastic cap from the centre of the left-hand side drive flanges, remove the circlip and washer, and withdraw the flanges with a suitable puller.
8   Engage 5th and reverse gears by removing the selector forks, then unscrew the 5th gear synchronizer retaining nut using a 12 mm Allen key. The bolt is very tight and an assistant will be required to hold the main casing.
9   Engage neutral, then unscrew the sleeve or prise out the locking plate from the end of the shift fork rod.
10 Unscrew the selector tube anti-clockwise from the 5th gear selector fork, but do not remove the selector rod.
11 Withdraw the 5th gear together with the synchronizer and selector fork from the mainshaft.
12 Extract the circlip from the end of the pinion shaft, then remove the 5th gear with a suitable puller.
13 Using a 5 mm Allen key, unscrew the bolts securing the mainshaft bearing retaining plate.
14 Unscrew the bolts attaching the main casing to the gear carrier housing, then use a puller to draw the main casing from the mainshaft bearing. (Refer to Section 4 paragraph 9 for alternative methods of removing the main casing). Recover the shim located against the bearing outer track. Remove the gasket and the magnet from the gear carrier housing.

17 Manual gearbox (5-speed) mainshaft, pinion shaft and differential – removal

1   Pull the selector fork rod from the gear carrier housing and withdraw the fork set sideways.
2   Extract the circlip from the end of the pinion shaft, then remove the mainshaft assembly from the gear carrier housing while removing the 4th gear from the pinion shaft.
3   Extract the remaining circlip from the pinion shaft and remove 3rd gear, 2nd gear, 2nd synchro ring and the needle bearing, using a puller if necessary.
4   Remove the reverse gear and shaft from the gear carrier housing.
5   Using a suitable puller, remove the 1st gear and 1st/2nd synchronizer from the pinion shaft, together with the 2nd gear needle bearing inner race. Remove the 1st gear needle bearing and thrust washer.
6   Unbolt the bearing retaining plate and remove the pinion shaft from the gear carrier housing. Note that the retaining plate incorporates the reverse gear stop which locates beneath the reverse gear.
7   Remove the remaining drive flange as described in Section 16, paragraph 7, then lift out the differential unit. Overhaul of the differential unit is best entrusted to a VW agent and should not be attempted by the home mechanic.

18 Manual gearbox (5-speed) housings – overhaul

1   The procedure is identical to that described in Sections 6 and 7, except that the end cover retaining the clutch release components is separate from the main casing.
2   To remove the clutch release components refer to Chapter 5.

19 Manual gearbox (5-speed) pinion shaft bearings – renewal

Refer to Section 8.

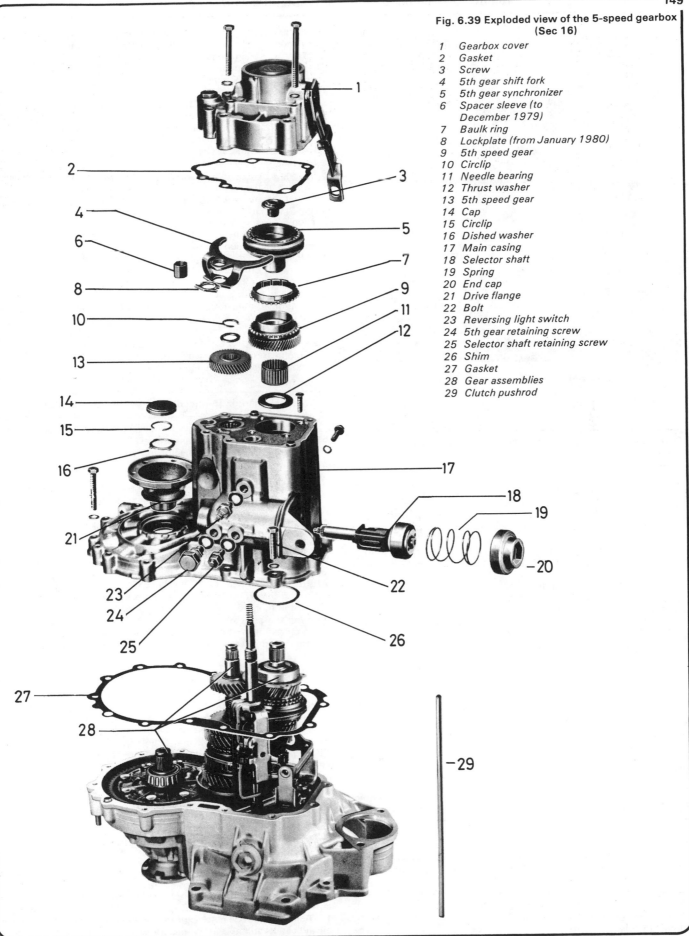

Fig. 6.39 Exploded view of the 5-speed gearbox (Sec 16)

1 Gearbox cover
2 Gasket
3 Screw
4 5th gear shift fork
5 5th gear synchronizer
6 Spacer sleeve (to December 1979)
7 Baulk ring
8 Lockplate (from January 1980)
9 5th speed gear
10 Circlip
11 Needle bearing
12 Thrust washer
13 5th speed gear
14 Cap
15 Circlip
16 Dished washer
17 Main casing
18 Selector shaft
19 Spring
20 End cap
21 Drive flange
22 Bolt
23 Reversing light switch
24 5th gear retaining screw
25 Selector shaft retaining screw
26 Shim
27 Gasket
28 Gear assemblies
29 Clutch pushrod

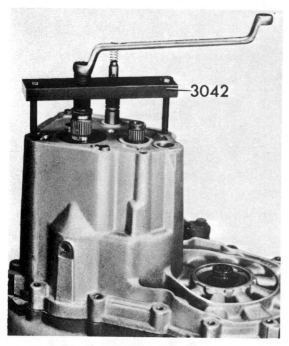

Fig. 6.40 Removing the main casing (Sec 16)

20 Manual gearbox (5-speed) mainshaft – dismantling and reassembly

1   Remove the 5th gear needle bearing and thrust washer.
2   Using a suitable puller, withdraw the ball-bearing from the mainshaft. On pre-May 1979 models the bearing inner race will remain on the shaft and must be removed with the 4th gear.
3   Remove the clamping plate, 4th gear and needle bearing, and 4th synchro ring.
4   Follow the procedure given in Section 9, paragraphs 3 to 9 inclusive, but disregarding the reference to 2nd and 3rd gear clearance.
5   Fit the 4th synchro ring, the needle bearing, and the 4th gear.
6   On pre-1979 models, press the mainshaft bearing inner race onto the mainshaft next to the 4th gear.
7   Locate the shim in the main casing, then press in the bearing with the inner race wide shoulder facing 4th gear (as applicable).
8   Fit the clamping plate to the main casing and tighten the bolts to the specified torque using a 5 mm Allen key.
9   Note that there is no adjustment for the mainshaft endfloat and that the bearing shim remains constant.

21 Manual gearbox (5-speed) synchroniser units – inspection

1   Refer to Section 10.
2   When assembling the 5th gear synchronizer, make sure that the longer ends of the sliding keys face the synchro ring.

22 Manual gearbox (5-speed) differential unit – inspection

Refer to Section 11.

23 Manual gearbox (5-speed) differential, pinion shaft and mainshaft – assembly

1   Refit the differential unit in the gear carrier housing.
2   Fit the right-hand drive flange followed by the spring washer, retaining circlip, and cap.

3   Fit the pinion shaft complete with taper bearings into the gear carrier housing and mesh it with the differential gear.
4   Fit the bearing retaining plate and tighten the bolts.
5   Locate the 1st gear thrust washer on the pinion shaft with its shoulder facing the bearing plate.
6   Fit the needle bearing and 1st gear, followed by the 1st synchro ring. Press on the 1st/2nd synchronizer, making sure that the sliding keys locate in the synchro ring cut-outs. Heat the synchronizer to 120°C (248°F) before fitting it.
7   Insert the reverse gear shaft complete with the gear into the gear carrier housing, and at the same time engage the gear with the relay lever jaw.
8   Using a metal tube, drive on the 2nd gear needle bearing inner race, then fit the needle bearing, 2nd synchro ring, and 2nd gear.
9   Heat the 3rd gear and press it on the pinion shaft with its shoulder facing 2nd gear. Fit the circlip and check the endplay as described in Section 12, paragraph 10.
10   Insert the mainshaft into the gear carrier housing and mesh the gears with the pinion shaft.
11   Heat the 4th gear and press it on the pinion shaft with its shoulder facing away from the 3rd gear. Fit the circlip.
12   Locate the selector fork rod spring in the gear carrier housing, then install the fork set. To do this engage the 1st/2nd fork in the synchro sleeve groove, then rotate the fork set around the pinion shaft and engage the 3rd/4th fork and the reverse fork with the relay lever.
13   Push the selector fork rod into the gear carrier housing, and align the slots in the forks to the neutral position.
14   The gear carrier housing and shafts are now ready for the assembly of the main casing.

24 Manual gearbox (5-speed) – reassembling the housings

1   Check that the reverse gear shaft is in the correct position (see Fig. 6.26) and set the geartrain in neutral. Make sure that the spring is located on the end of the selector fork rod.
2   Fit a new gasket on the gear carrier housing flange, and make sure that the magnet is in position.
3   Lower the main casing over the shafts and selector rod, then use metal tubing to drive the bearing inner race into the mainshaft while supporting the mainshaft on a block of wood.
4   Insert and tighten the reverse gear shaft lockbolt, then insert and tighten the bolts attaching the main casing to the gear carrier housing.
5   Check the mainshaft bearing retaining plate bolts for tightness.
6   Fit the 5th gear thrust washer on the mainshaft with the chamfer facing the bearing, followed by the needle bearing.
7   Heat the 5th gear to 100°C (212°F) and press it into the pinion shaft with the groove facing away from the main casing.
8   Fit the thrust washer and circlip to the pinion shaft.
9   With the selector fork engaged with the groove in the 5th gear synchronizer, fit the 5th gear, synchro ring, and synchronizer onto the mainshaft and selector fork extension together with the locking plate or sleeve.
10   Without displacing the selector fork rod, screw the selector tube into the fork, then screw it out until it projects by 5.0 mm (0.2 in) (see Fig. 6.45).
11   Coat the threads of the 5th gear synchronizer retaining nut with locking compound, then screw it into the mainshaft. Engage 5th and reverse gears by moving the selector forks, then tighten the nut to the specified torque using a 12 mm Allen key.
12   Engage neutral and insert the selector shaft with the gearbox on its side; insert a length of welding wire as shown in Fig. 6.46 to prevent the mechanism turning.
13   Fit the spring and tighten the selector shaft cover using a spark plug box spanner.
14   Insert and tighten the reversing light switch or fuel consumption indicator, the 5th gear retaining screw, and the selector shaft detent plunger or peg bolt.
15   Adjust the selector shaft detent plunger as described in Section 13, paragraph 9.
16   Adjust the 5th gear detent plunger as follows. With the gears in neutral remove the cap and loosen the locknut. Tighten the sleeve until the central plunger just starts to move, then loosen the sleeve $\frac{1}{3}$ of a turn and tighten the locknut.
17   Adjust the 5th gear selector fork as follows. Engage 5th gear with the aid of a lever if necessary, then press the synchronizer sleeve away

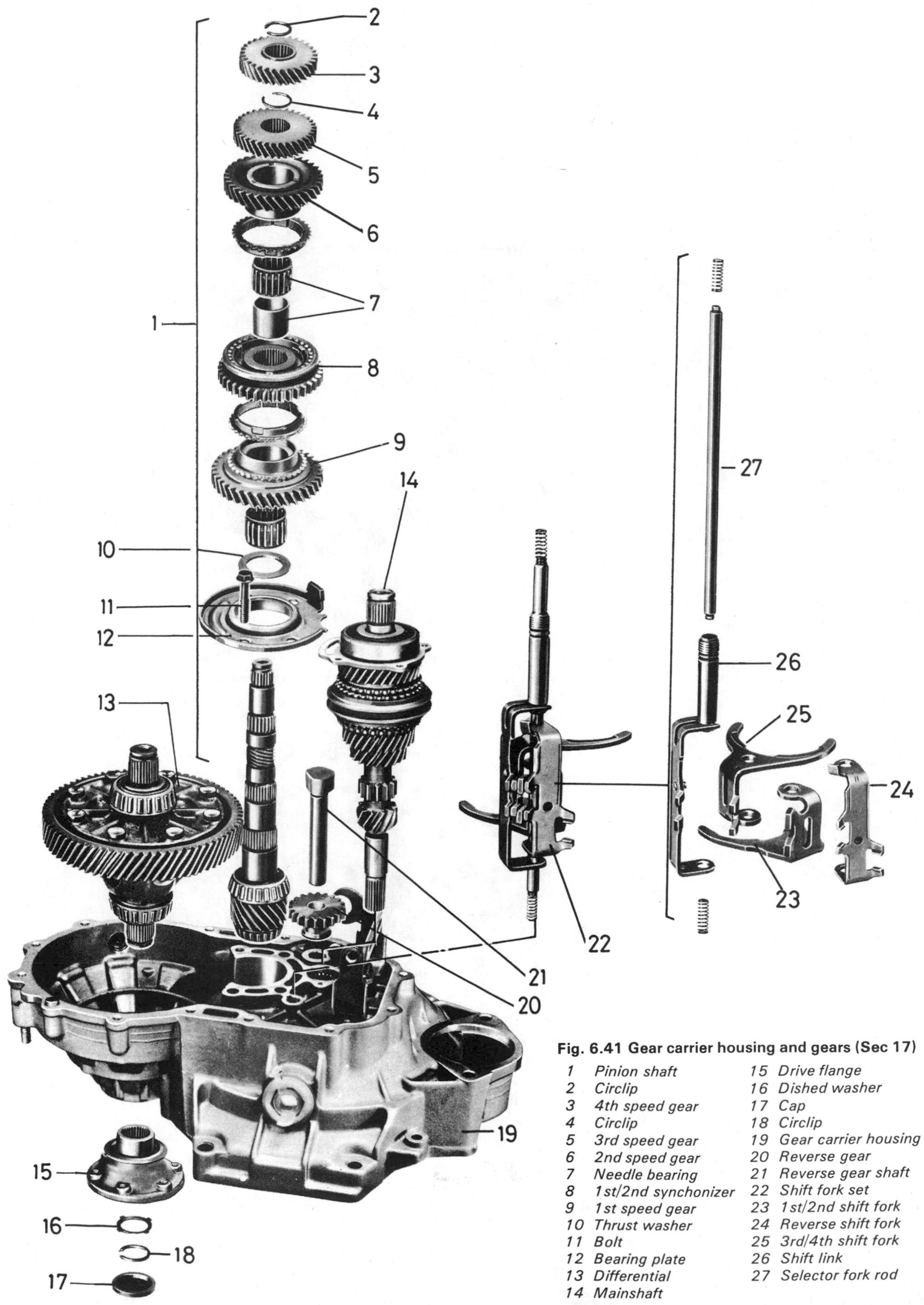

Fig. 6.41 Gear carrier housing and gears (Sec 17)

1	Pinion shaft	15	Drive flange
2	Circlip	16	Dished washer
3	4th speed gear	17	Cap
4	Circlip	18	Circlip
5	3rd speed gear	19	Gear carrier housing
6	2nd speed gear	20	Reverse gear
7	Needle bearing	21	Reverse gear shaft
8	1st/2nd synchonizer	22	Shift fork set
9	1st speed gear	23	1st/2nd shift fork
10	Thrust washer	24	Reverse shift fork
11	Bolt	25	3rd/4th shift fork
12	Bearing plate	26	Shift link
13	Differential	27	Selector fork rod
14	Mainshaft		

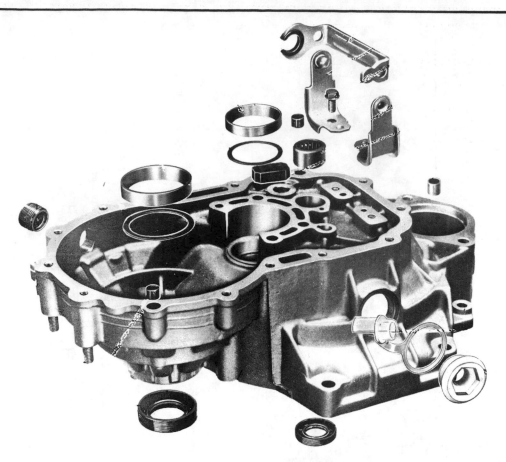

Fig. 6.42 Gear carrier housing components for 5-speed gearbox (Sec 18)

For component identification see Fig. 6.17

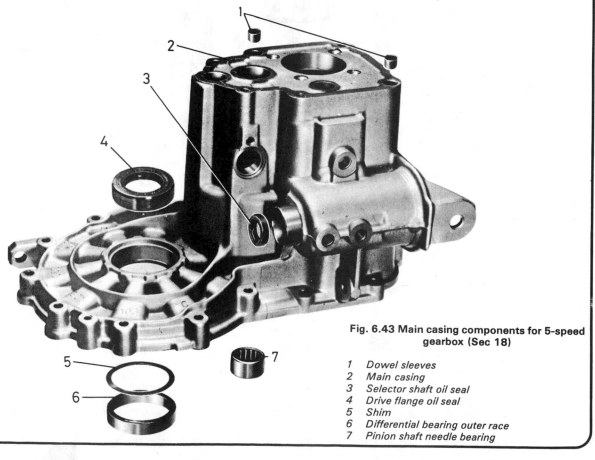

Fig. 6.43 Main casing components for 5-speed gearbox (Sec 18)

1 Dowel sleeves
2 Main casing
3 Selector shaft oil seal
4 Drive flange oil seal
5 Shim
6 Differential bearing outer race
7 Pinion shaft needle bearing

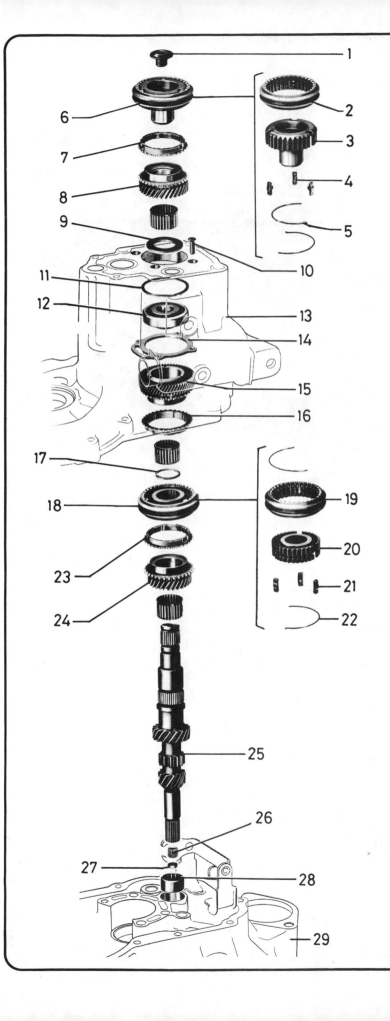

Fig. 6.44 Mainshaft components for 5-speed gearbox (Sec 20)

1   Screw
2   Sleeve
3   Hub
4   Locking key
5   Spring
6   5th gear synchonizer
7   Baulk ring
8   5th speed gear
9   Thrust washer
10 Screw
11 Shim
12 Ball-bearing
13 Main casing
14 Clamping plate
15 4th speed gear
16 Baulk ring
17 Circlip
18 3rd/4th synchronizer
19 Sleeve
20 Hub
21 Locking key
22 Spring
23 Baulk ring
24 3rd speed gear
25 Mainshaft
26 Bush
27 Seal
28 Needle bearing
29 Gear carrier housing

Fig. 6.45 Selector tube fitting dimension (X) (Sec 24)

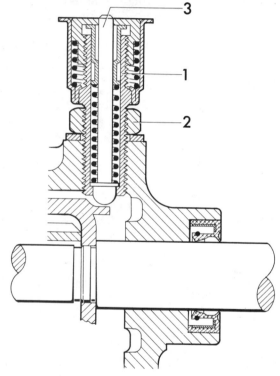

Fig. 6.47 Cross-section of 5th gear detent plunger (Sec 24)

1   Adjusting sleeve   3   Plunger
2   Locknut

from the gearbox to eliminate any play and check that the sleeve overlaps the hub by 1.0 mm (0.039 in) (see Fig. 6.48). If not, turn the selector tube as necesary.

18   Where a locking plate is fitted, clamp it in position as shown in Fig. 6.49 without tilting it. Where a sleeve is fitted, lock it by peening in two places with a blunt chisel (see Fig. 6.50), but make sure that the selector rod moves freely in the selector tube.

19   Fit the end cover to the main casing together with a new gasket and tighten the bolts.

20   Lubricate the clutch pushrod and insert it in the mainshaft.

21   Fit the left-hand drive flange followed by the spring washer, retaining circlip and cap.

25   Manual gearbox (5-speed) gearshift linkage and lever – adjustment, removal and refitting

The gearshift components fitted to the 5-speed gearbox are similar to those on the 4-speed downward pressure system. The adjustment

Fig. 6.46 Inserting the selector shaft (Sec 24)

A and arrow – welding wire

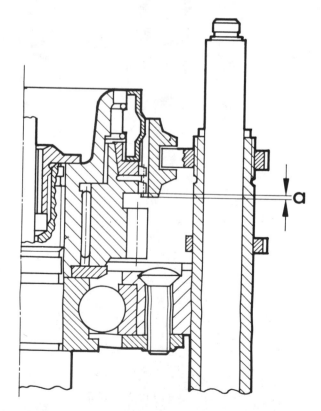

Fig. 6.48 5th gear selector fork adjustment dimension (a) (Sec 24)

procedure is given in Section 14, and the removal and refitting procedures in Section 15; however, the dimension 'a' in paragraph 9, Section 14, is 15 mm (0.6 in).

Fig. 6.49 Clamping the locking plate in position (Sec 24)

Fig. 6.50 Peening the 5th gear spacer sleeve (Sec 24)

a = 19 mm (0.75 in)

26 Automatic transmission – general description

The automatic transmission is of the 3-speed epicyclic geartrain type incorporating two multi-plate clutches, one multi-plate brake, and one brake band. A fluid filled torque converter transmits drive from the engine.

Three forward gears and one reverse are provided, with a kickdown facility for rapid acceleration during overtaking when an immediate change to a lower gear is required.

Due to the complex design of the automatic transmission, only the procedures described in the following Sections should be contemplated by the home mechanic. Further, if the unit develops a fault it should be tested by a VW agent while still in the car in order to verify the fault.

27 Automatic transmission – routine maintenance

1 At the specified intervals the automatic transmission fluid level should be checked and topped up if necessary. The check must be made with the engine warm and idling, with the selector lever in position 'N' (neutral) and the handbrake firmly applied.

2 With the car on a level surface, withdraw the dipstick and wipe it clean with a lint-free cloth. Reinsert it and withdraw it again; the level must be between the two marks on the dipstick. If not, top up the level through the dipstick tube using the specified fluid. Check for leaks if much topping-up is required.

3 Finally insert the dipstick and switch off the engine.

4 At the intervals given in Routine Maintenance the automatic transmission fluid must be renewed, and the oil pan and strainer cleaned (where applicable). Under extreme operating conditions the fluid should be changed at more frequent intervals. First jack up the car and support it on axle stands.

5 Remove the drain plug and drain the fluid into a suitable container. If there is no drain plug, loosen the oil pan front bolts, then unscrew the rear bolts and lower the pan in order to drain the fluid. Take care to avoid scalding if the engine has just been run.

6 Unbolt and remove the pan from the transmission and remove the gasket. Clean the inside of the pan.

October 1976 on models only

7 Unbolt the strainer cover and remove the strainer and gasket.

8 Clean the strainer and cover and dry thoroughly.

9 Refit the cover and strainer together with a new gasket and tighten the bolts.

All models

10 Refit the pan together with a new gasket and tighten the bolts.

11 Refill the transmission with the correct quantity of fluid. Run the engine to warm the fluid and recheck the fluid level as described in paragraphs 1 to 3.

Final drive

12 At the specified interval the automatic transmission final drive oil level should be checked. To do this, first wipe clean the area surrounding the filler/level plug.

13 Remove the filler/level plug and check the oil level, which should be up to the base of plug hole. If necessary, add oil of the specified type.

14 Refit the plug on completion.

Fig. 6.51 Automatic transmission dipstick location (Sec 27)

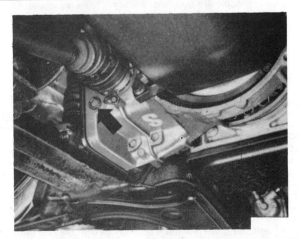

Fig 6.52 Filler/level plug on automatic transmission final drive (arrowed) (Sec 27)

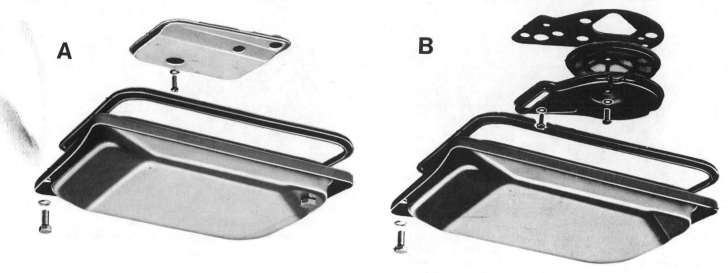

Fig. 6.53 Automatic transmission oil pan and strainer (Sec 27)

A Early models   B Later models

28 Automatic transmission – removal and refitting

1   Disconnect the battery earth strap and the starter cable from the battery. Undo the bolt holding the speedometer drive to the bellhousing and remove the speedo cable.
2   Refer to Section 2 and using a method suggested there support the engine. Ultimately the gearbox is lowered to the ground. The ideal would be to work over a pit.
3   Remove the upper engine/transmission bolts (2). Next remove the three nuts from the bracket holding the transmission to the frame of the car. This bracket must be removed while working under the car, it is on the right-hand side of the transmission if you stand at the side of the car and look over the transmission towards the engine. Sling the transmission to the support bar to take the weight.
4   Remove the transmission side carrier nut from the body. Undo the bolts and remove both driveshafts (Chapter 7).
5   Remove the starter motor (see Chapter 9). Tag the cables for easy reconnection. The third bolt is between the engine and the starter.
6   Remove the screws holding the small cover plate and the large cover plate over the driveplate.
7   Working through the hole left by the starter, locate and undo the three bolts holding the torque converter to the driveplate. These can be seen also in the gap left when the bottom cover plate is removed.
8   Set the selector lever to 'P' and disconnect the cable from the lever.
9   Remove the cable bracket and disconnect the accelerator cable and the pedal cable but do not alter the settings.
10 Now remove the side carrier from the transmission.
11 Undo the nuts and remove the torque strut from the left-hand side of the engine.
12 Remove the lower bolts securing the transmission to the engine.
13 The transmission may now be removed. Lift a little and push the LH drive shaft up and out of the way. Pull the transmission off the dowels and lower it gently, at the same time supporting the torque converter, which will fall out if not held in place in the transmission. There are two shafts and two sets of splines, be careful not to bend either of them or you will have a leaking torque converter.
14 The transmission is too heavy for one person to lift so a sling and tackle must be used. There is a convenient lifting eye on the converter housing.
15 Refitting is the reverse of removal. The pump driveshaft is inside the impeller shaft. It must be fully engaged with the pump splines, so that the converter is fully seated on the one-way clutch (Fig. 6.54). Make sure that the converter turns easily by hand.
16 Before tightening the mounting bolts check that the rear mounting is straight and that the other mountings are centralized (see Figs. 6.7, 6.8, and 6.9).
17 Adjust the selector cable, throttle cable, and pedal cable as

described in Sections 31 and 32. Refill the transmission with the correct quantity of fluid and recheck the fluid level as described in Section 27.
18 Remove the final drive filler/level plug and check that the oil level is to the bottom of the hole. If necessary top up the level with the specified oil, then refit the plug.

29 Automatic transmission – stall test

1   The stall test is used to check the performance of the torque converter and the results can also indicate certain faults in the automatic transmission.
2   Connect a tachometer to the engine, then run the engine until warm.
3   Finally apply the handbrake and footbrake, and select position 'D'.
4   Fully depress the accelerator pedal and record the engine speed, then release the pedal. *Do not continue the test for more than 20 seconds otherwise the torque converter will overheat.*
5   If the stall speed is higher than the speed given in the Specifications then the forward clutch or 1st gear one-way clutch may be slipping. Repeat the test in position '1'; if the stall speed is now correct the 1st gear one-way clutch is faulty, but if the speed is still too high, the forward clutch is faulty.
6   A stall speed approximately 200 rpm below the specified amount indicates poor engine performance, and the engine should therefore be tuned up as necessary.
7   If the stall speed is approximately 400 rpm below the specified amount, the torque converter stator one-way clutch is faulty and the torque converter should be renewed.
8   Switch off the engine and disconnect the tachometer.

30 Automatic transmission final drive oil seals – renewal

1   The final drive flange oil seals can be renewed with the transmission in the car. First disconnect the driveshaft with reference to Chapter 7 and tie it to one side – note that it will be necessary to disconnect the lower suspension arm on the left-hand side.
2   Prise off the cap and extract the circlip and spring washer from the drive flange. Withdraw the flange.
3   Prise the oil seal from the final drive housing and wipe clean the location.
4   Fill the space between the lips of the new seal with multi-purpose grease, then drive it fully into the housing using a suitable length of metal tube.
5   Fit the drive flange, spring washer and circlip, making sure that the circlip is fully entered. The use of tool VW391 may be required to do this.

6   Refit the cap, and the driveshaft with reference to Chapter 7.
7   With the car lowered to the ground, remove the final drive filler/level plug and check that the oil level is to the bottom of the hole. If necessary top up the level with the specified oil, then refit the plug.

31 Automatic transmission selector lever cable – adjustment

1   Unbolt the splash guard from under the transmission.

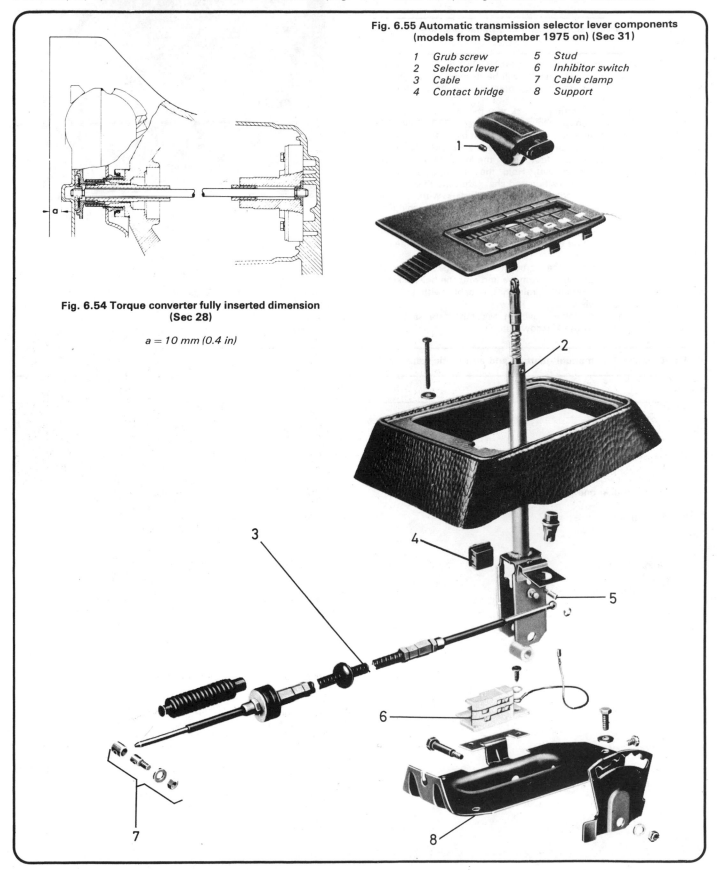

Fig. 6.54 Torque converter fully inserted dimension (Sec 28)

a = 10 mm (0.4 in)

Fig. 6.55 Automatic transmission selector lever components (models from September 1975 on) (Sec 31)

1	*Grub screw*	5	*Stud*
2	*Selector lever*	6	*Inhibitor switch*
3	*Cable*	7	*Cable clamp*
4	*Contact bridge*	8	*Support*

2   Move the selector lever to position 'P', then loosen the clamp nut at the transmission end of the cable and push the transmission lever towards the engine.

3   Tighten the clamp nut and refit the splash guard.

32 Automatic transmission throttle and pedal cables – adjustment

1   The cable arrangement is shown in Fig. 6.57. If the cables are not adjusted correctly, automatic upshifts will be delayed at part throttle and the automatic transmission main pressure will be excessive at idling.

2   Before making an adjustment check that the throttle cable is not twisted along its total length. On pre-November 1979 models the cable has varying resistance to bending and must be installed with the bends in the correct places. Later models have a Bowden cable.

3   To adjust the throttle cable first loosen the locknuts on the outer cable at the carburettor bracket. Hold the choke lever on the carburettor in the fully open position and check that the throttle valve is in the fully closed (idling) position. On models with the 1B3 carburettor make sure that the fast idle cam is not touching the adjusting screw.

4   Push the lever on the transmission fully anti-clockwise, then position the adjustment nuts at the carburettor end until the free play is just eliminated.

5   Tighten the locknuts at the carburettor bracket. To check the adjustment, it must be possible to remove and refit the ball socket on the transmission lever without straining the cable with the lever pushed fully anti-clockwise.

6   To adjust the pedal cable, have an assistant depress the accelerator pedal fully onto the kickdown stop.

Fig. 6.56 Automatic transmission selector lever cable adjustment (Sec 31)

1   Clamp nut   2   Lever

7   Loosen the locknut at the transmission end of the cable and turn the knurled nut to eliminate the free play with the transmission lever held fully clockwise.

8   Tighten the locknut.

33 Fault diagnosis – manual gearbox and automatic transmission

Symptom	Reason(s)
Manual gearbox	
Gearbox noisy in neutral	Mainshaft (input shaft) bearings worn
Gearbox noisy only when moving (in all gears)	Pinion shaft (output shaft) bearings worn Differential bearings worn
Gearbox noisy in only one gear	Worn, damaged, or chipped gear teeth
Jumps out of gear	Worn synchro hubs or baulk rings Worn selector shaft detent plunger or spring Worn selector forks
Ineffective synchromesh	Worn baulk rings or synchro hubs
Difficulty in engaging gears	Clutch fault Gearshift mechanism out of adjustment
Automatic transmission	
Shift speeds too high or too low	Throttle and pedal cables out of adjustment
Loss of drive	Fluid level too low Driveplate to torque converter bolts fallen out Internal fault
Erratic drive	Fluid level too low Dirty oil pan filter
Gear selection jerky	Fluid level too low Idle speed too high
Poor acceleration	Faulty torque converter Throttle and pedal cables out of adjustment

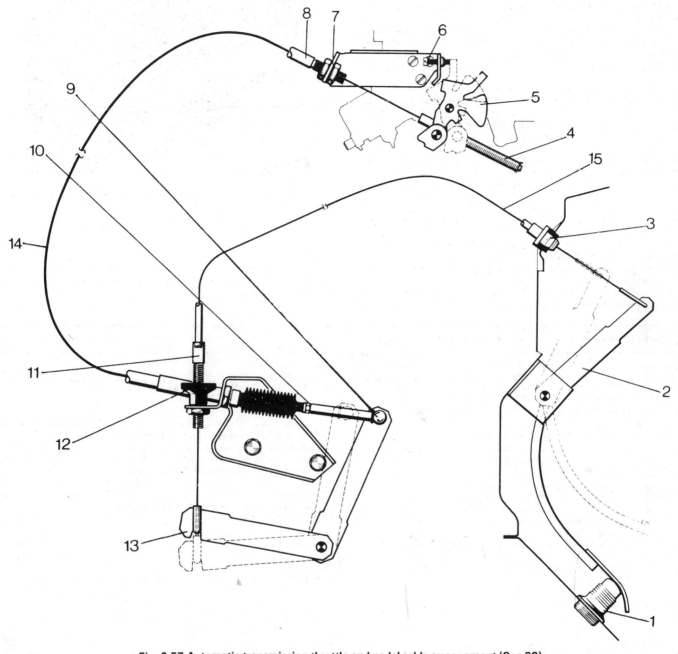

Fig. 6.57 Automatic transmission throttle and pedal cable arrangement (Sec 32)

1	Kickdown switch	6	Stop screw	10	Locknut	13	Gearbox lever
2	Accelerator pedal	7	Adjusting locknuts	11	Cable anchorage	14	Cable
3	Outer cable anchorage	8	Outer cable	12	Adjusting nut and	15	Cable
4	Spring	9	Balljoint		locknut		
5	Carburettor linkage						

Chapter 7 Driveshafts

Contents

Specifications

Driveshaft length
Left-hand (solid) .... 445.5 mm (17.539 in)
Right-hand (tubular) .... 658.0 mm (25.906 in)

Torque wrench settings

	lbf ft	Nm
Driveshaft to flange	33	45
Front hub nut:		
UK models	169	230
North American models	174	240

1 General description

Drive from the differential unit to the roadwheels is provided by two driveshafts. Each driveshaft has a constant velocity joint (CVJ) at each end, the inner end being flanged and secured to the final drive flange by bolts and the outer end being splined to the hub.

The left-hand driveshaft is of solid construction and is shorter than the tubular right-hand driveshaft.

2 Driveshaft – removal and refitting

1 Removal of the shaft does not present many problems. While the vehicle is standing on its wheels, undo the axle nut and slacken the roadwheel studs. Jack up the front wheels and support the vehicle on axle stands. Remove the roadwheel and turn the steering to full lock, left lock for the left shaft and right for the right shaft.

2 Using a splined tool remove the socket head bolts holding the inner CVJ to the final drive flange. Be careful to use a proper key for if the socket head is damaged the result will be time consuming to say the least. These bolts are quite tight.

3 Once all the bolts are removed the CVJ may be pulled away from the final drive and the shaft removed from the hub (photos). If difficulty is experienced, separate the lower suspension arm from the wheel bearing housing by removing the clamp bolt and pressing the suspension arm down. The suspension strut can then be pulled outwards and the driveshaft removed.

4 Refitting is the reverse of removal. Clean the splines carefully and smear a little molybdenum-based grease on them. Fit a new axle nut and tighten to the specified torque.

3 Driveshaft – dismantling and reassembly

1 Having removed the shaft from the car it may be dismantled for the individual parts to be checked for wear.

2 The rubber boots, clips and thrust washers may be renewed if necessary but the CV joints may only be renewed as complete assemblies. It is not possible to fit new hubs, outer cases, ball cages or balls separately for they are mated to a tolerance on manufacture; it is not possible to buy them either.

3 Start by removing the outer joint. Cut open the small diameter clip, release the large diameter clip, and pull the rubber boot from the CV joint.

4 There are two types of circlip fitted to the CV joint as shown in Fig. 7.2 – if the circlip is visible through the end of the joint, the early type joint is fitted.

2.3a Removing the driveshaft from the final drive flange

2.3b Removing the driveshaft from the hub

2.3c The driveshaft ready for dismantling

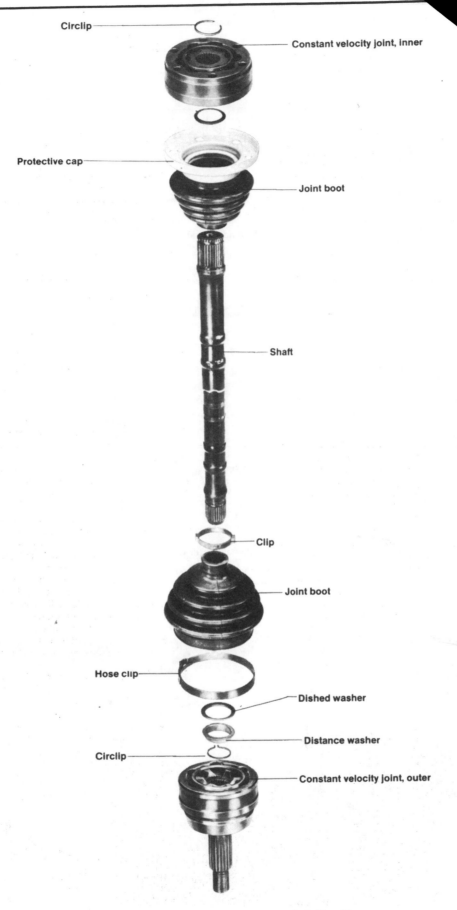

Fig. 7.1 Exploded view of a driveshaft (Sec 3)

Circlip

Constant velocity joint, inner

Protective cap

Joint boot

Shaft

Clip

Joint boot

Hose clip

Dished washer

Distance washer

Circlip

Constant velocity joint, outer

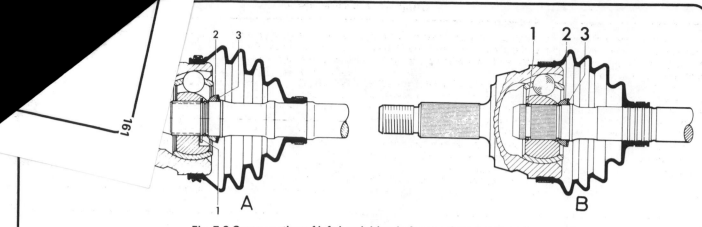

Fig. 7.2 Cross-section of left-hand driveshaft outer CV joint (Sec 3)

A   Early models
B   Later models

1   Circlip

2   Distance washer

3   Dished washer

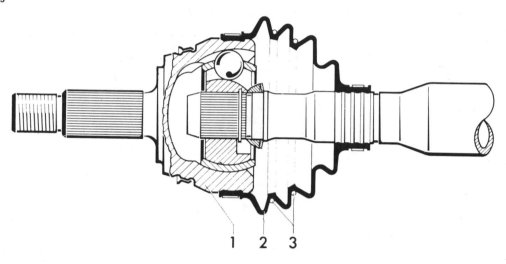

Fig. 7.3 Cross-section of early right-hand driveshaft outer CV joint on 81 kW engine models (Sec 3)

1   Outer ring

2   Rubber boot

3   Steel rings

Fig. 7.4 Removing early driveshaft outer CV joint. Open circlip 'A' and press in direction 'B' (Sec 3)

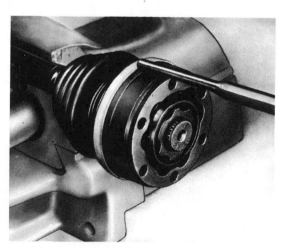

Fig. 7.5 Removing the plastic cap from driveshaft inner joint (Sec 3)

5   To remove the early type CV joint, open the circlip with a pair of circlip pliers and press the outer end of the joint inwards; this will force the ball hub away from the driveshaft, and enable the complete CV joint to be removed from the driveshaft.

6   To remove the later type CV joint, use a wooden mallet to drive the joint sharply from the driveshaft. If only the boot is to be renewed, it may be found easier to first remove the inner CV joint and then to remove and fit the boot from the inner end of the shaft.

7   With the outer CV joint removed mark the ball hub, cage, and housing in relation to each other. Remove the thrust washer (if fitted), dished washer, rubber boot, and clamp. Note that the rubber boot on the 81 kW engine is fitted with two steel support rings.

8   If the boot of the inner CV joint is damaged, or if the joint itself is faulty, it will be necessary to remove the joint from the inner end of the shaft. Use circlip pliers to remove the circlip from the end of the shaft and press off the CV joint. It will be necessary to ease the plastic cap away from the joint before pressing off the CV joint. The CV joint may now be set aside for inspection.

9   The CV joints should be washed clean and lightly oiled. Press the ball hub and cage out of the joint. Pivot the case through 90° to extract it. Examine the balls and ball tracks for scoring and wear. There should be a bright ring where the ball track runs round the joint but no further scoring. If excessively worn the joint should be renewed.

10   Assembly is a reversal of dismantling, but pack each joint with 90 grams of molybdenum disulphide based grease. Make sure that the dished washer is fitted as shown in Figs. 7.2 and 7.3. Always fit new clips to the rubber boots.

11   The shaft is now ready for refitting as described in Section 2.

4 Fault diagnosis – driveshafts

Symptom	Reason(s)
Vibration and noise on turns	Worn driveshaft joints
Noise on taking up drive	Worn drive flange and/or driveshaft splines Loose driveshaft-to-hub nut Worn driveshaft joints Loose roadwheel nuts

Chapter 8 Braking system

For modifications and information applicable to later models, see Supplement at end of manual

Contents

Specifications

System type ....

Four wheel hydraulic, disc front and drum rear. Dual hydraulic system diagonally connected, servo assistance on most models. Cable-operated handbrake on rear wheels

Front brakes

Disc diameter	239 mm (9.4 in)
Disc thickness (new):	
81 kW engine models	20 mm (0.79 in)
Except 81 kW engine models	12 mm (0.47 in)
Disc thickness (minimum):	
81 kW engine models	18 mm (0.71 in)
Except 81 kW engine models	10 mm (0.40 in)
Disc run-out (maximum)	0.06 mm (0.002 in)
Pad thickness (new):	
81 kW engine models	10 mm (0.40 in)
Except 81 kW engine models	14 mm (0.55 in)
Pad thickness (minimum, including backing plate, except on Kelsey-Hayes type)	7 mm (0.276 in)
Pad thickness (minimum, Kelsey-Hayes type, not including backing plate)	2 mm (0.08 in)

Rear brakes

Drum internal diameter:	
Manual adjustment and self-adjusting wedge type	180 mm (7.08 in)
Self-adjusting lever type	200 mm (7.87 in)
Lining thickness (new):	
Rivetted linings	5 mm (0.197 in)
Bonded linings	4 mm (0.157 in)
Wear limit:	
Rivetted linings	2.5 mm (0.1 in)
Bonded linings	1.0 mm (0.04 in)
Handbrake adjustment:	
Manual adjustment and self-adjusting wedge type	2 notches
Self-adjusting lever type	4 notches

Torque wrench settings

	lbf ft	Nm
Caliper to strut – UK models	44	60
Caliper to strut – US models	36	50
Disc to hub	5	7
Pad retainer (Girling)	14	20
Caliper guide pins (Kelsey-Hayes)	30	42
Backplate to axle	44	60
Wheel cylinder – UK models	11	15
Wheel cylinder – US models	7	10
Master cylinder	11	15
Brake hoses	7	10
Servo	15	21
Brake line union at master cylinder	15	21

1 General description

The braking system is of four wheel hydraulic dual circuit type, with discs at the front and drum brakes at the rear. The dual circuit system is of the diagonal type so that with the failure of one hydraulic circuit, one front and one rear brake remain operative. A direct-acting brake servo unit is fitted to most models.

The handbrake operates the rear brakes by cable, and on most models a warning light is provided on the instrument panel for the handbrake and low fluid level.

Note that the Kelsey-Hayes type caliper may also be referred to as the Mk 2 type caliper.

2 Routine maintenance

1 The brake fluid level should be checked every week and, if necessary, topped-up with the specified fluid to the maximum level mark (photo). The reservoir is translucent and the check can be made without removing the filler cap. Any fall in level should be investigated.

2 At the intervals given in Routine Maintenance at the beginning of this manual the front brake pad thickness should be checked and all four pads renewed if any one is below the specified minimum thickness.

3 At the specified service intervals the thickness of the rear brake shoe linings should also be checked and renewed, if necessary. Where applicable the rear brake shoes should be adjusted.

4 Inspect the hydraulic pipes and unions for chafing, leakage, cracks and corrosion and also check the condition of the brake servo vacuum hose.

5 At the less frequent intervals given, renew the brake fluid in the hydraulic system.

3 Rear brakes (manual) – adjustment

1 Jack up the rear of the car and support it on axle stands. Check the front wheels and release the handbrake.

2 On models fitted with a brake pressure regulator, press the lever towards the rear axle to release any residual pressure.

3 Remove the rubber plug from the adjuster hole in the backplate. Using a screwdriver, lever the adjuster wheel, teeth downwards (handle of the screwdriver upwards) until the lining binds in the drum (photo). Now back off the adjuster until the roadwheel will rotate without the drum touching the shoes.

4 Refit the rubber plug then adjust the opposite wheel in the same way.

4 Disc pads (Teves) – inspection and renewal

1 Brake pads wear more quickly than drum brake shoes, and they should be checked for wear at the intervals given in Section 2. The thickness of the pad, including the backing plate, must not be less than the dimension given in the Specifications. If the pads wear below this thickness then damage to the brake disc may result. Measure the pad thickness through the holes in the roadwheels as shown (photo).

2 The pads are different. The inner one is flat on both sides, the outer one has a slot cut in its outer face (photo) which engages with a boss on the caliper.

3 To remove the pads, jack up the front of the car and remove the wheels. Using a suitable drift tap out the pins securing the disc pads (photo). On some cars there may be a wire securing clip fitted round these pins (photo). This should be pulled off. If there is no clip the pins will have sleeves.

4 Remove the spreader and pull out the inner, direct pad (photos). If you are going to put the pads back then they must be marked so that they go back in the same place. Use a piece of wire with a hook on the

2.1 Removing the master cylinder filler cap (Scirocco)

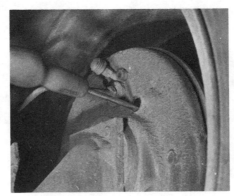

3.3 Adjusting the rear brake (manual adjustment type)

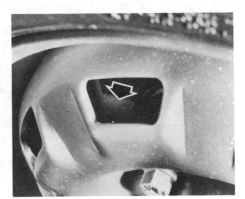

4.1 Checking disc pad wear (Teves). Pad is arrowed

4.2 Teves outer brake pad showing slot

4.3a Removing pad retaining pins (Teves)

4.3b Wire clip fitted to some pad retaining pins (Teves)

4.4a Removing the spreader ...

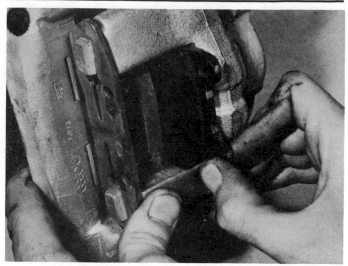

4.4b ... and inner brake pad (Teves)

4.5 Installing the outer brake pad (Teves)

4.6 Checking the caliper piston angle (Teves)

end to pull the pad out. Now lever the caliper over so that there is space between the disc and the outer pad, ease the pad away from the caliper onto the disc and lift it out.

5   Clean out the pad holder and check that the rubber dust cover is not damaged. Insert the outer pad and fit it over the projection on the caliper (photo). It will be necessary to push the piston in to insert the inner pad. This may cause the header tank to overflow unless action is taken to prevent it. Either draw some fluid out of the tank with a pipette or slacken the bleed screw. We prefer the first method, but do not suck the fluid out with a syphon. It is poisonous. Use a pipette that has been used for brake fluid only, not the battery hydrometer.

6   Push the piston in and check that the angle of the edges of the raised face of the piston is 20° to the face of the caliper (photo). Make a gauge out of cardboard as shown in the photo. If the angle is more or less, turn the piston until the angle is correct.

7   Insert the inner pad, fit the spreader and install the pins. Fit a new locking wire if the type of pin requires it.

8   Do not forget to shut the bleed screw (if it was opened) as soon as the piston has been forced back. We do not like this method because there is a chance of air entering the cylinder and we do not like spare brake fluid about on the caliper while working on the friction pads.

10 Work the footbrake a few times to settle the pistons, Now repeat the job for the other wheel.

11 Refit the roadwheels, lower to the ground and take the car for a test run.

5   Disc pads (Girling) – inspection and renewal

1   In general, the method is the same as for the Teves caliper with the following differences.

2   Lever off the pad spreader spring with a screwdriver, and pull out the pins with pliers after removing the screw which locks them in position.

3   Remove and refit the pads as with the Teves caliper. Install the pins and the locking screw. A repair kit for brake pads will include new pins and retainer so use them.

4   The pad spreader spring is pressed on. The arrow must point in the direction of rotation of the disc when the car is travelling forward.

6   Disc pads (Kelsey-Hayes) – inspection and renewal

1   Refer to Section 4, paragraph 1, but remove the roadwheel if necessary to check the pad thickness. Note that the measurement must **not** include the backing plate.

2   The inner and outer pads are different, the inner lining being

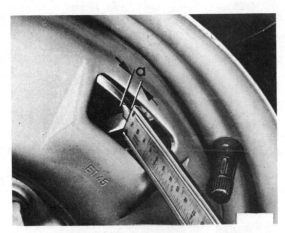

Fig. 8.1 Checking Girling disc pad thickness on models with steel wheels (Sec 5)

Fig. 8.2 Checking Girling disc pad thickness on models with alloy wheels (Sec 5)

Fig. 8.3 Removing the Girling disc pad spreader with screwdriver (Sec 5)

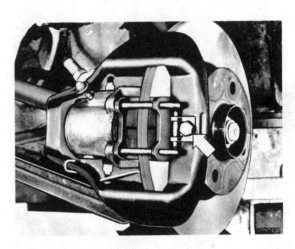

Fig. 8.4 Disc pad pin retaining screw location on Girling caliper (Sec 5)

Fig. 8.5 Removing Girling disc pad pin (Sec 5)

slightly smaller and chamfered at each end (photo).

3   To remove the pads, the front of the car must be jacked up and supported on axle stands, and the roadwheel removed. Apply the handbrake.

4   Unclip and remove the two anti-rattle springs (photo).

5   Using an Allen key, unscrew the guide pins from the caliper mounting bracket, then slide the caliper forwards and tie it to one side without straining the hydraulic hose (photos).

6   Remove the disc pads from the bracket (photos). Brush any accumulated dust and dirt from the bracket and inner cavities of the caliper, but take care not to inhale it as the lining dust is poisonous. Before fitting the new pads, the piston must be pushed back into the caliper – while doing this check that the hydraulic fluid will not overflow from the reservoir, and if necessary draw out some fluid with a pipette, or alternatively slacken the bleed nipple on the caliper temporarily to drain the excess fluid.

7   Fit the disc pads to the bracket with the chamfered pad on the inside (photo).

8   Slide the caliper over the pads, locating the upper notches on the bracket (photo), and tighten the guard pins. Note that the top guide pin is longer than the bottom pin.

9   Refit the anti-rattle springs, then depress the brake pedal several times to set the pads.

10 Refit the roadwheel, lower the car to the ground, and repeat the procedure on the remaining front wheel.

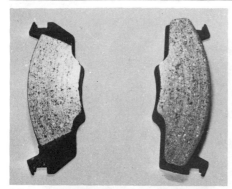
6.2 Inner (left) and outer (right) disc pads (Kelsey-Hayes)

6.4 Anti-rattle spring location (Kelsey-Hayes)

6.5a Removing the caliper guide pins (Kelsey-Hayes)

6.5b Removing the caliper (Kelsey-Hayes)

6.6a Removing the outer disc pad (Kelsey-Hayes) on a Golf

6.6b Removing the inner disc pad (Kelsey-Hayes) on a Golf

6.7 Disc pads fitted to the bracket (Kelsey-Hayes) on a Scirocco

6.8 Caliper locating shoulder (Kelsey-Hayes) on a Scirocco

7   Calipers, pistons, and seals (Teves) – removal, inspection and refitting

1   Support the front of the car on stands and remove the wheels.
2   If it is intended to dismantle the caliper then the brake hoses must be removed, plugged and tied out of the way. Refer to Section 19.
3   Mark the position of the brake pads and remove them (Section 4), if the caliper is to be dismantled.
4   Remove the two bolts holding the caliper to the stub axle. This should not be done while the caliper is hot.
5   Withdraw the caliper from the car and take it to a bench.
6   Refer to Fig. 8.6. A repair kit should be purchased for the overhaul of the caliper.
7   Ease the floating frame away from the mounting frame. Now press the brake cylinder and guide spring off the floating frame. The cylinder may now be removed.
8   Remove the retaining ring and the rubber boot. The next problem is to remove the piston which is probably stuck in the piston seal. The obvious way is to blow it out using air pressure in the hole which normally accommodates the hydraulic pressure hose. However, be careful. The piston may be stuck in the seal but when it does come out it will come quickly. Fit the cylinder in a vice with a piece of wood arranged to act as a stop for the piston. If you do not have a ready supply of compressed air, use a foot pump. If it will not come out that way then a trip to the local garage is indicated.
9   When the piston is out of the cylinder clean carefully the bore of the cylinder and the piston with brake fluid or methylated spirit.
10   It is difficult to define wear on the piston. When it has been cleaned it should have a mirror finish. Scratches or dull sections indicate wear. The inside of the bore must be clean with no scratches or distortion. If there is any doubt renew the whole unit. In any case renew the seal and dust excluder. Dip the cylinder in clean brake fluid. Coat the piston and seal with brake cylinder paste (ATE) and press the piston and seal into the cylinder. Use a vice with soft jaws. Install a new dust excluder and its retaining ring. Fit a new locating spring and

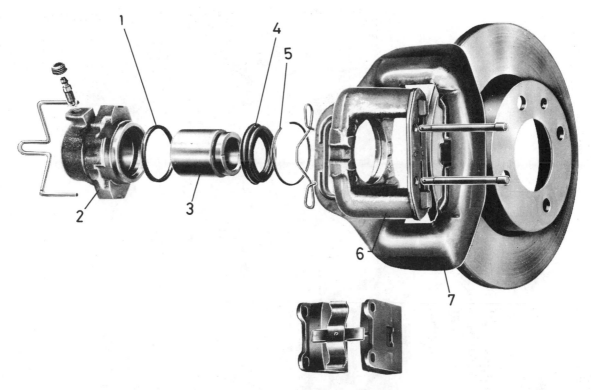

Fig. 8.6 Exploded view of the Teves brake caliper. Retaining pins and springs may differ on North American models (Sec 7)

1 O-ring seal	3 Piston	5 Circlip	7 Floating frame
2 Cylinder	4 Dust cap	6 Mounting frame	

knock the cylinder onto the floating frame with a brass drift.

11 Refit the floating frame to the mounting frame and set the piston recess at an inclination of 20° to the guide surface of the caliper as described in Section 4.

12 Bolt the mounting frame onto the stub axle and fit the pads. Refit the wheel and lower the car to the ground.

13 Top up the brake fluid reservoir and bleed the brakes as described in Section 20.

14 Road test the car to check the operation of the brakes.

8   Calipers, piston, and seals (Girling) – removal, inspection and refitting

1   Refer to Fig. 8.7. The general rules for overhaul are the same as for the Teves but the complication of the extra piston is more work.

2   Remove the cylinder and floating mounting from the stub axle and press them apart. Again use compressed air to dislodge the pistons and be careful that they do not come out suddenly. Clean the pistons and bore carefully. Use a Girling kit of seals and parts. Wash the cylinder and pistons with clean brake fluid and reassemble.

3   In this case the pistons and cylinder are bolted to the front suspension. The caliper sliding frame must move easily over the cylinder casting. Tighten the holding bolts to the specified torque. Note that the brake fluid hose union has a left-hand thread on later models – see Section 19.

9   Calipers, pistons, and seals (Kelsey-Hayes) – removal, inspection and refitting

1   Jack up the front of the car and support it on axle stands. Apply the handbrake and remove the roadwheel.

2   Loosen (but do not remove) the hydraulic fluid hose at the caliper.

3   Unclip and remove the two anti-rattle springs.

4   Using an Allen key, unscrew the guide pins from the caliper mounting bracket, then slide the caliper forward over the disc pads.

5   Unscrew the caliper from the hydraulic hose and plug the hose.

6   Position a length of wood across the caliper, then force the piston

out of its bore by using air pressure from a foot pump in the fluid aperture.

7   Prise the rubber dust seal from the caliper with a screwdriver, then using a non-metallic instrument, prise the rubber seal from the caliper bore.

8   If necessary unbolt the caliper bracket from the wheel bearing housing after removing the disc pads.

9   Clean the piston and caliper with methylated spirit and wipe dry. Examine the surfaces of the piston and bore for scoring and wear. If evident renew the complete caliper, but if the components are in good condition discard the seals and obtain a repair kit.

10 Commence reassembly by locating the seal in the caliper bore.

11 Smear the piston with a little brake cylinder paste; then locate the rubber dust seal on the piston with the sealing lip innermost.

12 Push the piston into the caliper and tap the dust seal into position with a soft metal drift.

13 Before refitting the caliper, remove the guide bolts and sleeves from the bushes and examine them for wear. If necessary press out the bushes and obtain a repair kit comprising new bushes and sleeves. Press in the new bushes and insert the sleeves and guide bolts.

14 Remove the plug and screw the caliper onto the hydraulic bore.

15 Refit the caliper bracket, if removed, and tighten the bolts. Fit the disc pads to the bracket with the chamfered pad on the inside.

16 Slide the caliper over the pads, locating the upper notches on the bracket, and tighten the guide pins. Note that the top guide pin is longer than the bottom pin.

17 Tighten the hydraulic fluid hose union to the caliper.

18 Refit the disc pad anti-rattle springs, refit the roadwheel, and lower the car to the ground.

19 Bleed the hydraulic system as described in Section 20.

10   Brake disc – removal, overhaul and refitting

1   Two thicknesses of disc may be fitted, as detailed in the Specifications. Note that the two different types are not interchangeable.

2   If the discs are worn excessively, they may be removed and reground by an engineering firm provided that the final thickness is not

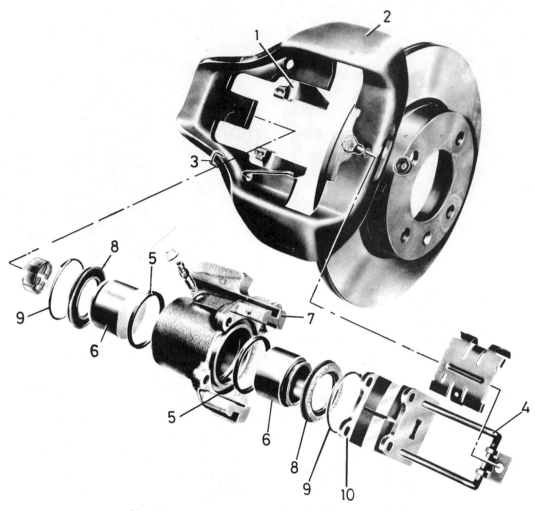

Fig. 8.7 Exploded view of the Girling brake caliper (Sec 8)

1	*Clip*	*5*	*Sealing rings*	*8*	*Dust caps*
2	*Frame*	*6*	*Pistons*	*9*	*Circlips*
3	*Retaining spring*	*7*	*Cylinder housing*	*10*	*Brake pads*
4	*Retaining pin*				

less than the specified minimum dimension.

3   Removal is quite simple. Remove the pads and calipers but do not disconnect the hydraulic hose. Hang the calipers out of the way.

4   The disc is held to the hub by one small screw. Remove this and the disc may be drawn off the hub for servicing.

5   If the vehicle has been left for a while and the discs have rusted seriously they can be salvaged by a VW agent without removing them from the vehicle. Special polishing blocks can be inserted in place of the pads and the wheels driven to polish the discs.

6   Machining the discs is a job which should be left to a specialist in a machine shop. It may be cheaper to buy a new disc. If a new disc is fitted then new pads should be installed, the old ones will have worn unevenly.

7   If one side is serviced then look at the situation on the other wheel. If the disc is in good condition fit a new set of pads or you will have problems later when the old pads wear.

8   Refitting is a reversal of the removal procedure.

11 Rear brake shoes (manual adjustment) – inspection and renewal

1   Slacken the roadwheel bolts. Chock the front wheels, jack up the rear of the car and support it on axle stands or other suitable supports. Release the handbrake lever and remove the roadwheel.

2   Take off the hub cap, remove the split pin and the locking cap. Undo the nut and pull the drum off the stub axle; the thrust washer and

wheel bearing will come with it. Set the drum on one side for inspection. It may be necessary to back off the adjuster as described in Section 3; if a brake pressure regulator is fitted, depress the lever to release the residual pressure.

3   The brake assembly is now exposed – do not depress the brake pedal from now on. Although one rubber plug and checking hole is provided in the backplate, it is recommended that the drum is always removed in order to inspect the lining thickness, as both shoes rarely wear uniformly.

4   Brush the dust from the brake drum, brake shoes, and backplate, but *do not* inhale it as it is injurious to health. Scrape any scale or rust from the drum. Check that the lining thickness on each shoe is not less than the specified minimum — if any one is less, renew all of the rear shoes as described in the following paragraphs.

5   Remove the large U-spring and unhook the two springs at the bottom of the brake shoes (photos). Take off the leaf springs from the steady pins (photo), and remove the shoes from the backplate. It will be necessary to unhook the handbrake cable to remove the shoes (photo).

6   The adjuster rod will come away with the shoes. The backplate may be removed if necessary with the stub axle by undoing the four bolts now accessible, after removing the wheel cylinder. If the wheel cylinder is being left in position, retain the pistons with an elastic band – check that there are no signs of fluid leakage and if necessary repair or renew the wheel cylinder as described in Section 14.

7   Refitting is a reversal of the removal procedure. Fit the handbrake cable to the trailing shoe lever, locate the shoes on the backplate and

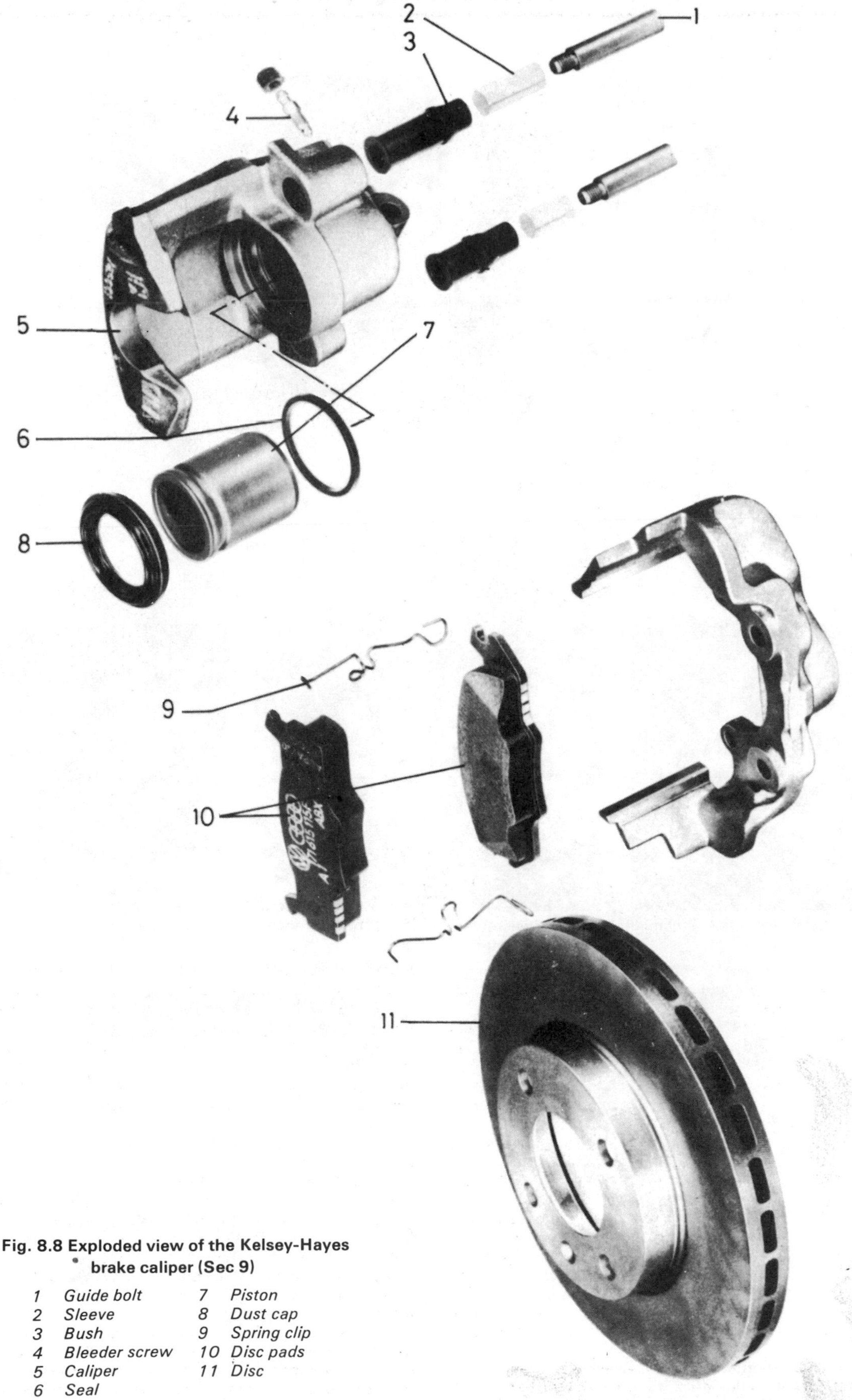

Fig. 8.8 Exploded view of the Kelsey-Hayes brake caliper (Sec 9)

1	Guide bolt	7	Piston
2	Sleeve	8	Dust cap
3	Bush	9	Spring clip
4	Bleeder screw	10	Disc pads
5	Caliper	11	Disc
6	Seal		

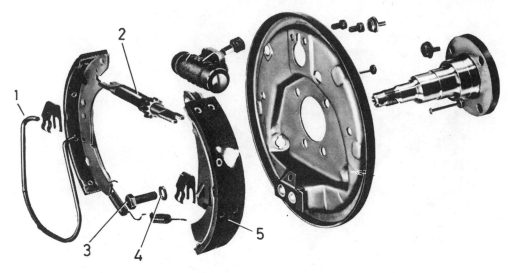

Fig. 8.9 Exploded view of rear brake with manual adjustment (Sec 11)

1　Return spring
2　Adjustable strut
3　Backplate retaining bolt
4　Spring washer
5　Brake shoe

11.5a Rear brake shoe configuration – manual adjustment

11.5b Lower return springs and bottom anchor (manual adjustment models)

11.5c Shoe steady spring (manual adjustment models)

11.5d Handbrake cable end (manual adjustment models)

11.8 The maximum regrinding diameter is marked on the brake drum

fit the leaf springs. Fit the bottom springs. Lever the shoes apart and fit the adjuster rod. Finally fit the U-spring.

8　Before refitting the brake drum, check it for wear and damage. Light scoring of the friction surface is normal but if excessive, it is recommended that the drums are renewed as a pair. After a high mileage the friction surface may become oval. Where this has occurred

it may be possible to grind the surface true, but this should only be carried out by a qualified engineering firm (photo).

9　Refit the drum and bearing and adjust the bearings as described in Chapter 10. Refit the roadwheel and adjust the brakes as described in Section 3.

10　Lower the car to the ground.

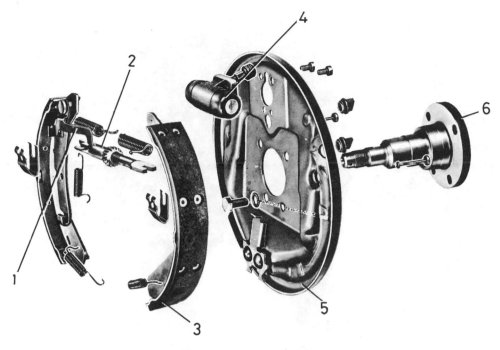

Fig. 8.10 Exploded view of rear brake with automatic adjustment (lever type) (Sec 12)

1	Lever	3	Brake shoes	5	Backplate
2	Strut	4	Wheel cylinder	6	Stub axle

Fig. 8.11 Method of releasing brake adjuster (drum removed)
(Sec 12)

12 Rear brake shoes (self-adjusting lever type) – inspection and renewal

1   Refer to Fig. 8.10. Proceed as in Section 11 up to the point where the drum is to be taken off. The automatic adjuster will have kept the lining right up to the drum and the adjuster must be turned through the hole in the backplate to slacken the linings back. Before this can be done the automatic adjuster lever must be pulled away from the gear. This is done by inserting a piece of wire with a hook on the end through a wheel bolt hole and pulling the lever back. You can see the approximate position from Fig. 8.11. Once the hook is in contact with the lever, the screwdriver through the hole in the backplate will tell you when the lever is clear of the gearwheel. Back the lining down enough to enable the drum to be withdrawn.
2   The method of dismantling is the same as detailed in Section 11 except that there is a pair of coil springs in place of the U-spring.
3   Assembly is the reverse of removal. Hold the automatic adjuster

lever away from the pushrod while doing the initial brake adjustment.
4   Adjust the wheel bearings as described in Chapter 10. Refit the roadwheel, lower the car to the ground, and operate the handbrake fully several times to set the shoes in their correct position.

13 Rear brake shoes (self-adjusting wedge type) – inspection and renewal

1   As with the previous types of rear brake, it is possible to remove a rubber plug and check the leading brake shoe lining thickness through the backplate. However, it is recommended that the drum is removed in order to make a more thorough inspection.
2   Proceed as in Section 11 up to the point where the drum is to be taken off. Using a screwdriver through a bolt hole in the drum, push the wedge upwards to retract the shoes, then withdraw the drum. Do not depress the brake pedal from now on.
3   Brush the dust from the brake drum, brake shoes, and backplate, but **do not** inhale it as it is injurious to health. Scrape any scale or rust from the drum. Check that the lining thickness on each shoe is not less

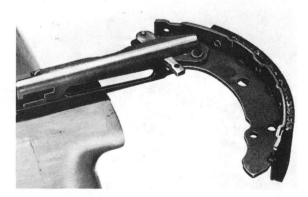

Fig. 8.12 Removing the wedge from the rear brake shoe (Sec 13)

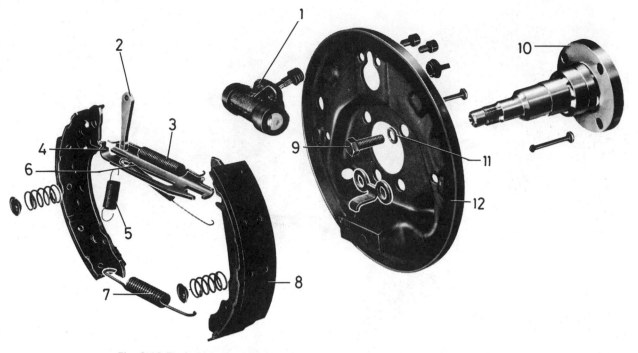

Fig. 8.13 Exploded view of the wedge type self-adjusting rear brakes (Sec 13)

1	Wheel cylinder	4 Pushrod	7 Lower return spring	10 Stub axle
2	Wedge	5 Spring	8 Brake shoe	11 Washer
3	Spring	6 Upper return spring	9 Backplate retaining bolt	12 Backplate

13.3 Rear brake shoes (self-adjusting wedge type)

13.4 Removing the brake shoe steady springs

13.5 Lower return spring location (self-adjusting wedge type)

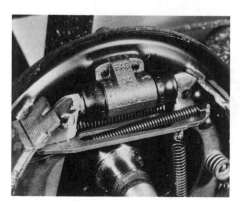

13.6a Strut, wedge and upper return spring location (right-hand side)

13.6b Wedge and spring location (left-hand side)

13.9 Checking the rear wheel cylinder for signs of hydraulic fluid leakage

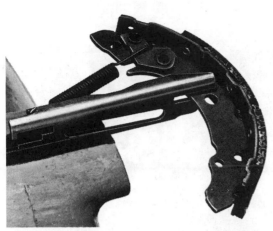

Fig. 8.14 Removing the rear brake shoe from the strut (Sec 13)

Fig. 8.15 Assembling the handbrake lever and shoe to the strut (Sec 13)

than the specified minimum – if any one is less, renew all of the rear shoes as described in the following paragraphs (photo).
4   Using a pair of pliers, depress the steady spring caps, turn them through 90°, and remove the cups and springs from the pins (photo).
5   Lever the brake shoes from the bottom anchor (photo).

6   Note the location of all the springs and the strut, then unhook the bottom return spring (photos).
7   Disengage the handbrake cable from the lever on the trailing brake shoe.
8   Release the brake shoes from the wheel cylinder, unhook the wedge spring and upper return spring, and withdraw the shoes.
9   Grip the strut in a vice and release the shoe, then remove the wedge and spring. The backplate and stub axle may be removed if necessary by unscrewing the four bolts after removing the wheel cylinder. Note the location of the return spring bracket, if fitted. If the wheel cylinder is being left in position, retain the pistons with an elastic band – check that there are no signs of fluid leakage and if necessary repair or renew the wheel cylinder as described in Section 14 (photo).
10 Refitting is a reversal of the removal procedure, noting that the lug on the wedge faces the backplate.
11 Check the brake drum for wear and damage as described in Section 11.
12 Refit the drum and bearing and adjust the bearings as described in Chapter 10. Refit the roadwheel and lower the car to the ground.
13 Fully depress the brake pedal once in order to set the shoes in their correct position.

14 Wheel cylinder – removal, overhaul and refitting

1   Remove the rear brake shoes as described in Sections 11, 12, or 13 as applicable (photo).
2   Where possible, remove the cap from the brake fluid reservoir and tighten it onto a sheet of thin polythene – this will reduce the loss of brake fluid in the subsequent procedure.
3   Unscrew the hydraulic pipe union from the rear of the cylinder (photo). Plug the end of the pipe.
4   Remove the securing screws and withdraw the wheel cylinder from the backplate.
5   To dismantle, remove the dust caps and blow the pistons out with low air pressure. Be careful when doing this that the pistons do not come out too quickly. Muffle the cylinder with a large piece of rag.
6   Wash the bores and pistons with clean brake fluid and examine for mirror finish and scratches. If there is any blemish discard the complete unit and fit a new one. Always fit new seals and dust caps. Coat them with a little brake cylinder paste before installing and make sure the seals are the right way round.
7   Refitting is a reversal of the removal procedure. Bleed the hydraulic system as described in Section 20 and road test the car to check the operation of the brakes.

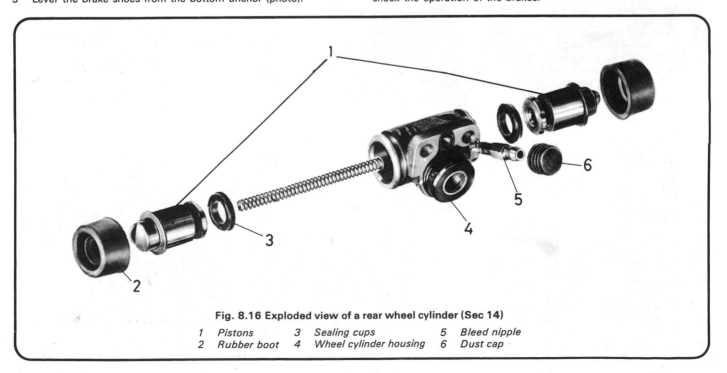

Fig. 8.16 Exploded view of a rear wheel cylinder (Sec 14)

1 Pistons	3 Sealing cups	5 Bleed nipple
2 Rubber boot	4 Wheel cylinder housing	6 Dust cap

14.1 Rear wheel cylinder and shoes (manual adjustment models)

14.3 Wheel cylinder hydraulic pipe connection and securing screws location on the rear backplate

15.1a Right-hand side brake bellcrank and rods (RHD Jetta model)

15.1b Left-hand side brake bellcrank assembly (RHD Scirocco model)

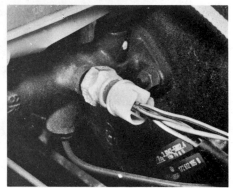

15.2 Stop-light switch location on the master cylinder (Scirocco)

15 Master cylinder – removal and refitting

1   The master cylinder is located on the front of the servo unit on the left-hand side of the car on all models, except for some US models not fitted with a servo. On the latter models the master cylinder is located directly on the bulkhead on the left-hand side of the car. On the right-hand drive models the foot pedal is connected to the servo by rods and levers (photos).
2   To remove the master cylinder, first disconnect the battery negative lead, and the wiring from the stop-light and fluid level switches on the master cylinder and fluid reservoir filler cap (photo).
3   Disconnect the hydraulic fluid pipes from the master cylinder and collect the fluid which will drain out in a suitable container.

Models without servo
4   Unscrew the mounting nuts and withdraw the master cylinder from the bulkhead and away from the pushrod. Recover the angle rubber sealing ring, or on some models the wedge plate and two sealing rings. Do not spill hydraulic fluid on the body paintwork.

Models with servo
5   Unscrew the mounting nuts and withdraw the master cylinder from the front of the servo unit. Recover the single rubber sealing ring. Do not spill hydraulic fluid on the body paintwork.

All models
6   Refitting is a reversal of the removal procedure but always fit a new sealing ring (or sealing rings), and tighten the mounting nuts to the specified torque. Where a wedge plate is fitted, the thicker side must be uppermost. Fill the brake fluid reservoir with fresh fluid (never re-use fluid removed from the system) and bleed the hydraulic system as described in Section 20.

Models without servo
7   After refitting, the foot pedal pushrod adjustment should be

checked. To do this, first check that the brake pedal is level with the clutch pedal when fully released. If not, loosen the locknut on the pedal stop adjusting bolt, turn the bolt in or out as necessary, then tighten the locknut. Now check the free play at the pedal pad which should be 2 to 4 mm (0.08 to 0.16 in). If necessary loosen the locknut and rotate the pushrod from inside the car until the free play is correct, then tighten the locknut.

16 Master cylinder – overhaul

1   Clean the outside of the cylinder thoroughly, then place it in a clean area for dismantling. Work only with clean hands. Obtain a repair kit and a quantity of fresh brake fluid in a clean container.
2   Unscrew and remove the stop-light switch(es).
3   Pull the fluid reservoir out of the rubber grommets, then prise the grommets from the cylinder.
4   Remove the stop screw and washer from the top of the cylinder (except on the Bendix non-servo type).
5   Remove the rubber boot (where fitted) from the end of the cylinder.
6   Push the piston inward slightly, then remove the retaining circlip – use a screwdriver to remove the three-cornered type, or circlip pliers to remove the round type. The contents of the cylinder can now be removed, but note the position of each item with reference to Figs. 8.18, 8.19 and 8.20 if necessary. If the secondary piston is difficult to remove, tap the cylinder on a block of wood.
7   Clean all the components in methylated spirit and examine them for wear and damage. In particular check the surfaces of the pistons and cylinder bore for scoring and corrosion. If evident, renew the complete master cylinder, but if in good condition, discard the seals and washers and fit the repair kit items. Check that all the ports in the cylinder are free and unobstructed.
8   Commence reassembly by fitting the new seals. VW make a special tapered mandrel (see Fig. 8.21) which fits on the end of the piston, and the seal is eased over the taper. The seals may be fitted

Fig. 8.17 Removing the three-cornered type clip from the master cylinder (Sec 16)

without this tool, but use the fingers only to manipulate them into position.

9   Assemble the two pistons with their associated parts, dipping the components in fresh brake fluid first. Ensure that the caps and seals are fitted correctly.

10 Assemble the remaining components using a reversal of the dismantling procedure. Where necessary, depress the pistons slightly before fitting the stop screw.

Fig. 8.18 Tapered mandrel for fitting new seals (Sec 16)

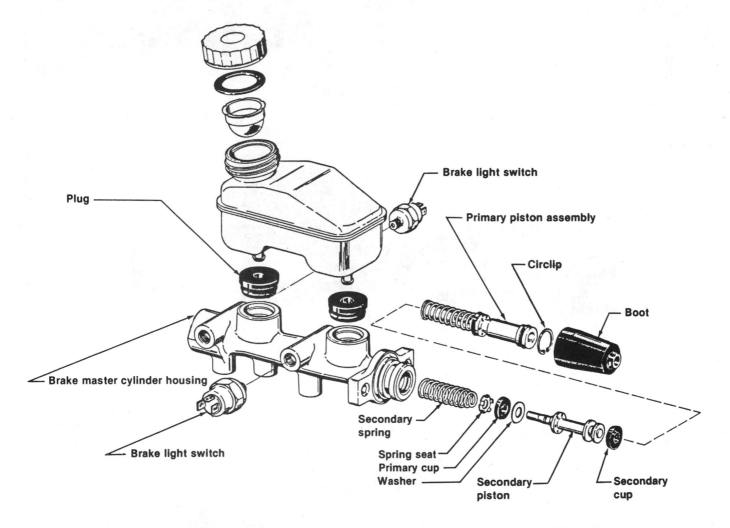

Fig. 8.19 Exploded view of the Bendix brake master cylinder on non-servo models (Sec 16)

Fig. 8.20 Exploded view of the Teves (ATE) or Shafer (FAG) brake master cylinder on non-servo models (Sec 16)

1 Boot
2 Circlip
3 Stop washer
4 Secondary cup
5 Pushrod piston
6 Cup washer
7 Primary cup
8 Support ring
9 Spring
10 Stop sleeve
11 Limit screw
12 Piston seal
13 Piston seal
14 Secondary piston
15 Cup washer
16 Primary cup
17 Support ring
18 Conical spring
19 Cylinder
20 Residual pressure valve (early models only)
21 Stop light switch
22 Washer
23 Plug
24 Stop screw
25 Brake fluid reservoir
26 Filter
27 Washer
28 Cap

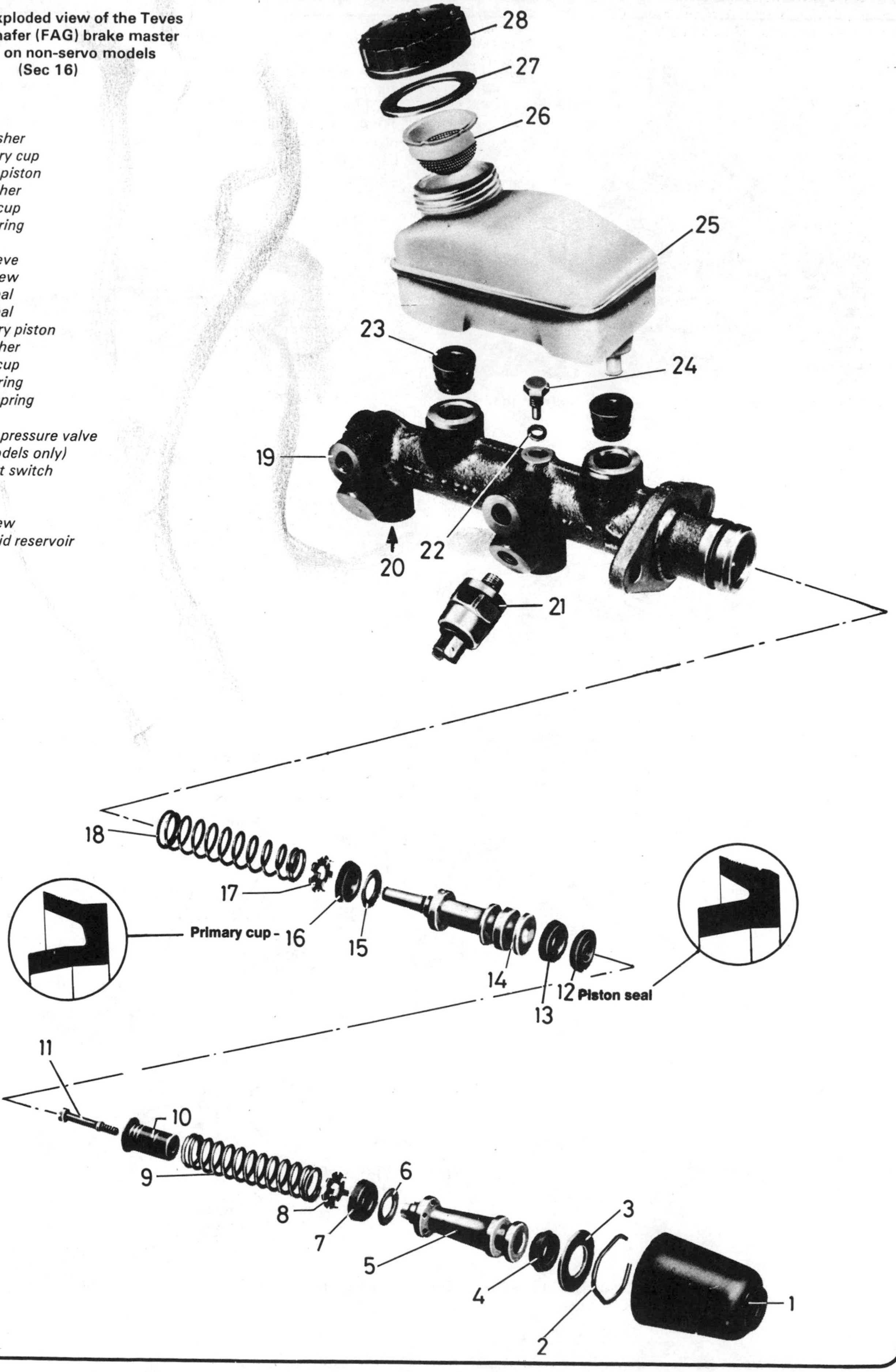

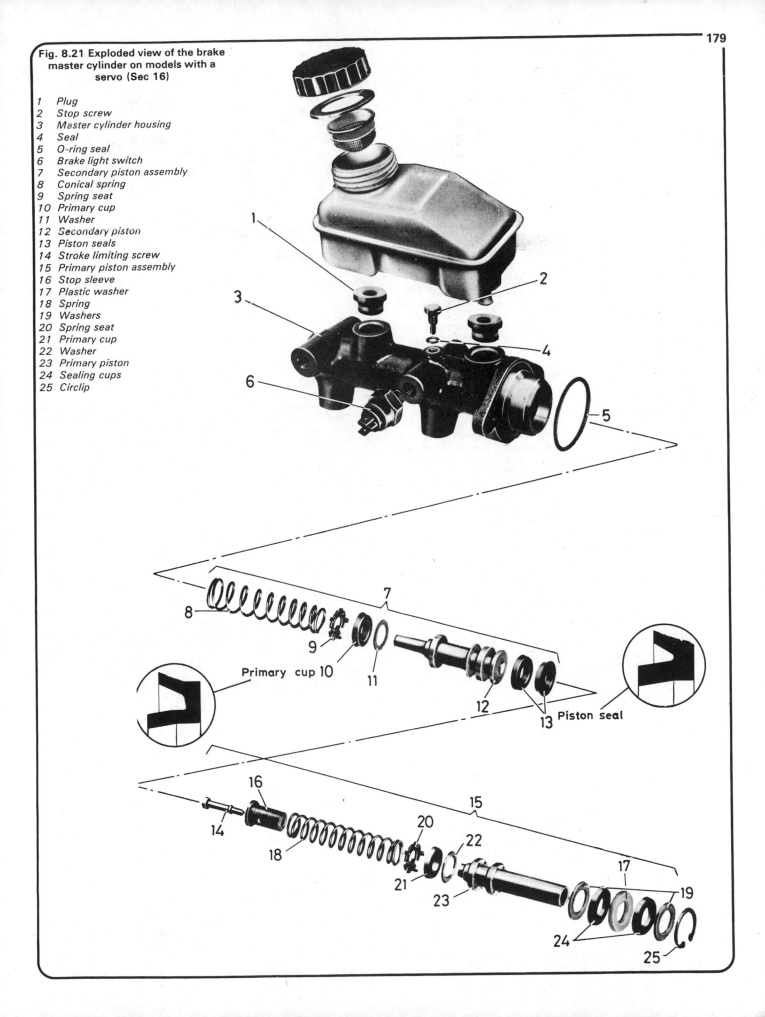

Fig. 8.21 Exploded view of the brake master cylinder on models with a servo (Sec 16)

1   Plug
2   Stop screw
3   Master cylinder housing
4   Seal
5   O-ring seal
6   Brake light switch
7   Secondary piston assembly
8   Conical spring
9   Spring seat
10   Primary cup
11   Washer
12   Secondary piston
13   Piston seals
14   Stroke limiting screw
15   Primary piston assembly
16   Stop sleeve
17   Plastic washer
18   Spring
19   Washers
20   Spring seat
21   Primary cup
22   Washer
23   Primary piston
24   Sealing cups
25   Circlip

Primary cup 10

Piston seal

17 Servo unit – testing, removal and refitting

1   If the brakes seem to need more or less pressure than normal, a check of the servo is indicated.

2   First of all trace the hoses and check their condition. There must be no leaks or obstructions.

3   Test the vacuum check valve. This is to be found in the vacuum line between the induction manifold and the servo. Remove it from the hose line and clean it carefully. There is an arrow on the valve. Blow into the valve in the direction of the arrow, the valve should open. Blow in the opposite direction and the valve must seat. The valve is there to stop pressure from the manifold, eg a backfire, arriving in the vacuum side of the servo, ie it is a non-return valve, so that the induction suction can only suck, and not blow.

4   If the servo is still not working correctly check that the filter and damping washer at the rear of the unit are not clogged with dust. If they are, renew them but note that the slots in each item must be offset 180° on reassembly.

5   To test the servo, first depress the brake pedal several times with the engine stopped. This will exhaust the vacuum in the unit. Now depress the pedal and hold it down. Start the engine and allow it to idle – if the servo unit is functioning correctly the pedal will move slightly towards the floor as the vacuum assistance commences.

6   To remove the servo first remove the master cylinder as described in Section 15.

7   Disconnect the vacuum hose from the unit.

8   If a return spring is fitted in the servo mounting bracket, remove the split pin and washer and withdraw the spring from the clevis.

9   Unscrew the servo unit mounting nuts.

10 On right-hand drive models withdraw the unit from the bracket until the clevis pin is visible. Pull out the clip and remove the clevis pin from the bellcrank. Recover the two washers. On left-hand drive models disconnect the clevis from the foot pedal inside the car.

11 On all models withdraw the servo unit from the car.

12 Refitting is a reversal of removal, with reference to Section 15 as necessary. On right-hand drive models check that the relay rods and levers are in good condition and lightly grease the pivot points; if the pivot pins and shafts are worn they should be renewed with stainless steel parts. On left-hand drive models set the pushrod clevis to the dimension shown in Fig. 8.26.

13 On some North American models equipped with fuel injection, an adjustable booster is fitted in the vacuum hose to provide a minimum vacuum of 11.8 in Hg. If the booster is suspect, check the vacuum with a vacuum gauge and adjust the screw as necessary after loosening the end locknut. The adjustment screw is located in the locknut and is accessible after disconnecting the hose.

18 Brake pressure regulator – description

1   A brake regulator is fitted in the rear brake circuit of some models and is located just in front of the rear axle to which it is attached by a spring. 1981 North American models built at Westmoreland are fitted with a brake regulator; this unit is located on the left-hand side of the engine compartment.

2   Both units limit the braking force applied to the rear brakes and effectively prevent the rear brakes locking under heavy braking conditions.

3   Adjustment or renewal of the regulator should be left to a VW agent since special equipment is required; it is not possible to adjust the proportioning valve.

4   When bleeding the hydraulic system of cars fitted with a pressure regulator, the lever of the regulator should be pressed toward the rear axle.

19 Hydraulic pipes and hoses – inspection and renewal

1   The magnitude of the pressure in the hydraulic lines is not generally realized. The test pressures are 100 kgf/cm² (1420 lbf/in²) for the front brakes. The normal pressure in the hydraulic system when the brakes are not in use is negligible. The pressure builds up quickly when the brakes are applied and remains until the pedal is released. Each driver will know how quick the build up is when equating it to the speed of his own reaction in an emergency brake application.

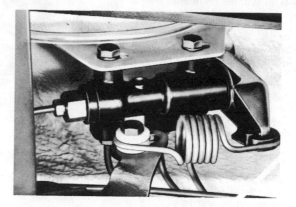

Fig. 8.22 The brake pressure regulator (Sec 18)

2   Research in the USA has shown that brake line corrosion may be expected to lead to failure after only 90 days exposure to salt spray such as is thrown up when salt is used to melt ice or snow. This in effect makes a four year old vehicle automatically suspect. It is possible to use pipe made of a copper alloy used in marine work called 'Kunifer 10' as a replacement. This is much more resistant to salt corrosion, but as yet is not a standard fitting.

3   All this should by now have indicated that pipes need regular inspection. The obvious times are in the autumn before the winter conditions set in, and in the spring to see what damage has been done.

4   Trace the routes of all the rigid pipes and wash or brush away accumulated dirt. If the pipes are obviously covered with some sort of underseal compound do not disturb the underseal. Examine for signs of kinks or dents which could have been caused by flying stones. Any instances of this means that the pipe section should be renewed, but **before actually taking it out read the rest of this Section.** Any unprotected sections of pipe which show signs of corrosion or pitting on the outer surface must also be considered for renewal.

5   Flexible hoses, running to each of the front wheels and from the underbody to each rear wheel should show no external signs of chafing or cracking. Move them about to see whether surface cracks appear. If they feel stiff and inflexible or are twisted they are nearing the end of their useful life. If in any doubt renew the hoses. Make sure also that they are not rubbing against the bodywork.

6   Before attempting to remove a pipe for renewal it is important to be sure that you have a replacement source of supply within reach if you do not wish to be kept off the road for too long. Pipes are often damaged on removal. If an official agency is near you may be reasonably sure that the correct pipes and unions are available. If not, check first that your local garage has the necessary equipment for making up the pipes and has the correct metric thread pipe unions available. The same goes for flexible hoses.

7   Where the couplings from rigid to flexible pipes are made there are support brackets and the flexible pipe is held in place by a U-clip which engages in a groove in the union (photo). The male union screws into it. Before getting the spanners on, soak the unions in penetrating fluid as there is always some rust or corrosion binding the threads. Whilst this is soaking in, place a piece of plastic film under the fluid reservoir cap (if possible) to minimise loss of fluid from the disconnected pipes. Hold the hexagon on the flexible pipe coupling whilst the union on the rigid pipe is undone. Then pull out the clip to release both pipes from the bracket. For flexible hose removal this procedure will be needed at both ends. For a rigid pipe the other end will only involve unscrewing the union from a cylinder or connector. When you are renewing a flexible hose, take care not to damage the unions of the pipes that connect into it. If a union is particularly stubborn be prepared to renew the rigid pipe as well. This is quite often the case if you are forced to use open-ended spanners. It may be worth spending a little money on a special pipe union spanner which is like a ring spanner with a piece cut out to enable it to go round the tube.

8   Note that later Girling calipers have a flexible hose union using a *left-hand thread*. The hose used with such a caliper is shorter and has an identification groove on the hexagon at the caliper end.

9   If you are having the new pipe made up, take the old one along to check that the unions and pipe flaring at the ends are identical.

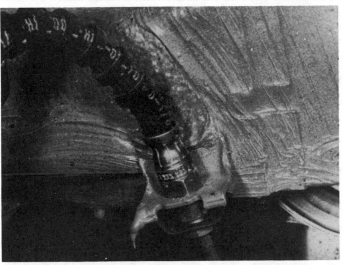

19.7 Front brake flexible hose and union

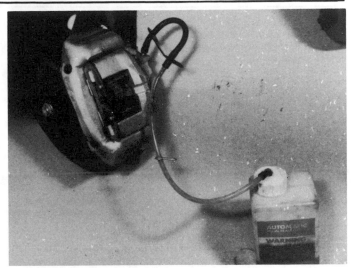

20.3a One-man brake bleeding kit in use

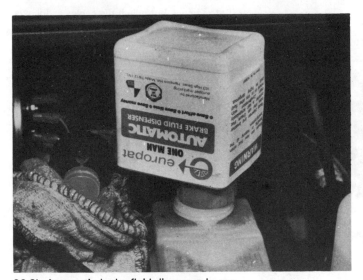

20.3b Automatic brake fluid dispenser in use

20.7 Front caliper bleed nipple and cap

10 Refitting of the hoses or pipes is a reversal of the removal procedure. Precautions and care are needed to make sure that the unions are correctly lined up to prevent cross-threading. This may mean bending the pipe a little where a rigid pipe goes into a fixture. Such bending must not, under any circumstances, be too acute or the pipe will kink and weaken.

11 When fitting flexible hoses take care not to twist them. This can happen when the unions are finally tightened unless a spanner is used to hold the end of the flexible hose and prevent twisting.

12 If a pipe is removed or a union slackened so that air can get into the system then the system must be bled as described in Section 20.

20 Hydraulic system – bleeding

1 The correct functioning of the brake hydraulic system is only possible after the removal of all air from the components and circuit; this is achieved by bleeding the system. Note that only clean unused brake fluid which has remained unshaken for at least 24 hours must be used.

2 If there is any possibility of incorrect fluid being used in the system, the brake lines and components must be completely flushed with fresh fluid and new seals fitted to the components.

3 There are a number of one-man, do-it-yourself, brake bleeding kits currently available from motor accessory shops. It is recommended that one of these kits should be used wherever possible as they greatly simplify the bleeding operation and also reduce the risk of expelled air and fluid being drawn back into the system (photos).

4 If one of these kits is not available then it will be necessary to gather together a clean jar and a suitable length of clear plastic tubing which is a tight fit over the bleed screw, and also to engage the help of an assistant.

5 Before commencing the bleeding operation, check that all rigid pipes and flexible hoses are in good condition and that all hydraulic unions are tight. Take great care not to allow hydraulic fluid to come into contact with the vehicle paintwork, otherwise the finish will be seriously damaged. Wash off any spilled fluid immediately with cold water. Where a servo is fitted, depress the brake pedal several times in order to dissipate the vacuum.

6 If hydraulic fluid has been lost from the master cylinder, due to a leak in the system, ensure that the cause is traced and rectified before proceeding further or a serious malfunction of the braking system may occur.

7 To bleed the system, clean the area around the bleed screw at the wheel cylinder to be bled (photo). If the hydraulic system has only been partially disconnected and suitable precautions were taken to prevent further loss of fluid, it should only be necessary to bleed that part of the system. However, if the entire system is to be bled, start at the right-hand rear wheel cylinder. Note that where a brake pressure regulator is fitted, the regulator lever should be pressed towards the rear axle

during the bleeding of the rear brakes.

8   Remove the master cylinder filler cap and top up the reservoir. periodically check the fluid level during the bleeding operation and top up as necessary.

9   If a one-man brake bleeding kit is being used, connect the outlet tube to the bleed screw and then open the screw half a turn. If possible position the unit so that it can be viewed from the car, then depress the brake pedal to the floor and slowly release it. The one-way valve in the kit will prevent dispelled air from returning to the system at the end of each stroke. Repeat this operation until clean hydraulic fluid, free from air bubbles, can be seen coming through the tube. Now tighten the bleed screw and remove the outlet tube.

10 If a one-man brake bleeding kit is not available, connect one end of the plastic tubing to the bleed screw and immerse the other end in the jar containing sufficient clean hydraulic fluid to keep the end of the tube submerged. Open the bleed screw half a turn and have your assistant depress the brake pedal to the floor and then slowly release it. Tighten the bleed screw at the end of each downstroke to prevent expelled air and fluid from being drawn back into the system. Repeat this operation until clean hydraulic fluid, free from air bubbles, can be seen coming through the tube. Now tighten the bleed screw and remove the plastic tube.

11 If the entire system is being bled the procedures described above should now be repeated at the left-hand rear wheel cylinder, followed by the right-hand front and left-hand front calipers. Do not forget to recheck the fluid level in the master cylinder at regular intervals and top up as necessary.

12 When completed, recheck the fluid level in the master cylinder, top

up if necessary and refit the cap. Check the 'feel' of the brake pedal which should be firm and free from any 'sponginess' which would indicate air still present in the system.

13 Discard any expelled hydraulic fluid as it is likely to be contaminated with moisture, air and dirt which makes it unsuitable for further use.

21 Handbrake lever and cables – removal, refitting and adjustment

1   To remove the lever first remove the plastic boot from the handbrake lever (photo).

2   Unscrew the locknut and adjusting nut from each cable and lift off the equalizer bar (photo).

3   Extract the clip from the pivot pin and push the pin out of the housing.

4   Withdraw the handbrake lever, leaving the cables in place.

5   To remove a cable first disconnect it from the handbrake lever as already described.

6   Remove the rear brake drum and disconnect the cable from the shoe operating lever as described in Section 11, 12 or 13. Detach the cable from the backplate.

7   Release the cable from the clips and withdraw it from under the car.

8   Refitting is a reversal of removal, but adjust the cables as follows after refitting the brake drums.

9   On manually adjusted rear brakes, first adjust the shoes as

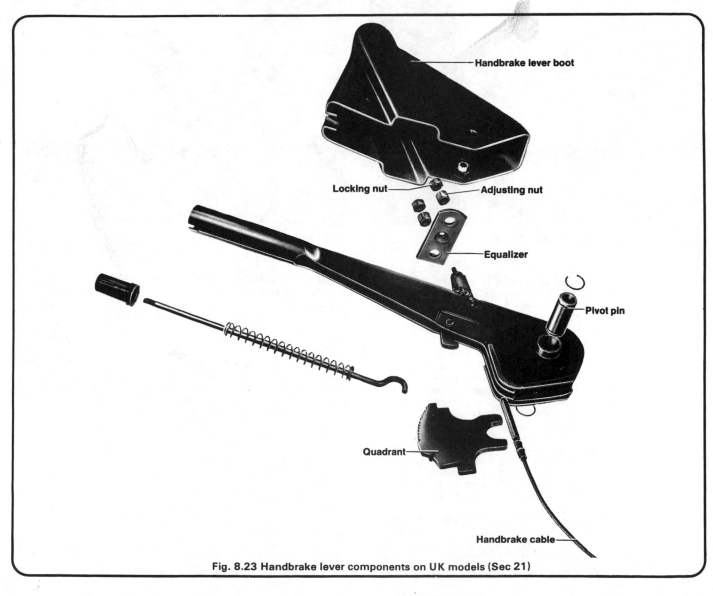

Fig. 8.23 Handbrake lever components on UK models (Sec 21)

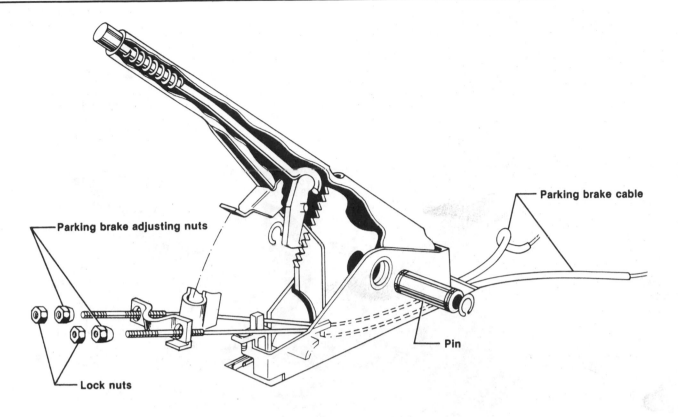

Fig. 8.24 Handbrake lever components on North American models (Sec 21)

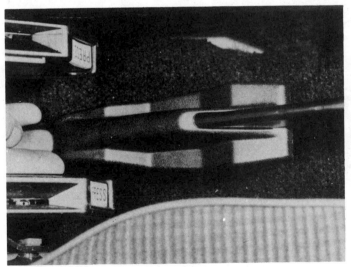

21.1 Removing the handbrake lever plastic boot

21.2 Handbrake lever and cables (early models)

described in Section 3. On self-adjusting brakes apply and release the handbrake lever several times (lever type), or fully depress the foot pedal once (wedge type).

10 Apply the handbrake lever by the number of notches given in the Specifications.

11 Loosen the locknuts and adjust the position of each cable adjusting nut so that each rear wheel is just locked and cannot be turned by hand.

12 Fully release the handbrake lever and check that each rear wheel can be rotated freely.

13 Tighten the locknuts and refit the plastic boot.

22 Brake pedal – removal and refitting

1 Working inside the car, disconnect the pushrod clevis from the brake pedal (photo). On early models and some later right-hand drive models, slide out the clip and remove the clevis pin – on all other models prise the combined clip and pin from the clevis.

2 On manual gearbox models remove the clutch pedal as described in Chapter 5, then remove the pivot shaft and withdraw the brake pedal.

3 On automatic transmission models slide out the clip, remove the

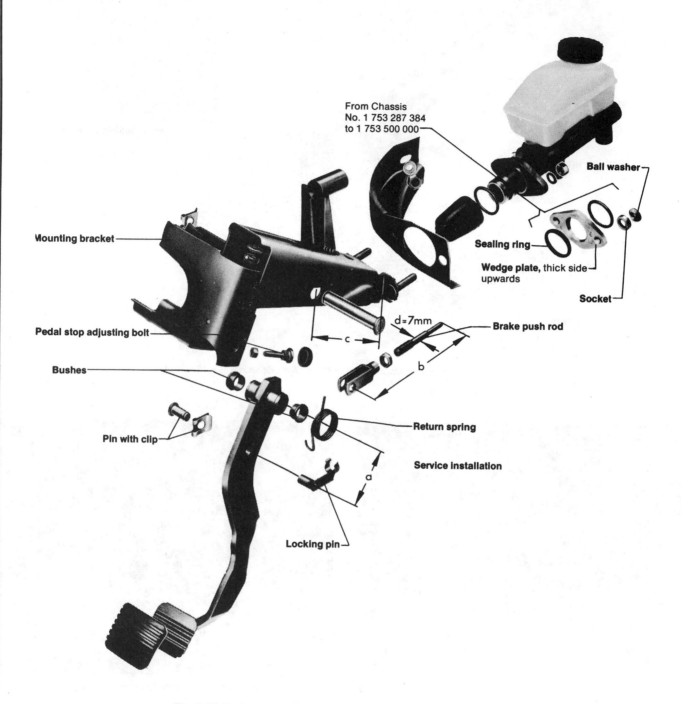

Mounting bracket

From Chassis
No. 1 753 287 384
to 1 753 500 000

Ball washer

Sealing ring

Wedge plate, thick side
upwards

Socket

Pedal stop adjusting bolt

d=7mm

c

b

Brake push rod

Bushes

Pin with clip

Return spring

Service installation

a

Locking pin

Fig. 8.25 Brake pedal components on non-servo models (Sec 22)

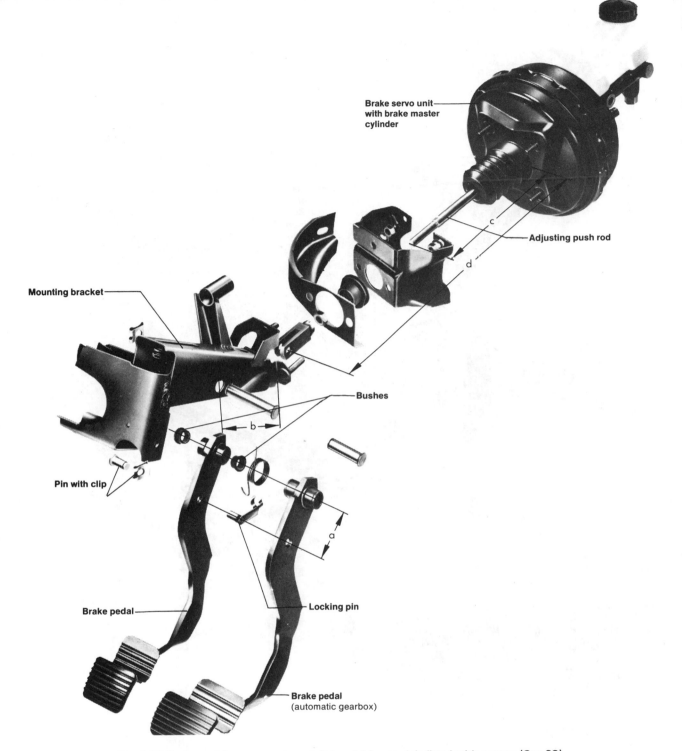

Fig. 8.26 Brake pedal components on left-hand drive models fitted with a servo (Sec 22)

	Dimension a	Dimension b	Dimension c	Dimension d
Up to chassis No 175 3 500 000/ 535 500 000	1.85 in (47 mm)	4.72 in (120 mm)	7.36 in (187 mm)	8.90 in (226 mm)
From chassis No 176 3 000 001/ 536 2 000 001	1.61 in (41 mm)	3.94 in (100 mm)	6.73 in (171 mm)	8.11 in (206 mm)
From chassis No 177 3 000 001/ 537 2 000 001 and all 81 kW engine models	1.69 in (43 mm)	3.94 in (100 mm)	6.93 in (176 mm)	8.11 in (206 mm)

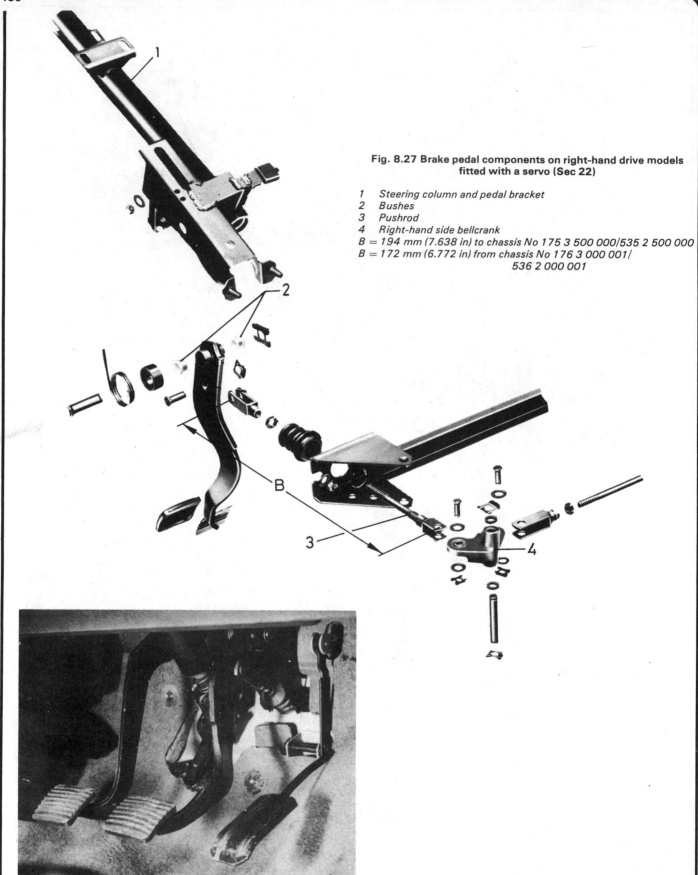

Fig. 8.27 Brake pedal components on right-hand drive models
fitted with a servo (Sec 22)

1   Steering column and pedal bracket
2   Bushes
3   Pushrod
4   Right-hand side bellcrank
$B = 194$ mm (7.638 in) to chassis No 175 3 500 000/535 2 500 000
$B = 172$ mm (6.772 in) from chassis No 176 3 000 001/
                                        536 2 000 001

22.1 Brake pedal and pushrod (later Golf models)

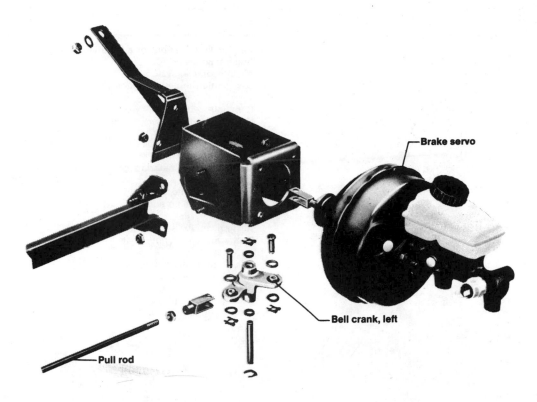

Fig. 8.28 Brake pedal connecting rod, left-hand side bellcrank and servo on right-hand drive models (Sec 22)

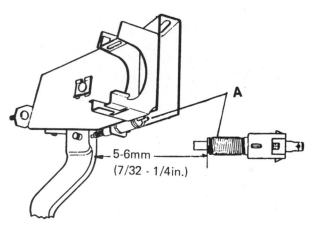

Fig. 8.29 Stop-light switch (A) adjustment on 1981 North American models built at Westmoreland (Sec 22)

pivot shaft, and withdraw the brake pedal. Note the location of the return spring.

4   On right-hand drive models fitted with a servo, note the spacer located on the right-hand side of the pedal.

5   Examine the pedal bushes and shaft for wear, and renew them if necessary. The bushes can be removed using a drift and new ones fitted by clamping in a vice.

6   Refitting is a reversal of removal, but lubricate the bushes with a little general-purpose grease.

7   On North American models fitted with a servo unit, make sure that the clevis and pin are located in the second hole in the pedal 2 in (51 mm) from the centre of the pivot shaft. On non-servo models adjust the pushrod as described in Section 15.

8   On 1981 North American models built at Westmoreland, adjust the stop-light switch so that it is 5 to 6 mm (0.20 to 0.24 in) from the brake pedal (Fig. 8.29).

23 Fault diagnosis – braking system

Symptom	Reason(s)
Excessive pedal travel	Rear brake shoes out of adjustment (as applicable) or worn Brake fluid leak Air in hydraulic system Lost motion in pedal linkage (RHD only)
Uneven braking and pulling to one side	Contaminated linings Seized wheel cylinder or caliper Incorrect adjustment (as applicable) Unequal tyre pressures Loose suspension anchor point Different lining materials on same axle
Brake judder	Worn drums and/or discs Loose suspension anchor point
Brake pedal feels spongy	Air in hydraulic system Faulty master cylinder seals
Excessive effort required to stop car	Servo unit faulty (as applicable) Seized wheel cylinder or caliper Incorrect lining material Contaminated linings New linings not yet bedded-in

Chapter 9 Electrical system

For modifications and information applicable to later models, see Supplement at end of manual

Contents

Specifications

General
System type	12 volt, negative earth
Battery capacity (amp hr)	27, 36, 45, 54 or 63

Alternator
Maximum output (amps)	35, 45, 55 or 65
Brush length (minimum)	5 mm (0.2 in)
Regulator voltage	12.5 to 14.5 volt
Stator resistance (ohms):	
Bosch:	
35 amp	0.25 to 0.28
45 amp	0.18 to 0.20
55 amp	0.14 to 0.16
65 amp	0.10 to 0.11
Motorola:	
35 amp	0.23 to 0.25
45 amp (up to March 1981)	0.27 to 0.3
45 amp (March 1981 on)	0.09 to 0.11
55 amp	0.15 to 0.17
65 amp	0.13 to 0.15
Rotor resistance (ohms):	
Bosch (except 65 amp)	3.4 to 3.75
Bosch (65 amp)	2.8 to 3.0
Motorola (except 65 amp)	3.9 to 4.3
Motorola (65 amp)	3.8 to 4.2

Starter motor
Type	Pre-engaged
Brush length (minimum)	13 mm (0.5 in)
Commutator diameter (minimum)	33.5 mm (1.319 in)
Commutator run-out (maximum)	0.05 mm (0.002 in)
Armature endplay:	
Type 023 and 023A	0.1 to 0.15 mm (0.004 to 0.006 in)
Type 023B	0.1 to 0.3 mm (0.004 to 0.012 in)

Fuses

Note: *The following tables are typical – refer to the fuse box lid if necessary*

Early UK models:

1	Left headlamp - low beam
2	Right headlamp - low beam
3	Left headlamp - high beam
4	Right headlamp - high beam
5	Rear window heater
6	Interior light - door switches
7	Brake light, glovebox light, cigar lighter
8	Turn signal and emergency flasher
9	Back-up light, horn
10	Rear window heater - warning light, headlamp washer circuit
11	Fresh air fan
12	Number plate lamps
13	Tail light right, parking light right, side marker front
14	Tail light left, parking light left, side marker front
15	Foglamps

Later UK and North American models:

1	Left headlamp - low beam
2	Right headlamp - low beam
3	Left headlamp - high beam, warning lamp
4	Right headlamp - high beam
5	Rear window heater
6	Emergency lights, stop-lights, radio (except North American models)
7	Interior light, cigarette lighter, clock
8	Turn signals
9	Reversing lights, horn, selector lever console (automatic transmission), automatic choke, inlet manifold heater, fuel cut-off valve
10	Fresh air blower
11	Windscreen wipers and washer pump, intermittent relay
12	Number plate lights
13	Sidelamp - right, tail lamp - right, side marker - right (North American models)
14	Sidelamp - left, tail lamp - left, side marker - left (North American models)
15	Radiator fan

In-line fuses are located above the fusebox for the following circuits . Foglight, rear window wiper, electric fuel pump (where applicable), air conditioner (where applicable), radio (North American models)

Bulbs

	Wattage
Headlamp	45/40 or 60/55
Sidelamp	4
Front and rear turn signal	21
Stop-lamp	21
Reversing lamp	21
Number plate light	4
Interior lamp	10
Glovebox	2
Warning lamps	1.2
Instrument lights	1.2
Foglamps (halogen)	55
Rear foglight	21

Torque wrench settings

	lbf ft	Nm
Starter motor:		
Manual gearbox models	33	46
Automatic transmission models	17	23
Wiper arm	4	5
Alternator	15	20
Alternator bracket	22	30

1 General description

The electrical system is of 12 volt negative earth type. The battery is charged by a belt-driven alternator which incorporates a voltage regulator. The starter motor is of pre-engaged type and incorporates four brushes; with this type of starter a solenoid moves the drive pinion into engagement with the ring gear before the starter motor is energised.

Although repair procedures are given in this Chapter, it may well be more economical to renew worn components as complete units.

2 Battery – removal and refitting

1   The battery is mounted on the left-hand side at the front of the engine compartment (photo). Remove the earth strap (negative) and the positive cable terminal. The battery is held in position by a clamp which fits over a rim at the base. A 13 mm socket spanner, preferably with an extension, is necessary to undo the clamp nut.

2   Installation is the reverse of the removal procedure. Smear the terminals with a little petroleum jelly. **Do not** use grease.

2.1 Battery location on a Scirocco

necessary, neither is it possible to measure the specific gravity of the electrolyte. Some such batteries have a built-in charge indicator; instructions concerning its interpretation are usually printed on the battery cover.

4 Battery – electrolyte replenishment

Note: *This Section is not applicable to maintenance-free batteries.*
1   If the battery has been fully charged but one cell has a specific gravity of 0.025, or more, less than the others it is most likely that electrolyte has been lost from the cell at some time and the acid over-diluted with distilled water when topping up.
2   In this case remove some of the electrolyte with a hydrometer and top up with fresh electrolyte. It is best to get this done at a service station, for making your own electrolyte is messy, dangerous, and expensive for the small amount you need. If you must do it yourself add 1 part of sulphuric acid (concentrated) to 2.5 parts of water. **Add the acid to the water**, not the other way round or the mixture will spit back as water is added to acid and you will be badly burnt. Add the acid a drop at a time to the water.
3   Having added fresh electrolyte, recharge and recheck the readings. In all probability this will cure the problem. If it does not, then there is a short-circuit somewhere.
4   Electrolyte must always be stored away from other fluids and should be locked up, not left about. If you have children this is even more important.

3 Battery – maintenance

1   The modern battery seldom requires topping up but nevertheless, the electrolyte level should be inspected weekly as a means of providing the first indication that the alternator is overcharging or that the battery casing has developed a leak.
2   When topping up is required, use only distilled water or melted ice from a refrigerator (frosting not ice cubes).
3   Acid should never be required if the battery has been correctly filled from new, unless spillage has occurred.
4   Inspect the battery terminals and mounting tray for corrosion. This is the white fluffy deposit which grows at these areas. If evident, clean it away and neutralise it with ammonia or baking soda. Apply petroleum jelly to the terminals and paint the battery tray with anti-corrosive paint.
5   With normal motoring, the battery should be kept in a good state of charge by the alternator and never need charging from a mains charger.
6   However, as the battery ages, it may not be able to hold its charge and some supplementary charging may be needed. Before connecting the charger, disconnect the battery terminals or better still, remove the battery from the vehicle.
7   An indication of the state of charge of a battery can be obtained by checking the electrolyte in each cell using a hydrometer. The specific gravity of the electrolyte for fully charged and fully discharged conditions at the electrolyte temperature indicated, is listed below.

Fully discharged	Electrolyte temperature	Fully charged
1.098	38°C (100°F)	1.268
1.102	32°C (90°F)	1.272
1.106	27°C (80°F)	1.276
1.110	21°C (70°F)	1.280
1.114	16°C (60°F)	1.284
1.118	10°C (50°F)	1.288
1.122	4°C (40°F)	1.292
1.126	−1.5°C (30°F)	1.296

8   There should be very little variation in the readings between the different cells, but if a difference is found in excess of 0.025 then it will probably be due to an internal fault indicating impending battery failure. This assumes that electrolyte has not been spilled at some time and the deficiency made up with water only.
9   The cells have individual filler/vent caps on the battery fitted as original equipment. The battery plates should always be covered to a depth of 6.0 mm (0.25 in) with electrolyte.
10 Keep the top surface of the battery casing dry.
11 Where a 'maintenance-free' battery is fitted, no topping up is

5 Battery – charging

1   In winter time when heavy demand is placed upon the battery such as starting from cold, and much electrical equipment is continually in use, it is a good idea occasionally to have the battery fully charged from an external source at the rate of 3.5 to 4 amps. Always disconnect it from the car electrical circuit when charging.
2   Continue to charge the battery at this rate until no further rise in specific gravity is noted over a four hour period.
3   Alternatively, a trickle charger, charging at the rate of 1.5 amps, can be safely used overnight. Disconnect the battery from the car electrical circuit before charging or you will damage the alternator.
4   Specially rapid 'boost' charges which are claimed to restore the power of the battery in 1 to 2 hours can cause damage to the battery plates through overheating.
5   While charging the battery note that the temperature of the electrolyte should never exceed 100°F (37.8°C).
6   Make sure that your charging set and battery are set to the same voltage.
7   'Maintenance-free' batteries must only be trickle charged and may require twice the charging period of a normal battery.

6 Alternator – maintenance and special precautions

1   Periodically wipe away any dirt which has accumulated on the outside of the unit, and also check that the plug is pushed firmly on the terminals. At the same time check the tension of the drivebelt and adjust it if necessary as described in Chapter 2.
2   Take extreme care when making electrical circuit connections on the car, otherwise damage may occur to the alternator or other electrical components employing semiconductors. Always make sure that the battery leads are connected to the correct terminals. Before using electric arc welding equipment to repair any part of the car, disconnect the battery leads and alternator multi-plug. Disconnect the battery leads before using a mains charger. Never run the alternator with the multi-plug or a battery lead disconnected.

7 Alternator – removal and refitting

1   Disconnect the battery negative lead.
2   Pull the multi-plug from the rear of the alternator and disconnect the wiring support.
3   Loosen the adjustment link bolts and the mounting pivot bolt, using an Allen key where necessary (photo).
4   Swivel the alternator downward and slip the drivebelt from the

7.3 Alternator location

8 Alternator – testing

1   The following method is recommended by the manufacturers, although it requires the use of a battery cut-out switch and a variable resistance in addition to an ammeter, voltmeter, and tachometer. If this equipment is not available, a simpler method may be employed using one of the compact multi-testers available from accessory shops – in this case follow the instructions with the instrument.

2   Connect up the circuit as shown in Fig. 9.1. The variable resistance should be capable of consuming up to 500 watts, the ammeter should have a 0 to 40 amp scale, and the voltmeter a 0 to 20 volt scale.

3   Start the engine and run it at 3000 rpm, then adjust the variable resistance so that the ammeter reading is 20 amps.

4   Open the battery cut-out switch in order to isolate the battery.

5   Adjust the resistance so that the ammeter reads 25 amps with the 35 amp alternator, 30 amps with the 45 amp alternator, 35 amps with the 55 amp alternator, and 40 amps with the 65 amp alternator.

6   Read the voltmeter – it should be between 12.5 and 14.5 volts.

7   If the voltmeter reading is outside these limits close the cut-off switch, stop the engine and replace the alternator regulator with a new one (or a borrowed one). Repeat the test. If the desired 12.5 to 14.5 volts are obtained then the old regulator is faulty. If not then the alternator is faulty and must be changed. It seems a lot to do for little reward but the only other way is to take the alternator to an official agent for testing.

9 Alternator (Bosch) – overhaul

1   The regulator is fitted into the alternator housing. Remove the small screws and it may be removed. Refer to Figs. 9.2 and 9.3.

2   Inside it will be seen the two slip ring brushes. These must be free in the guides and protrude at least 5 mm (0.2 in). The brushes may be renewed by unsoldering the leads from the regulator, fitting new brushes and resoldering the leads.

3   Undo the pulley nut and remove the pulley, the spacer ring, the large washer and the fan. Note which way the fan fits to make assembly easier. There is an arrow showing the direction of rotation.

4   Remove the bracket from the housing which held the wiring plug and if not already removed, take away the regulator (photo).

5   Undo the housing bolts and separate the components. The rotor will stay in the endplate and the housing bearing will stay on the shaft (photo). Have a good look at the various components. Clean off all the dust using a soft brush and then wipe clean. Any smell of burnt carbon

alternator pulley, water pump pulley, and crankshaft pulley.

5   Remove the adjustment and pivot bolts and washers and withdraw the alternator from the engine. Note that early models are equipped with rubber mounting bushes, whereas later models have a rigid mounting.

6   On models equipped with air conditioning, check the compressor drivebelt tension and if necessary adjust it before fitting the water pump/alternator drivebelt. This is particularly necessary where the compressor position must be altered in order to adjust the drivebelt tension since this alters the water pump/alternator drivebelt tension.

7   Refitting is a reversal of removal, but before tightening the mounting and adjustment bolts, tension the drivebelt as follows. Where a rigid mounting is fitted, slightly loosen the bracket bolts. Lever the alternator upward until the correct tension is achieved (see Chapter 2 Specifications). The alternator must only be levered at the drive end bracket. On models with air conditioning, the drivebelt can be tensioned using a screwdriver as shown in Fig. 2.6, Chapter 2. Tighten the adjustment link bolts followed by the pivot bolt, and bracket bolts (where applicable), then recheck the tension.

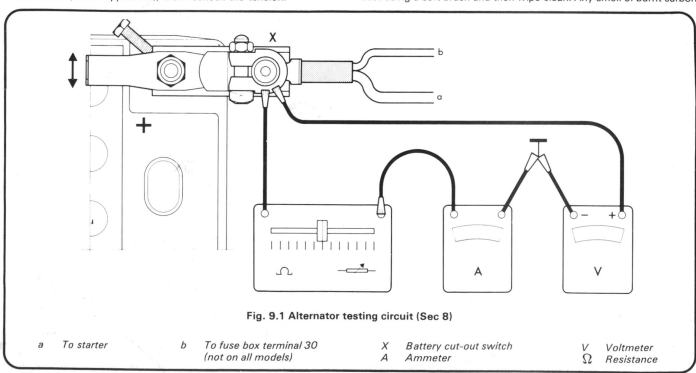

Fig. 9.1 Alternator testing circuit (Sec 8)

a To starter	*b* To fuse box terminal 30 (not on all models)	*X* Battery cut-out switch *A* Ammeter	*V* Voltmeter Ω Resistance

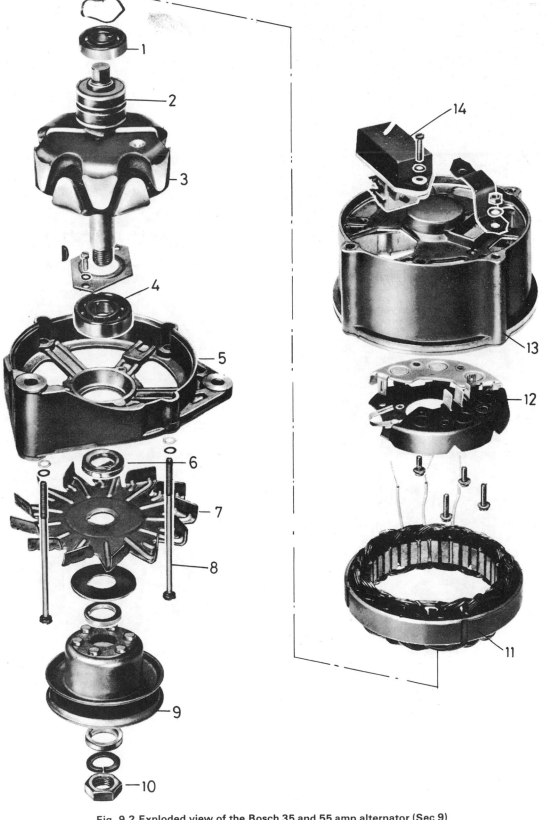

Fig. 9.2 Exploded view of the Bosch 35 and 55 amp alternator (Sec 9)

1	Bearing	4	Bearing	8	Through bolt	12	Diode plate
2	Slip rings	5	Endplate	9	Pulley	13	Alternator housing
3	Claw pole rotor with	6	Spacer ring	10	Nut	14	Regulator with carbon
	field windings	7	Fan	11	Stator with windings		brushes

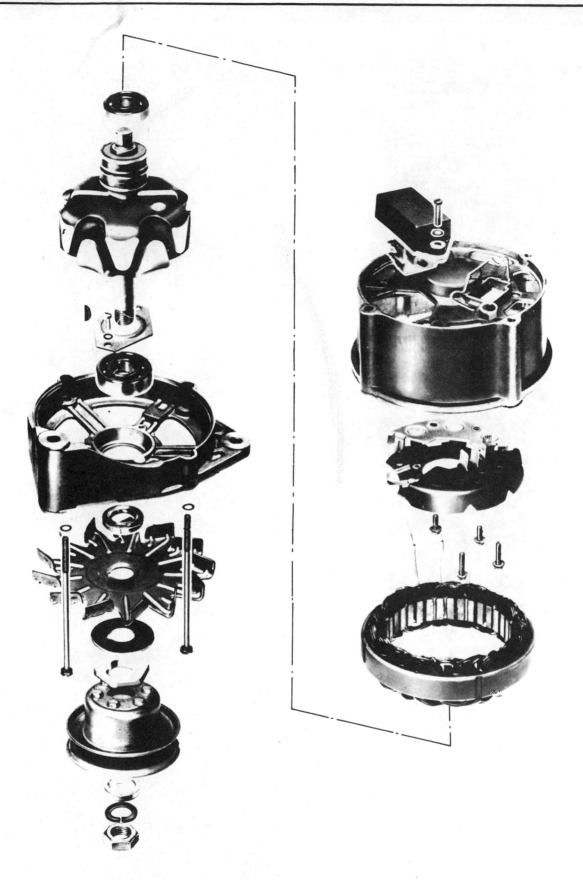

Fig. 9.3 Exploded view of the Bosch 45 and 65 amp alternator (Sec 9)

See Fig. 9.2 for component identification

Fig. 9.4 Bosch regulator and bushes, showing wear dimension (a) and soldering points (arrowed) (Sec 9)

9.4 Alternator voltage regulator and brushes

9.5 Endplate and rotor on a Bosch alternator

or signs of overheating must be investigated. Check the slip rings for burning, scoring and ovality. Check the bearings. At this point you must make up your mind whether to do the repair yourself, or whether to take the alternator to a specialist. If you have the tools and skill, it is possible to renew the bearings, renew the diode carrier complete, clean up the slip rings and to fit a new rotor or stator. It is not possible to repair the winding, renew individual diodes, renew the slip rings or repair the fan.

6   The rotor may be removed from the endplate by using a mandrel press. Then take the screws out of the cover over the endplate bearing and press the bearing out of the frame. The slip ring end bearing may be pulled off using an extractor on the inner race. If you pull on the outer race the bearing will be scrapped. Renew the bearings if necessary.

7   The slip rings may be cleaned up with fine glasspaper (not emery paper).

8   Test the rotor electrically. Check the insulation resistance between the slip rings and the shaft. This must be infinity. If it is not there is a short-circuit and the rotor must be renewed. Get an auto-electrical specialist to confirm your findings first. Check the resistance of the winding. Measure this between slip rings. It should be as specified. If there is an open-circuit or high resistance, then again the rotor must be renewed.

9   The stator and the diode carrier are connected by wires. Make a simple circuit diagram so that you know which wire goes to which diode and then unsolder the connections. This is a delicate business as excess heat will destroy the diode and possibly the winding. Grip the wire as close as possible to the soldered joint with a pair of long-nosed pliers and use as small a soldering iron as possible (photo).

10   The stator winding may now be checked. First check that the insulation is sound. The resistance between the leads and the frame must be infinity. Next measure the resistance of the winding. It should be as specified. A zero reading means a short-circuit, and of course a high or infinity reading, an open-circuit.

11   The diode carrier may now be checked. Each diode should be checked in turn. Use a test lamp or an ohmmeter. Current must flow only one way; ie, the resistance measured one way must be high and the other way (reverse the leads), low. Keep the current down to 0.8 amps and do not allow the diode to heat up. If the resistance both ways is a high one, then the diode is open-circuited, a low one, short-circuited. If only one diode is defective the whole assembly (diode plate) must be renewed.

12   Reconnect the stator winding to the diode circuit, again be careful not to overheat the diode, and reassemble the stator and diode carrier to the housing.

13   A new diode carrier or a new stator may be fitted, but be careful to get the correct parts.

14   Assembly is the reverse of dismantling. Be careful to assemble the various washers correctly.

9.9 Diode plate on a Bosch alternator

10 Alternator (Motorola) – overhaul

1   Refer to Figs. 9.5 and 9.6. It will be seen that although the construction is basically the same as the Bosch generator the Motorola differs considerably in detail.

2   The stator and rotor have the same form as those of the Bosch but the cover, housing and diode plate are of different construction. The earth strap is bolted to the cover, not the hinge as in the case of the Bosch.

3   The same principles apply for overhaul. The rotor should be checked for earth short-circuit and continuity. The resistance between

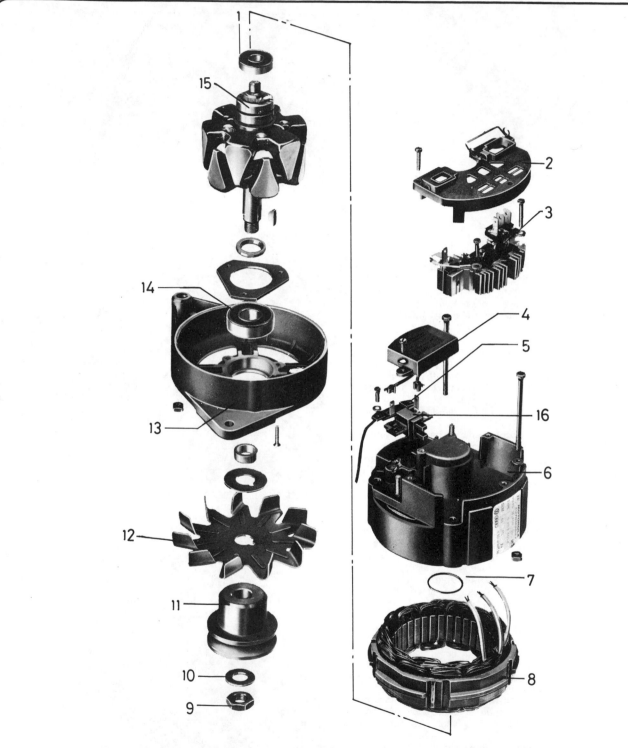

Fig. 9.5 Exploded view of the Motorola 35, 55 and 65 amp alternator (Sec 10)

1	Bearing	5	Connector plate D+	9	Nut	13	Endplate
2	Cover plate	6	Housing	10	Thrust washer	14	Bearing
3	Diode plate	7	O-ring	11	Pulley	15	Rotor
4	Voltage regulator	8	Stator	12	Fan	16	Brush gear

slip rings must agree with the Specifications. Bearings may be drawn off with a puller and renewed if necessary.

4   The stator may be disconnected from the diode plate and the winding tested for open and short-circuit. The resistance should agree with the Specifications.

5   Once isolated the diode plate may be tested, as in Section 9, and a new one fitted if required. It is not recommended that any attempt be made to replace diodes.

6   The routing of the 'D+' wire inside the cover is important. It must be fitted in the two sets of clips provided or it will become involved with the rotor.

7   The voltage regulator connections must be checked. The green wire goes to 'DF' and the red wire to 'D+'.

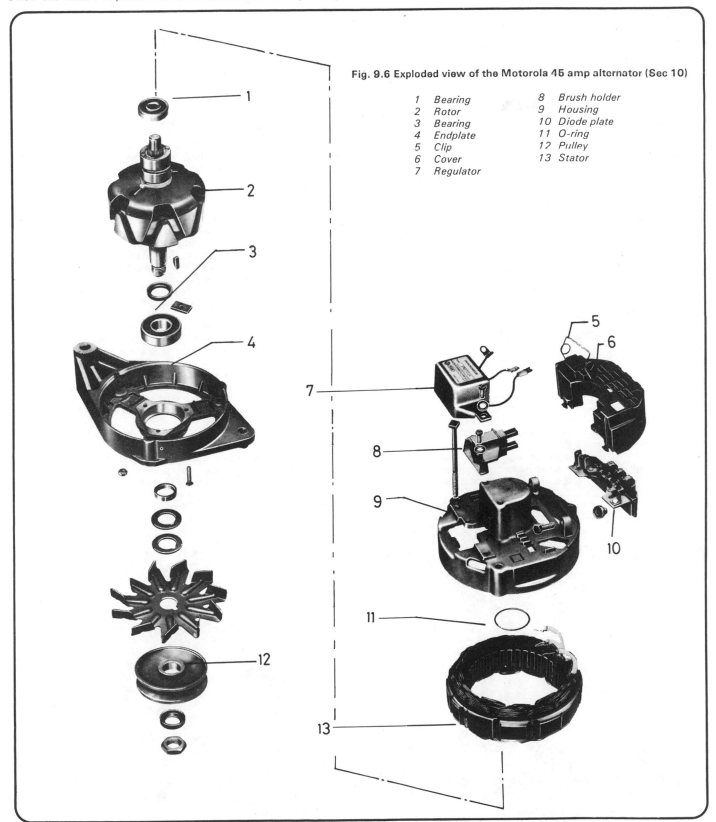

Fig. 9.6 Exploded view of the Motorola 45 amp alternator (Sec 10)

1	Bearing	8	Brush holder
2	Rotor	9	Housing
3	Bearing	10	Diode plate
4	Endplate	11	O-ring
5	Clip	12	Pulley
6	Cover	13	Stator
7	Regulator		

11 Starter motor – testing in the car

1   If the starter motor fails to operate, first check the condition of the battery by switching on the headlamps. If they glow brightly, then gradually dim after a few seconds, the battery is in an uncharged condition.

2   If the battery is in good condition, check the starter motor main terminal and the engine earth cable for security. Check the terminal connections on the starter solenoid located on top of the starter.

3   If the starter still fails to turn, use a voltmeter or 12 volt test lamp and leads to check that current is reaching the uppermost terminal on the solenoid. Connect one lead to earth and the other to the terminal, when a reading should be obtained or the test lamp should glow.

4   With the ignition switched on and the ignition key in the starting position, check that current is reaching the remaining lower solenoid terminal. If a voltmeter is being used, there should not be any significant voltage drop across the solenoid, otherwise a bad connection within the solenoid is indicated.

5   If current at the correct voltage is available at the starter motor supply lead yet it does not operate, the starter motor is faulty.

6   A sticking solenoid can sometimes be freed temporarily by tapping it smartly with a light hammer. If the problem is recurrent, the motor should be removed for examination.

12 Starter motor – removal and refitting

1   Disconnect the battery negative lead.

2   Disconnect the supply lead from the starter solenoid (photo).

3   Pull the ignition and (where fitted) the resistance wires from the solenoid terminals, noting their location.

4   Unscrew the nuts and bolts securing the starter motor to the gearbox and engine; on automatic transmission models, remove the clip.

5   Withdraw the starter motor (photo) – if necessary remove the mounting bracket.

6   Refitting is a reversal of removal. Tighten the mounting bolts to the specified torque.

13 Starter motor – overhaul

1   Clean the exterior of the starter motor before starting to dismantle it. Refer to Figs. 9.7 and 9.8.

2   Remove the connector strip terminal nut and from the other end remove the bolts holding the solenoid to the mounting bracket. Now lift the solenoid pullrod so that it is clear of the operating lever and remove the solenoid.

3   At the front end of the starter is a cap held by two screws. Remove this and under it there is a shaft with a circlip and shims. Remove the circlip and shims.

4   Now remove the through-bolts and remove the cover.

5   The brushgear is now visible. Lift the brushes out of the holder and remove the brush holder. The starter body holding the field coils may now be separated from the endplate. This will leave the armature still in the mounting bracket.

6   To remove the mounting bracket from the drive end of the shaft, first push back the stop ring (where fitted) with a suitable tube so that the circlip underneath (where fitted) may be released from its groove. It is now possible to remove the mounting bracket and pinion from the shaft.

7   Finally remove the operating lever pin from the mounting bracket and remove the pinion assembly.

8   Clean and examine the pinion, shaft and lever and inspect for wear. If possible run the armature between centres in a lathe and check that the shaft is not bent. Check the fit of the drive pinion on the shaft. Check that the pinion will revolve in one direction only (one-way clutch) and that the teeth are not chipped.

9   Examine the commutator. Clean off the carbon with a rag soaked in petrol or trichlorethylene. Minor scoring may be removed with fine emery paper. Deep scoring must be removed by machining in a lathe. Commutator copper is harder than the commercial grade, and requires the lathe tool to be ground differently. Unless you have had instruction on machining commutators we suggest that the skimming and under-cutting be left to the expert. The minimum diameter for the commutator is given in the Specifications.

10   Test the armature electrically. Check the insulation between the armature winding and the shaft. To do this connect the negative terminal of the ohmmeter to the shaft and place the positive probe on each commutator segment in turn.

11   Burning on the commutator is usually a sign of an open-circuited winding. If you have access to a 'growler' have the armature checked for short-circuits.

12   Inspect the field windings for signs of abrasion or stiff and damaged insulation, particularly where the leads leave the coil. Check the field coil for short-circuit to the pole piece and for open-circuits. Renew if necessary.

13   The brushes must be at least $\frac{1}{2}$ in (13 mm) long and must slide easily in the holder. There are two schools of thought about brush renewal. One says that the entire field coil must be renewed, or the brushplate with the armature current brushes. The VW/Audi method is somewhat different.

14   Pull the brushes out of the holders, hold them away from the winding and crush the old brush with a powerful pair of pliers until the lead is free from the brush. Clean the end of the lead and prepare it for soldering. The new brush, obtainable from official agents, is drilled and has a tinned insert. Push the end of the lead into the drilling and splay it out, then solder the brush to the lead.

15   If it is your first attempt at soldering it could be better to get expert

12.2 Starter motor, showing supply leads

12.5 Removing the starter motor

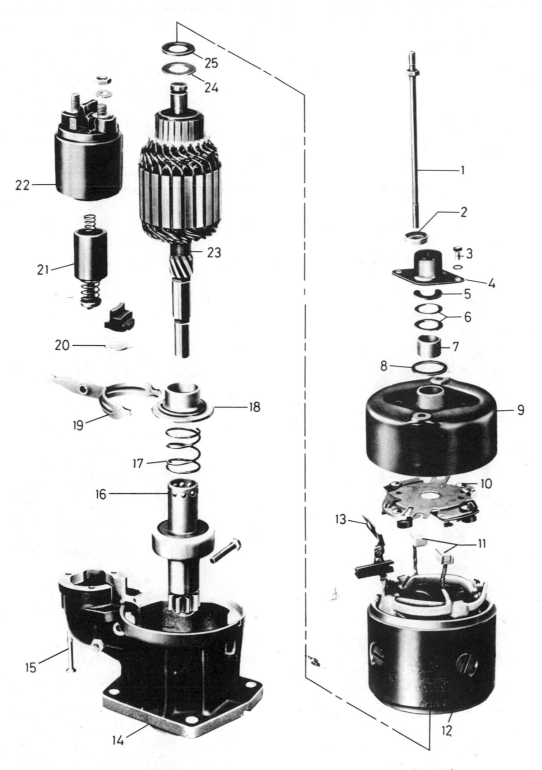

Fig. 9.7 Exploded view of the type 023 and 023A starter motor (Sec 13)

1	Housing screw (through bolt)	8	Washer	15	Solenoid switch screw	21 Solenoid plunger
2	Cupped washer	9	Housing	16	Drive pinion	22 Solenoid
3	End cap screw	10	Brush plate	17	Spring	23 Armature
4	End cap	11	Brushes	18	Bush	24 Shim
5	Circlip	12	Stator	19	Operating lever	25 Washer
6	Shims	13	Terminal tag for solenoid (field winding)	20	Disc (lug toward armature)	
7	Bush	14	Mounting bracket			

help. Use a large soldering iron (250 watts plus); do not let any of the solder creep along the wire and file off any surplus. Do not let the lead get too hot, or damage will occur to the field coils. Use a flat pair of pliers to hold the lead as close to the brush as possible while soldering. These will act as a heat sink and will also stop the solder getting in the core of the lead.

16 One final word about brushes. Check that you can get new ones before crushing the old ones!

17 Assembly is the reverse of dismantling. Fit the drive pinion and operating lever to the mounting bracket. Fit the drive pinion to the armature shaft. Fit a new lockring (circlip) and install the stop ring (groove towards the outside) over the lockring (where applicable).

Check that the stop ring will revolve freely on the shaft. It fits on the armature shaft outside the pinion.

18 Fit the starter body over the armature to the mounting bracket. See that the tongue on the body fits in the cut-out of the mounting bracket and that the body seats properly on the rubber seating. Smear a little joint compound round the joint before assembly.

19 Fit the two washers onto the armature shaft and install the brush holder over the commutator. This we found easier to write about than to do. In order to get the holder in place with the brushes correctly assembled we found that we didn't have enough fingers so we cut two lengths of wire and bent them to hold up the brush springs while the brushes were fitted over the commutator (photo). Once the four

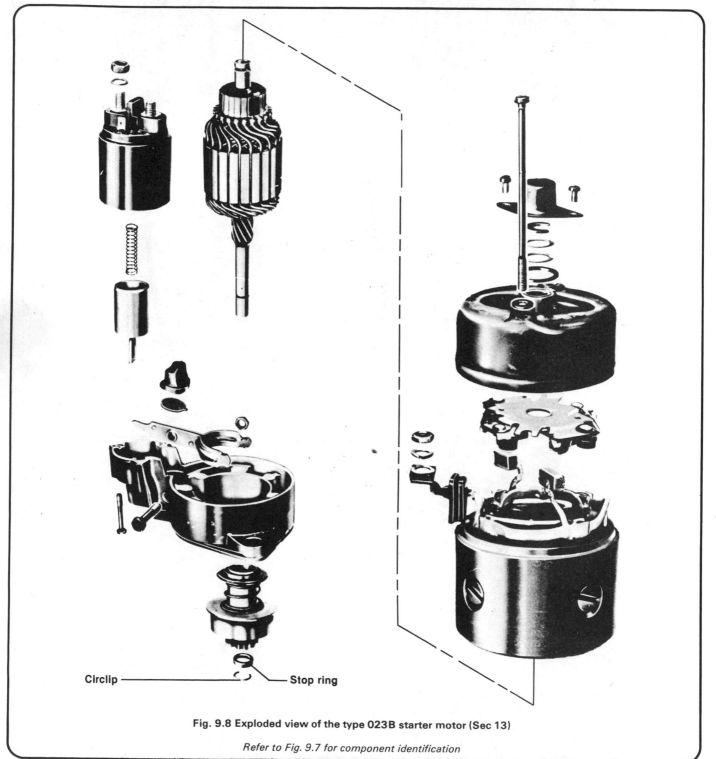

Circlip ——————   —— Stop ring

Fig. 9.8 Exploded view of the type 023B starter motor (Sec 13)

Refer to Fig. 9.7 for component identification

13.19 Using a piece of wire (arrowed) to hold the starter motor brush springs

14.6a Fuse and relay board on an early Golf

14.6b Fuse and relay board on a 1977 Golf. Relays: A – dipswitch, B – heated rear window, C – intermittent wiper/washer, D – hazard warning

brushes are in place the wires may be withdrawn.

20 Wipe the end of the shaft and oil it, then fit the end cover onto the housing and install the through-bolts. Again seal the joint, and seal the ends of the through-bolts. Now refit the shims and the circlips. If a new armature has been fitted the endplay must be checked. It should be as given in the Specifications – if necessary select shims to give the correct endplay.

21 Check that the solenoid lead grommet is in place and refit the solenoid. Use a seal compound on the joint faces, move the pinion to bring the operating lever to the opening and reconnect the pullrod. Seat the solenoid firmly on the mounting bracket in the sealing compound and install the bolts. Reconnect the wire to the starter body.

22 The starter may now be refitted to the car.

23 The pinion end of the shaft fits into a bearing in the gearbox housing and this can be checked only when the transmission is dismantled. The commutator end of the shaft fits into a bearing bush in the endplate. The old bush may be pressed out if necessary and a new one pressed in, but soak the new bush in oil for a minimum of five minutes before installing it.

14 Fuses and relays – general

1 The fuses are located in the fuse box beneath the left-hand side of the dash panel. Access to them is gained by lifting the transparent cover.

2 The function of each fuse is given in the Specifications.

3 To remove a fuse, depress the upper contact spring and lift the fuse out.

4 Always renew a fuse with one of similar rating, and never renew it more than once without finding the source of the trouble.

5 Fit the fuse with the metal strip facing outwards. Check that the contacts are free of any corrosion and clean them up with emery tape if necessary.

6 Relays are plugged into the upper part of the fuse panel (photos). If a component served by a relay fails to operate, always remember that it could be the relay at fault. A defective relay must be renewed, no repair being possible.

15 Direction indicators and hazard flasher system – general

1 The direction indicators are controlled by the left-hand column switch.

2 A switch on the facia board operates all four flashers simultaneously, and although the direction indicators will not work when the ignition is switched off, the emergency switch overrides this and the flasher signals continue to operate.

3 All the circuits are routed through the relay on the console and its fuse.

4 If the indicators do not function correctly, a series of tests may be done to find which part of the circuit is at fault.

5 The most common fault is in the flasher lamps, defective bulbs, and dirty or corroded contacts or mountings. Check these first, then test the emergency switch. Remove it from the circuit and check its

operation. If the switch is in good order refit it and again turn on the emergency lights. If nothing happens then the relay is not functioning properly and it should be renewed. If the lights function on emergency but not on operation of the column switch then the wiring and column switch are suspect (see Section 16).

16 Steering column switches – removal and refitting

1 There are four switches on the steering column:

   (a) *The horn switch in the centre of the steering wheel*

   (b) *The turn signal/headlight dip and flasher lever on the left of the column*

   (c) *The windscreen wiper/washer control lever on the right of the column*

   (d) *The steering lock/starter switch on the lower right of the column (see Section 17)*

2 Before commencing dismantling, remove the earth strap from the battery.

3 To remove the horn pad simply pull or prise it upwards. It takes a very strong pull, but it does come off that way. Remove the wire connection (photo). Undo the nut and remove the steering wheel.

4 Cross-head screws hold the two halves of the cover for the column switches together. Remove these and take the lower half of the cover away (photo). The various components of the switches are now visible.

5 From below the switch pull out the three multi-pin plugs. There is one for each lever switch and one for the starter switch (photo). They will go back only one way so there is no need to mark them. Undo the screws which hold the wiper/turn signal switch assemblies in place and lift the complete switch away (photos). Note that on pre-1977 models the switch wiring is located in guide rails which are held together with plastic hooks. The guide rails are clipped to the bottom of the wiper switch.

6 The action of the lever switches may now be tested. If the switch does not move decisively and there is slackness in the linkage, then the switch must be renewed.

7 Assembly is the reverse of removal. When refitting the steering wheel be careful to align the cancelling lug in the right place or the switch levers will be damaged. The roadwheels should be in the straight-ahead position, the turn signal switch in the neutral position and the lug to the right.

17 Ignition and steering lock switch – removal and refitting

1 Disconnect the battery negative terminal.

2 Remove the steering column switches as described in Section 16.

3 To remove the lock and key on early models, pull out the locking plate with a pair of pliers, insert and turn the ignition key clockwise approximately one thickness of the key, then withdraw the lock and key.

4 On all other models it is necessary to drill a 3.0 mm (0.11 in) diameter hole on the lock housing at the location shown in Fig. 9.12 or 9.13. Do not drill into the lock cylinder. Insert a length of stout wire through the hole and depress the spring-tensioned retaining peg; the

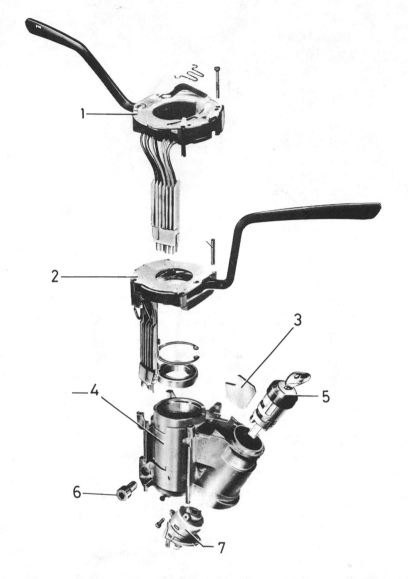

Fig. 9.9 Steering column switch components – models up to July 1976 (Sec 16)

1 Turn signal switch
2 Wiper switch
3 Lockplate
4 Housing
5 Lock cylinder
6 Screw
7 Ignition/starter switch

16.3 Disconnecting the wire from the horn pad

16.4 Removing the steering column lower shroud

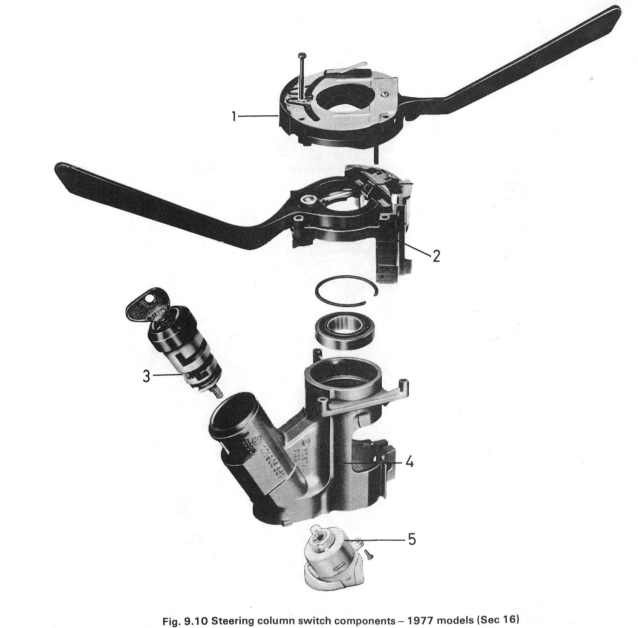

Fig. 9.10 Steering column switch components – 1977 models (Sec 16)

1   Turn signal switch   3   Lock cylinder   5   Ignition/starter switch
2   Dip and flasher switch   4   Housing

16.5a Disconnecting the multi-plug from the column switch

16.5b Remove the screws ...

16.5c ... followed by the steering column switch

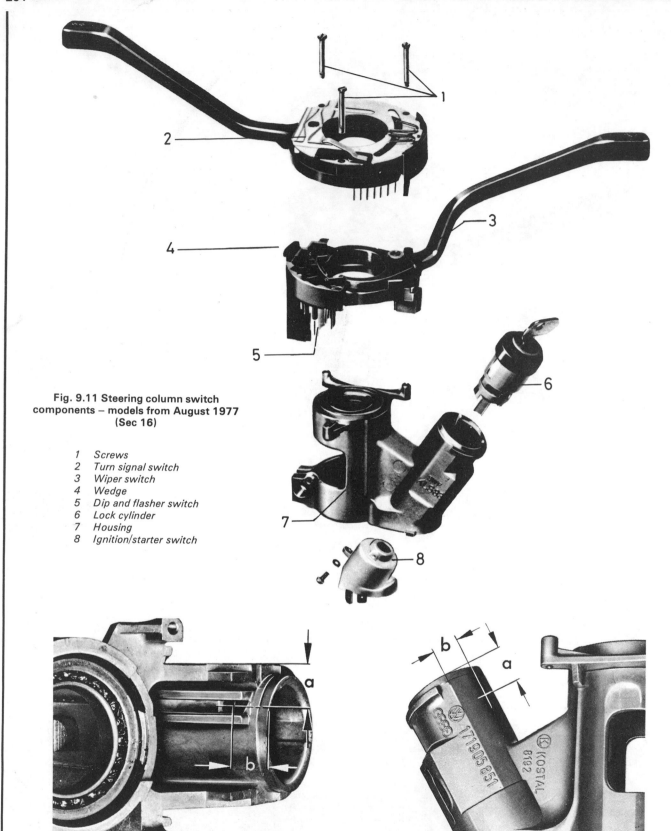

Fig. 9.11 Steering column switch components – models from August 1977 (Sec 16)

1 Screws
2 Turn signal switch
3 Wiper switch
4 Wedge
5 Dip and flasher switch
6 Lock cylinder
7 Housing
8 Ignition/starter switch

Fig. 9.12 Drilling point for removal of lock cylinder on early models (Sec 17)

a and b = 11 mm (0.43 in)

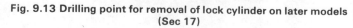

Fig. 9.13 Drilling point for removal of lock cylinder on later models (Sec 17)

a = 12 mm (0.47 in)   *b = 10 mm (0.39 in)*

cylinder can now be removed with the ignition key. Renew the lock cylinder if it is faulty.

5   To remove the switch, first withdraw the switch housing from the top of the steering column after unscrewing the socket head bolt. Remove the retaining screw and withdraw the switch.

6   Refitting is a reversal of removal, but with the early type, peen the locking plate into position to retain it.

18 Switches (facia) – removal, testing and refitting

1   Disconnect the battery negative lead.
2   Remove the instrument panel as described in Section 19.
3   Move up the dovetail clips and withdraw the switch from the surround on early models, or depress the spring clips on the sides of the switch on later models (photos).
4   The switches cannot be repaired, and if one is proved faulty after testing with a meter or test lamp, it must be renewed.
5   Refitting is a reversal of removal.

19 Instrument panel – removal, inspection and refitting

1   Disconnect the battery negative lead.
2   Remove the steering wheel with reference to Chapter 10. This is not essential but will facilitate subsequent operations (photo). Where fitted remove the lower facia panels, knee bar, and shelf.

All except May 1981 on Scirocco models
3   If no radio is fitted, prise out the cubby hole (photo).
4   Pull off the heater control knobs (photo).
5   Prise out the heater trim plate on pre-1981 models, and the switch surround (where fitted) on 1981 on models (photo).
6   If a radio is fitted, prise off the control knobs, remove the surrounds, then reach under the radio and depress the two side clips. Ease the radio out from the front of the facia, and disconnect the earth and supply wires, speaker plug, and aerial plug (photos).

18.3a Disconnecting the wires from the facia switches

18.3b Removing a facia switch

18.3c Note the clips on the sides of the facia switches

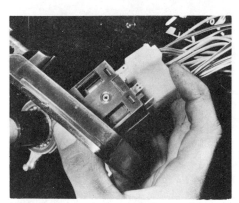

18.3d Reconnecting a multi-plug to a facia switch

19.2 Instrument panel with steering wheel removed on an early Golf

19.3 Removing the cubby hole

19.4 Removing the heater control knobs

19.5 Removing the switch surround on a 1981 model

19.6a Removing the radio outer surround ...

19.6b ... inner surround ...

19.6c ... and radio

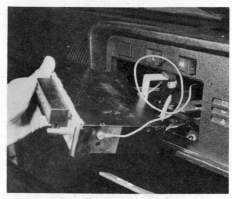

19.6d Removing the radio on an early Golf

19.7a Removing the instrument panel surround centre screw ...

19.7b ... side screw ...

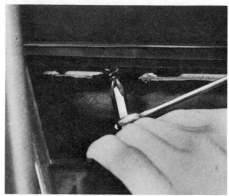

19.7c ... and inner screw. Note use of hexagonal bit and spanner

19.9a Removing an instrument panel retaining screw

19.9b Instrument panel multi-plug

19.15a Instrument panel for a late Golf model

19.15b Instrument panel for a late Jetta model

19.16a Rear view of the instrument panel on a late Golf model

19.16b Rear view of the instrument panel on a late Jetta model

1981 on models

7 Remove the screws retaining the instrument panel surround in position (where fitted). Note that, one is located above the heater control position (photos). On May 1981 on Scirocco models, lever out the facia clips.

8 Withdraw the surround and disconnect the multi-plugs, wiring and bulbs from the switches, together with the vacuum hose for the gearchange and consumption indicator (where fitted).

9 Remove the retaining screws and withdraw the instrument panel sufficiently to disconnect the multi-plug and speedometer cable (photos). On Westmoreland models a single screw is located behind the instrument panel.

10 Withdraw the instrument panel from the facia.

Pre-1981 models

11 Reach up behind the instrument panel and disconnect the speedometer cable.

12 Remove the glovebox (if fitted).

13 Remove the retaining screw from the rear of the instrument panel and withdraw the unit from the facia sufficiently to disconnect the multi-plugs.

14 Withdraw the instrument panel from the facia.

All models

15 With the instrument panel removed, the instruments, warning bulbs, and printed circuit can be dismantled from the casing if necessary (photos).

16 The printed circuit should be examined, preferably using a magnifying glass. Any defects will show up as breaks or short-circuits, in which case the printed circuit must be renewed (photos).

17 The various circuits can be tested for continuity using a test lamp and leads or a meter.

18 Refitting is a reversal of removal.

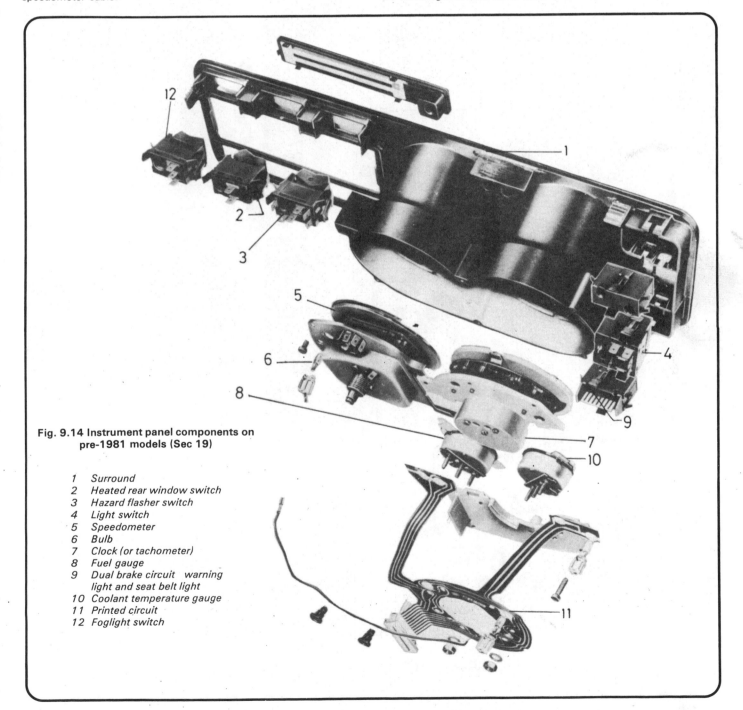

Fig. 9.14 Instrument panel components on pre-1981 models (Sec 19)

1   Surround
2   Heated rear window switch
3   Hazard flasher switch
4   Light switch
5   Speedometer
6   Bulb
7   Clock (or tachometer)
8   Fuel gauge
9   Dual brake circuit warning light and seat belt light
10 Coolant temperature gauge
11 Printed circuit
12 Foglight switch

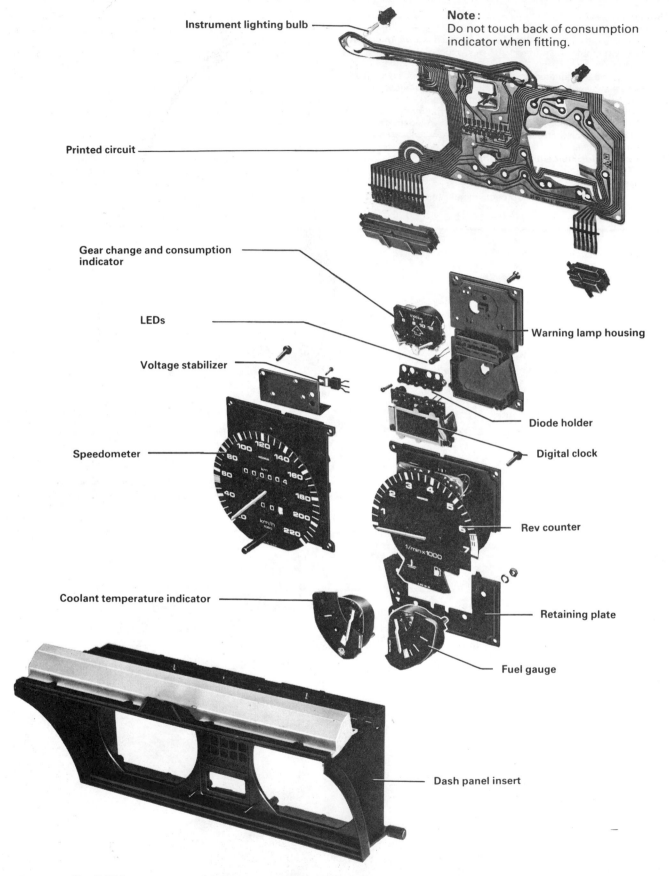

Instrument lighting bulb

Note:
Do not touch back of consumption indicator when fitting.

Printed circuit

Gear change and consumption indicator

LEDs

Voltage stabilizer

Speedometer

Coolant temperature indicator

Warning lamp housing

Diode holder

Digital clock

Rev counter

Retaining plate

Fuel gauge

Dash panel insert

Fig. 9.15 Instrument panel components on May 1981 on Scirocco models with tachometer (Sec 19)

20 Temperature gauge – testing

1   The temperature gauge is not fitted to all models; on some models a yellow flashing light emitting diode (LED) indicates that the engine is not at normal operating temperature, and a red flashing LED indicates that the engine is overheating. All 1981 on models are fitted with a temperature gauge incorporating a red flashing LED for overheating.

2   If the gauge is giving inaccurate readings, first carry out the easiest test which is to check the sender unit. Pull the wire off the sender and using a 12V 6 watt bulb as a series resistance, and with the ignition switched on, touch the bulb centre pin to earth momentarily. Have someone watch the gauge. It should move right across the scale. It is essential to have the bulb in series with the wire or you may damage the gauge. If there is no reading then press a bit harder with your contact. Still no reading, then either the wiring or the gauge are at fault. Check the fuse, if there is one in the circuit for your vehicle. If there is still no reading then the gauge must be extracted for testing separately.

3   If there is a reading then the gauge is not at fault but the sender is suspect. To test the gauge for accuracy disconnect the sender and fit resistances in its place. Ordinary radio resistances will do. A 47 ohm resistance should indicate that the engine is hot. Replace this with a 150 ohm resistance and the needle should move to the middle zone. Finally use a 270 ohm resistor and the needle should register 'cold'.

4   If the gauge still gives inaccurate readings, test the voltage stabilizer for correct output. To do this, remove the instrument panel as described in Section 19 and locate the voltage stabilizer which is connected to the printed circuit by three tabs. The centre tab is earth and the outer tabs are marked +E (plus in) and +A (plus out). With the +E terminal energised, the voltage between the +A and earth terminals should be 10 ± 0.5 volts. If not, renew the unit.

5   If the gauge is receiving the correct voltage from the stabilizer, and the sender unit and wiring are functioning correctly but the gauge is still inaccurate, it should be renewed.

21 Fuel gauge – testing

1   The handbook states that when the needle of the fuel gauge reaches the reserve mark there is about one gallon of fuel in the tank. It is important therefore that the gauge is accurate.

2   There is a very good way of checking the reserve mark. Buy one gallon of petrol, empty the petrol tank, put in the one gallon and check the reading against the reserve tank. If it is possible to arrange to fill the tank from empty to full, one gallon at a time, a piece of thin cardboard fitted to the face of the gauge glass may be marked at each gallon and you will know exactly how much fuel is in the tank at all times.

3   If the gauge is not reading then a simple test is required. A 47 ohm resistor and a 0-12V meter are needed. Underneath the car at the rear on the right-hand side of the petrol tank is the combined fuel hose and fuel gauge wires entry. Switch on the ignition and measure the voltage across the terminals. If there is no voltage pull off the terminal of the wire to the gauge and check the voltage between that terminal and earth. If there is now a reading the sender unit is at fault. Check that

the other wire is in fact connected securely to earth. If there is still no reading then either the wiring or the gauge is faulty. Check that all the fuses are in order.

4   If the sender unit is faulty then the tank must be drained. Remove the hose clip(s) and pull off the hose(s). Disconnect the battery earth strap and disconnect the wires from the sender unit. Turn the locking plate until the unit can be withdrawn from the tank, and then remove the fuel pipe and sender unit. There is little that can be done to the sender unit, it is best to take it to an expert, who may be able to repair it or supply a new one.

5   To test the accuracy of the gauge, if it is working, disconnect the gauge wires at the sender unit and insert a 47 ohm resistance between them. Switch on the ignition and the gauge should register full. Replace this with a 100 ohm and then a 220 ohm resistor in turn and the needle should be on the second mark and then the reserve mark respectively.

6   If the gauge still gives inaccurate readings, test the voltage stabilizer as described in Section 20, paragraph 4.

22 Courtesy light switch – removal and refitting

1   Disconnect the battery negative lead.

2   Open the door and locate the courtesy light switch. Remove the single screw and withdraw the switch (photo).

3   Disconnect the supply wire and tie a loose knot in it to prevent it dropping into the pillar. Remove the switch.

4   Refitting is a reversal of removal.

23 Headlamps and bulbs – removal and refitting

UK models (bulb type)

1   To remove the bulb, open the bonnet and pull the connector and rubber cover (if fitted) from the rear of the headlamp. On some models it is necessary to remove a small rubber grommet and a large cover first (photos).

2   Turn the retaining ring or cap anti-clockwise and withdraw it (photos).

3   On some headlights, hinge the spring clip outward (photo).

4   On all models lift the bulb from the reflector, but do not touch the glass with the fingers if the bulb is to be re-used (photos).

5   Refitting is a reversal of removal, but make sure that the lug on the bulb engages the recess in the reflector. Make sure that the rubber cover is pressed firmly into position.

6   To remove the reflector first remove the radiator grille as described in Chapter 11, and remove the bulb as described in paragraphs 1 to 4.

7   On round headlamp models remove the retaining screws (**not** the beam adjusting screws) and withdraw the lamp from the front. The frame and reflector are held together by clamps which must be turned to separate the parts, although it is better to renew them as an assembly (photos).

8   On rectangular headlamp models, turn the plastic nuts through 90° from inside the engine compartment, then withdraw the lamp from the front (photo).

9   Refitting is a reversal of removal, but adjust the headlamps as described in Section 25.

22.2 Removing the courtesy light switch

23.1a Removing the headlamp bulb connector on a Scirocco model

23.1b Removing the headlamp bulb connector ...

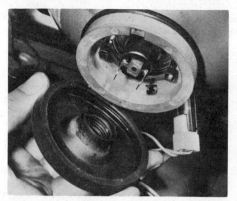

23.1c ... and rubber cover on a late Jetta model

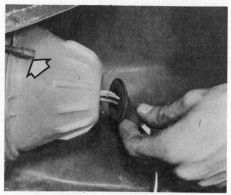

23.1d Rear of the headlamp on some Golf models showing (arrowed) beam adjustment screw

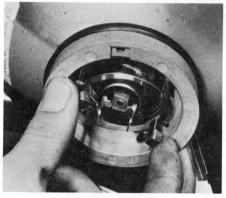

23.2a Removing the headlamp bulb retaining ring

23.2b Removing the headlamp bulb rear cap

23.3 Showing headlamp bulb retaining spring clip

23.4a Removing the headlamp bulb on a Scirocco model

23.4b Removing the headlamp bulb on a Jetta model

23.7a Removing the headlamp on a Golf model

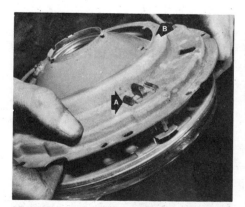

23.7b Fastener clip 'A' and beam adjusting screw 'B' on a Golf model

23.8 Removing the headlamp reflector on a Jetta model

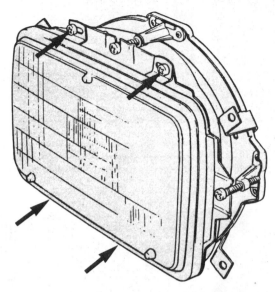

Fig. 9.16 Headlight retaining ring screw locations on a Westmoreland Rabbit model (Sec 23)

North American models (sealed beam type)

10 On 1981 on Rabbit models, remove the headlight trim (4 screws) – on all other models remove the radiator grille as described in Chapter 11.

11 Remove the screws and withdraw the headlight retaining ring. **Do not** alter the beam adjustment screws.

12 Withdraw the sealed beam unit and pull off the wiring connector.

13 Refitting is a reversal of removal, but make sure that the glass lugs engage with the cut-outs in the support.

24 Lamp bulbs – renewal

Front parking light (UK models)

1 The front parking light is located on the headlamp reflector and its wiring is connected to the headlamp wiring. On dual headlamp models it is located on the outer headlamps.

2 Removal of the bulb on dual headlamp models is identical to the removal of the headlamp bulb described in Section 23.

3 On all other models, turn the bulb holder fully anti-clockwise and withdraw it from the reflector, then depress and twist the bulb to remove it (photo).

Front parking light (North American models)

4 Where the light is located in the bumper, remove the lens (two screws), depress the bulb and turn it anti-clockwise to remove it.

5 Where the light is beside the headlight, pull out the bulb holder into the engine compartment – on some models, squeeze the plastic lugs together. Depress the bulb and turn it anti-clockwise to remove it.

Front indicator lamps

6 Where the lamp is located in the bumper, remove the lens (two screws), depress the bulb and turn it anti-clockwise to remove it (photos). Check the gasket before refitting the lens.

7 Where the lamp is beside the headlight, remove the rubber cover and pull out the bulb holder into the engine compartment – on some models squeeze the plastic lug(s). Depress the bulb and turn it anti-clockwise to remove it (photo).

Rear light cluster

8 The bulbs are removed from inside the car. First unscrew the knurled knob and remove the cover, if fitted (photo).

9 On 1981 on Rabbit and North American Scirocco models, depress the spring clip, turn the bulb holder anti-clockwise one quarter of a turn and withdraw the bulb holder.

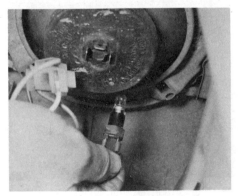

24.3 Removing a front parking light bulb

24.6a Removing the front indicator lamp lens ...

24.6b ... and bulb on a Golf model

24.7 Removing a front indicator lamp bulb on a Jetta model

24.8 Removing the rear light cluster cover on a Scirocco model

24.10a Rear light cluster bulb holder location ...

24.10b ... and removal on a Golf model

24.10c Rear light cluster retaining lugs location on a Jetta model

24.10d Rear light cluster bulb holder location ...

24.10e ... and removal on a Scirocco model

24.10f Rear light cluster bulb holder on an early Golf model

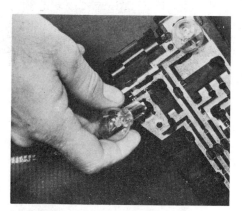

24.11 Removing a rear light cluster bulb

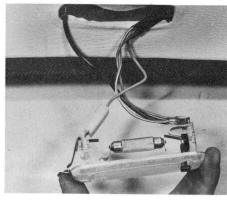

24.12 Interior lamp removed from headlining

24.15 Removing the number plate lamp screws ...

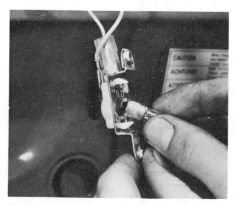

24.16 ... and bulb on a Jetta model

24.19a Removing an instrument panel warning lamp bulb on a Golf model ...

24.19b ... and on a Jetta model

10 On all other models depress the lugs and withdraw the bulb holder (photos).
11 Depress and twist the bulbs as necessary to remove them (photo).

Interior lamp

12 Depress the spring clip, if fitted, then prise the lamp from the roof, taking care not to damage the headlining (photo).
13 Extract the festoon type bulb from the spring contacts.
14 When refitting, insert the switch end of the lamp first, then press the opposite end until the spring clip is fully engaged.

Number plate lamp

15 Open the tailgate/boot lid, then remove the two screws and lift off the lens and cover (photo).
16 Extract the bulb holder if necessary. Depress and twist the bulb to remove it (photo).
17 When refitting, make sure that the wires are not trapped and that the lens lug is correctly located.

Instrument panel warning lamps

18 Remove the instrument panel as described in Section 19.
19 Twist the bulb holder and remove it from the instrument panel (photos).
20 Pull the wedge type bulb from the bulb holder.

Choke warning lamp

21 This warning lamp is located on the right-hand side of the instrument panel on certain 1981 on models.
22 To remove the bulb, remove the instrument panel surround with reference to Section 19.
23 Pull the wedge type bulb from the multi-plug (photo).

Hazard warning switch lamp

24 Remove the switch as described in Section 18.
25 Pull the bulb from the holder (photo).

Side marker lamps

26 On Jetta models open the bonnet or boot lid, pull out the bulb holder, and withdraw the bulb.
27 On all other models remove the screws and withdraw the lamp. Remove the bulb holder by turning it or depressing the lugs (as applicable), then withdraw the bulb.

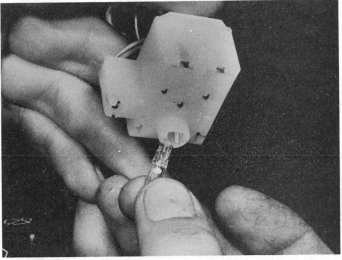

24.23 The choke warning lamp bulb

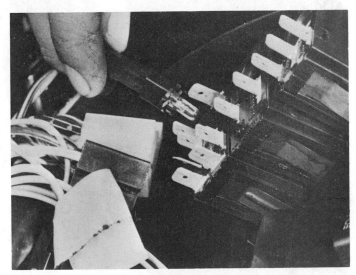

24.25 The hazard warning switch lamp bulb

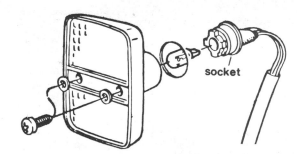

Fig. 9.17 Side marker lamp components (Sec 24)

25 Headlamps – alignment

1 Depending on the model, the headlamps are adjusted from within the engine compartment, or alternatively from the front of the car by inserting a screwdriver between the radiator grille and the headlamp.
2 Two adjustment screws are provided, one for the vertical setting and the other for the lateral setting.
3 It is recommended that the headlamp beams are adjusted by your dealer, but in an emergency the following procedure may be used.
4 Set the car on level ground with tyres correctly inflated, approximately 10 metres (33 feet) in front of, and at right-angles to, a wall or garage door. The vehicle should be normally laden.
5 Draw a horizontal line on the wall or door at headlamp centre height. Draw a vertical line corresponding to the centre-line of the car, then measure off a point either side of this, on the horizontal line, corresponding with the headlamp centres.
6 Switch on the main beam and check that the areas of maximum illumination coincide with the headlamp centre marks on the wall. If not, turn the adjustment screws as necessary.

26 Fuse and relay panel – removal and refitting

1 Disconnect the battery negative lead.
2 Remove the retaining screws and withdraw the panel to expose the multi-plug connectors.
3 Disconnect the multi-plug connectors and remove the panel.
4 The wiring diagrams show the various terminals on the panel which will be of assistance when tracing a fault.
5 Refitting is a reversal of removal.

27 Horn, testing, removal and refitting

1 The horn(s) are located on the front crossmember in front of the engine (photos).
2 If the horn fails to operate, first check that the relevant fuse is intact and is firmly fitted between the contacts.
3 Using a test lamp and leads, or a voltmeter, check that current is reaching the horn from the supply wire (usually yellow and black) with the ignition switched on. If not, the supply wire is faulty.

27.1a Twin horns on a Golf model

27.1b Single horn on a Jetta model

28.6 Speedometer cable end (arrowed) with instrument panel removed

29.1a Wiper blade and arm fastening

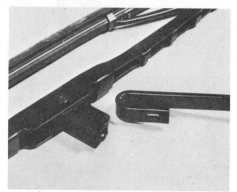

29.1b Dismantled wiper blade and arm

29.2a Wiper arm retaining nut location

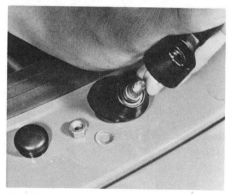

29.2b Removing the wiper arm from the spindle

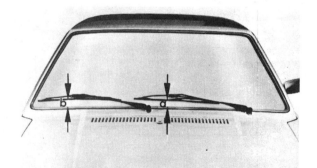

Fig. 9.18 Windscreen wiper blade parked positions – LHD shown (Sec 29)

a = 35 mm (1.38 in) for Golf/Rabbit/Jetta, or 25 mm (1.0 in) for Scirocco with two blades
b = 65 mm (2.56 in) for Golf/Rabbit/Jetta, or 30 mm (1.18 in) for Scirocco with two blades

4   If current is reaching the supply wire, use the same method to check that current is reaching the horn output terminal. If not, the horn is faulty. If it is, but the horn fails to operate, have an assistant operate the horn push, then turn the adjusting screw (if fitted) until the horn operates satisfactorily.

5   If the horn still fails to operate after making the previous tests, connect a wire between the output terminal and earth. If the horn now operates, a fault exists in the horn push or wiring. Use the same method as previously described to trace the fault.

6   To remove the horn, first disconnect the battery negative lead.

7   Disconnect the horn input and output wires.

8   Unbolt the horn from the mounting bracket.

9   Refitting is a reversal of removal.

28 Speedometer head and cable – removal and refitting

1   Disconnect the battery negative lead.

2   Remove the instrument panel as described in Section 19.

3   Unscrew the two retaining screws and remove the speedometer head from the rear of the instrument panel. On some models it will be necessary to remove the voltage stabilizer.

4   Refitting is a reversal of removal, but where fitted, make sure that the cardboard washers are located beneath the retaining screw heads. If these are left out, damage may occur to the voltage stabilizer and speedometer – if necessary replacements can be made out of ordinary cardboard.

5   To remove the speedometer cable, remove the retaining screw at the transmission end and withdraw it from the drivegear. Take care that the gear remains in place so that it cannot become lost or fall into the transmission.

6   With the cable disconnected from the speedometer head, pull it through the grommet hole and withdraw the cable from the car (photo).

7   Refitting is a reversal of removal, but make sure that the cable is positioned with the minimum amount of curving. On Scirocco models the cable must be attached to a plastic retainer near the bulkhead in order to prevent it touching the clutch cable. Do not grease the cable at the head end as this may cause the needle to stick.

29 Wiper blades and arms – renewal

1   To remove a wiper blade, depress the clip with a screwdriver and slide the blade from the arm (photos). On some models it may be possible to renew the wiper rubber separately. Where the type is fitted, use pliers to squeeze the support rail, then withdraw the rubber.

2   To remove a wiper arm, first prise off the cover with a screwdriver, then unscrew the retaining nut. Lever the arm off the shaft, being careful not to damage the paintwork (photos).

3   When refitting a wiper arm and blade assembly, locate it in the position shown in Figs. 9.18, 9.19 or 9.20, with the wiper motor in the parked position.

30 Windscreen wiper mechanism – removal and refitting

1   Remove the wiper arm(s) and blade(s) as described in Section 29.

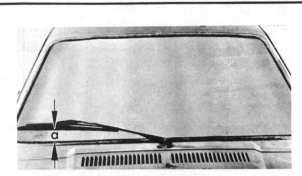

Fig. 9.19 Windscreen wiper blade parked position for Scirocco with single blade – LHD shown (Sec 29)

a = 55 mm (2.17 in)

Fig. 9.20 Tailgate wiper blade parked position (Sec 29)

a = 30 mm (1.18 in)

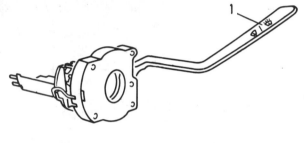

Fig. 9.21 Windscreen wiper mechanism components (Sec 30)

1   Windscreen wiper switch
2   Wiper blade
3   Wiper arm
4   Intermittent action relay
5   Linkage
6   Frame
7   Wiper motor

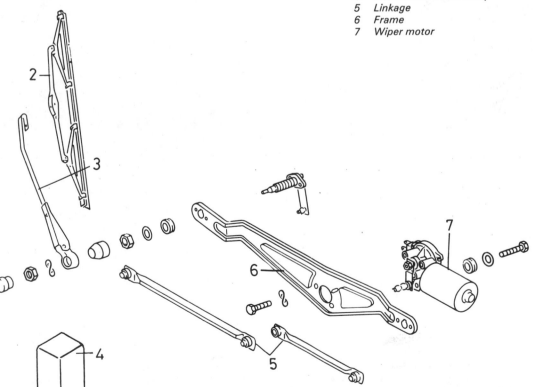

30.5 Wiper motor on a Scirocco model

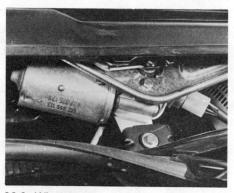
30.6a Wiper motor on a Golf model

30.6b Wiper motor and frame on a Golf model

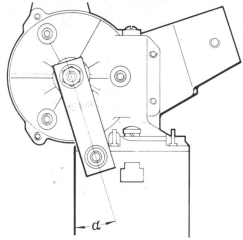
Fig. 9.22 Wiper motor crank parked position for RHD models
(Sec 30)

Angle = 20°

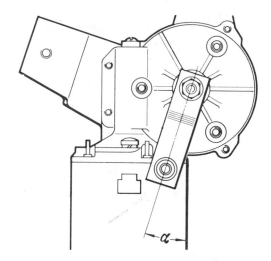
Fig. 9.23 Wiper motor crank parked position for LHD models
(Sec 30)

Angle = 20°

2   Disconnect the battery negative lead, then remove the cover from
each spindle and unscrew the retaining nuts.
3   Where fitted, unclip the thin plastic guard from the bulkhead.
4   Disconnect the multi-plug.
5   On Scirocco models with a single wiper arm, unscrew the nut and
remove the crank from the motor, then unbolt the motor from the
frame (photo). Remove the linkage and spindle.
6   On all other models, remove the mounting bolt and withdraw the
motor and frame (photos). Separate the frame from the motor by
unscrewing the two bolts.
7   Examine the frame, levers and pivots for wear and renew them if
necessary. Where applicable do not remove the crank from the motor
unless the motor is to be renewed. If it is removed, connect the multi-
plug to the motor before refitting it, switch on the motor then switch
it off. With the motor now stopped in its parked position, refit the crank
in the position shown in Figs. 9.22 or 9.23
8   Refitting is a reversal of removal, but lubricate all moving parts
with general purpose grease. When refitting the crank to Scirocco
models with one wiper, set the motor shaft to its parked position by
switching on the motor then switching it off, then refer to Fig. 9.24.
9   Refer to Section 29 for the refitting of the wiper arm(s) and
blade(s).

31 Tailgate wiper motor – removal and refitting

1   Disconnect the battery negative lead.
2   Remove the wiper arm and blade as described in Section 29.
3   Remove the cover from the spindle and unscrew the retaining nut.
Remove the spacer.
4   Prise the inspection panel from the tailgate lower edge, and
disconnect the wiring at the loom (photo). Note that the two wires

Fig. 9.24 Wiper motor crank parked position for Scirocco models
with one wiper (Sec 30)

1   LHD models   2   RHD models

must never be interchanged as this will damage an internal diode on
early models.
5   Unscrew the mounting bolts, disengage the motor assembly from
the mechanism, and withdraw it through the aperture.
6   Unbolt the mechanism from the tailgate.
7   Refitting is a reversal of removal, but make sure that the motor is
in its parked position as shown in Figs. 9.26 and 9.27 before fitting it.

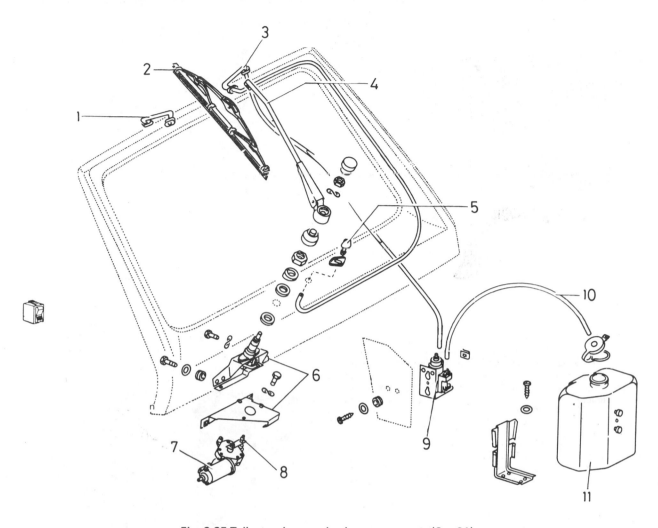

Fig. 9.25 Tailgate wiper mechanism components (Sec 31)

1	Wiring grommet	4	Wiper arm
2	Wiper blade	5	Jet
3	Water hose grommet	6	Spindle and frame

7	Wiper motor	10	Hose
8	Crank	11	Reservoir
9	Washer pump		

31.4 Tailgate wiper motor on a Scirocco model

Fig. 9.26 Tailgate wiper motor crank parked position for Golf/Rabbit/Jetta models (Sec 31)

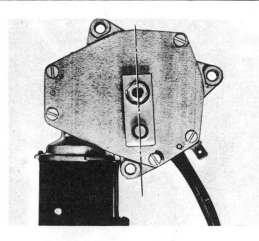

Fig. 9.27 Tailgate wiper motor crank parked position for Scirocco models (Sec 31)

32 Washer jets – adjustment

1   Periodically the washer jets should be adjusted so that the water spray is directed toward the points shown in Fig. 9.28. The tailgate jet should be adjusted to direct spray into the centre of the wiped area.
2   Where headlight washers are fitted, direct the spray into the shaded areas shown in Fig. 9.29
3   The washer pumps are located by the reservoirs (photo).

33 Radios and tape players – installation

A radio or tape player is an expensive item to buy, and will only give its best performance if fitted properly. It is useless to expect concert hall performance from a unit that is suspended from the dashpanel by string with its speaker resting on the back seat or parcel shelf! If you do not wish to do the fitting yourself, there are many in-car entertainment specialists who will do the fitting for you.

Make sure the unit purchased is of the same polarity as the vehicle (ie negative earth). Ensure that units with adjustable polarity are correctly set before commencing the fitting operations.

It is difficult to give specific information with regard to fitting. However, the following paragraphs give guidelines to follow, which are relevant to all installations.

Radios

Most radios are a standardised size of 7 in wide by 2 in deep. This ensures that they will fit into the radio aperture provided in the car.

Some radios will have mounting brackets provided, together with instructions; others will need to be fitted using drilled and slotted metal strips, bent to form mounting brackets. These strips are available from most accessory shops. The unit must be properly earthed by fitting a separate earthing lead between the casing of the radio and the vehicle frame.

Use the radio manufacturer's instructions when wiring the radio into the vehicle's electrical system. If no instructions are available, refer to the relevant wiring diagram to find the location of the radio feed connection in the vehicle's wiring circuit. A 1 to 2 amp in-line fuse must be fitted in the radio's feed wire; a choke may also be necessary (see the following Section).

The type of aerial used, and its fitted position, is a matter of personal preference. In general, the taller the aerial the better the reception. It is best to fit a fully retractable aerial; especially if a mechanical car-wash is used or if you live in an area where cars tend to be vandalised. In this respect, electric aerials which are raised and lowered automatically when switching the radio on or off are convenient, but are more likely to give trouble than the manual type.

When choosing a site for the aerial, the following points should be considered:

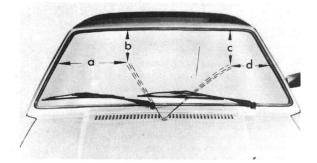

Fig. 9.28 Windscreen washer jet adjusting dimensions. LHD shown, RHD is mirror image (Sec 32)

Scirocco:
a = 400 to 500 mm (15.7 to 19.7 in)
b = 235 to 285 mm (9.3 to 11.2 in)
c = 325 to 375 mm (12.8 to 14.8 in)
d = 150 to 250 mm (5.9 to 9.8 in)

All models except Scirocco:
a = 170 to 270 mm (6.7 to 10.6 in)
b = 275 to 325 mm (10.8 to 12.8 in)
c = 305 to 355 mm (12.0 to 14.0 in)
d = 230 to 330 mm (9.1 to 13.0 in)

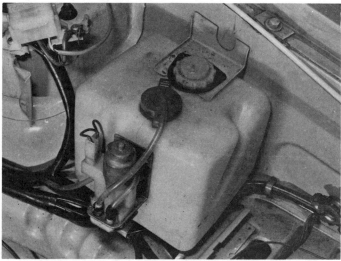

32.3 Windscreen washer reservoir location, showing pump location

(a) *The aerial lead should be as short as possible; this means that the aerial should be mounted at the front of the vehicle*
(b) *The aerial must be mounted as far away from the distributor and HT leads as possible*
(c) *The part of the aerial which protrudes beneath the mounting point must not foul the roadwheels, or anything else*
(d) *If possible, the aerial should be positioned so that the coaxial lead does not have to be routed through the engine compartment*
(e) *The plane of the panel on which the aerial is mounted should not be so steeply angled that the aerial cannot be mounted vertically (in relation to the end-on aspect of the car). Most aerials have a small amount of adjustment available*

Having decided on a mounting position, a relatively large hole will have to be made in the panel. The exact size of the hole will depend upon the specific aerial being fitted, although generally, the hole required is of $\frac{3}{4}$ in diameter. A tank-cutter of the relevant diameter is the best tool to use for making the hole. This tool needs a small

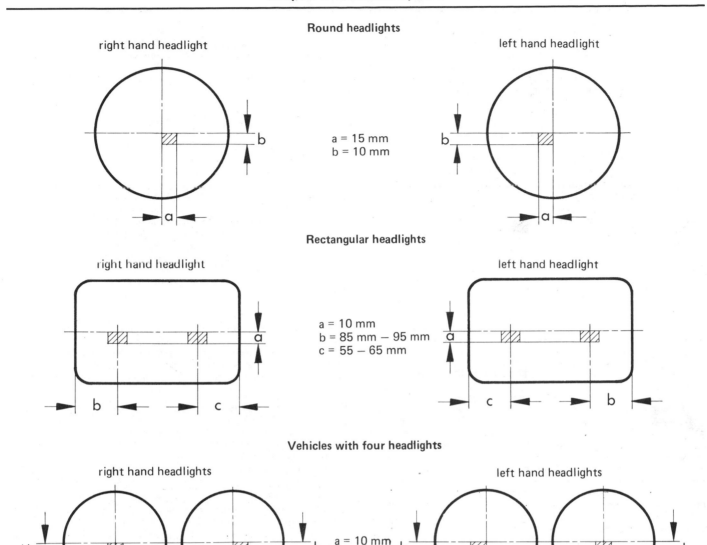

Fig. 9.29 Headlight washer adjusting dimensions (Sec 32)

diameter pilot hole drilled through the panel, through which the tool clamping bolt is inserted. When the hole has been made the raw edges should be de-burred with a file and then painted to prevent corrosion.

Fit the aerial according to the manufacturer's instructions. If the aerial is very tall, or if it protrudes beneath the mounting panel for a considerable distance, it is a good idea to fit a stay beneath the aerial and the vehicle frame. This stay can be manufactured from the slotted and drilled metal strips previously mentioned. The stay should be securely screwed or bolted in place. For best reception, it is advisable to fit an earth lead between the aerial and the vehicle frame.

It will probably be necessary to drill one or two holes through bodywork panels in order to feed the aerial lead into the interior of the car. Where this is the case, ensure that the holes are fitted with rubber grommets to protect the cable and to stop possible entry of water.

Positioning and fitting of the speaker depends mainly on its type. Generally, the speaker is designed to fit directly into the aperture already provided in the car. Where this is the case, fitting the speaker is just a matter of removing the facia panel from the aperture and screwing or bolting the speaker in place. Take great care not to damage the speaker diaphragm whilst doing this. It is a good idea to fit a gasket beneath the speaker frame and the mounting panel. In order to prevent vibration, some speakers will already have such a gasket fitted.

When connecting a rear mounted speaker to the radio, the wires should be routed through the vehicle beneath the carpets or floor mats, preferably along the side of the floorpan where they will not be trodden on by passengers. Make the relevant connections as directed by the radio manufacturer.

By now you will have several yards of additional wiring in the car, use PVC tape to secure this wiring out of harm's way. Do not leave electrical leads dangling. Ensure that all new electrical connections are properly made (wires twisted together will not do) and completely secure.

The radio should now be working, but before you pack away your tools, it will be necessary to trim the radio to the aerial. Follow the radio manufacturer's instructions regarding this adjustment.

Tape players

Fitting instructions for both cartridge and cassette stereo tape players are the same, and in general the same rules apply as when fitting a radio. Tape players are not usually prone to electrical interference like radios, although it can occur, so positioning is not so critical. If possible, the player should be mounted on an even-keel. Also it must be possible for a driver wearing a seat belt to reach the unit in order to change or turn over tapes.

For the best results from speakers designed to be recessed into a panel, mount them so that the back of the speaker protrudes into an enclosed chamber within the car (eg door interiors).

To fit recessed type speakers in the front doors, first check that there is sufficient room to mount a speaker in each door without it fouling the latch or window winding mechanism. Hold the speaker against the skin of the door and draw a line around the periphery of the speaker. With the speaker removed, draw a second cutting line within the first to allow enough room for the entry of the speaker back, but at the same time providing a broad seat for the speaker flange. When you are sure that the cutting-line is correct, drill a series of holes around its periphery. Pass a hacksaw blade through one of the holes and then cut through the metal between the holes until the centre section of the panel falls out.

De-burr the edges of the hole and then paint the raw metal to prevent corrosion. Cut a corresponding hole in the door trim panel, ensuring that it will be completely covered by the speaker grille. Now drill a hole in the door edge and a corresponding hole in the door surround. These holes are to feed the speaker leads through, so fit grommets. Pass the speaker leads through the door trim, door skin and out through the holes in the side of the door and door surround. Refit the door trim panel and then secure the speaker to the door using self-tapping screws. If the speaker is fitted with a shield to prevent water dripping on it, ensure that this shield is at the top.

34 Radios and tape players – suppression of interference (general)

To eliminate buzzes and other unwanted noises costs very little and is not as difficult as sometimes thought. With a modicum of common sense and patience, and following the instructions in the following paragraphs, interference can be virtually eliminated.

The first cause for concern is the generator. The noise this makes over the radio is like an electric mixer and the noise speeds up when the engine is revved. (To prove the point, remove the fanbelt and try it). The remedy for this is simple; connect a 1.0 mf to 3.0 mf capacitor between earth (probably the bolt that holds down the generator base) and the *output* terminal on the alternator. This is most important for if it is connected to the other terminal, the generator will probably be damaged permanently (see Fig. 9.30).

A second common cause of electrical interference is the ignition system. Here a 1.0 mf capacitor must connected between earth and the SW or + terminal on the coil (see Fig. 9.31). This may stop the tick-tick sound that comes over the speaker. Next comes the spark itself.

There are several ways of curing interference from the ignition HT system. One is the use of carbon-cored HT leads as original equipment. Where copper cable is used then resistive spark plug caps must be used (see Fig. 9.32). These should be of about 10 000 to 15 000 ohm resistance. If, due to lack of room, these cannot be used, an alternative is to use in-line suppressors. If the interference is not too bad, it may be possible to get away with only one suppressor in the coil to distributor line. If the interference does continue (a clacking noise), then modify all HT leads.

At this stage it is advisable to check that the radio is well earthed, also the aerial and to see that the aerial plug is pushed well into the set and that the radio is properly trimmed (see preceding Section). In addition, check that the wire which supplies the power to the set is as short as possible and does not wander all over the car.

At this point, the more usual causes of interference have been suppressed. If the problem still exists, a look at the cause of interference may help to pinpoint the component generating the stray electrical discharges.

The radio picks up electromagnetic waves in the air. Some are made by regular broadcasters and some, which we do not want, are made by the car itself. The home made signals are produced by stray electrical discharges floating around in the car. Common producers of these signals are electrical motors, ie the windscreen wipers, electric screen washers, electric window winders, heater fan or an electric aerial if fitted. Other sources of interference are flashing turn signals and instruments. The remedy for these cases is shown in Fig. 9.33 for an electric motor whose interference is not too bad and Fig. 9.34 for

instrument suppression. Turn signals are not normally suppressed. In recent years, radio manufacturers have included in the live line of the radio, in addition to the fuse, an in-line choke. If your circuit lacks one of these, put one in as shown in Fig. 9.35.

All the foregoing components are available from radio stores or accessory stores. If you have an electric clock fitted, this should be suppressed by connecting a 0.5 mf capacitor directly across it as shown for a motor in Fig. 9.33.

If after all this you are still experiencing radio interference, first assess how bad it is, for the human ear can filter out unobtrusive unwanted noises quite easily. But if you are still adamant about eradicating the noise, then continue.

As a first step, a few experts seem to favour a screen between the radio and the engine. This is OK as far as it goes, literally! The whole set is screened anyway and if interference can get past that then a small piece of aluminium is not going to stop it.

A more sensible way of screening is to discover if interference is coming down the wires. First, take the live lead; interference can get between the set and the choke (hence the reason for keeping the wires short). One remedy here is to screen the wire and this is done by buying screened wire and fitting that. The loudspeaker lead could be screened also to prevent pick-up getting back to the radio although this is unlikely.

Now for the really impossible cases, here are a few tips to try out. Where metal comes into contact with metal, an electrical disturbance is caused which is why good clean connections are essential. To remove interference due to overlapping or butting panels, you must bridge the join with a wide braided earth strap (like that from the frame to the engine/transmission). The most common moving parts that could create noise and should be strapped are, in order of importance:

(a) *Silencer to frame*
(b) *Exhaust pipe to engine block and frame*
(c) *Air cleaner to frame*
(d) *Front and rear bumpers to frame*
(e) *Steering column to frame*
(f) *Bonnet and boot lids to frame*
(g) *Hood frame to bodyframe on soft tops*

These faults are most pronounced when the engine is idling or labouring under load. Although the moving parts are already connected with nuts, bolts, etc, these do tend to rust and corrode, this creating a high resistance interference source.

If you have a ragged sounding pulse when mobile, this could be wheel or tyre static. This can be cured by buying some anti-static powder and sprinkling inside the tyres.

If the interference takes the shape of a high pitched screeching noise that changes its note when the car is in motion and only comes now and then, this could be related to the aerial, especially if it is of the telescopic or whip type. This source can be cured quite simply by pushing a small rubber ball on top of the aerial as this breaks the electric field before it can form; but it would be much better to buy yourself a new aerial of a reputable brand. If, on the other hand, you are getting a loud rushing sound every time you brake, then this is brake static. This effect is most prominent on hot dry days and is cured only by fitting a special kit, which is quite expensive.

In conclusion, it is pointed out that it is relatively easy and therefore cheap, to eliminate 95 per cent of all noise, but to eliminate the final 5 per cent is time and money consuming. It is up to the individual to decide if it is worth it. Please remember also, that you cannot get a concert hall performance out of a cheap radio.

Finally, players and eight track players are not usually affected by car noise but in a very bad case, the best remedies are the first three suggestions plus using a 3 to 5 amp choke in the live line and in incurable cases, screening the live and speaker wires.

Note: *If your car is fitted with electronic ignition, then it is not recommended that either the spark plug resistors or the ignition coil capacitor be fitted as these may damage the system. Most electronic ignition units have built in suppression and should, therefore, not cause interference.*

35 Wiring diagrams – description

1   The wiring diagrams included at the end of this Chapter are of the current flow type, where each wire is shown in the simplest line form

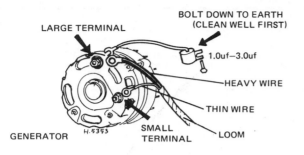

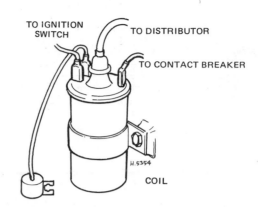

Fig. 9.30 The correct way to connect a capacitor to the alternator (Sec 34)

Fig. 9.31 The capacitor must be connected to the ignition switch side of the coil (Sec 34)

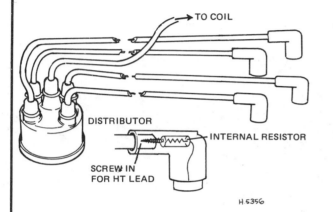

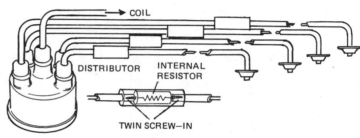

Fig. 9.32 Ignition HT lead suppressors (Sec 34)

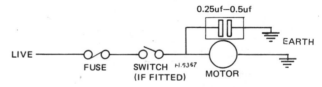

Fig. 9.33 Correct method of suppressing electric motors (Sec 34)

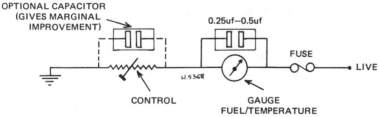

Fig. 9.34 Method of suppressing gauges and their control units (Sec 34)

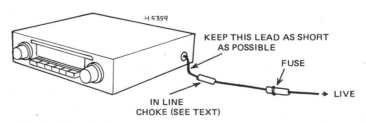

Fig. 9.35 An 'in-line' choke should be fitted into the live supply lead as close to the unit as possible (Sec 34)

without crossing over the wires.

2   The fuse/relay panel is at the top of the diagram and the combined letter/figure numbers appearing on the panel terminals refer to the multi-plug connector in letter form and to the terminal in figure form.

3   Internal connections through electrical components are shown by a single line.

4   The encircled numbers along the bottom of the diagram indicate the earthing connecting points as given in the legend.

36 Fault diagnosis – electrical system

Symptom	Reason(s)
Starter fails to turn engine	Battery discharged or defective Battery terminal and/or earth leads loose Starter motor connections loose Inhibitor switch defective (automatic transmission) Starter solenoid faulty Starter brushes worn or sticking Starter commutator dirty or worn Starter field coils earthed
Starter turns engine very slowly	Battery discharged Starter motor connections loose Starter brushes worn or sticking
Starter noisy	Pinion or flywheel ring gear teeth badly worn Mounting bolts loose
Battery will not hold charge for more than a few days	Battery defective internally Electrolyte level too low Battery terminals loose Alternator drivebelt slipping Alternator or regulator faulty Short-circuit draining battery
Ignition light stays on	Alternator faulty Alternator drivebelt broken
Ignition light fails to come on	Warning bulb blown Faulty wiring Alternator faulty
Instrument readings increase with engine speed	Voltage stabilizer faulty
Fuel or temperature gauge gives no reading	Wiring open-circuit Sender unit faulty
Fuel or temperature gauge gives maximum reading all the time	Wiring short-circuit Gauge or sender faulty
Lights inoperative	Bulb blown Fuse blown Battery discharged Switch faulty Wiring open-circuit Bad earth connection due to corrosion
Failure of component motor	Commutator dirty or burnt Armature faulty Brushes sticking or worn Armature bearings dry or misaligned Field coils faulty Fuse blown Wiring loose or broken
Failure of an individual component	Wiring loose or broken Fuse blown Bad wiring or earth connection Switch faulty Component faulty Relay faulty (if applicable)

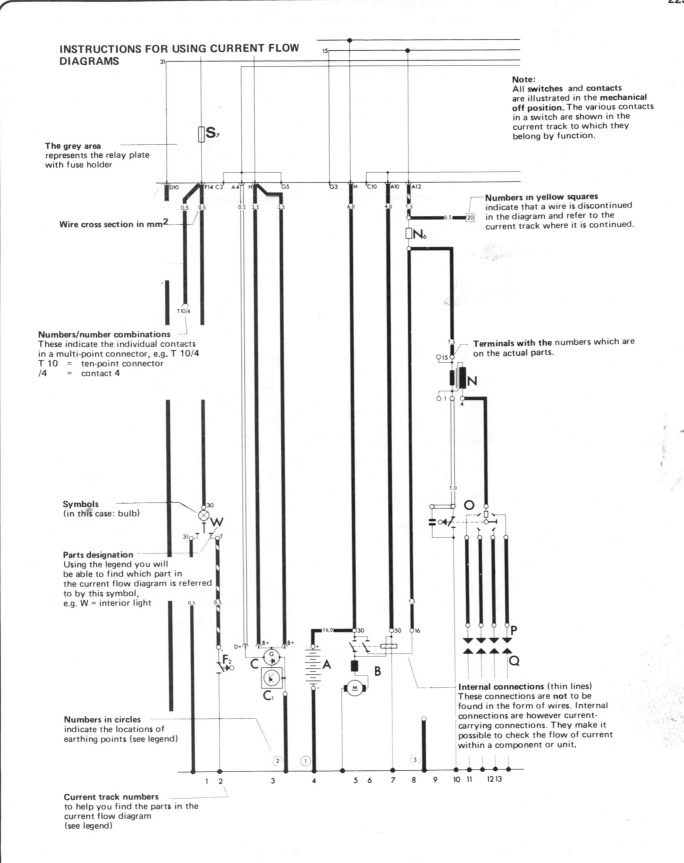

INSTRUCTIONS FOR USING CURRENT FLOW DIAGRAMS

Note:
All **switches** and **contacts** are illustrated in the **mechanical off position.** The various contacts in a switch are shown in the current track to which they belong by function.

The grey area represents the relay plate with fuse holder

Wire cross section in mm²

Numbers in yellow squares indicate that a wire is discontinued in the diagram and refer to the current track where it is continued.

Numbers/number combinations
These indicate the individual contacts in a multi-point connector, e.g. T 10/4
T 10 = ten-point connector
/4 = contact 4

Terminals with the numbers which are on the actual parts.

Symbols (in this case: bulb)

Parts designation
Using the legend you will be able to find which part in the current flow diagram is referred to by this symbol, e.g. W = interior light

Internal connections (thin lines)
These connections are **not** to be found in the form of wires. Internal connections are however current-carrying connections. They make it possible to check the flow of current within a component or unit.

Numbers in circles indicate the locations of earthing points (see legend)

Current track numbers to help you find the parts in the current flow diagram (see legend)

Fig. 9.36 Instructions for using wiring diagrams

INSTRUCTIONS FOR USING WIRING DIAGRAMS

Specimen legend
The same part designations are used in all current flow diagrams.

eg: A is always used for the battery or N for the ignition coil.

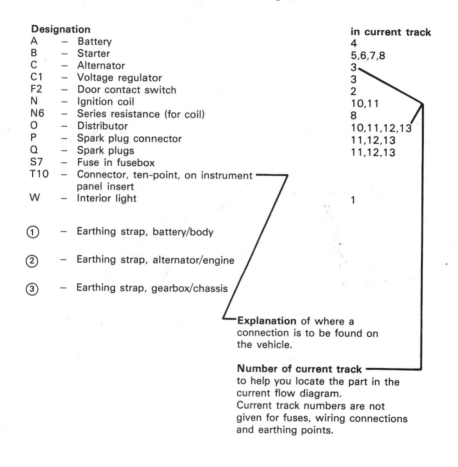

Designation		in current track
A	– Battery	4
B	– Starter	5,6,7,8
C	– Alternator	3
C1	– Voltage regulator	3
F2	– Door contact switch	2
N	– Ignition coil	10,11
N6	– Series resistance (for coil)	8
O	– Distributor	10,11,12,13
P	– Spark plug connector	11,12,13
Q	– Spark plugs	11,12,13
S7	– Fuse in fusebox	
T10	– Connector, ten-point, on instrument panel insert	
W	– Interior light	1

① – Earthing strap, battery/body

② – Earthing strap, alternator/engine

③ – Earthing strap, gearbox/chassis

Explanation of where a connection is to be found on the vehicle.

Number of current track to help you locate the part in the current flow diagram. Current track numbers are not given for fuses, wiring connections and earthing points.

Fig. 9.36 (contd) Instructions for using wiring diagrams

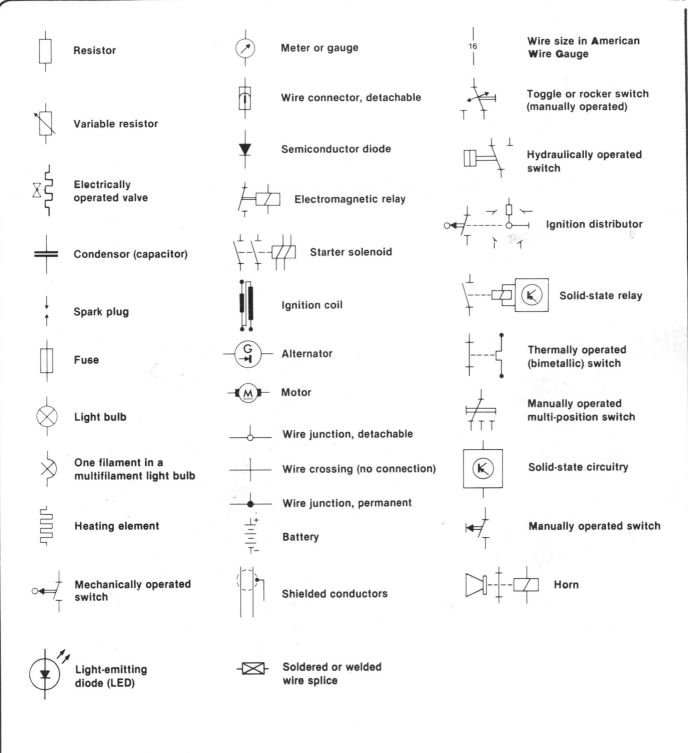

Resistor

Variable resistor

Electrically operated valve

Condensor (capacitor)

Spark plug

Fuse

Light bulb

One filament in a multifilament light bulb

Heating element

Mechanically operated switch

Light-emitting diode (LED)

Meter or gauge

Wire connector, detachable

Semiconductor diode

Electromagnetic relay

Starter solenoid

Ignition coil

Alternator

Motor

Wire junction, detachable

Wire crossing (no connection)

Wire junction, permanent

Battery

Shielded conductors

Soldered or welded wire splice

16 Wire size in American Wire Gauge

Toggle or rocker switch (manually operated)

Hydraulically operated switch

Ignition distributor

Solid-state relay

Thermally operated (bimetallic) switch

Manually operated multi-position switch

Solid-state circuitry

Manually operated switch

Horn

Terminal Number Code

30 = power from battery, always 'hot'
15 = power when ignition is ON
50 = power only when cranking
X = power when key is ON
    (looses power when cranking)
31 = ground

Color Code

Black	— BK	Green	— G
Brown	— BR	Light Green	— LT. G
Clear	— CL	Blue	— BL
Red	— R	Violet	— V
Yellow	— Y	Gray	— GY
		White	— W

Wire Connector Code

T1 — single
T2 — double
T3 — 3-point
T10 — 10-point
T18 — 18-point

Fig. 9.36 (contd) Key to symbols used in wiring diagrams

Key to Fig. 9.37. Numbers in triangles are connections to diagnostic test socket

Description			Current track
A	–	Battery	3
B	–	Starter	4-6
C	–	Alternator	1,2
C1	–	Regulator	2
D	–	Ignition/starter switch	17-20
E1	–	light switch	65-67
E2	–	Turn signal switch	55
E3	–	Emergency flasher switch	51-59
E4	–	Headlight dimmer switch	93
E9	–	Fresh air fan switch	8,9
E15	–	Rear window defogger switch	83
E20	–	Instrum. panel light switch	68
E22	–	Windshield wiper intermittent switch	88-91
E24	–	Safety belt lock contact, left	18
E25	–	Safety belt lock contact, right	18
F	–	Brake light switch	36,37
F1	–	Oil pressure switch	46
F2	–	Door contact buzzer switch, switch, left	16,17
F3	–	Door contact switch, right	15
F4	–	Back-up light switch warning light	40
F9	–	Parking brake warning light switch	28
F18	–	Radiator fan thermoswitch	99
F24	–	Elapsed mileage switch CAT light	30
F27	–	Elapsed mileage switch/EGR light	29
G	–	Fuel gauge sending unit	48
G1	–	Fuel gauge	21
G2	–	Coolant temperature sending unit	47
G3	–	Coolant temperature gauge	22
G7	–	TDC marker unit	24
G20	–	Temperature sensor for catalytic converter	33
H	–	Horn button	39
H1	–	Horn	38
J	–	Headlight dimmer relay	93-95
J2	–	Emergency flasher relay	53-55
J9	–	Rear window defogger relay	81,82
J34	–	Safety belt warning system relay	16-20
J42	–	Relay for catalytic converter (behind dash)	32,33
K1	–	Headlight high beam warning light	98
K2	–	Alternator warning light	25
K3	–	Oil pressure warning light	24
K5	–	Turn signal warning light	26
K6	–	Emergency flasher warning light	58
K7	–	Dual circuit brake/parking brake/safety belt warning light	27-29
K10	–	Rear window defogger warning light	84
K21	–	Catalytic converter warning light	31
K22	–	EGR warning light	30
L1	–	Left headlight, high/low beam	94,96
L2	–	Right headlight, high/low beam	95,97
L10	–	Instrument panel light	68-70
L15	–	Ashtray light	11

Description			Current track
L16	–	Heater lever light	60
L28	–	Cigarette lighter bulb	12
M1	–	Parking light, left front	74
M2	–	Tail light, right	79
M3	–	Parking light, right front	77
M4	–	Tail light, left	76
M5	–	Turn signal, left front	61
M6	–	Turn signal, left rear	62
M7	–	Turn signal, right front	63
M8	–	Turn signal, right rear	64
M9	–	Brake light, left	44
M10	–	Brake light, right	45
M11	–	Side marker, front	73,78
M12	–	Side marker, rear	75,80
M16	–	Back-up light, left	42
M17	–	Back-up light, rear	43
N	–	Ignition coil	34
N1	–	Automatic choke	85
N3	–	Electromagnetic cut-off valve	84
N6	–	Ballast resistor	34
O	–	Ignition distributor	34,35
P	–	Spark plug connectors	35,36
Q	–	Spark plugs	42,43
S1 to S14	–	Fuses on fuse/relay panel	
U1	–	Cigarette lighter	13
V	–	Windshield wiper motor	86,87
V2	–	Fresh air fan	9
V5	–	Windshield washer pump	92
V7	–	Radiator fan	99
W	–	Interior light	14
W6	–	Glove compartment light	10
X	–	License plate light	71,72
Y	–	Clock	66
Z1	–	Rear window defogger heat, element	81

Wire connectors

T	–	Behind dashboard
T1a	–	Single, behind dashboard
T1b	–	Single, behind dashboard
T1c	–	Single, in engine compartment
T1d	–	Single, engine compartment, front left
T1e	–	Single, engine compartment, front right
T1f	–	Single, trunk
T1g	–	Single, trunk, right rear
T1h	–	Single, trunk, left rear
T2a	–	Double, engine compartment
T2b	–	Double, behind dashboard
T2c	–	Double, behind dashboard
T2d	–	Double, behind dashboard
T3a	–	3-point, engine compartment, left front
T3b	–	3-point, engine compartment, right front
T12	–	12 point, on dashboard cluster
T20	–	Test socket

Ground connectors

①	–	Battery to body
②	–	Alternator to engine
⑩	–	Instrument cluster
⑪	–	Body
⑮	–	Engine compartment, front left
⑯	–	Engine compartment, front right

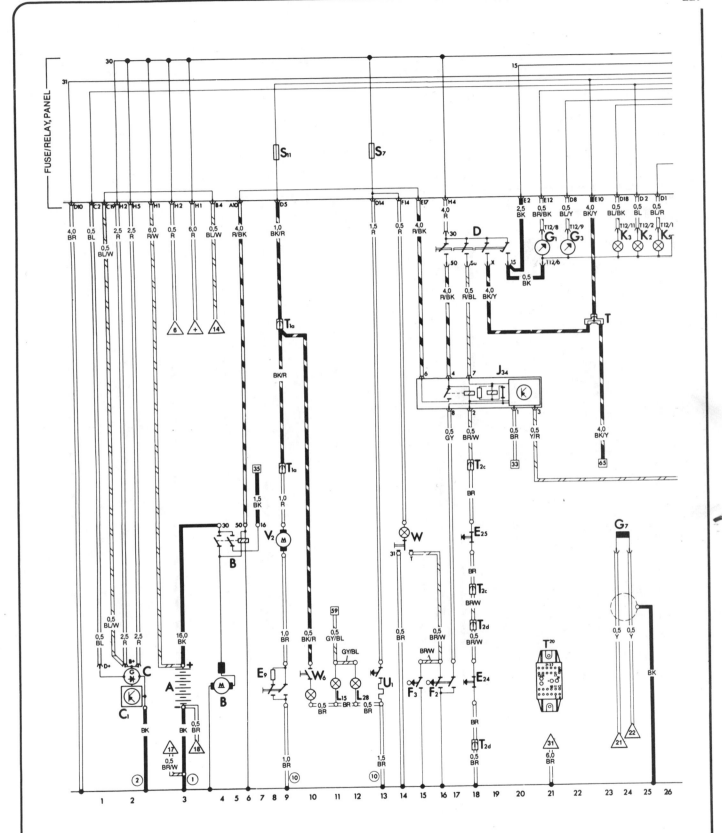

Fig. 9.37 Wiring diagram (typical) for pre-1977 Rabbit models. For key see page 226

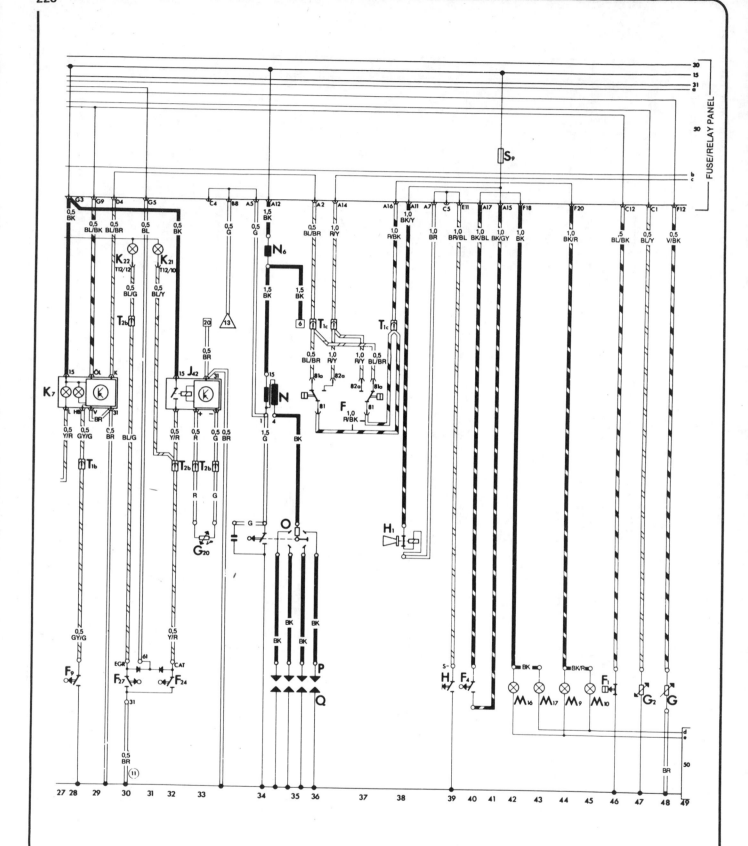

Fig. 9.37 (contd) Wiring diagram (typical) for pre-1977 Rabbit models. For key see page 226

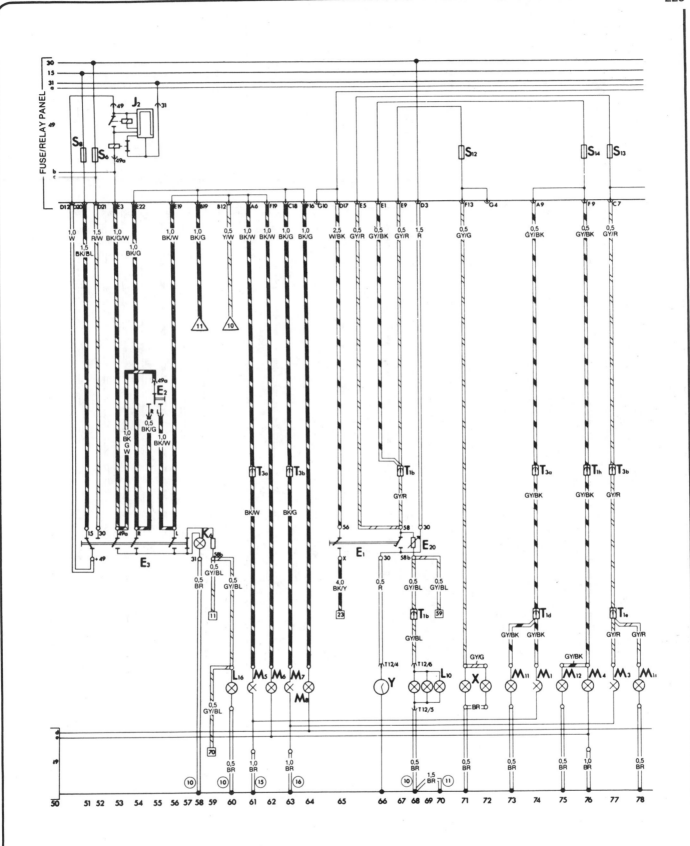

Fig. 9.37 (contd) Wiring diagram (typical) for pre-1977 Rabbit models. For key see page 226

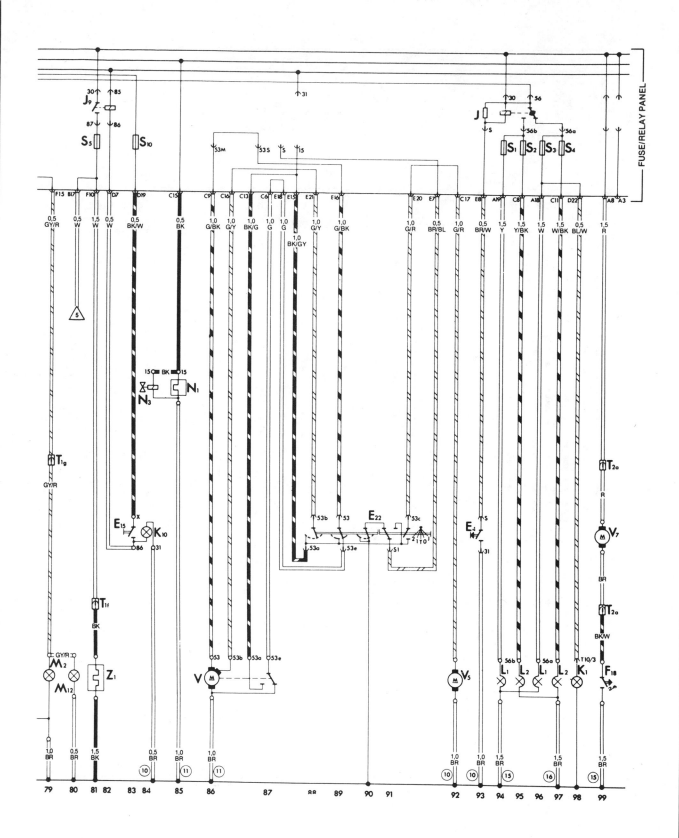

Fig. 9.37 (contd) Wiring diagram (typical) for pre-1977 Rabbit models. For key see page 226

Key to Fig. 9.38. Numbers in triangles are connections to diagnostic test socket

Description		Current track
A	– Battery	2
B	– Starter motor	3,4
C	– Alternator	1
C1	– Regulator	1
D	– Ignition/starter switch	10-14
E1	– Light switch	58,60
E2	– Turn signal switch	46
E3	– Emergency flasher switch	42-48
E4	– Headlight dimmer switch	93
E9	– Fresh air fan switch	78,79
E15	– Rear window defogger switch	91
E20	– Instrument panel light switch	61
E22	– Windshield wash/wipe intermittent switch	84-88
E24	– Safety belt lock contact, left	11
F	– Brake light switch	36,37
F1	– Engine oil pressure switch	39
F2	– Door switch/buzzer, left	107,108
F3	– Door switch/buzzer, right	106
F4	– Back-up light switch	31
F9	– Parking brake warning light switch	22
F18	– Radiator fan thermoswitch	102
F24	– Elapsed mileage switch/ CAT light	25
F25	– Throttle valve micro switch	9
F26	– Thermotime switch for cold start	30
F27	– Elapsed mileage switch/ EGR light	23
F37	– Thermoswitch for secondary stage	31
G	– Fuel gauge sending unit	41
G1	– Fuel gauge	15
G2	– Coolant temperature. sending unit	40
G3	– Coolant temperature gauge	16
G5	– Tachometer	18
G7	– to TDC sensor	18
G14	– Voltmeter	77
G20	– Temp. sensor for CAT converter	26
H	– Horn button	36
H1	– Horn	33,34
J	– Headlight dimmer switch	93-95
J2	– Emergency flasher relay	44-46
J4	– Horn relay	35,36
J6	– Voltage stabilizer	15
J9	– Rear window defogger relay	90
J31	– Wiper intermittent relay	82-84
J34	– Safety belt warning relay	11-15
J42	– Relay for CAT converter (behind dash)	25-28
K1	– Headlight high beam warning light	101
K2	– Alternator charging warning light	19
K3	– Oil pressure warning light	18
K5	– Turn signal warning light	20
K6	– Emergency flasher warning light	49
K7	– Dual circuit brake/parking brake/safety belt warning light	21,22
K10	– Rear window defogger light	92
K21	– CAT converter warning light	24
K22	– EGR warning light	23
L1	– Left headlight, high/low beam	94, 96
L2	– Right headlight, high/low beam	95,100
L8	– Clock light	65
L10	– Instrument panel light	61-63
L15	– Ashtray light	52
L16	– Fresh air lever light	50
L17	– Left headlight, high beam	98
L18	– Right headlight, high beam	99
L25	– Voltmeter light	64
L28	– Cigarette lighter light	53
M1	– Parking light, front left	70
M2	– Tail light, right	75
M3	– Parking light, front right	73

Description		Current track
M4	– Tail light, left	72
M5	– Turn signal, front left	54
M6	– Turn signal, rear left	55
M7	– Turn signal, front right	56
M8	– Turn signal, rear right	57
M9	– Brake light, left	38
M10	– Brake light, right	37
M11	– Side marker lights, front	69,74
M12	– Side marker lights, rear	71,76
M16	– Back-up light, left	32
M17	– Back-up light, right	33
N	– Ignition coil	6
N1	– Automatic choke	30
N3	– Electro-magnetic cut-off valve	29
N6	– Ballast resistor	6
N18	– EGR valve	9
N38	– Diverter valve for air injection	28
O	– Ignition distributor	6,8
P	– Spark plug connectors	8
Q	– Spark plugs	8
S1 to S15	– Fuses on fuse/relay panel	
U1	– Cigarette lighter	104
V	– Windshield wiper motor	81,82
V2	– Fresh air fan	79
V5	– Windshield wiper pump	89
V7	– Radiator cooling fan	102
W	– Interior light	105
W3	– Trunk light	66
W6	– Glove compartment light	80
X	– License plate light	67,68
Y	– Clock	59
Z1	– Rear window defogger light	90

Wire connectors

T	–	Single, behind dashboard
T1a	–	Single, in engine compartment front left
T1b	–	Single, in engine compartment front right
T1c	–	Single, behind dashboard
T1d	–	Single, in engine compartment
T1e	–	Single, in engine compartment
T1f	–	Single, in engine compartment
T1g	–	Single, behind dashboard
T1h	–	Single, behind dashboard
T1i	–	Single, behind dashboard
T1k	–	Single, behind dashboard
T1l	–	Single, behind dashboard
T1m	–	Single, behind dashboard
T1n	–	Single, in trunk
T1o	–	Single, behind dashboard
T1p	–	Single, behind dashboard
T1q	–	Single, behind dashboard
T1f	–	Single, behind dashboard
T1s	–	Single, in trunk
T1t	–	Single, in trunk, left
T1v	–	Single, in trunk, right
T2a	–	Double, in engine compartment front
T2b	–	Double, in engine compartment on firewall
T2c	–	Double, behind dashboard
T2d	–	Double, behind dashboard
T2e	–	Double, in engine compartment
T2f	–	Double, on frame, left
T3	–	3-point, behind dashboard
T12	–	12-point, instrument cluster
T20	–	Diagnosis socket

Ground connectors

①	–	Battery to body
②	–	Alternator to engine
⑩	–	Instrument cluster
⑪	–	Dashboard
⑮	–	Engine compartment front left
⑯	–	Engine compartment front right

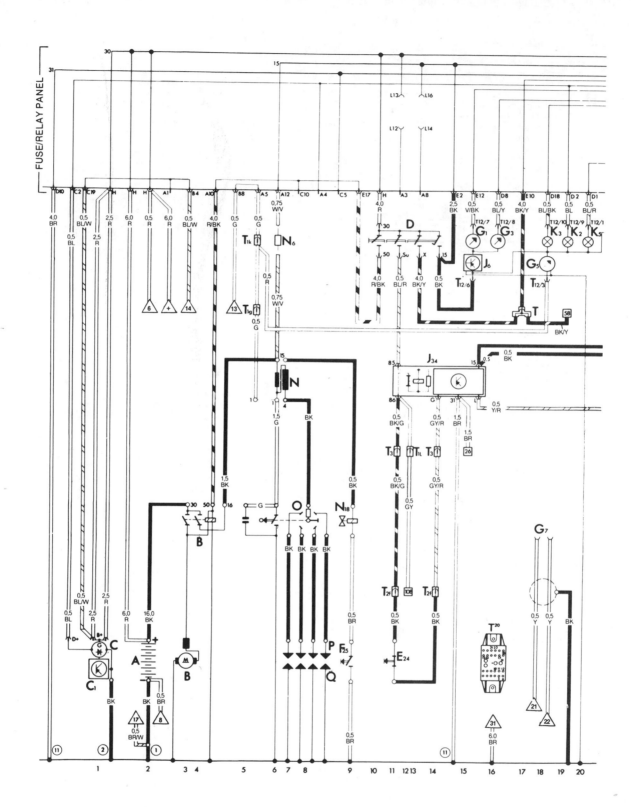

Fig. 9.38 Wiring diagram (typical) for pre-1977 Scirocco models. For key see page 231

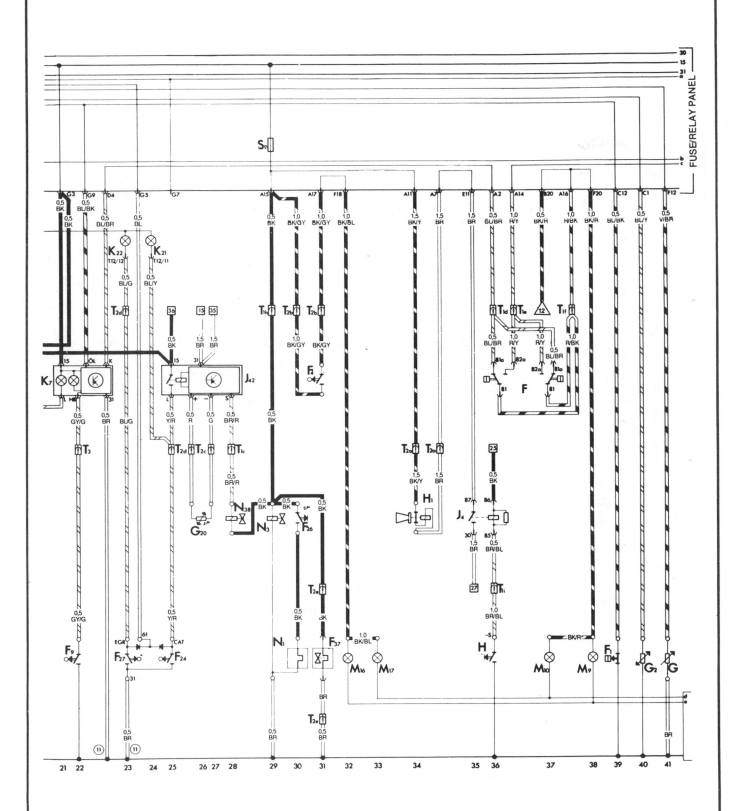

Fig. 9.38 (contd) Wiring diagram (typical) for pre-1977 Scirocco models. For key see page 231

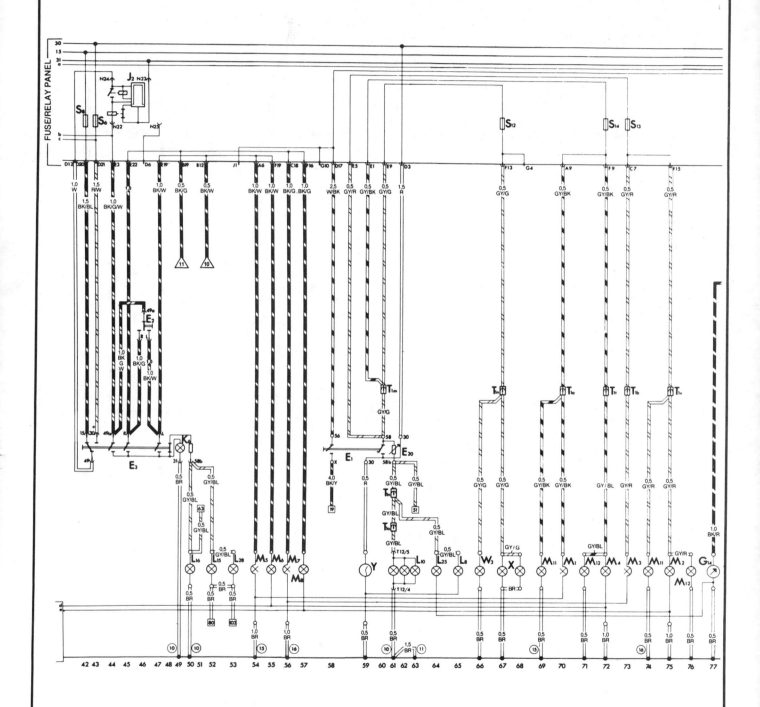

Fig. 9.38 (contd) Wiring diagram (typical) for pre-1977 Scirocco models. For key see page 231

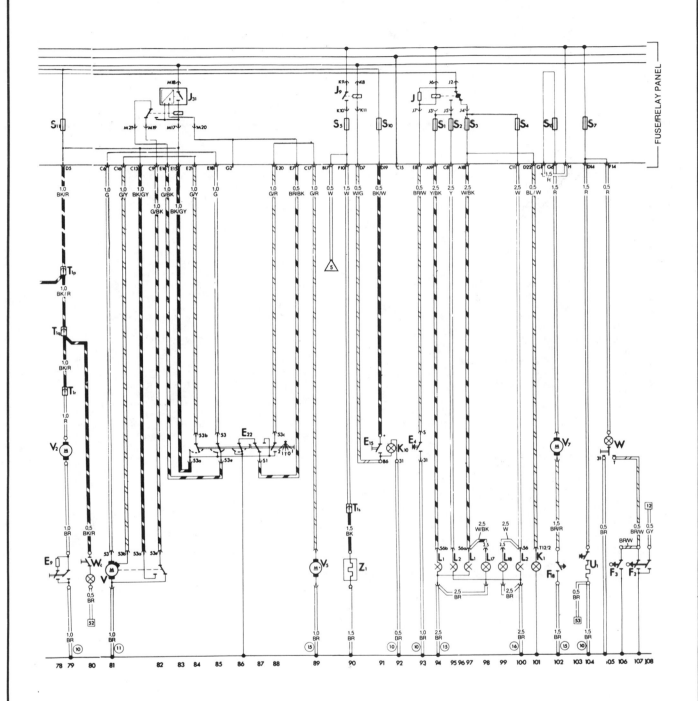

Fig. 9.38 (contd) Wiring diagram (typical) for pre-1977 Scirocco models. For key see page 231

Key to Fig. 9.39

Description		Current track
A	– Battery	2
B	– Starter motor	10-12
C	– Alternator	1
C1	– Regulator	1
D	– Ignition/starter switch	17-20
E1	– Light switch	81-84
E2	– Turn signal switch	61
E3	– Emergency flasher switch	57-65
E4	– Headlight dimmer/flasher switch	79,80
E5	– Fresh air fan switch	94,95
E15	– Rear window defogger switch	97,98
E20	– Instrument panel lights switch	83
E22	– Windshield washer/wiper intermittent switch	101-105
E24	– Safety belt switch, left	38
F	– Brake light switch	43,44
F1	– Engine oil pressure switch	28
F2	– Door switch/buzzer, front left	54,55
F3	– Door switch, front right	53
F4	– Back-up light switch	32
F9	– Parking brake warning light switch	42
F18	– Radiator fan thermoswitch	107
F26	– Thermoswitch/cold start valve	8
F29	– Elapsed mileage switch/ EGR light (not for Canada)	27
G	– Fuel gauge sending unit	30
G1	– Fuel gauge	21
G2	– Coolant temperature sending unit	29
G3	– Coolant temperature gauge	22
G5	– Tachometer	23
G6	– electrical fuel pump	7
G8	– Engine oil temperature sending unit	37
G9	– Engine oil temperature gauge	37
H	– Horn button	36
H1	– Dual horn	34,35
J2	– Emergency flasher relay	59-61
J4	– Dual horn relay	35,36
J6	– Voltage stabilizer	21
J17	– Electric fuel pump relay	4-10
J31	– Windscreen washer/wiper intermittent relay	100-103
J34	– Safety belt warning relay	38,39
J59	– Load reducing relay – X terminal	15,16
K1	– Headlight high beam warning light	78
K2	– Alternator charging warning light	25
K3	– Engine oil pressure warning light	24
K5	– Turn signal warning light	26
K6	– Emergency flasher warning light	64
K7	– Dual circuit brake/parking brake warning light	41
K10	– Rear window defogger warning light	98
K19	– Safety belt warning light	40
K22	– EGR warning light (not for Canada)	27
L1	– Left headlight, low/ high beam	72,74
L2	– Right headlight, low/ high beam	73,77
L8	– clock light	51
L10	– instrument panel light	65-67
L15	– Ashtray light	48
L17	– Left headlight, high beam	75
L18	– Right headlight, high beam	76
L24	– Engine oil temperature gauge light	50

Description		Current track
L28	– Cigarette lighter light	47
M1	– Left front parking light	88
M2	– Right tail light	92
M3	– Right front parking light	91
M4	– Left tail light	90
M5	– Left front turn signal	68
M6	– Left rear turn signal	69
M7	– Right front turn signal	70
M8	– Right rear turn signal	71
M9	– Brake light, left	45
M10	– Brake light, right	44
M12	– Rear side marker lights	89,93
M16	– Back-up light, left	33
M17	– Back-up light, right	34
N	– Ignition coil	14,15
N6	– Ballast resistor wire	14
N9	– Control pressure regulator	3
N17	– Cold start valve	8
N21	– Auxiliary air regulator	3
N23	– Fresh air ballast resistor	94
O	– Ignition distributor	16
P	– Spark plug connectors	16
Q	– Spark plugs	16
S1 to S14	– fuses in fuse box	
S20	– fuse for fuel pump	
U1	– Cigarette lighter	46
V	– Windshield wiper motor	99,100
V2	– Fresh air fan	95
V5	– Windshield washer pump	106
V7	– Radiator cooling fan	107
W	– Interior light	52,53
W3	– Trunk light	87
X	– License plate light	85,86
Y	– Clock	56
Z	– Rear window defogger element	96

Wire connectors

T	– Next to relay panel	
T1a	– Single, in engine compartment	
T1b	– Single, behind dashboard	
T1c	– Single, behind dashboard	
T1d	– Single, behind dashboard	
T1e	– Single, behind dashboard	
T1f	– Single, behind dashboard	
T1g	– Single, behind dashboard	
T1h	– Single, next to fuse/relay panel	
T1i	– Single, next to fuse/relay panel	
T1j	– Single, next to fuse/relay panel	
T1l	– Single, in trunk, right	
T1m	– Single, in trunk, left	
T1n	– Single, in trunk, left	
T1k	– Single, behind dashboard	
T2	– Double, in engine compartment	
T2b	– Double, behind dashboard	
T2c	– Double, in engine compartment	
T3	– 3-point, behind dashboard	
T4a	– 4-point, behind dashboard	
T12	– 12-point, on instrument cluster	

Ground connectors

①	– Battery/body/engine
②	– Alternator/engine
⑩	– Instrument cluster
⑪	– Steering column bracket
⑭	– Footwell, right
⑩	– Instrument cluster
⑪	– Steering column bracket
⑮	– Engine compartment front left
⑯	– Engine compartment front right
⑰	– Trunk
⑳	– Steering gear

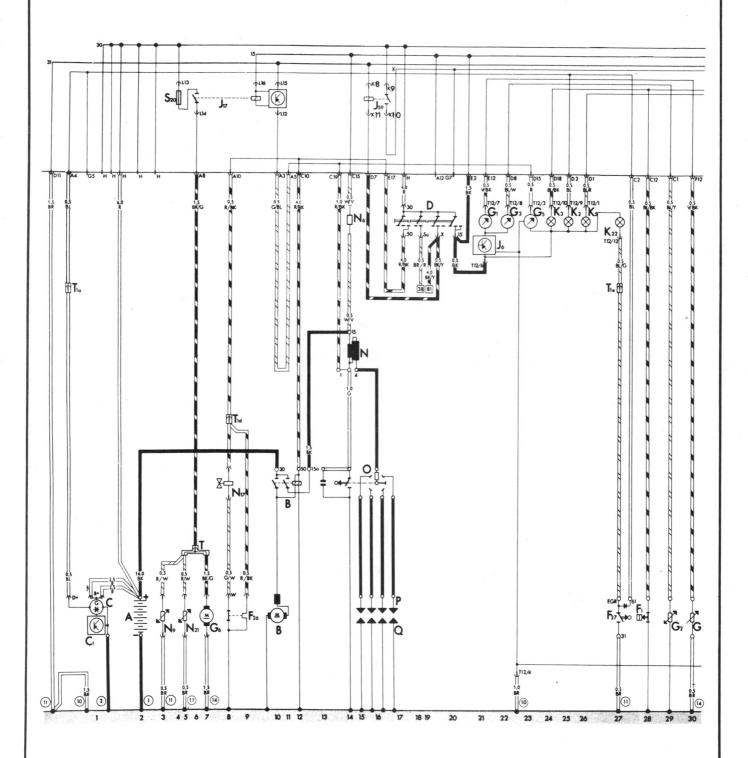

Fig. 9.39 Wiring diagram (typical) for 1977/78 Rabbit and Scirocco models. For key see page 236

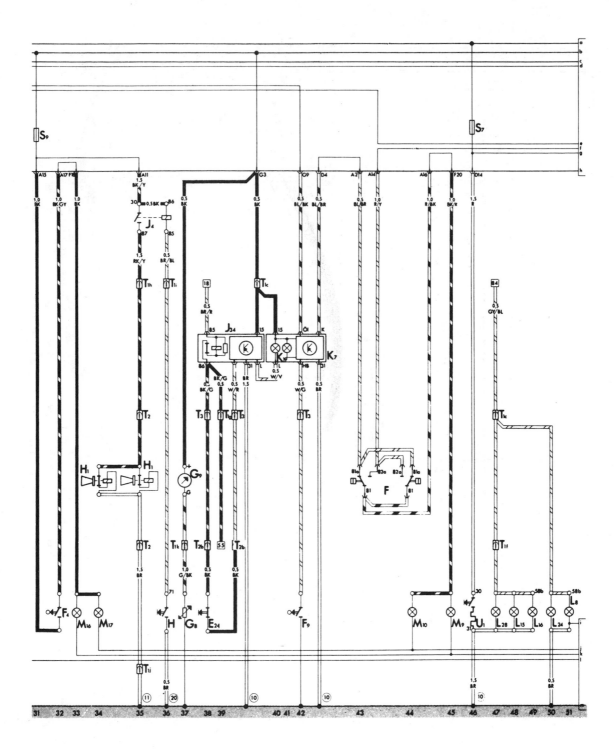

Fig. 9.39 (contd) Wiring diagram (typical) for 1977/78 Rabbit and Scirocco models. For key see page 236

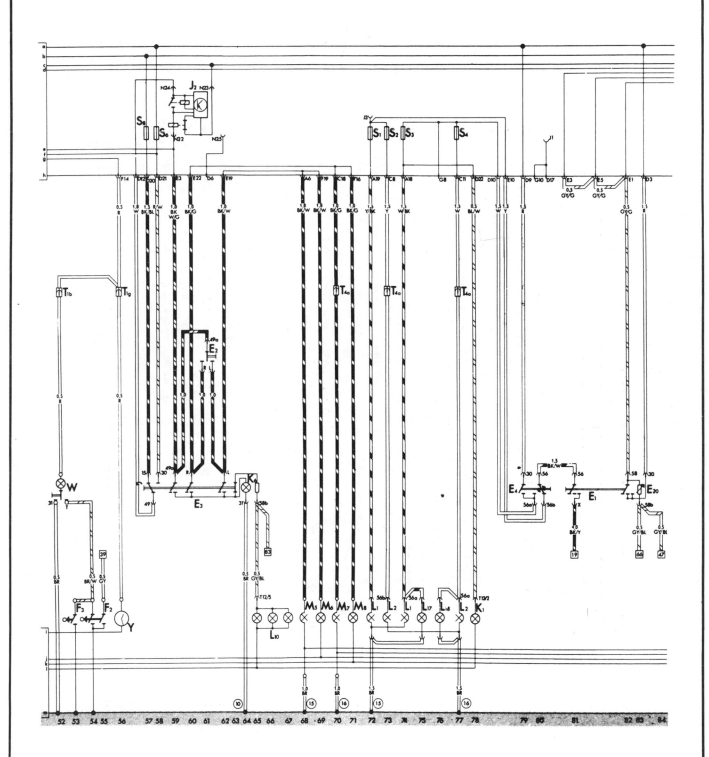

Fig. 9.39 (contd) Wiring diagram (typical) for 1977/78 Rabbit and Scirocco models. For key see page 236

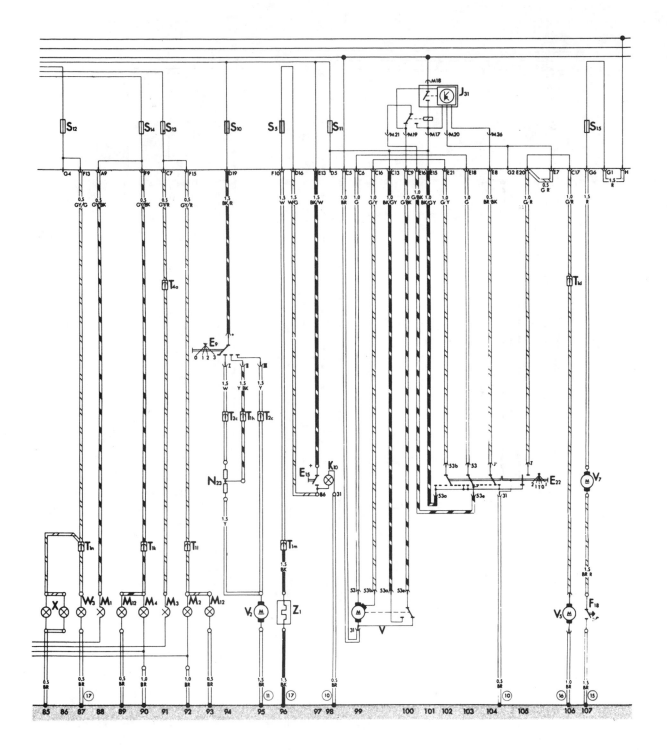

Fig. 9.39 (contd) Wiring diagram (typical) for 1977/78 Rabbit and Scirocco models. For key see page 236

Key to Fig. 9.40

Description	Current track
Alternator	3
Alternator charging light	24
Ashtray light	53
Auxiliary air regulator	6
Back-up lights	35-36
Back-up light switch	34
Ballast resistance wire	11
Battery	4
Cigarette lighter	48
Cigarette lighter light	52
Cold start valve	14
Control pressure regulator	5
Coolant temperature light	29
Coolant temperature switch	32
Door switch (right)	44
Door switch/buzzer (left)	45-46
EGR elapsed mileage switch (inoperative in Canada)	29-30
EGR light (inoperative in Canada)	29
Emergency flasher relay	51-53
Emergency flasher switch	49-56
Emergency flasher indicator light	55
Fresh air fan	86
Fresh air fan speed control resistors	84
Fresh air fan switch	84-86
Fuel gauge	20
Fuel level sensor	33
Fuel pump	7
Fuel pump relay	5-10
Fuses S1-S15, on fuse/relay panel (under dash) S20 (on fuel pump relay)	
Headlights	63-66
Headlight dimmer/flasher switch	68-69
Heater lever light	54
High beam indicator light	67
Horn	36
Horn button	37
Ignition coil	11
Ignition/starter switch	15-19
Ignition distributor	12-13
Instrument panel lights	56-58
Instrument panel light switch/dimmer	72
Interior lights	43-44
License plate lights	74-75
Light switch	70-73
Load reduction relay	70-71
Oil pressure switch	31
Oil pressure warning light	23
Parking brake indicator light	24-28
Parking brake indicator light switch	27
Parking light, left	77
Parking light, right	80
Radiator fan	42
Radiator fan thermal switch	42
Radio	100
Rear window defogger	87
Rear window defogger indicator light	89
Rear window defogger switch	88-89
Seat belt/relay	15-20
Seat belt warning light	25
Shift console light (auto.trans)	29
Side marker lights, front	76-81
Side marker lights, rear	78-83
Spark plug suppressors	12-13
Spark plugs	12-13
Starter	8-10
Stop-lights	40-41
Stop-light switch	38-39
Tail light, left	79
Tail light, right	82
Thermal time switch	14-15
Turn signal lights	59-62

Description	Current track
Turn signal switch	53
Turn signal indicator light	25
Voltage regulator	3
Voltage stabilizer	20
Windshield washer pump	99
Windshield wiper motor	90-93
Windshield wiper switch	94-98

Wire connectors		Current track
T	Cable adaptor, engine compartment	6-7
T1a	In engine compartment	2
T1b	In engine compartment, front left	77
T1c	In engine compartment, front right	80
T1d	Behind instrument panel	99
T1e	Behind instrument panel	29
T1f	Behind instrument panel	15
T1g	Behind instrument panel	47
T1h	Behind instrument panel	85
T1i	Behind instrument panel	27
T1j	Behind instrument panel	15
T1k	In luggage compartment, left rear	79
T1l	In luggage compartment, right rear	82
T1m	In luggage compartment, left rear	87
T1p	Behind instrument panel	97
T2a	In engine compartment, front left	59,77
T2b	In engine compartment, front right	61,80
T2c	Behind instrument panel	84,86
T2d	Behind instrument panel	16
T2e	Behind instrument panel	16
T2f	Behind instrument panel	15
T2g	Behind instrument panel, right of steering column	49
T3	Behind instrument panel, right of steering column	48,52
T4	In engine compartment	61,64,66,80
T14	On rear of instrument panel	20,21,23,24,25 29,47,56,67

Ground connectors

① — From battery to body

② — From alternator to engine

⑩ — On steering column support

⑪ — On steering column support

⑫ — In luggage compartment, rear

⑬ — On dome light

⑭ — Middle body member, rear

⑮ — In engine compartment, front left

⑯ — In engine compartment, front right

⑰ — On steering column

⑱ — On tail light cover, left

⑲ — On tail light cover, right

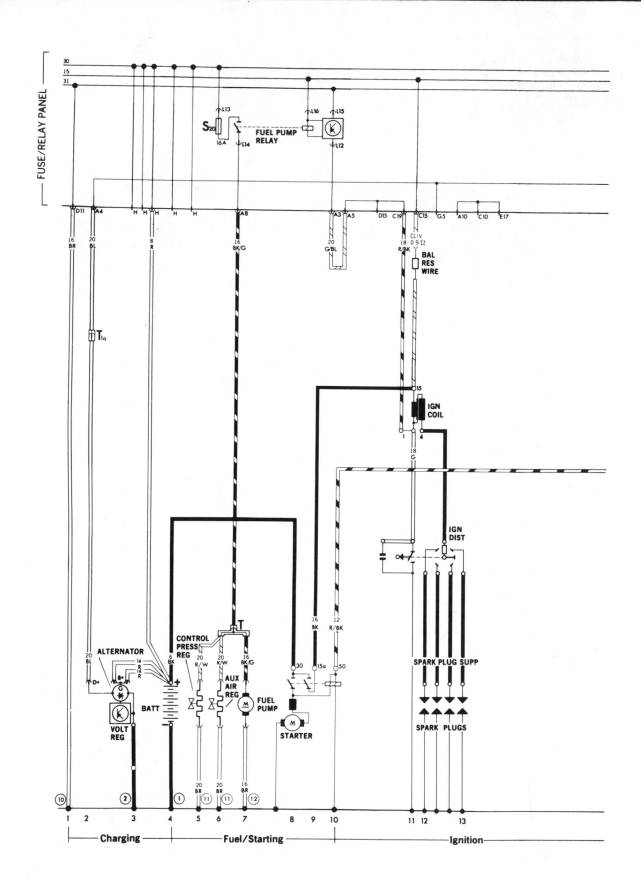

Fig. 9.40 Wiring diagram for 1979 Rabbit Custom and Basic models. For key see page 241

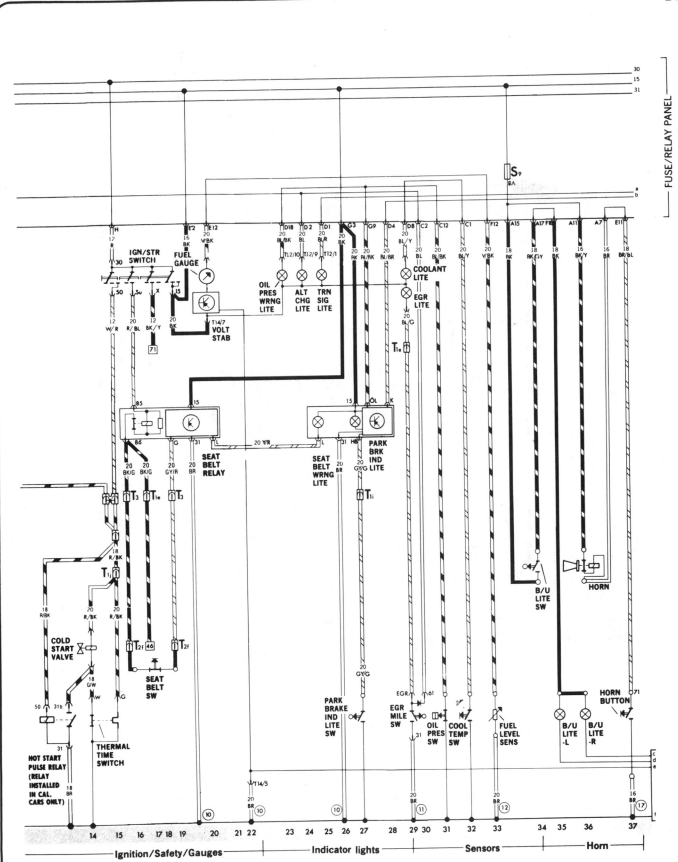

Fig. 9.40 (contd) Wiring diagram for 1979 Rabbit Custom and Basic models. For key see page 241

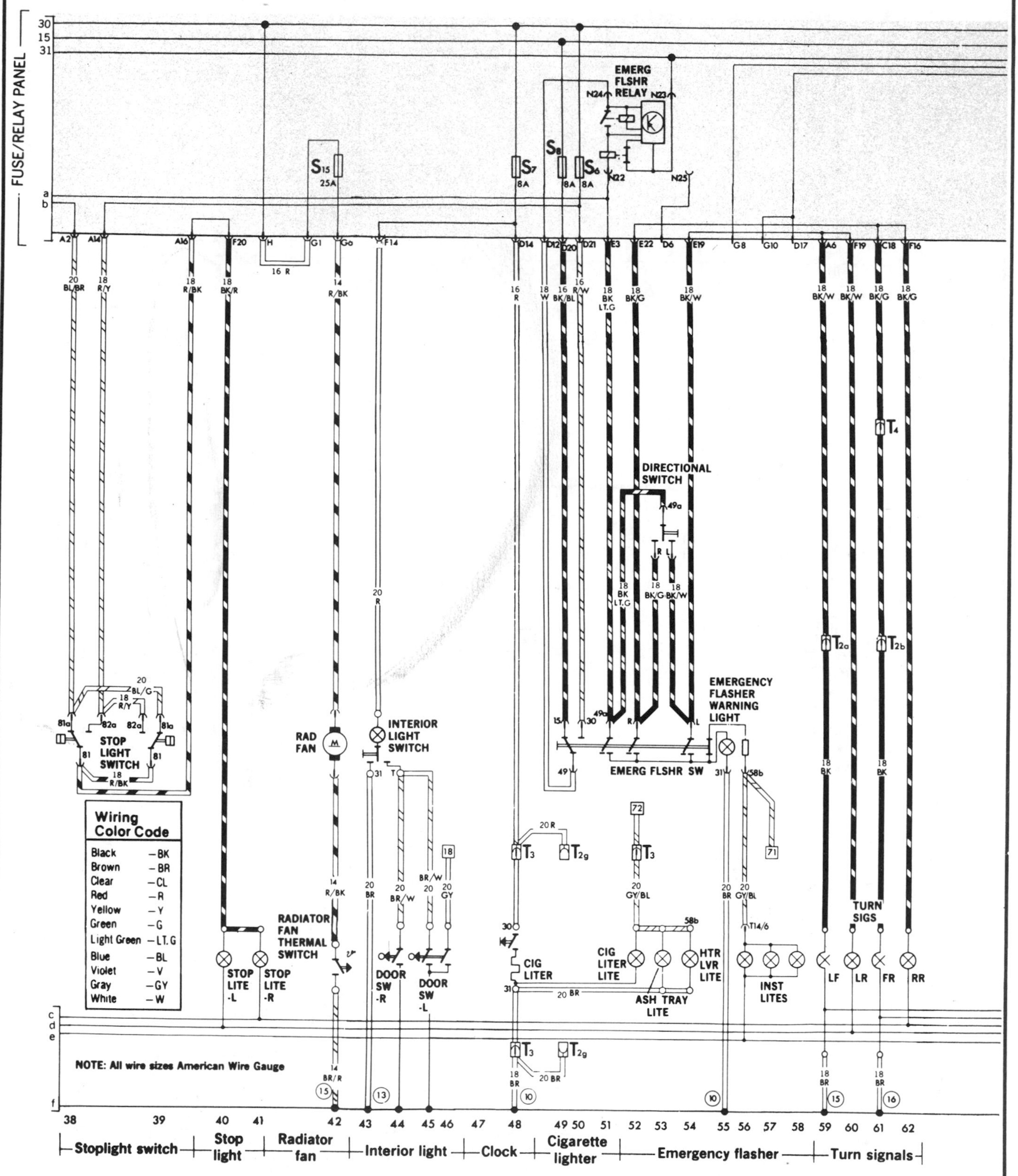

Fig. 9.40 (contd) Wiring diagram for 1979 Rabbit Custom and Basic models. For key see page 241

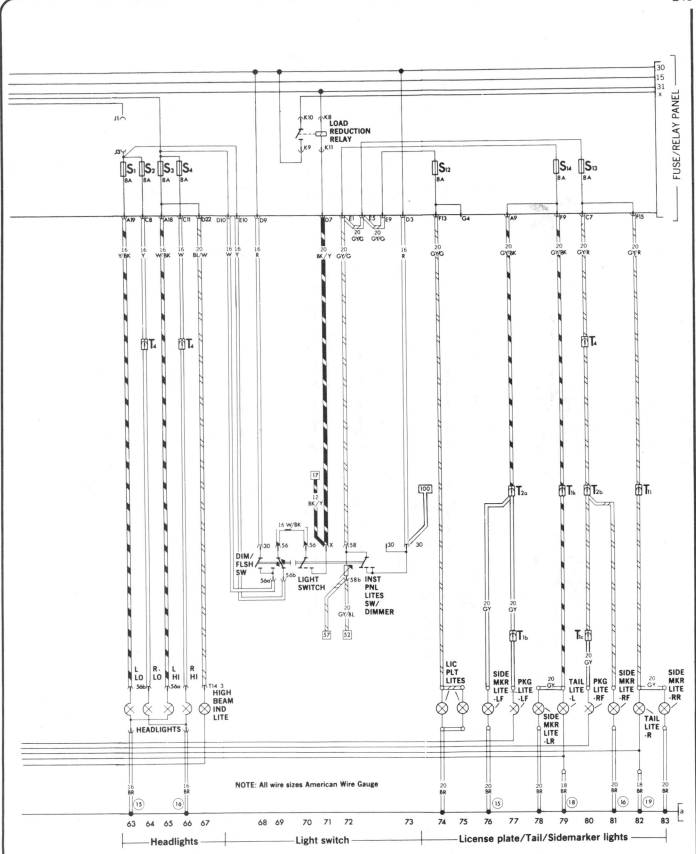

Fig. 9.40 (contd) Wiring diagram for 1979 Rabbit Custom and Basic models. For key see page 241

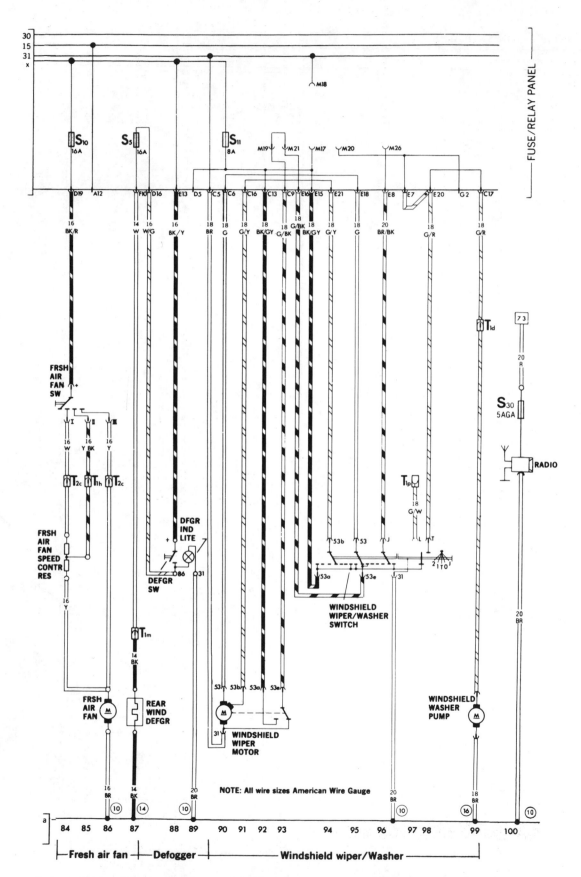

Fig. 9.40 (contd) Wiring diagram for 1979 Rabbit Custom and Basic models. For key see page 241

Key to Fig. 9.41

Description	Current track
Alternator	3
Alternator charging light	24
Ashtray light	53
Auxiliary air regulator	6
Back-up lights	35-36
Back-up light switch	34
Ballast resistance wire	11
Battery	4
Cigarette lighter	48
Cigarette lighter light	52
Clock	47
Cold start valve	14
Control pressure regulator	5
Coolant temperature gauge	21
Coolant temperature sensor	32
Door switch (right)	44
Door switch/buzzer (left)	45-46
EGR elapsed mileage switch (inoperative in Canada)	29-30
EGR light (inoperative in Canada)	29
Emergency flasher relay	51-53
Emergency flasher switch	49-56
Emergency flasher indicator light	55
Fresh air fan	86
Fresh air fan speed control resistors	84
Fresh air fan switch	84-86
Fuel gauge	20
Fuel level sensor	33
Fuel pump	7
Fuel pump relay	5-10
Fuses S1-S15, on fuse/relay panel (under dash) S20 (on fuel pump relay)	
Headlights	63-66
Headlight dimmer/flasher switch	68-69
Heater lever light	54
High beam indicator light	67
Horn	36
Horn button	37
Ignition coil	11
Ignition/starter switch	15-19
Ignition distributor	12-13
Instrument panel lights	56-58
Instrument panel light switch/dimmer	72
Interior lights	43-44
License plate lights	74-75
Light switch	70-73
Load reduction relay	70-71
Oil pressure switch	31
Oil pressure warning light	23
Parking brake indicator light	24-28
Parking brake indicator light switch	27
Parking light, left	77
Parking light, right	80
Radiator fan	42
Radiator fan thermal switch	42
Radio	100
Rear window defogger	87
Rear window defogger indicator light	89
Rear window defogger switch	88-89
Seat belt/starter lock-out relay	15-20
Seat belt switch, left	16
Seat belt switch, right	16
Seat belt warning light	25
Shift console light (auto.trans)	29
Side marker lights, front	76-81
Side marker lights, rear	78-83
Spark plug suppressors	12-13
Spark plugs	12-13
Starter	8-10
Stop-lights	40-41
Stop-light switch	38-39
Tail light, left	79
Tail light, right	82

Description	Current track
Thermal time switch	14-15
Turn signal lights	59-62
Turn signal switch	53
Turn signal indicator light	25
Voltage regulator	3
Voltage stabilizer	20
Windshield washer pump	99
Windshield wiper motor	90-93
Windshield wiper switch	94-98

Wire connectors		Current track
T	– Cable adaptor, engine compartment	6-7
T1a	– In engine compartment	2
T1b	– In engine compartment, front left	77
T1c	– In engine compartment, front right	80
T1d	– Behind instrument panel	99
T1e	– Behind instrument panel	29
T1f	– Behind instrument panel	15
T1g	– Behind instrument panel	47
T1h	– Behind instrument panel	85
T1i	– Behind instrument panel	27
T1j	– Behind instrument panel	15
T1k	– In luggage compartment, left rear	79
T1l	– In luggage compartment, right rear	82
T1m	– In luggage compartment, left rear	87
T1p	– Behind instrument panel	97
T2a	– In engine compartment, front left	59,77
T2b	– In engine compartment, front right	61,80
T2c	– Behind instrument panel	84,86
T2d	– Behind instrument panel	16
T2e	– Behind instrument panel	16
T2f	– Behind instrument panel	15
T2g	– Behind instrument panel, right of steering column	49
T3	– Behind instrument panel, right of steering column	48,52
T4	– In engine compartment	61,64,66,80
T14	– On rear of instrument panel	20,21,23,24,25 29,47,56,67

Ground connectors

1	–	From battery to body
2	–	From alternator to engine
10	–	On steering column support
11	–	On steering column support
12	–	In luggage compartment, rear
13	–	On dome light
14	–	Middle body member, rear
15	–	In engine compartment, front left
16	–	In engine compartment, front right
17	–	On steering column
18	–	On tail light cover, left
19	–	On tail light cover, right

248

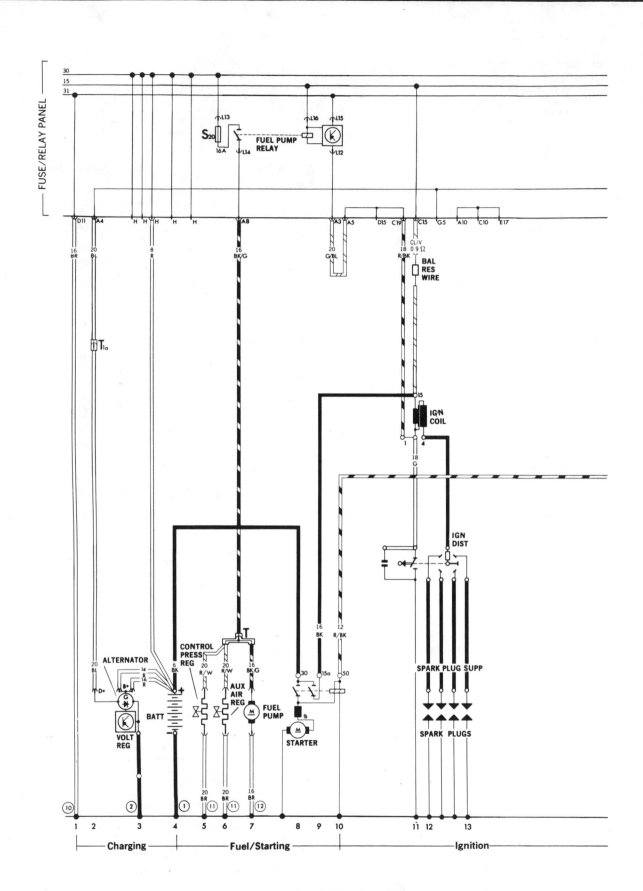

Fig. 9.41 Wiring diagram for 1979 Rabbit Deluxe. For key see page 247

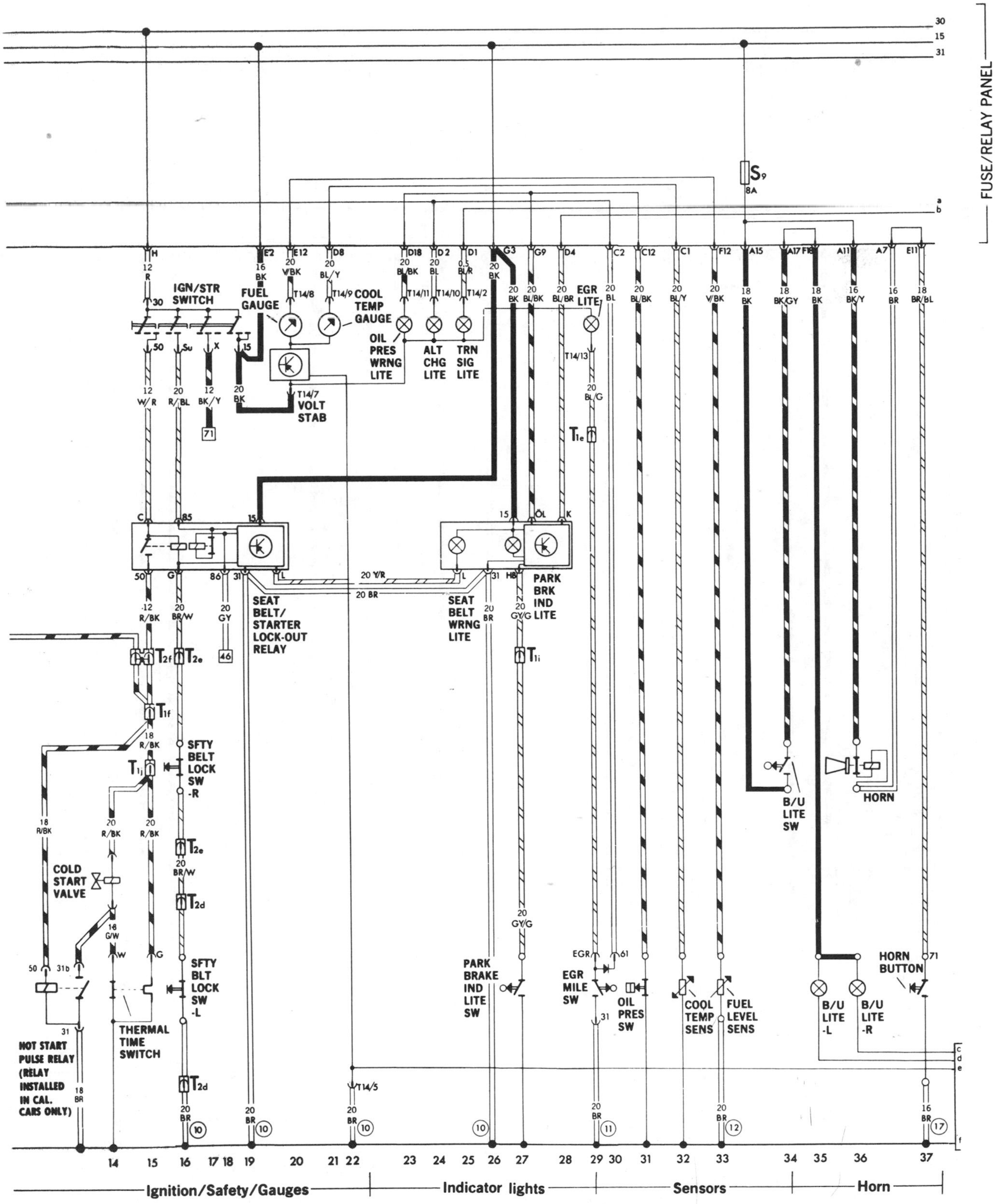

FUSE/RELAY PANEL

30
15
31

S₉
8A

a
b

H · IGN/STR SWITCH · E2 FUEL GAUGE · E12 · D8 · COOL TEMP GAUGE · D18 · D2 · D1 · G3 · G9 · D4 · C2 · C12 · C1 · F12 · A15 · A17 F18 · A11 · A7 · E11

12 R
30
16 BK
20 V/BK · T14/8
20 BL/Y · T14/9
20 BL/BK · T14/11
20 BL · T14/10
0.5 BL/R · T14/2
20 BK
20 BL/BK
20 BL/BR
20 BL
20 BL/BK
20 BL/Y
20 V/BK
18 BK
18 BK/GY
18 BK
16 BK/Y
16 BR
18 BR/BL

50 · Su · X · 15
12 W/R · 20 R/BL · 12 BK/Y · 20 BK

OIL PRES WRNG LITE · ALT CHG LITE · TRN SIG LITE · EGR LITE

71

T14/7 VOLT STAB

20 BL/G
T14/13
T1e

15 · 15 · ÖL · K

C · 85 · 50 · G · 86 · 31

SEAT BELT/STARTER LOCK-OUT RELAY

20 Y/R · 20 BR

PARK BRK IND LITE

-12 R/BK · 20 BR/W · 20 GY

SEAT BELT WRNG LITE · 20 BR · 20 GY/G

T2f · T2e

46

T1i

T1f

18 R/BK

SFTY BELT LOCK SW -R

T1j · 18 R/BK · 20 R/BK · 20 R/BK

COLD START VALVE

T2e · 20 BR/W

T2d

20 GY/G

16 G/W · W · G

50 · 31b · SFTY BLT LOCK SW -L

PARK BRAKE IND LITE SW

EGR MILE SW

EGR/ · 61 · 31

OIL PRES SW

COOL TEMP SENS · FUEL LEVEL SENS

HORN

B/U LITE SW

HORN BUTTON · 71

31 · THERMAL TIME SWITCH

T2d

HOT START PULSE RELAY (RELAY INSTALLED IN CAL. CARS ONLY)

18 BR

B/U LITE -L · B/U LITE -R

c
d
e

20 BR ⑩ · 20 BR ⑩ · 20 BR ⑩ · ⑩ · 20 BR ⑪ · 20 BR ⑫ · 16 BR ⑰

T14/5 · T14/5

f

14 · 15 · 16 · 17 · 18 · 19 · 20 · 21 · 22 · 23 · 24 · 25 · 26 · 27 · 28 · 29 · 30 · 31 · 32 · 33 · 34 · 35 · 36 · 37

Ignition/Safety/Gauges — Indicator lights — Sensors — Horn

Fig. 9.41 (contd) Wiring diagram for 1979 Rabbit Deluxe. For key see page 247

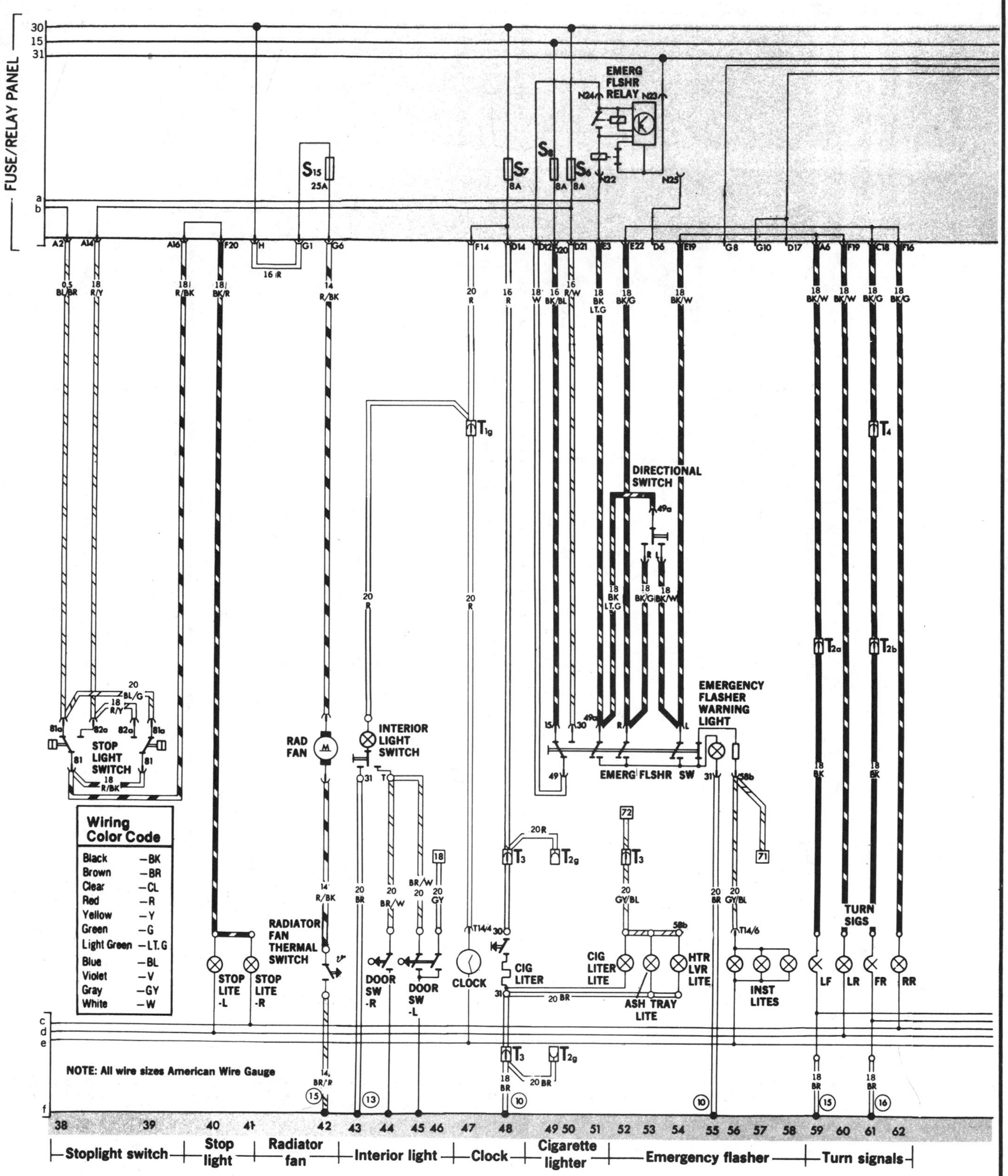

Fig. 9.41 (contd) Wiring diagram for 1979 Rabbit Deluxe. For key see page 247

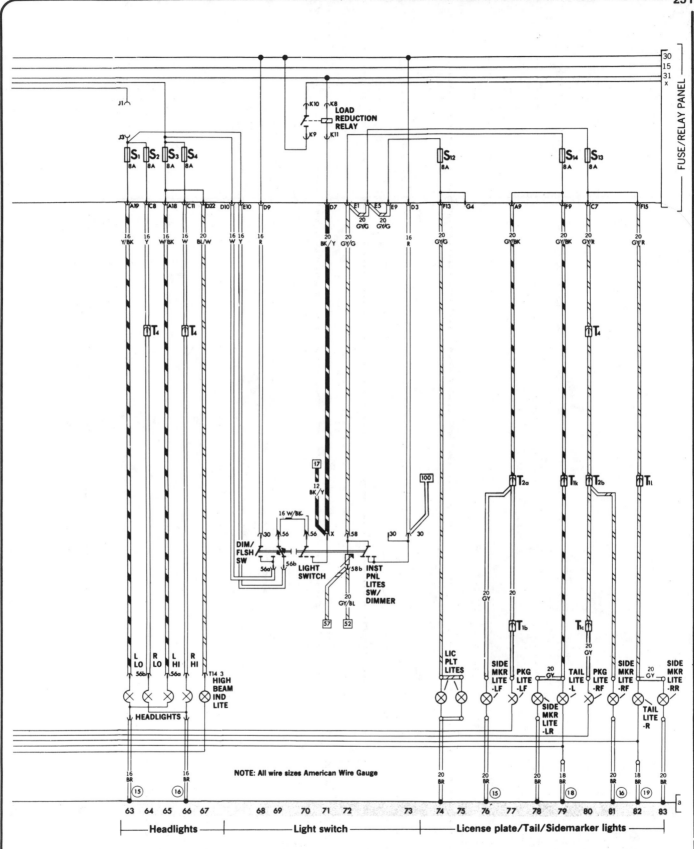

Fig. 9.41 (contd) Wiring diagram for 1979 Rabbit Deluxe. For key see page 247

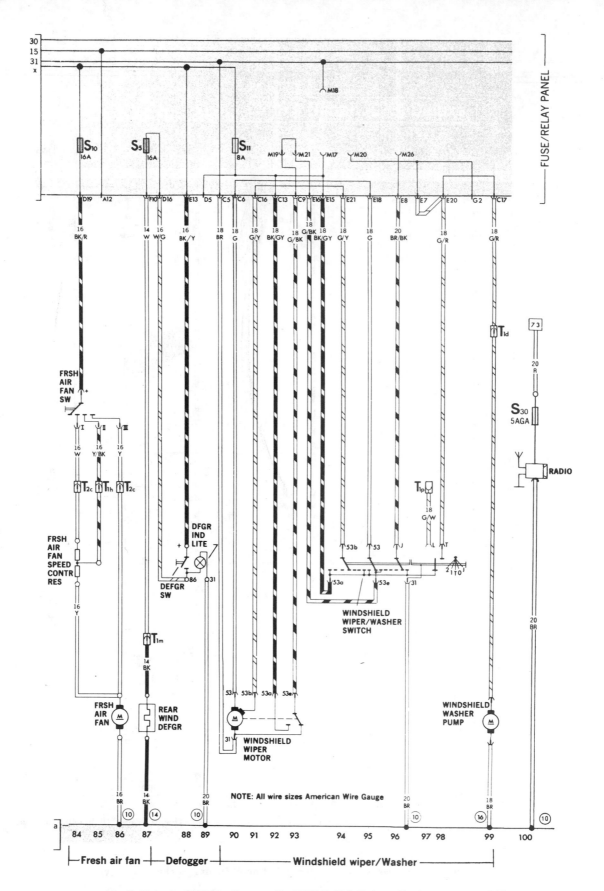

Fig. 9.41 (contd) Wiring diagram for 1979 Rabbit Deluxe. For key see page 247

Key to Fig. 9.42

Description	Current track
Alternator	3
Alternator charging light	24
Ashtray light	53
Auxiliary air regulator	6
Back-up lights	35-36
Back-up light switch	34
Ballast resistance wire	11
Battery	4
Cigarette lighter	48
Cigarette lighter light	52
Clock	47
Cold start valve	14
Control pressure regulator	5
Coolant temperature gauge	21
Coolant temperature sensor	32
Door switch (right)	44
Door switch/buzzer (left)	45-46
EGR elapsed mileage switch (inoperative in Canada)	29-30
EGR light (Inoperative in Canada)	29
Emergency flasher relay	51-53
Emergency flasher switch	49-56
Emergency flasher indicator light	55
Fresh air fan	86
Fresh air fan speed control resistors	84
Fresh air fan switch	84-86
Fuel gauge	20
Fuel level sensor	33
Fuel pump	7
Fuel pump relay	5-10
Fuses S1-S15, on fuse/relay panel (under dash) S20 (on fuel pump relay)	
Headlights	63-66
Headlight dimmer/flasher switch	68-69
Heater lever light	54
High beam indicator light	67
Horn	36
Horn button	37
Ignition coil	11
Ignition/starter switch	15-19
Ignition distributor	12-13
Instrument panel lights	56-58
Instrument panel light switch/dimmer	72
Interior lights	43-44
License plate lights	74-75
Light switch	70-73
Load reduction relay	70-71
Oil pressure switch	31
Oil pressure warning light	23
Parking brake indicator light	24-28
Parking brake indicator light switch	27
Parking light, left	77
Parking light, right	80
Radiator fan	42
Radiator fan thermal switch	42
Rear window defogger	87
Rear window defogger indicator light	89
Rear window defogger switch	88-89
Seat belt/starter lock-out relay	15-20
Seat belt switch, left	16
Seat belt switch, right	16
Seat belt warning light	25
Shift console light (auto.trans)	29
Side marker lights, front	76-81
Side marker lights, rear	78-83
Spark plug suppressors	12-13
Spark plugs	12-13
Starter	8-10
Stop-lights	40-41
Stop-light switch	38-39
Tail light, left	79
Tail light, right	82
Thermal time switch	14-15

Description	Current track
Turn signal lights	59-62
Turn signal switch	53
Turn signal indicator light	25
Voltage regulator	3
Voltage stabilizer	20
Windshield washer pump	99
Windshield wiper motor	90-93
Windshield wiper switch	94-98

Wire connectors		Current track
T	— Cable adaptor, engine compartment	6-7
T1a	— In engine compartment	2
T1b	— In engine compartment, front left	77
T1c	— In engine compartment, front right	80
T1d	— Behind instrument panel	99
T1e	— Behind instrument panel	29
T1f	— Behind instrument panel	15
T1g	— Behind instrument panel	47
T1h	— Behind instrument panel	85
T1i	— Behind instrument panel	27
T1j	— Behind instrument panel	15
T1k	— In luggage compartment, left rear	79
T1l	— In luggage compartment, right rear	82
T1m	— In luggage compartment, left rear	87
T1p	— Behind instrument panel	97
T2a	— In engine compartment, front left	59,77
T2b	— In engine compartment, front right	61,80
T2c	— Behind instrument panel	84,86
T2d	— Behind instrument panel	16
T2e	— Behind instrument panel	16
T2f	— Behind instrument panel	15
T2g	— Behind instrument panel, right of steering column	49
T3	— Behind instrument panel, right of steering column	48,52
T4	— In engine compartment	61,64,66,80
T14	— On rear of instrument panel	20,21,23,24,25 29,47,56,67

Ground connectors

① — From battery to body

② — From alternator to engine

⑩ — On steering column support

⑪ — On steering column support

⑫ — In luggage compartment, rear

⑬ — On dome light

⑭ — Middle body member, rear

⑮ — In engine compartment, front left

⑯ — In engine compartment, front right

⑰ — On steering column

⑱ — On tail light cover, left

⑲ — On tail light cover, right

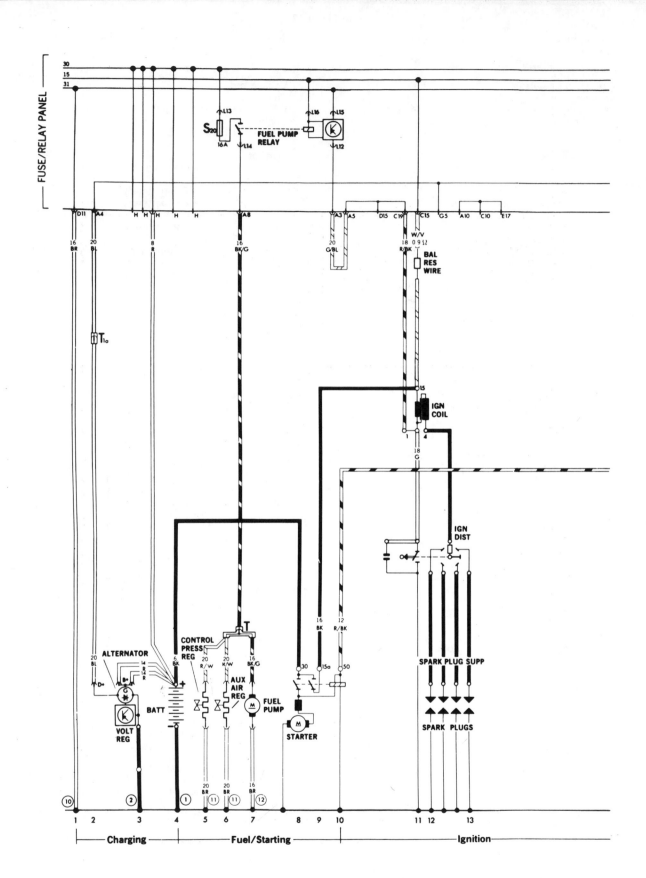

Fig. 9.42 Wiring diagram for 1979 Rabbit Custom and Deluxe – Canadian models. For key see page 253

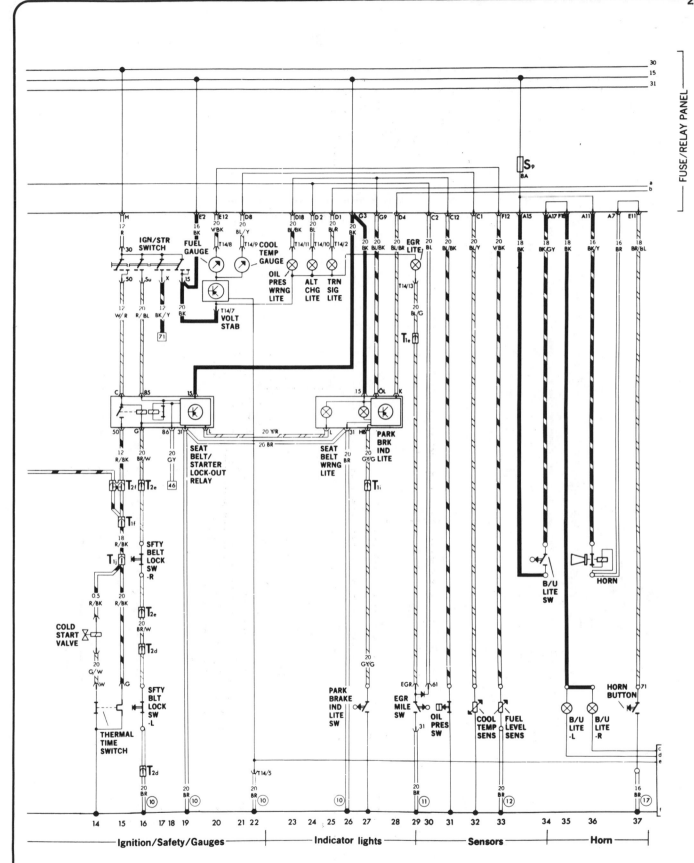

Fig. 9.42 (contd) Wiring diagram for 1979 Rabbit Custom and Deluxe – Canadian models. For key see page 253

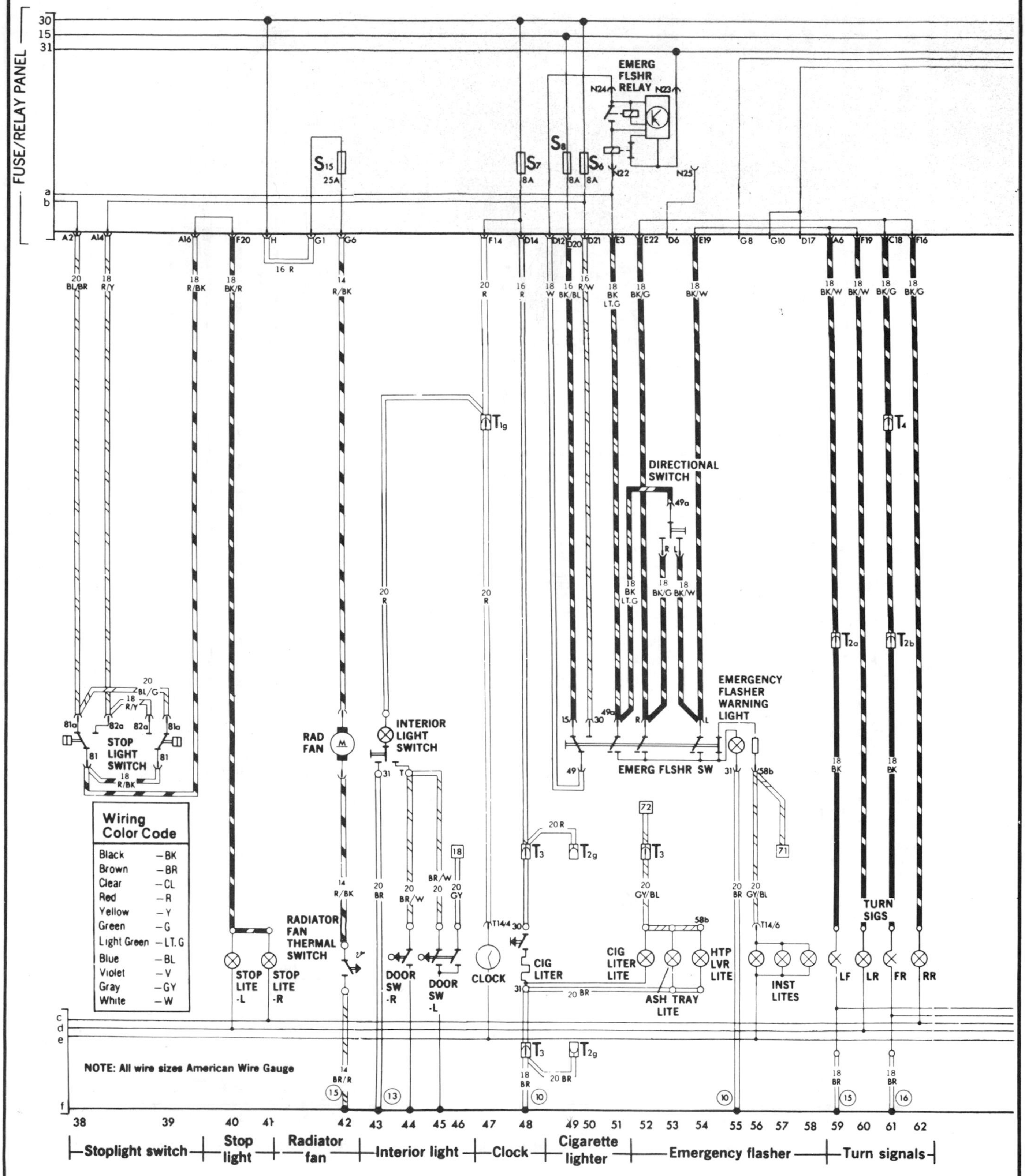

FUSE/RELAY PANEL

30
15
31

EMERG FLSHR RELAY
N24 N23
N22 N25

S15 25A
S7 8A
S8
S6 8A 8A

a
b

A2 A14 A16 F20 H G1 G6 F14 D14 D12 D20 D21 E3 E22 D6 E19 G8 G10 D17 A6 F19 C18 F16

16 R

20 BL/BR | 18 R/Y | 18 R/BK | 18 BK/R | 14 R/BK | 20 R | 16 R | 18 W | 16 BK/BL | 16 R/W | 18 BK LT.G | 18 BK/G | 18 BK/W | 18 BK/W | 18 BK/W | 18 BK/G | 18 BK/G

T1g

T4

DIRECTIONAL SWITCH
49a
R L

18 BK LT.G
18 BK/G
18 BK/W

20 R
20 R
20 R

T2a
T2b

EMERGENCY FLASHER WARNING LIGHT

L5
30
49a
30
R
L

49
31
58b
71

18 BK
18 BK

20 BL/G
18 R/Y
82a 82a
81a
81a
81
81
STOP LIGHT SWITCH
18 R/BK

RAD FAN
M

INTERIOR LIGHT SWITCH
31
T

BR/W

18

EMERG FLSHR SW

72

T3
T2g
T3

20 R
20 GY/BL
20 BR GY/BL

58b
T14/6

TURN SIGS

Wiring Color Code

Black	— BK
Brown	— BR
Clear	— CL
Red	— R
Yellow	— Y
Green	— G
Light Green	— LT.G
Blue	— BL
Violet	— V
Gray	— GY
White	— W

RADIATOR FAN THERMAL SWITCH

14 R/BK
20 BR
20 BR/W
20 GY
T14/4 30

STOP LITE -L
STOP LITE -R
DOOR SW -R
DOOR SW -L
CLOCK
31
CIG LITER
31
20 BR
CIG LITER LITE
ASH TRAY LITE
HTP LVR LITE
INST LITES
LF LR FR RR

c
d
e

NOTE: All wire sizes American Wire Gauge

14 BR/R
15
13
18 BR
T3
10
20 BR
T2g
10
18 BR
15
18 BR
16

f

38 39 40 41 42 43 44 45 46 47 48 49 50 51 52 53 54 55 56 57 58 59 60 61 62

Stoplight switch | Stop light | Radiator fan | Interior light | Clock | Cigarette lighter | Emergency flasher | Turn signals

Fig. 9.42 (contd) Wiring diagram for 1979 Rabbit Custom and Deluxe – Canadian models. For key see page 253

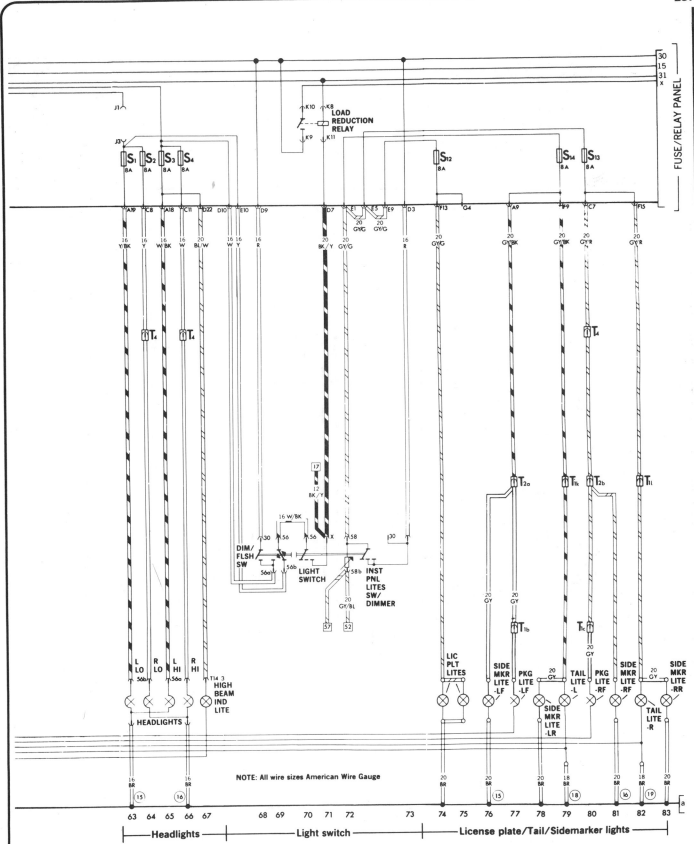

NOTE: All wire sizes American Wire Gauge

Fig. 9.42 (contd) Wiring diagram for 1979 Rabbit Custom and Deluxe – Canadian models. For key see page 253

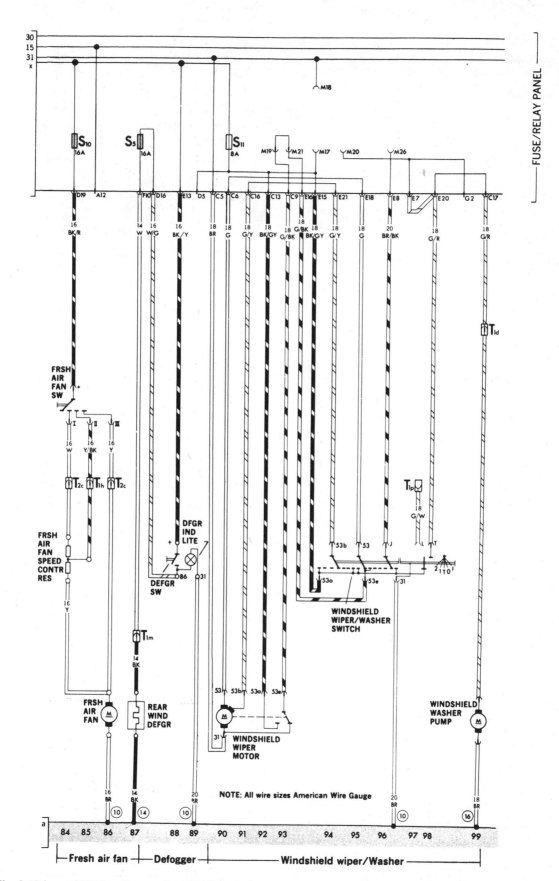

Fig. 9.42 (contd) Wiring diagram for 1979 Rabbit Custom and Deluxe – Canadian models. For key see page 253

Key to Fig. 9.43

Description	Current track
Alternator	3
Alternator charging light	24
Ashtray light	53
Auxiliary air regulator	6
Back-up lights	35-36
Back-up light switch	34
Ballast resistance wire	11
Battery	4
Cigarette lighter	48
Cigarette lighter light	52
Clock	47
Cold start valve	14
Control pressure regulator	5
Coolant temperature light	29
Coolant temperature switch 32	
Door switch (right)	44
Door switch/buzzer (left)	45-46
EGR elapsed mileage switch (inoperative in Canada)	29-30
EGR light (inoperative in Canada)	29
Emergency flasher relay	51-53
Emergency flasher switch	49-56
Emergency flasher indicator light	55
Fresh air fan	86
Fresh air fan speed control resistors	84
Fresh air fan switch	84-86
Fuel gauge	20
Fuel level sensor	33
Fuel pump	7
Fuel pump relay	5-10
Fuses S1-S15, on fuse/relay panel (under dash) S20 (on fuel pump relay)	
Headlights	63-64
Headlight dimmer/flasher switch	68-69
Heater lever light	54
High beam indicator light	67
Horn	36
Horn button	37
Ignition coil	11
Ignition/starter switch	15-19
Ignition distributor	12-13
Instrument panel lights	56-58
Instrument panel light switch/dimmer	72
Interior lights	43-44
Intermittent wiper relay	93
License plate lights	74-75
Light switch	70-73
Load reduction relay	70-71
Oil pressure switch	31
Oil pressure warning light	23
Oil temperature gauge	23
Parking brake indicator light	24-28
Parking brake indicator light switch	27
Parking light, left	77
Parking light, right	80
Radiator fan	42
Radiator fan thermal switch	42
Rear window defogger	87
Rear window defogger indicator light	89
Rear window defogger switch	88-89
Seat belt/starter lock-out relay	15-20
Seat belt switch, left	16
Seat belt switch, right	16
Seat belt warning light	25
Shift console light (auto.trans)	29
Side marker lights, rear	78-83
Spark plug suppressors	12-13
Spark plugs	12-13
Starter	8-10
Stop-lights	40-41
Stop-light switch	38-39
Tachometer	23
Tail light, left	79
Tail light, right	82

Description	Current track
Thermal time switch	14-15
Turn signal lights	59-62
Turn signal switch	53
Turn signal indicator light	25
Trunk signal indicator light	25
Trunk light	73
Voltage regulator	3
Voltage stabilizer	20
Windshield washer pump	99
Windshield wiper motor	90-93
Windshield wiper switch	94-98

Wire connectors — Current track

		Current track
T	Cable adaptor, engine compartment	6-7
T1a	In engine compartment	2
T1b	In engine compartment, front left	77
T1c	In engine compartment, front right	80
T1d	Behind instrument panel	99
T1e	Behind instrument panel	29
T1f	Behind instrument panel	15
T1g	Behind instrument panel	47
T1h	Behind instrument panel	85
T1i	Behind instrument panel	27
T1j	Behind instrument panel	15
T1k	In luggage compartment, left rear	79
T1l	In luggage compartment, right rear	82
T1m	In luggage compartment, left rear	87
T1p	Behind instrument panel	97
T2a	In engine compartment, front left	59,77
T2b	In engine compartment, front right	61,80
T2c	Behind instrument panel	84,86
T2d	Behind instrument panel	16
T2e	Behind instrument panel	16
T2f	Behind instrument panel	15
T2g	Behind instrument panel, right of steering column	49
T3	Behind instrument panel, right of steering column	48,52
T4	In engine compartment	61,64,66,80
T14	On rear of instrument panel	20,21,23,24,25 29,47,56,67

Ground connectors

- ① — From battery to body
- ② — From alternator to engine
- ⑩ — On steering column support
- ⑪ — On steering column support
- ⑫ — In luggage compartment, rear
- ⑬ — On dome light
- ⑭ — Middle body member, rear
- ⑮ — In engine compartment, front left
- ⑯ — In engine compartment, front right
- ⑰ — On steering column
- ⑱ — On tail light cover, left
- ⑲ — On tail light cover, right

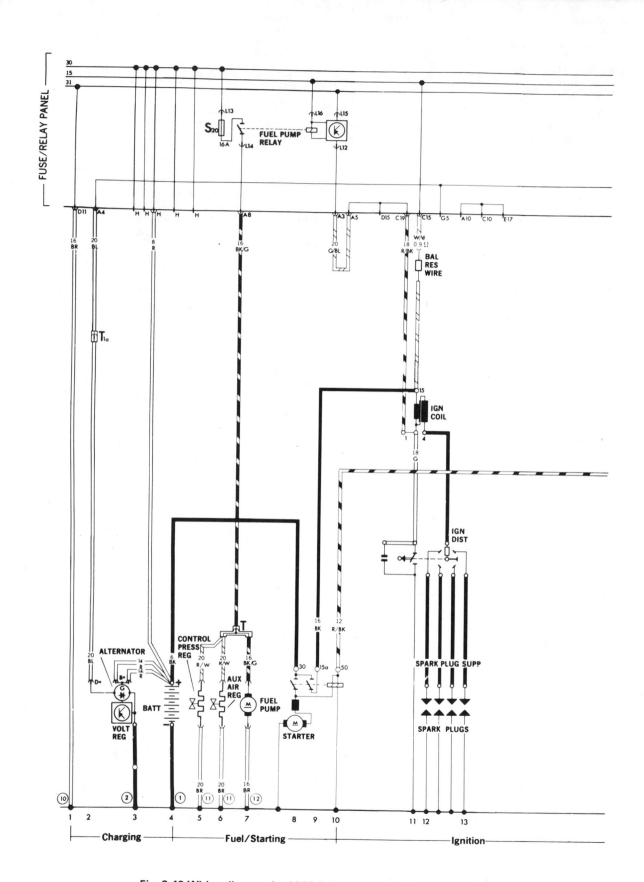

Fig. 9.43 Wiring diagram for 1979 Scirocco models. For key see page 259

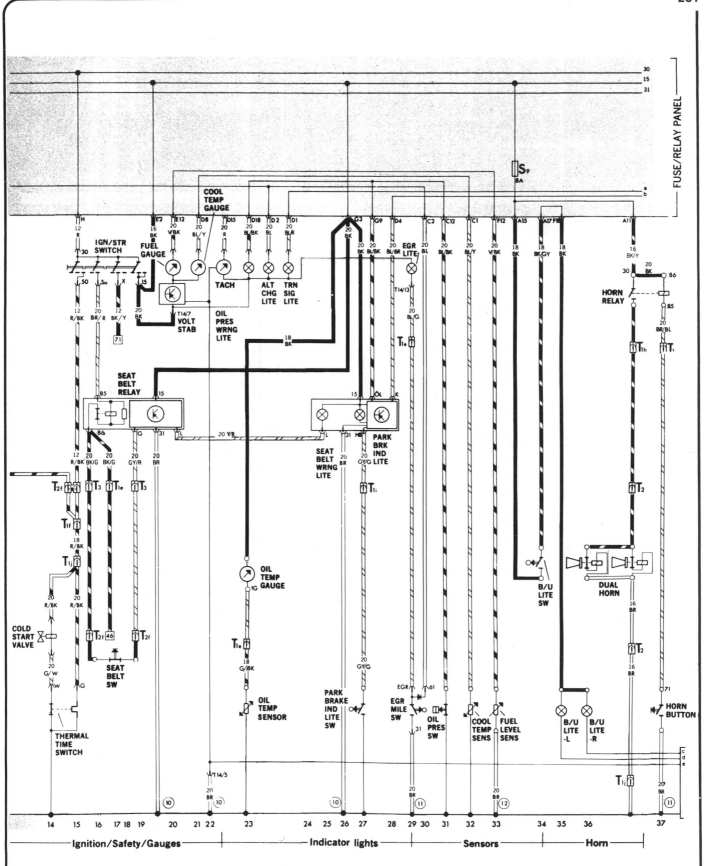

Fig. 9.43 (contd) Wiring diagram for 1979 Scirocco models. For key see page 259

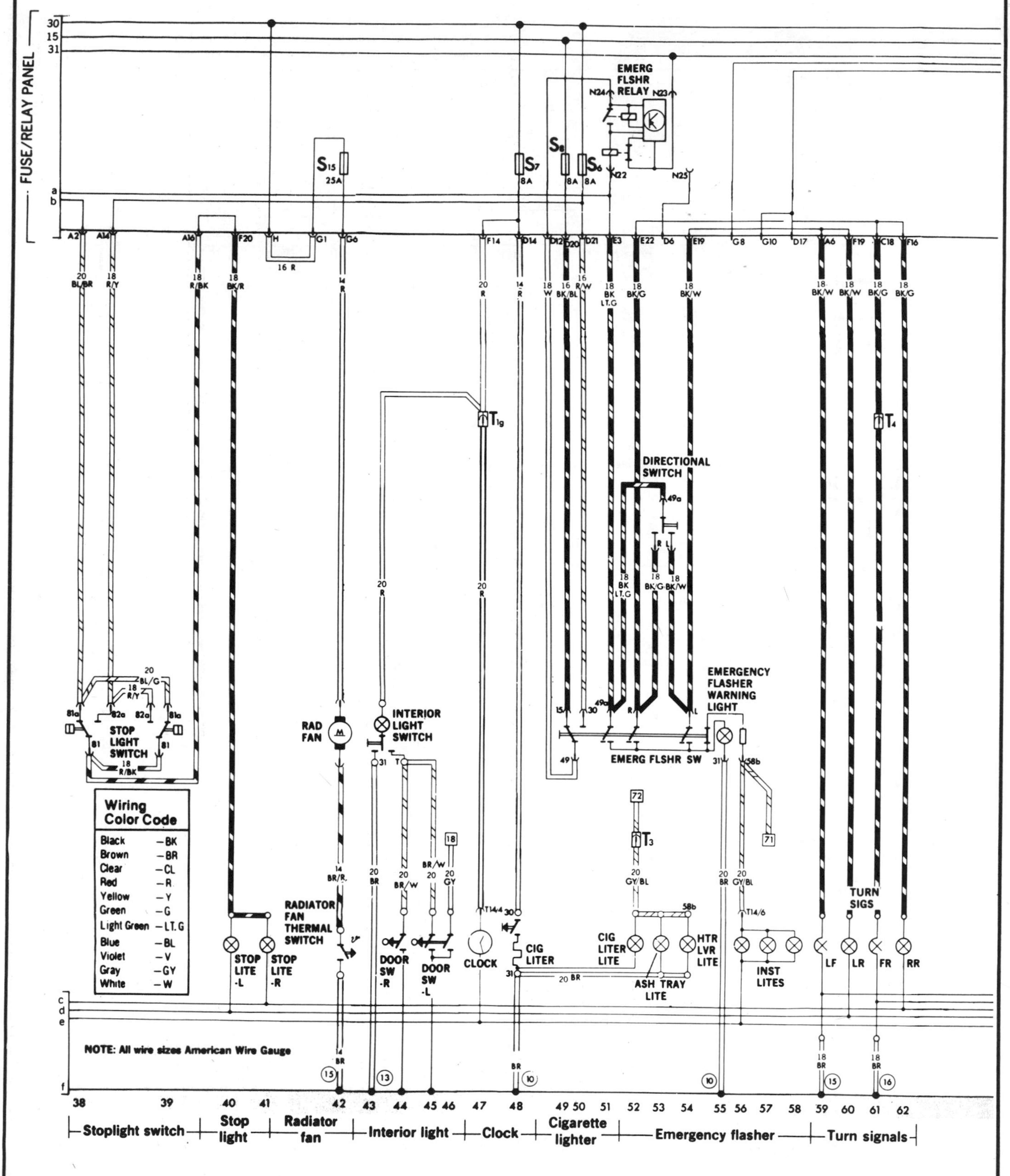

FUSE/RELAY PANEL

30
15
31

EMERG FLSHR RELAY

N24 N23

N22 N25

S15
25A

S7
8A

S8

S6
8A 8A

A2 A14 A16 F20 H G1 G6 F14 D14 D12 D20 D21 E3 E22 D6 E19 G8 G10 D17 A6 F19 C18 F16

20
BL/BR

18
R/Y

18
R/BK

18
BK/R

16 R

14
R

20
R

14
R

18
W

16
BK/BL

16
R/W

18
BK
LT.G

18
BK/G

18
BK/W

18
BK/W

18
BK/W

18
BK/G

18
BK/G

T1g

T4

DIRECTIONAL SWITCH

49a

R R

18
BK
LT.G

18 18
BK/G BK/W

20
R

20
R

EMERGENCY FLASHER WARNING LIGHT

15 30 49 R L

49 EMERG FLSHR SW 31 58b

20
BL/G

18
R/Y

18
R/Y

81a 82a 82a 81a

STOP LIGHT SWITCH

81 81

18
R/BK

72

T3

71

Wiring Color Code

Black – BK
Brown – BR
Clear – CL
Red – R
Yellow – Y
Green – G
Light Green – LT.G
Blue – BL
Violet – V
Gray – GY
White – W

RAD FAN
M

INTERIOR LIGHT SWITCH

31 T

14
BR/R.

20
BR

20
BR/W

BR/W

20
GY

20
R

T14.4 30

20
GY/BL

20
BR

20
GY/BL

T14/6

RADIATOR FAN THERMAL SWITCH

STOP LITE -L

STOP LITE -R

DOOR SW -R

DOOR SW -L

CLOCK

31

CIG LITER

31

CIG LITER LITE

ASH TRAY LITE

HTR LVR LITE

58b

INST LITES

TURN SIGS

LF LR FR RR

c
d
e

NOTE: All wire sizes American Wire Gauge

f

14
BR

15

13

20 BR

BR

10

10

18
BR

15

18
BR

16

38 39 40 41 42 43 44 45 46 47 48 49 50 51 52 53 54 55 56 57 58 59 60 61 62

Stoplight switch — Stop light — Radiator fan — Interior light — Clock — Cigarette lighter — Emergency flasher — Turn signals

Fig. 9.43 (contd) Wiring diagram for 1979 Scirocco models. For key see page 259

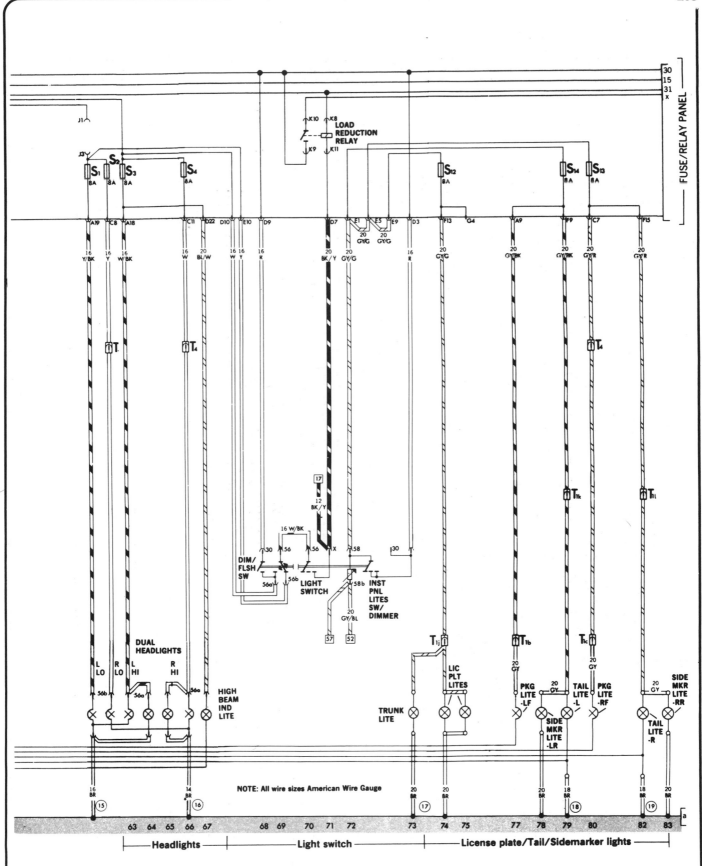

Fig. 9.43 (contd) Wiring diagram for 1979 Scirocco models. For key see page 259

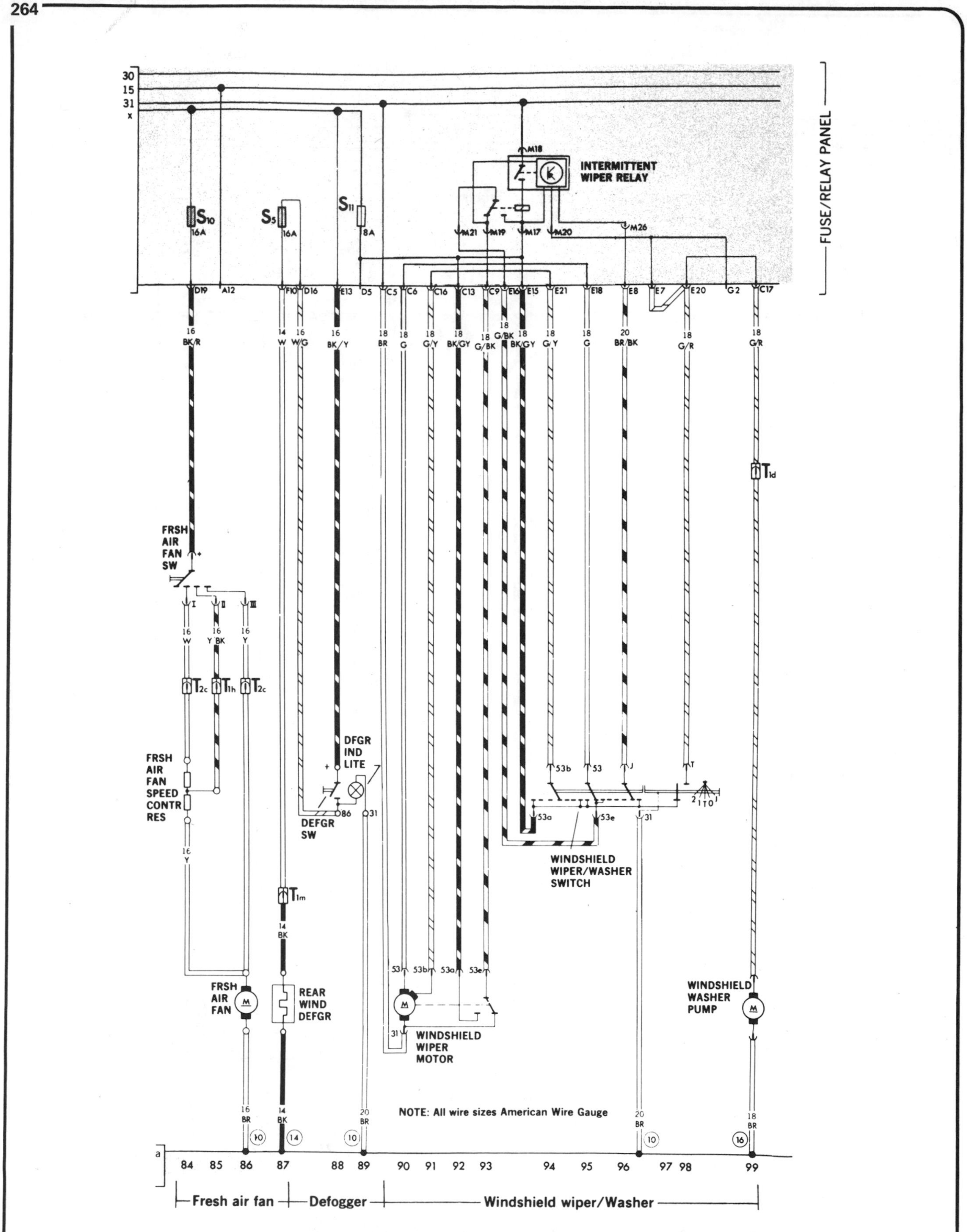

FUSE/RELAY PANEL

INTERMITTENT WIPER RELAY

FRSH AIR FAN SW

FRSH AIR FAN SPEED CONTR RES

DFGR IND LITE

DEFGR SW

WINDSHIELD WIPER/WASHER SWITCH

FRSH AIR FAN

REAR WIND DEFGR

WINDSHIELD WIPER MOTOR

WINDSHIELD WASHER PUMP

NOTE: All wire sizes American Wire Gauge

Fresh air fan — Defogger — Windshield wiper/Washer

Fig. 9.43 (contd) Wiring diagram for 1979 Scirocco models. For key see page 259

Key to Fig. 9.44

Description	Current track
Alternator	3
Alternator charging light	24
Ashtray light	53
Auxiliary air regulator	6
Back-up lights	35–36
Back-up light switch	34
Ballast resistance wire	11
Battery	4
Cigarette lighter	48
Cigarette lighter light	52
Cold start valve	14
Control pressure regulator	5
Coolant temperature light	29
Coolant temperature switch	32
Door switch (right)	44
Door switch/buzzer (left)	45–46
EGR elapsed mileage switch (inoperative in Canada)	29–30
EGR light (inoperative in Canada)	29
Emergency flasher relay	51–53
Emergency flasher switch	49–56
Emergency flasher indicator light	55
Fresh air fan	86
Fresh air fan speed control resistors	84
Fresh air fan switch	84–86
Fuel gauge	20
Fuel level sensor	33
Fuel pump	7
Fuel pump relay	5–10
Fuses S–S15, on fuse/relay panel (under dash) S20 (on fuel/pump relay)	
Headlights	63–66
Headlight dimmer/flasher switch	68–69
Heater lever light	54
High beam indicator light	67
Horn	36
Horn button	37
Ignition coil	11
Ignition/starter switch	15–19
Ignition distributor	12–13
Instrument panel lights	56–58
Instrument panel light switch/dimmer	72
Interior lights	43–44
License plate lights	74–75
Light switch	70–73
Load reduction relay	70–71
Oil pressure switch	31
Oil pressure warning light	23
Parking brake indicator light	24–28
Parking brake indicator light switch	27
Parking light, left	77
Parking light, right	80
Radiator fan	42
Radiator fan thermal switch	42
Radio	100
Rear window defogger	87
Rear window defogger indicator light	89
Rear window defogger switch	88–89
Seat belt/relay	15–20
Seat belt warning light	25
Shift console light (auto. trans.)	29
Side marker lights, front	76–81
Side marker lights, rear	78–83
Spark plug suppressors	12–13
Spark plugs	12–13
Starter	8–10
Stop-lights	40–41
Stop-light switch	38–39
Tail light, left	79
Tail light, right	82
Thermal time switch	14–15
Turn signal lights	59–62

Description	Current track
Turn signal switch	53
Turn signal indicator light	25
Voltage regulator	3
Voltage stabilizer	20
Windshield washer pump	99
Windshield wiper motor	90–93
Windshield wiper switch	94–98

Wire connectors		Current track
T	Cable adaptor, engine compartment	6–7
T1a	In engine compartment	2
T1b	In engine compartment, front left	77
T1c	In engine compartment, front right	80
T1d	Behind instrument panel	99
T1e	Behind instrument panel	29
T1f	Behind fuse/relay panel	15
T1g	Behind instrument panel	47
T1h	Behind instrument panel	85
T1i	Behind instrument panel	27
T1j	Behind instrument panel	15
T1k	In luggage compartment, left rear	79
T1l	In luggage compartment, right rear	82
T1m	In luggage compartment, left rear	87
T1p	Behind instrument panel	97
T2a	In engine compartment, front left	59,77
T2b	In engine compartment, front right	61,80
T2c	Behind instrument panel	84,86
T2d	Behind instrument panel	16
T2e	Behind instrument panel	16
T2f	Behind instrument panel	15
T2g	Behind instrument panel, right of steering column	49
T3	Behind instrument panel, right of steering column	48,52
T4	In engine compartment	61,64 66,80
T14	On rear of instrument panel	20,21,23, 24,25,29, 47,56,67

Ground connectors

①	From battery to body
②	From alternator to engine
⑩	On steering column support
⑪	On steering column support
⑫	In luggage compartment, rear
⑬	On dome light
⑭	Middle body member, rear
⑮	In engine compartment, front left
⑯	In engine compartment, front right
⑰	On steering column
⑱	On tail light cover, left
⑲	On tail light cover, right

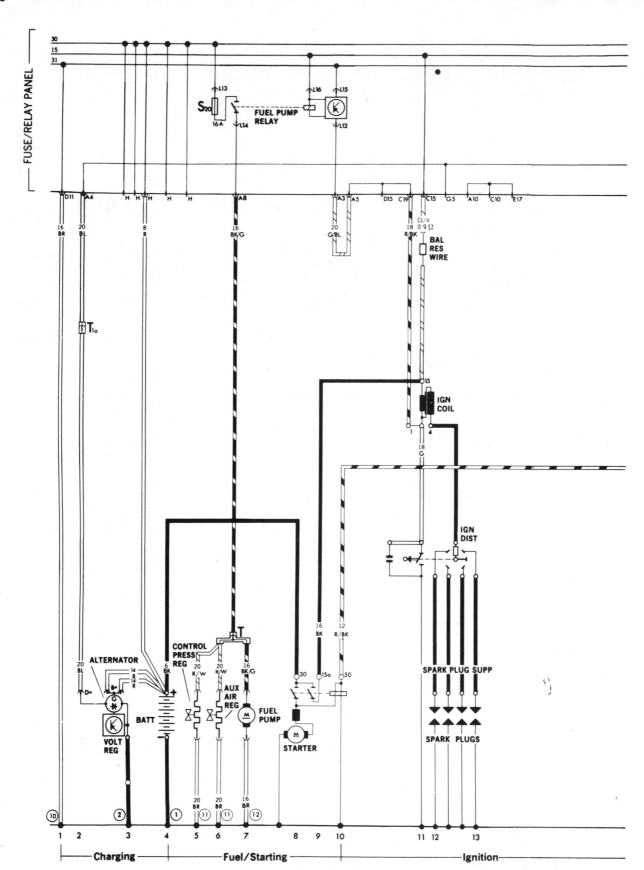

Fig. 9.44 Wiring diagram for 1980 Rabbit Basic and Custom, and Pick-up Truck. For key see page 265

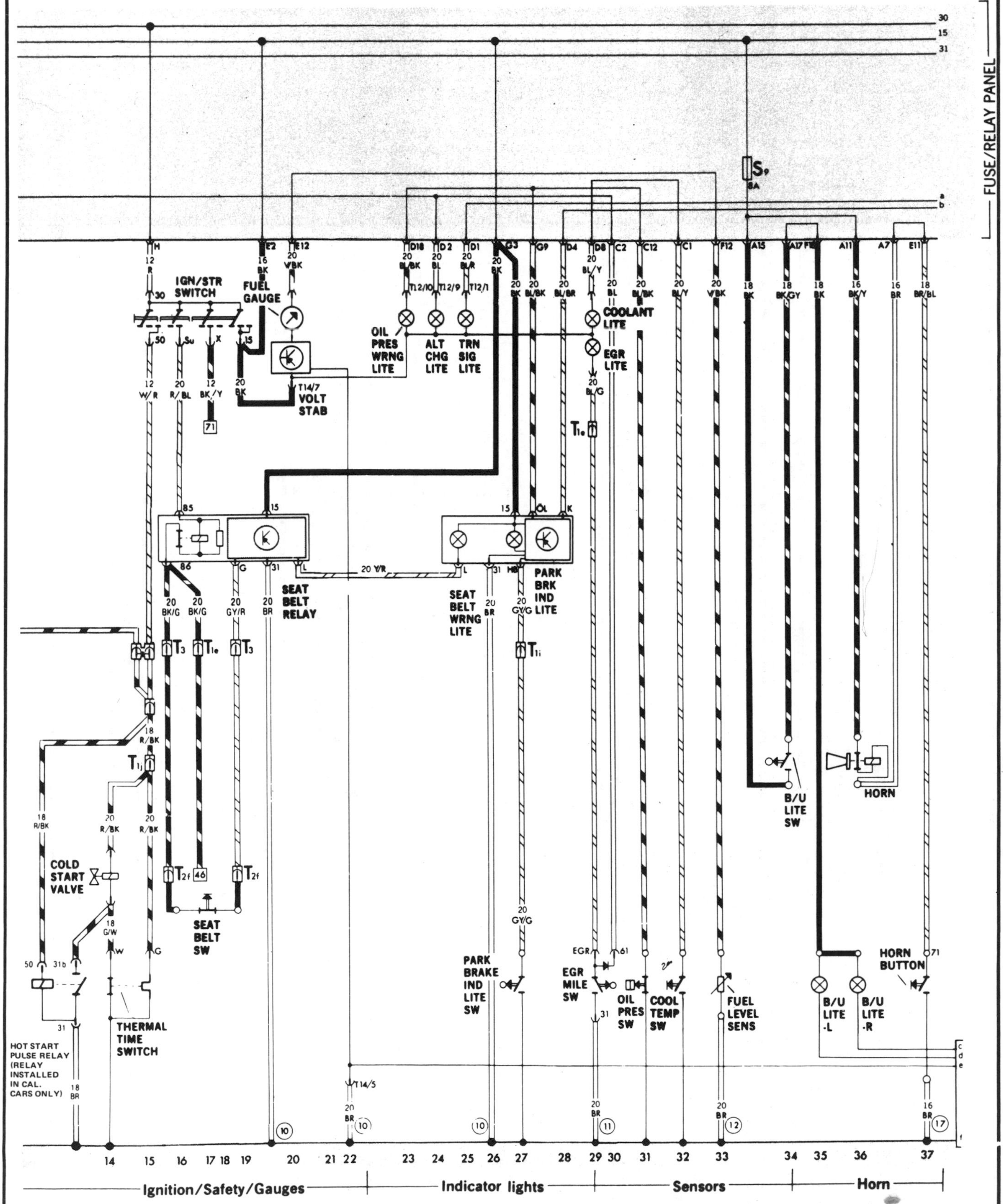

Fig. 9.44 (contd) Wiring diagram for 1980 Rabbit Basic and Custom, and Pick-up Truck. For key see page 265

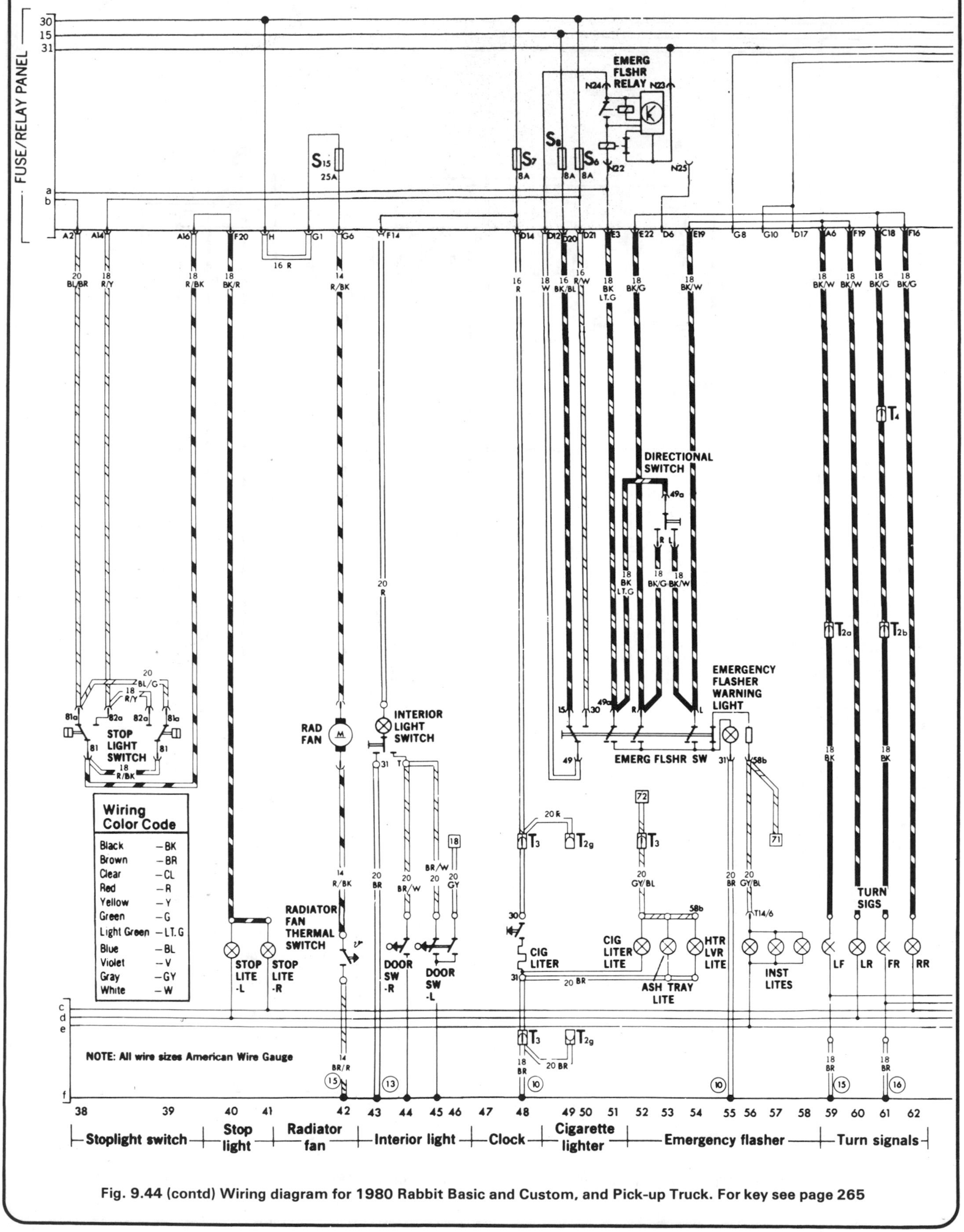

FUSE/RELAY PANEL

30
15
31

EMERG FLSHR RELAY

N24 N23

S15
25A

S7 S8 S6
8A 8A 8A

N22 N25

a
b

A2 A14 A16 F20 H G1 G6 F14 D14 D12 D20 D21 E3 E22 D6 E19 G8 G10 D17 A6 F19 C18 F16

16 R

20   18   18   18   14   16   18 16 R/W 18   18   18   18   18   18   18
BL/BR   R/Y   R/BK BK/R   R/BK   R   W BK/BL   BK   BK/G   BK/W   BK/W BK/W BK/G BK/G
                                                        LT.G

T4

DIRECTIONAL SWITCH

49a

R L

18   18 18
BK   BK/G BK/W
LT.G

20
R

EMERGENCY FLASHER WARNING LIGHT

T2a T2b

INTERIOR LIGHT SWITCH

20
BL/G
18
R/Y

81a 82a 82a 81a

STOP LIGHT SWITCH

81 81

18
R/BK

RAD FAN

31 T

LS 30 49a R L

49

EMERG FLSHR SW

31 58b

T3 T2g

72

T3

71

20   20 20 20
BR/W   BR/W GY

18

20
GY/BL

20 20
BR GY/BL

T14/6

18
BK

18
BK

Wiring Color Code

Black — BK
Brown — BR
Clear — CL
Red — R
Yellow — Y
Green — G
Light Green — LT.G
Blue — BL
Violet — V
Gray — GY
White — W

RADIATOR FAN THERMAL SWITCH

14
R/BK

DOOR SW -R

DOOR SW -L

30

CIG LITER

31   20 BR

CIG LITER LITE

58b

HTR LVR LITE

ASH TRAY LITE

INST LITES

STOP LITE -L STOP LITE -R

TURN SIGS

LF LR FR RR

c
d
e

NOTE: All wire sizes American Wire Gauge

BR/R

14
R/BK

T3 T2g

18   20 BR
BR

f

15   13   10   10   15 16

38 39 40 41 42 43 44 45 46 47 48 49 50 51 52 53 54 55 56 57 58 59 60 61 62

Stoplight switch | Stop light | Radiator fan | Interior light | Clock | Cigarette lighter | Emergency flasher | Turn signals

Fig. 9.44 (contd) Wiring diagram for 1980 Rabbit Basic and Custom, and Pick-up Truck. For key see page 265

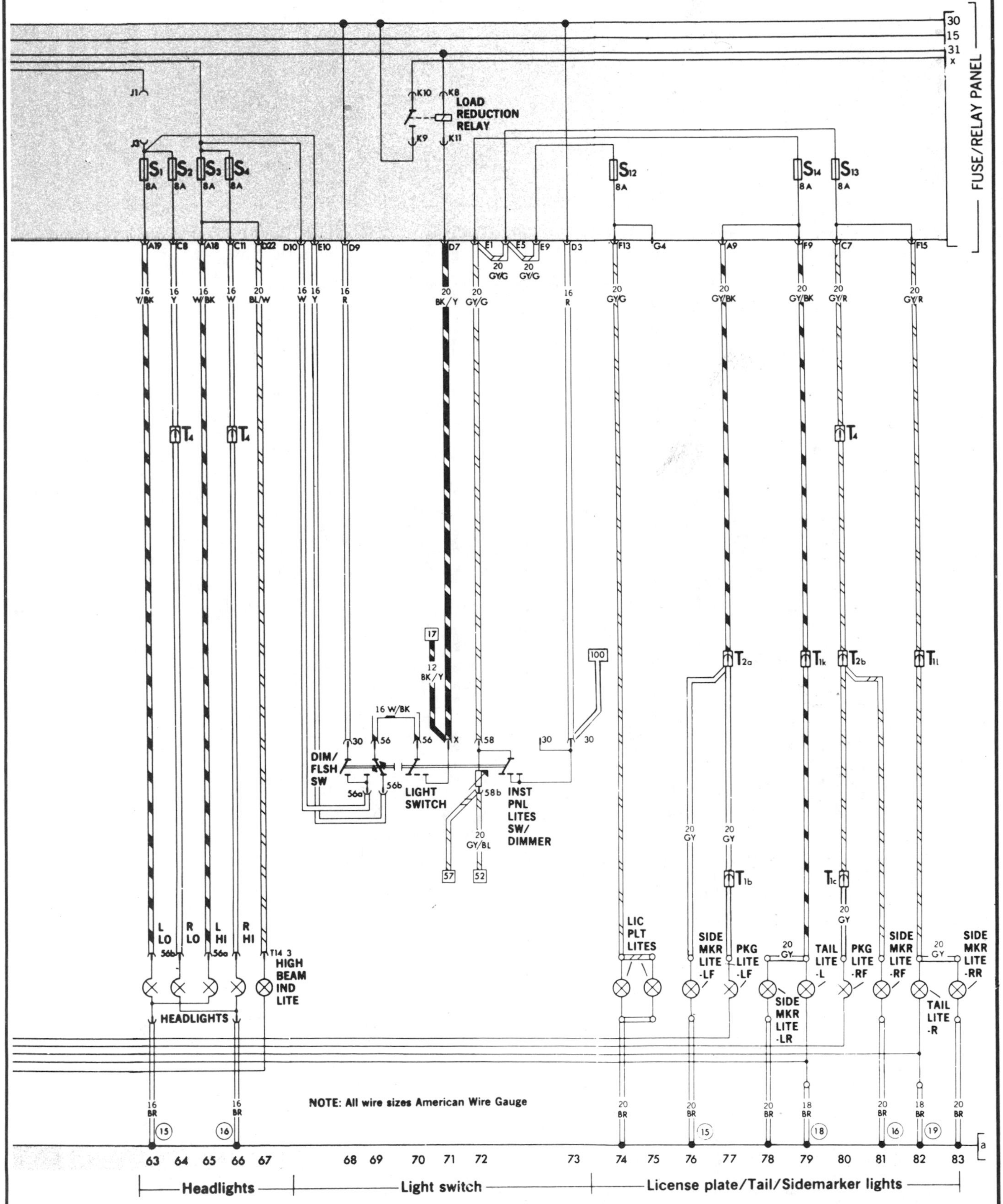

Fig. 9.44 (contd) Wiring diagram for 1980 Rabbit Basic and Custom, and Pick-up Truck. For key see page 265

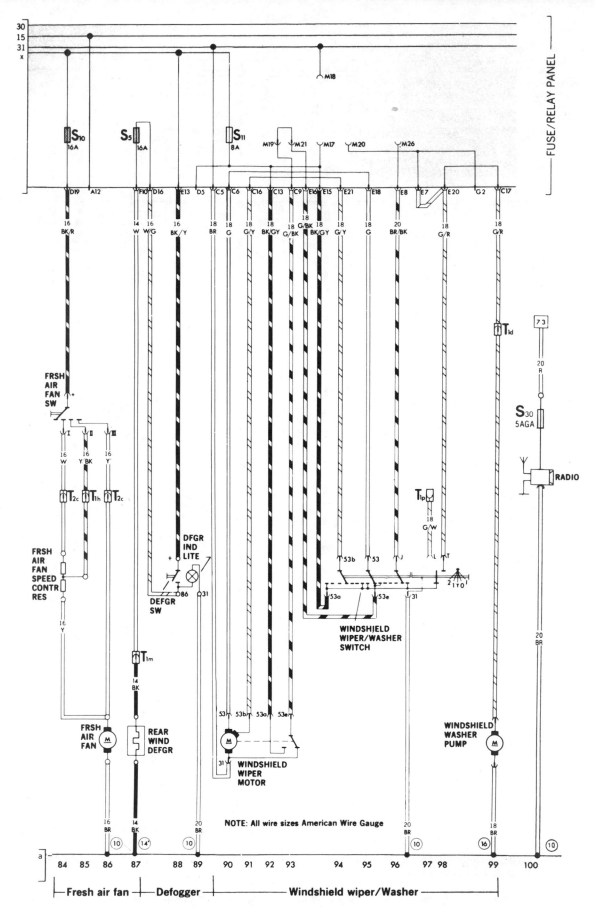

NOTE: All wire sizes American Wire Gauge

Fig. 9.44 (contd) Wiring diagram for 1980 Rabbit Basic and Custom, and Pick-up Truck. For key see page 265

Key to Fig. 9.45

Description	Current track
Alternator	3
Alternator charging light	24
Ashtray light	53
Auxiliary air regulator	6
Back-up lights	35–36
Back-up light switch	34
Ballast resistance wire	11
Battery	4
Cigarette lighter	48
Cigarette lighter light	52
Clock	47
Cold start valve	14
Control pressure regulator	5
Coolant temperature light	21
Coolant temperature sensor	32
Door switch (right)	44
Door switch/buzzer (left)	45–46
EGR elapsed mileage switch	29–30
(inoperative in Canada)	
EGR light (inoperative in Canada)	29
Emergency flasher relay	51–53
Emergency flasher switch	49–56
Emergency flasher indicator light	55
Fresh air fan	86
Fresh air fan speed control resistors	84
Fresh air fan switch	84–86
Fuel gauge	20
Fuel level sensor	33
Fuel pump	7
Fuel pump relay	5–10
Fuses S1–S15, on fuse/relay panel	
(under dash) S20 (on fuel/pump relay)	
Headlights	63–66
Headlight dimmer/flasher switch	68–69
Heater lever light	54
High beam indicator light	67
Horn	36
Horn button	37
Ignition coil	11
Ignition/starter switch	15–19
Ignition distributor	12–13
Instrument panel lights	56–58
Instrument panel light switch/dimmer	72
Interior lights	43–44
License plate lights	74–75
Light switch	70–73
Load reduction relay	70–71
Oil pressure switch	31
Oil pressure warning light	23
Parking brake indicator light	24–28
Parking brake indicator light switch	27
Parking light, left	77
Parking light, right	80
Radiator fan	42
Radiator fan thermal switch	42
Radio	100
Rear window defogger	87
Rear window defogger indicator light	89
Rear window defogger switch	88–89
Seat belt/starter lock-out relay	15–20
Seat belt switch, left	16
Seat belt switch, right	16
Seat belt warning light	25
Shift console light (auto. trans.)	29
Side marker lights, front	76–81
Side marker lights, rear	78–83
Spark plug suppressors	12–13
Spark plugs	12–13
Starter	8–10
Stop-lights	40–41
Stop-light switch	38–39
Tail light, left	79
Tail light, right	82

Description	Current track
Thermal time switch	14–15
Turn signal lights	59–62
Turn signal switch	53
Turn signal indicator light	25
Voltage regulator	3
Voltage stabilizer	20
Windshield washer pump	99
Windshield wiper motor	90–93
Windshield wiper switch	94–98

Wire connectors		Current track
T	– Cable adaptor, engine compartment	6–7
T1a	– In engine compartment	2
T1b	– In engine compartment, front left	77
T1c	– In engine compartment, front right	80
T1d	– Behind Instrument panel	99
T1e	– Behind instrument panel	29
T1f	– Behind fuse/relay panel	15
T1g	– Behind instrument panel	47
T1h	– Behind instrument panel	85
T1i	– Behind instrument panel	27
T1j	– Behind instrument panel	15
T1k	– In luggage compartment, left rear	79
T1l	– In luggage compartment, right rear	82
T1m	– In luggage compartment, left rear	87
T1p	– Behind instrument panel	97
T2a	– In engine compartment, front right	59,77
T2b	– In engine compartment, front right	61,80
T2c	– Behind instrument panel	84,86
T2d	– Behind instrument panel	16
T2e	– Behind instrument panel	16
T2f	– Behind instrument panel	15
T2g	– Behind instrument panel, right of steering column	49
T3	– Behind instrument panel, right of steering column	48,52
T4	– In engine compartment	61,64 66,80
T14	– On rear of instrument panel	20,21,23, 24,25,29, 47,56,67

Ground connectors

①	– From battery to body
②	– From alternator to engine
⑩	– On steering column support
⑪	– On steering column support
⑫	– In luggage compartment, rear
⑬	– On dome light
⑭	– Middle body member, rear
⑮	– In engine compartment, front left
⑯	– In engine compartment, front right
⑰	– On steering column
⑱	– On tail light cover, left
⑲	– On tail light cover, right

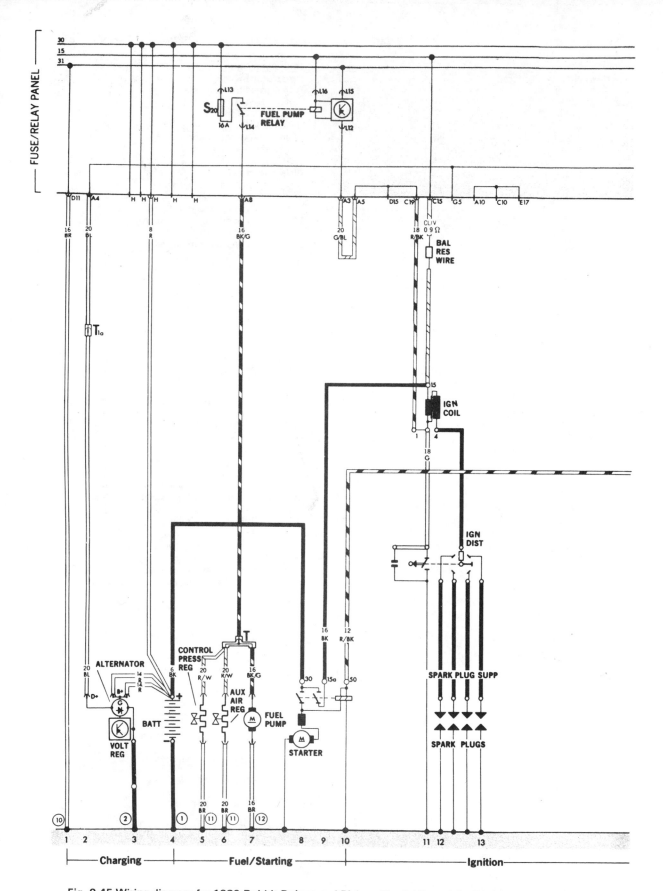

Fig. 9.45 Wiring diagram for 1980 Rabbit Deluxe and Pick-up Truck LX models. For key see page 271

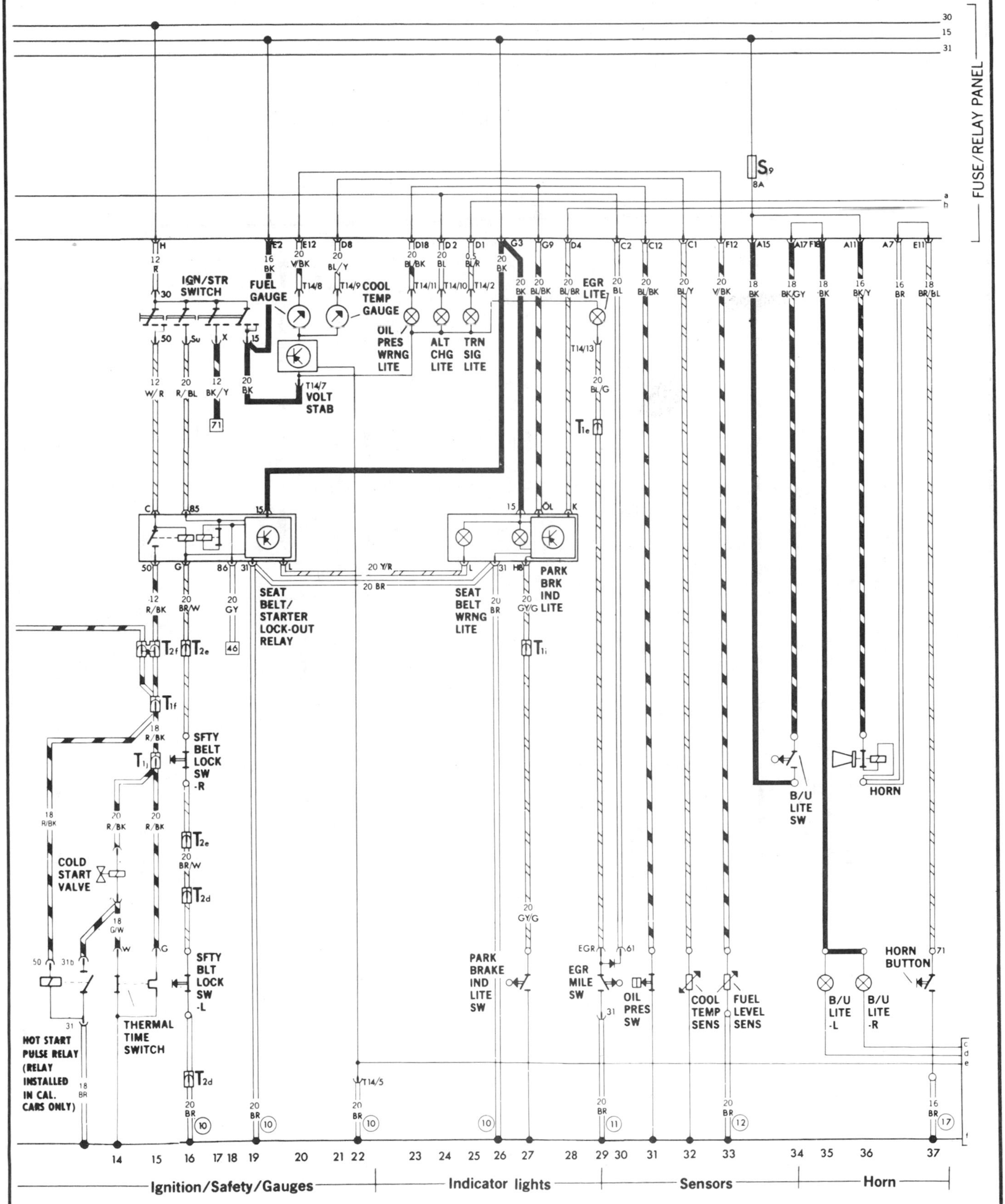

Fig. 9.45 (contd) Wiring diagram for 1980 Rabbit Deluxe and Pick-up Truck LX models. For key see page 271

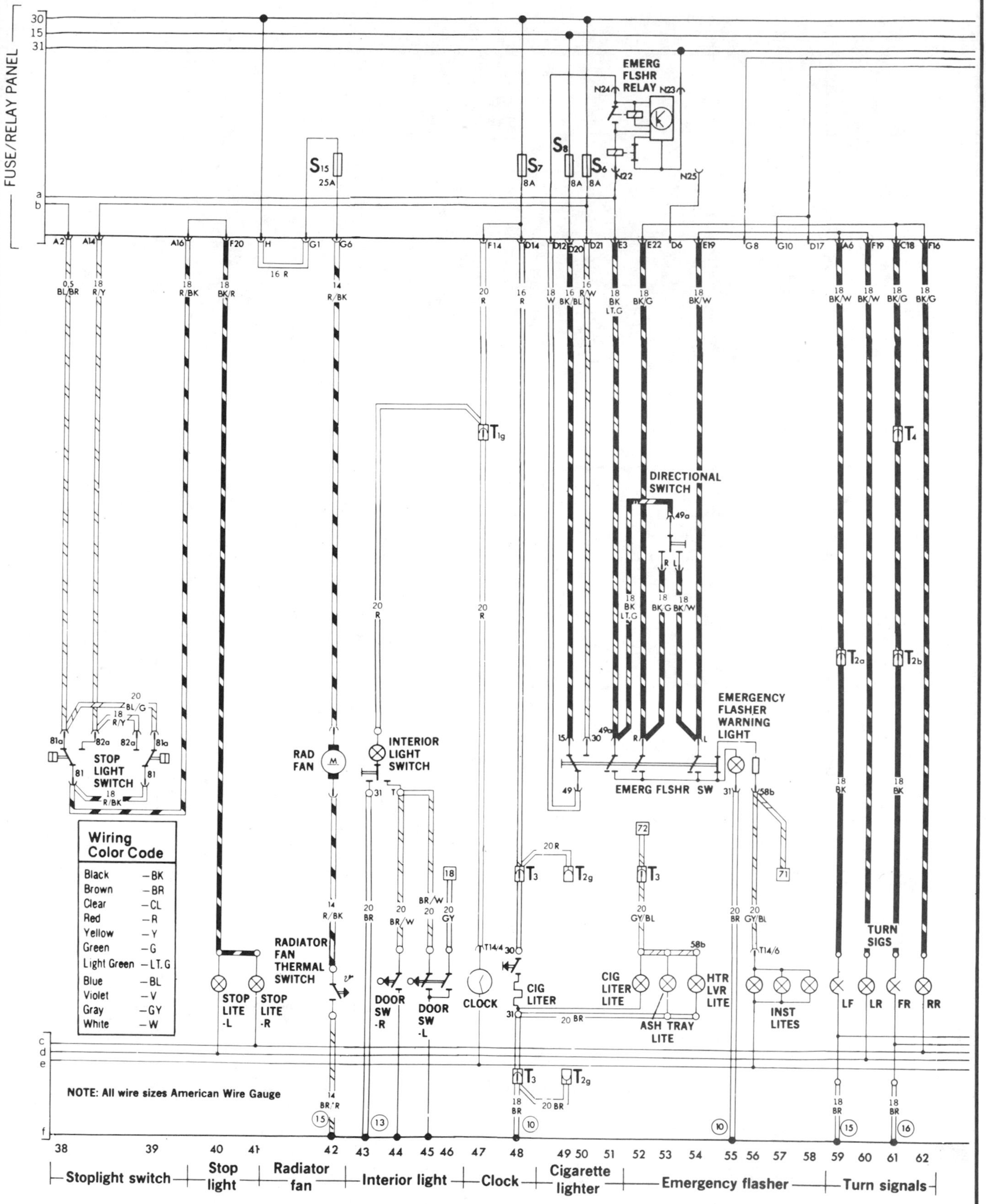

274

FUSE/RELAY PANEL

30
15
31

EMERG FLSHR RELAY

N24 N23
K
N22 N25

S15 25A   S7 8A S8 S6 8A

a
b

A2 A14 A16 F20 H G1 G6   F14 D14 D12 D20 D21 E3 E22 D6 E19 G8 G10 D17 A6 F19 C18 F16

0.5 BL/BR N R/Y 18 R/BK 18 BK/R 16 R 14 R/BK   20 R 16 R 18 W 16 BK/BL 16 R/W 18 BK LT.G 18 BK/G 18 BK/W   18 BK/W 18 BK/W 18 BK/G 18 BK/G

16 R

T1g   T4

DIRECTIONAL SWITCH
49a
R L
18 BK LT.G 18 BK G 18 BK/W

20 R   20 R

EMERGENCY FLASHER WARNING LIGHT

15 30 R L

20 BL/G
18 R/Y
20 82a 82a 20
81a   81a
81 81
STOP LIGHT SWITCH
18 R/BK

49 30 R L

49   EMERG FLSHR SW   31 58b

20 BK/G BK/W

T2a   T2b

18 BK   18 BK

RAD FAN INTERIOR LIGHT SWITCH

31 T

Wiring Color Code
Black —BK
Brown —BR
Clear —CL
Red —R
Yellow —Y
Green —G
Light Green —LT. G
Blue —BL
Violet —V
Gray —GY
White —W

14 R/BK

BR/W
20 BR
BR/W 20 20 GY
18

72   71
T3   T3
20 R   T2g

20 GY/BL 20 BR GY/BL

RADIATOR FAN THERMAL SWITCH

STOP LITE -L STOP LITE -R DOOR SW -R DOOR SW -L CLOCK CIG LITER CIG LITER LITE HTR LVR LITE INST LITES

T14/4 30   58b   T14/6

ASH TRAY LITE   TURN SIGS

LF LR FR RR

20 BR

c
d
e

NOTE: All wire sizes American Wire Gauge

14 BR/R   T3   T2g   18 BR 18 BR

18 BR 20 BR

(15) (13)   (10)   (10) (15) (16)

f
38 39 40 41 42 43 44 45 46 47 48 49 50 51 52 53 54 55 56 57 58 59 60 61 62

Stoplight switch — Stop light — Radiator fan — Interior light — Clock — Cigarette lighter — Emergency flasher — Turn signals

Fig. 9.45 (contd) Wiring diagram for 1980 Rabbit Deluxe and Pick-up Truck LX models. For key see page 271

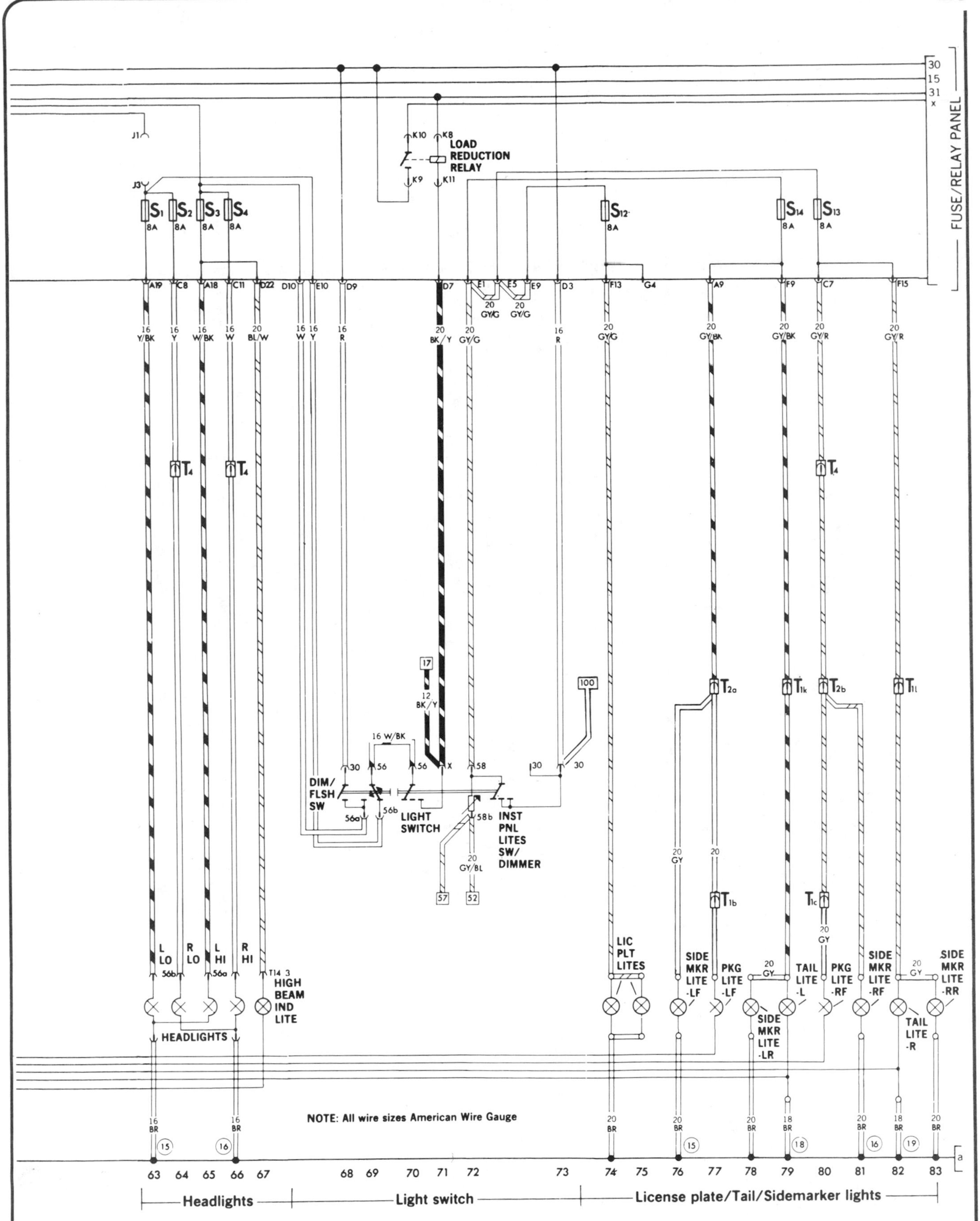

Fig. 9.45 (contd) Wiring diagram for 1980 Rabbit Deluxe and Pick-up Truck LX models. For key see page 271

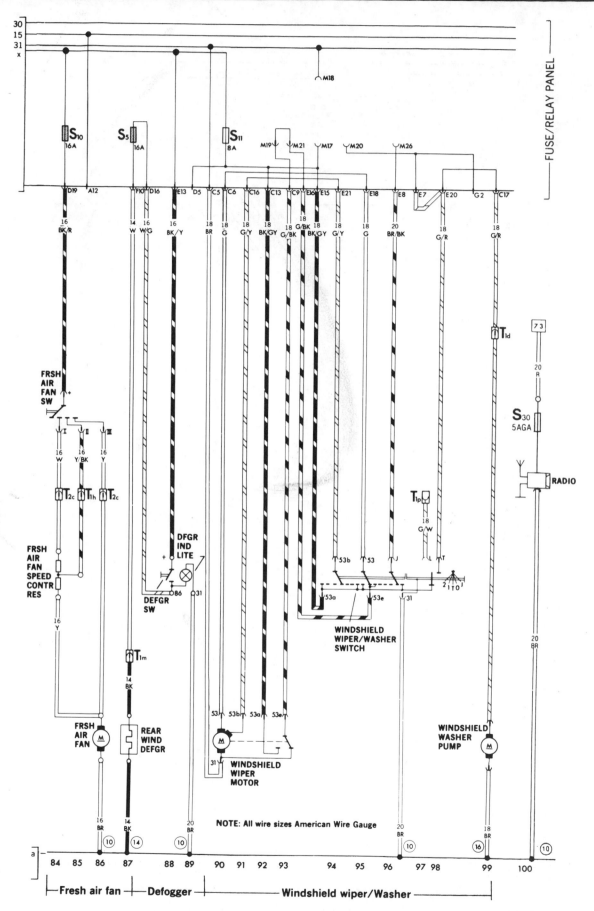

NOTE: All wire sizes American Wire Gauge

Fig. 9.45 (contd) Wiring diagram for 1980 Rabbit Deluxe and Pick-up Truck LX models. For key see page 271

Key to Fig. 9.46

Description	Current track
Alternator	2–3
Alternator charging light	31
Air conditioner control lever light	60
Ashtray light	61
Auxiliary air regulator	17
Back-up light, left	40
Back-up light, right	41
Back-up light switch	39
Ballast resistor	9
Ballast resistor, fresh air fan	112
Battery	4
Cigarette lighter	63
Cigarette lighter light	62
Clock	57
Clock illumination light	58
Cold start valve	15
Coolant over-temperature indicator	29
Coolant temperature indicator	27
Coolant temperature sensor	36
Cut-out relay (load reduction)	81–82
Door switch (right)	55
Door switch/buzzer (left)	53–54
EGR elapsed mileage indicator	34–35
EGR indicator light	33
Electric fuel pump	19
Emergency flasher light	80
Emergency flasher relay	77–79
Emergency flasher switch	76–81
Fog light connector	101
Fresh air fan	113
Fresh air fan switch	112–113
Fuel gauge	25
Fuel gauge sender unit	38
Fuel pump relay	18–20
Fuses S1-S15, on fuse/relay panel	–
S31 fuel pump fuse on fuel/pump relay	–
Glove compartment light	105
Headlight, high beam left	102
Headlight, high beam right	101
Headlight, low left	97–99
Headlight, low right	98–100
Headlight dimmer switch	95–96
High beam indicator light	103
Horn, double tone	41–42
Horn button	44
Horn relay, double tone	43–44
Ignition coil	9
Ignition distributor	8–12
Ignition/starter switch	21–24
Instrument panel lights	81–83
Instrument panel light switch/dimmer	86
Interior lighting	56
License plate lights	88–89
Light switch	83–86
Luggage compartment light	87
Oil pressure switch	37
Oil pressure warning light	30
Oil temperature indicator	46
Oil temperature indicator light	59
Oil temperature sensor	45
Parking brake switch	65–66
Parking brake indicator light	48
Parking brake light switch	47
Parking light, left	90
Parking light, right	93
Radiator fan	104
Radiator fan thermoswitch	104
Rear window defogger	69
Rear window defogger indicator light	71
Rear window defogger switch	70
Seat belt buzzer switch, left	52
Seat belt warning light	49
Seat belt warning relay	50–52
Side marker light, rear	92–95
Spark plugs	10–12
Spark plug connector	10–12
Starter	5–6
Stop-light, left	91

Description	Current track
Stop-light, right	94
Stop-light, left	68
Stop-light, right	67
Stop-light switch	64
Tachometer	26
Thermal time switch	13–14
Turn signal light, front left	72
Turn signal light, rear left	73
Turn signal light, front right	74
Turn signal light, rear right	75
Turn signal indicator light	32
Turn signal switch	78
Voltage regulator	3
Voltage regulator	25
Warm air regulator	16
Windshield washer motor/pump	111
Windshield washer/wiper intermittent relay	107–108
Windshield wiper intermittent selector switch	108–110
Windshield wiper motor	106–107

Wire connectors

T	– Cable adaptor behind instrument panel
T1a	– Single, behind instrument panel
T1b	– Single, behind instrument panel
T1c	– Single, engine compartment, left headlight
T1d	– Single, near relay panel
T1e	– Single, behind instrument panel
T1f	– Single, behind instrument panel
T1g	– Single, behind instrument panel
T1h	– Single, luggage compartment, rear left
T1j	– Single, behind instrument panel
T1k	– Single, left engine compartment, near main brake cylinder
T1l	– Single, behind instrument panel
T1m	– Single, luggage compartment, rear left
T1n	– Single, behind instrument panel
T1o	– Single, behind instrument panel
T1p	– Single, behind instrument panel
T1r	– Single, behind instrument panel
T1s	– Single, near left stop-light
T1t	– Single, near right stop-light
T1u	– Single, behind instrument panel
T2a	– Double, engine compartment, near double horn
T2b	– Double, behind instrument panel
T2c	– Double, near main brake cylinder
T2d	– Double, engine compartment, near right headlight
T2e	– Double, engine compartment fixed to coolant hose
T2f	– Double, behind instrument panel
T2g	– Double, under drivers seat
T2h	– Double, behind instrument panel
T3a	– Three-point, engine compartment, near left headlight
T3b	– Three-point, behind instrument panel
T4	– Four-point, behind instrument panel
T14	– Fourteen-point, instrument panel

Ground connectors

①	– Battery to body
②	– Alternator to engine
⑨	– Fuse/relay panel
⑩	– Steering column support
⑫	– Rear baggage compartment
⑭	– Rear roof middle support
⑮	– From isolated tubing, front harness
⑰	– Steering column
⑱	– Tail light cover, left
⑲	– Tail light cover, right

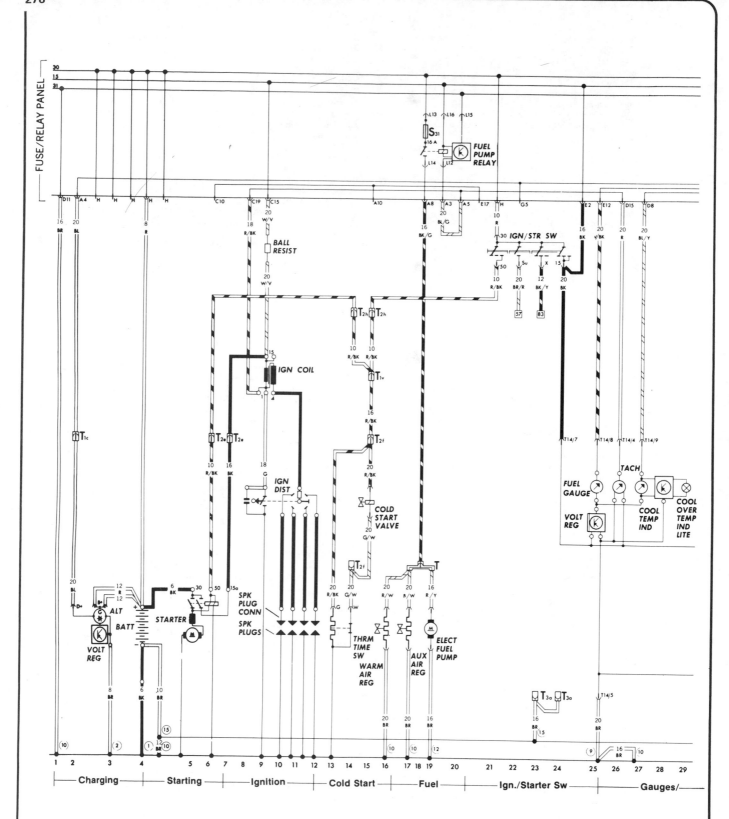

Fig. 9.46 Wiring diagram for 1980/81 Scirocco and 1980 Jetta models (except California). For key see page 277

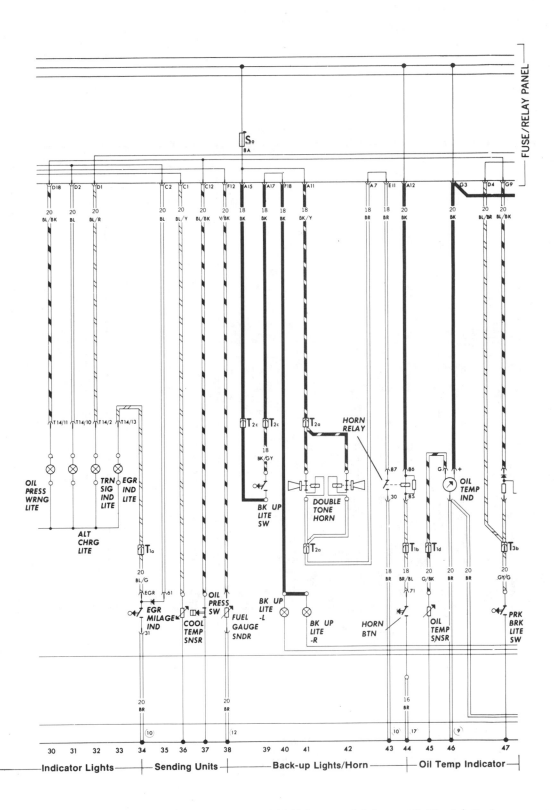

Fig. 9.46 (contd) Wiring diagram for 1980/81 Scirocco and 1980 Jetta models (except California). For key see page 277

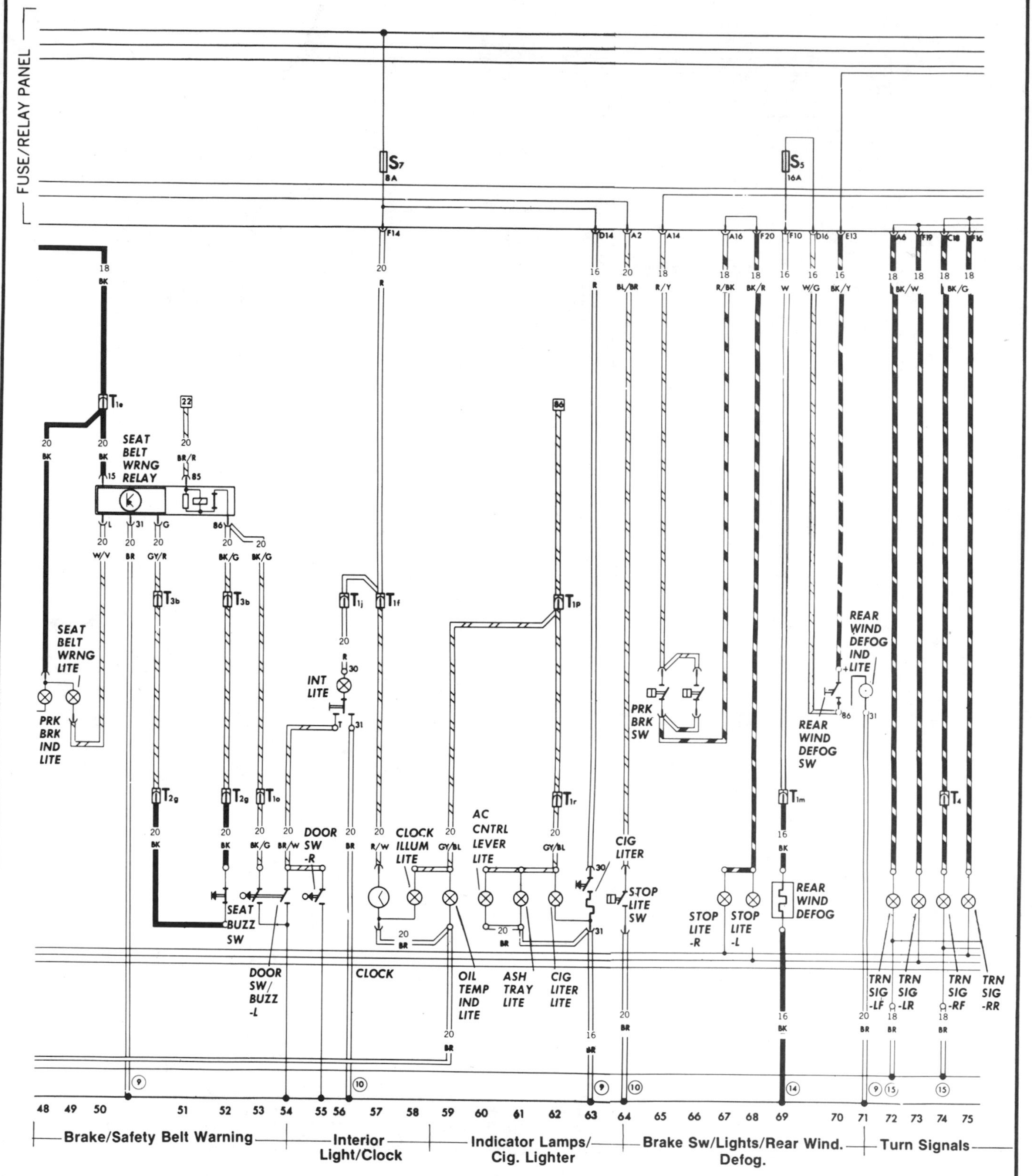

FUSE/RELAY PANEL

S7
8A

S5
16A

F14

D14 A2 A14 A16 F20 F10 D16 E13 A6 F19 C18 F16

18
BK

20
R

16 20 18 18 18 16 16 16 18 18 18 18
R BL/BR R/Y R/BK BK/R W W/G BK/Y BK/W BK/G

T1a

22
20
BR/R

SEAT BELT WRNG RELAY

T1a 15
85

86

31 G
L

86

20 20 20 20 20
W/V BR GY/R BK/G BK/G

SEAT BELT WRNG LITE

T3b T3b T1j T1f

REAR WIND DEFOG IND +LITE

B6

T1p

PRK BRK IND LITE

INT LITE

R 30

31

PRK BRK SW

REAR WIND DEFOG SW

86 31

T2g T2g T1a

DOOR SW -R

CLOCK ILLUM LITE

AC CNTRL LEVER LITE

CIG LITER

T1r

STOP LITE SW

T1m

REAR WIND DEFOG

T4

20 20 20 20
BK BK BK/G BR/W BR

R/W GY/BL GY/BL

30

BK

SEAT BUZZ SW

DOOR SW/ BUZZ -L

CLOCK

OIL TEMP IND LITE

ASH TRAY LITE

CIG LITER LITE

31

20
BR

STOP LITE -R

STOP LITE -L

REAR WIND DEFOG

TRN SIG -LF

TRN SIG -LR

TRN SIG -RF

TRN SIG -RR

20
BR

16
BR

20
BR

16
BK

20
BR

18
BR

18
BR

48 49 50 51 52 53 54 55 56 57 58 59 60 61 62 63 64 65 66 67 68 69 70 71 72 73 74 75

| Brake/Safety Belt Warning | Interior Light/Clock | Indicator Lamps/ Cig. Lighter | Brake Sw/Lights/Rear Wind. Defog. | Turn Signals |

Fig. 9.46 (contd) Wiring diagram for 1980/81 Scirocco and 1980 Jetta models (except California). For key see page 277

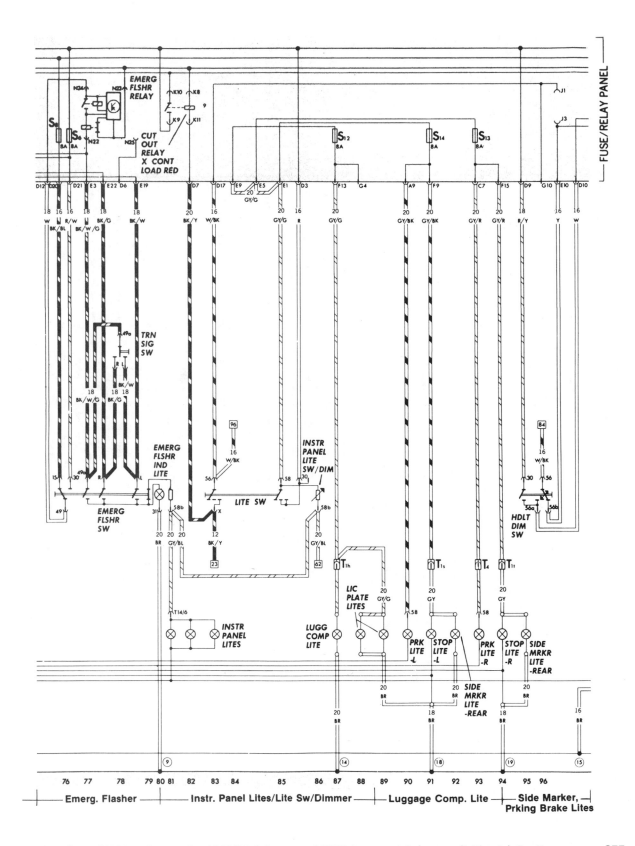

Fig. 9.46 (contd) Wiring diagram for 1980/81 Scirocco and 1980 Jetta models (except California). For key see page 277

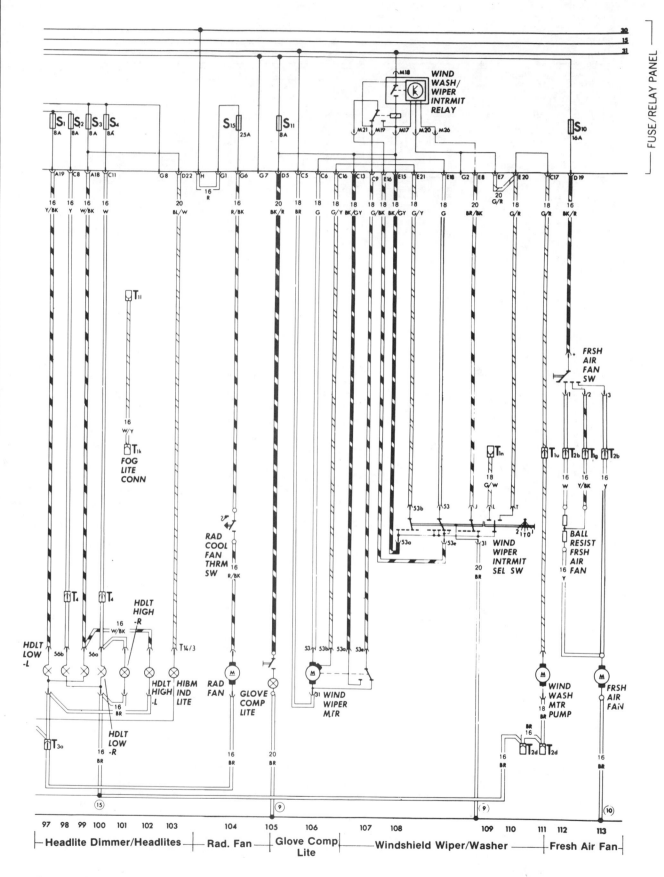

Fig. 9.46 (contd) Wiring diagram for 1980/81 Scirocco and 1980 Jetta models (except California). For key see page 277

Key to Fig. 9.47

Description	Current track	Description	Current track
Alternator	2–3	Stop-light, right	68
Alternator charging light	31	Stop-light switch	66–67
Ashtray light	62	Tachometer	26
Auxiliary air regulator	17	Tail light, left	97
Back-up light, left	40	Tail light, right	93
Back-up light, right	41	Thermal time switch	13–14
Back-up light switch	39	Turn signal, front left	73
Ballast resistance wire	9	Turn signal, rear left	75
Brake control light	65	Turn signal indicator light	32
Cigarette lighter	64	Turn signal, rear left	74
Cigarette lighter light	63	Turn signal, rear right	76
Clock	57	Turn signal switch	79
Clock light	58	Voltage regulator	2–3
Cold start valve	15	Voltage stabilizer	25
Control-pressure regulator	16	Voltmeter	56
Coolant temperature gauge	27	Voltmeter light	59
Coolant temperature sensor	36	Windshield washer pump	113
Coolant thermoswitch fan	105	Windshield wiper motor	106–108
Coolant temperature warning light	29	Windshield wiper switch	109–112
Door switch/buzzer (left)	50–51	Windshield wiper wash/wipe relay	107–110
Door switch, right	52		
Dual brake-circuit warning light and parking brake indicator light	46	**Wire connectors**	
EGR elapsed-mileage switch	34–35	T – Wire adaptor behind instrument panel	
EGR light	33	T1a – Single, behind instrument panel	
Emergency flasher indicator light	80	T1b – Single, behind instrument panel	
Emergency flasher relay	78–79	T1c – Single, engine compartment, next to left headlight	
Emergency flasher switch	77–81	T1d – Single, in engine compartment, front left	
Fuel gauge	25	T1e – Single, in engine compartment, front left	
Fuel level sensor	38	T1f – Single, in engine compartment, front right	
Fuel pump	19	T1g – Single, behind instrument panel	
Fuel pump relay	18–20	T1h – Single, in luggage compartment, rear left	
Fuses S1-S15, on fuse/relay panel		T1k – Single, in engine compartment, front right	
S37 for fuel pump (on fuel pump relay)		T1l – Single, next to fuse/relay panel	
Fresh air blower switch	114–115	T1m – Single, in luggage compartment, rear left	
Fresh air fan	115	T1n – Single, behind instrument panel	
Fresh air fan resistor	114	T1o – Single, behind instrument panel	
Headlight, left	100–102	T1s – Single, next to tail light, left	
Headlight, right	101–103	T1t – Single, next to tail light, left	
High beam indicator light	104	T1u – Single, behind instrument panel	
Horn	41–42	T1v – Single, behind instrument panel	
Horn button	44	T2a – 2-point, in engine compartment, next to horn	
Horn relay	43–44	T2b – 2-point, behind instrument panel	
Ignition coil	9	T2c – 2-point, behind instrument panel	
Ignition distributor	10–12	T2e – 2-point, behind instrument panel	
Ignition/starter switch	21–24	T2f – 2-point, behind instrument panel	
Instrument panel lights	85–87	T2g – 2-point, below driver's seat	
Instrument panel light switch/dimmer	87	T2h – 2-point, behind instrument panel	
Interior light	52–53	T3a – 3-point, behind instrument panel	
License plate light	98–90	T3b – 3-point, behind instrument panel	
Light switch	83–87	T3c – 3-point, in engine compartment, front right	
Load-reduction relay	81–82	T4 – 4-point, behind instrument panel	
Luggage compartment light	88	T4a – 4-point, in engine compartment, front left	
Luggage compartment light switch	88	T14 – 14-point, on dashboard cluster	
Oil pressure warning light	30		
Oil temperature gauge	55		
Oil temperature gauge light	60		
Oil temperature sensor	54		
Parking brake indicator-light switch	45	**Ground connectors**	
Parking light, front left	97	① – From battery to body/transmission	
Parking light, front right	95	② – From alternator to engine	
Parking light switch	98–99	⑩ – On steering column support	
Radiator fan	105	⑪ – On steering column support	
Radio connection	63	⑫ – In luggage compartment	
Rear window defogger	70	⑭ – On roof support, rear center	
Rear window defogger indicator light	72	⑮ – In wiring harness, front	
Rear window defogger switch	71–72	⑰ – On steering gear	
Seat belt/starter lock-out relay	47–49	⑱ – Rear panel, left	
Seat belt switch, left	49	⑲ – Rear panel, right	
Seat belt warning light	46		
Side marker lights, front	92–96		
Side marker lights, rear	114		
Spark plugs	10–12		
Spark plug suppressors	10–12		
Starter	5–6		
Stop-light, left	69		

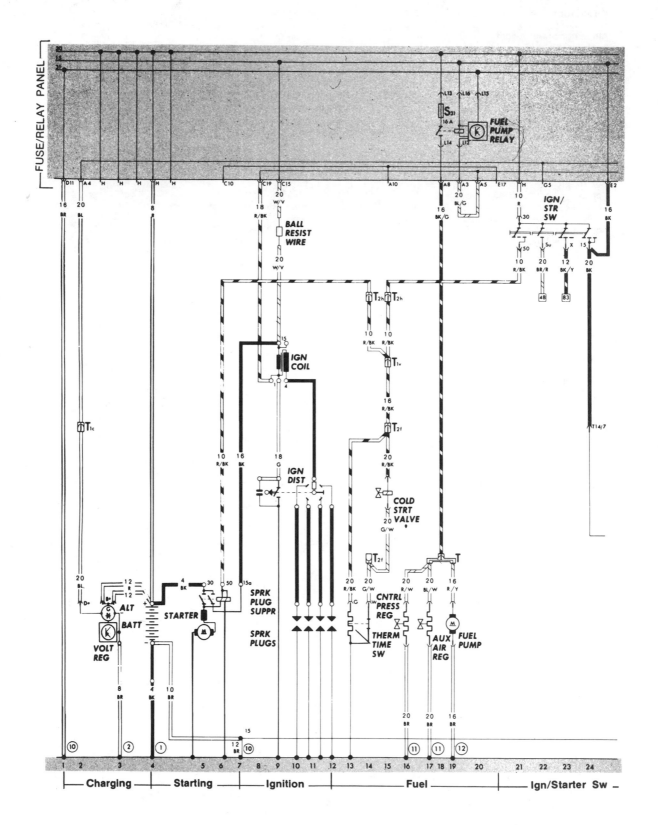

Fig. 9.47 Wiring diagram for 1980 Rabbit Convertible (except California) and 1980 Canadian Rabbit Deluxe models. For key see page 283

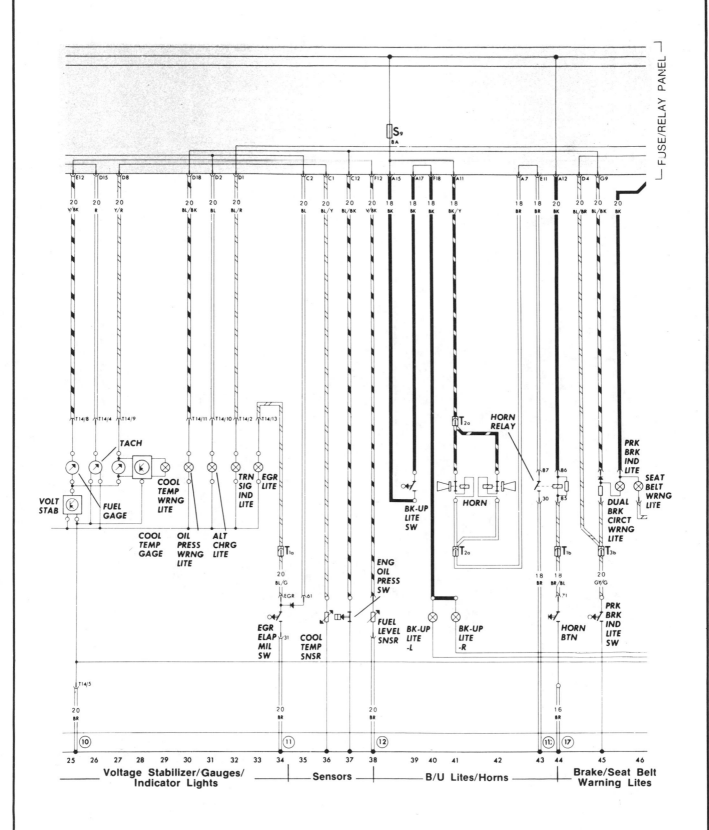

Fig. 9.47 (contd) Wiring diagram for 1980 Rabbit Convertible (except California) and 1980 Canadian Rabbit Deluxe models.
For key see page 283

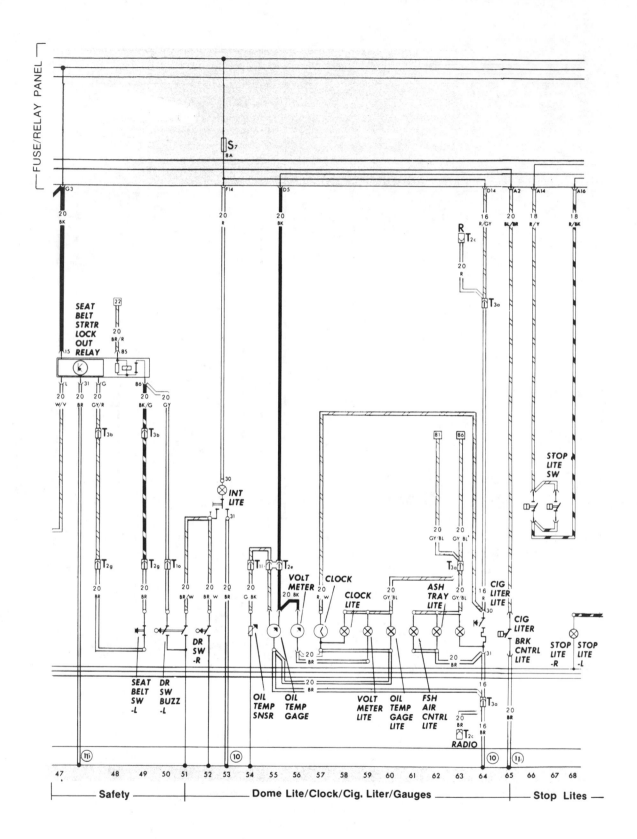

Fig. 9.47 (contd) Wiring diagram for 1980 Rabbit Convertible (except California) and 1980 Canadian Rabbit Deluxe models. For key see page 283

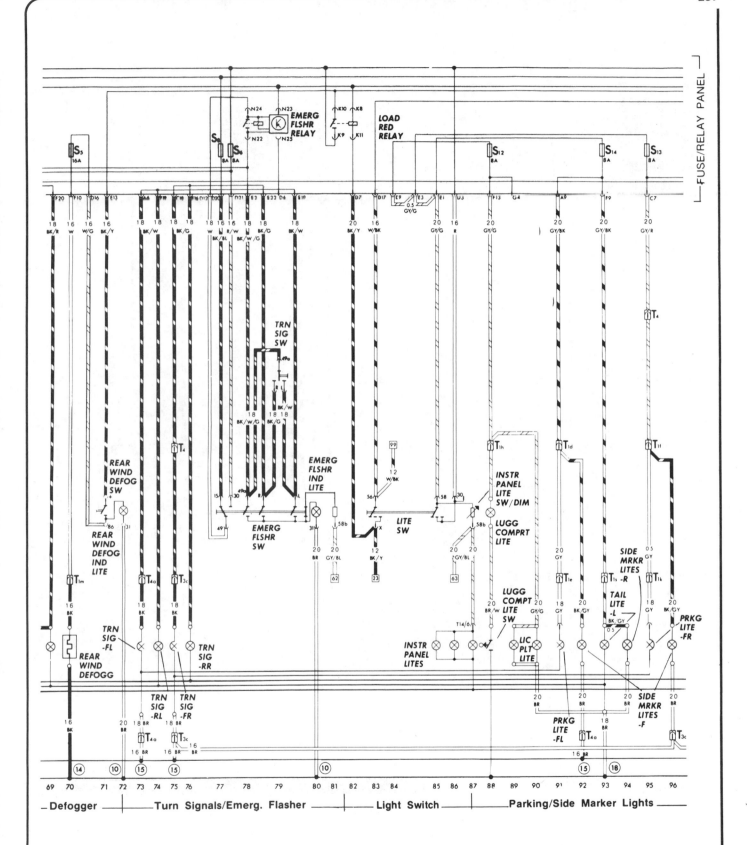

Fig. 9.47 (contd) Wiring diagram for 1980 Rabbit Convertible (except California) and 1980 Canadian Rabbit Deluxe models.
For key see page 283

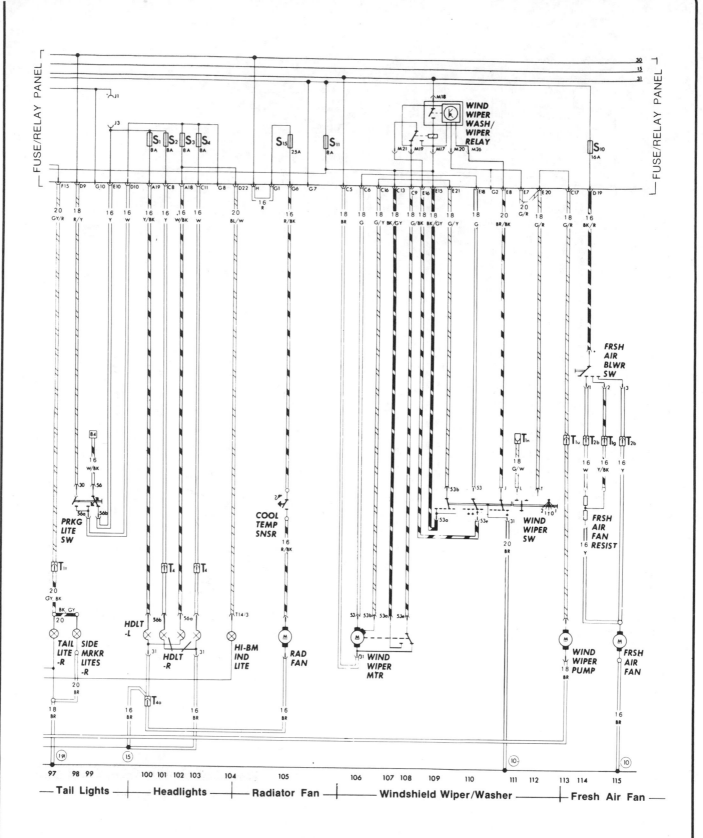

Fig. 9.47 (contd) Wiring diagram for 1980 Rabbit Convertible (except California) and 1980 Canadian Rabbit Deluxe models.
For key see page 283

Key to Fig. 9.48

Description	Current track	Description	Current track
Alternator	2	Ignition/starter switch	32
Alternator charging light	35	Ignition distributor	9
Ashtray light	54	Ignition module	11
Auxiliary air regulator	17	Instrument panel lights	54
Back-up lights	60	Interior light	64
Back-up light switch	60	License plate lights	55
Battery	4	Load reduction relay	33
Brake proportioning valve	36	Oil pressure switch	38
Bulb check relay	39	Oil pressure warning light	38
Cigarette lighter	84	Oxygen sensor control unit	23
Cigarette lighter light	54	Oxygen sensor frequency valve	33
Clock	68	Oxygen sensor relay	21
Cold start valve	29	Oxygen sensor thermal switch	23
Control pressure regulator	16	Parking brake indicator light	35
Coolant temperature gauge	26	Parking brake indicator light switch	35
Coolant temperature sensor	39	Parking – side marker lights	48
Door switch (right)	64	Radiator fan	15
Door switch/buzzer (left)	63	Radiator fan relay	14
EGR elapsed mileage switch	35	Radiator fan thermal switch	14
EGR light	35	Radio	90
Emergency flasher relay	72	Rear window defogger	78
Emergency flasher switch	72	Rear window defogger switch	78
Emergency flasher indicator light	54	Seat belt relay	40
Fresh air fan	77	Seat belt switch	40
Fresh air fan speed control resistors	76	Seat belt warning light	38
Fresh air fan switch	77	Shift console light (auto. trans.)	54
Fuel gauge	27	Side marker lights, rear	50
Fuel level sensor	27	Spark plug suppressors	9
Fuel pump	18	Spark plugs	9
Fuel pump relay	19	Starter	5
Fuse links	2	Stop-lights	57
Glovebox light	66	Stop-light switch	57
Headlights	47	Tail light	52
Headlight switch	50	Thermal time switch	29
Headlight dimmer/flasher switch	47	Trunk light	67
Heater lever light	54	Turn signal lights	72
High beam indicator light	54	Turn signal switch	72
Horn	44	Turn signal indicator light	35
Horn button	45	Voltage regulator	2
Horn relay	44	Voltage stabilizer	27
Hot start pulse relay	28	Windshield washer pump	81
Idle stabilizer	12	Windshield wiper motor	83
Ignition coil	8	Windshield wiper switch	83

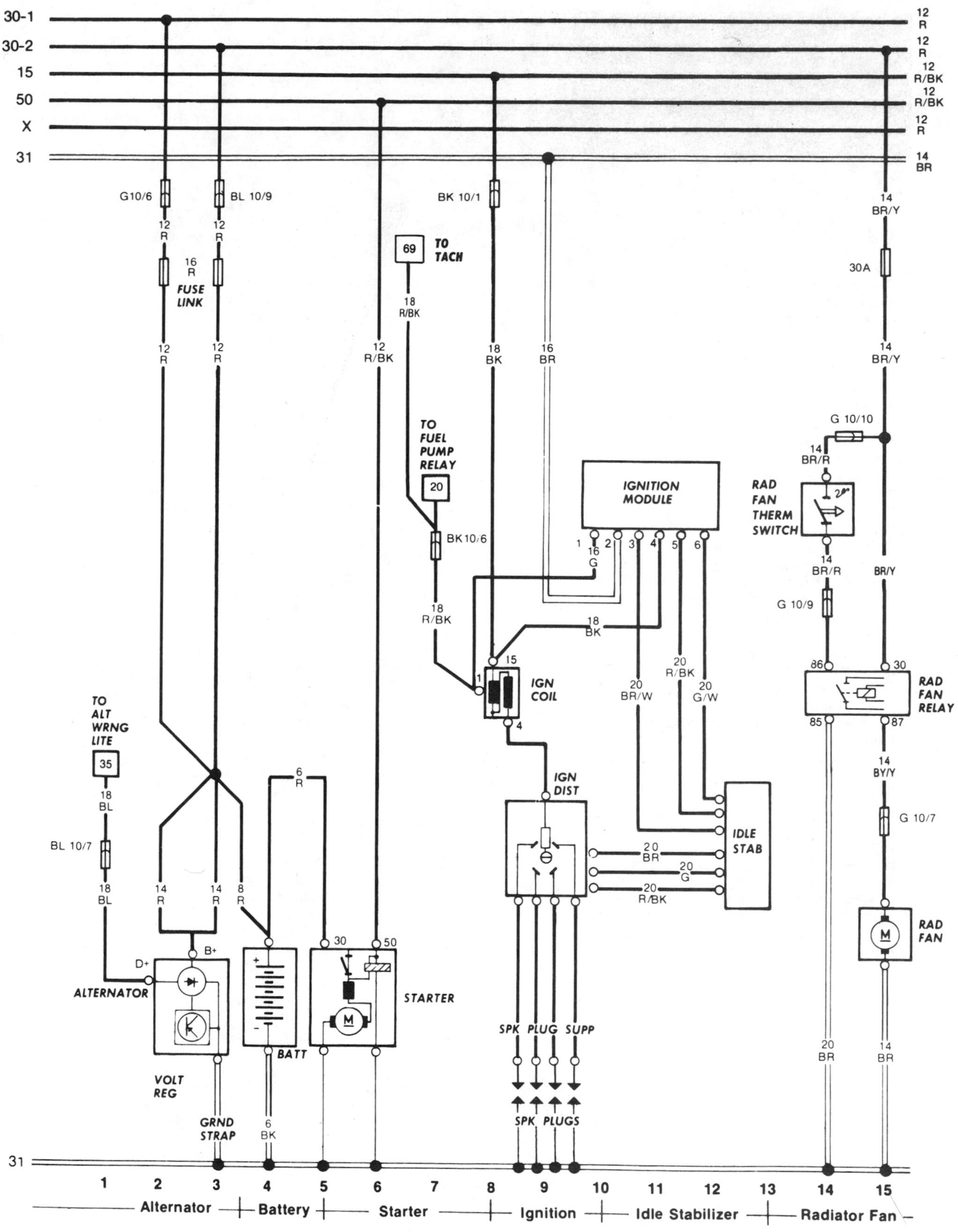

30-1
30-2
15
50
X
31

12 R
12 R
12 R/BK
12 R/BK
12 R
14 BR

G10/6
BL 10/9
BK 10/1
14 BR/Y

12 R
12 R
16 R
FUSE LINK
12 R

69 TO TACH

18 R/BK

30A

12 R
12 R
12 R/BK
18 BK
16 BR
14 BR/Y

TO FUEL PUMP RELAY

20

G 10/10
14 BR/R

RAD FAN THERM SWITCH

IGNITION MODULE

14 BR/R

BK 10/6

1 16 G 2   3   4   5   6

18 BK

G 10/9

BR/Y

TO ALT WRNG LITE

35

18 BL

15

86   30

BL 10/7

1   IGN COIL

20 BR/W   20 R/BK   20 G/W

RAD FAN RELAY

18 BL

4

85   87

BL 10/7

6 R

IGN DIST

14 BY/Y

D+   B+

20 BR

20 G

IDLE STAB

G 10/7

18 BL

14 R   14 R   8 R

20 R/BK

ALTERNATOR

30   50

RAD FAN

M

VOLT REG

BATT

STARTER

SPK PLUG SUPP

GRND STRAP

6 BK

SPK PLUGS

20 BR   14 BR

31

1   2   3   4   5   6   7   8   9   10   11   12   13   14   15

Alternator — Battery — Starter — Ignition — Idle Stabilizer — Radiator Fan

Fig. 9.48 Wiring diagram for 1981 Rabbit (except Convertible) and Pick-up Truck models. For key see page 289

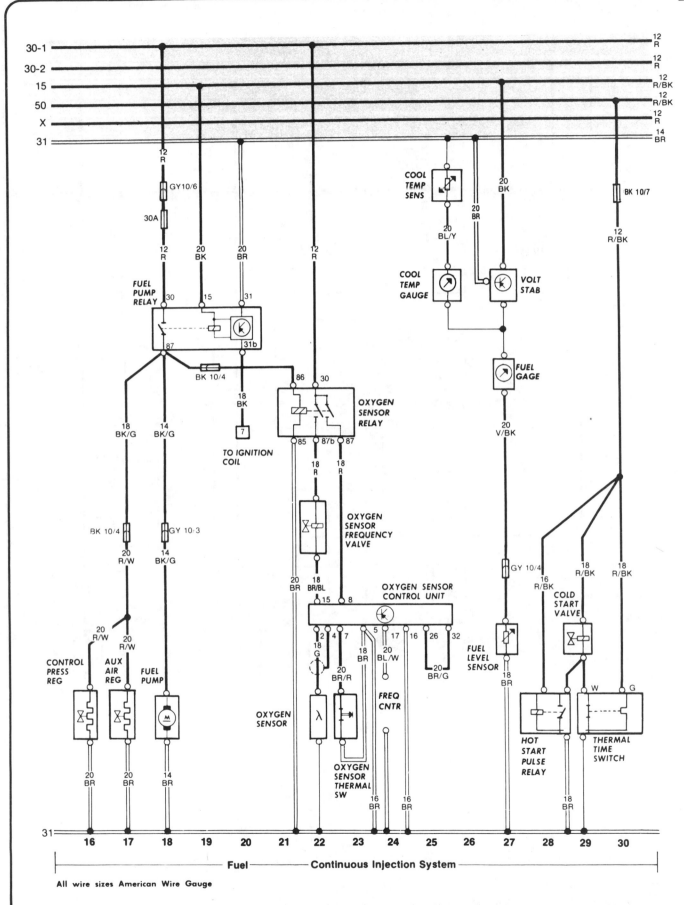

Fig. 9.48 (contd) Wiring diagram for 1981 Rabbit (except Convertible) and Pick-up Truck models. For key see page 289

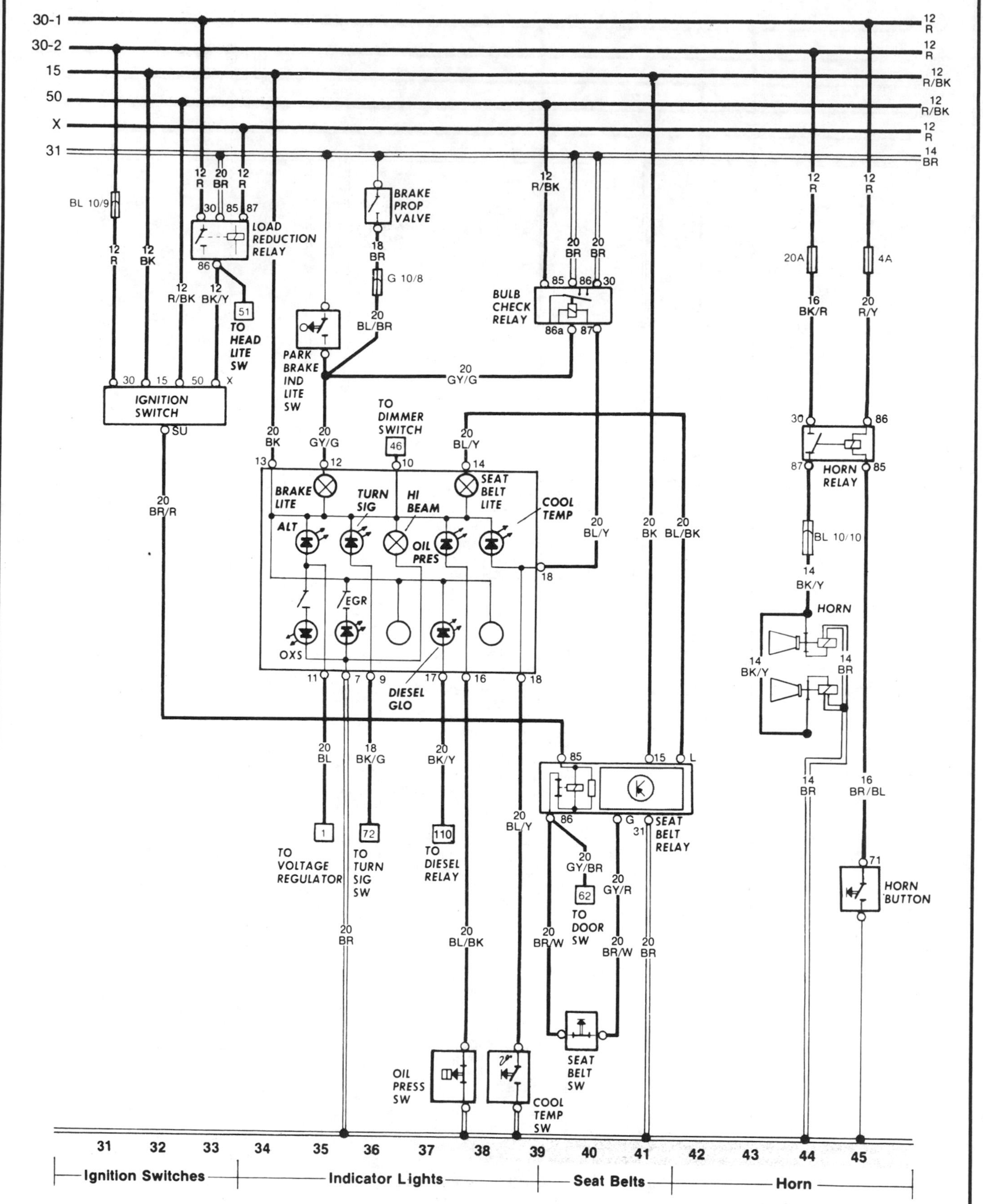

All wire sizes American Wire Gauge

Fig. 9.48 (contd) Wiring diagram for 1981 Rabbit (except Convertible) and Pick-up Truck models. For key see page 289

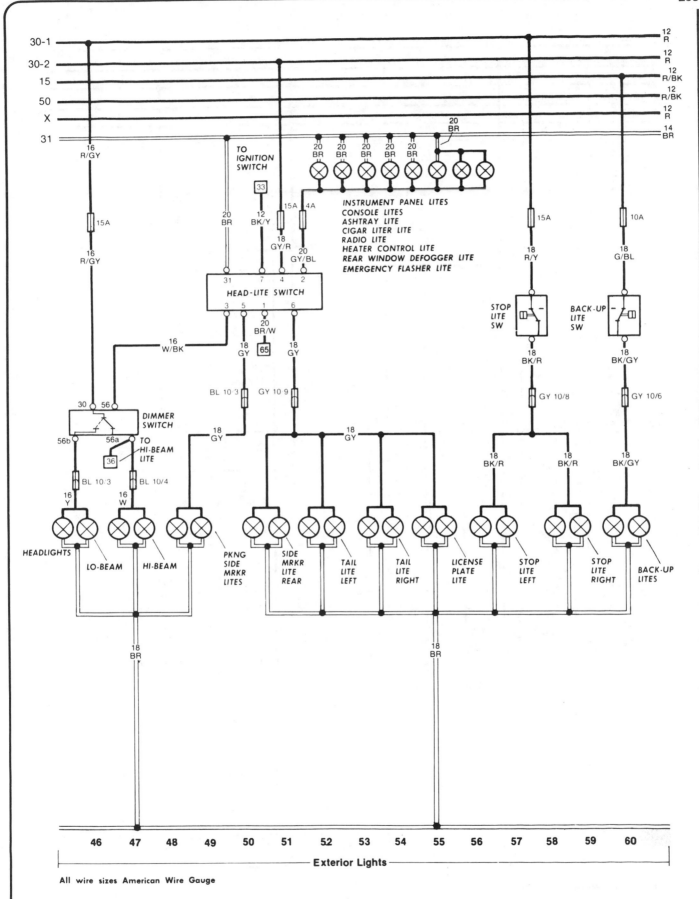

Fig. 9.48 (contd) Wiring diagram for 1981 Rabbit (except Convertible) and Pick-up Truck models. For key see page 289

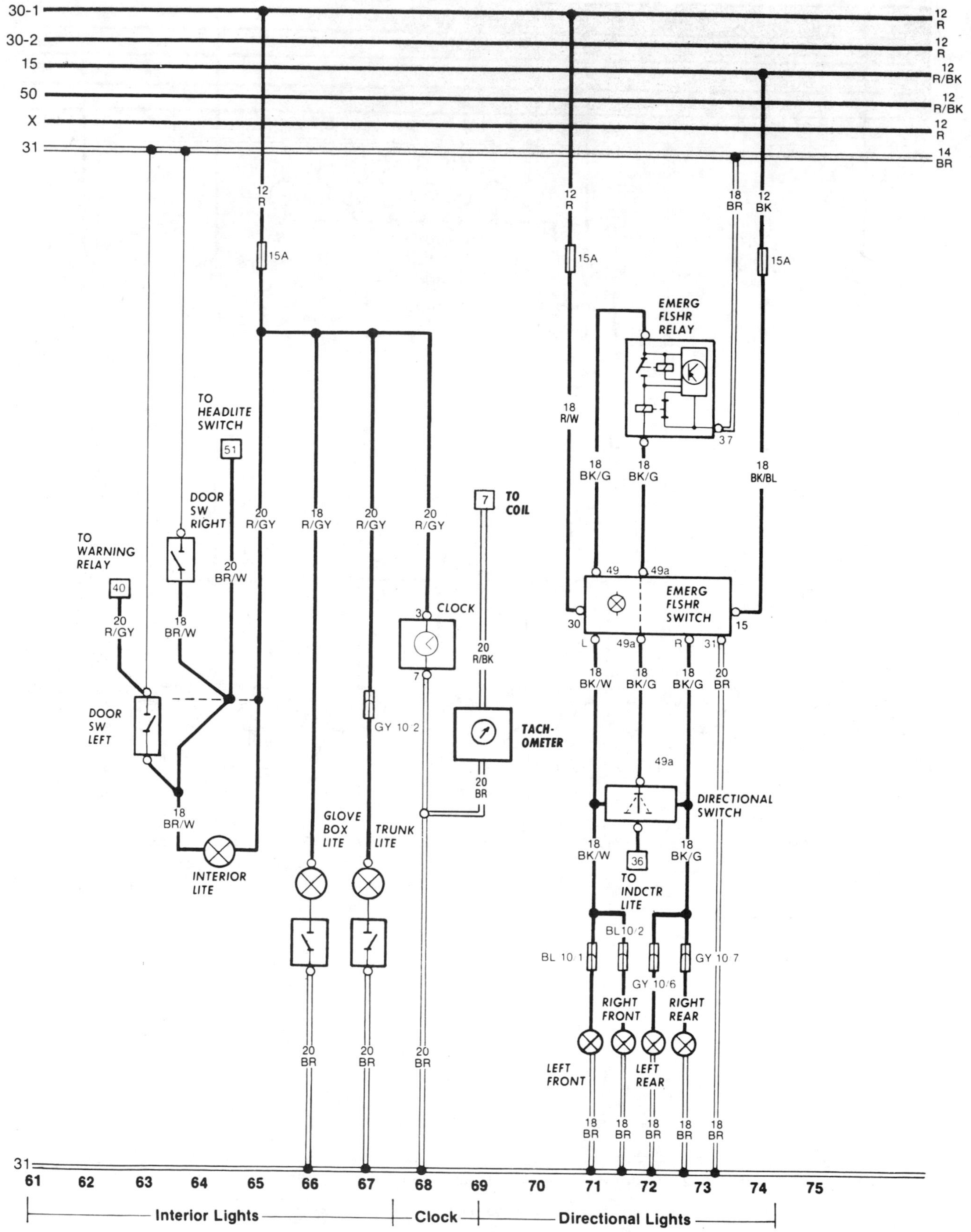

30-1

30-2

15

50

X

31

12 R

12 R

12 R/BK

12 R/BK

12 R

14 BR

12 R

15A

12 R

15A

18 BR

12 BK

15A

EMERG FLSHR RELAY

TO HEADLITE SWITCH

51

18 R/W

20 R/GY

18 R/GY

20 R/GY

20 R/GY

7 TO COIL

18 R/W

18 BK/G

18 BK/G

18 BK/BL

37

DOOR SW RIGHT

20 BR/W

3 CLOCK

TO WARNING RELAY

40

20 R/GY

18 BR/W

CLOCK

20 R/BK

49 49a

EMERG FLSHR SWITCH

30

L

49a

R

31

15

DOOR SW LEFT

7

TACH-OMETER

18 BK/W

18 BK/G

18 BK/G

20 BR

GY 10 2

20 BR

18 BR/W

GLOVE BOX LITE

TRUNK LITE

49a

DIRECTIONAL SWITCH

INTERIOR LITE

18 BK/W

36

TO INDCTR LITE

18 BK/G

BL 10/2

BL 10 1

GY 10/6

GY 10 7

RIGHT FRONT

RIGHT REAR

20 BR

20 BR

20 BR

LEFT FRONT

LEFT REAR

31

18 BR

18 BR

18 BR

18 BR

18 BR

61   62   63   64   65   66   67   68   69   70   71   72   73   74   75

Interior Lights ─── Clock ── Directional Lights

All wire sizes American Wire Gauge

Fig. 9.48 (contd) Wiring diagram for 1981 Rabbit (except Convertible) and Pick-up Truck models. For key see page 289

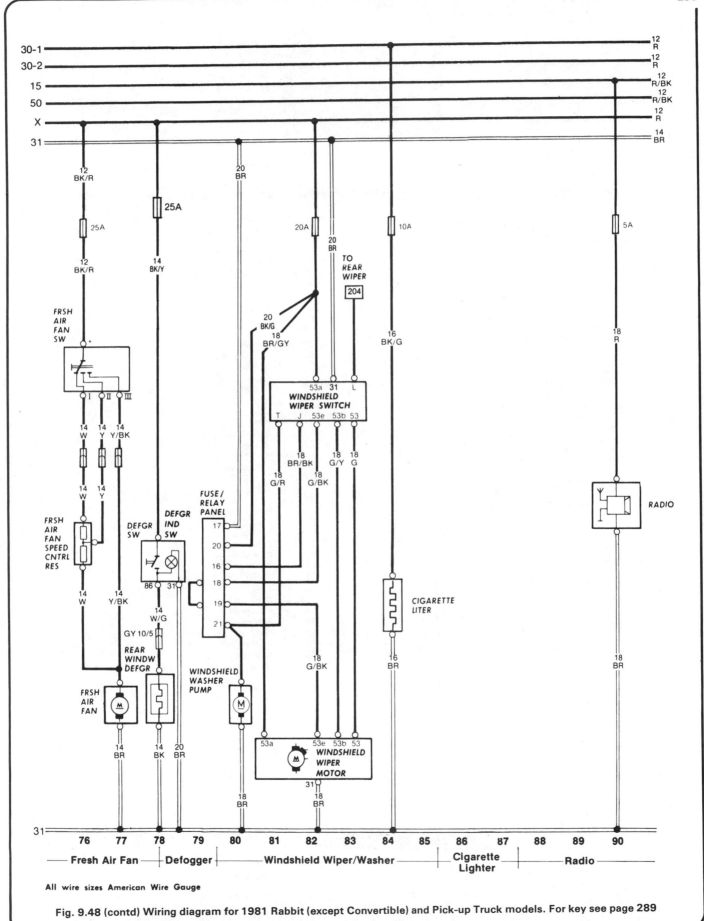

All wire sizes American Wire Gauge

Fig. 9.48 (contd) Wiring diagram for 1981 Rabbit (except Convertible) and Pick-up Truck models. For key see page 289

Key to Fig. 9.49

Description	Current track
Alternator	2–3
Alternator charging indicator light	33
Auxiliary air regulator	20
Back-up light, left	43
Back-up light, right	45
Back-up light switch	42
Battery	4
Brake fluid level warning switch	61
Brake light, left	64
Brake light, right	63
Brake light switch	62–63
Brake warning light	47
Cigarette lighter	58
Cigarette lighter light	59
Clock	60
Cold start valve	25
Control pressure regulator	19
Coolant overheat warning light	31
Coolant temperature gauge	30
Coolant temperature sender	40
Door switch, left front, with buzzer contact	51–52
Door switch, left rear	53
Door switch, right front	55
Door switch, right rear	54
Electronic ignition control unit	6–10
Emergency flasher indicator light	74
Emergency flasher pilot light	76
Emergency flasher relay	71–72
Emergency flasher switch	69–75
Frequency valve	17
Fresh air fan	114
Fresh air fan series resistor	113
Fresh air fan switch	113–114
Fuel gauge	29
Fuel gauge sender	23
Fuel pump	22
Fuel pump fuse (on fuel pump relay)	–
Fuel pump relay	13–14
Fuse S1-S15 on fuse/relay panel (under dash)	–
Hall generator	8–9
Headlight dimmer switch/flasher	96–97
Headlight, high beam, left inner	104
Headlight, high beam, left outer	101
Headlight, high beam, right inner	103
Headlight, high beam, right outer	102
Headlight, low beam, left outer	99
Headlight, low beam, right outer	100
Heater/fresh air controls light	57
High beam indicator light	36
Horn	44
Horn button	46
Ignition coil	10–11
Ignition distributor	10–12
Ignition/starter switch	25–28
Interior light, front	55–56
Instrument panel lights	83–85
Instrument panel light switch	85
License plate light	87–88
Light switch	82–85
Light switch light	80
Load reduction relay	80–81
Oil pressure light	35
Oil pressure switch	41
OXS control unit (behind dash, on right)	13–17
OXS elapsed mileage switch	38–39
OXS (oxygen) sensor	13
OXS voltage supply relay	16–18
OXS warning light	37
Parking brake indicator light switch	47
Parking light, left	89
Parking light, right	93
Radiator fan motor	105
Radiator fan thermoswitch	105
Radio ground connector	58
Radio power connector	70
Rear window defogger	79
Rear window defogger indicator light	77
Rear window defogger switch	78
Seat belt safety switch, left	50

Description	Current track
Seat belt warning/interlock relay	48–51
Seat belt warning light	47
Side marker light, left front	90
Side marker light, left rear	92
Side marker light, right front	94
Side marker light, right rear	96
Spark plugs	10–12
Spark plug connectors	10–12
Starter	5–6
Tail light, left	91
Tail light, right	95
Thermoswitch for OXS system	14
Thermotime switch	24
Trunk light (convertible only)	86
Trunk light switch (convertible only)	86
Turn signal indicator light	34
Turn signal, left front	65
Turn signal, left rear	66
Turn signal, right front	67
Turn signal, right rear	68
Turn signal switch	72
Voltage regulator	2–3
Voltage stabilizer	29
Windshield washer pump motor	112
Windshield wiper intermittent switch	108–111
Windshield wiper motor	106–107
Windshield wiper/washer intermittent relay	108–110

Wire connectors

T	–	Behind dash, near fuse/relay panel
T1a	–	Behind dash
T1b	–	Behind dash
T1c	–	In engine compartment, left side
T1d	–	Near left headlight
T1e	–	Near left headlight
T1f	–	Near right headlight
T1g	–	Behind dash
T1h	–	In trunk, left rear
T1k	–	Near right headlight
T1m	–	In trunk, left rear
T1n	–	Behind dash
T1p	–	Behind dash
T1u	–	Behind dash
T1v	–	Behind dash
T1y	–	In engine compartment, on fuel line
T2b	–	Behind dash
T2c	–	Behind dash
T2f	–	Behind dash
T2g	–	Behind dash
T2l	–	Under dash, left side
T2m	–	Behind dash
T3a	–	Behind dash
T3b	–	Behind dash
T3c	–	Behind dash
T3d	–	Near right headlight
T4	–	Near right headlight
T4q	–	Near left headlight
T14	–	On instrument cluster

Ground connectors

①	–	Ground cable, battery to transmission
②	–	Ground cable, alternator to engine block
⑦	–	On cold start valve
⑧	–	On cold start valve
⑩	–	On fuse/relay panel mounting
⑬	–	On rear panel, left
⑭	–	On steering column
⑮	–	Insulated ground wire, engine compartment
⑯	–	Insulated ground wire, on instrument cluster
⑱	–	On rear panel, center
⑲	–	On rear roof crossmember, center

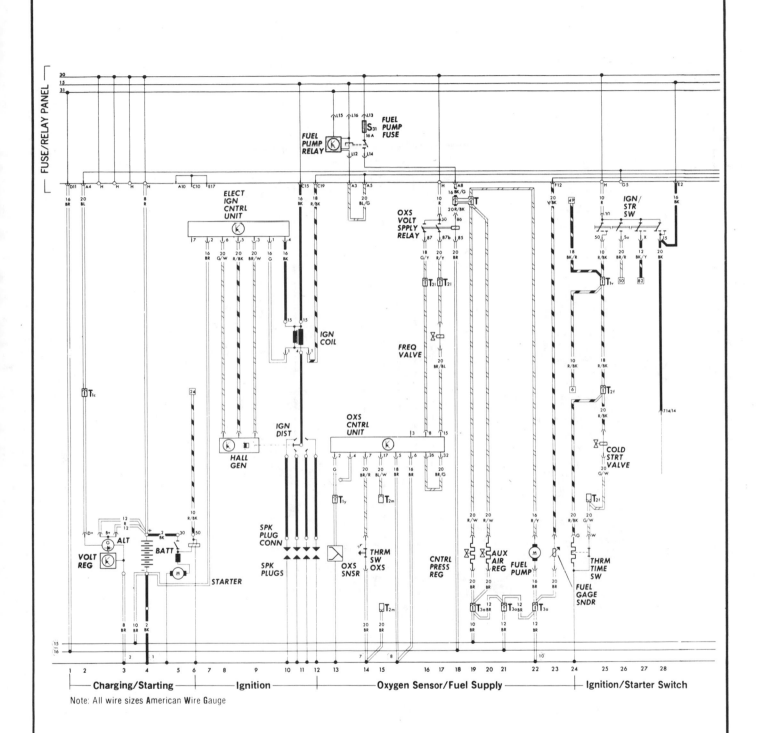

Fig. 9.49 Wiring diagram for 1981 Rabbit Convertible and Jetta models (except California). For key see page 296

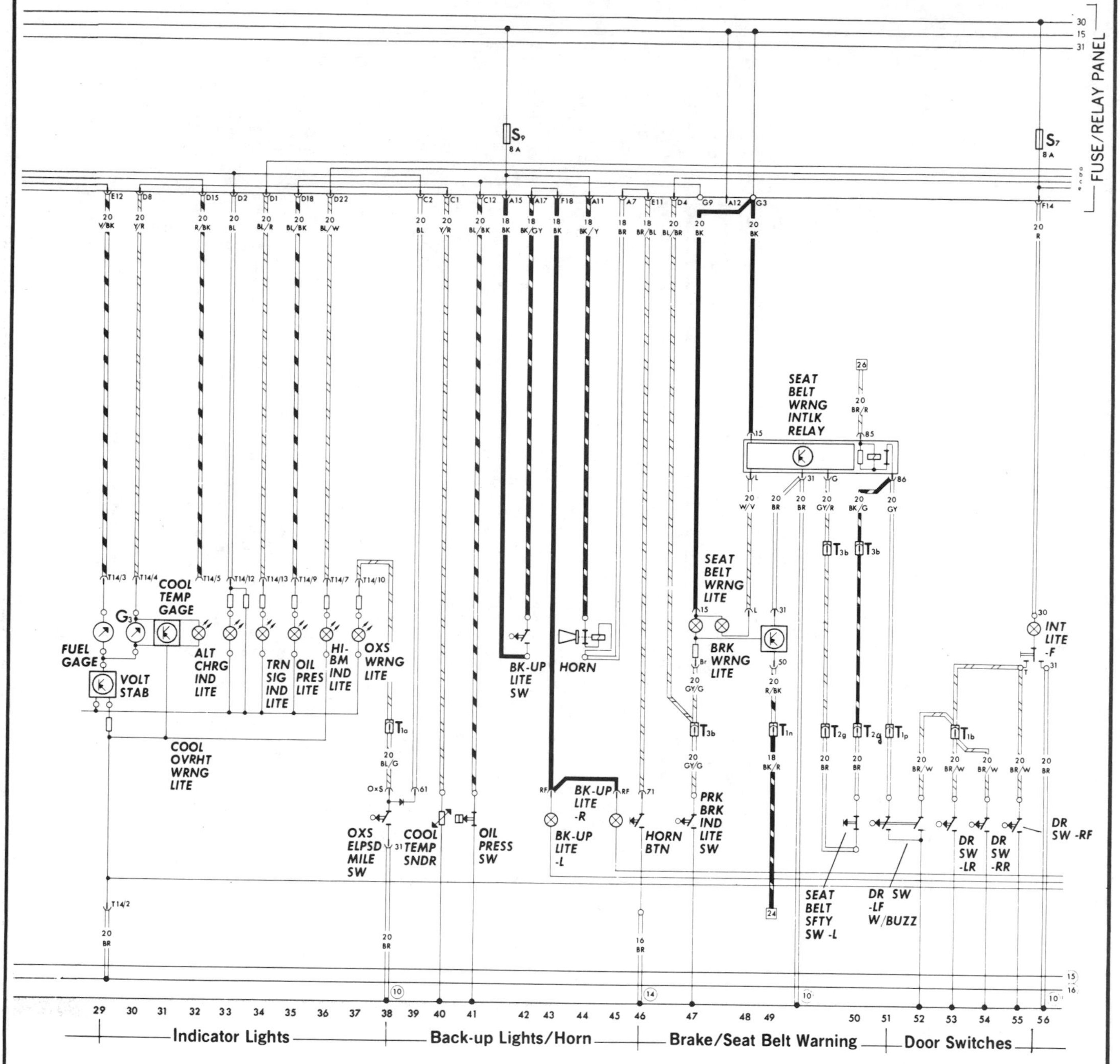

FUSE/RELAY PANEL

30
15
31

S9
8 A

S7
8 A

E12 | D8 | D15 | D2 | D1 | D18 | D22 | C2 | C1 | C12 | A15 | A17 | F18 | A11 | A7 | E11 | D4 | G9 | A12 | G3 | F14

20 V/BK | 20 Y/R | 20 R/BK | 20 BL | 20 BL/R | 20 BL/BK | 20 BL/W | 20 BL | 20 Y/R | 20 BL/BK | 18 BK | 18 BK/GY | 18 BK | 18 BK/Y | 18 BR | 18 BR/BL | 20 BL/BR | 20 BK | 20 BK | 20 R

SEAT BELT WRNG INTLK RELAY

26
20 BR/R

85

L | 31 | G

86

20 W/V | 20 BR | 20 BR | 20 GY/R | 20 BK/G | 20 GY

T3b | T3b

SEAT BELT WRNG LITE

15 | L | 31

T14/3 | T14/4 | T14/5 | T14/12 | T14/13 | T14/9 | T14/7 | T14/10

COOL TEMP GAGE

FUEL GAGE | G3 | ALT CHRG IND LITE | TRN SIG IND LITE | OIL PRES LITE | HI-BM IND LITE | OXS WRNG LITE

BK-UP LITE SW

HORN

BRK WRNG LITE

20 GY/G | 20 R/BK

VOLT STAB

COOL OVRHT WRNG LITE

T1a

20 BL/G

OXS ELPSD MILE SW | COOL TEMP SNDR | OIL PRESS SW

OXS | 61

RF | BK-UP LITE -R | RF | 71

BK-UP LITE -L

HORN BTN | PRK BRK IND LITE SW

T3b | T1n | T2g | T2g | T1p | T1b

20 GY/G | 18 BK/R | 20 BR | 20 BR | 20 BR/W | 20 BR/W | 20 BR/W | 20 BR/W | 20 BR

SEAT BELT SFTY SW -L | DR SW -LF W/BUZZ | DR SW -LR | DR SW -RR | DR SW -RF

INT LITE -F

30

T | 31

24

T14/2

20 BR

20 BR

16 BR

15
16

10 | 14 | 10 | 10

29 30 31 32 33 34 35 36 37 38 39 40 41 42 43 44 45 46 47 48 49 50 51 52 53 54 55 56

├── Indicator Lights ──┤├── Back-up Lights/Horn ──┤├── Brake/Seat Belt Warning ──┤├── Door Switches ──┤

Fig. 9.49 (contd) Wiring diagram for 1981 Rabbit Convertible and Jetta models (except California). For key see page 296

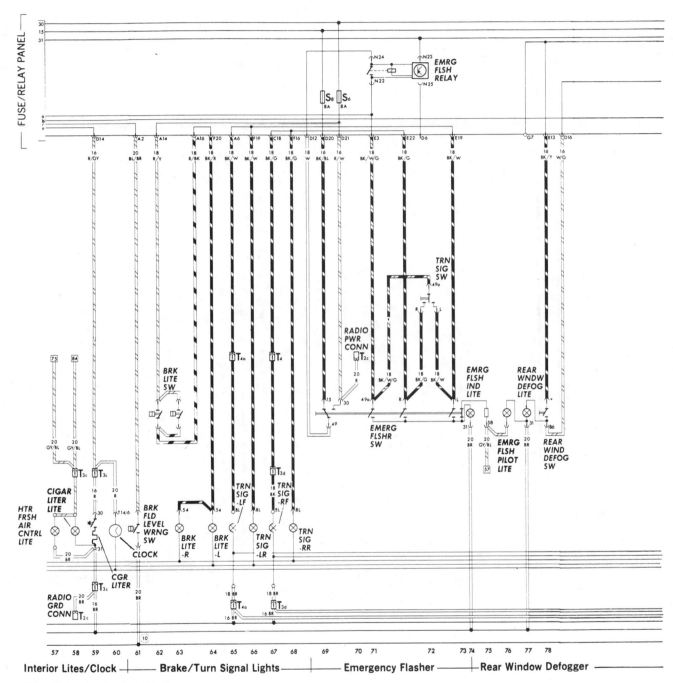

Fig. 9.49 (contd) Wiring diagram for 1981 Rabbit Convertible and Jetta models (except California). For key see page 296

Note: All wire sizes American Wire Gauge

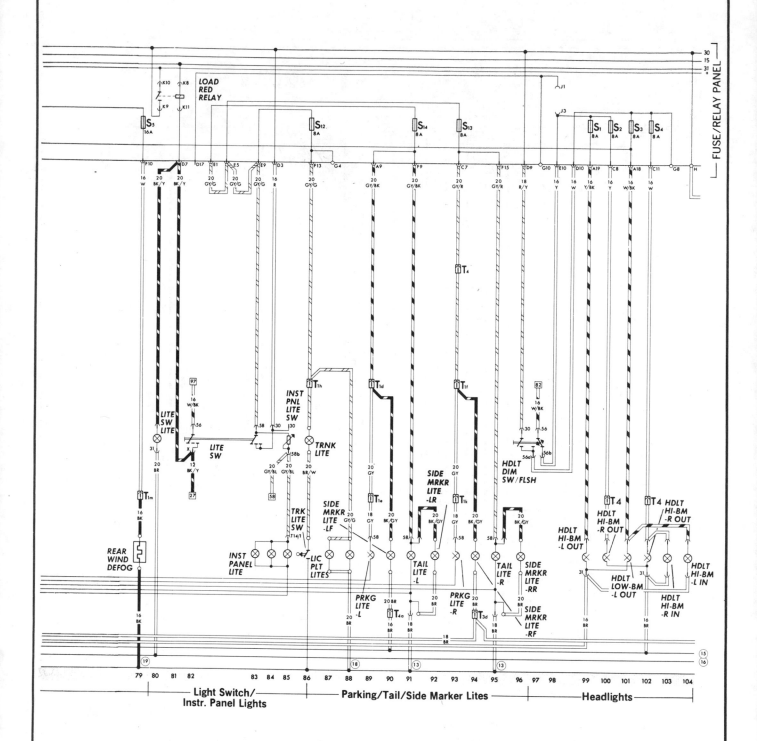

Fig. 9.49 (contd) Wiring diagram for 1981 Rabbit Convertible and Jetta models (except California). For key see page 296

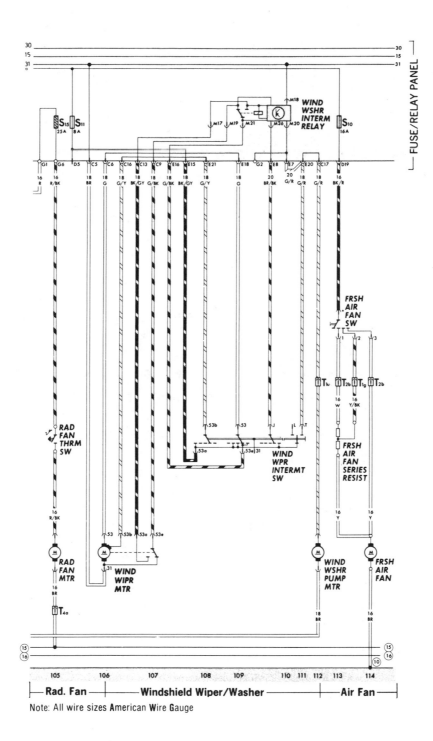

Fig. 9.49 (contd) Wiring diagram for 1981 Rabbit Convertible and Jetta models (except California). For key see page 296

Key to Fig. 9.50

Description	Current track
Starter	6,7,8
Starter cutout and back-up light switch	3,4,5
Selector lever light	4
Back-up light, left	1
Back-up light, right	1

Wire connectors

T1a	– connector, single, behind dashboard	8
T2a	– connector, double, behind dashboard	8

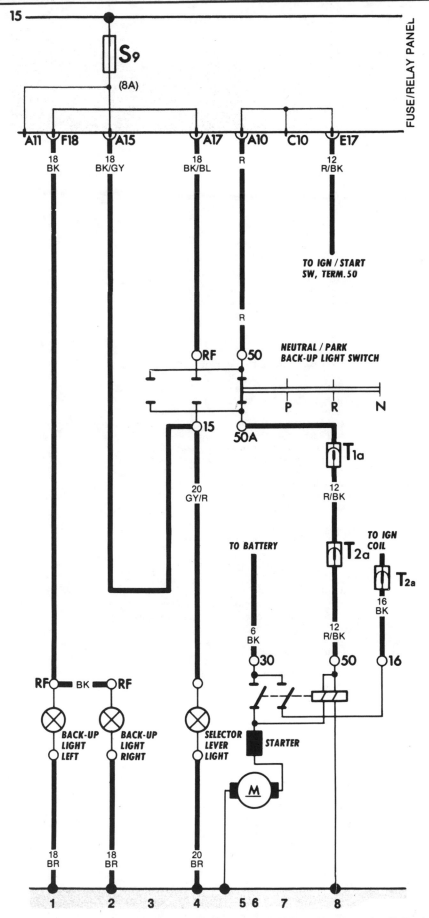

Fig. 9.50 Additional wiring diagram for automatic transmission (except 1981 Westmoreland). For key see page 302

Key to Fig. 9.51

Description	Current track
Air conditioner blower motor	2
Air conditioner fan speed control	1
Air conditioner relay (on steering column support)	3–7
Air conditioner switch (on lever for temp switch)	4
Compressor clutch	6
Coolant fan motor	9
Coolant in fan thermoswitch	8
Evaporator fan relay (on steering column support)	4,5
Fuse 15 for coolant fan	7
Fuse 23 for air conditioner (above fuse/relay board)	4
Hi-temp compressor cut-out switch (Diesel only)	6
Load reduction relay	2,3
Temperature switch	5
Two-way valve (CIS)	5

Wire connectors

T1 — Single connector, engine compartment
T1a — Single connector, next to steering column support
T1b — Single connector, engine compartment
T1c — Single connector, on compressor
T1d — Vacant
T1e — Single connector, engine compartment, left
T2 — Double connector, behind dash, center
T6 — 6-point connector, behind dash

Ground connectors

(10) — On steering column support

(16) — Engine compartment, right

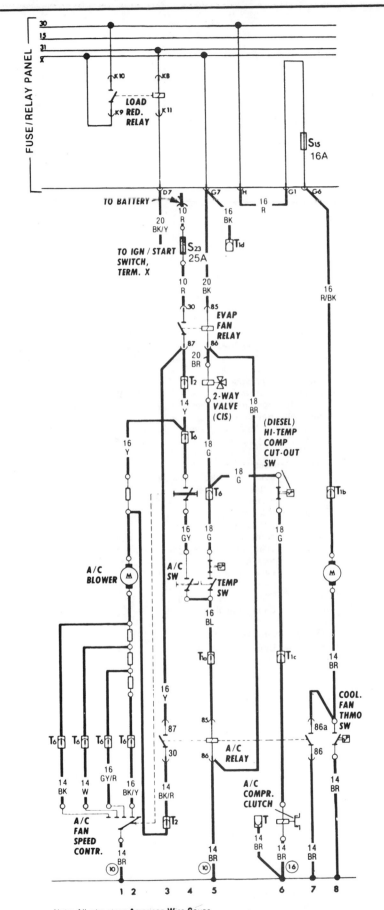

Note: All wire sizes American Wire Gauge

Fig. 9.51 Additional wiring diagram for air conditioner (1979 models). For key see page 304

Key to Fig. 9.52

Description	Current track
Fuse 11 for wiper/washer system	1
Fuse 30 for rear wiper motor (in-line under dash)	8
Motor for rear washer pump	5
Motor for rear wiper	8,9
Relay for rear wiper/washer (above fuse/relay panel)	7,8
Windshield wiper switch with intermittent operation	2–6

Wire connectors

T1g	–	Wire connector, single, in left rear of luggage compartment	9
T1h	–	Wire connector, single, in left rear of luggage compartment	8
T1i	–	Wire connector, single, in rear lid	9
T1k	–	Wire connector, single, in rear lid	8
T1o	–	Wire connector, single, behind dashboard	5

Ground connectors

⑩	–	Behind dashboard	7

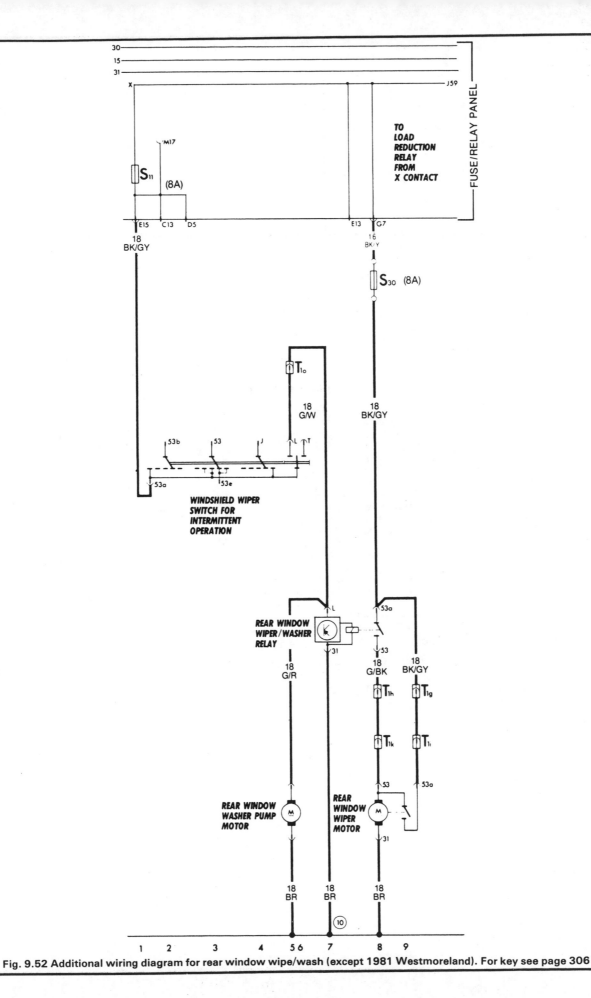

Fig. 9.52 Additional wiring diagram for rear window wipe/wash (except 1981 Westmoreland). For key see page 306

Key to Fig. 9.53

Description	Current track
Dual horns	1
Fuse S9 (8A)	1
Horn relay	1
Horn switch	2

Wire connectors

T2 — Double connector near horns

Ground connector

⑳ — On steering column support

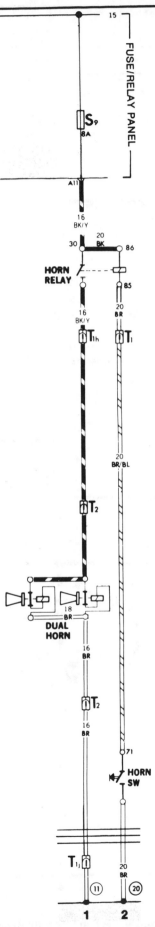

Fig. 9.53 Additional wiring diagram for dual horns (except 1981 Westmoreland). For key see page 308

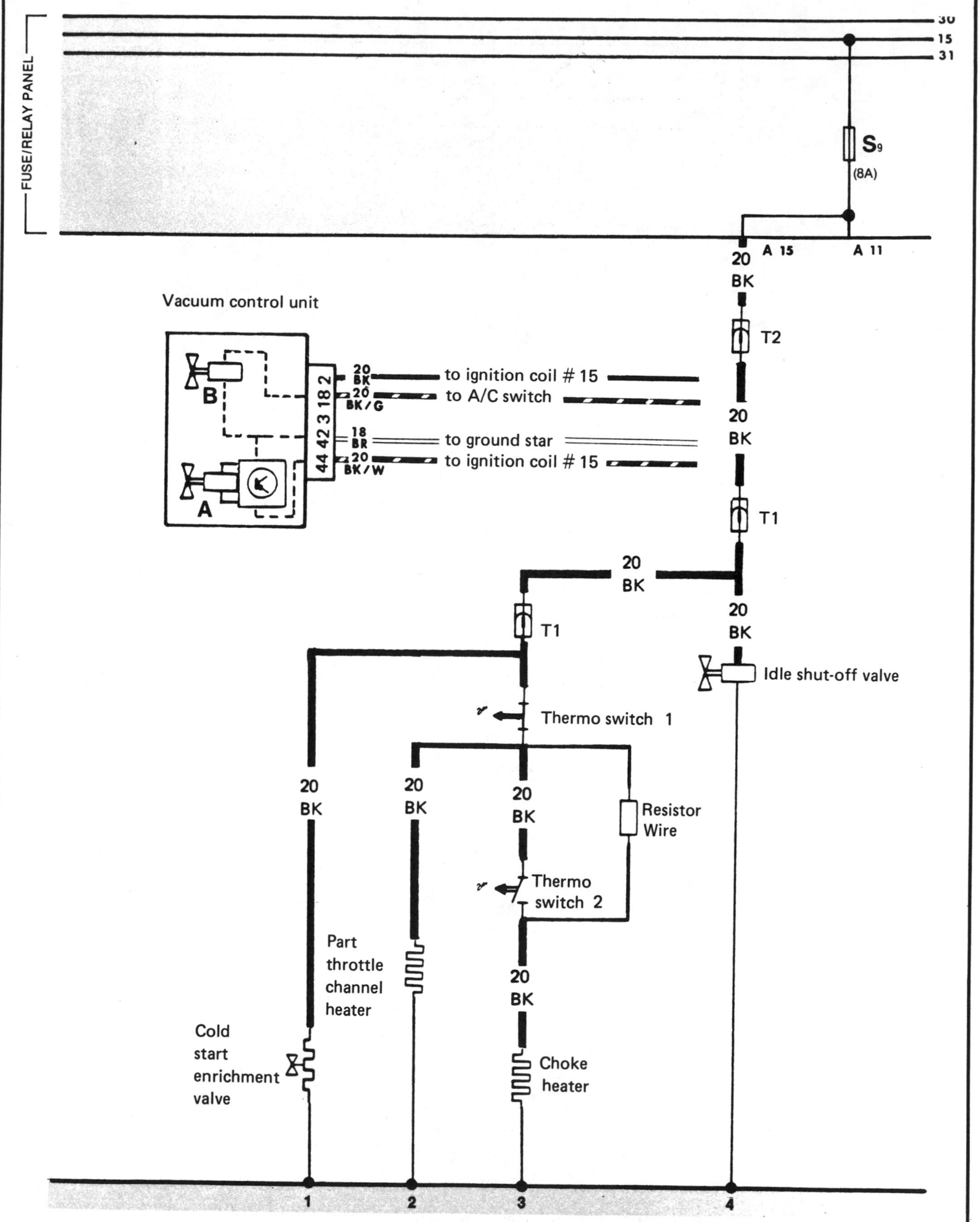

Fig. 9.54 Additional wiring diagram for carburettor (1980 models)

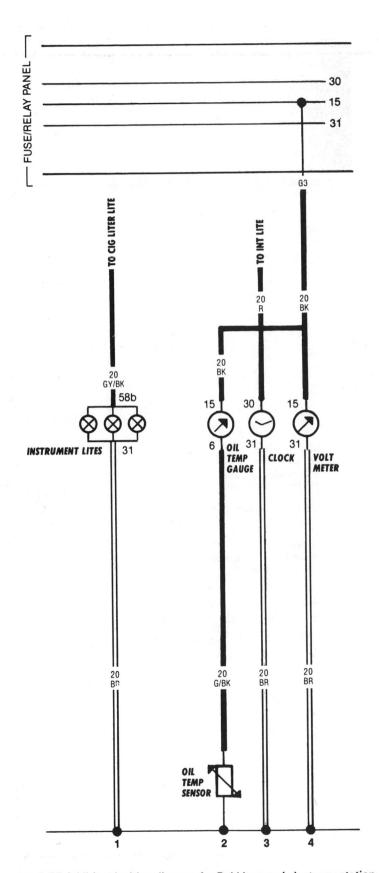

Fig. 9.55 Additional wiring diagram for Rabbit console instrumentation

Key to Fig. 9.56

Description	Current track
A/C Blower motor	1
A/C compressor clutch	6
A/C fan speed control	1
A/C relay	1–6
A/C temperature switch	6
Micro switch	4
Series resistor	1
Radiator fan	7
Rad fan temperature switch	7
Two way valve	5

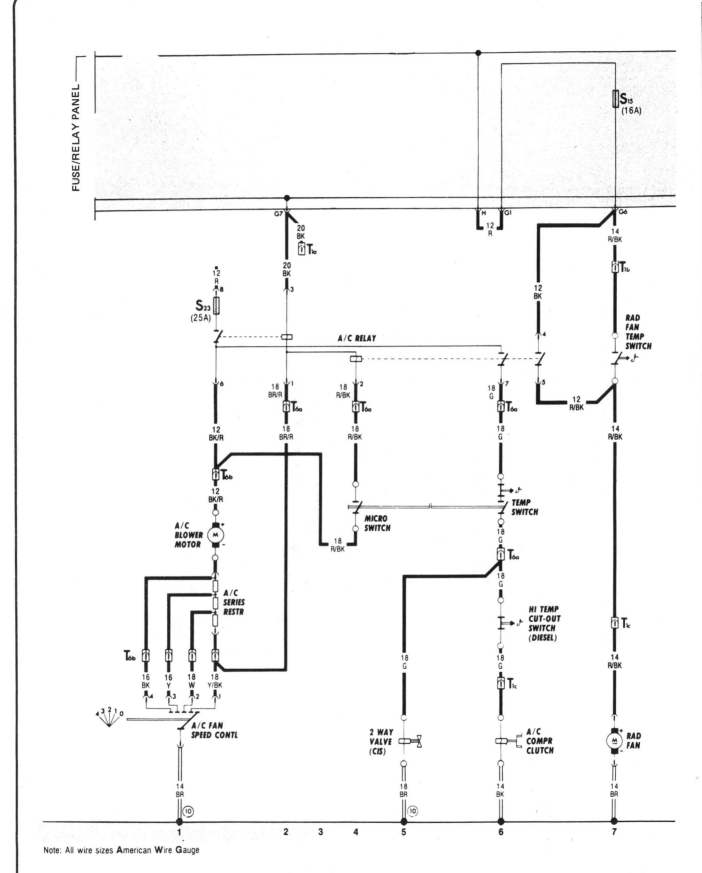

Note: All wire sizes **A**merican **W**ire **G**auge

Fig. 9.56 Additional wiring diagram for air conditioner on 1980 models (except US Rabbit). For key see page 312

Key to Fig. 9.57

Description	Current track
A/C blower motor	1
A/C compressor clutch	6
A/C fan speed control	1
A/C relay	1–6
A/C temperature switch	6
Hi temperature cut-out	6
Micro switch	4
Series resistor	1
Radiator fan	7
Rad fan temperature switch	7
Two-way valve	5

Wire connectors

T1b	–	Single connector – engine comp. L
T1c	–	Single connector – engine comp. L
T6a	–	6-point connector behind dash
T6b	–	6-point connector behind dash

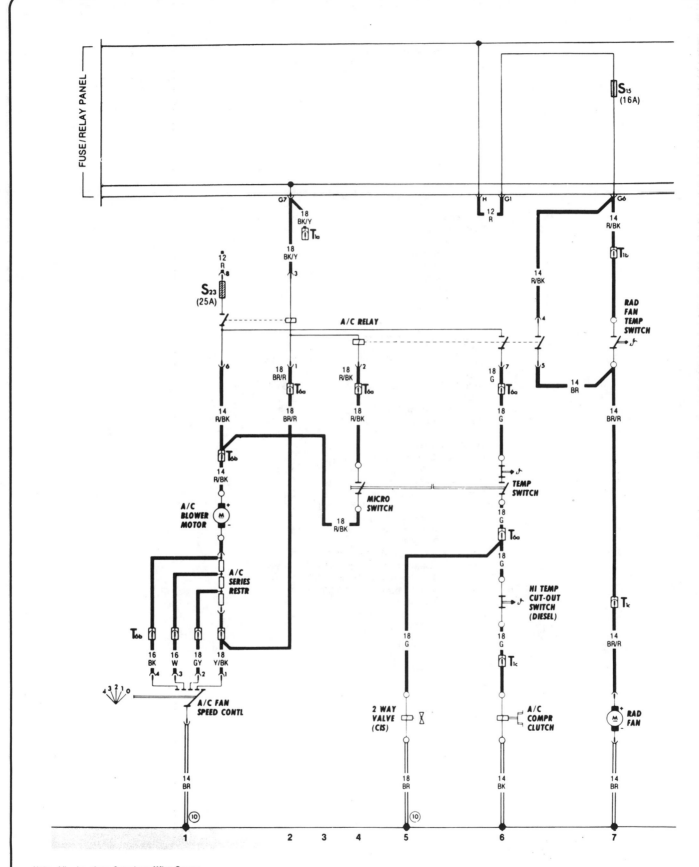

Note: All wire sizes **A**merican **W**ire **G**auge

Fig. 9.57 Additional wiring diagram for air conditioner on 1980 models (US Rabbit). For key see page 314

Key to Fig. 9.58

Description	Current track
Cold start valve	26
Distributor	7–10
Hall sender unit	3–5
Hot start relay	24–25
Idle stabilizer (California only)	3–5
Ignition coil	8–9
Ignition control unit	1–8
Oxygen sensor	15
Oxygen sensor control light	23
Oxygen sensor control unit (behind dashboard on right)	15–21
Oxygen sensor elapsed mileage switch	22–23
Oxygen sensor relay	14–16
Oxygen sensor thermal switch	16
Spark plugs	7–10
Spark plug connector	7–10
Thermal time switch	27–28

Wire connectors

T	– Cable adaptor behind dashboard	12–14
T1a	– Single, behind dashboard	23
T1v	– Single, behind dashboard	24
T1w	– Single, behind dashboard	24
T1y	– Single, clamped to fuel line in engine compartment	15
T2f	– Double, right side in engine compartment	26
T2h	– Double, behind dashboard	24,25
T2l	– Double, behind dashboard	15,16
T2m	– Double, behind dashboard in right side	18
T14	– Fourteen point, on dashboard	23

Ground connectors

⑦ – On cold start valve

⑧ – On cold start valve

⑨ – Near relay/fuse box

⑩ – Steering column support

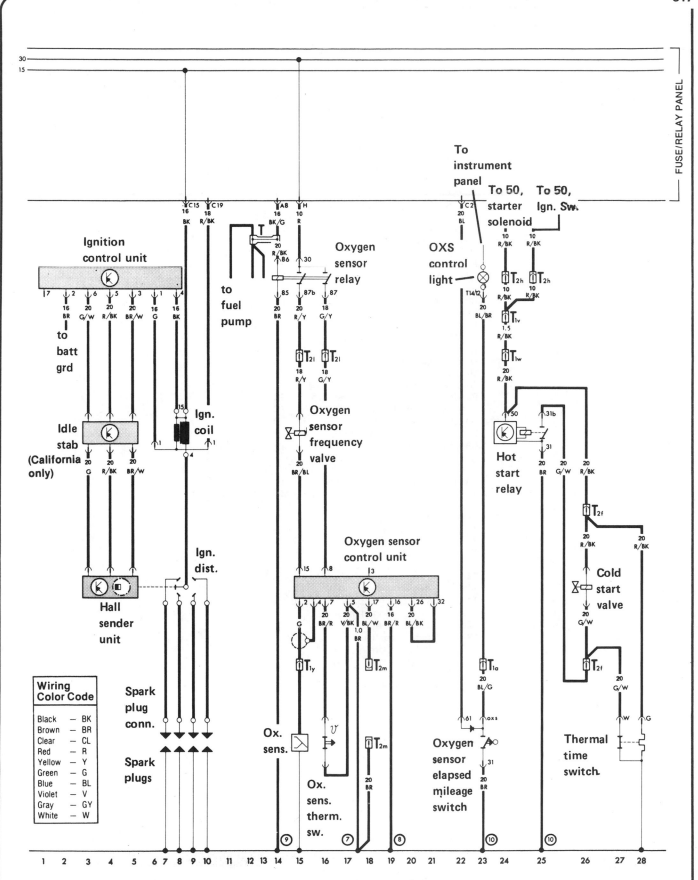

Fig. 9.58 Additional wiring diagram for oxygen sensor system (except 1981 Rabbit Convertible and Jetta, California models). For key see page 316

Key to Fig. 9.59

Description	Current track
Brake warning light	23
Cold start valve	37
Door switch, left front, with buzzer contact	26–28
Electronic ignition control unit	1–8
Frequency valve	15
Hall generator	3–5
Hot start pulse relay	31–34
Idle stabilizer	3–5
Ignition coil	8
Ignition distributor	7–10
Ignition/starter switch	29–35
Interior light, front	26
OXS control unit (behind dash, on right)	15–21
OXS elapsed mileage switch	20
OXS (oxygen) sensor	15
OXS voltage supply relay	14–16
OXS warning light	20
Parking brake indicator light switch	23
Seat belt switch, left	30
Seat belt switch, right	30
Seat belt warning/interlock relay	25–31
Seat belt warning light	24
Spark plugs	7–10
Spark plug connectors	7–10
Thermoswitch for OXS systems	16
Thermotime switch	38–39

Wire connectors

T	–	behind dash
T1	–	behind dash
T1a	–	behind dash
T1b	–	behind dash
T1c	–	behind dash
T1d	–	behind dash
T1y	–	in engine compartment, on fuel line
T2a	–	behind dash, right side
T2b	–	behind dash, left side
T2f	–	behind dash
T2l	–	behind dash
T2m	–	behind dash

Ground connectors

⑦ – On cold start valve

⑧ – On cold start valve

⑩ – On fuse/relay panel mounting

⑩ – Insulated ground wire on instrument cluster

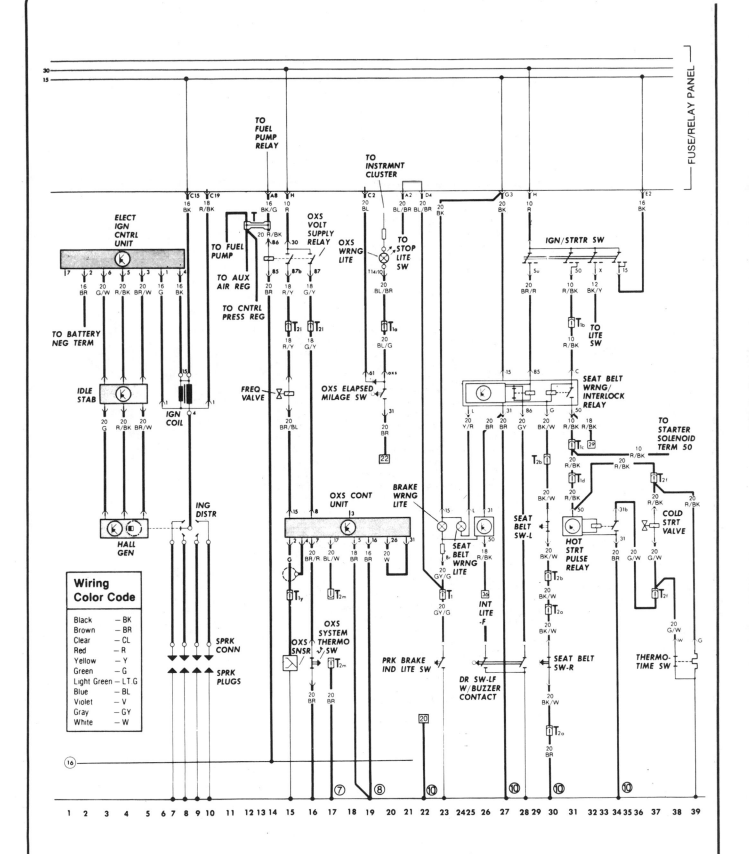

Fig. 9.59 Additional wiring diagram for oxygen sensor system (1981 Rabbit Convertible, Scirocco and Jetta, California models only). For key see page 318

Key to Fig. 9.60

Wire connectors

T1v   –   Single, behind dash
T1w   –   Single, behind dash
T2f   –   2 point, behind dash
T2h   –   2 point, behind dash

Ground connectors

⑩   –   On steering column

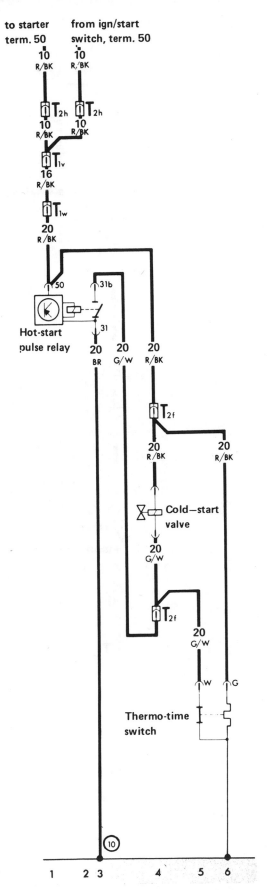

Fig. 9.60 Additional wiring diagram for hot start pulse relay. For key see page 320

Fig. 9.61 Additional wiring diagram for glove compartment light (1980 Jetta models)

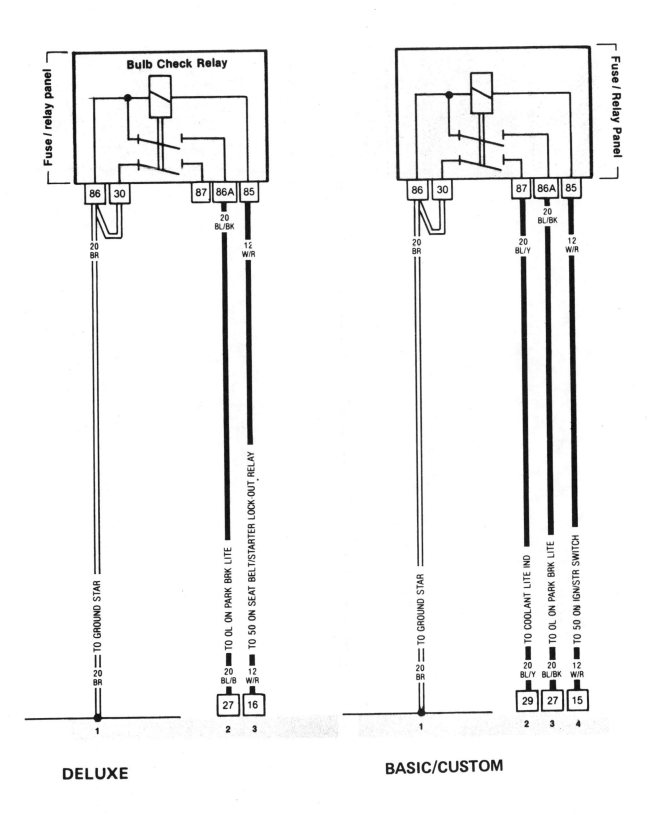

Fig. 9.62 Additional wiring diagram for bulb check circuit (1980 models). Relay is energized only while starter is activated

Key to Fig. 9.63

Description	Current track
Air conditioner fuse (25A)	310
Ambient temperature switch	312
Arc suppressor	310
Blower motor	308
Blower motor relay	308
Compressor clutch	312
On-off switch	312
Protective diode	313
Speed control switch	309
Speed control resistors	310
Thermostat	312
Vacuum retard valve	310

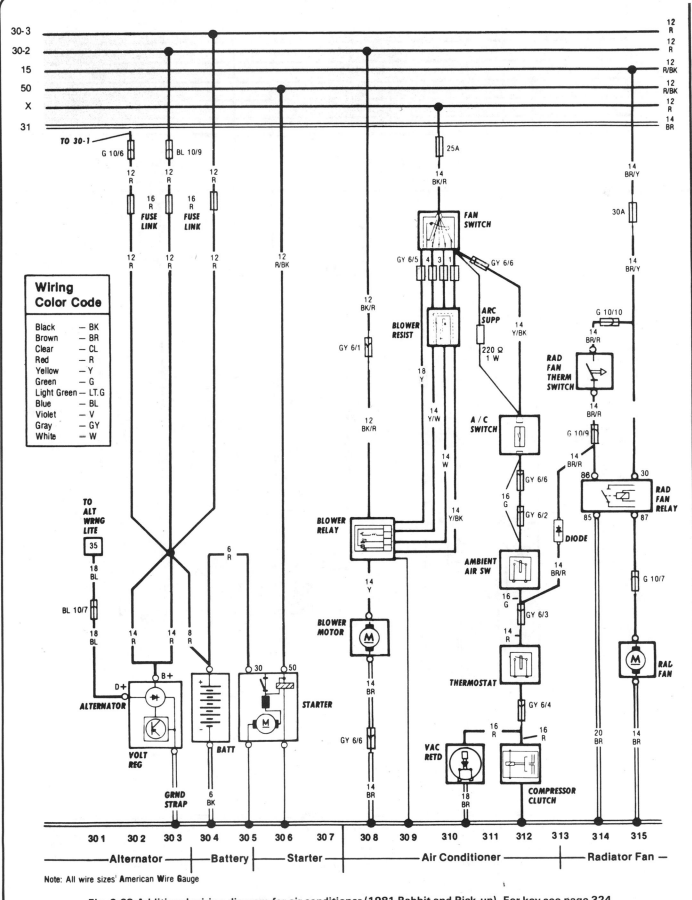

Fig. 9.63 Additional wiring diagram for air conditioner (1981 Rabbit and Pick-up). For key see page 324

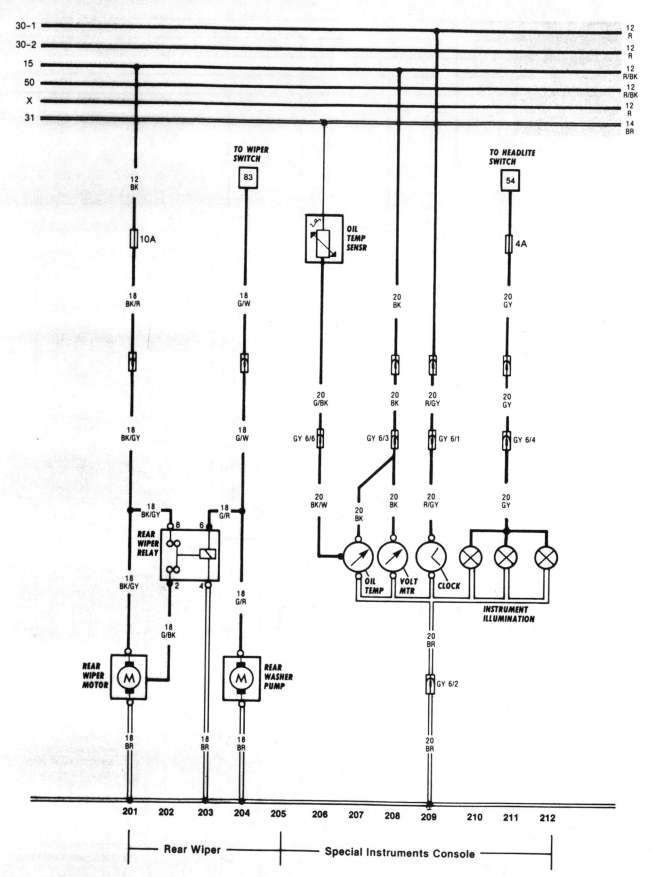

Fig. 9.64 Additional wiring diagram for rear wash/wipe and instrumentation (1981 Rabbit and Pick-up)

Key to Fig. 9.65

Wire connectors		Current track
T1a	– Single, vacant for optionals (on fuse relay panel)	3
T1b	– Single, in engine compartment, left side	6
T1c	– Single, in engine compartment, left side	5
T6a	– Six-point, behind instrument panel	1,2,4,5
T6b	– Six-point, behind instrument panel	1

Ground connectors

⑩	– On steering column support	1

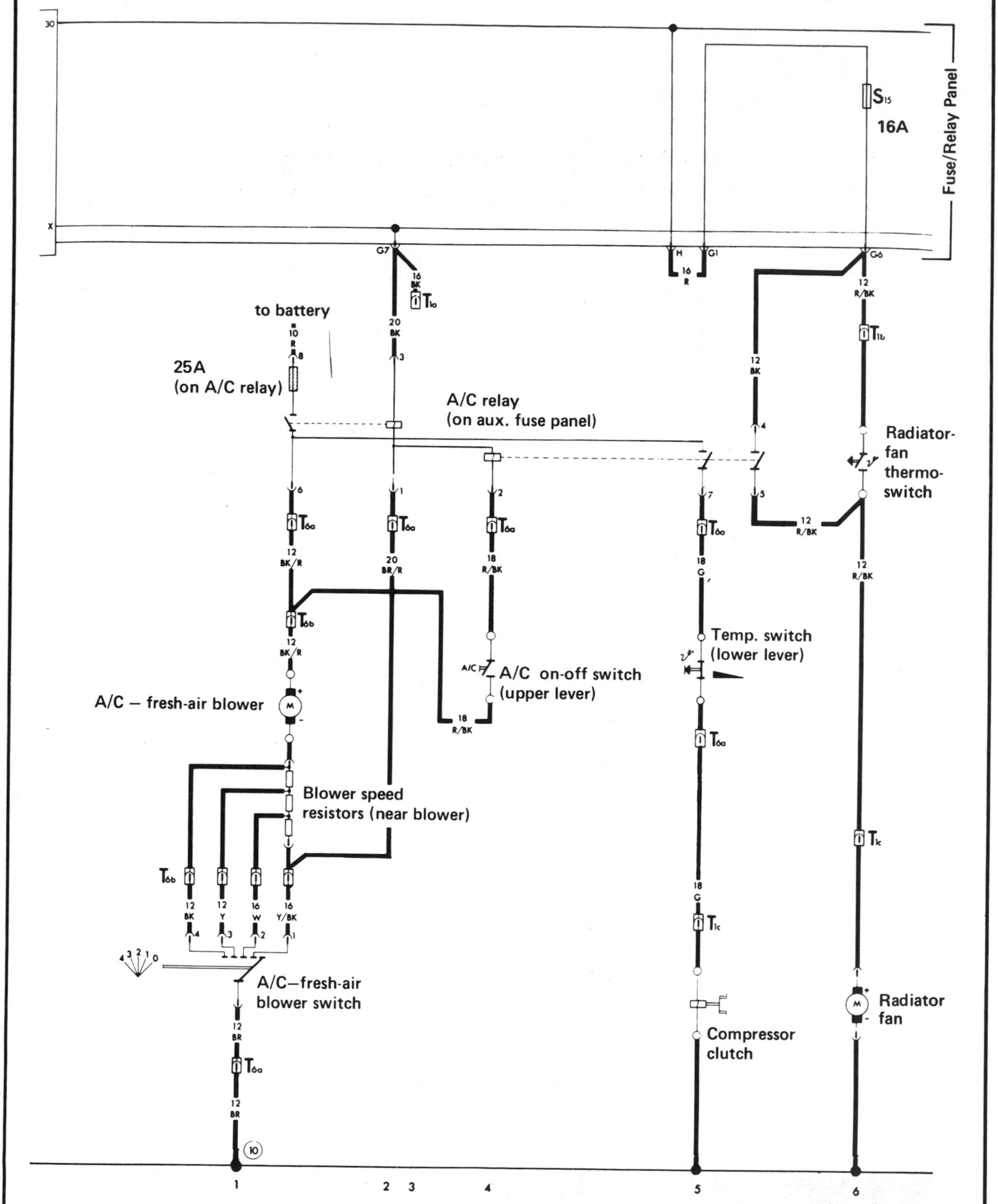

Fuse/Relay Panel

30

S₁₅
16A

X

G7

16
BK
T_{1a}

to battery

20
BK
3

10
R
8

25A
(on A/C relay)

A/C relay
(on aux. fuse panel)

16
R

G1

G6

12
R/BK
T_{1b}

12
BK

4

Radiator-
fan
thermo-
switch

6
T_{6a}

1
T_{6a}

2
T_{6a}

7
T_{6a}

5

12
R/BK

12
BK/R

20
BR/R

18
R/BK

18
G

12
R/BK

T_{6b}

12
BK/R

A/C — fresh-air blower

M

A/C
A/C on-off switch
(upper lever)

18
R/BK

Temp. switch
(lower lever)

T_{6a}

Blower speed
resistors (near blower)

T_{6b}

12
BK

12
Y

16
W

16
Y/BK

4   3   2   1

4 3 2 1 0

A/C—fresh-air
blower switch

12
BR

T_{6a}

12
BR

18
G
T_{1c}

Compressor
clutch

T_k

Radiator
fan

M

1   2   3   4   5   6

Fig. 9.65 Additional wiring diagram for air conditioner (1981 Rabbit Convertible, Scirocco and Jetta). For key see page 327

Chapter 10 Suspension and steering

For modifications and information applicable to later models, see Supplement at end of manual

Contents

Specifications

Front suspension

Type	Independent, MacPherson strut and lower wishbone, coaxial coil spring and integral telescopic double-acting shock absorber

Rear suspension

Type (except Pick-up)	Trailing arms and double spring leaf crossmember, MacPherson type strut, coaxial coil spring and integral shock absorber
Type (Pick-up)	Tubular dead axle, semi-elliptical leaf springs, and telescopic shock absorbers
Rear wheel camber (non-adjustable):	
All models with 81 kW engine	-1° 15′ ± 25′
Golf/Rabbit up to chassis No 176 3 241690 and Scirocco up to chassis No 536 2 031722	-1° ± 35′
Golf/Rabbit from chassis No 176 3 241691, Scirocco from chassis No 536 2 031723, and Jetta	-1° 15′ ± 35′
Pick-up	0° ± 1°
Maximum difference between sides	40′
Rear wheel toe-in (non-adjustable):	
All models with 81 kW engine	+20′ ± 20′
Golf/Rabbit up to chassis No 176 3 241690 and Scirocco up to chassis No 536 2 031722	+10′ ± 30′
Golf/Rabbit from chassis No 176 3 241691, Scirocco from chassis No 536 2 031723, and Jetta	+20′ ± 20′
Pick-up	0° ± 1°
Maximum deviation from alignment	30′

Steering

Type	Rack-and-pinion
Overall ratio	17.32:1
Steering wheel turns, lock-to-lock	3.5
Camber – wheels straight-ahead:	
Except 81 kW models	+20′ ± 30′
Maximum difference between sides	1°
81 kW models	+20′ ± 20′
Maximum difference between sides	30′
Castor (non-adjustable)	1° 50′ ± 30′
Maximum difference between sides	1°
Toe-out	0.5 to 3 mm (0.020 to 0.118 in) or equivalent angles of 5′ to 30′

Wheels
Type .... Perforated steel disc, optional light alloy
Size .... 4½J x 13 or 5J x 13, alloy 5½J x 13

Tyres
Size .... 145 x 13, 155 x 13, 145SR x 13, 155SR x 13 78S, 175/70 HR/SR x 138 OH/S radial; 5.95 x 13, 6.15 x 13 crossply

Pressures – bar (psi)	Front	Rear
UK models:		
Half load	1.7 (24)	1.7 (24)
Full load	1.8 (26)	2.2 (31)
North American models:		
Half load	1.8 (26)	1.8 (26)
Full load (Jetta)	1.9 (28)	2.3 (33)
Full load (except Jetta)	1.8 (26)	2.1 (30)

Torque wrench settings

	lbf ft	Nm
Front suspension		
Strut to body	14	20
Strut bearing to piston rod	58	80
Wheel bearing housing to strut	58	80
Tie-rod to strut	22	30
Bottom balljoint to wheel bearing housing:		
M8	22	30
M10	36	50
Bottom balljoint to wishbone	18	25
Driveshaft nut:		
UK models	169	230
North American models	174	240
Front wishbone bolt	73	100
Rear wishbone bolt or nut	33	5
Anti-roll bar to wishbone	18	25
Rear suspension (except Pick-up)		
Shock absorber mounting – upper	25	35
Shock absorber mounting – lower	33	45
Spring upper seat to piston rod	14	20
Mounting to rear axle:		
UK models	51	70
North American models	43	60
Mounting to body	33	45
Anti-roll bar bracket	22	30
Rear suspension (Pick-up)		
Spring U-bolt	29	40
Shock absorber bolt	29	40
Spring front eyebolt	68	95
Spring shackle bolt	45	62
Wheels		
Wheel bolts	66	90
Steering		
UJ to steering gear	22	30
UJ to column	22	30
Steering wheel	36	50
Steering gear to body (to July 1977)	14	20
Steering gear to body (from August 1977)	22	30
Tie-rod to steering gear	29	40
Tie-rod locknut	36	50

1 General description

The front suspension is of independent MacPherson strut type, incorporating coil springs and integral shock absorbers.

The rear suspension, except on pick-up models, is of trailing arm type and the arms are connected at their front ends by a spring leaf crossmember. The rear ends incorporate mountings for the Mac-Pherson type struts.

On pick-up models the rear suspension comprises a tubular dead axle and two semi-elliptical leaf springs. Two telescopic shock absorbers are attached to the axle and body mountings.

The steering is of rack-and-pinion type, located behind the front wheels. The steering shaft, which connects the steering column to the steering gear, is located at an angle as a safety feature. If the steering gear is pushed back as the result of an accident, the angle of the shaft ensures that the steering column moves to one side instead of into the passenger compartment.

Some of the illustrations in this Chapter show left-hand drive components, in particular with reference to the steering gear. Unless otherwise stated, it can be assumed that right-hand drive components are similar.

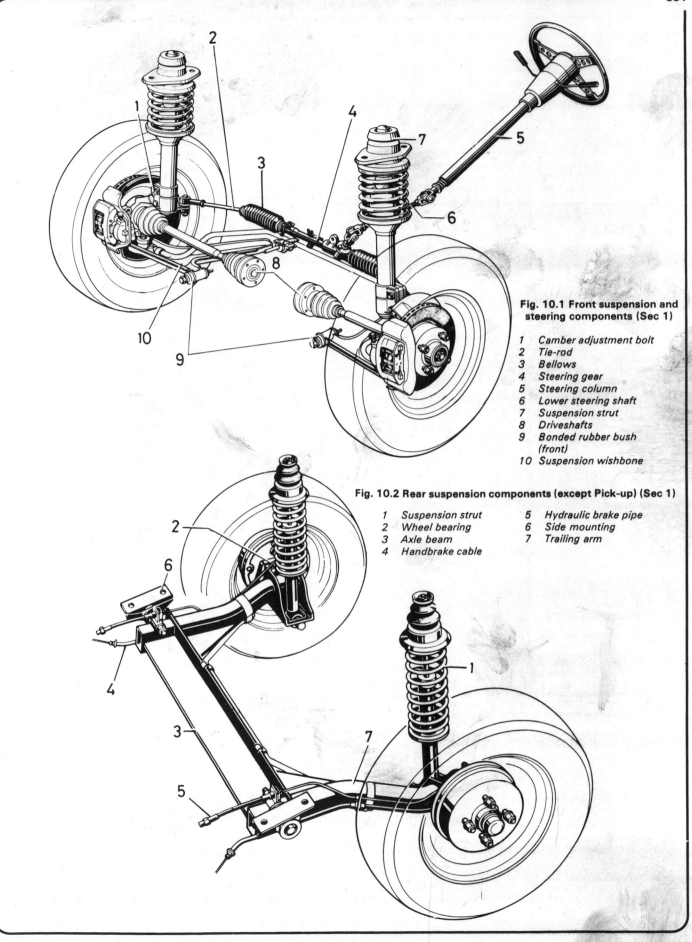

Fig. 10.1 Front suspension and steering components (Sec 1)

1   Camber adjustment bolt
2   Tie-rod
3   Bellows
4   Steering gear
5   Steering column
6   Lower steering shaft
7   Suspension strut
8   Driveshafts
9   Bonded rubber bush
    (front)
10 Suspension wishbone

Fig. 10.2 Rear suspension components (except Pick-up) (Sec 1)

1   Suspension strut   5   Hydraulic brake pipe
2   Wheel bearing   6   Side mounting
3   Axle beam   7   Trailing arm
4   Handbrake cable

2 Routine maintenance

1   At the specified intervals (see Routine Maintenance), the steering and suspension balljoints should be checked for wear. To do this, lever or pull the joint in and out – if the clearance exceeds 2.5 mm (0.098 in) on a suspension balljoint, or if there is any play at all on a steering tie-rod end, renew the balljoint.
2   At the same time check the balljoint dust covers and renew them if they are split.
3   Similarly check the bellows in the steering gear, and also check the steering gear free play – adjust if necessary as described in Section 27.
4   Frequently check the tyres for wear, damage and deterioration.

Renew any tyres which are worn below the legal limit. Tyre pressures should be checked weekly, or before a long journey.

3 Front suspension strut – removal and refitting

1   There are several ways in which the strut may be removed, depending on the reason for removal and the tools available. If it is possible to remove the component without disturbing the axle nut or the camber, so much the better.
2   If only the coil or shock absorber are to be removed, refer to paragraph 9.
3   Apply the handbrake, then jack up the front of the car and support it on axle stands. Remove the roadwheel. Remove the socket-headed

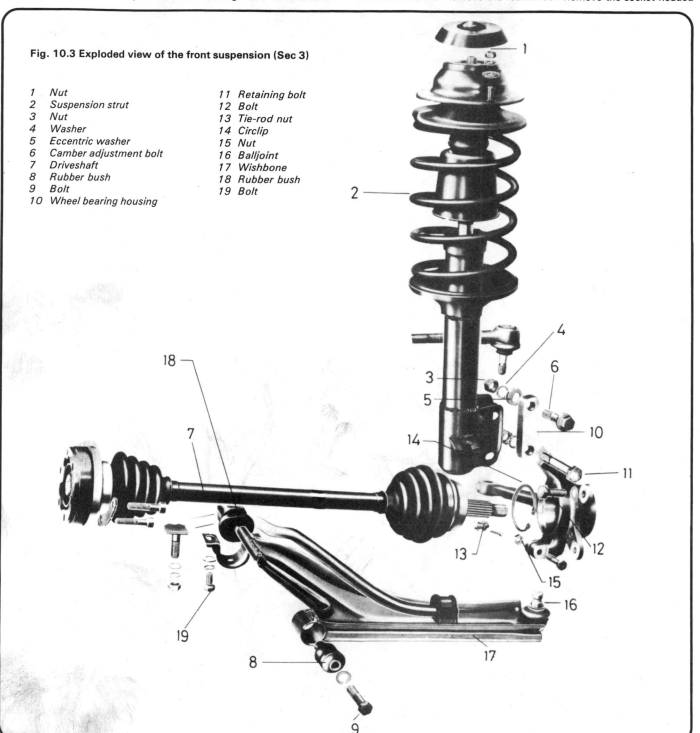

Fig. 10.3 Exploded view of the front suspension (Sec 3)

1   Nut
2   Suspension strut
3   Nut
4   Washer
5   Eccentric washer
6   Camber adjustment bolt
7   Driveshaft
8   Rubber bush
9   Bolt
10 Wheel bearing housing
11 Retaining bolt
12 Bolt
13 Tie-rod nut
14 Circlip
15 Nut
16 Balljoint
17 Wishbone
18 Rubber bush
19 Bolt

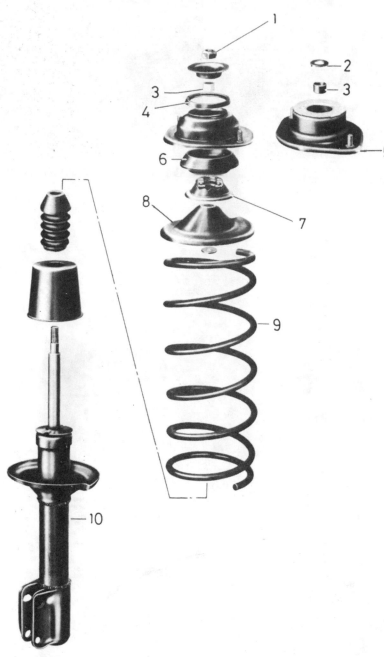

Fig. 10.4 Exploded view of the front suspension strut on pre-1980 models (Sec 3)

1   Nut
2   Washer
3   Spacer sleeve
4   End collar
5   Bearing
6   Rubber damper
7   Strut bearing
8   Spring seat
9   Coil spring
10 Shock absorber

bolts, disconnect the inner CV joint from the flange, and cover it with a polythene bag. Remove the brake caliper with reference to Chapter 8 and hang it to one side.

4   Remove the clamp bolt from the wheel bearing housing which holds the steering balljoint in place and separate the wishbone from the wheel bearing housing (photo). Undo the tie-rod securing nut and using a puller, break the tie-rod balljoint.

5   Remove the two nuts holding the top of the suspension strut to the bodyframe inside the engine compartment (photo). Lower the strut from the frame and take it away complete with driveshaft.

6   The coil spring must be held in compression while the top nut on the rod is removed. To do this, obtain a spring compressor from a tool hire agent or garage. The piston rod must be held while undoing the nut. On early models use an Allen key in the hexagonal hole in the top of the rod. On later models the rod has flats to fit a spanner.

7   Remove the coil spring and test the shock absorber as in Section 5.

8   If the shock absorber is to be removed then the camber angle must be upset. To be able to reassemble the strut with the correct camber angle proceed as follows. Locate the top bolt holding the shock absorber clamp to the wheel bearing housing. This is an eccentric bolt. Mark the relative position of the bolt head to the clamp by two centre-punch marks (photos). Unscrew the camber adjusting bolt and the lower bolt and remove them. Open the clamp with a lever and extract the shock absorber.

9   It is possible to extract the strut without undoing the driveshaft or wishbone. Remove the bolts from the clamp as in paragraph 8, disconnect the top of the strut from the body as in paragraph 5, prise the clamp apart and push the wheel bearing housing off the strut. Lower the strut and remove it (photo).

10   Assembly is the reverse of removal. Refit the shock absorber and coil spring to the wheel bearing housing. The spring must be compressed to start the securing nut. Torque the nut to the specified figure. Adjust the camber eccentric correctly. Push the top of the piston rod through the wing into the engine compartment and secure it correctly.

11   Refit the steering balljoint and wishbone to the wheel bearing housing, refit the tie-rod balljoint and then refit the driveshaft to the final drive.

12   If you removed the caliper this must be refitted. Refit the wheel and lower to the ground.

13   This may seem a lot of work but it does avoid struggling with the

3.4 Steering balljoint and clamp bolt location

3.5 Front suspension strut upper mounting nut locations (A)

3.8a Camber adjusting bolt (A) and centre-punch marks

3.8b Camber adjusting bolt components

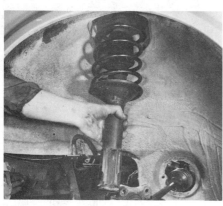

3.9 Removing the front suspension strut

Fig. 10.5 Exploded view of the front suspension strut on 1980 on models (Sec 3)

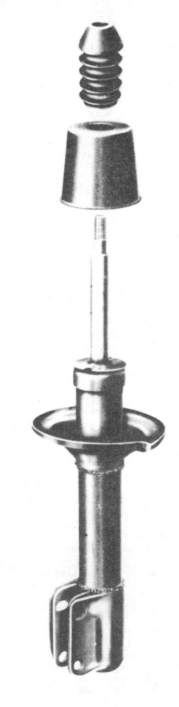

Fig. 10.6 Using a spring compressor on the front coil spring (Sec 3)

axle nut. If you removed the camber eccentric bolt have the camber angle checked to make sure you assembled the bolt correctly.

4 Front coil springs – inspection and renewal

1 If a rattling noise is heard from the coil spring on pre-November 1979 models, especially when travelling over rough ground, this may be due to the top and bottom coils moving in the seats. Where this occurs, obtain some special sleeving from a VW agent and fit it over the end coils of the spring.

2 When removed, the coil spring should be examined for damage, deterioration, and fractures. If possible compare its free length with a new spring. Renew the spring where necessary, but make sure the new spring is the correct one for the particular model.

3 As from November 1979 the upper end of the coil spring is turned in to form a smaller diameter, and the upper and lower spring seats are modified to accommodate the new spring. The coil springs are coded with paint spots and must only be renewed with springs of the identical code.

5 Front shock absorbers – inspection and renewal

1 A defective shock absorber will upset the steering and braking so

it should be attended to right away. Apart from steering and braking dificulties it usually complains audibly as it operates.

2 A quick and reliable test is done by pushing the car down on the front corner and releasing the pressure sudenly. The car should return to its correct level without oscillation. Any oscillation indicates that the shock absorber is empty.

3 A small leak may be discounted. Large leaks must be attended to at once.

4 The shock absorber removed from the suspension strut should be held by the cylinder body in a vice. Push the piston rod right down and then pull it right out. There should be a firm, even, resistance to movement throughout the stroke in both directions. If there is not then the unit is defective. If you are not sure take it to the VW agent and ask for it to be tested against a new one.

5 There is no repair, only renewal. It is not necessary to renew both shock absorbers if only one is faulty but it **must** be replaced by one of the same part number.

6 The method of removal and refitting is given in Section 3.

6 Front suspension wishbone (manual gearbox models) – removal, overhaul and refitting

1 Two patterns of wishbone have been fitted. On early models the steering balljoint was fastened to the wishbone by two M8 bolts and nuts. On later models the bolts were replaced by three 7 mm rivets. Replacement balljoints to the later types are fitted by drilling out the rivets with a 6 mm drill and fastening the new one in with three 7 mm bolts and nuts. If the old type needs a new balljoint then the outer holes of the new balljoint must be enlarged to 8.3 mm diameter and the joint fitted with two 8 mm bolts and nuts with spring washers.

2 Apart from fitting a new balljoint the pivot bushes may be renewed if worn. To do this properly the wishbone must be removed from the vehicle.

3 Accident damage to the wishbone may result in the camber angle being altered and rapid tyre wear. Check the underside for kinks and wrinkles and check that the front and profile sides are straight, using a straight-edge or an engineer's square (photo).

4 Although the wishbone may be removed with the roadwheel in place, it is easier and safer to support the vehicle on axle stands and remove the front wheel. Support the wheel hub with a jack. Undo the clamp bolt holding the steering balljoint to the wheel bearing housing, disconnect the anti-roll bar (where fitted), and lower the wishbone as far as possible. Remove the nuts or bolts holding the U-clip and rear pivot, hold the wishbone level and undo and extract the front hinge bolt. Remove the wishbone from the vehicle (photos).

5 The rubber bush at the rear may be pressed off and after the pivot has been cleaned up a new one tapped into place with a hammer.

6 The front bush is a little more difficult. The simple way to press out the bush is to use a two arm puller. Fit a 10 mm bolt through the bush from the inside surface and push on the bolt with the puller centre bolt as shown in the diagram (Fig. 10.7), so that the bush is driven out from the wishbone. Smear the bore with a little brake grease and push a new bush in from the outside. If the bush has three lugs on it, these must face the front of the car. When fully home, the bush protrudes past the bore of the wishbone so that the wishbone must be supported with a piece of tube large enough to allow the bush to slide inside it.

6.3 Checking the wishbone with a straight-edge

6.4a Suspension wishbone rear mounting

6.4b Suspension wishbone front mounting

6.4c The suspension wishbone

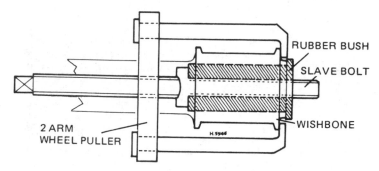

Fig. 10.7 Method of removing the front wishbone bush (Sec 6)

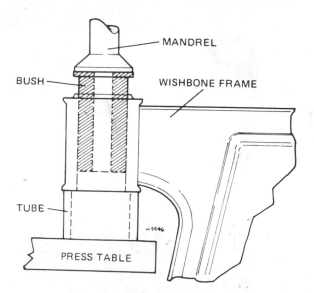

Fig. 10.8 Method of fitting the front wishbone bush (Sec 6)

A diagram shows this arrangement (Fig. 10.8).

7   With the older type of wishbone the steering balljoint may be removed, without disconnecting the wishbone from the vehicle, by unbolting it; the removal of the riveted version presents difficulties. It is possible to remove the rivets without dismantling the wishbone from the vehicle but it is equally possible to let the drill run out and enlarge the hole as well as remove the rivets. We recommend the removal of the wishbone and the drilling out accurately under a pillar drill with the

wishbone clamped in position on the drill table. Fit the new balljoint as described in paragraph 1.

8   When refitting the wishbone to the vehicle great care must be taken not to destroy the thread of the nut which holds the front hinge bolt in position. The bolt must be tightened to the specified torque. If this torque is not attainable then a new nut must be fitted and as the nut is welded **inside** the front crossmember the replacement of it is a major task only possible in a fully equipped workshop by professionals who have the right equipment. It involves opening up of the front crossmember – you have been warned! VW recommend the use of a new bolt with a lockwasher fitted under its head.

9   Before installing the wishbone try the new bolt in the nut. Make sure it screws in easily. Remove it and position the wishbone in the correct place. Install the U-clip for the back hinge but do not tighten it. Next try the front bolt and ease the wishbone until the bolt engages the thread in the nut easily. Keep the wishbone in that position, remove the bolt, fit the washer and install the bolt. Tighten to the specified torque and then adjust the back bearing again. Check that the wishbone moves easily about the hinge bolts. Then tighten the rear hinge clip bolts or nuts. Check that the wishbone moves easily about the hinge bolts with no tight spots.

10 Finally refit the steering balljoint to the wheel bearing housing, and the anti-roll bar (where fitted) to the wishbone. Remove the jack from under the housing, refit the wheel and lower the vehicle to the ground.

7   Front suspension wishbone (automatic transmission models) – removal, overhaul and refitting

1   On automatic transmission models the front pivot bolt on the left-hand side wishbone is not accessible without carrrying out the following work. Proceed generally as in Section 6 to the point where the front pivot bolt is to be removed.

2   Support the engine, either with a hoist or beam from above, or with a jack below (use wooden packing) and remove the front left mounting, the securing nut for the rear mounting and the engine steadying strut (the front one). Now lift the engine until the front wishbone bolt may be removed.

3   Refitting is a reversal of the removal procedure.

8   Front wheel bearing housing – removal and refitting

1   Unscrew the axle nut with the car on the ground, then jack up the front of the car and support it on axle stands. Apply the handbrake and remove the roadwheel.

2   Disconnect the steering tie-rod balljoint with reference to Section 23.

3   Unscrew the clamp bolt, then push the wishbone and balljoint from the wheel bearing housing.

4   Remove the brake caliper and suspend it out of the way, referring to Chapter 8. Unscrew the cross-head screw and withdraw the brake disc.

5   At this point there is a choice of procedure. Either remove the strut complete by unscrewing the upper mounting nuts, or unbolt the wheel bearing housing from the strut. If the latter method is used, mark the camber adjusting bolt for position before removing it, then pull the housing from the driveshaft splines.

6   Refitting is a reversal of removal, but fit a new axle nut and tighten it to the specified torque. Bleed the brakes if the hydraulic line was disconnected, and have the camber angle adjusted if the wheel bearing housing was separated from the strut.

9   Front wheel bearings – renewal

1   Remove the front wheel bearing housing as described in Section 8.

2   Using a press, force the hub out of the wheel bearings. If a press is not available use a suitable size shouldered drift, but take care not to damage the hub splines.

3   Unbolt the backplate from the wheel bearing housing.

4   Using a two-legged puller, pull the bearing inner track from the hub.

5   Extract the circlips from the wheel bearing housing, then press out the bearing outer track.

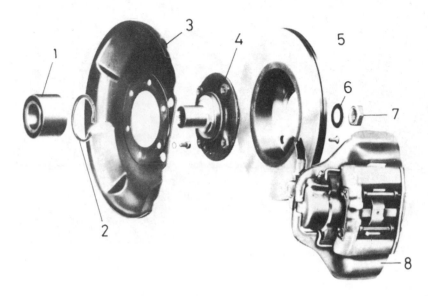

Fig. 10.9 Front hub and wheel bearing components (Sec 9)

1 Wheel bearing
2 Circlip
3 Backplate
4 Hub
5 Disc
6 Thrust washer
7 Axle nut
8 Brake caliper

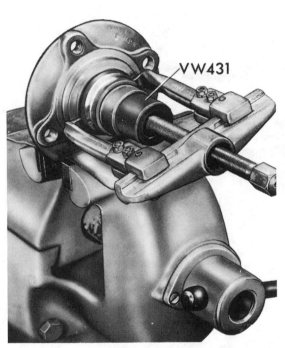

Fig. 10.10 Removing the wheel bearing inner race (Sec 9)

10.4 Anti-roll bar (rear) mounting clamp

6 Clean all components with paraffin and wipe dry. The bearing must not be re-used and should therefore be discarded.
7 Insert the outer circlip in the wheel bearing housing, then press in the bearing using a metal tube on its outer track. Insert the inner circlip.
8 Place the hub upright and locate the wheel bearing housing on top with its inner face upwards.
9 Using a metal tube on the inner track, press the bearing fully onto the hub.
10 Refit the wheel bearing housing as described in Section 8.

10 Anti-roll bar – removal and refitting

1 Jack up the front or rear of the car and support it on axle stands. Apply the handbrake or chock the front roadwheels as applicable.
2 On the front anti-roll bar, disconnect the mountings from the suspension wishbones.
3 On the rear anti-roll bar, bend down the tabs and tap off the

retaining clips located on the ends of the bar beneath the trailing arms. Remove the straps and mounting rubbers.
4 On both front and rear anti-roll bars, unbolt the mountings and withdraw the anti-roll bar (photo).
5 Examine the components for wear and damage, in particular the mounting rubbers, and renew them as necessary.
6 Refitting is a reversal of removal.

11 Rear wheel bearings – adjustment

1 Jack up the rear of the car and support it on axle stands. Chock the front wheels and release the handbrake.
2 Lever off the dust cap, remove the split pin, and withdraw the nut locking ring (photo).
3 Slacken the hub nut, then tighten it while turning the wheel to settle the bearings.
4 Now slacken off the hub nut again, then tighten it until the thrust washer can be removed slightly with a screwdriver (photo). **Do not twist or lever the screwdriver to obtain movement.**
5 Refit the nut locking ring and a new split pin.
6 Half fill the dust cap with lithium-based grease and tap it into position on the hub.
7 Lower the car to the ground.

11.2 Removing rear wheel bearing dust cap

11.4 Checking rear wheel bearing adjustment

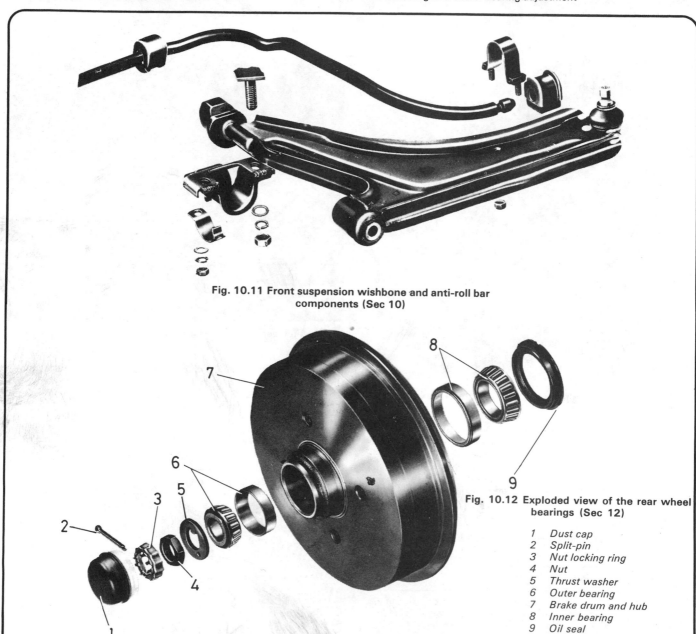

Fig. 10.11 Front suspension wishbone and anti-roll bar components (Sec 10)

Fig. 10.12 Exploded view of the rear wheel bearings (Sec 12)

1 Dust cap
2 Split-pin
3 Nut locking ring
4 Nut
5 Thrust washer
6 Outer bearing
7 Brake drum and hub
8 Inner bearing
9 Oil seal

12.2a Rear wheel bearing split pin and locking ring

12.2b Rear wheel bearing adjusting nut

12.3a Removing a rear wheel bearing oil seal

12.3b Removing the inner rear wheel bearing outer track

12.3c Removing the outer rear wheel bearing outer track

12.8 Installing the outer rear wheel bearing and thrust washer

12 Rear wheel bearings – removal and refitting

1   Slacken the wheel bolts, jack up the rear wheel, support the vehicle on an axle stand and remove the wheel.
2   Remove the hub grease cap, remove the split pin and locking ring (photo). Undo the adjusting nut (photo). Slacken the brake adjusters (Chapter 8), and remove the brake drum. The thrust washer and the outer bearing complete will come away with the drum together with the oil seal and the inner bearing.
3   Remove the oil seal and tap the bearings out of the brake drum with a drift (photos). Clean the drum and stub axle and oil them lightly. Wash the bearings in clean paraffin and then swill out all residue with more clean paraffin. Dry them carefully with a non-fluffy rag.
4   Examine the tracks of the races for scoring or signs of overheating. If these are present then the complete bearing should be renewed. Inspect the roller bearings carefully, there should be no flats or burrs. Spin the inner race in the outer race. Any roughness indicates undue wear and the bearing should be renewed. Once a bearing begins to wear the wear accelerates rapidly and may be the cause of damage to the stub axle or drum so if you are in doubt get an expert opinion.
5   Examine the oil seal; if there is any damage or sign of hardening renew it anyway. Failure of an oil seal will mean contamination of the brake shoes and the minimum penalty will be new shoes on **both** rear wheels.
6   If all the items are correct and the stub axle bearing surfaces and brake drum bore are in good order then proceed to assemble the hub.
7   Pack the taper bearings with a lithium-based grease, and smear the stub axle with a light film of grease. Fit the inner race, the inner bearing and the oil seal into the brake drum. Press the seal into place, tap it home with a rubber hammer taking care that it is squarely seated.
8   Fit the drum to the stub axle then the outer race and finally the thrust washer (photo). Fit the nut and adjust the bearing as in Section 11. Fit the locking ring and a new split pin. Refit the dust cap, refit the wheel and test the bearing by spinning the wheel. Lower the vehicle to the ground.

13 Rear stub axle (except Pick-up) – removal, inspection and refitting

1   Apart from scoring on the bearing surface or ovality due to excessive bearing wear, the only other defect to check on the stub axle is distortion due to bending. This could happen if the vehicle has been in an accident or has been driven heavily laden at excessive speed over rough ground.
2   The effect of a bent stub axle will be excessive tyre wear due to the wrong camber angle and possibly incorrect toe-in. These angles are small with fine limits and, in our opinion, not measurable without the proper equipment. If irregular tyre wear occurs the owner is advised to have these angles checked right away.
3   Alternatively the stub axle may be removed, bolted to a lathe face plate and checked for alignment with a dial gauge. The allowable run-out is 0.25 mm (0.010 in).
4   To remove the stub axle proceed as in Section 12 and remove the brake drum and bearings. The brake backplate and stub axle are held to the axle beam by four bolts. These may only be accessible after the brake shoes have been removed (see Chapter 8). Remove the shoes if necessary and then the four bolts. The backplate and wheel cylinder may be moved out of the way to extract the stub axle (photo). If necessary, disconnect the brake line from the wheel cylinder and plug it to prevent leakage of hydraulic fluid.
5   Refitting is a reversal of removal, but make sure that the joint faces of the stub axle and axle beam are clean and free from burrs before assembly. Bleed the brakes as described in Chapter 8 if the brake line has been disconnected.

14 Rear suspension strut (except Pick-up) – removal and refitting

1   Open the boot lid or tailgate and lift the parcel shelf (as applicable). On each side of the body on top of the wheel arches are plastic caps. Remove these to reveal the upper anchorage nuts of the suspension struts (photo).

13.4 Removing the rear stub axle from the backplate

14.1 Rear suspension strut upper mounting (Jetta)

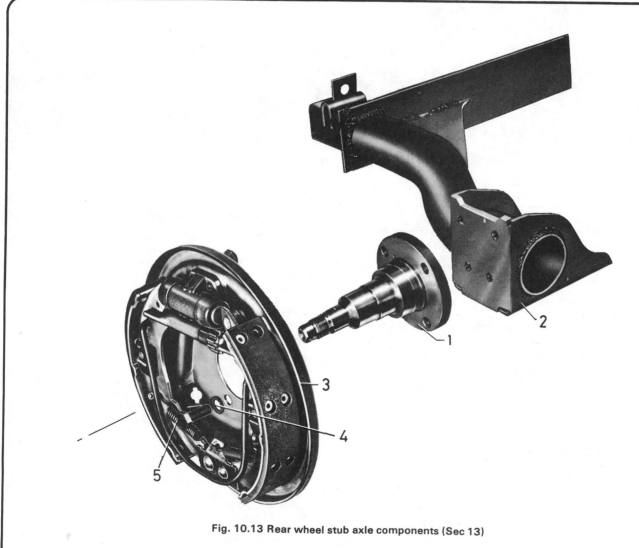

Fig. 10.13 Rear wheel stub axle components (Sec 13)

1   Stub axle
2   Axle beam
3   Backplate
4   Spring washer
5   Retaining bolt

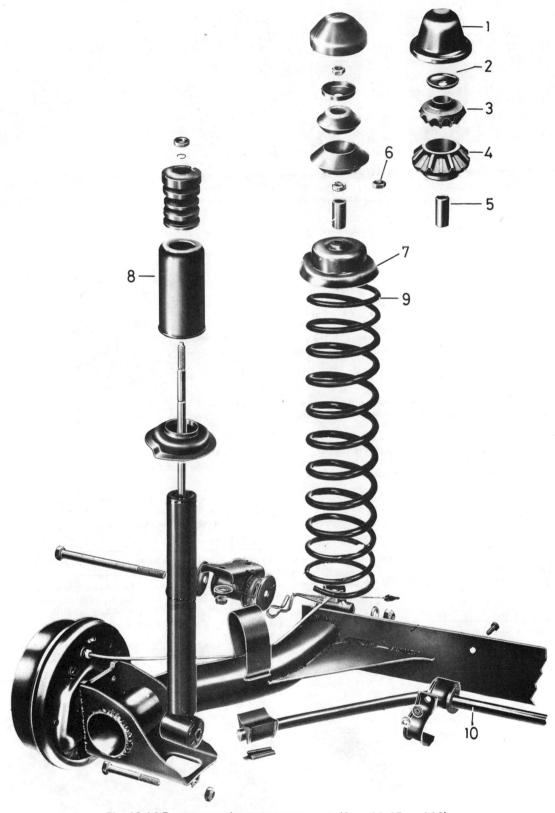

Fig. 10.14 Rear suspension strut components (Secs 14, 15, and 16)
Note: *Items 1 to 6 are fitted to 1978 on models*

1	Plastic cap	5	Spacer sleeve	8	Protective tube
2	Plate	6	Alternative hexagon nut	9	Coil spring
3	Upper bush	7	Spring cap	10	Anti-roll bar
4	Lower bush				

14.3 Rear suspension strut lower mounting

14.4a Removing the rear suspension strut

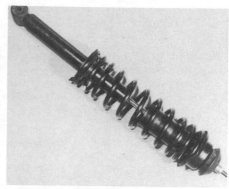

14.4b The rear suspension strut

2   Lift the rear of the vehicle and support the body on axle stands. The best place for this is the recommended lifting place just forward of the wheel.

3   Remove the nut from the bolt holding the shock absorber to the trailing arm and tap out the bolt (photo). It may be necessary to take the weight of the hub to extract this bolt. If the bolt fouls the brake drum then the brake backplate must be removed (Section 13).

4   Once the bottom anchorage is clear, remove the nut holding the top of the shock absorber piston inside the body and lower the suspension strut (photos). This needs two people; one to undo the nut and one to hold the strut. Note the location of the upper washer and bushes.

5   Refitting is a reversal of the removal procedure.

15 Rear suspension strut (except Pick-up) – dismantling and reassembly

1   The spring is held in compression by a special slotted nut (an ordinary nut may be found instead on some models). It is not necessary to clamp the spring with a compressor – mount the strut in a vice as shown in Fig. 10.15.

2   If the special slotted nut is fitted, a corresponding tool will be required to remove it.

3   Unscrew the nut while holding the shock absorber piston rod stationary with a spanner.

4   Withdraw the spacer, upper seat, and coil spring.

5   Remove the washer and circlip from the piston rod, followed by the rubber buffer and protective tube.

6   Reassembly is a reversal of dismanting, but tighten the upper nut to the specified torque.

16 Rear shock absorbers (except Pick-up) – inspection and renewal

1   A defective shock absorber usually makes a rumbling noise as the car goes over rough surfaces. A quick test to confirm this suspicion is to press the rear of the car down on the suspected side and release it sharply. The car should rise and settle at once, if it oscillates at all the shock absorber is not working correctly. A small leakage of fluid round the piston seal is normal and need cause no worry, but a large leakage indicates that the shock absorber must be changed. There is no repair possible.

2   Remove and dismantle the suspension strut as in Sections 14 and 15. Hold the lower portion of the shock absorber in a vice with the piston rod in a vertical position. Pull the rod right up and press it down again. The force required in each direction should be even and equal. Repeat this test several times. If the stroke is uneven or jerky then the unit must be replaced with a new one.

3   Examine the lower anchorage. The bush must be a good fit on the locating bolt, and the rubber mounting in good condition. If either of these are faulty, enquire whether a new bush and mounting are available from the VW stores. Should this be so get a new locating bolt at the same time. Press the bush out of the eye with a little rubber grease or soap before pressing the mounting home and be careful to enter it squarely. This must be done on a flypress or in a large vice, do

Fig. 10.15 Rear suspension strut mounted in a vice, showing holding flats (arrowed) and special tool (Sec 15)

not attempt to hammer it in. Alternatively, an arrangement of a draw bolt with a nut and two large washers may be used.

4   Refit the shock absorber with reference to Sections 14 and 15.

17 Rear axle (except Pick-up) – removal and refitting

1   If the rear axle beam is distorted the entire rear suspension must be removed. It is not possible to remove the pivot bolts from the mountings as the bolts foul the body (photo).

2   Support the vehicle body on axle stands and remove the rear

17.1 Rear axle pivot and mounting (except Pick-up)

wheels. Remove the brake drums and dismantle the brake shoes to free the handbrake cables (Chapter 8). Unclip the handbrake outer cables from the trailing arms.

3 Disconnect the hydraulic brake lines and plug the hoses to prevent dirt or grit entering the system.

4 Support the rear axle with a jack, then unscrew the mounting nuts. If you have the misfortune to shear one of the studs then the stud must be drilled out and the resultant hole tapped for a 10 mm thread. Use an 8 mm drill and be careful to drill exactly in the centre of the stud. We advise caution. Unless you have experience in this type of work get a trained mechanic to do it for you. If you drill in the wrong place, the result will be very expensive. After tapping the hole fit a 10 mm bolt x 40, tensile class 10.9.

5 Working inside the car, remove the caps and unscrew the strut upper mounting nuts – have an assistant support the trailing arms at the same time.

6 Lower the rear axle to the ground and withdraw it from under the car.

7 Unscrew the hinge bolts and remove the mountings from the rear axle, noting the location of the washers. Remove the handbrake cable clips if necessary.

8 Remove the anti-roll bar (if fitted), stub axles and struts if necessary, with reference to the relevant Section of this Chapter.

9 Refitting is a reversal of removal, but before tightening the mounting pivot bolts refer to Fig. 10.16. Remember to adjust the handbrake and bleed the hydraulic system as described in Chapter 8.

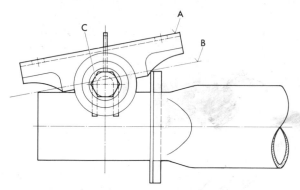

Fig. 10.16 Rear axle pivot bush tightening diagram (Sec 17)
Edge 'A' to be parallel with line 'B' before tightening nut 'C'

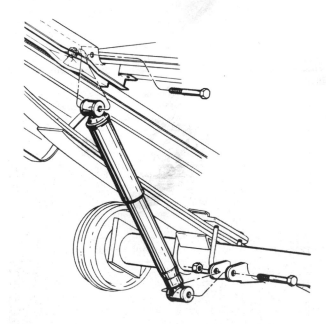

Fig. 10.17 Pick-up rear shock absorber and mountings (Sec 18)

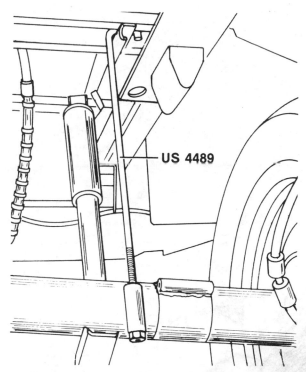

Fig. 10.18 Pick-up rear axle support tool (Sec 18)

18 Rear shock absorber (Pick-up) – inspection and renewal

1 Check the shock absorber with reference to Section 16, paragraph 1.

2 To remove the shock absorber, jack up the rear of the vehicle and support it on axle stands.

3 Note that the mounting bolt heads face inward, then unscrew the nuts, remove the bolts, and withdraw the shock absorber. If necessary make a tool similar to that shown in Fig. 10.18 to tension the springs before removing the shock absorber.

4 To test the shock absorber, mount it vertically in a vice and move the upper section fully up and down. If the resistance is uneven the shock absorber is faulty and must be renewed.

5 Check the mounting bushes for wear and deterioration, and if evident renew the complete unit.

6 Refitting is a reversal of removal.

19 Rear spring (Pick-up) – removal and refitting

1 Jack up the rear of the vehicle and support it with axle stands placed beneath the body. Chock the front wheels and use a trolley jack to support the end of the axle.

2 Detach the handbrake cable from the spring bracket and cut the support strap.

3 Unscrew and remove the shock absorber lower mounting bolt.

4 Unscrew the U-bolt nuts. Withdraw the U-bolts from the axle, and the spring plate from the spring. Note the location of the spring plate.

5 Loosen the upper and lower shackle bolt nuts. Note that the bolt heads face in opposite directions.

6 If the left-hand side spring is being removed, remove the rear exhaust system with reference to Chapter 3.

7 Support the spring, then remove the lower shackle bolt and the front spring bolt. Withdraw the spring from the vehicle.

8 Examine the spring for wear and damage, and renew it if necessary. Check the front mounting and the rear shackle bushes. To remove and fit a front bush use two piece of metal tubing, a long bolt and a nut, or alternatively a press.

9 Refitting is a reversal of removal, but delay tightening the mounting nuts until the weight of the vehicle is on the spring. Make sure the the spring location pin enters the hole in the axle mounting bracket.

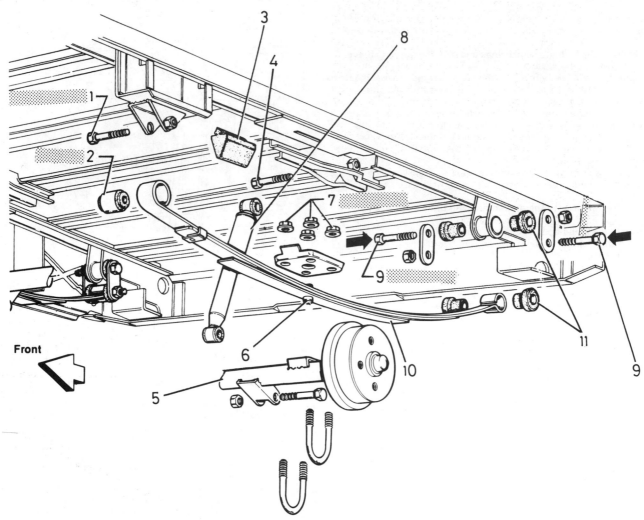

Fig. 10.19 Pick-up rear spring components (Sec 19)

1	Front spring bolt	4	Bolt
2	Mounting bush	5	Rear axle
3	Bump stop	6	Centre pin

7	Nuts	10	Rear spring
8	Shock absorber	11	Bushes
9	Shackle bolts		

20 Rear axle (Pick-up) – removal and refitting

1   Jack up the rear of the vehicle and support it with axle stands placed beneath the body. Chock the front wheels and use a trolley jack to support the axle.

2   Disconnect the handbrake cable at the handbrake lever with reference to Chapter 8.

3   Detach the handbrake cables from the side-members and the spring brackets. Remove the cable straps and pull the cables from the tube leading to the lever.

4   Unhook the brake cable equalizer spring, noting its location.

5   Where possible, remove the brake fluid reservoir filler cap and tighten it down onto a piece of polythene sheet – this will reduce the loss of hydraulic fluid in the subsequent procedure.

6   Disconnect and plug the hydraulic brake line from the rear axle.

7   Unscrew the brake equalizer pivot bolt, and remove the brake hose bracket from the axle.

8   Unscrew and remove the shock absorber lower mounting bolts.

9   Unscrew the U-bolt nuts and withdraw the U-bolts from the axle and the spring plates from the springs. Note the location of the spring plates.

10 Support the axle, then lower the trolley jack. Withdraw the rear axle from under the vehicle.

11 If necessary remove the brake shoes from the rear axle with reference to Chapter 8.

12 Refitting is a reversal of removal, but delay tightening the

mounting nuts until the weight of the vehicle is on the springs. Make sure that the spring location pins enter the holes in the axle mounting brackets. Bleed the brakes and adjust the handbrake as described in Chapter 8.

21 Steering wheel – removal and refitting

1   Disconnect the battery earth lead to avoid accidental short-circuits. The horn pad pulls off, after a struggle, to expose the steering column nut. Disconnect the lead, undo the nut and pull the wheel off the splines (photo). Do not thump the steering wheel.

2   When refitting the wheel be careful to install the wheel in the central position with the roadwheels straight-ahead.

3   Do not forget to reconnect the battery earth lead.

22 Steering column – removal, overhaul and refitting

1   One of three types of steering column may be fitted as shown in Figs. 10.20, 10.21 and 10.22. The early type is secured rigidly, but on later models the bottom of the column is retained to the pedal bracket by a leaf spring which is displaced in the event of an accident, enabling the steering shaft to move sideways. This arrangement was again improved on later models by adding a collapsible inner column.

2   To remove the column first disconnect the battery negative lead and remove the steering wheel as described in Section 21.

21.1 Removing the steering wheel nut

3   Where fitted, remove the panel from the bottom of the steering column.

4   Remove the steering column switches as described in Chapter 9, then prise out the spacer sleeve.

5   On models with a column incorporating a lower mounting bracket, remove the pedal connections (for the clutch pedal refer to Chapter 5 and for the brake pedal refer to Chapter 8).

6   On models with a column incorporating a leaf spring, depress the retaining spring with a screwdriver and withdraw the leaf spring.

7   On all models remove the nuts or bolts from the mounting brackets. Where shear head bolts have been fitted, it will be necessary to drill off the heads and unscrew the threaded portions, or use a centre punch to unscrew them.

8   Unscrew the nut and remove the bolt clamping the universal joint to the steering column. Remove the steering column and tube from the car.

9   To remove the column shaft from the tube, first remove the spring and spring seat, then extract the shaft from the top of the tube. If the steering column bearing has to be renewed, it can be pushed out and a new bearing pressed in. If necessary prise the spacer sleeve from the top of the column using a screwdriver, and remove the mounting ring from the outer column.

10   Clean all the components and examine them for wear and damage, renewing them as necessary.

11   Refitting is a reversal of removal. Where a mounting ring is fitted to the outer column, heat it in hot water and press it onto the bottom of the inner column until it is 31 mm (1.2 in) from the end of the column.

12   Where a slotted bush is fitted to the outer column, make sure that the lug is engaged in the hole in the column – tap it in with a hammer if necessary.

13   Press on the top spacer sleeves until the distance from the top of the column to the top of the spacer sleeve is 41.5 mm (1.63 in). This will set the gap between the steering wheel and the column switch at 2 to 4 mm (0.08 to 0.16 in). Fig. 10.23 shows the measurement. Tighten the shear bolts until the heads break off.

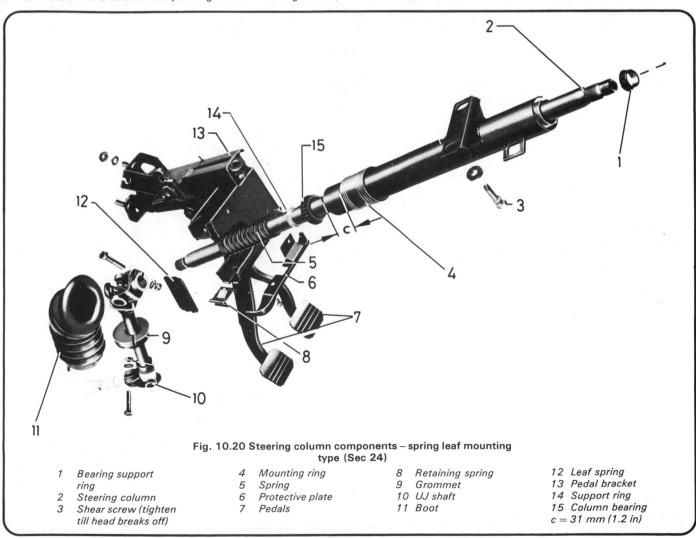

Fig. 10.20 Steering column components – spring leaf mounting type (Sec 24)

1 Bearing support ring	4 Mounting ring	8 Retaining spring	12 Leaf spring
2 Steering column	5 Spring	9 Grommet	13 Pedal bracket
3 Shear screw (tighten till head breaks off)	6 Protective plate	10 UJ shaft	14 Support ring
	7 Pedals	11 Boot	15 Column bearing

c = 31 mm (1.2 in)

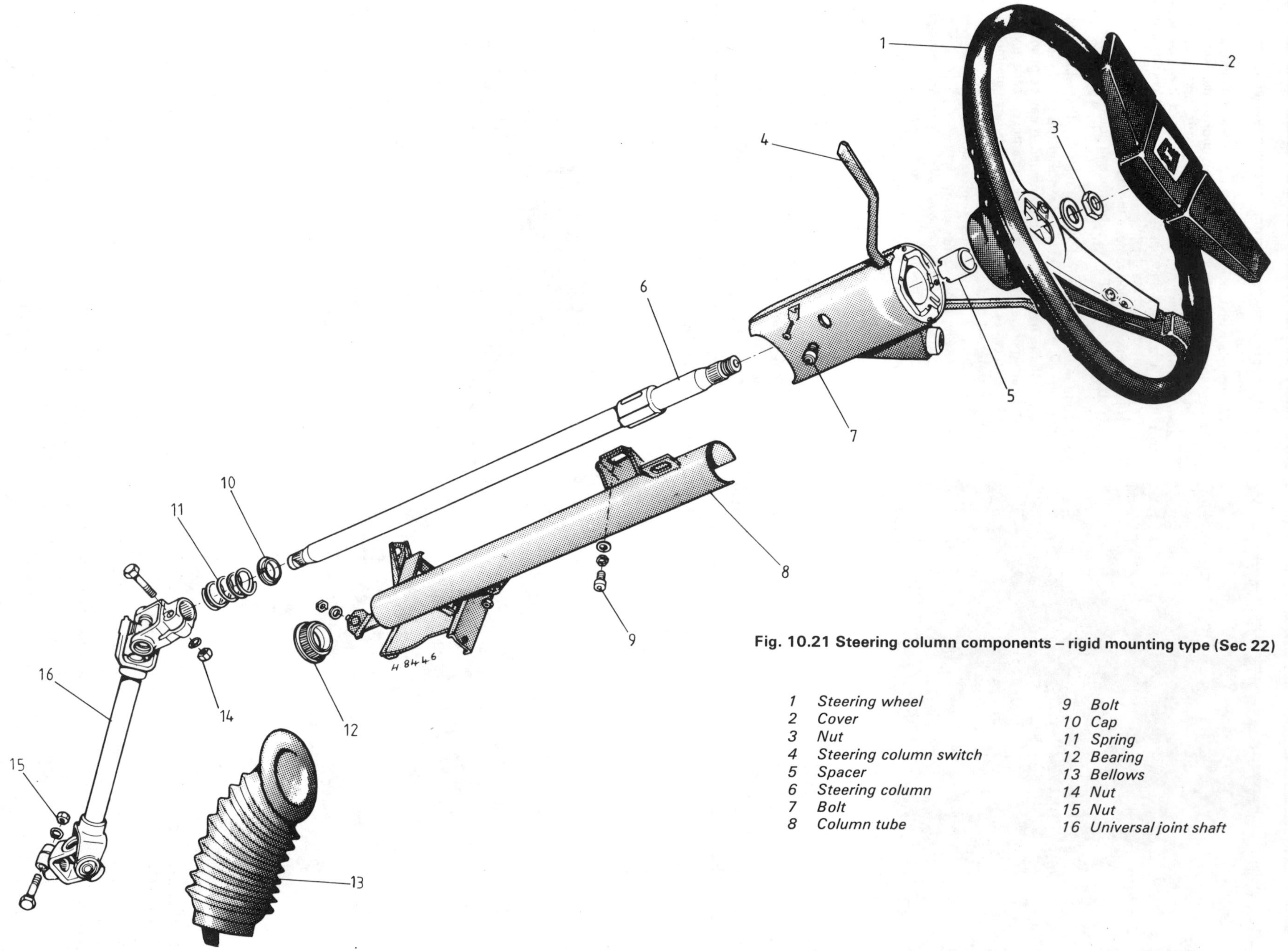

Fig. 10.21 Steering column components – rigid mounting type (Sec 22)

1 Steering wheel	9 Bolt
2 Cover	10 Cap
3 Nut	11 Spring
4 Steering column switch	12 Bearing
5 Spacer	13 Bellows
6 Steering column	14 Nut
7 Bolt	15 Nut
8 Column tube	16 Universal joint shaft

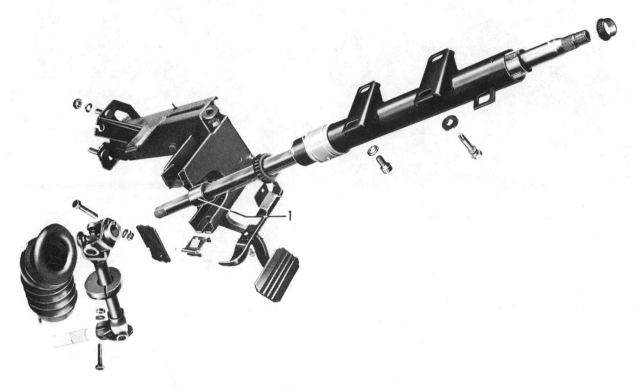

Fig. 10.22 Steering column components – telescopic type (Sec 22)

1   Bush

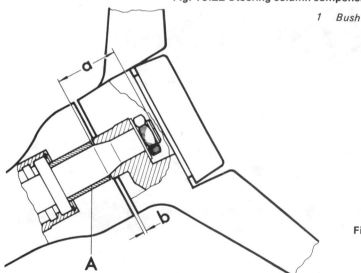

Fig. 10.23 Steering column spacer sleeve (A) adjustment
dimensions (Sec 22)

a = 41.5 mm (1.63 in)   b = 2.0 to 4.0 mm (0.08 to 0.16 in)

Fig. 10.24 Slotted bush (1) fitted to steering column (2) on 1976
on models (Sec 22)
Arrow shows slot in column over which the bush is fitted

23 Tie-rod end balljoint – removal and refitting

1   On new vehicles the left-hand tie-rod is made in one piece and is
not adjustable. The right-hand one is made of two pieces which screw
together so that its length may be altered to adjust the wheel
alignment.
2   When a new tie-rod is required to replace the left-hand rod the
solid type is not supplied, an adjustable one is provided which must be
adjusted to suit the length of the original solid rod.
3   The tie-rods must be positioned correctly on the steering gear
rack. To check this they must first be removed and the rack positioned
centrally so that it protrudes equally from each side of the casing. Note

that the pinion end datum is the back (inside) of the flange.
4   When the rack is correctly set the tie-rods should be screwed on
to the dimensions given in paragraph 8 below (photo). Once the rods
are set to the correct dimension the locknuts should be tightened and
the rubber gaiters fitted in position.
5   The outer ends of the tie-rods are attached to the steering arms by
balljoints (photo). These joints are pre-packed with lubricant. If the
rubber seal perishes and the balljoint becomes worn, a new tie-rod end
must be fitted (on original left-hand side rods the complete rod must
be renewed).
6   To renew a tie-rod end, mark the position of the locknut and then
slacken the locknut. Remove the split pin and castellated nut attaching
the balljoint to the steering arm. Use a balljoint separator to disconnect
the balljoint from the steering arm (photo). Screw the new tie-rod end
onto the tie-rod in the same position and tighten the locknut. Fit the
balljoint to the steering arm, then tighten the securing nut to the
specified torque and fit the split pin.
7   Wheel alignment should always be adjusted on the right-hand tie-
rod.

23.4 Steering tie-rod inner balljoint

23.5 Steering tie-rod end and balljoint

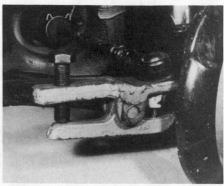

23.6 Removing a tie-rod end balljoint from the steering arm with a separator

8   The tie-rod fitting dimensions are as follows:

Protrusion of rack (see Fig. 10.26) – Equal
Tie-rod inner balljoint setting (see Fig. 10.27):

	a	b
Manual gearbox models –	*69 mm (2.7 in)*	*69 mm (2.7 in)*
Automatic transmission models –	*67 mm (2.6 in)*	*69 mm (2.7 in)*

Left-hand side tie-rod length (see Fig. 10.25) – 379 mm (14.92 in)
Right-hand side initial tie-rod lengths (see Fig. 10.25):
    Manual gearbox models – 379 mm (14.92 in)
    Automatic transmission models – 381 mm (15.0 in)

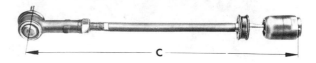

Fig. 10.25 Basic tie-rod adjustment dimension C (Sec 23)

Fig. 10.26 Steering rack in central position (Sec 23)

a = a

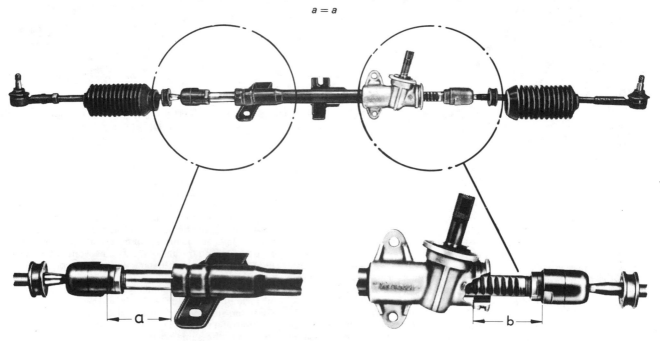

Fig. 10.27 Tie-rod inner balljoint setting dimensions. For a and b see text (Sec 23)

24 Steering rack gaiter – renewal

1 Jack up the front of the car and support it on axle stands. Apply the handbrake and remove the relevant front roadwheel.
2 Remove the split pin from the tie-rod end, unscrew the castellated nut, and use a balljoint separator to disconnect the balljoint from the steering arm.
3 Remove the clips (where fitted) and pull the gaiter from the rack and tie-rod mounting. Carefully ease the gaiter over the tie-rod end.
4 Lubricate the contact surfaces of the new gaiter with steering gear lubricant, then ease the gaiter into position and refit the clips as necessary.
5 Refit the tie-rod end balljoint as described in Section 23.

25 Wheel alignment – checking and adjusting

1 Accurate wheel alignment is essential for good steering and slow tyre wear. Before checking it, make sure that the car is unladen and that the tyres are correctly inflated.

2 Position the car on level ground with the wheels in the straight-ahead position, then roll the car backwards 12 ft (4 m) and forwards again.
3 Using a wheel alignment gauge, check that the front wheel toe-out dimension is as given in the Specifications.
4 If adjustment is necessary, loosen the tie-rod end locknut (right-hand side) and release the gaiter outer clip (where fitted).
5 Rotate the tie-rod until the alignment is correct, then tighten the locknut. Check that the gaiter is not distorted, then refit the clip where necessary with the end lugs uppermost.

26 Steering gear – removal and refitting

1 The steering gear is located in the engine compartment behind the engine. First jack up the front of the car and support it on axle stands. Apply the handbrake and remove the front roadwheels.
2 Remove the clips (where fitted) and pull the rubber gaiters from the steering gear to expose the tie-rod inner balljoints. Loosen the locknuts and unscrew the balljoints. Move the tie-rods to one side, then remove the locknuts.

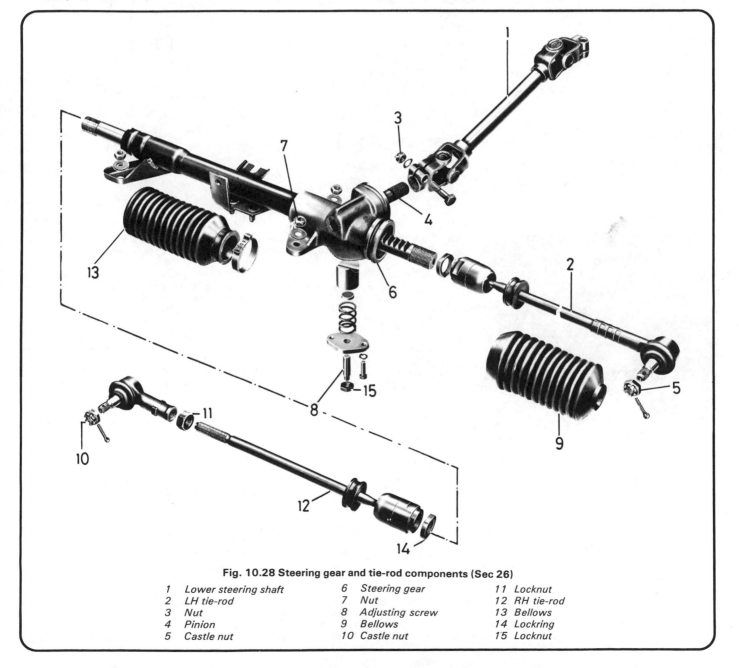

Fig. 10.28 Steering gear and tie-rod components (Sec 26)

1	Lower steering shaft	6	Steering gear	11	Locknut
2	LH tie-rod	7	Nut	12	RH tie-rod
3	Nut	8	Adjusting screw	13	Bellows
4	Pinion	9	Bellows	14	Lockring
5	Castle nut	10	Castle nut	15	Locknut

Fig. 10.29 Steering gear mounting components on 1978 on models (Sec 26)

1 Steering gear	5 U-clamp
2 Rubber bush	6 Washer
3 Rubber bush	7 Washer
4 U-clamp	8 Nuts

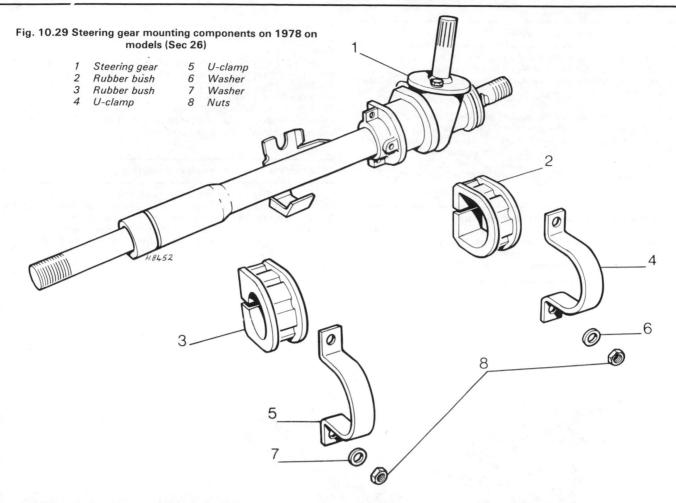

26.3 Steering shaft universal joint

3   Push back the rubber boot from the universal joint and remove the clamp bolt from the lower universal joint (photo).
4   On manual gearbox models, working beneath the car disconnect the bracket which attaches the gearchange linkage to the steering gear.
5   On pre-1978 models, remove the mounting nuts from the studs. On 1978 on models, unscrew the nuts and remove the mounting U-clamps.

6   On all models lift the steering gear and withdraw it from the universal joint shaft. Remove the steering gear through the right-hand side wheel arch.
7   Refitting is a reversal of removal. Where a new steering gear is being fitted to an automatic transmission model, bend up the gearchange linkage bracket approximately 45°. On 1978 on models, make sure that the rubber mounting bushes are in good condition. When fitting the universal joint shaft, take care that the recess on the pinion shaft aligns with the clamp bolt hole. Fit the clamp bolt loosely before tightening the mounting nuts. Adjust the gearchange linkage (where applicable) with reference to Chapter 6, and adjust the tie-rod inner balljoints to the dimensions given in Section 23. Finally check and if necessary adjust the front wheel alignment with reference to Section 25.

27 Steering gear – adjustment

1   The steering gear is not repairable; if it is damaged or worn beyond adjustment, a complete new assembly must be fitted.
2   The only adjustment is the play between the rack and the pinion, which is controlled by an adjustment screw.
3   The adjustment screw is located behind the gear assembly and is therefore difficult to reach.
4   If rattling noises are heard coming from the steering gear when the vehicle goes over rough surfaces then it must be adjusted. To do this first jack up the front of the car and set it on axle stands. Undo the adjuster locknut and back off the adjuster a little. Now tighten it until it touches the thrust washer, you will note more resistance at this point. Hold the adjuster in this position and tighten the locknut (photo).
5   A creaking sound from the rack and pinion denotes lack of lubrication. Move the steering to full lock and pull back the rubber rack cover on the extended side, wipe the grease away and spray on Molykote 321 R. Allow this to dry for ten minutes and then apply a thin film of lithium based grease and refit the rubber cover.

Fig. 10.30 Bending the gearchange linkage bracket on automatic transmission models (Sec 26)

27.4 Adjusting the steering gear

6   When correctly adjusted there should be a natural self-centering force when cornering; this will not be as strong as in cars with conventional steering geometry. If this is absent and the steering is stiff then the pinion is binding on the rack and should be adjusted.

28 Roadwheels and tyres – general

1   Clean the insides of the roadwheels whenever they are removed. If necessary, remove any rust and repaint them.
2   At the same time remove any flints or stones which may have been embedded in the tyres. Examine the tyres for damage and splits. Where the depth of tread is almost down to the legal minimum renew them.
3   The wheels should be rebalanced halfway through the life of the tyres to compensate for loss of rubber.
4   Check and adjust the tyre pressures regularly and make sure that the dust caps are correctly fitted. Remember to also check the spare tyre.
5   Rotation of tyres to even out wear is not nowadays normal practice. If it is wished to do this, note that radial tyres should only be moved from front to rear or vice versa on the same side of the car, **not** from one side to the other.

39 Fault diagnosis – suspension and steering

Symptom	Reason(s)
Excessive play in steering	Worn rack-and-pinion or tie-rods
	Worn tie-rod end balljoints
	Worn wishbone balljoints
	Worn suspension bushes
Wanders or pulls to one side	Incorrect wheel alignment
	Worn tie-rod end balljoints
	Worn wishbone balljoints
	Uneven tyre pressures
	Worn shock absorber
	Braking system fault
Heavy or stiff steering	Seized balljoint
	Incorrect wheel alignment
	Low tyre pressures
	Lack of lubricant in rack-and-pinion
Wheel wobble and vibration	Roadwheels out of balance
	Roadwheels damaged
	Worn shock absorbers
	Worn wheel bearings
Excessive tyre wear	Incorrect wheel alignment
	Worn shock absorbers
	Incorrect tyre pressures
	Roadwheels out of balance

Chapter 11 Bodywork and fittings

For modifications and information applicable to later models, see Supplement at end of manual

Contents

1 General description

The body is of all-steel unit construction with impact-absorbing front and rear crumple zones which take the brunt of any accident, leaving the passenger compartment with minimum distortion. The front crumple zones take the form of two corrugated box sections in the scuttle and firewall (bulkhead).

In the UK the Golf is available as a hatchback in two or four-door versions, or as a convertible. The Scirocco is a sports streamlined version of the Golf. In North America the Golf is called the Rabbit and in addition a pick-up version is available.

The Jetta is the four-door 'notchback' version, incorporating a conventional boot lid.

On all models the front wings are bolted to the body and can easily be renewed in the event of damage.

2 Maintenance – bodywork and underframe

The general condition of a vehicle's bodywork is the one thing that significantly affects its value. Maintenance is easy but needs to be regular. Neglect, particularly after minor damage, can lead quickly to further deterioration and costly repair bills. It is important also to keep watch on those parts of the vehicle not immediately visible, for instance the underside, inside all the wheel arches and the lower part of the engine compartment.

The basic maintenance routine for the bodywork is washing – preferably with a lot of water, from a hose. This will remove all the loose solids which may have stuck to the vehicle. It is important to flush these off in such a way as to prevent grit from scratching the finish. The wheel arches and underframe need washing in the same way to remove any accumulated mud which will retain moisture and tend to encourage rust. Paradoxically enough, the best time to clean the underframe and wheel arches is in wet weather when the mud is thoroughly wet and soft. In very wet weather the underframe is usually cleaned of large accumulations automatically and this is a good time for inspection.

Periodically, except on vehicles with a wax-based underbody protective coat, it is a good idea to have the whole of the underframe of the vehicle steam cleaned, engine compartment included, so that a thorough inspection can be carried out to see what minor repairs and renovations are necessary. Steam cleaning is available at many garages and is necessary for removal of the accumulation of oily grime which sometimes is allowed to become thick in certain areas. If steam cleaning facilities are not available, there are one or two excellent grease solvents which can be brush applied. The dirt can then be simply hosed off. Note that these methods should not be used on vehicles with wax-based underbody protective coating or the coating will be removed. Such vehicles should be inspected annually, preferably just prior to winter, when the underbody should be washed down and any damage to the wax coating repaired. Ideally, a completely fresh coat should be applied. It would also be worth considering the use of such wax-based protection for injection into door panels, sills, box sections, etc, as an additional safeguard against rust damage.

After washing paintwork, wipe off with a chamois leather to give an unspotted clear finish. A coat of clear protective wax polish will give added protection against chemical pollutants in the air. If the paintwork sheen has dulled or oxidised, use a cleaner/polisher combination to restore the brilliance of the shine. This requires a little effort, but such dulling is usually caused because regular washing has been neglected. Care needs to be taken with metallic paintwork, as special non-abrasive cleaner/polisher is required to avoid damage to the finish. Always check that the door and ventilator opening drain holes and pipes are completely clear so that water can be drained out. Bright work should be treated in the same way as paintwork. Windscreens and windows can be kept clear of the smeary film which often appears by the use of a proprietary glass cleaner. Never use any form of wax or other body or chromium polish on glass.

3 Maintenance – upholstery and carpets

1   Mats and carpets should be brushed or vacuum cleaned regularly to keep them free of grit. If they are badly stained remove them from the vehicle for scrubbing or sponging and make quite sure they are dry before refitting. Seats and interior trim panels can be kept clean by wiping with a damp cloth. If they do become stained (which can be more apparent on light coloured upholstery) use a little liquid detergent and a soft nail brush to scour the grime out of the grain of the material. Do not forget to keep the headlining clean in the same way as the upholstery. When using liquid cleaners inside the vehicle do not over-wet the surfaces being cleaned. Excessive damp could get into the seams and padded interior causing stains, offensive odours or even rot. If the inside of the vehicle gets wet accidentally it is worthwhile taking some trouble to dry it out properly, particularly where carpets are involved. *Do not leave oil or electric heaters inside the vehicle for this purpose.*

2.4a Clearing a door drain hole

2.4b Clearing a sill rear drain hole

2.4c Clearing a sill side drain hole

4 Minor body damage – repair

The photographic sequences on pages 358 and 359 illustrate the operations detailed in the following sub-sections.

Repair of minor scratches in bodywork

If the scratch is very superficial, and does not penetrate to the metal of the bodywork, repair is very simple. Lightly rub the area of the scratch with a paintwork renovator, or a very fine cutting paste, to remove loose paint from the scratch and to clear the surrounding bodywork of wax polish. Rinse the area with clean water.

Apply touch-up paint to the scratch using a fine paint brush; continue to apply fine layers of paint until the surface of the paint in the scratch is level with the surrounding paintwork. Allow the new paint at least two weeks to harden: then blend it into the surrounding paintwork by rubbing the scratch area with a paintwork renovator or a very fine cutting paste. Finally, apply wax polish.

Where the scratch has penetrated right through to the metal of the bodywork, causing the metal to rust, a different repair technique is required. Remove any loose rust from the bottom of the scratch with a penknife, then apply rust inhibiting paint to prevent the formation of rust in the future. Using a rubber or nylon applicator fill the scratch with bodystopper paste. If required, this paste can be mixed with cellulose thinners to provide a very thin paste which is ideal for filling narrow scratches. Before the stopper-paste in the scratch hardens, wrap a piece of smooth cotton rag around the top of a finger. Dip the finger in cellulose thinners and then quickly sweep it across the surface of the stopper-paste in the scratch; this will ensure that the surface of the stopper-paste is slightly hollowed. The scratch can now be painted over as described earlier in this Section.

Repair of dents in bodywork

When deep denting of the vehicle's bodywork has taken place, the first task is to pull the dent out, until the affected bodywork almost attains its original shape. There is little point in trying to restore the original shape completely, as the metal in the damaged area will have stretched on impact and cannot be reshaped fully to its original contour. It is better to bring the level of the dent up to a point which is about $\frac{1}{8}$ in (3 mm) below the level of the surrounding bodywork. In cases where the dent is very shallow anyway, it is not worth trying to pull it out at all. If the underside of the dent is accessible, it can be hammered out gently from behind, using a mallet with a wooden or plastic head. Whilst doing this, hold a suitable block of wood firmly against the outside of the panel to absorb the impact from the hammer blows and thus prevent a large area of the bodywork from being 'belled-out'.

Should the dent be in a section of the bodywork which has a double skin or some other factor making it inaccessible from behind, a different technique is called for. Drill several small holes through the metal inside the area – particularly in the deeper section. Then screw long self-tapping screws into the holes just sufficiently for them to gain a good purchase in the metal. Now the dent can be pulled out by pulling on the protruding heads of the screws with a pair of pliers.

The next stage of the repair is the removal of the paint from the damaged area, and from an inch or so of the surrounding 'sound' bodywork. This is accomplished most easily by using a wire brush or

abrasive pad on a power drill, although it can be done just as effectively by hand using sheets of abrasive paper. To complete the preparation for filling, score the surface of the bare metal with a screwdriver or the tang of a file, or alternatively, drill small holes in the affected area. This will provide a really good 'key' for the filler paste.

To complete the repair see the Section on filling and re-spraying.

Repair of rust holes or gashes in bodywork

Remove all paint from the affected area and from an inch or so of the surrounding 'sound' bodywork, using an abrasive pad or a wire brush on a power drill. If these are not available a few sheets of abrasive paper will do the job just as effectively. With the paint removed you will be able to gauge the severity of the corrosion and therefore decide whether to renew the whole panel (if this is possible) or to repair the affected area. New body panels are not as expensive as most people think and it is often quicker and more satisfactory to fit a new panel than to attempt to repair large areas of corrosion.

Remove all fittings from the affected area except those which will act as a guide to the original shape of the damaged bodywork (eg headlamp shells etc). Then, using tin snips or a hacksaw blade, remove all loose metal and any other metal badly affected by corrosion. Hammer the edges of the hole inwards in order to create a slight depression for the filler paste.

Wire brush the affected area to remove the powdery rust from the surface of the remaining metal. Paint the affected area with rust inhibiting paint; if the back of the rusted area is accessible treat this also.

Before filling can take place it will be necessary to block the hole in some way. This can be achieved by the use of zinc gauze or aluminium tape.

Aluminium or plastic mesh is probably the best material to use for a large hole. Cut a piece to the approximate size and shape of the hole to be filled, then position it in the hole so that its edges are below the level of the surrounding bodywork. It can be retained in position by several blobs of filler paste around its periphery.

Aluminium tape should be used for small or very narrow holes. Pull a piece off the roll and trim it to the approximate size and shape required, then pull off the backing paper (if used) and stick the tape over the hole; it can be overlapped if the thickness of one piece is insufficient. Burnish down the edges of the tape with the handle of a screwdriver or similar, to ensure that the tape is securely attached to the metal underneath.

Bodywork repairs – filling and re-spraying

Before using this Section, see the Sections on dent, deep scratch, rust holes and gash repairs.

Many types of bodyfiller are available, but generally speaking those proprietary kits which contain a tin of filler paste and a tube of resin hardener are best for this type of repair. A wide, flexible plastic or nylon applicator will be found invaluable for imparting a smooth and well contoured finish to the surface of the filler.

Mix up a little filler on a clean piece of card or board – measure the hardener carefully (follow the maker's instructions on the pack) otherwise the filler will set too rapidly or too slowly.

Using the applicator apply the filler paste to the prepared area; draw the applicator across the surface of the filler to achieve the correct contour and to level the filler surface. As soon as a contour that approximates to the correct one is achieved, stop working the paste — if you carry on too long the paste will become sticky and begin to 'pick up' on the applicator. Continue to add thin layers of filler paste at twenty-minute intervals until the level of the filler is just proud of the surrounding bodywork.

Once the filler has hardened, excess can be removed using a metal plane or file. From then on, progressively finer grades of abrasive paper should be used, starting with a 40 grade production paper and finishing with 400 grade wet-and-dry paper. Always wrap the abrasive paper around a flat rubber, cork, or wooden block — otherwise the surface of the filler will not be completely flat. During the smoothing of the filler surface the wet-and-dry paper should be periodically rinsed in water. This will ensure that a very smooth finish is imparted to the filler at the final stage.

At this stage the 'dent' should be surrounded by a ring of bare metal, which in turn should be encircled by the finely 'feathered' edge of the good paintwork. Rinse the repair area with clean water, until all of the dust produced by the rubbing-down operation has gone.

Spray the whole repair area with a light coat of primer — this will show up any imperfections in the surface of the filler. Repair these imperfections with fresh filler paste or bodystopper, and once more smooth the surface with abrasive paper. If bodystopper is used, it can be mixed with cellulose thinners to form a really thin paste which is ideal for filling small holes. Repeat this spray and repair procedure until you are satisfied that the surface of the filler, and the feathered edge of the paintwork are perfect. Clean the repair area with clean water and allow to dry fully.

The repair area is now ready for final spraying. Paint spraying must be carried out in a warm, dry, windless and dust free atmosphere. This condition can be created artificially if you have access to a large indoor working area, but if you are forced to work in the open, you will have to pick your day very carefully. If you are working indoors, dousing the floor in the work area with water will help to settle the dust which would otherwise be in the atmosphere. If the repair area is confined to one body panel, mask off the surrounding panels; this will help to minimise the effects of a slight mis-match in paint colours. Bodywork fittings (eg chrome strips, door handles etc) will also need to be masked off. Use genuine masking tape and several thicknesses of newspaper for the masking operations.

Before commencing to spray, agitate the aerosol can thoroughly, then spray a test area (an old tin, or similar) until the technique is mastered. Cover the repair area with a thick coat of primer; the thickness should be built up using several thin layers of paint rather than one thick one. Using 400 grade wet-and-dry paper, rub down the surface of the primer until it is really smooth. While doing this, the work area should be thoroughly doused with water, and the wet-and-dry paper periodically rinsed in water. Allow to dry before spraying on more paint.

Spray on the top coat, again building up the thickness by using several thin layers of paint. Start spraying in the centre of the repair area and then, using a circular motion, work outwards until the whole repair area and about 2 inches of the surrounding original paintwork is covered. Remove all masking material 10 to 15 minutes after spraying on the final coat of paint.

Allow the new paint at least two weeks to harden, then, using a paintwork renovator or a very fine cutting paste, blend the edges of the paint into the existing paintwork. Finally, apply wax polish.

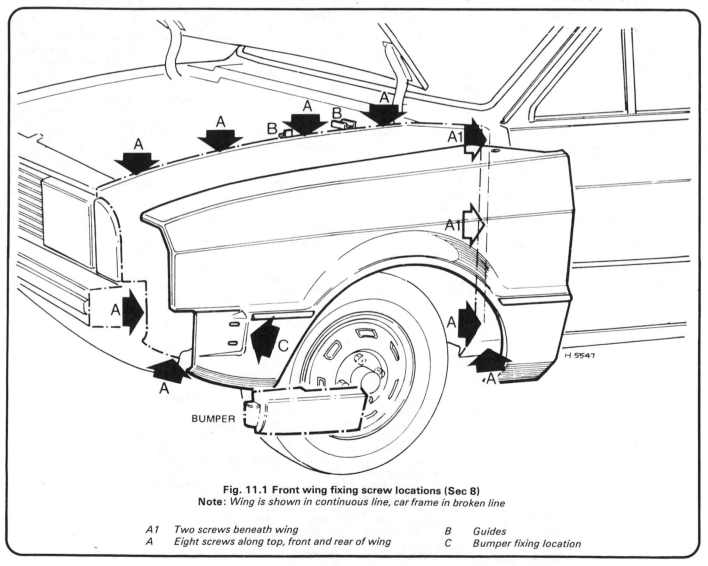

Fig. 11.1 Front wing fixing screw locations (Sec 8)
Note: *Wing is shown in continuous line, car frame in broken line*

A1 *Two screws beneath wing*	B *Guides*
A *Eight screws along top, front and rear of wing*	C *Bumper fixing location*

5 Major body damage – repair

Where serious damage has occurred or large areas need renewal due to neglect, it means certainly that completely new sections or panels will need welding in and this is best left to professionals. If the damage is due to impact, it will also be necessary to completely check the alignment of the bodyshell structure. Due to the principle of construction, the strength and shape of the whole car can be affected by damage to one part. In such instances the services of a VW agent with specialist checking jigs are essential. If a body is left misaligned, it is first of all dangerous as the car will not handle properly, and secondly uneven stresses will be imposed on the steering, engine and transmission, causing abnormal wear or complete failure. Tyre wear may also be excessive.

6 Maintenance – hinges and locks

1   Oil the hinges and check straps of the bonnet, tailgate or boot lid and doors, with a drop or two of light oil at regular intervals (see Routine Maintenance).
2   At the same time, lightly oil the bonnet release mechanism and all door locks.
3   Do not attempt to lubricate the steering lock.

7 Door rattles – tracing and rectification

1   Check first that the door is not loose at the hinges, and that the latch is holding the door firmly in position. Check also that the door lines up with the aperture in the body. If the door is out of alignment, adjust it as described in Section 23.
2   If the latch is holding the door in the correct position but the latch still rattles, the lock mechanism is worn and should be renewed.
3   Other rattles from the door could be caused by wear in the window operating mechanism, interior lock mechanism, or loose glass channels

8 Front wings – removal and refitting

1   A badly damaged front wing may be removed complete and replaced by a new one. The wing is secured with 10 fixing screws. Refer to Fig. 11.1 in which the locations of the screws are shown. Those marked 'A1' are under the wing and not easily accessible.
2   It will be necessary to remove the side bumper before removing the wing. The screws fastening the wing are fitted very tightly and may not come out without considerable force. Do not use an impact screwdriver or you will distort the frame. It may be necessary to grind off the heads and drill out the shanks.
3   Once all the screws are out, the wing may be levered away pulling it out of the guides. If it does not come out easily it may be necessary to warm the line of the joint with a blowlamp to melt the adhesive underseal. Be careful how you do this, for apart from the fire risk to the car the adhesive is also imflammable.
4   When removing, lever the wing away from the wheel housing and the door pillar, work it to-and-fro, pulling it forwards to the front of the car a little.
5   Clean up the frame and paint with inhibitor if any rust is present.

Use a good sealing tape along the line of the bolts before installing the wing, and once the wing is securely in place treat the underside with underseal compound. Refer to Section 4 for respraying techniques.

9 Radiator grille – removal and refitting

1   On early models the radiator grille is held in position by eight screws located or shown in Fig. 11.2. On later models some of the screws are replaced by plastic clips.
2   On Jetta models the radiator grille is secured by screws and plastic clips located as shown in Fig. 11.3.
3   In order to remove a plastic clip, the central locking dowel must be pulled out (photo). If this proves difficult, drill a small hole in the dowel and use a self-tapping screw to extract it.
4   On Jetta models, the headlamp surrounds are removed separately from the grille, and the grille must be lifted from the lower guides (photos).
5   Refitting is a reversal of removal.

10 Tailgate, strut and lock (Hatchback models) – removal and refitting

1   Disconnect the battery negative lead.
2   Open the tailgate and remove the straps which support the rear shelf. Disconnect the gas-filled support strut from the tailgate, where fitted. Have an assistant support the tailgate.
3   Ease the headlining back to uncover the hinge securing bolts. Slacken the hinge bolts using an impact screwdriver.
4   Disconnect the wiring to the heated rear window/rear wiper and disconnect the washer hose (where fitted).
5   Remove the hinge bolts and lift away the tailgate.
6   Refitting is a reversal of removal, but before tightening the hinge bolts, close the tailgate and check that it is central within the body aperture and that the lock works correctly. If necessary adjust the tailgate with the bolts hand tight.
7   If the gas-filled support strut is to be renewed, it is important to fit the correct type. If the strut body has one identification groove on it, the body end must be attached to the tailgate, but if the body has two grooves, the body end must be attached to the aperture.
8   The lock is secured to the bottom of the tailgate by three cross-head screws (photos). No repair to the lock is possible – if it is faulty, renew it.

11 Boot lid and lock (Jetta models) – removal and refitting

1   Disconnect the battery negative lead.
2   Disconnect the number plate lamp wiring at the connector.
3   Mark the position of the bolts securing the hinges to the boot lid (photo).
4   With the help of an assistant, unscrew the bolts and withdraw the boot lid.
5   The boot lock and striker pin are each secured by two cross-head screws, but when removing the lock it will be necessary to unhook the connecting rod (photos).
6   Refitting is a reversal of removal, but make sure that the boot lid is central within the aperture and adjust its position on the hinge bolts if necessary. To adjust the boot lock striker, loosen the mounting

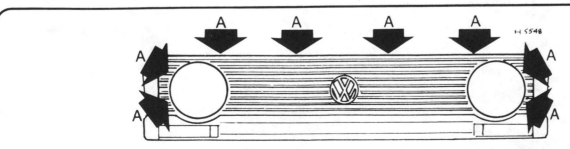

Fig. 11.2 Radiator grille fixing screw locations (A) on early models (Sec 9)

Fig. 11.3 Locations of radiator grille retaining clips (1) and screws (2) on Jetta models (Sec 9)

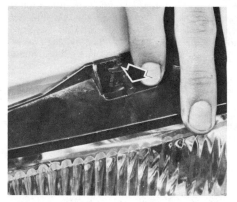

9.3 A radiator grille plastic clip showing locking dowel (arrowed)

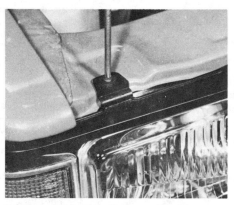

9.4a Removing a headlamp surround upper ...

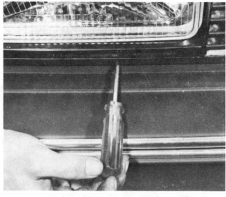

9.4b ... and lower retaining screw (Jetta)

9.4c Removing a headlamp surround (Jetta)

10.8a Outer view of the tailgate lock

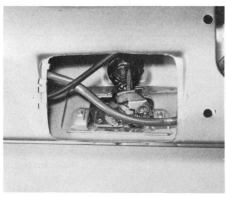

10.8b Inner view of the tailgate lock

Fig. 11.4 Single groove type gas-filled tailgate strut (Sec 10)

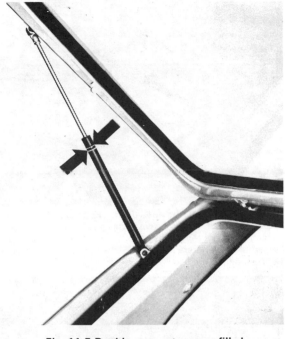

Fig. 11.5 Double groove type gas-filled tailgate strut (Sec 10)

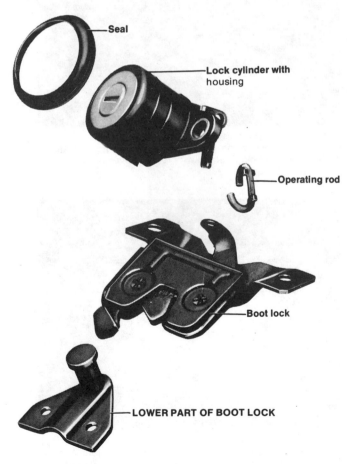

Fig. 11.6 Boot lid lock components on Jetta models (Sec 11)

Seal — Lock cylinder with housing — Operating rod — Boot lock — LOWER PART OF BOOT LOCK

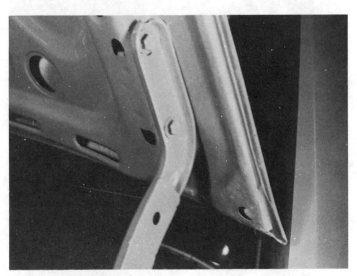

11.3 Boot lid hinge (Jetta)

screws, then tighten them sufficiently to hold the striker in position. Fully close the boot lid, then open it and fully tighten the screws. Adjust the stop rubbers if necessary.

12 Tailgate handle and latch (Pick-up models) – removal and refitting

1   Open the tailgate and unscrew the three inner bolts.
2   Disconnect the latch rods from the handle and withdraw the handle.
3   Unscrew the retaining bolts and withdraw the latches together with the rods.
4   Refitting is a reversal of removal, but in order to reconnect the latch rods to the handle, it may be helpful to completely remove the tailgate and depress the latch by standing the tailgate on end.

This sequence of photographs deals with the repair of the dent and paintwork damage shown in this photo. The procedure will be similar for the repair of a hole. It should be noted that the procedures given here are simplified — more explicit instructions will be found in the text

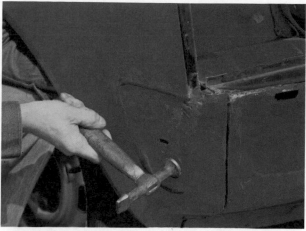

In the case of a dent the first job — after removing surrounding trim — is to hammer out the dent where access is possible. This will minimise filling. Here, the large dent having been hammered out, the damaged area is being made slightly concave

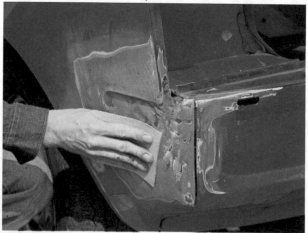

Now all paint must be removed from the damaged area, by rubbing with coarse abrasive paper. Alternatively, a wire brush or abrasive pad can be used in a power drill. Where the repair area meets good paintwork, the edge of the paintwork should be 'feathered', using a finer grade of abrasive paper

In the case of a hole caused by rusting, all damaged sheet-metal should be cut away before proceeding to this stage. Here, the damaged area is being treated with rust remover and inhibitor before being filled

Mix the body filler according to its manufacturer's instructions. In the case of corrosion damage, it will be necessary to block off any large holes before filling — this can be done with aluminium or plastic mesh, or aluminium tape. Make sure the area is absolutely clean before ...

... applying the filler. Filler should be applied with a flexible applicator, as shown, for best results; the wooden spatula being used for confined areas. Apply thin layers of filler at 20-minute intervals, until the surface of the filler is slightly proud of the surrounding bodywork

Initial shaping can be done with a Surform plane or Dreadnought file. Then, using progressively finer grades of wet-and-dry paper, wrapped around a sanding block, and copious amounts of clean water, rub down the filler until really smooth and flat. Again, feather the edges of adjoining paintwork

The whole repair area can now be sprayed or brush-painted with primer. If spraying, ensure adjoining areas are protected from over-spray. Note that at least one inch of the surrounding sound paintwork should be coated with primer. Primer has a 'thick' consistency, so will find small imperfections

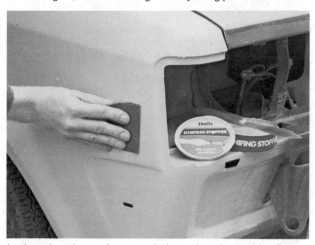

Again, using plenty of water, rub down the primer with a fine grade wet-and-dry paper (400 grade is probably best) until it is really smooth and well blended into the surrounding paintwork. Any remaining imperfections can now be filled by carefully applied knifing stopper paste

When the stopper has hardened, rub down the repair area again before applying the final coat of primer. Before rubbing down this last coat of primer, ensure the repair area is blemish-free – use more stopper if necessary. To ensure that the surface of the primer is really smooth use some finishing compound

The top coat can now be applied. When working out of doors, pick a dry, warm and wind-free day. Ensure surrounding areas are protected from over-spray. Agitate the aerosol thoroughly, then spray the centre of the repair area, working outwards with a circular motion. Apply the paint as several thin coats

After a period of about two weeks, which the paint needs to harden fully, the surface of the repaired area can be 'cut' with a mild cutting compound prior to wax polishing. When carrying out bodywork repairs, remember that the quality of the finished job is proportional to the time and effort expended

11.5a Boot lid lock ...

11.5b ... and striker pin (Jetta)

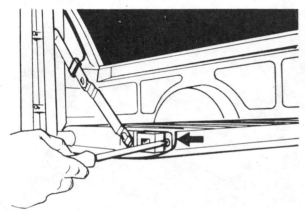

Fig. 11.7 Removing a tailgate latch (arrowed) on Pick-up models
(Sec 12)

13 Rear lid (Convertible models) – removal and refitting

1   Open the rear lid, mark the position of the hinges, then unscrew
the hinge nuts and withdraw the rear lid.
2   If necessary remove the lock and cylinder from the lid.
3   Refitting is a reversal of removal. Make sure that the lock and
cylinder linkage are correctly aligned. If necessary adjust the lid
centrally in the body aperture by loosening the hinge nuts slightly, then
tighten the nuts; it may also be necessary to adjust the position of the
striker.

14 Bumpers – removal and refitting

UK models

1   The front bumper consists of a crossmember and two side pieces
on early models. The sections are fitted to each other and the wings
by studs and nuts. To remove the bumper, first disconnect the
indicator lamp wiring and unscrew the stud nuts. Withdraw the side
pieces, then unbolt the centre section from the underframe.
2   Later models are fitted with a similar centre section to which is
attached a single plastic covering. To remove this type, use a
screwdriver to prise the side covering from each wing, disconnect the
bumper lamp wires (where fitted) and headlamp washer tubing (where
fitted) (photo), and unbolt the centre section from the underframe. The
plastic covering is obtainable as a separate item, but a press will be
required to attach it to the centre section.
3   Removal of the rear bumper is similar to that for the front, except

that there are no lighting or washer connections (photo). As from May
1981 side guides are fitted to Scirocco models; to remove this type,
unscrew the bracket bolts from within the rear compartment and slide
the bumper from the car.
4   Refitting is a reversal of removal.

North American models

5   With the exception of some Pick-up models, the bumpers incorporate impact absorbers. To remove this type, unscrew the absorber mounting bolts from within the engine compartment or rear
compartment, disconnect the lighting wiring as necessary, and
withdraw the bumper from the car. The overriders and side caps may
then be removed and the impact absorbers unbolted. On Jetta models,
a further impact strip is attached to the body with plastic clips.
6   To remove the bumper on Pick-up models, unbolt the brackets
from the body – disconnect the lighting wiring as necessary. The side
caps, impact strip and brackets can then be removed, but note the
location of spacers between the bumper and brackets.
7   Refitting is a reversal of removal.

15 Bonnet – removal and refitting

1   The bonnet, or engine compartment cover, is hinged at the rear
and held shut by a lock operated from inside the vehicle. It is held to
the hinge by two bolts on each side (photo). Remove these, and it may
be lifted off and taken away. Two people are needed to lift it, not
because it is heavy but to avoid scratching the paint. Do not forget to
disconnect the plastic tube from the windscreen washer jet (photo).
2   Refitting is a reversal of removal, but check that the bonnet is level
with the surrounding bodywork. If necessary adjust its position at the
hinge bolts.

16 Bonnet cable and lock – removal, refitting and adjustment

1   Working inside the car, unscrew the two cross-head retaining
screws and release the bonnet lock handle from the left-hand side
panel. On some models it may be necessary to remove the centre
cover under the facia and the glovebox.
2   Disconnect the cable at the lock end after removing the radiator
grille (Section 9). On 1981 on Scirocco models there is no need to
remove the grille.
3   Bend the clamping plate in the operating handle outwards, and
remove the handle from the cable.
4   Withdraw the cable from the car.
5   Refitting is a reversal of removal, but make sure that the cable is
routed free of strain without any sharp curves. To adjust the cable, pull
it through the clamp on the lock as far as possible, then, with the lever
fully released, tighten the clamp screw and bend the excess cable over.

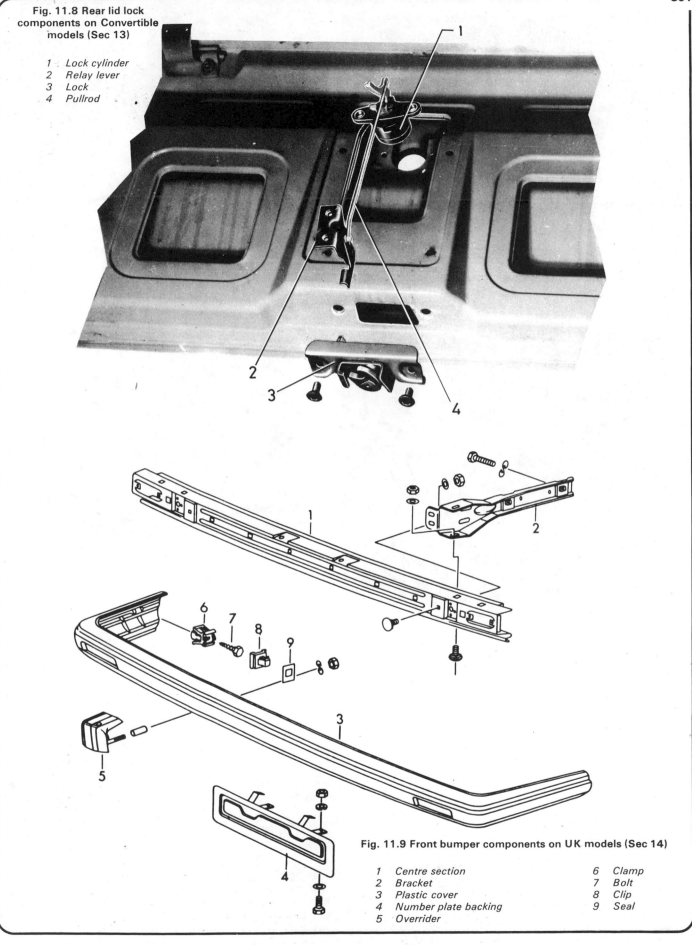

Fig. 11.8 Rear lid lock components on Convertible models (Sec 13)

1 Lock cylinder
2 Relay lever
3 Lock
4 Pullrod

Fig. 11.9 Front bumper components on UK models (Sec 14)

1 Centre section
2 Bracket
3 Plastic cover
4 Number plate backing
5 Overrider
6 Clamp
7 Bolt
8 Clip
9 Seal

14.2 Headlamp washer jet on front bumper (Golf/Rabbit)

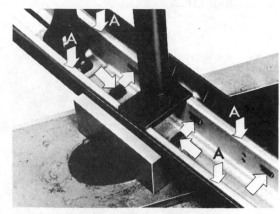

Fig. 11.10 Using a press to fit the plastic cover to the bumper. Arrows 'A' indicate direction of pressure – remaining arrows indicate the location lugs (Sec 14)

14.3 Rear bumper retaining bolt location (Jetta)

Fig. 11.11 Bumper guide fitted to later Scirocco models (Sec 14)

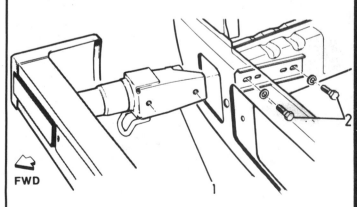

FWD

Fig. 11.12 Front bumper components on North American models (Sec 14)

1   Impact absorber   2   Bolts

15.1a A bonnet hinge (Scirocco)

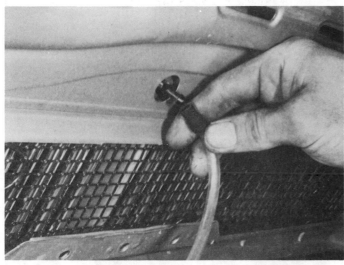

15.1b Windscreen washer jet and supply tube location on the bonnet (Scirocco)

Fig. 11.13 Bonnet lock cable adjusting screw – arrowed – on all models except 1981 on Scirocco (Sec 16)

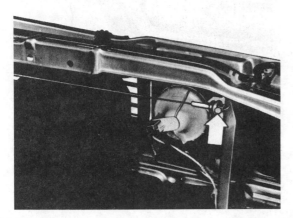

Fig. 11.14 Bonnet lock cable adjusting screw – arrowed – on 1981 on Scirocco models (Sec 16)

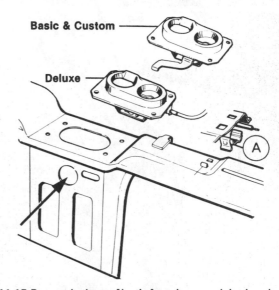

Fig. 11.15 Bonnet locks on North American models showing cable clip (A) and access hole (arrowed) (Sec 16)

16.7 Bonnet lock upper half (Jetta)

6   To remove the bonnet lock, remove the radiator grille (Section 9) and disconnect the cable.

7   Unscrew the two retaining bolts and lift the lock assembly from the crossmember. The top half of the lock can be removed from the bonnet by unscrewing the two bolts (photo). Note that on some later models the lock may be secured with pop rivets, in which case they must be drilled out, and new ones installed when refitting.

8   Refitting is a reversal of removal, but adjust the cable as described in paragraph 5. If necessary, adjust the length of the upper striking pin until the front edge of the bonnet is level with the wings.

17 Door interior trim – removal and refitting

1   With the window shut, note the position of the window regulator handle. Using a screwdriver prise the plastic cover from the handle, then remove the retaining screw and slide the handle from the shaft (photo).

2   Remove the door pull. To do this on early Golf/Rabbit models, prise up the end covers and slide them to the centre of the strap, then remove the retaining screws (photo). On models with an angled door pull, remove the lower cross-head retaining screws, swivel the door pull upwards through 90° and withdraw it from the trim (photos). On 1981 on Scirocco models, remove the two screws and withdraw the door pull downward. On all other models remove the cross-head screws and withdraw the door pull (photo).

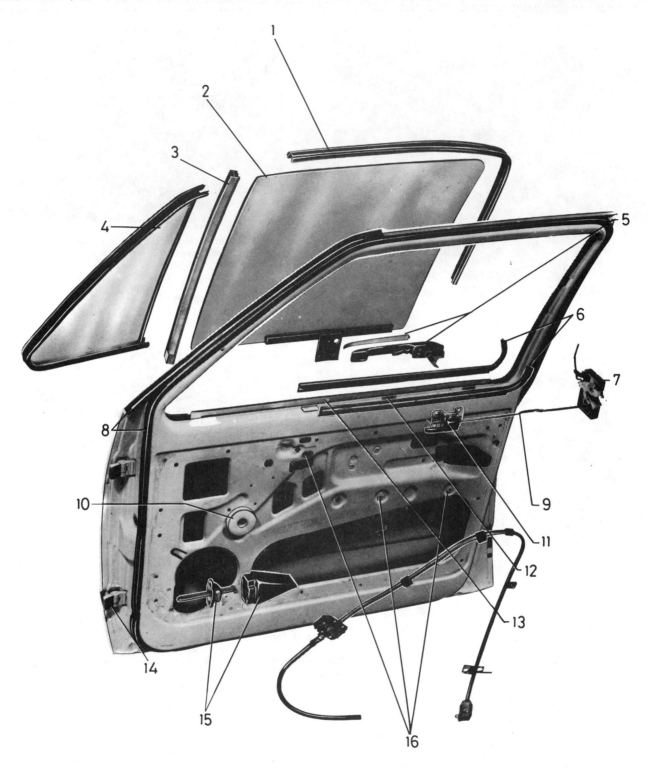

Fig. 11.16 Exploded view of the front door on Golf, Rabbit and Jetta models (Sec 17)

1 Window channel	5 Exterior handle	9 Connecting link	13 Seal clips
2 Glass	6 Window seals	10 Seal	14 Hinge
3 Guide rail	7 Door lock	11 Remote handle	15 Check strap
4 Corner window	8 Door seals	12 Trim clips	16 Expanding nuts and clips

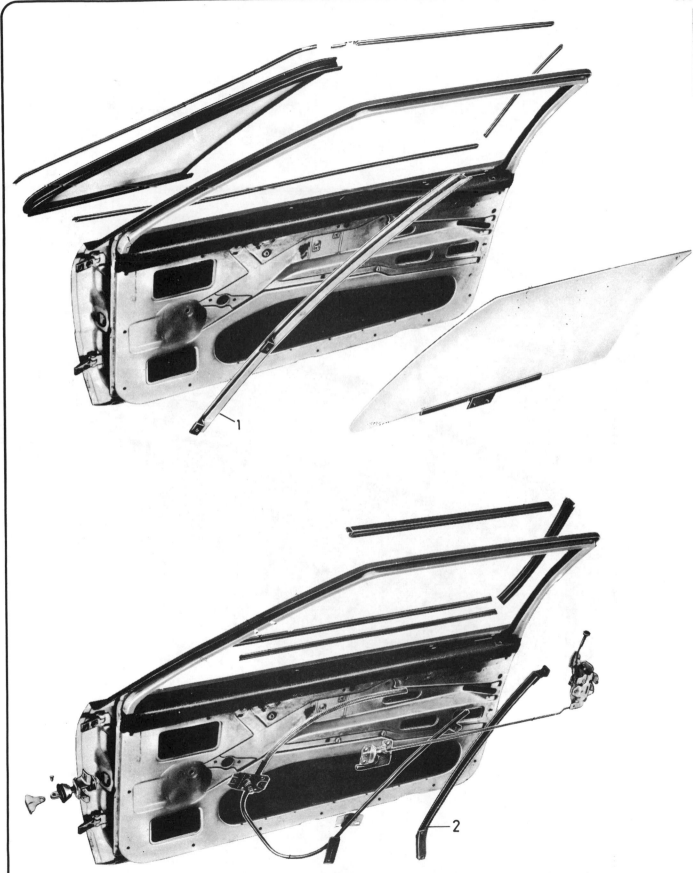

Fig. 11.17 Exploded view of the front door on Scirocco models up to May 1981 (Sec 17)

1   *Window glass front guide*   2   *Window glass rear guide*

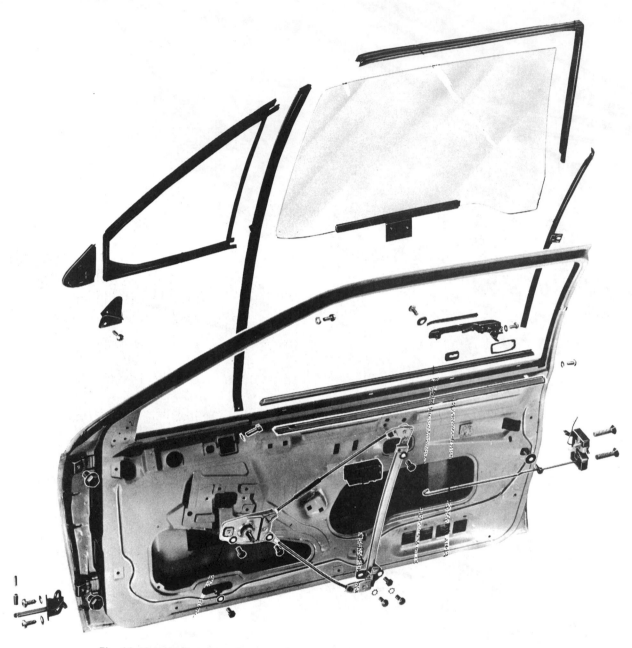

Fig. 11.18 Exploded view of the front door on May 1981 on Scirocco models (Sec 17)

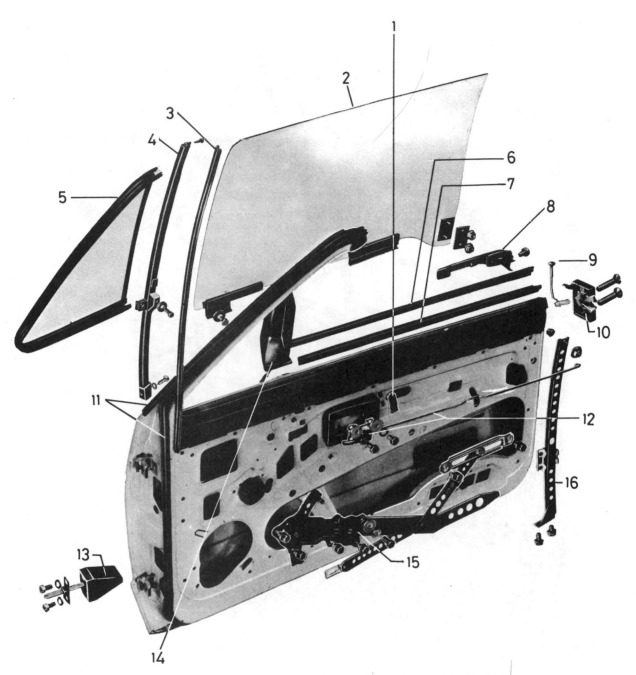

Fig. 11.19 Exploded view of the front door on Convertible models (Sec 17)

1	Lifter stop	5	Corner window	9	Locking knob	13	Check strap
2	Window glass	6	Outer seal	10	Door lock	14	Exterior mirror
3	Front window channel	7	Inner seal	11	Seal	15	Window regulator
4	Guide rail	8	Exterior handle	12	Remote control	16	Guide rail

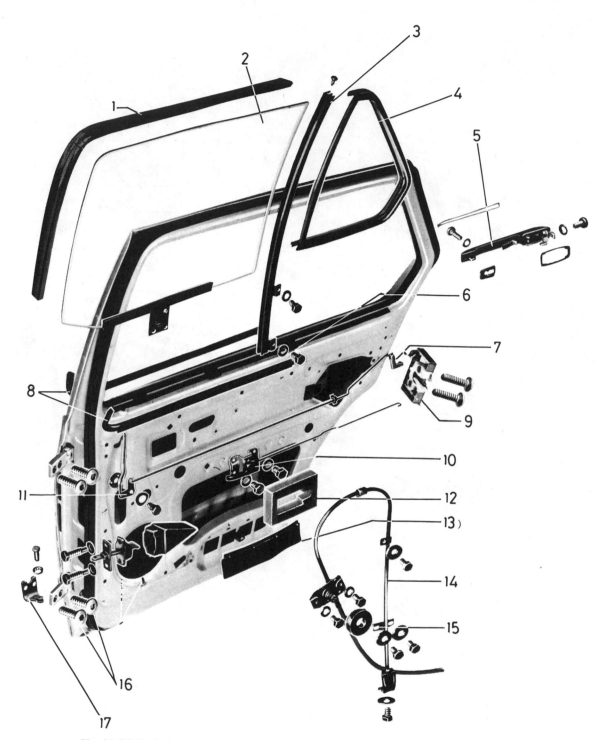

Fig. 11.20 Exploded view of the rear door on Golf, Rabbit, and Jetta models (Sec 17)

1	Window channel	6	Clips	10	Remote handle	14	Window regulator
2	Glass	7	Sleeve	11	Bellcrank lever	15	Seal
3	Guide rail	8	Window seals	12	Seal	16	Hinge bolts
4	Corner window	9	Door lock	13	Check flap	17	Bracket
5	Exterior handle						

Fig. 11.21 Front door trim panel components on Jetta models (Sec 17)

1 Locking knob	3 Screws and covers	5 Window regulator handle
2 Surround	4 Trim panel	6 Armrest and door pull

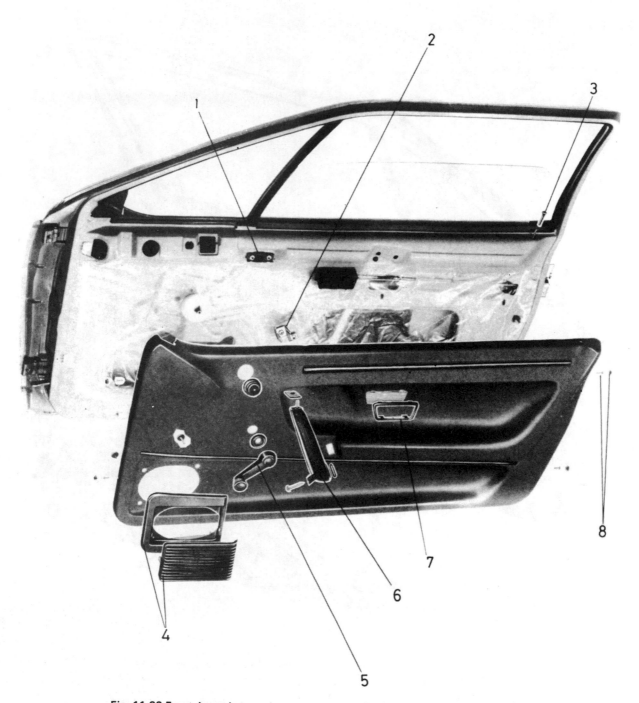

Fig. 11.22 Front door trim panel components on 1981 on Scirocco models (Sec 17)

1	Clip	5	Window regulator handle
2	Clip	6	Door pull
3	Locking knob	7	Escutcheon
4	Loudspeaker trim	8	Screws

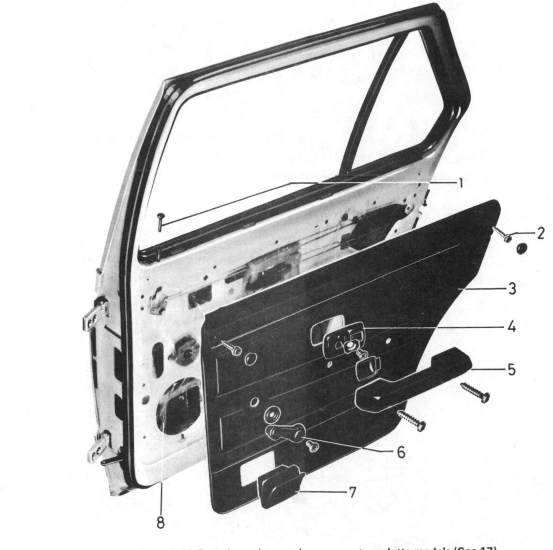

Fig. 11.23 Rear door trim panel components on Jetta models (Sec 17)

1	Locking knob	5	Armrest and door pull
2	Screws	6	Window regulator handle
3	Trim panel	7	Ashtray
4	Surround	8	Plastic sheet

17.1 Removing a window regulator handle

17.2a Removing an early type door pull

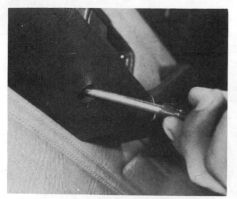
17.2b Removing an angled door pull lower screw ...

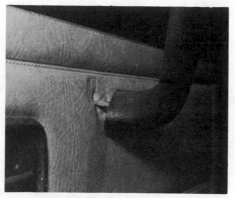
17.2c ... and disconnecting the upper retainer

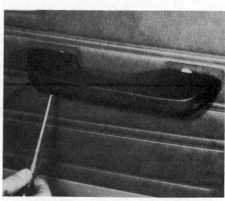
17.2d Removing a standard door pull

17.4a Removing the interior door handle recessed cover ...

17.4b ... and surround

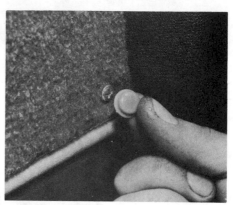
17.6a Removing door interior trim cap ...

17.6b ... and retaining screw

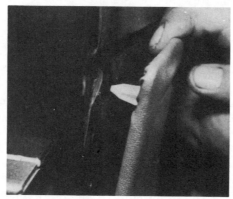
17.7 Door interior trim retaining clip

17.8 Front door with trim removed (Jetta)

18.3 Door lock on pre-October 1976 models

18.5 Door lock on October 1976 on models

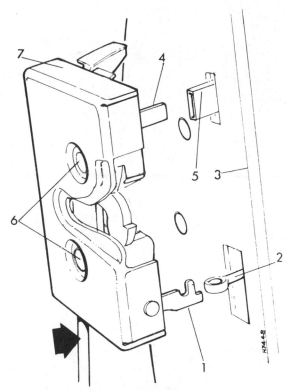

Fig. 11.24 Removing the door lock on October 1976 on models (Sec 18)

1 Remote control lever in pulled out position	4 Control lever 1
2 Remote control rod	5 Sleeve for control lever 1
3 Door face	6 Holes for securing screws
	7 Lock body

3   Unscrew and remove the locking knob where necessary.
4   On 1981 on Scirocco models, slide the interior door handle escutcheon rearward and withdraw it. On all other models prise out the recessed cover, remove the screw and withdraw the escutcheon (photos).
5   Where fitted, prise off the cover and remove the mirror, adjusting knobs and escutcheon.
6   Where fitted on late models, prise off the caps and unscrew the four trim retaining screws (photos).
7   Using a wide-bladed screwdriver inserted between the trim and the door, prise out the retaining clips (photo).
8   Withdraw the trim panel (photo). If fitted, disconnect the wiring to the loudspeaker.
9   Refitting is a reversal of removal, but make sure that the plastic sheeting is correctly positioned before mounting the trim on the door.

---

18   Door lock – removal and refitting

Pre-October 1976 models and May 1981 on Scirocco models

1   Remove the interior trim (Section 17). Remove the plastic cover from the face of the door. Press the clips off the linkage inside the door.
2   Remove the two screws, holding the remote control lever in the centre of the door, disengage the long link and then disconnect it from the lock (where applicable).
3   Undo the two screws holding the lock to the door and remove the lock through the door opening (photo).
4   When assembling make sure the door handle operating lever engages with the lock operating lever.

October 1976 on models (except 1981 on Scirocco)

5   As from October 1976, it is not necessary to remove the door

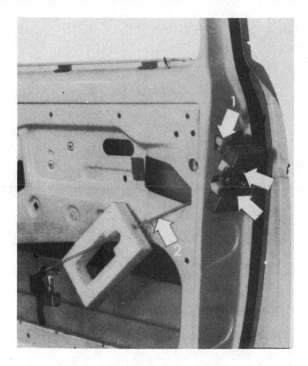

Fig. 11.25 Door lock remote control (Sec 19)

1   Control lever
2   Connecting link
Arrows indicate screw holes

interior trim in order to remove the door lock (photo).
6   Open the door and set the lock in the locked position, either by moving the interior knob or by turning the exterior key.
7   If the rear door lock is being removed, move the child safety lock catch to the unlocked position.
8   Using a hexagon key, unscrew the retaining screws and withdraw the lock approximately 12 mm (0.5 in) to expose the operating lever.
9   Retain the operating lever in the extended position by inserting a screwdriver through the hole in the bottom of the lock.
10   Unhook the remote control rod from the operating lever and pull the upper lever from the sleeve. Withdraw the lock from the door.
11   Refitting is a reversal of removal, but remember to set the lock in the locked position first.

---

19   Door lock remote control – removal and refitting

1   Remove the door interior trim as described in Section 17.
2   Where necessary remove the door lock as described in Section 18.
3   Unbolt the remote control handle from the door and where applicable unhook it from the control rod (photo) – on 1981 on Scirocco models pull out the retaining cleat, then slide the handle forward to remove it.
4   Refitting is a reversal of removal, but make sure that any sound-deadening foam is positioned correctly on the control rod.

---

20   Door exterior handle – removal and refitting

1   Open the door and remove the retaining screw located above the door lock (photo).
2   Prise the plastic insert from the handle and remove the second cross-head retaining screw. Note that early Golf/Rabbit models do not have the screw.
3   If the driver's side handle is being removed, make sure that it is unlocked.
4   Withdraw the handle from the door – if necessary push the handle forward, withdraw it a little, then remove it rearward (photo).
5   Refitting is a reversal of removal.

19.3 Door lock remote control handle

20.1 Door exterior handle retaining screw

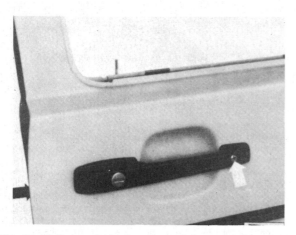

Fig. 11.26 Door exterior handle retaining screw locations –
arrowed (Sec 20)

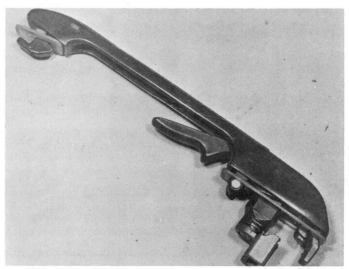

20.4 The door exterior handle

21 Window regulator – removal and refitting

1   Remove the interior trim as described in Section 17.
2   Temporarily refit the window regulator handle and lower the
window until the lifting plate is visible (photo).
3   Remove the bolts securing the regulator to the door and the bolts
securing the lifting plate to the window channel.
4   Unclip the regulator from the door and remove it through the
aperture.
5   Refitting is a reversal of removal, but ensure that the cable is
adequately lubricated with grease, and if necessary adjust the position
of the regulator so that the window moves smoothly.

22 Windows – removal and refitting

Door windows
1   Remove the window regulator as described in Section 21.
2   With the window fully lowered, unclip the inner and outer
mouldings from the window aperture.
3   Remove the window channel abutting the corner window. To do
this, remove the retaining bolts and screws, and on some models drill
out the lower rivet.
4   Unclip the window seals and remove the corner window.
5   Lift the window glass from the door.
6   Refitting is a reversal of removal, with reference to Section 21 as

21.2 Door window channel and lifting plate

necessary. A rivetting tool will be required where the window channel is secured with a rivet. If the glass is being renewed, make sure that the lift channel is positioned in the same position as on the old glass.

Windscreen and fixed glass
7 The average owner is strongly advised to leave windscreen removal and refitting to a VW agent or windscreen specialist. The fitting charge is negligible compared with the expense which will be incurred if a new screen is broken by unskilled handling!

23 Doors – removal and refitting

1 The front door hinges on early models are secured to the pillar with shallow socket headed bolts which are very difficult to undo unless the special tools are available. They are also in an awkward position. If the socket heads are damaged and the hexagon hole is converted into a round one then you are in serious trouble, as it will be necessary to drill the bolt and extract it with a special bolt extractor. For this reason we recommend that door hinges should be undone by professionals with the correct equipment. However, if you can undo these bolts the door is easily removed.
2 The rear door hinges on all models are also secured with socket-headed bolts, but the front door hinges on later models have ordinary bolts.
3 Take the pin out of the check strap, slacken the hinge bolts, have someone hold the door while you remove the bolts, and lift the door away (photos). Check the weatherstrip and fit a new one, if necessary.
4 When installing the door first remove the door striker bolt from the frame. You cannot adjust the hinge while this is in place. Fit the door to the pillar and tighten the hinge bolts enough to hold the door in place. Close the door and check that the gap all round the edge is symmetrical. Adjust the hinge until it is correct then tighten the hinge bolts fully. Refit the striker bolt.

24 Remote controlled exterior mirror – removal and refitting

1 Remove the door interior trim panel as described in Section 17, and pull back the plastic sheeting.
2 On the early crank type, remove the countersunk screws securing the mirror to the door and withdraw the mirror together with the reinforced plate. From the door interior panel unscrew the three retaining bolts and withdraw the remote control lever and bracket together with the anti-rattle foam.
3 On the later cable type, unscrew the nut and press the adjusting knob out of the door – some models may have a retaining ring instead of a nut. Remove the screws from the mirror head and withdraw the mirror and knob together with the cable from the door.
4 Refitting is a reversal of removal

25 Knee bar (Jetta models) – removal and refitting

1 Disconnect the battery negative lead.
2 Remove the three cross-head screws from the centre console, remove the gear lever knob and boot, then withdraw the console.
3 Detach the ashtray/cigarette lighter assembly and disconnect the wiring.
4 Remove the cross-head screws on either side, then lower the knee bar and remove it from the car.
5 Refitting is a reversal of removal.

26 Sunroof – removal, refitting and adjustment

All models except Scirocco
1 Open the sunroof about one-third, remove the screws, and withdraw the wind deflector.
2 Remove the handle, finger plate, and cable drive assembly.
3 Unclip the headlining from the front of the sunroof, then close the sunroof and push the headlining into the roof.
4 Remove the front guides, rear leaf springs, and rear support plates.
5 Lift the sunroof from the car. If necessary remove the cable guides and cables and remove the headlining panel.

23.3a Outer view of the door check strap

23.3b Inner view of the door check strap

6 With the sunroof removed, use a flexible cable to check that the water drain channels on Jetta models are clear (Fig. 11.32). Where the control cables incorporate fabric, lubricate them with oil; otherwise use high melting-point grease.
7 Refitting is a reversal of removal, but adjust the height of the sunroof with the weatherseal removed. The front of the sunroof should be level with, or up to 1 mm (0.04 in) lower than, the roof; the rear should be level with, or up to 1 mm (0.04 in) higher than, the roof. To adjust the front of the sunroof, loosen the mounting screws, turn the adjusting screws as necessary, then tighten the mounting screws. To adjust the rear of the sunroof, remove the leaf springs, loosen the adjusting screws, reposition the sunroof; then tighten the screws and refit the leaf springs.

Scirocco models
8 Open the sunroof and pull the release pins.
9 Pull the sunroof rearward until the front guides are released, then lift out the sunroof.
10 Refer to paragraph 6 for cleaning the water channels and lubricating the cables.
11 Refitting is a reversal of removal, but the following checks and adjustments should be made.
12 To check that the sunroof is centred the sunroof must be removed, the weatherseal removed, and the sunroof refitted. With the sunroof

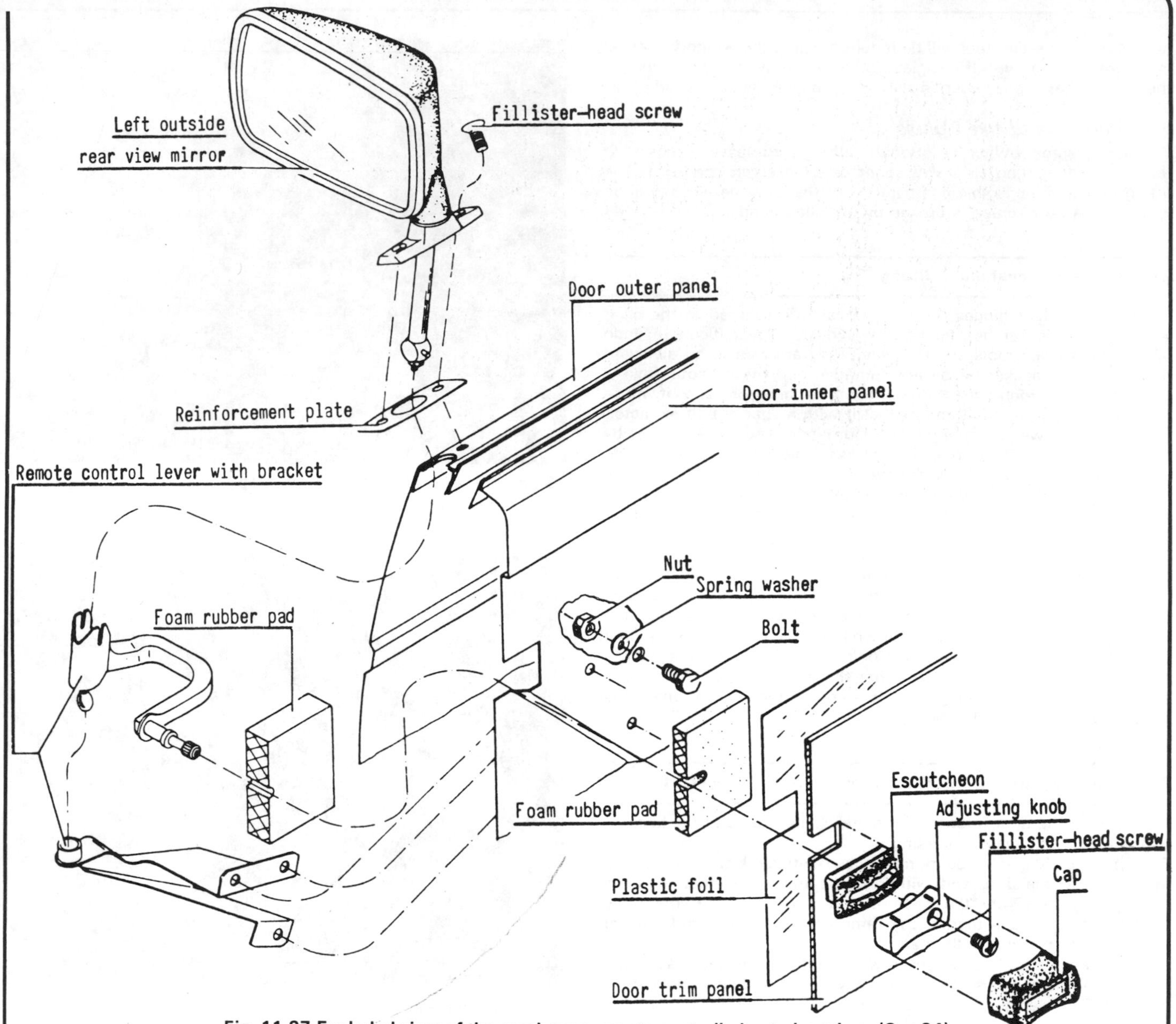

Left outside rear view mirror

Fillister—head screw

Door outer panel

Door inner panel

Reinforcement plate

Remote control lever with bracket

Foam rubber pad

Nut
Spring washer
Bolt

Foam rubber pad

Escutcheon
Adjusting knob
Fillister—head screw
Cap

Plastic foil

Door trim panel

Fig. 11.27 Exploded view of the crank type remote controlled exterior mirror (Sec 24)

Rear view mirror

Fillister head screw

Adjustment knob

Bellows

Lock nut

Mirror mounting packing

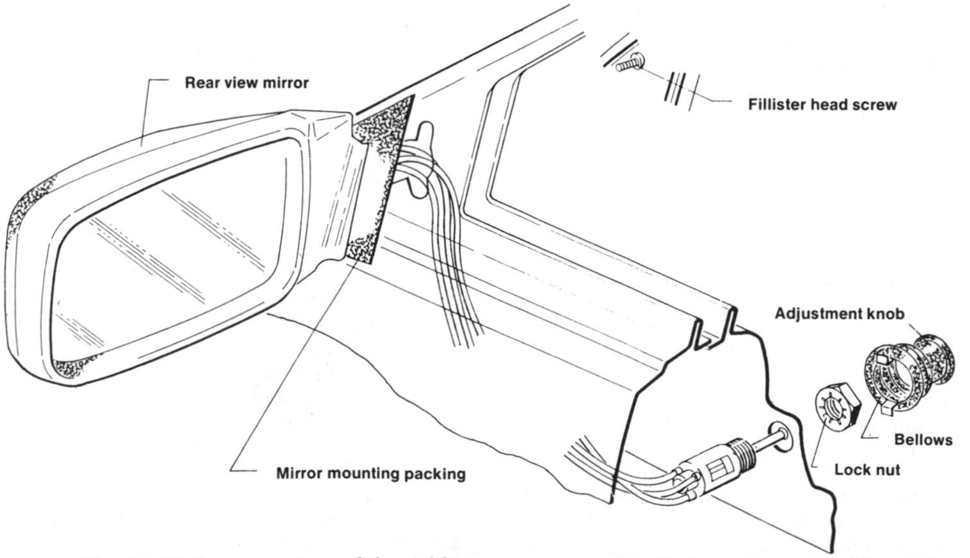

Fig. 11.28 Cutaway view of the cable type remote controlled exterior mirror (Sec 24)

Fig. 11.29 Removing the ashtray/cigarette lighter assembly from the knee bar on Jetta models (Sec 25)

1   Multi-plug   2   Bulb housings

closed the front clearance should be 4.0 to 3.6 mm (0.16 to 0.14 in). If not, remove the sunroof and cable drive, loosen the stop plate screws, reposition the stop plates, tighten the screws, and refit the cable drive.

13 To adjust the cables the sunroof and cables must be removed. With the levers pulled up and the guide blocks forward, turn the cable drive fully clockwise then refit the components.

14 Adjustment of the sunroof height is similar to that described in paragraph 7, but the front guide must be repositioned to adjust the front, and the sunroof tilted for access to the rear adjusting screws.

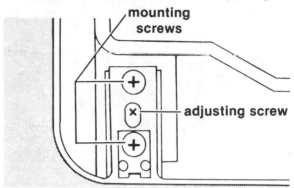

Fig. 11.30 Sunroof front adjustment on Golf, Rabbit, and Jetta models (Sec 26)

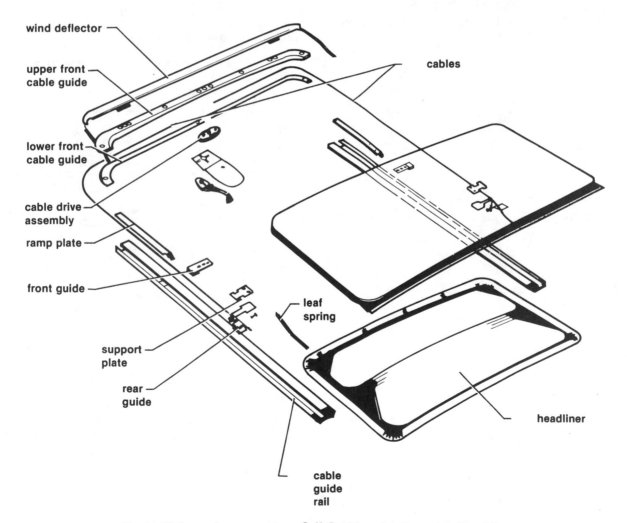

Fig. 11.31 Sunroof components on Golf, Rabbit, and Jetta models (Sec 26)

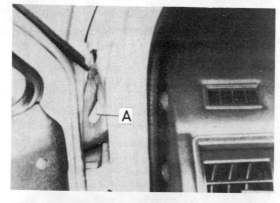

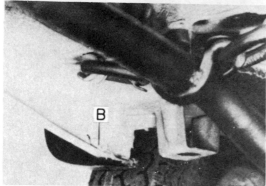

Fig. 11.32 Front (A) and rear (B) sunroof drain hoses on Jetta models (Sec 26)

Rear

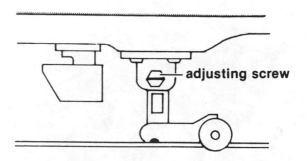

Fig. 11.33 Sunroof rear adjustment on Golf, Rabbit, and Jetta models (Sec 26)

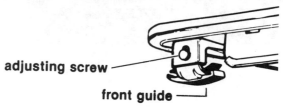

Fig. 11.34 Sunroof front adjustment on Scirocco models (Sec 26)

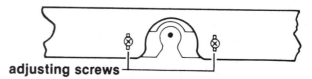

Fig. 11.35 Sunroof rear adjustment on Scirocco models (Sec 26)

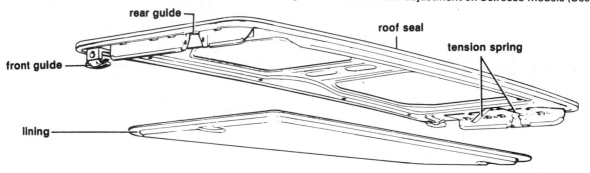

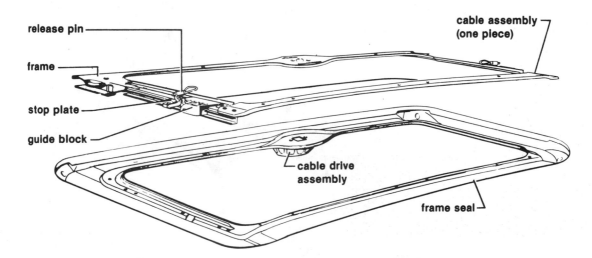

Fig. 11.36 Sunroof components on Scirocco models (Sec 26)

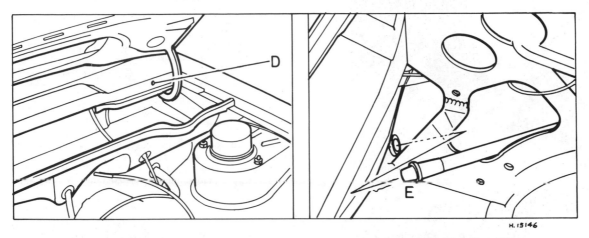

Fig. 11.37 Front (D) and rear (E) sunroof drain outlets on Scirocco models (Sec 26)

27 Top frame assembly (Convertible) – removal and refitting

1   Open the top about 30 cm (12 in).
2   Bend open the headlining tabs beneath the luggage compartment lining and detach the headlining.
3   Disconnect the wiring from the heated rear window.

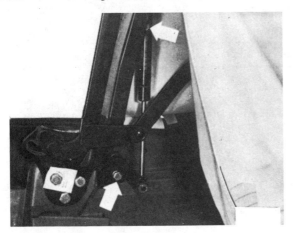

Fig. 11.38 Top frame strut upper circlip and lower bolt locations on Convertible models (Sec 27)

Fig. 11.39 Removing the tensioning wire (arrowed) on Convertible models (Sec 27)

4   Remove the rear window frame hinges and remove the frame lower cover.
5   Detach the rear trim by removing the screws and disconnecting the press studs.
6   Close the top and remove the gas-filled struts. To do this, remove the lower bolts and the upper circlips.
7   Release the tensioning wire from each side, using an open-ended spanner to prevent it twisting.
8   Pull the cover from the channels with the tensioning wire and remove the screws to detach the lower part of the headlining.
9   Unbolt the brackets to release the corner straps.
10 Remove the beading and trim screws, then unbolt the main hinges and withdraw the top frame assembly.
11 Refitting is a reversal of removal, but an assistant will be required to refit the tensioning wire into the channels using a wooden drift (see Fig. 11.40). If necessary carry out the following adjustments.
12 Check that the front of the top frame contacts the header panel evenly when shut – if not, adjust the hooks after loosening the locknuts.
13 Check that the cover contacts the top of the roll bar correctly – if not, turn the eccentric bolts on either side as necessary.
14 Check that the door windows contact the top seals correctly; to adjust the windows loosen the guide bolts at the bottom of the door and move the channels in or out as necessary. If the windows are not

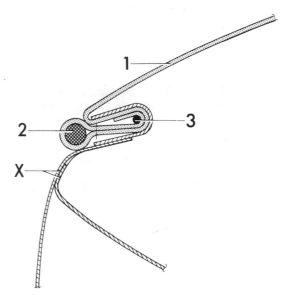

Fig. 11.40 Cross-section of rear cover fold on top frame assembly on Convertible models (Sec 27)

X	Body	2	Plastic cable
1	Cover	3	Tensioning wire

Fig. 11.41 Top frame front hook adjustment (arrowed) on Convertible models (Sec 27)

Fig. 11.42 Top frame cover to roll bar adjustment on Convertible models (Sec 27)

1	Eccentric bolt	A-B Adjustment

Fig. 11.43 Window to cover adjustment (1-2) on Convertible models (Sec 27)

parallel with the top, reposition the adjusting bolts after removing the trim panel. Fore-and-aft movement of the windows is also possible by adjusting the lower channel bolts. Similar adjustments are also possible on the rear side windows.

28 Seats – removal and refitting

Front seats
1   At the back of the runners are small caps, lever these off the runners. Now look under the seat. There is an extra clip which must be removed and then the seat can be pushed toward the rear. When refitting, fit the spring clips in the upper slide, install the seat from the rear guiding the adjusting lever into the latch bolt mountings. Refit the covers on the runners.

Rear seats
2   Remove the mounting screws (where fitted) from the front of the cushion, and pull off the plastic covers (photo).
3   Lift the rear of the cushion to disengage the wire hooks (where fitted) from the floor, then withdraw the cushion. On 1981 on Convertible models, disengage the central tab.
4   On Convertible models unscrew the backrest mounting bolts; on other models prise the upper hooks from the backrest panel (photo).
5   Lift the backrest from the car. The rear seat belt mountings (if fitted) are now exposed (photos).
6   Refitting is a reversal of removal, but on pre-1981 Convertible models, engage the rear seat cushion in the right-hand side first, then press it into the left-hand side retainer.

29 Heater controls – removal and refitting

1   The control unit is located in the centre of the dashboard. It is accessible after the radio has been removed or, on cars without a radio, the cubby hole. Once the radio, or cubby hole, is extracted the control unit may be seen. Disconnect the battery earth strap.
2   Pull off the control knobs and unclip the trim panel.
3   Remove the two cross-head screws holding the control unit, and it may be eased forwards.
4   Note the location of the control cables, then unclip and disconnect them (photo). The control assembly can now be removed.
5   Refitting is a reversal of removal. On 1977 on models note the two detents (Fig. 11.46) for positioning the control and cut-off levers in the closed position. With the two levers in this position, close the control and cut-off flaps, then fit the clips to the cables.

30 Heater unit and fan motor – removal and refitting

Note: *The following paragraphs describe the pre-1977 heater, however the later heater is similar*
1   Refer to Figs. 11.47 and 11.48. The heater cover may be removed from the back of the engine compartment by extracting the two plastic pegs or screws (photos). This gives access to the cut-off flap and its actuating lever. Disconnect the cable and unhook one pivot of the cut-off flap. The flap may now be removed.
2   The fan motor is inside the throat of the inlet to the fresh air housing and may be lifted out. Disconnect the fan cable by pulling off the clip.
3   The housing is held to the body by two metal clips which are difficult to locate and even more difficult to release. In the centre of the clip is a tongue or retaining spring. This must be pressed in and the clip will come undone. There is a clip on each side of the housing. Once these are free the housing can be drawn off the heat exchanger. The large air ducts to the dashboard outlets pull out of the housing.
4   The heat exchanger must be removed after the fresh air housing. Two pipes go through the double grommet and are connected to hoses. It will be necessary to drain the radiator before these hoses are disconnected.
5   Refitting is a reversal of removal. Fitting the clip is tricky – the tab of the clip should be pushed into the retainer on the fresh air housing and the housing lifted squarely until the spring clicks into position.
6   Unless the heat exchanger leaks, the control cables break or the fan motor fails to work, it is best to leave the heater well alone. The

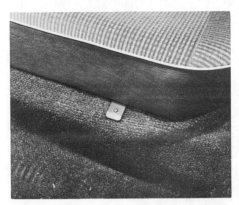

28.2 A rear seat cushion mounting screw (Jetta)

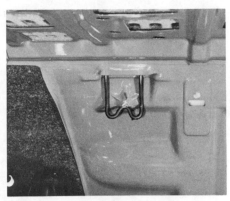

28.4 Rear seat backrest upper hook ...

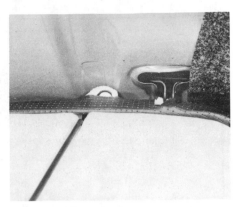

28.5a ... and lower hook

28.5b Rear seat belts with seats removed (Jetta)

28.5c A rear seat belt side anchorage (Jetta)

28.5d Rear seat belt reel location in the boot compartment (Jetta)

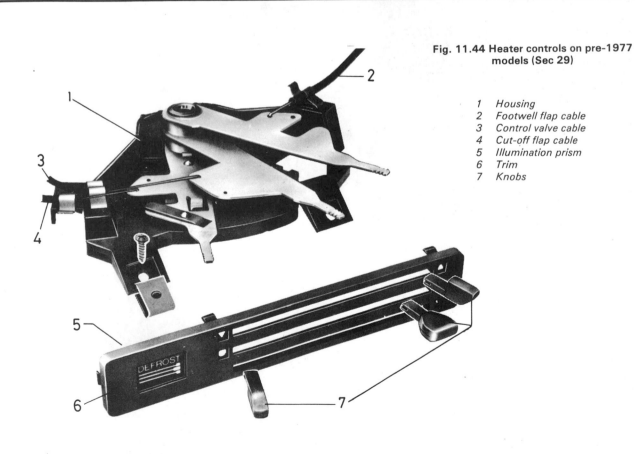

Fig. 11.44 Heater controls on pre-1977 models (Sec 29)

1 Housing
2 Footwell flap cable
3 Control valve cable
4 Cut-off flap cable
5 Illumination prism
6 Trim
7 Knobs

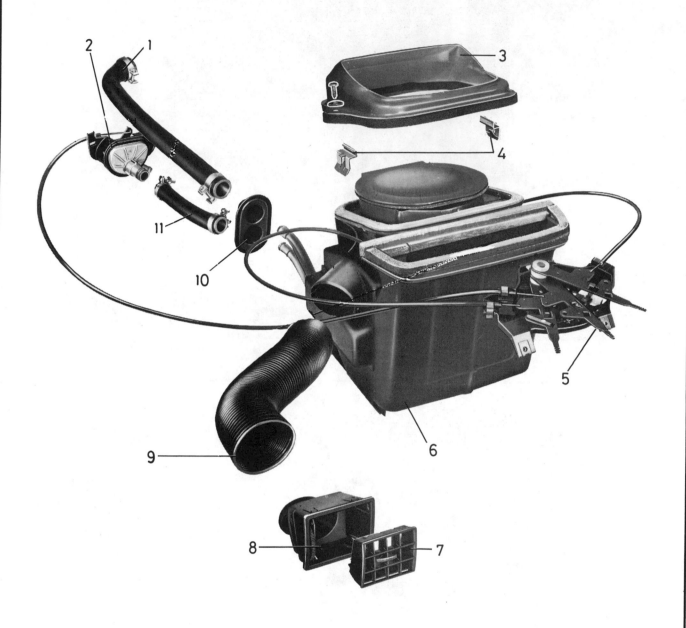

Fig. 11.45 Heater external components on pre-1977 models (Sec 29)

1 Heater hose to cylinder head	4 Clips	7 Air outlet	10 Grommet
2 Control valve	5 Heater controls	8 Fresh air vent	11 Heater hose to control valve
3 Heater cover	6 Housing	9 Air outlet	

29.4 Heater temperature control valve located in the engine compartment (arrowed). Note control cable connection

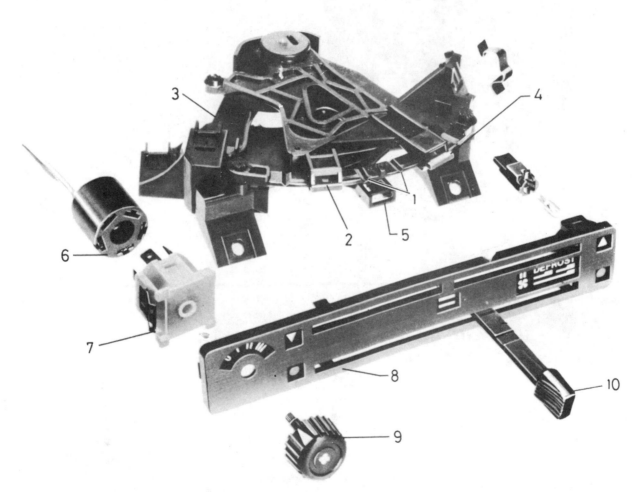

Fig. 11.46 Heater controls on 1977 on models (Sec 29)

1	Detents	6	Plug
2	Control flap lever	7	Switch
3	Fresh air and heater control	8	Trim
4	Cut-off flap lever	9	Knob
5	Regulating valve lever	10	Knob

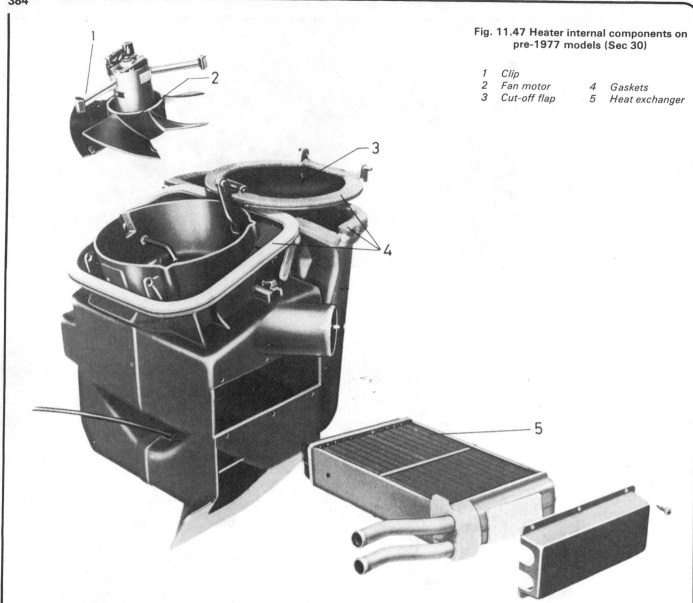

**Fig. 11.47 Heater internal components on
pre-1977 models (Sec 30)**

1 Clip
2 Fan motor
3 Cut-off flap
4 Gaskets
5 Heat exchanger

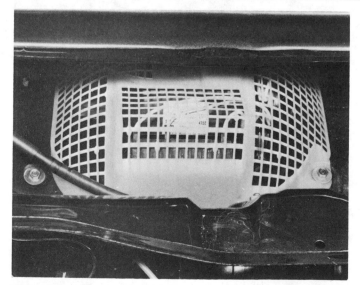

30.1a Heater cover location (Golf)

30.1b Heater location (Scirocco)

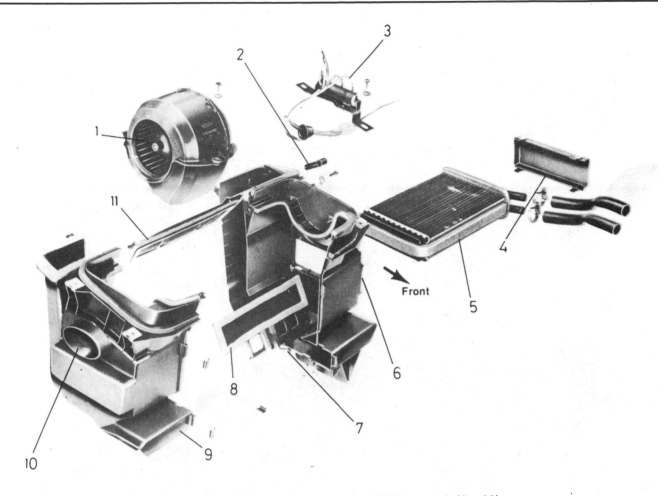

Fig. 11.48 Heater internal components on 1977 on models (Sec 30)

1 Rotary fan unit	7 Control flap clamp
2 Lever	8 Control flap
3 Series resistance	9 Housing half
4 Cover	10 Hose connection
5 Heat exchanger	11 Cut-off flap
6 Housing half	

dismantling and reassembly is not a long job but you can get into trouble trying to get the housing clips off and on and unless the job is done carefully the housing may crack or split.

31 Air conditioning system – general

1 The unit works on exactly the same principle as a domestic refrigerator, having a compressor, a condenser and an evaporator. The condenser is attached to the car radiator system. The compressor, belt-driven from the crankshaft pulley, is installed on a bracket on the engine. The evaporator is installed in a housing under the dashboard which takes the place of the normal fresh air housing. The housing also contains a normal heat exchanger unit for warming the intake air. The evaporator has a blower motor to circulate cold air as required.

2 The system is controlled by a unit on the dashboard similar to the normal heater control in appearance.

3 The refrigerant used is difluorodichloromethane (CF_2CL_2 more commonly known as Frigen F12 or Freon F12. It is a dangerous substance in unskilled hands. As a liquid it is very cold and if it touches the skin there will be cold burns and frostbite. As a gas it is colourless and has no odour. Heavier than air, it displaces oxygen and can cause asphyxiation if pockets of it collect in pits or similar workplaces. It does not burn, but even a lighted cigarette causes it to break down into constituent gases, some of which are poisonous to the extent of being fatal. So if you have an air-conditioner and your car catches fire, you have an additional problem.

4 We strongly recommend that even trained refrigeration mechanics do not adjust the system unless they have had instruction by VW. We suggest that the system is left entirely alone, except for the adjustment of the compressor drivebelt, which should have 5 to 10 mm (0.2 to 0.4 in) deflection in the centre when depressed by the thumb. See Chapter 2 for adjustment procedures.

5 Removal and refitting of the air conditioner compressor is straightforward as can be seen from Fig. 11.50 but the refrigerant circuit **must not be opened**. The compressor must be placed on the side of the engine compartment when removing the engine, but only move it to the point where the flexible refrigerant hoses are in no danger of being stretched.

6 When a situation arises which calls for the removal of one of the air conditioning system components, have the system discharged by your VW agent or a qualified refrigeration engineer. Similarly have the system recharged by him on completion.

7 During the winter period operate the air conditioner for a few minutes each week to keep the system in good order.

8 Periodically, clean the condenser of dirt and insects, either by washing with a cold water hose or by air pressure. Use a soft bristle brush to assist removal of dirt jammed in the condenser fins.

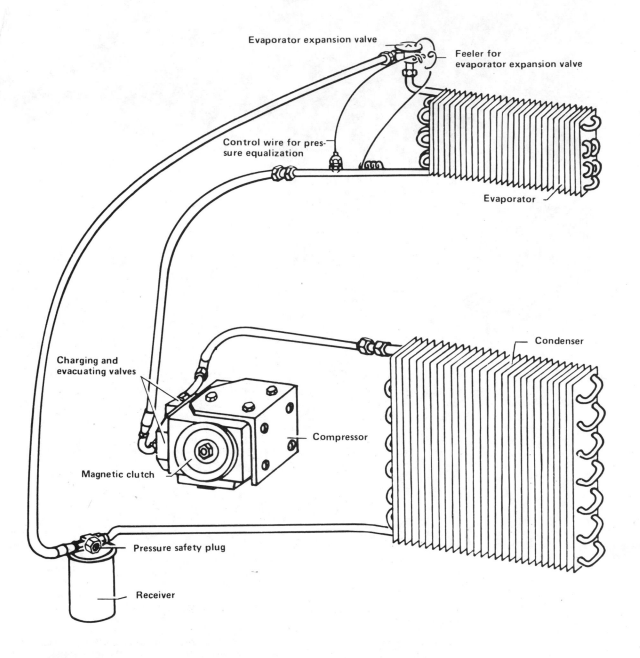

Fig. 11.49 Diagrammatic layout of the air conditioning system (Sec 31)

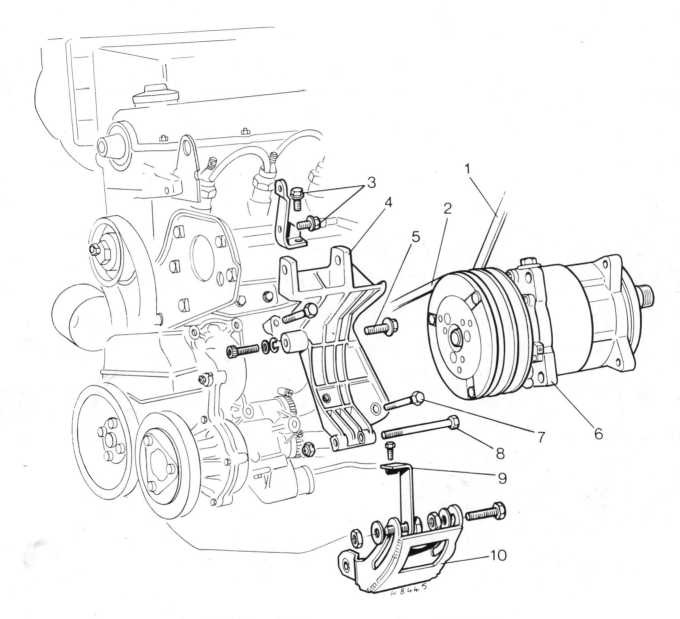

Fig. 11.50 Air conditioning compressor and mounting (Sec 31)

1 Alternator drivebelt
2 Water pump and compressor
   drivebelt
3 Bolts
4 Bracket
5 Bolt

6 Compressor – bolt must
   be at top
7 Bolt
8 Bolt
9 Hose bracket
10 Tensioner

Chapter 12 Supplement:
Revisions and information on later models

Contents

1   Introduction

This supplement contains changes to vehicle specification and modifications which affect servicing and/or repairs to Golf, Rabbit, Jetta and Pick-up models from 1982 on. Changes which affect earlier models are also included and this is stated where applicable.

In order to use the Supplement to the best advantage it is suggested that it is referred to before the main Chapters of the Manual: this will ensure that any relevant information can be noted and incorporated within the procedures given in Chapters 1 to 11. Time and cost will therefore be saved and the particular job will be completed correctly.

2   Specifications

The specifications listed below are revisions of, or supplementary to, the main Specifications listed at the beginning of each Chapter
Engine
1715 cc engine
Valve timing (nil valve clearance, at 1 mm valve lift):
    Inlet opens .... 1° BTDC
    Inlet closes .... 37° ABDC
    Exhaust opens .... 42° BBDC
    Exhaust closes .... 2° ATDC

1780 cc engine
The specifications are the same as for the 1588 cc engine listed in Chapter 1, except for the following differences

General
Engine code:
    UK models .... DX
    North American models .... JH
Bore .... 81.0 mm (3.19 in)
Stroke .... 86.4 mm (3.40 in)
Compression ratio:
    Engine code DX .... 10.0 : 1
    Engine code JH .... 8.5 : 1

Crankshaft
Crankpin diameter (standard) .... 47.80 mm (1.883 in)
Crankpin undersizes .... 47.55, 47.30 and 47.05 mm (1.873, 1.863 and 1.853 in)
Crankshaft endfloat (maximum) .... 0.25 mm (0.010 in)

Pistons
Piston diameter (standard) .... 80.98 mm (3.190 in)
Piston oversizes .... 81.23 and 81.48 mm (3.200 and 3.210 in)

Valves
Inlet valve head diameter .... 38.0 mm (1.497 in)
Exhaust valve head diameter .... 33.0 mm (1.300 in)
Valve timing (nil valve clearance, at 1 mm valve lift):
    Inlet opens .... 6° BTDC
    Inlet closes .... 49° ABDC
    Exhaust opens .... 45° BBDC
    Exhaust closes .... 8° ATDC

Torque wrench settings

	lbf ft	Nm
Crankshaft sprocket:		
M12 x 1.5 bolt	59	80
M14 x 1.5 bolt	148	200
Cylinder head bolts:		
M10-12 point socket head bolts:		
Stage 1	29	40
Stage 2	40	55
Stage 3	47	65
Stage 4	Tighten further by $\frac{1}{4}$ turn	
M11-12 point socket head bolts:		
Stage 1	29	40
Stage 2	44	60
Stage 3	Tighten further by $\frac{1}{2}$ turn	
Connecting rod big-end nuts (see text):		
M9 x 1 rigid bolt	33	45
M8 x 1 stretch bolt, notched retaining nuts:		
Stage 1	22	30
Stage 2	Tighten further by $\frac{1}{2}$ turn	
Oil pressure switch:		
Tapered thread	8	11
Cylindrical thread	18	25

Fuel and exhaust systems
Carburettor data – Solex 1B3, October 1981 onward
The data given in Chapter 3 is still applicable, except for the following
Carburettor number:
    Engine code JB
        Manual .... 055 129 025 J
        Automatic .... 055 129 025 K
    Engine code GH .... 055 129 025 L

K-Jetronic Continuous Injection System (CIS) data
Idling speed – UK models:
    Electronic ignition with Digital Idling Stabilization (DIS):
        1588 cc, 1981 on .... 750 to 850 rpm
        1780 cc, 1982 on .... 900 to 1000 rpm
    Electronic ignition without Digital Idling Stabilization (DIS):
        All models, 1981 on .... 900 to 1000 rpm

CO content (volume %):

	USA except California	California	Canada
UK 1780 cc models .... 0.5 to 1.5			
North American models:			
1982 on except Pick-up	0.3 to 3.0	0.3 to 3.0	1.5 maximum (manual), 0.9 maximum (automatic)
1982 on Pick-up	1.0 to 2.0	0.3 to 3.0	1.5 maximum (manual), 0.9 maximum (automatic)

System pressures:
   Holding pressure after 10 mins:
      Fuel accumulator suffix C or D ....   2.6 bar (37.7 lbf/in^2)
   Holding pressure after 20 mins:
      Fuel accumulator suffix C or D ....   2.4 bar (34.8 lbf/in^2)
System pressure – August 1979 onward ....   4.7 to 5.4 bar (68.1 to 78.3 lbf/in^2)

Ignition system
Ignition timing (static or idle)

UK models:
   1780 cc, engine code DX, 1982 onward ....   6° BTDC
North American models:
   1983 US Rabbit and Jetta with manual transmission, and
   Pick-up for California with manual transmission ....   6° BTDC
   1983 US Rabbit and Jetta wth automatic transmission, and Pick-up
   for California with automatic transmission ....   3° ATDC
   1983 Pick-up with manual transmission (except California) ....   3° ATDC
   1983 Canada models ....   3° ATDC
   1984 Rabbit and Jetta, 1715 cc with manual transmission ....   6° BTDC
   1984 Rabbit and Jetta, 1715 cc with automatic transmission ......   3° ATDC
   1984 Rabbit and Jetta, 1780 cc ....   6° BTDC

Spark plug types

UK models:
   1780 cc, engine code DX, 1982 onward ....   Bosch W6DO
    Beru 14-6 DU
    Champion N79Y

North American models:
   1980, US models ....   Bosch WR7DS
    Beru RS-35
    Champion N8GY

   1980, Canada models ....   Bosch W8D or W145 T30
    Beru 14-8D or 145/14/3A
    Champion N10Y

   1981 to 1984, 1715 cc US models except California ....   Bosch W7D or W175 T30
    Beru 14-7D or 175/14/3A
    Champion N8Y

   1981 to 1984, 1715 cc California models ....   Bosch WR7DS or W7DT
    Beru RS35 or 14-7DT
    Champion N8GY

   1981 to 1982, Canada models ....   Bosch W7D or W175 T30
    Beru 14-7D or 175/14/3A
    Champion N8Y

   1983, Canada models ....   Bosch W8D or W145 T30
    Beru 14-8D or 145/14/3A
    Champion N10Y

   1983, 1780 cc US models except Pick-up ....   Bosch W7DT or WR7DS
    Beru RS35
    Champion N8GY

   1983, Pick-up models:
     With oxygen sensors ....   Bosch WR7DS
     Beru RS35
     Champion N8GY

     Without oxygen sensors ....   Bosch W7D or W175 T30
     Beru 14-7D or 175/14/3A
     Champion N8Y

   1984, 1780 cc US models ....   Bosch WR7DS
    Beru RS35
    Champion N8GY or N281BY

   1984, Canada models ....   Bosch W8DO
    Beru 14-8DO
    Champion N8IY

Spark plug electrode gap

All models except UK 1780 cc ....   0.6 to 0.8 mm (0.024 to 0.032 in)
UK 1780 cc ....   0.8 to 0.9 mm (0.032 to 0.035 mm)

Manual gearbox
Gear ratios (5-speed gearbox)
All 1780 cc models:

1st	3.45 : 1 (11/38)
2nd	2.12 : 1 (17/36)
3rd	1.44 : 1 (27/39)
4th	1.13 : 1 (31/35)
5th:	
Up to August 1983, gearbox codes 7G and 2H	0.91 : 1 (34/31)
From August 1983, gearbox codes 9A, 4Y and 4K	0.89 : 1 (47/42)
Reverse	3.17 : 1 (12/38)
Final drive:	
UK models up to August 1983, gearbox code 7G	3.65 : 1 (17/62)
UK models from August 1983, gearbox code 9A	3.66 : 1 (18/66)
North American models up to August 1983, gearbox code 2H	3.93 : 1 (16/63)
North American models from August 1983, gearbox code 4K	3.94 : 1 (17/67)

Braking system
Torque wrench settings

	lbf ft	Nm
Brake caliper-to-strut (M10 x 30) locking bolt	52	70

Electrical system
Fuses
Note: *The following table applies to UK models from 1983 onward – for North American models refer to the information stamped on the fusebox below each fuse*

Fuse No	Current rating (amps)	Circuits protected
1	30	Radiator fan
2	10	Brake lights
3	15	Cigarette lighter, radio, clock, interior light
4	15	Hazard flasher lights
5	15	Fuel pump
6	15	Foglights (main current)
7	10	Left-hand side and tail lights
8	10	Right-hand side and tail lights
9	10	Right-hand headlamp main beam and main beam warning lamp
10	10	Left-hand headlamp main beam
11	15	Windscreen wipers/washers
12	15	Coolant level monitor
13	15	Heated rear window
14	20	Fresh air fan
15	20	Reversing lights, automatic transmission selector lever illumination
16	15	Horn (single)
17	10	Automatic choke and idling cut-off valve, electric manifold heater
18	15	Horn (dual tone), headlight washer, brake warning lamp
19	10	Turn signals
20	10	Number plate light, glovebox light, foglights (switch current)
21	10	Left-hand headlamp dipped beam
22	10	Right-hand headlamp dipped beam
Additional 10 amp fuse in separate holder above fusebox		Rear foglight

Suspension and steering
Power assisted steering pump drivebelt tension
Deflection midway between crankshaft and power steering pump pulleys .... 10 to 12 mm (0.4 to 0.5 in)

Torque wrench settings

	lbf ft	Nm
Power steering pump to bracket	11	15
Power steering pump bracket to engine	14	20
Pulley to power steering pump	14	20
Power steering gear retaining U-clamp nuts	22	30
Tie-rod to steering rack	51	70
Tie-rod end balljoint to steering arm	22	30
Fluid pipe unions	30	40

3 Engine

Cylinder head – revised bolt tightening procedure
1   On later engines two different sizes of cylinder head retaining bolts are used; according to engine type and power output. Both types are of the 12-point socket-head variety and can only be used once. Therefore new bolts **must be** obtained whenever the cylinder head is removed.

2   The revised tightening procedure and torque settings for both bolt sizes are given in the Specifications and are applicable to all engines fitted with these bolts. Note that no further tightening of the bolts is necessary during maintenance or after repairs.

Connecting rod cap bolts and nuts – modifications
3   The retaining bolts used to secure the connecting rod caps to the connecting rods may now be either conventional M9 x 1 rigid bolts and nuts or M8 x 1 'stretch' bolts with notched retaining nuts. Figs.

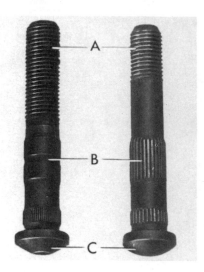

Fig. 12.1 Connecting rod bolt types (Sec 3)

Left M8x1 'stretch' bolt   Right M9x1 rigid bolt

A, B and C Differences between bolt types

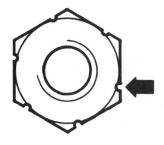

Fig. 12.2 Connecting rod nuts for use with 'stretch' bolts (Sec 3)

Arrow indicates identification notches

12.1 and 12.2 show the distinguishing features of the two types. The tightening procedure and torque setting has been altered for the 'stretch' bolt, so correct identification of the type fitted is essential before reassembly.

Inlet and exhaust valves – modifications

4   From approximately May 1981 the inlet and exhaust valve stems, split collets and spring caps have been modified, as shown in Fig. 12.3. Three grooves instead of one are machined in the valve stem and the split collets have been changed accordingly. The spring cap used with these modified parts has an additional chamfer on its inner circumference. The modified components may be fitted in complete or part sets when carrying out repairs to earlier engines, but each modified valve must only be installed with its associated modified collets and cap.

Valve clearances – adjustment

5   From approximately August 1982 the distance between the inlet valve and exhaust valve has been increased and VW tool 2078 is now required to push the tappets down for removal of the tappet disc. Alternatively the home made tools described in Chapter 1, Section 23 may still be used. The remainder of the adjustment procedure is unaffected by this modification.

1780 cc engine – description

6   From approximately August 1982 a larger engine of 1780 cc displacement was introduced for both UK and North American models. Apart from the larger capacity resulting from an increase in the cylinder bore diameter and piston stroke, and other related changes as

listed in the Specifications, the engine is essentially the same as the earlier 1588 cc unit. The maintenance and repair procedures described in Chapter 1 and earlier in this Supplement are therefore also applicable to the 1780 cc engine.

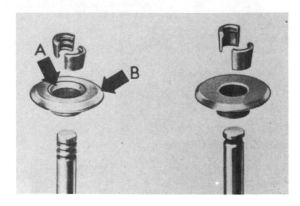

Fig. 12.3 Inlet and exhaust valve identification (Sec 3)

Left Later type   Right Early type

A and B Chamfers on spring cap

4   Fuel and exhaust systems

Solex carburettors – revisions

1   Certain minor modifications have been made to the design of the Solex 1B3 carburettor fitted to 1457 cc UK models from approximately October 1981. These are mainly concerned with the arrangement of the jets and internal drillings and passages and do not affect maintenance and servicing operations. Note, however, that when adjusting the position of the enrichment tube, a gap of 0.7 to 1.3 mm (0.03 to 0.05 in) must now exist between the bottom end of the tube and the upper surface of the choke valve (Fig. 12.4).

2   An inlet manifold preheater is also used on later installations using the 1B3 carburettor. This is an electric heating element which is bolted to the underside of the manifold and increases fuel vaporisation during cold start warm-up conditions. The preheater is controlled by a thermoswitch located in the manifold coolant circuit. This arrangement is shown in Fig. 12.5.

Fig. 12.4 Enrichment tube adjustment dimension – Solex 1B3 carburettor (Sec 4)

a = 0.7 to 1.3 mm (0.03 to 0.05 in)

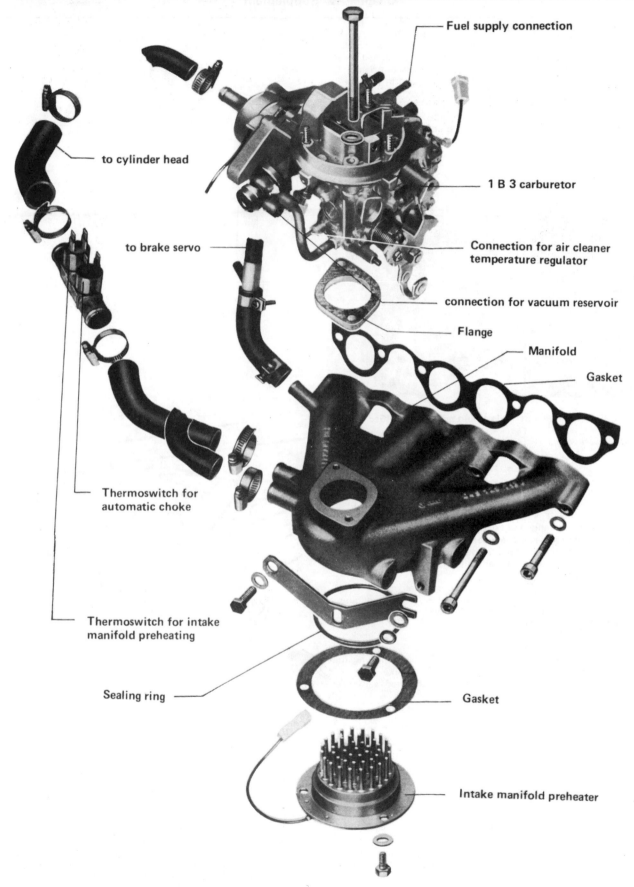

Fuel supply connection

to cylinder head

1 B 3 carburetor

to brake servo

Connection for air cleaner temperature regulator

connection for vacuum reservoir

Flange

Manifold

Gasket

Thermoswitch for automatic choke

Thermoswitch for intake manifold preheating

Sealing ring

Gasket

Intake manifold preheater

Fig. 12.5 Inlet manifold and carburettor layout – Solex 1B3 carburettor, October 1981 on (Sec 4)

Continuous Injection System (CIS) – adjustments

3   The adjustment procedures described in Chapter 3, Section 28 apply also to later models, but where the settings have altered these are given in the Specifications at the beginning of this Supplement.
4   In addition to the test and setting conditions listed in Chapter 3, Section 28, the crankcase breather hose should be disconnected at the valve cover on all UK models. Additionally, on 1985 model Golf Convertibles with 1780 cc engine, the headlamps should remain switched off and the hose from the idling speed boost valve to the manifold (Fig. 12.6) should be squeezed shut.

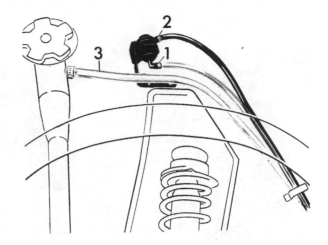

Fig. 12.7 Fuel tank gravity valve connections (Sec 4)

1 and 2 Hose connections at gravity valve   3   Large breather pipe

Fig. 12.6 Air hose layout – idle speed boost circuit (Sec 4)

*1 and 2 Boost valves   3   Boost valve-to-manifold
                                     air hose*

Fuel tank and components – modifications

5   During the course of production various alterations have been carried out to the fuel tank components, mainly concerned with the location, quantity and arrangement of breather, vent and fuel lines. The modifications are numerous and vary considerably according to model, engine size and operating territory. In the main the information given in Chapter 3 is still applicable, and any changes can be noted during removal as a guide to refitting.
6   A major revision of the fuel tank arrangement was made in 1984 which is applicable to models fitted with fuel injected engines. Removal and refitting instructions are as follows.
7   Disconnect the battery negative terminal.
8   Jack up the rear of the car and support it on axle stands. Chock the front wheels.
9   Drain the fuel tank by using a syphon, or by disconnecting the bottom filler hose. **Caution:** Ensure adequate ventilation.
10 Remove the access panel located under the right-hand rear wheel arch.
11 Disconnect the large breather pipe from the filler neck.
12 Pull the gravity valve down without disconnecting the two hoses (Fig. 12.7).
13 Detach the fuel pump bracket from the body and lower the pump.
14 Undo the tank retaining bolt, detach the hose from the fuel pump and detach the blue hose from the fuel return line (Fig. 12.8).
15 Disconnect both flexible brake hoses from the rear axle (see Chapters 8 and 10).
16 Detach the rear axle from the body on both sides (see Chapter 10) lower it carefully and allow it to hang on the handbrake cable guides.
17 Detach the rubber mounting rings from the exhaust main silencer.
18 Pull the hose from the filler neck of the tank.
19 Support the tank with a jack, undo the remaining retaining bolts or screws and carefully lower the tank.
20 When sufficient clearance exists, disconnect the fuel gauge sender unit connector.
21 Lower the tank fully, detach the breather pipes and remove the tank.
22 Refitting is the reverse sequence to removal, but bleed the braking system, as described in Chapter 8, on completion.

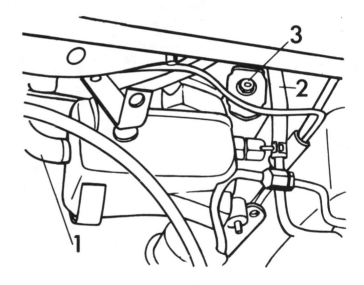

Fig. 12.8 Fuel tank and fuel pump details (Sec 4)

*1   Fuel pump hose   3   Tank retaining bolt
2   Fuel pump return
    line (blue)*

Exhaust system – general

23 Retaining clips are used to secure the exhaust front pipe to the manifold on later engines with carburettor induction. A special tool (VW 3049A) is specified for the removal and refitting of the clips (Fig. 12.9), but if care is taken a stout screwdriver or bar can be used instead. Ensure that the clips are not damaged or distorted during removal and renew them if necessary. Also renew the flange sealing ring if it is damaged or leaking.
24 When refitting the retaining clips, engage their upper ends in the manifold slots, push up firmly on the front pipe and lever the lower ends into place on the pipe flange.

Fig. 12.9 VW special tool for exhaust front pipe retaining clip removal (Sec 4)

The adjusting side (arrowed) must face down

Fig. 12.10 Ignition timing adjustment – models with Digital Idling Stabilization (Sec 5)

Disconnect connectors at DIS switch unit and join together (arrows)

5 Ignition system

Ignition timing – adjustment

1   On models equipped with Digital Idling Stabilization (DIS) it is first necessary to disconnect the DIS switch unit before adjusting the ignition timing. To do this, switch off the ignition, pull the two connectors off the DIS switch unit and join them together (Fig. 12.10).
2   The ignition timing can now be adjusted using the procedure described in Chapter 4, Section 11. On completion of the adjustment, switch off the engine and reconnect the two plugs to the DIS switch unit.

Thermo-pneumatic valve – general

3   On 1780 cc engines equipped with a thermo-pneumatic valve in the distributor vacuum line the test settings are the same as for the 1.6 litre, 55 kW automatic engine given in Chapter 4, Section 14.

6 Manual gearbox

Gearbox (4-speed) – modifications

1   From approximately August 1982 certain modifications have been carried out to the gearchange linkage to improve gear selection and engagement. A removable cap is now provided in the rubber boot at the base of the gear lever to facilitate adjustment of the linkage. In addition the shift rod support bearing is now of one-piece construction and the size of the rubber ball on the relay lever has been increased. Apart from these modifications the repair and adjustment procedures described in Chapter 6 remain unchanged.
2   The two circlips that secure the shift fork shaft in the shift fork set have been deleted on later gearboxes and in their place are two small springs, one at each end of the shaft (Fig. 12.11). This arrangement

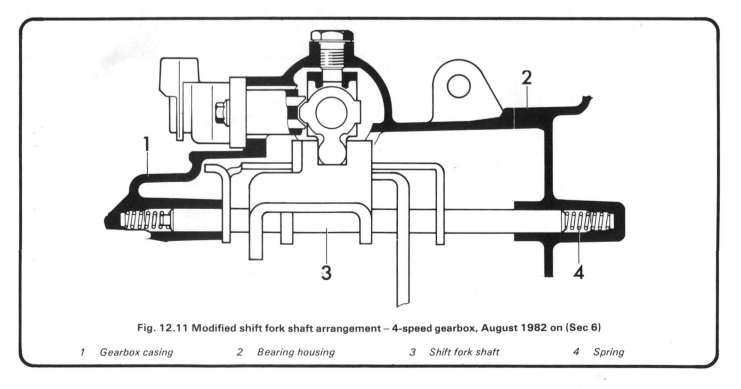

Fig. 12.11 Modified shift fork shaft arrangement – 4-speed gearbox, August 1982 on (Sec 6)

1 Gearbox casing	2 Bearing housing	3 Shift fork shaft	4 Spring

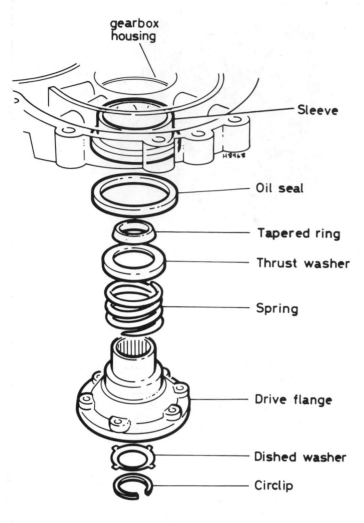

Fig. 12.12 Differential drive flange modifications – 4- and 5-speed gearboxes, March 1981 on (Sec 6)

allows the shaft to 'float' between the two springs, as in the 5-speed gearbox.

3   From approximately March 1981 the differential drive flange location has been modified on certain gearboxes. A spring, thrust ring and sleeve are fitted behind each flange to provide a location which is free of play, thus reducing drive train noise. This modification does not affect the drive flange removal or refitting procedures, but note the location of the modified components when carrying out repairs to the gearbox. The sleeve should always be renewed during gearbox overhaul and can be removed by tapping in one edge with a punch then withdrawing the sleeve with pliers. The new sleeve can be fitted by tapping it in using a hammer and tube of suitable diameter.

Gearbox (5-speed) – modifications

4   The modifications described above to the gearchange linkage and differential drive flanges are also applicable to the 5-speed gearbox.

---

7   Braking system

Brake caliper and pads (Kelsey-Hayes) – modifications

1   From February 1984 certain models may be fitted with a modified Kelsey-Hayes disc brake assembly with a closed caliper mounting bracket (Fig. 12.13). The procedures described in Chapter 8 for the earlier Kelsey-Hayes assembly are still applicable, apart from the following.

2   The previously used guide pins have been replaced by guide sleeves with socket-headed bolts and the pad retaining springs have been changed to metal strips (Figs. 12.14 and 12.15). When refitting the pads, locate the metal strips in the mounting bracket first followed by the pads. Slide the caliper over the pads just sufficiently to start the socket-headed bolts, otherwise the metal strips can become distorted. With the caliper in place the bolts can be tightened fully.

Brake caliper retaining bolts – modifications

3   From October 1981 flanged locking bolts to secure the brake caliper to the stub axle have been progressively introduced to replace the previously used conventional hex head bolt (Fig. 12.16). The bolt holes in the brake caliper have been provided with a 45° chamfer on their internal circumference when used with the new type bolt (Fig. 12.17).

4   The flanged locking bolt may be used with earlier calipers, but it will be necessary to chamfer the bolt holes accordingly. This may be done with a countersunk drill bit or suitable scraper. The earlier hex head bolts **must not** be used on calipers with chamfered bolt holes.

5   A revised torque wrench setting is applicable to the locking bolt and this is given in the Specifications at the beginning of this Supplement.

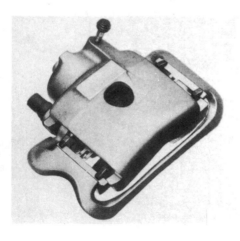

Fig. 12.13 Later type (left) and early type (right) Kelsey-Hayes disc brake caliper (Sec 7)

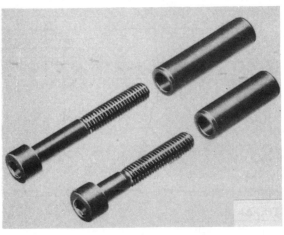 

Fig. 12.14 Kelsey-Hayes caliper guide sleeves with socket-headed bolts (left) and early type guide pins (right) (Sec 7)

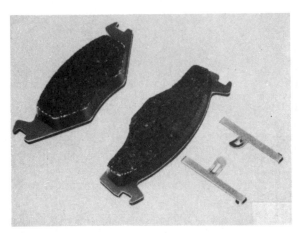 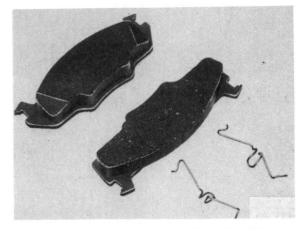

Fig. 12.15 Kelsey-Hayes disc brake pads with pad retaining strips (left) and retaining springs (right) (Sec 7)

Fig. 12.16 Brake caliper retaining bolt details (Sec 7)

Fig. 12.17 Caliper bolt hole chamfers (arrowed) for use with flanged locking bolts (Sec 7)

1   Later type flanged locking bolt   2   Early type conventional bolt

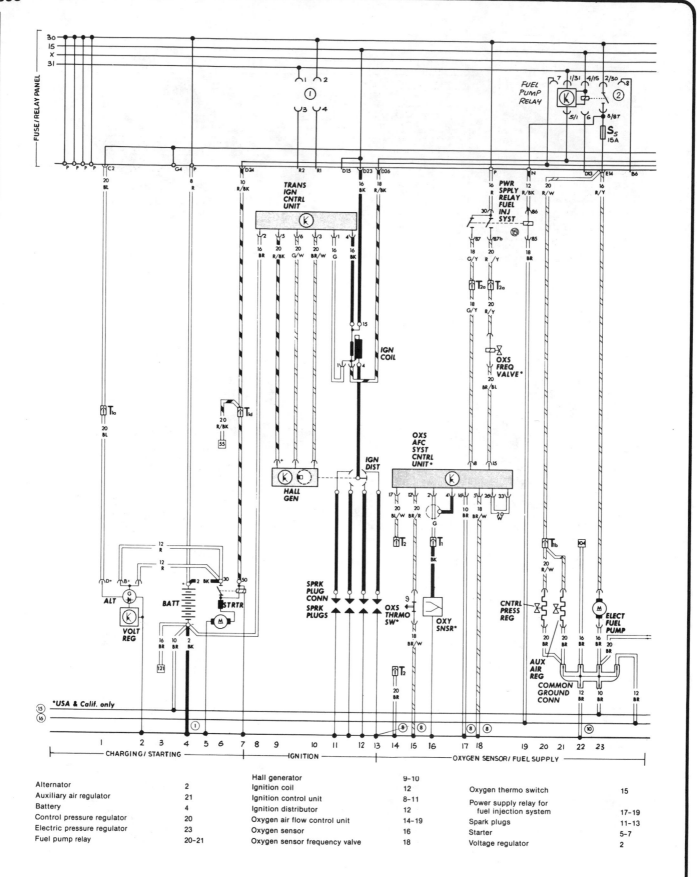

Fig. 12.18 Wiring diagram for 1983 and 1984 Jetta and Rabbit Convertible models

Alternator	2	Hall generator	9–10	
Auxiliary air regulator	21	Ignition coil	12	Oxygen thermo switch
Battery	4	Ignition control unit	8–11	Power supply relay for
Control pressure regulator	20	Ignition distributor	12	fuel injection system
Electric pressure regulator	23	Oxygen air flow control unit	14–19	Spark plugs
Fuel pump relay	20–21	Oxygen sensor	16	Starter
		Oxygen sensor frequency valve	18	Voltage regulator

Oxygen thermo switch — 15
Power supply relay for fuel injection system — 17–19
Spark plugs — 11–13
Starter — 5–7
Voltage regulator — 2

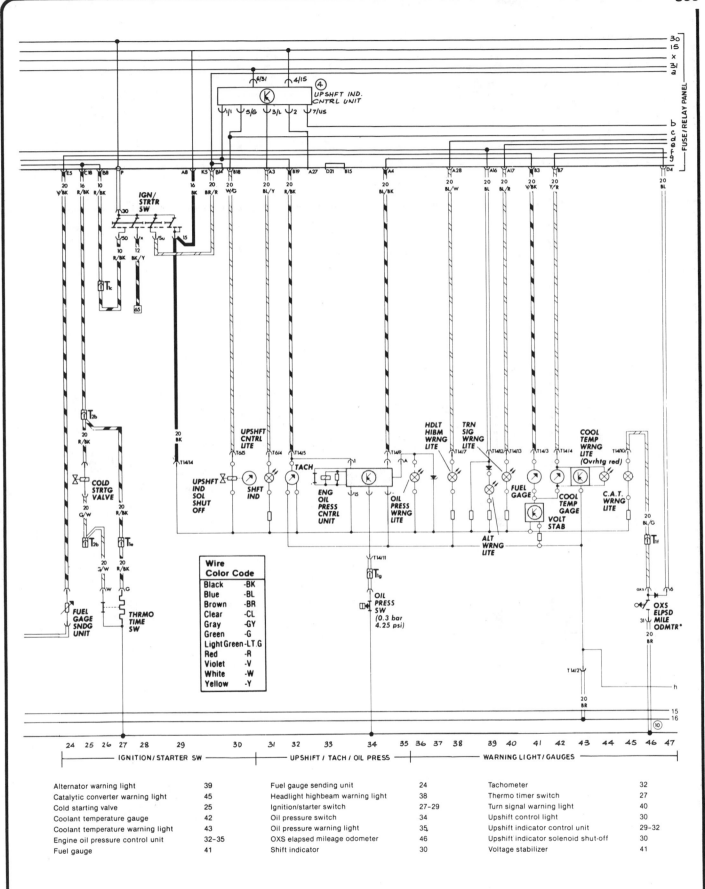

Fig. 12.18 Wiring diagram for 1983 and 1984 Jetta and Rabbit Convertible models (continued)

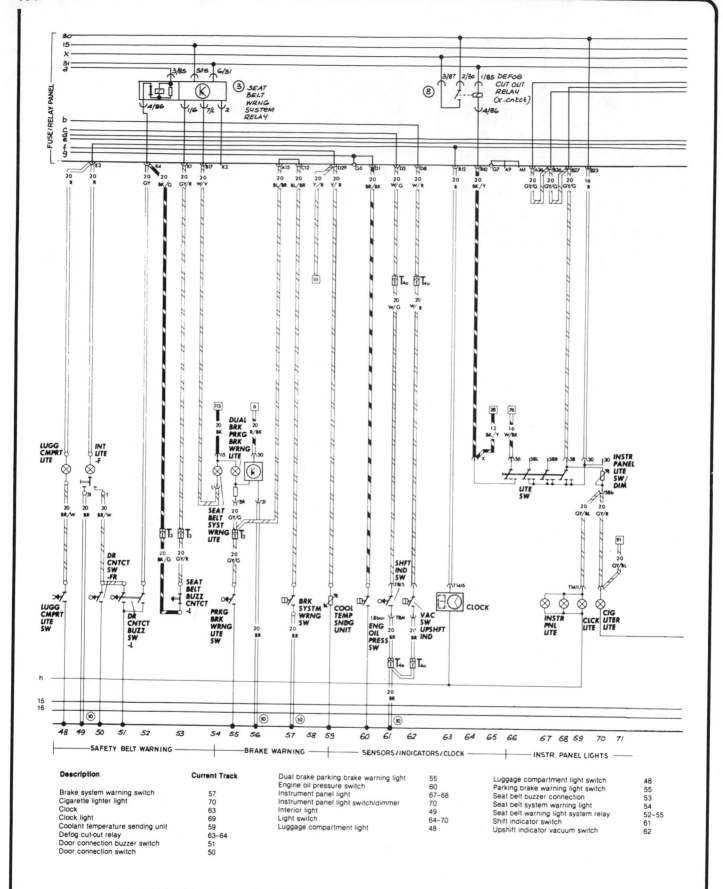

Fig. 12.18 Wiring diagram for 1983 and 1984 Jetta and Rabbit Convertible models (continued)

Description	Current Track				
Brake system warning switch	57	Dual brake parking brake warning light	55	Luggage compartment light switch	48
Cigarette lighter light	70	Engine oil pressure switch	60	Parking brake warning light switch	55
Clock	63	Instrument panel light	67-68	Seat belt buzzer connection	53
Clock light	69	Instrument panel light switch/dimmer	70	Seat belt system warning light	54
Coolant temperature sending unit	59	Interior light	49	Seat belt warning light system relay	52-55
Defog cut-out relay	63-64	Light switch	64-70	Shift indicator switch	61
Door connection buzzer switch	51	Luggage compartment light	48	Upshift indicator vacuum switch	62
Door connection switch	50				

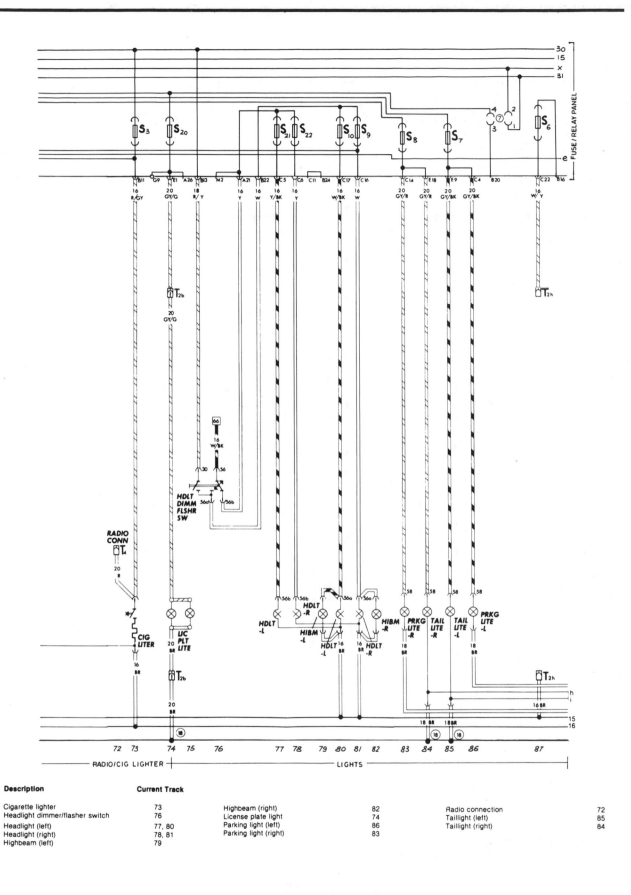

Fig. 12.18 Wiring diagram for 1983 and 1984 Jetta and Rabbit Convertible models (continued)

Description	Current Track				
Cigarette lighter	73	Highbeam (right)	82	Radio connection	72
Headlight dimmer/flasher switch	76	License plate light	74	Taillight (left)	85
Headlight (left)	77, 80	Parking light (left)	86	Taillight (right)	84
Headlight (right)	78, 81	Parking light (right)	83		
Highbeam (left)	79				

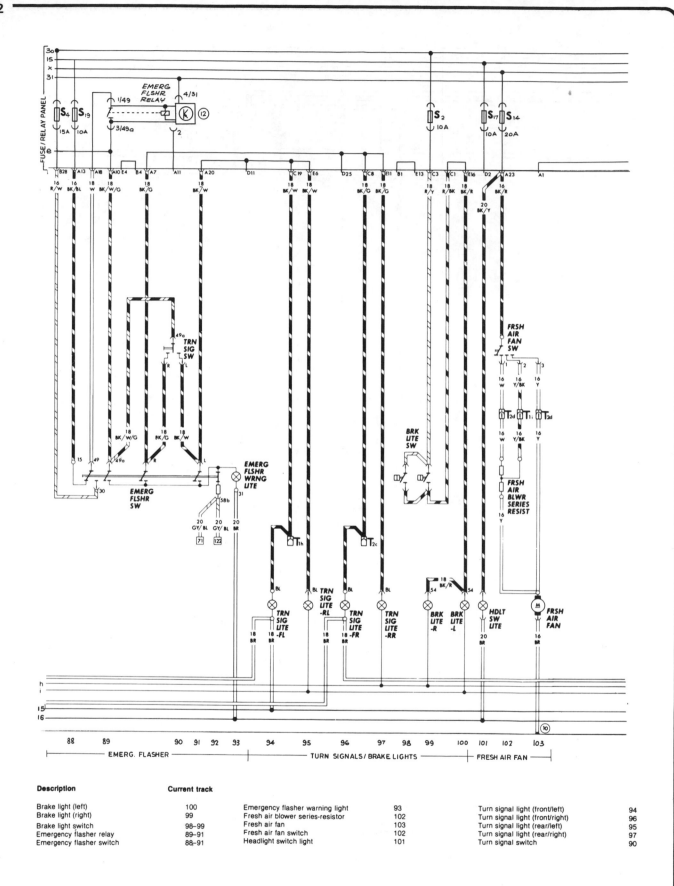

Fig. 12.18 Wiring diagram for 1983 and 1984 Jetta and Rabbit Convertible models (continued)

Description	Current track				
Brake light (left)	100	Emergency flasher warning light	93	Turn signal light (front/left)	94
Brake light (right)	99	Fresh air blower series-resistor	102	Turn signal light (front/right)	96
Brake light switch	98–99	Fresh air fan	103	Turn signal light (rear/left)	95
Emergency flasher relay	89–91	Fresh air fan switch	102	Turn signal light (rear/right)	97
Emergency flasher switch	88–91	Headlight switch light	101	Turn signal switch	90

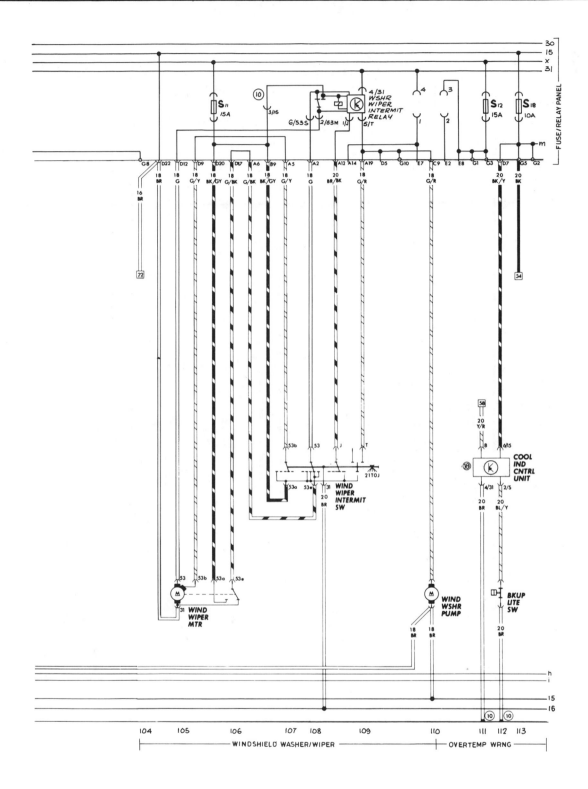

Description	Current Track				
Back-up light switch	112	Windshield washer pump	110	Windshield wiper intermittent switch	108
Coolant indicator control unit	112	Windshield wiper intermittent relay	107–109	Windshield wiper motor	105

Fig. 12.18 Wiring diagram for 1983 and 1984 Jetta and Rabbit Convertible models (continued)

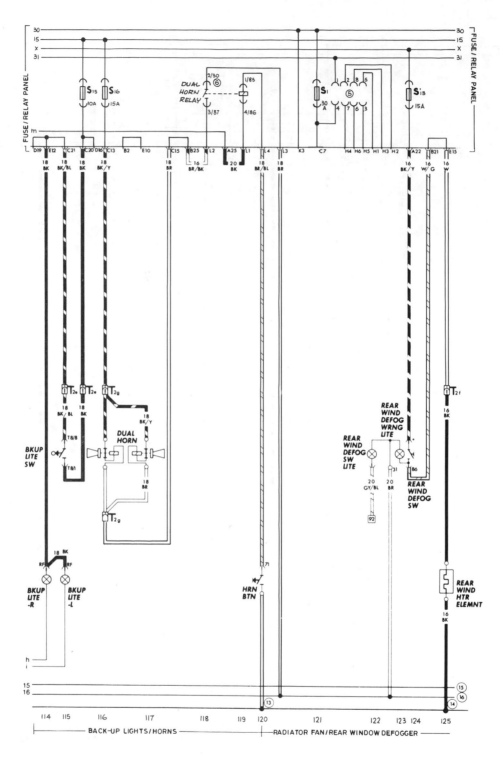

Description

Description	Current Track				
Back up light (left)	115	Dual horns	116–117	Rear window defog switch	124
Back up light (right)	114	Horn button	120	Rear window defog switch light	122
Back up light switch	115	Rear window heating element	125	Rear window defog warning light	123
Dual horn relay	118–119				

Fig. 12.18 Wiring diagram for 1983 and 1984 Jetta and Rabbit Convertible models (continued)

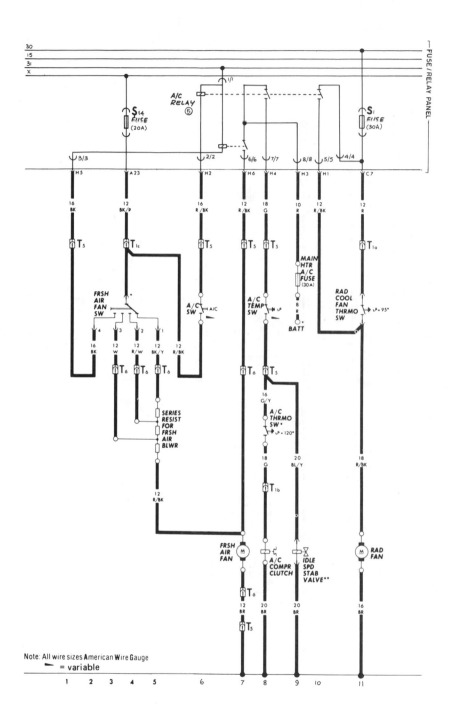

Fig. 12.18 Wiring diagram for 1983 and 1984 Jetta and Rabbit Convertible models (continued)

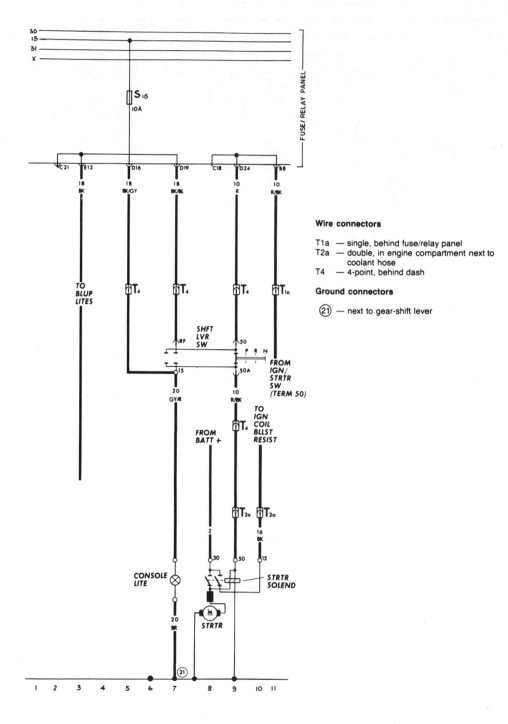

Fig. 12.18 Wiring diagram for 1983 and 1984 Jetta and Rabbit Convertible models (continued)

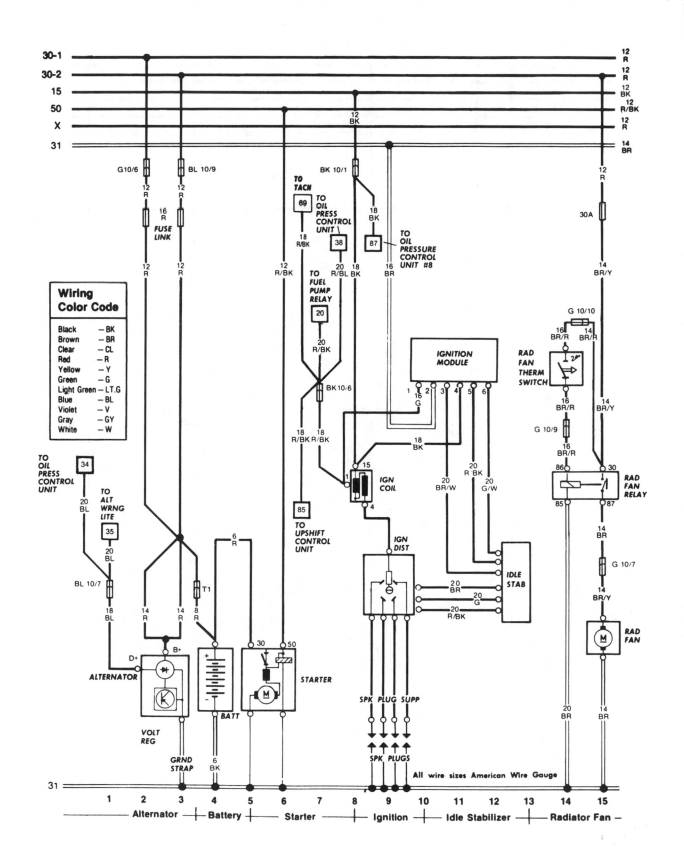

Fig. 12.19 Wiring diagram for 1982, 1983 and 1984 Rabbit and 1982 and 1983 Pick-up models

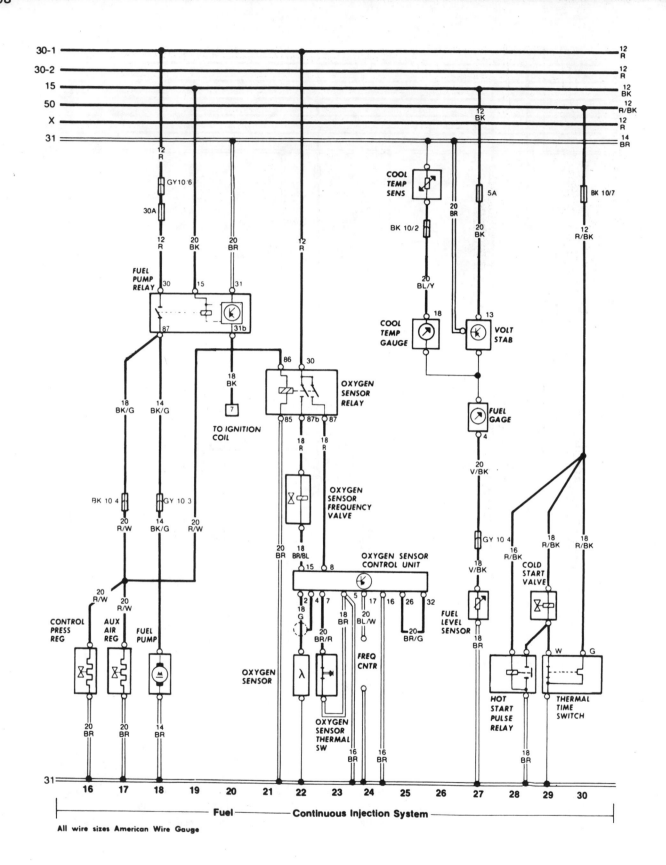

Fig. 12.19 Wiring diagram for 1982, 1983 and 1984 Rabbit and 1982 and 1983 Pick-up models (continued)

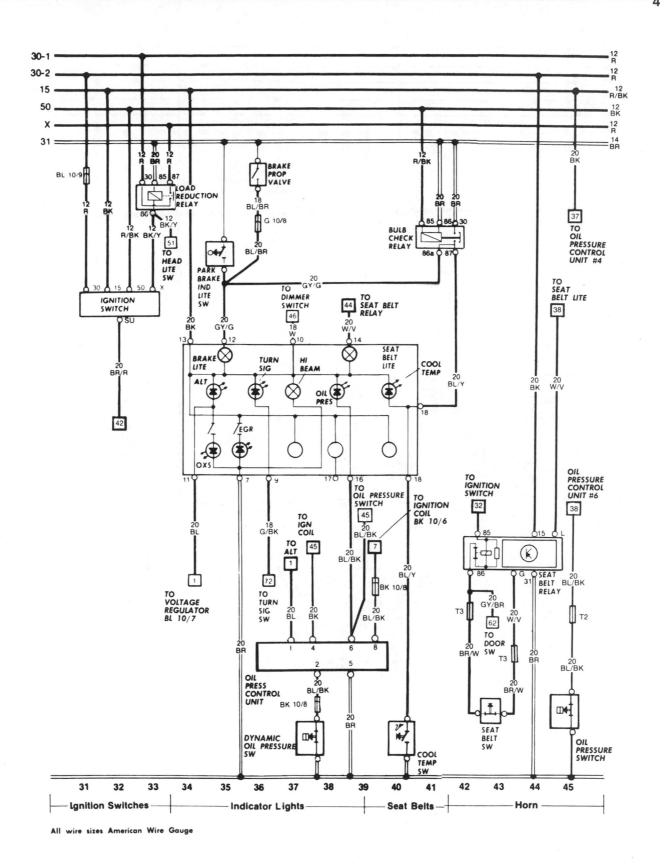

Fig. 12.19 Wiring diagram for 1982, 1983 and 1984 Rabbit and 1982 and 1983 Pick-up models (continued)

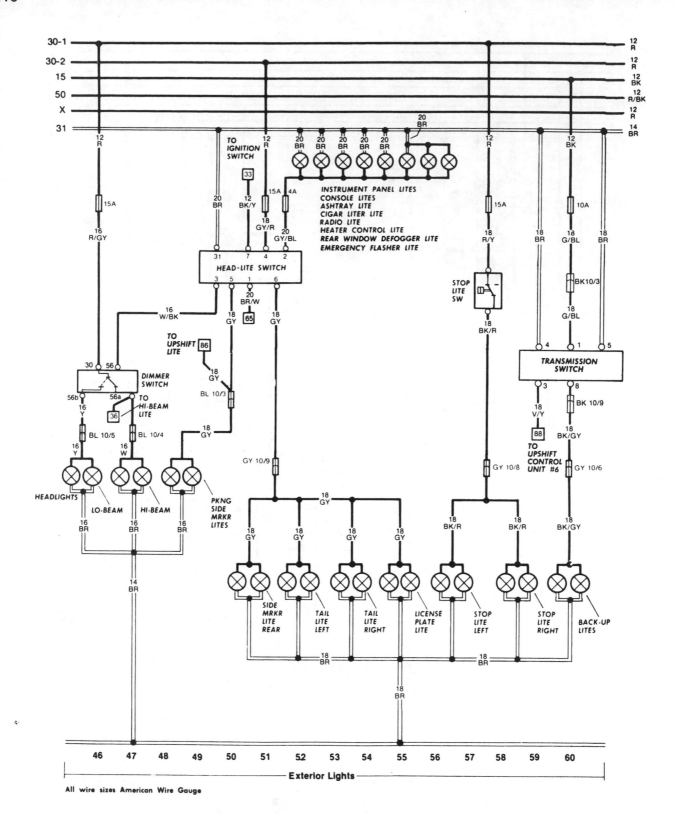

Fig. 12.19 Wiring diagram for 1982, 1983 and 1984 Rabbit and 1982 and 1983 Pick-up models (continued)

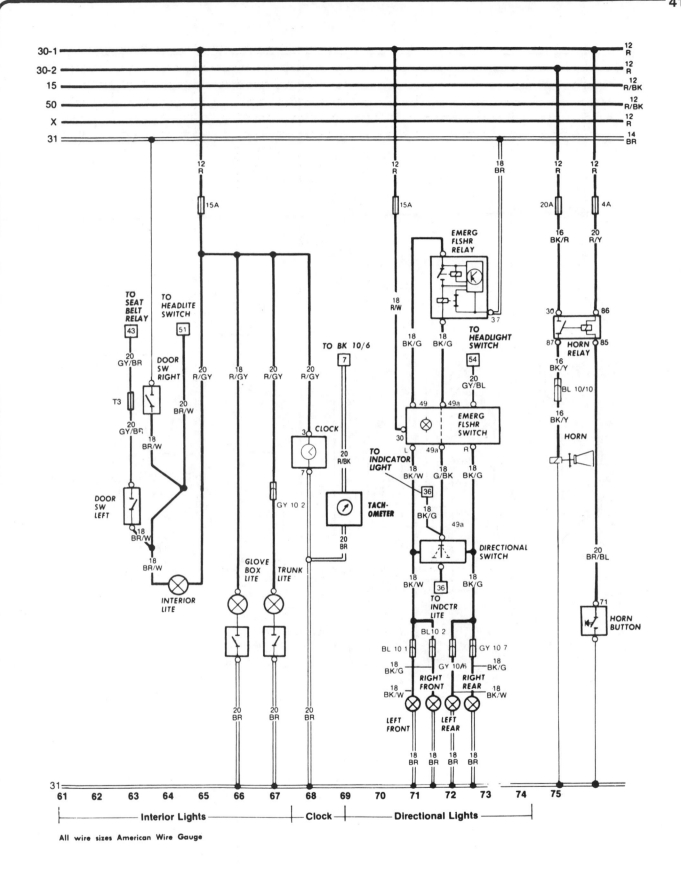

Fig. 12.19 Wiring diagram for 1982, 1983 and 1984 Rabbit and 1982 and 1983 Pick-up models (continued)

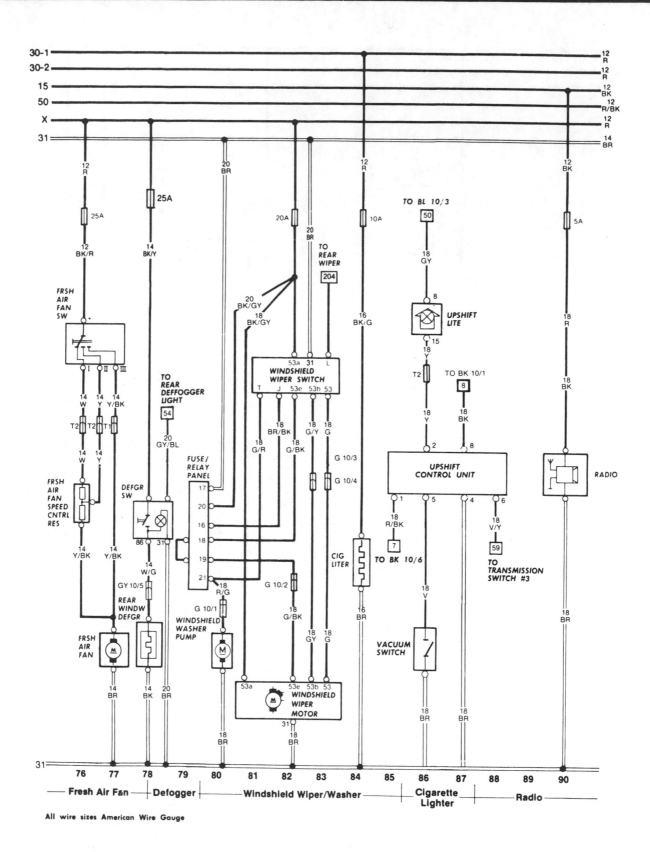

Fig. 12.19 Wiring diagram for 1982, 1983 and 1984 Rabbit and 1982 and 1983 Pick-up models (continued)

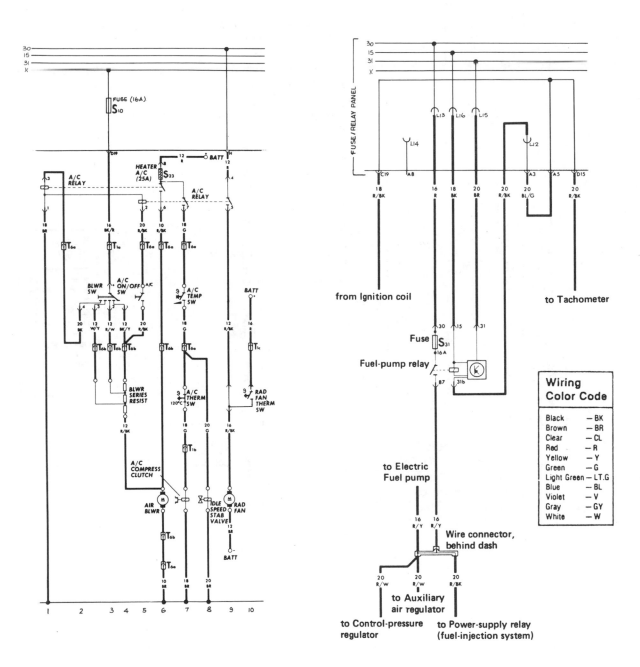

Fig. 12.20 Additional wiring diagram for 1982 Jetta and Rabbit Convertible air conditioning and fuel pump relay

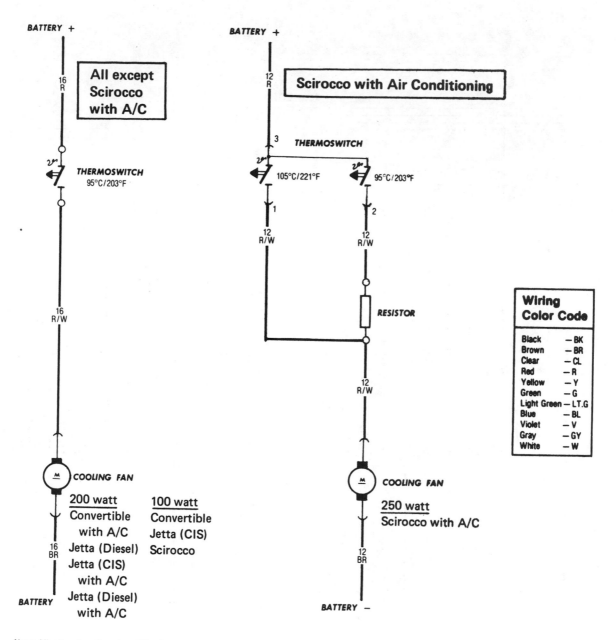

BATTERY +

16 R

All except Scirocco with A/C

THERMOSWITCH
95°C/203°F

16 R/W

COOLING FAN

200 watt
Convertible
  with A/C
Jetta (Diesel)
Jetta (CIS)
  with A/C
Jetta (Diesel)
  with A/C

100 watt
Convertible
Jetta (CIS)
Scirocco

16 BR

BATTERY —

BATTERY +

12 R

Scirocco with Air Conditioning

3 **THERMOSWITCH**

105°C/221°F   95°C/203°F

1   2

12 R/W   12 R/W

RESISTOR

12 R/W

COOLING FAN

250 watt
Scirocco with A/C

12 BR

BATTERY —

Wiring Color Code

Black	— BK
Brown	— BR
Clear	— CL
Red	— R
Yellow	— Y
Green	— G
Light Green	— LT.G
Blue	— BL
Violet	— V
Gray	— GY
White	— W

Note: All wire sizes American Wire Gauge

Fig. 12.21 Additional wiring diagram for 1982 Rabbit, Jetta, Scirocco and Pick-up radiator fan

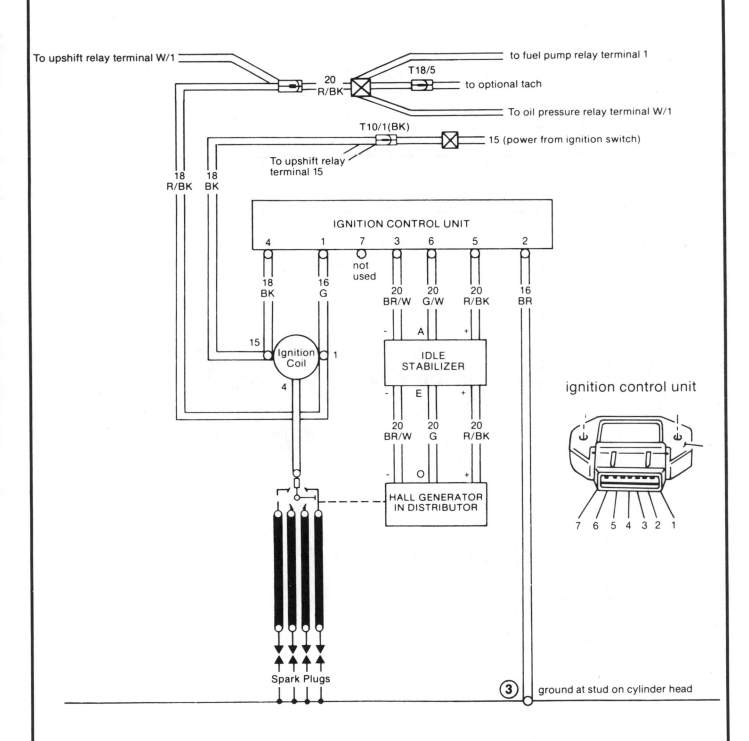

Fig. 12.22 Additional wiring diagram for 1982, 1983 and 1984 ignition systems

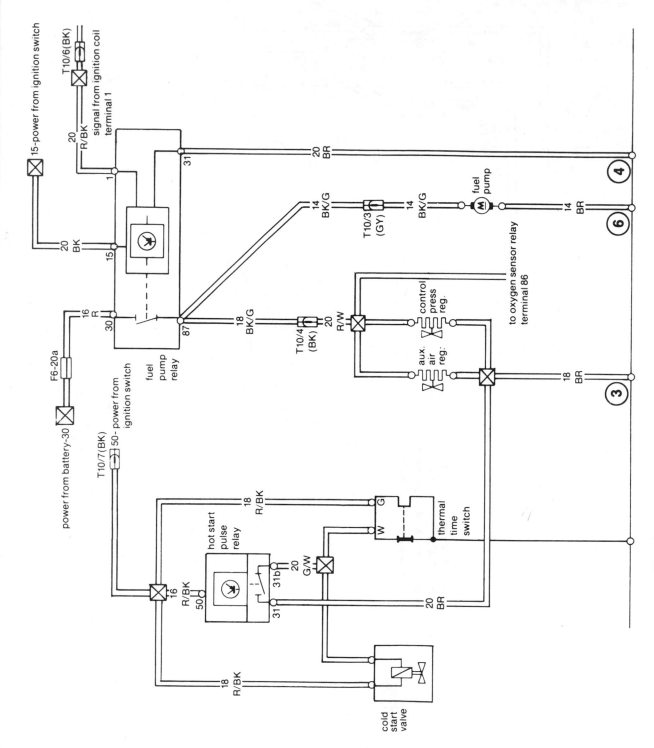

Fig. 12.23 Additional wiring diagram for 1982, 1983 and 1984 fuel injection system

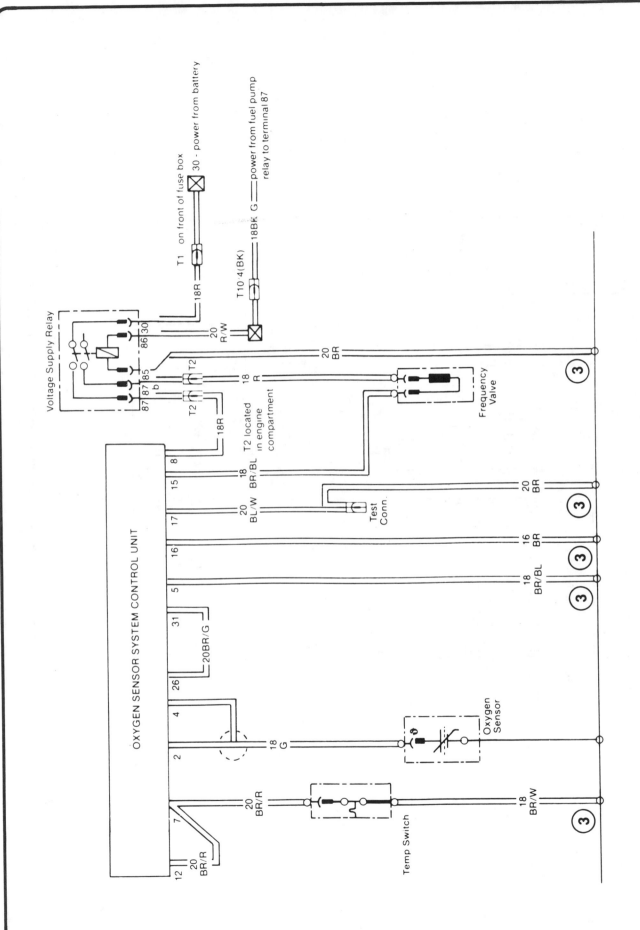

Fig. 12.24 Additional wiring diagram for 1982 and 1983 oxygen sensor system (except Rabbit GTi models)

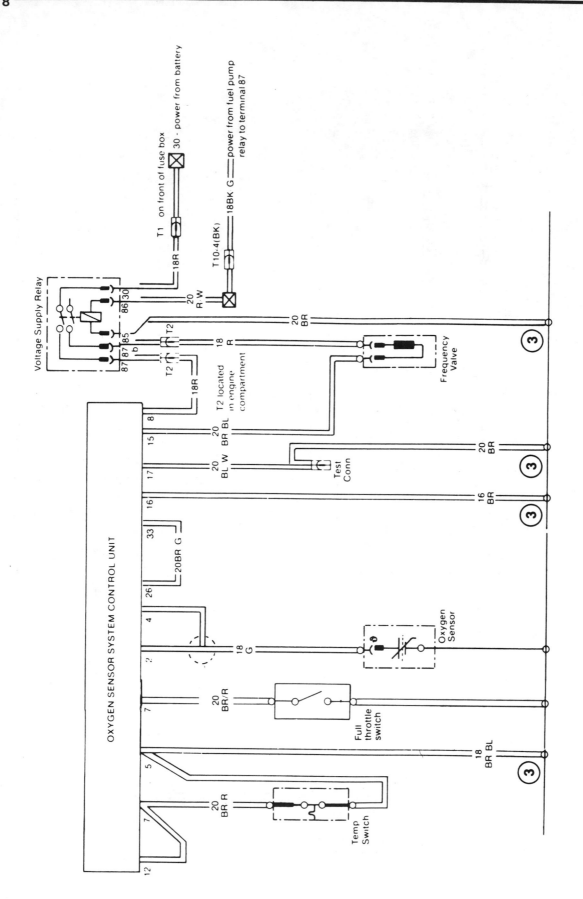

Fig. 12.25 Additional wiring diagram for 1983 oxygen sensor system (Rabbit GTi models)

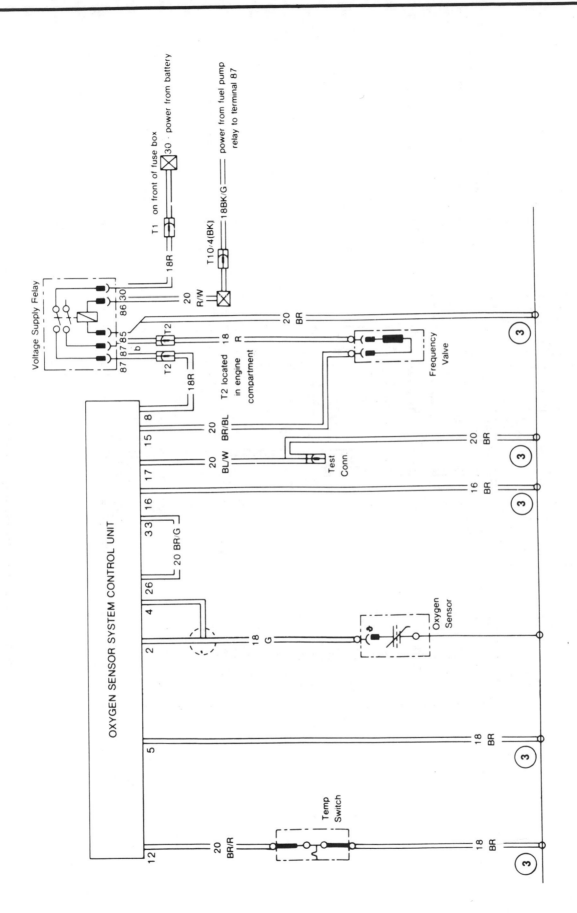

Fig. 12.26 Additional wiring diagram for 1984 oxygen sensor system (except Rabbit GTi and California models)

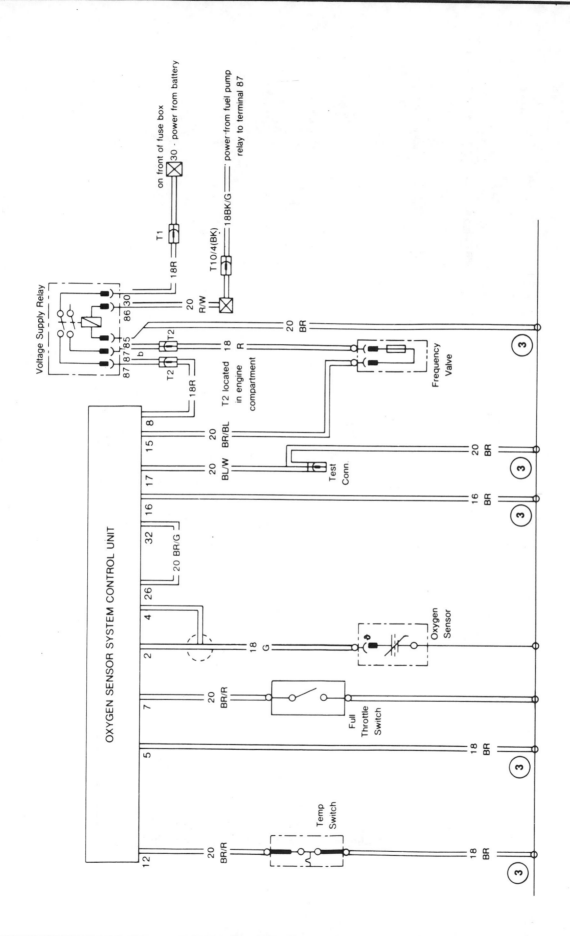

Fig. 12.27 Additional wiring diagram for **1984 oxygen sensor system** (Rabbit GTi and California models)

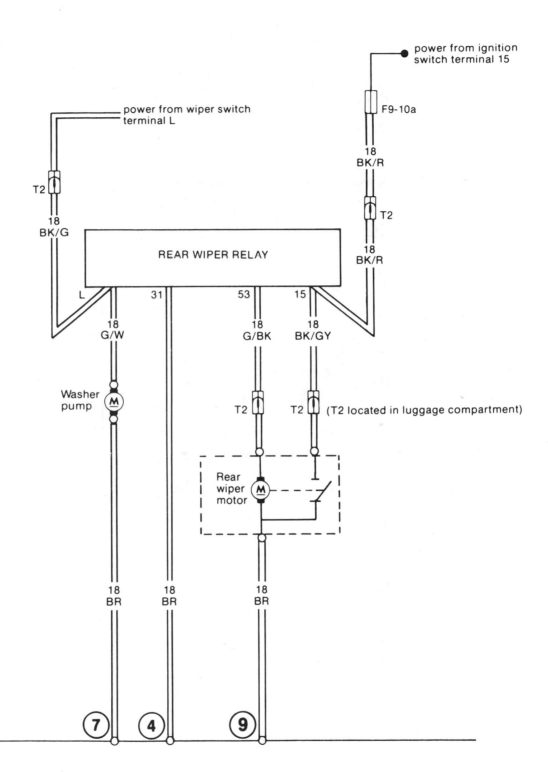

power from ignition switch terminal 15

F9-10a

18 BK/R

T2

18 BK/R

power from wiper switch terminal L

T2

18 BK/G

REAR WIPER RELAY

L   31   53   15

18 G/W

18 G/BK

18 BK/GY

Washer pump

T2   T2   (T2 located in luggage compartment)

Rear wiper motor

18 BR

18 BR

18 BR

7   4   9

Fig. 12.28 Additional wiring diagram for 1983 and 1984 rear window wiper/washer

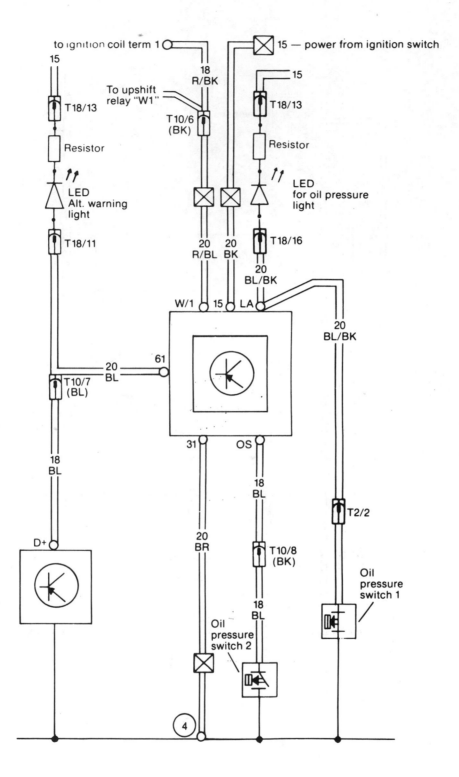

Fig. 12.29 Additional wiring diagram for 1983 and 1984 oil pressure warning system

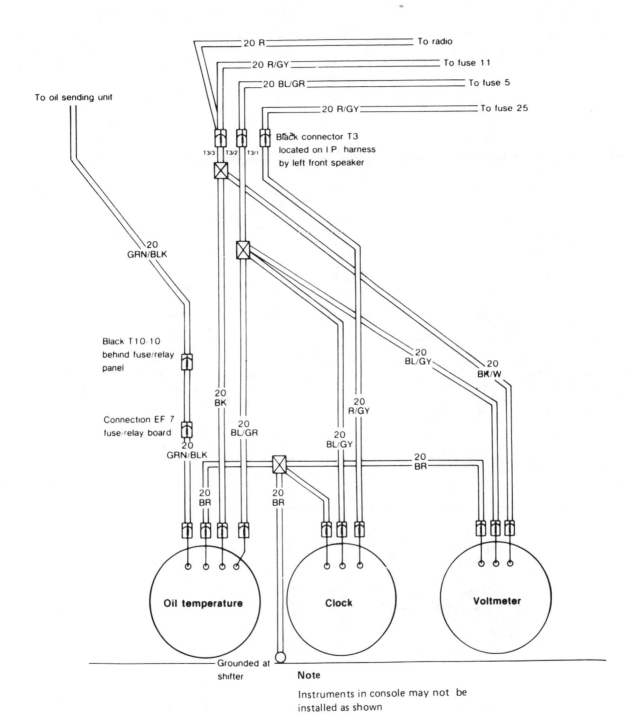

Fig. 12.30 Additional wiring diagram for 1983 and 1984 console illumination (Rabbit GTi models)

8   Electrical system

Fuses and relays — general

1   From January 1983 a revised fusebox and relay plate is fitted to all models. The new layout comprises 22 flat fuses, 11 relay positions on the relay plate and 6 relays on adaptors. The fuse ratings and circuits protected are given in the Specifications at the beginning of this Supplement. The location and number of relays used varies considerably according to model, year, options fitted and export territory, but are shown on the relevant wiring diagrams at the end of this Section.

Multi-function indicator — description

2   A multi-function indicator is available as standard or optional equipment on 1780 cc models from August 1982 on.
3   The unit is essentially a trip computer consisting of an electronic analyser and digital display unit capable of showing seven different functions.
4   The electronic analyser receives information on engine speed, load, temperature and vehicle mileage from sensors incorporated into the various vehicle systems. This information is processed by the analyser and is displayed in digital form on command from the driver.
5   The display unit is located in the centre of the instrument panel with some of the sensors and related components attached at the rear.
6   All the components are sealed units and cannot be dismantled for repair. They can, however, be removed and refitted during dismantling of the instrument panel using the procedures described in Chapter 9. Testing of the multi-function indicator, its circuits and components should be entrusted to a VW dealer as special test equipment and a specific procedure are necessary.

9   Suspension and steering

Power-assisted steering — general

1   Power-assisted steering is available as optional equipment on certain Rabbit GTi and Jetta GLi North American models.
2   The steering gear is of the conventional rack and pinion type and is similar in external appearance to the manual equipment apart from the hydraulic pipes and connections. Pressure for the system is supplied by a vane type pump mounted on the side of the engine and driven by a vee-belt from the crankshaft pulley.

Power steering pump drivebelt — removal, refitting and adjustment

3   The power steering pump drivebelt also drives the engine water pump on models with power-assisted steering. Both the water pump and power steering pump are rigidly mounted on the engine so that adjustment of the belt is by shims between the inner and outer halves of the power steering pump pulley. By subtracting shims the two halves fit closer together, effectively increasing the diameter of the pulley thus reducing slack in the belt. Adding shims has the opposite effect.
4   To remove the drivebelt, undo the three nuts and washers securing the spare shims, adjusting shims and pulley halves to the water pump. Lift off the shims and pump halves, but note the number of shims fitted between the pulley halves. The drivebelt can now be removed.
5   If the original belt is to be refitted, place the pulley inner half and the original number of shims over the pump studs. If a new belt is being fitted use one or two additional shims initially.
6   Slip the drivebelt over the pulleys then fit the pump pulley outer half, spare shims, nuts and washers. If the pulley outer half is difficult to fit turn the pump shaft so that one of the studs is towards the crankshaft then fit the nut finger tight. Turn the pulley so that each stud in turn is toward the crankshaft pulley and fit the nuts.
7   With all the nuts in place turn the crankshaft as necessary and tighten each nut in turn when it is towards the crankshaft pulley. Tighten the nuts to the specified torque, checking that the belt is sitting squarely in the vee of the pulley.
8   When all the nuts are tight, check that the belt deflection is as given in the Specifications. If not, repeat the above procedure, adding or subtracting shims as necessary.

Power steering pump — removal and refitting

9   Remove the pump drivebelt, as described previously in this Section.
10   Place a suitable container beneath the pump, then slacken the fluid feed hose clip at the uppermost connection on the pump. Detach the pump and allow all the fluid to drain into the container.
11   Disconnect the pressure and return hoses from the pump then protect the pump connections and hose ends against dirt ingress. Discard all the fluid drained from the reservoir.
12   Undo the nuts and bolts securing the pump to the pump mounting bracket and withdraw the pump from the engine.
13   If a new pump is to be fitted it will be necessary to transfer the pulley mounting flange from the old pump, as new pumps are not

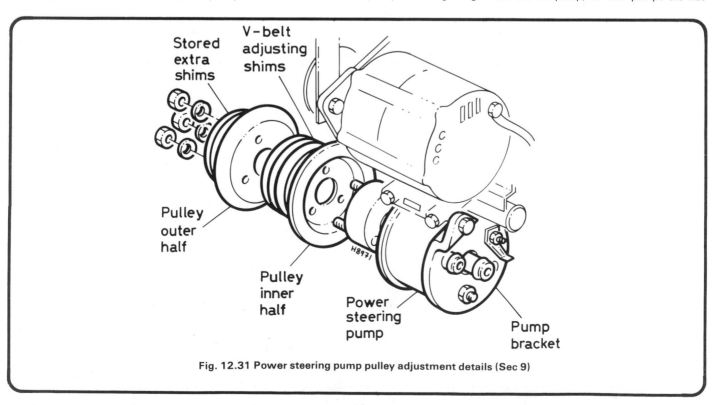

Fig. 12.31 Power steering pump pulley adjustment details (Sec 9)

supplied with a flange. To do this, support the underside of the flange on a press bed and press out the pump shaft. Position the flange on the new pump and using a suitable bolt or threaded bar, nut and washer screwed into the centre of the pump shaft, draw the flange into place.

14 Refitting the pump and hoses is the reverse sequence to removal, but observe the relevant torque wrench settings. Fit and adjust the drivebelt as described earlier in this Section.

15 With the pump and drivebelt installed, fill the reservoir with fresh fluid of the correct type up to the Full Cold mark on the filler cap dipstick.

16 Start the engine and allow it to idle. Add fluid to the reservoir until the level remains constant. Have an assistant turn the steering quickly, but without excessive force, from lock to lock. Add fluid as necessary until the level remains constant and no further air bubbles appear. **Do not** allow the pump to run dry during this operation and **do not** hold the steering on full lock for more than 5 seconds.

17 Finally, with the engine idling and the steering in the straight-ahead position, check the level once more, top up if necessary then refit the cap securely.

Power-assisted steering gear – removal and refitting

18 Jack up the front of the car and support it on axle stands. Remove both front roadwheels.

19 Mark the position of the left-hand tie-rod end balljoint on the tie-rod then slacken the retaining locknut.

20 Extract the split pins and unscrew the castellated nuts securing the tie-rod end balljoints to the steering arms. Release the balljoints using a balljoint separator tool. Unscrew the left-hand balljoint and remove it from the tie-rod.

21 Place a suitable container beneath the power steering pump and disconnect the fluid feed hose from the pump upper connection. Disconnect the pressure and return hoses and allow the fluid to drain into the container. Discard the drained fluid and protect the disconnected hoses and connections against dirt ingress.

22 On models with manual gearboxes, release the gearchange linkage from the steering gear.

23 Release the boot at the base of the steering column and undo the nut and clamp bolt securing the universal joint shaft to the steering gear pinion shaft.

24 Disconnect the fluid pressure hose at the pipe connector adjacent to the steering gear pinion housing. Disconnect the fluid return hose at the pinion housing union.

25 Undo the retaining nuts and bolts and remove the gearbox rear mounting completely.

26 Remove the exhaust front pipe at the manifold and exhaust system then withdraw the pipe.

27 Undo the U-shaped retaining clamps securing the steering gear to the body, ease the assembly away from the universal joint shaft then withdraw the unit from the car.

28 Refitting the steering gear is the reverse sequence to removal, bearing in mind the following points.

(a) Centre the steering gear before fitting by ensuring that the rack protrudes from the housing by equal amounts on both sides (it may be necessary to release the rubber boots to check this)

(b) Ensure that the steering gear is centered, and the steering wheel spokes are horizontal before fitting and tightening the universal joint shaft clamp bolt

(c) Refit the tie-rod end balljoint to the position marked during removal

(d) Tighten all retaining nuts and bolts to the specified torque, where applicable, and use new split pins to secure the tie-rod end balljoint nuts

(e) Fill and bleed the system on completion, as described in paragraphs 15 to 17 of this Section

(f) Check the front wheel alignment, as described in Chapter 10

Power steering gear tie-rod – removal and refitting

29 Jack up the front of the car and support it on axle stands. Remove the relevant front roadwheel.

30 Extract the split pin and unscrew the castellated nut securing the tie-rod end balljoint to the steering arm. Release the balljoint from the arm using a balljoint separator tool.

31 Release the retaining clips and slide the rubber boot down the tie-rod to expose the inner balljoint.

32 Using a suitable spanner, unscrew the tie-rod inner balljoint housing and remove the tie-rod assembly from the rack. Note that the

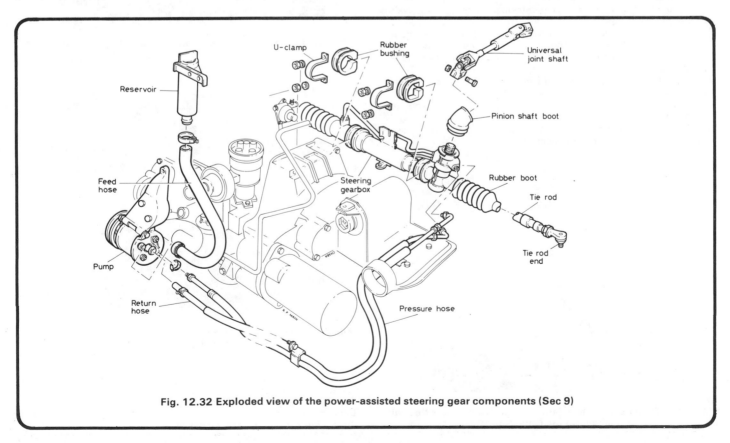

Fig. 12.32 Exploded view of the power-assisted steering gear components (Sec 9)

balljoint housing is likely to be quite tight due to the thread locking agent used during assembly.

33 If the rubber boot is to be renewed it will be necessary to remove the tie-rod outer balljoint and locknut, but mark their positions on the tie-rod first.

34 Refitting is the reverse sequence to removal, but use a thread locking agent on the threads of the inner balljoint housing. Tighten the tie-rod end castellated nut to the specified torque and use a new split pin. If the tie-rod end was removed the front wheel alignment should be checked, as described in Chapter 10.

Fault diagnosis — power-assisted steering

35 The majority of faults associated with power-assisted steering are caused by incorrect pump drivebelt tension, incorrect fluid levels or contaminated fluid. If the power assistance is weak or irregular or if there are unusual noises from the pump or rack and pinion assembly, check these items first, as described earlier in this Section.

36 Fluid leaks from the system can often be cured by attention to the pipes, hoses and unions. Fluid leakage from the rubber boots on the tie-rods would indicate a more serious problem such as failed seals within the unit itself. These problems and any others which cannot be cured by attending to the previously stated items will require the services of a VW dealer. To trace accurately internal faults on the steering gear, special test equipment is necessary and this is beyond the scope of the average home mechanic. Repair and overhaul of the pump or steering gear is not possible, and in all probability a confirmed fault will mean a new complete assembly is required.

---

10 Bodywork and fittings

Facia — removal and refitting

1 On Golf, Rabbit and Jetta models from 1981 on the facia is removed as follows. The procedure for earlier models is similar with only minor differences.

2 Refer to Chapter 9 and remove the instrument panel.

3 Working in the instrument panel opening, undo the two screws securing the heater controls in place.

4 Withdraw the ashtray and ashtray insert, disconnect the electrical connections and remove the insert.

5 Undo the four centre console retaining screws and move the console rearward.

6 On models equipped with a manually operated choke control, carefully tap out the pin securing the choke knob to the choke cable. Unscrew the cable retaining ring and remove the cable from the facia by pushing it inwards.

7 Depress the upper and lower retaining tags and carefully lever the fresh air vents out of the facia at each end.

8 Undo the screws and remove the left-hand and right-hand cubby hole/oddment trays from under the facia.

9 Refer to the illustration and detach the multi-plug connector and unscrew the screw in the radio aperture.

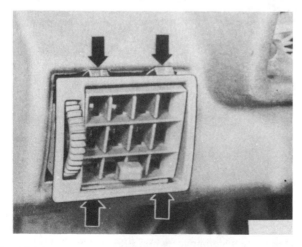

Fig. 12.33 Depress the tags (arrowed) and remove the fresh air vents from the facia (Sec 10)

Fig. 12.34 Left-hand cubby hole/oddment tray retaining screw locations (arrowed) (Sec 10)

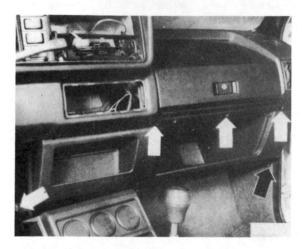

Fig. 12.35 Right-hand cubby hole/oddment tray retaining screw locations (arrowed) (Sec 10)

Fig. 12.36 Remove the screw (arrowed) and disconnect the multi-plug (F) (Sec 10)

10 Undo the two screws at each end of the facia and the two lower screws each side of the radio aperture.

11 Lift the facia up out of its retaining clips and remove it sideways through the door aperture.

12 Refitting is the reverse sequence to removal.

General repair procedures

Whenever servicing, repair or overhaul work is carried out on the car or its components, it is necessary to observe the following procedures and instructions. This will assist in carrying out the operation efficiently and to a professional standard of workmanship.

Joint mating faces and gaskets

Where a gasket is used between the mating faces of two components, ensure that it is renewed on reassembly, and fit it dry unless otherwise stated in the repair procedure. Make sure that the mating faces are clean and dry with all traces of old gasket removed. When cleaning a joint face, use a tool which is not likely to score or damage the face, and remove any burrs or nicks with an oilstone or fine file.

Make sure that tapped holes are cleaned, and keep them free of jointing compound if this is being used unless specifically instructed otherwise.

Ensure that all orifices, channels or pipes are clear and blow through them, preferably using compressed air.

Oil seals

Whenever an oil seal is removed from its working location, either individually or as part of an assembly, it should be renewed.

The very fine sealing lip of the seal is easily damaged and will not seal if the surface it contacts is not completely clean and free from scratches, nicks or grooves. If the original sealing surface of the component cannot be restored, the component should be renewed.

Protect the lips of the seal from any surface which may damage them in the course of fitting. Use tape or a conical sleeve where possible. Lubricate the seal lips with oil before fitting and, on dual lipped seals, fill the space between the lips with grease.

Unless otherwise stated, oil seals must be fitted with their sealing lips toward the lubricant to be sealed.

Use a tubular drift or block of wood of the appropriate size to install the seal and, if the seal housing is shouldered, drive the seal down to the shoulder. If the seal housing is unshouldered, the seal should be fitted with its face flush with the housing top face.

Screw threads and fastenings

Always ensure that a blind tapped hole is completely free from oil, grease, water or other fluid before installing the bolt or stud. Failure to do this could cause the housing to crack due to the hydraulic action of the bolt or stud as it is screwed in.

When tightening a castellated nut to accept a split pin, tighten the nut to the specified torque, where applicable, and then tighten further to the next split pin hole. Never slacken the nut to align a split pin hole unless stated in the repair procedure.

When checking or retightening a nut or bolt to a specified torque setting, slacken the nut or bolt by a quarter of a turn, and then retighten to the specified setting.

Locknuts, locktabs and washers

Any fastening which will rotate against a component or housing in the course of tightening should always have a washer between it and the relevant component or housing.

Spring or split washers should always be renewed when they are used to lock a critical component such as a big-end bearing retaining nut or bolt.

Locktabs which are folded over to retain a nut or bolt should always be renewed.

Self-locking nuts can be reused in non-critical areas, providing resistance can be felt when the locking portion passes over the bolt or stud thread.

Split pins must always be replaced with new ones of the correct size for the hole.

Special tools

Some repair procedures in this manual entail the use of special tools such as a press, two or three-legged pullers, spring compressors etc. Wherever possible, suitable readily available alternatives to the manufacturer's special tools are described, and are shown in use. In some instances, where no alternative is possible, it has been necessary to resort to the use of a manufacturer's tool and this has been done for reasons of safety as well as the efficient completion of the repair operation. Unless you are highly skilled and have a thorough understanding of the procedure described, never attempt to bypass the use of any special tool when the procedure described specifies its use. Not only is there a very great risk of personal injury, but expensive damage could be caused to the components involved.

Conversion factors

Length (distance)

Inches (in)	X	25.4	= Millimetres (mm)	X	0.0394	= Inches (in)
Feet (ft)	X	0.305	= Metres (m)	X	3.281	= Feet (ft)
Miles	X	1.609	= Kilometres (km)	X	0.621	= Miles

Volume (capacity)

Cubic inches (cu in; in³)	X	16.387	= Cubic centimetres (cc; cm³)	X	0.061	= Cubic inches (cu in; in³)
Imperial pints (Imp pt)	X	0.568	= Litres (l)	X	1.76	= Imperial pints (Imp pt)
Imperial quarts (Imp qt)	X	1.137	= Litres (l)	X	0.88	= Imperial quarts (Imp qt)
Imperial quarts (Imp qt)	X	1.201	= US quarts (US qt)	X	0.833	= Imperial quarts (Imp qt)
US quarts (US qt)	X	0.946	= Litres (l)	X	1.057	= US quarts (US qt)
Imperial gallons (Imp gal)	X	4.546	= Litres (l)	X	0.22	= Imperial gallons (Imp gal)
Imperial gallons (Imp gal)	X	1.201	= US gallons (US gal)	X	0.833	= Imperial gallons (Imp gal)
US gallons (US gal)	X	3.785	= Litres (l)	X	0.264	= US gallons (US gal)

Mass (weight)

Ounces (oz)	X	28.35	= Grams (g)	X	0.035	= Ounces (oz)
Pounds (lb)	X	0.454	= Kilograms (kg)	X	2.205	= Pounds (lb)

Force

Ounces-force (ozf; oz)	X	0.278	= Newtons (N)	X	3.6	= Ounces-force (ozf; oz)
Pounds-force (lbf; lb)	X	4.448	= Newtons (N)	X	0.225	= Pounds-force (lbf; lb)
Newtons (N)	X	0.1	= Kilograms-force (kgf; kg)	X	9.81	= Newtons (N)

Pressure

Pounds-force per square inch (psi; lbf/in²; lb/in²)	X	0.070	= Kilograms-force per square centimetre (kgf/cm²; kg/cm²)	X	14.223	= Pounds-force per square inch (psi; lbf/in²; lb/in²)
Pounds-force per square inch (psi; lbf/in²; lb/in²)	X	0.068	= Atmospheres (atm)	X	14.696	= Pounds-force per square inch (psi; lbf/in²; lb/in²)
Pounds-force per square inch (psi; lbf/in²; lb/in²)	X	0.069	= Bars	X	14.5	= Pounds-force per square inch (psi; lbf/in²; lb/in²)
Pounds-force per square inch (psi; lbf/in²; lb/in²)	X	6.895	= Kilopascals (kPa)	X	0.145	= Pounds-force per square inch (psi; lbf/in²; lb/in²)
Kilopascals (kPa)	X	0.01	= Kilograms-force per square centimetre (kgf/cm²; kg/cm²)	X	98.1	= Kilopascals (kPa)

Torque (moment of force)

Pounds-force inches (lbf in; lb in)	X	1.152	= Kilograms-force centimetre (kgf cm; kg cm)	X	0.868	= Pounds-force inches (lbf in; lb in)
Pounds-force inches (lbf in; lb in)	X	0.113	= Newton metres (Nm)	X	8.85	= Pounds-force inches (lbf in; lb in)
Pounds-force inches (lbf in; lb in)	X	0.083	= Pounds-force feet (lbf ft; lb ft)	X	12	= Pounds-force inches (lbf in; lb in)
Pounds-force feet (lbf ft; lb ft)	X	0.138	= Kilograms-force metres (kgf m; kg m)	X	7.233	= Pounds-force feet (lbf ft; lb ft)
Pounds-force feet (lbf ft; lb ft)	X	1.356	= Newton metres (Nm)	X	0.738	= Pounds-force feet (lbf ft; lb ft)
Newton metres (Nm)	X	0.102	= Kilograms-force metres (kgf m; kg m)	X	9.804	= Newton metres (Nm)

Power

Horsepower (hp)	X	745.7	= Watts (W)	X	0.0013	= Horsepower (hp)

Velocity (speed)

Miles per hour (miles/hr; mph)	X	1.609	= Kilometres per hour (km/hr; kph)	X	0.621	= Miles per hour (miles/hr; mph)

Fuel consumption*

Miles per gallon, Imperial (mpg)	X	0.354	= Kilometres per litre (km/l)	X	2.825	= Miles per gallon, Imperial (mpg)
Miles per gallon, US (mpg)	X	0.425	= Kilometres per litre (km/l)	X	2.352	= Miles per gallon, US (mpg)

Temperature

Degrees Fahrenheit = (°C x 1.8) + 32   Degrees Celsius (Degrees Centigrade; °C) = (°F - 32) x 0.56

*It is common practice to convert from miles per gallon (mpg) to litres/100 kilometres (l/100km), where mpg (Imperial) x l/100 km = 282 and mpg (US) x l/100 km = 235

Index

Printed by
J H Haynes & Co Ltd
Sparkford Nr Yeovil
Somerset BA22 7JJ England